Cw

To

A History ......
hope chimes a
chord,
love,

Ann
xx
xx

Jinglin' Geordie's Legacy

—

A HISTORY OF GEORGE HERIOT'S
HOSPITAL AND SCHOOL

Jinglin' Geordie's Legacy

—

A HISTORY OF GEORGE HERIOT'S
HOSPITAL AND SCHOOL

—

Brian R W Lockhart

TUCKWELL PRESS
2003

First published in 2003 by
Tuckwell Press Ltd
The Mill House
Phantassie
East Linton
East Lothian EH40 3DG
Scotland

ISBN 1-86232-257-0

British Library Cataloguing-in-Publication Data
A Catalogue record for this book is available
on request from the British Library

Layout and design by Mark Blackadder

Printed and bound by ·
The Cromwell Press, Trowbridge, Wiltshire

Contents

Acknowledgements

It seems strange that a school with a history as colourful as that of Heriot's has not had a monograph devoted to it since the 1870s, and even that was a second revision of a work first produced in 1845. Certainly great names in its more recent past were well equipped to take on the task and it seems unfortunate that William McL. Dewar, that doyen of Headmasters, did not turn his extensive talents to writing its history. It was he who influenced my own career most, although it was the later Headmaster, Keith Pearson, who persuaded me to take on what had probably become 'unfinished business' for me. As a former pupil of the Secondary Department of the School and Principal Teacher of History at Heriot's between 1972 and 1981 I did not take much persuading.

I owe many personal debts of gratitude to those who have helped and encouraged me take forward this work. The Heriot Trust staff, of the late Craigie Dougan, Fraser Simm, Sandy Wake and Charlotte Mckay, were always helpful, patient and understanding while I consulted the original documents held at Lauriston Place. I am also grateful to the staff of the National Archives of Scotland, the National Library of Scotland, the Edinburgh Room of the Edinburgh Public Library and the Librarians of the Universities of Edinburgh, Glasgow, Aberdeen, Oslo and Leipzig. Material was also obtained from the Royal Commission on the Ancient and Historical Monuments of Scotland (RCAHMS) in Edinburgh, the Library of Watson's College, the City Archivist's Department in Edinburgh, the Royal High School, and Hutchesons' Grammar School. Thanks also to Mrs Hermione Tennant, who allowed me to visit Innes House and examine its records, and John Brims of the Archives Department of Central Regional Council. For their translations of Norwegian and German my thanks go to Mrs Solweig McCulloch and Catriona Lockhart respectively.

A number of former pupils have been helpful to me in reminiscing about their time at school, and in this regard I wish to thank in particular Professor Roy MacGregor and Ronnie Cramond CBE. Former staff also have been extremely supportive and I thank the number who completed my questionnaire. My thanks to two former Headmasters, Mr Allan McDonald and Mr Keith Pearson, who spent time with me talking about their time at Heriot's. The Governors of George Heriot's Trust have been similarly supportive of this venture and I wish to express my thanks for the wise counsel given by Professor Hector L. Macqueen.

I wish to thank Professor Alastair Rowan, Principal of the Edinburgh College of Art, for his comments on Chapter 2. Professor Alan Smith, formerly of the History Department of the University of Glasgow, along with my former pupil and close friend Dr Gordon Millar of Geneva, both of whom read very early drafts of the book, gave me much useful advice for its improvement. I am happy to take responsibility for its final contents.

Thanks go to Mr Douglas Urquhart for his photography.

Tuckwell Press and in particular John Tuckwell have been helpful especially in the later stages of production. My Secretary, Ann Gannon, has proved invaluable and I warmly acknowledge her help. Finally, this work would not have been completed without unstinting support and encouragement from my wife, Fiona, and our two daughters, Joanne and Catriona, and son, Ross.

The book is dedicated to Helen and George Lockhart for introducing me to Heriot's in the first place and giving me such affectionate encouragement.

BRIAN R W LOCKHART

CHAPTER ONE

George Heriot and his Bequest

George Heriot was born into an established family in his 'mother Citie'[1] of Edinburgh. Although he and his father before him were natives of the metropolis, the family hailed from Trabroun in the parish of Lauder in Berwickshire. The family property of under 400 acres there had been acquired by John Heriot, from Archibald, Earl of Douglas, brother of James I, on 18 July 1423 for the yearly fee of one penny Scots money, in return for military service. In the charter confirmed early the following year by the King, John was designated 'Esquire', son and heir of James Heriot, of Nudre-Marschele, the Earl's 'lovite confederate'. At some point these lands of Trabroun had been forfeited for certain alleged acts of treason, for on 8 May 1515 they were restored to Andrew Heriot by James V, with the consent of the Duke of Albany, Protector, and of Parliament.[2] By the 1540s James Heriot of Trabroun was a supporter of collaboration with the English, suggesting a degree of sympathy with the Reformation,[3] and remained so in the revolutionary times of 1559–60[4] and during the pro-English Ruthven Raid of August 1582.[5]

The exact connection of the goldsmith Heriots of Edinburgh with the Trabroun Heriots is not known but it seems that George Heriot, a goldsmith and the grandfather of the Founder of Heriot's Hospital, was related to them.[6] His expertise was called upon by James V in 1531 when Heriot mended one of the king's silver flagons[7] – a sign of a growing respect for the reputation of the Heriot family. During the later sixteenth century the family was connected to the nobility and country gentry – Elizabeth Heriot being the mother of Thomas Hamilton, Earl of Haddington, President of the Court of Session and Secretary of State to James VI and I,[8] while Agnes Heriot was the mother of George Buchanan, historian and tutor of the same king. In October 1560 James Heriot married Isabel, daughter of the eminent Sir Richard Maitland of Lethington, and eight years later Helen Heriot, daughter of the Laird of Trabroun, married Sir Thomas Craig of Riccarton, the important Scottish jurist.[9] Ownership of the lands of Trabroun appears to have remained in the family until sold by James Heriot in 1611. The Heriots then moved to Elvingstone,[10] Haddington, in the parish of Gladsmuir in East Lothian, which

‡   1

the family in turn called Trabroun after their original land in Berwickshire.

George Heriot, having gained royal favour, is mentioned in the Burgh of Edinburgh Accounts as a shopkeeper in Edinburgh in the 1540s and 1550s and was probably the first of the family to settle in the capital.[11] He married Christian Kyle, and their son, George Heriot senior, was born in the town in 1540 and was admitted as a burgess of the town on 4 August 1562. He was successful early in life, becoming a member of the town council in 1565–6 (and again in 1567–8, 1575–6 and 1579–80). During these disturbed times, in which supporters of Mary, Queen of Scots and her son, James, vied for political control, Heriot senior appears to have been one of the 'Queen's men'[12] and lost his position as deacon of his craft for serving in the town during its occupation in June 1569. It seems that, despite a decade of John Knox and Protestant dominance, the Edinburgh establishment split and quite a number of the respectable older, conservative, wealthy merchants supported Mary: Heriot senior certainly did so.[13] However, with Regent Morton pursuing a conciliatory policy, Heriot appears to have regained his position relatively quickly, and was certainly firmly re-established by 1583–4.[14]

Heriot senior served as Deacon-Convener of the Incorporated Trades of Edinburgh on five different occasions (1590, 1593, 1594, 1606 and 1607)[15] and repeatedly represented the Town as a Commissioner in the Scottish Parliament[16] and in the Convention of Estates.[17] His municipal activities were varied and extensive: determining the prices of wine and timber in December 1590 and also goldsmith regulations eight months later, while complaining to the King about the export of wool in August 1595[18] and being called in to deal with a dispute in the herring trade in Dunbar in September 1602,[19] standing surety for the Mint in January 1593/4 and John Rae when he was elected 'regent of humanity' in the College in December 1597, while setting the Kirk rent in December 1595 and recovering Town debts from the nobility in February 1595/6.[20] He was also consulted on the princess's baptism in September 1596, the division of the Town into eight parishes in June 1597 and a banquet proposed for the French Ambassador in September 1599.[21] Heriot helped develop Sciennes Yards in January 1597/8,[22] advised the King on changes to St Giles,[23] was one of the Masters of Work appointed for the building of the new Tolbooth in February 1600 and some three years later organised the collection for those sick from pestilence in Prestonpans and North Berwick.[24] One of his last public acts was to repair the town mace in June 1608.[25]

Perhaps Heriot's prominence is most ably demonstrated in

George Heriot senior (1540-1610) was successful as a goldsmith in Edinburgh and played a prominent part in municipal affairs. In 1596 he was involved in persuading James VI that Edinburgh should retain its part in the administration of justice.

his part in the events of 17 December 1596. James VI was renowned for his fondness for episcopacy, wishing to promote a Protestantism that rejected, on the one hand, Papal authority and, on the other, Presbyterian church government. Tempers ran high as the leading churchman, Andrew Melville, attacked James VI personally[26] and the St Andrews minister David Black was summoned before the Privy Council to explain his extreme statements.[27] A sermon by Walter Balcanquall in St Giles excited the populace[28] who reacted by protesting against the King and breaking into a meeting James VI was holding with his Council at the Tolbooth. The ensuing tumult was quelled by the Lord Provost, Sir Alexander Hume, but the King and his advisers withdrew to Linlithgow, declaring Edinburgh unfit for the ministration of justice.[29] The burgesses of the City stood to lose much if the Town was deprived of its status as legal and judicial centre, not to mention the loss of the Court. Four of Edinburgh's most eminent burgesses, including Heriot senior, were chosen to go to Linlithgow to plead with and pacify James.[30] They appear to have been successful for the King returned in triumph on 1 January 1597 to a tranquil city.[31]

On his death in late 1610 his sons, George and David, had a fine memorial erected in Greyfriars' Churchyard.[32] It cost the princely sum of 500 merks[33] and rests to this day against the east wall of the Churchyard.[34] Heriot senior left ten children: three by Elizabeth Balderstone – George (Founder of Heriot's Hospital), Patrick and Margaret; and seven surviving by his second wife, Christian Blaw – David, James (baptised 30 September 1598), Marion, Janet, Sibilla (baptised 25 June 1607), Christian and Thomas (baptised at Holyrood Church[35] on 29 July 1603).[36]

We know little of George Heriot's early life other than that he was born in June 1563[37] and that he received a proper education given his father's position, a fact confirmed by his letters and other surviving documents. He was apprenticed to James Inglis, goldsmith,[38] and showed early determination to strike out in business on his own. He was fortunate in his timing – the trade of goldsmith was growing in status from its origins as the equal of hammermen or common smiths. On 20 August 1581 the goldsmiths were incorporated by the Edinburgh magistrates and had their privileges confirmed on 3 January 1586.[39] This was almost exactly contemporaneous with Heriot's conclusion of a marriage contract on 14 January 1586 with Christian, daughter of the deceased Edinburgh merchant, Simon Marjoribanks. Heriot senior agreed to contribute 1000 merks with an additional 500 merks for 'the setting up of an

A memorial to George Heriot senior rests against the east wall of Greyfriars' Churchyard. It was erected by his sons, George, the Founder, and David. It was restored by the School's Governors in 1913.

buith to him furnissing of his clething to his mariage and of wark lumes and utheris necessaris requisite to ane buith'.[40] Husband and wife were also to receive the annual interest, at the rate of 10%, on 1075 merks lent to the Town. This generous settlement was clearly of great benefit to George Heriot: within a month his new financial stability enabled him to take on William, youngest son of Peter Arnott of Balcormo, on payment of £100 Scots for a seven-year apprenticeship.[41] Heriot's position and status were confirmed when he was admitted into the Incorporation of Goldsmiths on 28 May 1588.

By September 1590 George and Christian were living in a tenement in Fishmarket Close, and by October 1596[42] he was working in his buith (or kram) at the Lady's Steps at the north-east corner of St Giles' Cathedral.[43] His father's financial backing plus his own hard work and perseverance led to the purchase of larger seven-foot-square premises at the west end of the Cathedral with back windows looking into Beth's Wynd.[44] Heriot had his name carved in stone above the door as his sign[45] and his booth had a forge and bellows, with a hollow stone, fitted with a stone cover or lid, which was used as a receptacle for, and a means of extinguishing, the fire-embers at night. He became increasingly important in Edinburgh: on 1 April 1590 he was chosen as one of the four ensign bearers of the Town for the 'wawpounschawing',[46] while on 6 October 1591 he was elected to the town council. Business boomed and he took on another apprentice and servant, David Gray, youngest brother of Thomas Gray, on 13 February 1592.[47]

In other respects Heriot was also fortunate: he was developing his business during a period of peace and at a time when there was a revolution in available materials as the global trade in diamonds, rubies and emeralds opened up. With such advantages he built up his business and was soon serving a number of significant personages: on 1 September 1593 Francis, the Earl Bothwell, great admiral of Scotland, received 24 gold jewelled buttons from Heriot.[48] However, his real stroke of fortune was coming to the attention of Queen Anna (of Denmark), the Consort since 1589 of James VI, who proved a compulsive spendthrift whose extravagance became renowned. Anna seems to have been impressed with Heriot – perhaps it was her initial meeting with him and his father as Town representatives in April 1592,[49] perhaps it was his discretion – but whatever it was, Heriot benefited. He began supplying Anna with jewels as early as May 1593[50] and this probably hastened his election to the post of Deacon of Goldsmiths in October of the same year. This, in turn, ensured a wide role for him in municipal affairs. He was involved in solving merchant disputes, in inspecting the High School and reporting on reforms needed in July 1594 and was consulted on the national issue of the suppression of papist lands in the north.[51] Moreover, he was prominent in the financial backing behind the founding of the Society of Brewers in 1596.[52]

Heriot's extensive resources and his willingness to give Queen Anna extended credit led to a steady stream of transactions (with Heriot usually only receiving part-payment for his services) and his appointment, on 17 July 1597, by writ of the Privy Seal issued at Dunfermline, as goldsmith to the Queen 'for all the dayis of his life',[53] replacing the Frenchman, Clei.[54] Letters detailing his appointment survive,[55] and on 27 July it was publicly proclaimed by 'sound of trumpet' at the Mercat Cross of Edinburgh in the High Street. Anna had a large household to maintain and, having grown up in the wealthier state of Denmark, she had developed expensive tastes. Moreover, her generous nature led to her bestowing jewellery on bringers of good tidings or indeed anyone doing her a service, however slight, and she was probably building up her jewel collection from a very low base.[56] This was good news for Heriot who supplied her needs, acting as her banker, making her loans, taking her jewels as security and even buying them for her when her finances deteriorated.

Heriot patiently and painstakingly recorded all his transactions. Anna constantly promised prompt payment for his work but almost always failed to live up to her promises. As a result, she had to assign specific jewels to Heriot, who was authorised to pledge, commit and mortgage them in any form or manner so long as they were returned to the Crown when the debt was finally repaid. Heriot, therefore, used jewels as security, or even rented them out, not necessarily in their existing form.[57] Periodically, James intervened if the situation seemed to be getting out of hand: on 13 June 1599 he instructed Lord Newbattle to pay immediately from taxes the money owing Heriot so that Anna's jewels could be taken out of pawn. Payment was to be made by John Preston of Fenton Barns out of 'that sowme destinat to the dispatche of our Ambassadour to France'.[58] At other times Heriot, having held royal jewels in pawn in return for cash advances, disposed of them himself to trade. Although it could be suggested that Heriot could not fail to succeed given the prevailing practice and need to give gifts as a symbol of status, a predecessor, exasperated by royal non-payment, had absconded with some of Anna's less valuable jewels and on his capture had been executed as a warning to his fellow-craftsmen to resist temptation even when experiencing royal injustice.[59] Being a goldsmith did not automatically mean success, as the fate of others showed. James Mossman and James Cockie had been hanged in 1573 for protracting the civil war;[60] Thomas Foulis, one of his immediate predecessors and contemporaries, who was heavily involved with James VI's money, had come badly unstuck in January 1598 as a result of a 'deliberately engineered royal bankruptcy'.[61] Whatever Heriot did, he did it well, and through his ability he succeeded where others before him had singularly failed.

Having been re-elected Deacon of Goldsmiths,[62] Heriot supplied the King, James VI, with 1500 crowns worth of jewels.[63] This explains the reference to 'remembering the gude service done to thair Majesties be George Heriote'[64] when the King appointed Heriot one of his own jewellers on 4 April 1601. By then Heriot was already significant to James: he had been given a chamber in Holyrood by the King in June 1599 in order to carry on his business,[65] was supplied with a departing gift to give to the French Ambassador in August 1599[66] and on 18 February 1600 was one of the agents who received Elizabeth's annual annuity to James.[67] Although this was another step forward, Heriot still had his loyalty to Anna. In July 1601 her finances were so strained that she had to return 'ane Imerod set about with dyamontis and rubeis In forme of ane fedder'.[68] At other times she could not repay all of her outstanding debts to him. On 7 June 1602 Anna repaid only part of 3927 crowns owed and handed over 'ane greit dyamant set in ane schattoun[69] of gold' to clear another 1000. Not wishing to part with more jewels, Anne deposited with Heriot 'ane jewall conteining threescore and threttene dyamondts' as a pledge for repayment of the remaining 927 crowns.[70]

It has been estimated that during the ten years before the Union of the Crowns between England and Scotland in 1603 Heriot's bills for Anna's jewels alone amounted to over £50,000 sterling.[71] Astronomical though these figures were, she was to continue purchases on such a scale long after 1603.[72] Increasingly indispensable to the royal household, he became one of at least six jewellers to Prince Henry, and to Prince Charles, born respectively in February 1594 and November 1600.

On 1 December 1601 Heriot figured as a member of a syndicate of eleven commissioned by the government to issue a new Scottish currency to replace the very debased one in use. They paid £45,889 9s. 6d Scots in return for the profits gained from one year from this process.[73] In 1603 he was referred to as one of the 'tacksmen' (farmers) of the customs. Heriot was goldsmith, moneylender and pawnbroker and in January 1603 he was holding the title deeds of the Chapel Royal in Stirling as James resorted to raising money against crown property[74] and Papal Bulls. However, one of his central functions was again to the fore just after James had departed south. Anna, taking advantage of her husband's absence to make yet another vain attempt to win control of her son, Prince Henry, from his traditional custodian, the Earl of Mar, needed money quickly to visit him in Stirling Castle. Still in existence is a note in her hand, according to one source the first extant[75] written in Scottish dialect, asking her faithful goldsmith for help: 'Gordg Heriott, I ernestlie dissyr youe present to send me tua hundrethe pundes vithe all expidition becaus I man hest me auay present lie. Anna R.'[76]

The death of Elizabeth I in 1603 and the accession of James VI of Scotland as James I of the united kingdoms meant the transfer of the Scottish court to London. Heriot was needed as never before to supply the jewellery to King, Queen and nobility to prepare them for this change. Indeed, between June and August 1603 Heriot provided Anna with jewels at places as far apart as York[77] and Windsor,[78] while in September and October of the same year he supplied her at Woodstock and Hampton Court, one item being 'a tablet for the Kinge of Denmarks portraict with fourskore and tenne Diamonds'.[79]

Like many other leading Scots, Heriot followed his sovereigns south and became part of the large Scottish community in London which became so detested by the English establishment that James had to take steps to check the flow and even repatriate some of the fortune-hunters.[80] Heriot was too useful to suffer such a fate. His acute business sense was seen in his 'nott of thingis left'[81] in Edinburgh and his twenty specific instructions to his servants which included finding 'sume skilfull joyner to taike downe the walnut buird bed and dressour standis in my upper hall' and transport them to London.[82] Other furniture, he ordered, was to be sold off at specific prices, and if his desired prices could not be achieved, he refused to countenance selling but instead ordered the items to be brought to London.[83]

Within a short time of his arrival in the capital Heriot had opened a shop near the Royal Exchange and his royal connections ensured that his services were soon in great demand.[84] Although only one of three royal jewellers appointed in May 1603, and only one of many others, Heriot grew wealthy as Anna added to her jewellery collection[85] and 'James tried to deck his dynasty in symbols of majesty far transcending the jewels available to ordinary mortals'.[86] Over a long period Heriot's detailed and meticulous accounts[87] confirm the pattern of events. Anna's habits in England were similar to those she had adopted in Scotland. After a time of building up debt she would pawn jewels to ensure future repayment or would partially repay the debt and deposit more pledges for the balance.[88] Only very occasionally did Anna settle her debt in full.

If business life for Heriot was successful then personal matters brought sorrows. His wife, Christian, died around 1603, and there seems to have been no surviving issue from the marriage. Writing later in the seventeenth century, Sir Robert Sibbald was to claim in his 'Scotia Illustrata'[89] that two sons of George and Christian were drowned while journeying by sea to London, but no other contemporary source mentions this. However, Sibbald may have been correct, for George Heriot had at least four children,[90] but none seems to have survived long. Given the tragic circumstances of losing wife and children in a comparatively short period, it is not surprising that Heriot himself certainly felt the need to begin a new family. Having determined on a good marriage, he returned to Scotland and on 26 September 1608[91] contracted to marry Alison, eldest daughter of James Primrose, a successful lawyer who had been Clerk to the Privy Council since 1602. Alison was only sixteen, George was forty-five. Despite the disparity in ages his new wife was to exhibit a level of maturity far beyond her years and she appears to have proved an amiable and able partner. The marriage contract made provision for James Primrose to pay Heriot 5000 merks to ensure Alison was provided with 'clethying and jewallis' suitable to her station. In turn Heriot was to add 20,000 merks to be employed in purchasing land or annual rents for their mutual advantage. The marriage was registered on 24 August 1609.[92] Unfortunately Alison was to die prematurely on 16 April 1612. Heriot was devastated, especially as she was pregnant with their first child at the time of her death. He had a monument erected over her remains in the south aisle of the choir of St Gregory's parish church in London.[93]

Meantime, business continued in such volume that Heriot could not procure sufficient workmen to execute the orders placed with him. In this instance the royal connection was to prove advantageous. A Royal Proclamation was issued by Thomas Howard, Earl of Suffolk on 15 March 1609 calling upon all Mayors, Sheriffs, JPs etc in the two kingdoms to help Heriot secure the assistance he required 'for the better expediting' of 'worke for Hir Ma[jesty]'s use & service'.[94]

Soon Queen Anna was facing another of her periodic financial crises. In May 1609 she had received goods from Heriot worth 1000 guineas, but as she did not have the money to pay for them and had bought some diamond pendants and a large supply of ambergris, civet and musk worth the same amount, she ordered Heriot to pawn certain of her jewels 'of which she had lost conceit'.[95] Having resorted to such a 'humiliating practice', she remained 'melancholy and dispirited in the winter of 1609'[96] as her difficulties mounted. As before, James intervened, in December 1609 drawing £20,000 sterling immediately from the public purse to pay her debts to Heriot and others,[97] and her annual allowance was increased by £3,000 from the customs. However, by November 1611 her debts were as bad as ever.[98]

Anna's extravagance continued undiminished and as she increased her debt to George Heriot, he found himself financially overstretched. Being hard pressed by his own creditors and needing to raise money in a hurry, he turned to Adam Lawtie, a cousin and his factor in Edinburgh, to raise the requisite capital firstly by applying to his father-in-law, James Primrose, for some bonds belonging to Heriot which Primrose was holding. A lengthy and difficult correspondence between the two followed.[99] Primrose refused to hand over the documents, maintaining that a third of the property which Heriot possessed at the time of his wife's death would 'fall and appertaine to his bairnis'.[100] To prevent a family feud, Heriot offered in September 1612 to repay the 5000 merks paid as 'tocher' by Primrose under the marriage contract. Primrose reacted by claiming that he should be reimbursed for the nearly 10,000 merks expended by him on the wedding. This attempt to press Heriot for money to benefit the junior members of the Primrose family[101] led the former to insist on paying only what was legally due. It took over a year before Primrose accepted in November 1613 that he could gain no more than Heriot's original offer of 5000 merks. Even then the dispute between them continued until September 1616 when it was finally settled by the intervention of Lord Binning who persuaded Primrose to offer an apology. By this time Heriot seemed indifferent – he was just recovering from a 'heavye disease' and was hoping 'to have yet some small respitt of my lyfe'.[102]

Experiencing difficulty in raising money quickly in Edinburgh, Heriot turned to their Majesties themselves and petitioned both King and Queen for payment of outstanding debts. He pressed James for the payment of £18,000 sterling due in February 1611, reminding him of his twenty-four years' service 'without havinge ever sought or obtained any recompence for the same, as uthers of his professione and meaner deserte hes had'.[103] The sovereigns went some way to easing Heriot's immediate problems and he was able to pay off creditors in Spain and Portugal, sources of his regular supplies of precious stones and jewellery.

Anna still demanded unusual and ambitious pieces from Heriot. In November 1616 he produced a sword with a gold hilt, handle and chape, set with 428 diamonds, along with a diamond-set tablet for a picture and a round gold chain with 180 diamonds, which in total cost £1,910 sterling.[104] On the 18th of that month Heriot reckoned that Anna's outstanding debts were £4,529 sterling.[105] This was five months after he had estimated that James owed him £10,091 sterling – some of it secured in jewels but much on 'forbearance' – interest on debts which despite royal promises had remained unpaid for up to five years.[106] Financial repayment always proved a problem. During the royal fiscal embarrassment of 1616–7 Heriot was the largest and most pressing creditor but received only a small proportion of the sum outstanding.[107] Soon

Anna was forced to transfer her annual rent of £5000 from the customs revenue to Heriot over three years to repay part of her debt. This, however, only scratched the surface of the problem and Heriot was soon stressing again his financial difficulties: tactfully and cleverly he claimed that without relief 'I must undoubtedlye perish which I hope her gratious Ma[jes]tie will not suffer in regaird of my long and loyall service'. He concluded this appeal by offering to return all the Queen's jewels held by him in pawn if she would 'assigne me to fower years of the sugers . . . which notwithstandinge as God knows will fall short of what I have payed and must paye for the forbearance of the same'.[108] It was ironic that he was successful on 4 December 1620 in having the sugar farm leased to him, for Anna had died in the previous year.[109]

With old age approaching and his health declining, it was clear that Heriot, even if he did return to Edinburgh for a visit, would never live again in his property in Fishmarket Close. He therefore instructed his lawyer, James Lawtie,[110] to sell his house there in September 1615. However, legal problems over the ownership of its gallery and kitchen led to a case in the burgh court which Heriot lost. Temporarily he felt he had been 'grossley wronged' by the town,[111] a feeling heightened by the disappointing price he subsequently obtained for the property. In pique he postponed a planned visit to Edinburgh and turned his wrath on Lawtie, accusing him of appropriating part of the money.[112] Lawtie angrily denied the charges but did apologise for money lost in the delay in investing the profits. Heriot remained dissatisfied on all points, indeed 'in any that I haiv wretein to you this thre years'.[113] Lawtie was forced to defend himself against malicious gossip relayed to Heriot by those envious of his position[114] and assured Heriot in December 1621 that he had not bought various properties such as Pilrig and Gosford in East Lothian because he had no warrant to do so and 'bargains neir Edinburghe are hard'.[115]

As Heriot was already an owner of a town house in The Strand in St Martin-in-the-Fields and a country estate at Roehampton in the parish of Putney, it is not surprising that he wished to invest in Scotland. It was common practice for successful goldsmiths and merchants to acquire extensive landholding as security against the enormous debts of their aristocratic clients.[116] He seems already to have owned a gable-ended house with windows looking westwards along the Burgh Loch.[117] In September 1622 Heriot corresponded with Adam Lawtie regarding estates in Broughton and Pilrig which were on the market : three months later he was thinking about buying land in the Canongate and Canonmills. However, his deteriorating health prevented a personal inspection and he failed to get around to concluding any deals.

From 1622 the royal attempts to ally with Spain led to a determination to display an unprecedented scale of splendour, and Heriot was not one to pass up such an opportunity. Prince Charles and his retinue demanded not only heart-shaped diamond rings and bejewelled lockets for miniatures needed for a royal wooing but also buttons and other dress accessories in gold and silver.[118] Heriot's accounts refer often to delivery to Robert Hossie to be taken to Spain. Showing great business acumen, Heriot appears to have reduced his risks considerably by taking existing royal jewels in pledge as security for payment and on 9 March 1623 he accepted delivery, from Walter Alexander, gentleman usher to the prince, of sealed jewel and diamond boxes.[119]

The pace of work did not slacken as James determined to impress Spain. An order for jewels in early March 1623 was ready within two weeks.[120] Heriot even assisted with their packaging and 'sat up day and night to get them completed'.[121] A month later on 22 April he was making up thirteen diamonds from the king's secret jewel house as a jewel for the Marquis Inijosa, whose arrival, as Ambassador Extraordinary of Spain, was imminent. Heriot was also involved in their presentation on 6 May.[122]

With his health declining further, Heriot increasingly sought to give his relatives a degree of financial independence. The irregular support he had given to his sister, Margaret, was formalised in August 1618,[123] while he was paying off the debts of his niece, Janet Scott, some four months earlier.[124] He was soon helping his nephew, George Scott,[125] and another relative, Catherine Robson,[126] to whom he gave an annual pension in 1620 of £24 sterling. He took ill again in September 1623 and in a letter to Adam Lawtie expressed his fear that his niece, Franchischetta, daughter and only child of his late brother Patrick, could inherit his property contrary to his wishes.[127] Lawtie in his reply sought to reassure Heriot, who accepted that the law would ensure that his final wishes would be carried out. Heriot, seemingly satisfied, drew up a Disposition and Assignation of his property, dated 3 September 1623,[128] and followed it up with his Last Will and Testament of 10 December 1623. His health worsened rapidly and George Heriot died on 12 February 1624. He was interred in his own parish church of St Martin-in-the-Fields eight days later.[129] A large congregation, with nobility prominent, heard Rev Dr Walter Balcanquall, Dean of Rochester, pronounce Heriot's funeral oration, extolling 'his piety towards God, his love of country, his boundless liberality to his relations, his munificence to the poor, his honesty in acquiring his fortune, his wisdom in disposing of it, and his other private virtues, fidelity, probity, humanity, grave decorum, and perfect command of his temper'.[130]

By any standards Heriot was a great financial success, leaving over

£50,000 sterling. [131] Perhaps he was fortunate not to have lived longer and to have had to face the end of the economic boom in the 1630s,[132] but during his lifetime his success was based on his ability to develop a consumer-credit system with built-in controls. He never allowed any credit situation he was involved in to get totally out of hand: he let his customers go so far into debt and then he retrieved the position by forcing the pawning or pledging of items to ensure long-term security. This required special business skills which ensured his survival and success, while others failed to walk this difficult tightrope. George Heriot was not the precursor of modern bankers taking deposits,[133] for he was a more traditional goldsmith – a moneylender and pawnbroker. However, the credit club he developed in the early seventeenth century allowed James and Anna to practise self-indulgence on a massive scale.[134]

In his Disposition composed at the Strand 'nair London' Heriot assigned his property to the town of Edinburgh and first mentioned his desire to found a Hospital – 'And forsameikle as I intend be god's grace In the zeal of pietie to found and erect ane publick, pious and charitable work within the same burgh of Edinburgh to the glorie of god for the public weill and ornament of the said burgh of Edinburgh and for the honour and due regaird which I have and bears to my native soyl and mother Citie of Edinburgh forsaid'.[135] Further, it was to be 'in imitation'[136] of Christ's Hospital, which had been founded by Edward VI in 1552 to deal with the burgeoning problem of orphans[137] and foundlings in London in a period of rapid inflation and a crumbling welfare system. Three hundred and eighty children had been admitted to Christ's immediately, and within months they were dressed in the Blue Coats which had clearly made a great impression on Heriot.[138] For the London Hospital the Crown provided the land and buildings in the form of the recently dissolved Grey Friars Monastery in Newgate Street, while City individuals and livery companies provided the cash. By Heriot's time Christ's Hospital was firmly established as an orphanage as well as a school for the poorer classes[139] with a steady trickle of 'Old Blues' reaching Oxford and Cambridge.

The success story of Christ's was one which Heriot was anxious to repeat in Britain's other capital after the Union of the Crowns. To ensure this he decided to give land – 'my great tenements of land biggit and waist with the yards and pertinents' between Gray's Close and Todrick's Wynd[140] – to the town council for the Hospital building and left the bulk of his estate to ensure its financial success. He determined that the Hospital, whose name was to be left to those carrying his intentions into effect, was 'for edification, nourishing and upbringing of youth being poor orphans and fatherless children of decayit burgesses and friemen[141] of the said burgh destitute and left without means'.[142] The recipients of his benefaction were to be maintained with food, lodging and clothing, and be kept within the Hospital or sent daily to the Town's Grammar School[143] until reaching 15 years of age when they would if capable go on to college or be apprenticed to some honest trade or occupation.[144] To ensure the Hospital was properly administered Heriot determined that it should be inextricably bound up with the administration of the City, for the Provost, Baillies and Council were to be the 'administrators, directors, guyders, governors and rulers'[145] of the institution, with the ministers of the Town to be its 'overseers, inspectors and visitors'.[146] He hoped also to encourage others to follow his example and found other charitable works.[147] However, if the administrators failed in their task and were held to be guilty of maladministration or tried to sell the building, they were to forfeit all rights.[148]

In his Disposition a number of legacies to his closest relatives were specified[149] and Heriot intimated that others would be contained in a later Will. However, the description of the Hospital in the Disposition occupied 22 lines, while it only obtained six lines in his Will. The rules for the government of the Hospital were to be left to the Statutes.

Three months later on 10 December 1623 Heriot, although 'weak of body', finalised his Will with 'guid and perfyte rememberence'.[150] It went further in detailing the specific bequests which Heriot left to his nearest and dearest. His niece, Franchischetta,[151] was given 500 merks, while legacies were left to his stepbrothers – James, who succeeded him as court jeweller to Charles I on 21 September, 1627, and Thomas, his stepmother Christian Blaw, his stepsisters, Christian, Sibilla (Isobel), Janet and Marion, relations on the Primrose side, and his servants.[152] He also provided for his natural daughters – Elizabeth Band (born 1613) and Margaret Scott (born 1619).[153] He left £20 sterling to the poor of the French Reformed Congregation of London, where Gilbert Primrose[154] was a preacher, and £10 sterling to the poor of St Martin-in-the-Fields. Importantly, he nominated as executors of his Will his 'very loving and kynd friends'[155] – Robert Johnstone, lawyer and gentleman; William Terrie,[156] goldsmith; and Gideon De Laune, apothecary, and bequethed them 100 merks sterling each.[157] Added to them were James Maxwell of the Bed Chamber, Revd Dr Walter Balcanquall, Master of the Savoy,[158] and Walter Alexander, gentleman usher to the Prince of Wales, who as 'worthie guid freindis' were to be 'overseers' or 'supervisors'.[159] All of them were also given legacies – that of Maxwell larger than the others, suggesting a prime role for him in the recovery of debts needed before the Hospital could begin.

After all these arrangements the residue of his estate was to go 'towards the founding and erecting of an Hospital within the said Town of Edinburgh in perpetuitie'.[160] This Hospital was 'for the maintainence, relief, bringing up and education of so many poor fatherless boys, friemen's sons of that town of Edinburgh' [161] as his legacy could cope with. 'And my will and mynd is that the said hospitall sall be there erected and governed and the said fatherless children ordered taught and guyded by such institutions, ordinances and directions and in suche maner and forms as sall be digested, limitate, appoyntit or sett down in a certane buik or writing framed and ordanyed for that purpose either by myself in my lifetyme and signed with my hand or be the said Mr Doctor Balcanquall after my death and signed by his hand and delivered unto the said provost, baillies, Ministers and Counsell of the aforsaid town of Edinburgh',[162] who in turn were to be the Governors of the Hospital.[163]

The executors were given six months to draw up a true Inventory of Heriot's debts and accounts and deliver to the town council all surpluses. If the latter body failed to carry out Heriot's instructions, it was now specified that the monies should be given over to the maintenance of poor scholars at St Andrews,[164] Scotland's oldest university.

As death approached, Heriot thought further about the complex arrangements that he had set out. On 21 January 1624[165] he added a codicil to his Will. In it he determined on an even more pivotal role for Balcanquall.[166] He was requested to repair as soon as possible to Edinburgh after Heriot's death and was given 'absolute power to treit and conclude',[167] with the Provost and elected representatives of Edinburgh, the arrangements for the Hospital. Balcanquall was to ensure Heriot's Will was put into effect in all regards. As an incentive he was given a further £100 sterling, the second instalment of which was only to be paid when the Hospital was 'fullie and absolutlie finischit'. If Balcanquall failed in this task, provision was made to ensure others (who included Robert Balcanquall, minister of Tranent) would take his place. Heriot also added a number of other bequests, the most significant of which was the maintenance of ten bursars in the College of Edinburgh at £5 sterling each per annum.[168] Although these were later to assume some significance, it can be argued that their inclusion in the codicil was something of an afterthought.

The leading executor, Robert Johnstone, wrote from London on 23 February 1624 informing the town council of Edinburgh of the death of Heriot and his stipulated arrangements. Although he estimated the legacy left to the Town to be about £11,000 sterling for erecting and maintaining the 'hospitall for orphans', Johnstone suggested that the final figure could be even greater once all the expenses, other legacies and debts had been finalised. Appreciating the delicacy of the situation, he assured the Council that all three executors were 'honest men' and it could 'expecte faire dealing' from them. No jewels, which made up the bulk of the estate, would be disposed of until the Council was satisfied with the valuation arrangements. He awaited further instructions.[169]

The town council of Edinburgh met on 5 March 1624 to discuss the implications of the Will and to appoint a delegation with power to meet the executors. After all, George Heriot's large legacy was 'an event of great importance to the Council'.[170] It delegated John Hay, advocate and Town Clerk of the City, as its commissioner 'with full power'[171] to act on its behalf. With Heriot's three executors and three overseers all in England, Hay travelled immediately to London: by the end of the month he had returned and reported back to another Council meeting. Hay gave over the details of the Assignation and Disposition and the 'particular Contracts, bands and sums of money therein contained'.[172] He had completed his first task. However, the scale of the problems still to be overcome was alluded to in a letter from Robert Johnstone on 22 March. He had delivered Heriot's assignations and full inventories to Hay but he asked the town council to take charge of discharging debts and legacies, so relieving the executors of 'a heavie burden' and avoiding 'all jealousie' which could result from disposing of the jewels at values which were the subject of varying opinion. Johnstone stressed the need to avoid delay, which would result in clamour and discontentment. Meantime, the executors had given them exact inventories and sealed all cabinets with keys in several men's custodies to prevent fraud or deceit.[173]

At the same time on 22 March Balcanquall wrote from Savoy, pleased with the choice of Hay whom he deemed 'so skillfull and faithfull a commissioner'. He was anxious that the town council should go ahead 'with all possible speed' with purchasing land and he hoped for more than £20,000 sterling for the charitable institution. He also asked that he be kept informed 'from tyme to tyme' of the progress being made.[174] Given such encouragement, the town council commissioned Hay along with John Maknacht, merchant, and Gilbert Kirkwood, Deacon of the Goldsmiths, on 30 March 1624 to 'ask, demand, levy, recover and receive'[175] from Heriot's executors all moveable goods, estate papers and sums of money left to the Town. They were given powers of attorney with full authority to appraise, auction and sell all property given over.

The first Inventory was ready by 28 April. It involved rubies, opals, emeralds, sapphires, diamonds – in the form of garters, pendants, hatbands, bracelets, necklaces, rings – and the total appraised value, according to Jacob Hardnet, Simon Gibbon and David Papillon, three well-known London jewellers, was £12,137. 12/10 sterling.[176] This was a working stock, with many loose stones – and as such was more than one-third of Heriot's net worth – kept in his house at Roehampton, resulting from Heriot's reliance on a high level of reserve to gain personal credit, employ workmen or buy expensive materials.

A more problematic issue for Hay was the Inventory of Debts owed to Heriot. It was calculated that James VI and I had incurred debts of £8,875. 17/4[177] during 1622–3; that the Duke of Buckingham, the King's favourite, had borrowed £2,566.10/7[178] to finance a Spanish trip; and that a number of other debts owed by nobility and gentry amounted to £20,718. -/6.[179] The recovery of these debts was to prove a stumbling block to the rapid realisation of the wish to build a hospital. The distance between London and Edinburgh also aggravated the situation, with Hay having to go to and fro to expedite his commission. To help Hay, Sir Robert Johnstone was asked to speak to the King and Buckingham's executors about debt repayment.[180]

The passage of time and lack of up-to-date information began to worry Balcanquall in the Savoy. He wrote on 26 June 1624 to the town council to find out what was happening. He complained that he had 'receaved none answers' despite his previous appeal to be kept informed of progress and was concerned that the executors (of whom he was not one) kept their proceedings secret from the overseers, Heriot's relations and friends. The first he knew of jewels being sold was when James Heriot complained to him that the executors had sold a jewel at too low a price. Balcanquall wanted reassurance about the transactions between the town council and executors,[181] as he jealously guarded the special position Heriot had given him.

Further correspondence of the time also highlighted the distrust felt on all sides. The executors were soon embroiled in a wrangle with Heriot's old servants. Accusations and counter-accusations began to circulate. William Adamson, who claimed in a letter of July 1624 to have served George Heriot for four and a half years 'without any staine, blame or imputatione', was perhaps jealous of his master's generosity to other servants,[182] and wrote to the town council firstly on 16 April 1624 attacking Johnstone whom he accused of making 'ciphers' of the other executors and overseers.[183] In another letter on 31 July 1624 he claimed that despite his co-operation with John Hay, Johnstone had accused him of falsifying accounts and hiding an inventory book. Although such claims were never proved, Adamson was forced to wait to have his claims for house and funeral expenses paid. Eventually he turned to the High Court of Chancery and on 16 March 1626 the executors were ordered to pay the outstanding sum of £16 to him.[184]

In his correspondence Adamson also warned the executors that Heriot's niece and her husband were on their way from Italy to try to overturn the Disposition. The town council appreciated the danger and on 11 October 1624 it ordered Hay to go to London to negotiate with Franchischetta, 'allegdit neice',[185] and her husband, John Cesaris (Crerar), who had arrived from Genoa. Both parties appreciated the problems. Hay had complications enough in trying to persuade the executors to speed up their transactions without a long wrangle with relatives of Heriot which would delay the process further. Crerar understood that Heriot had specifically provided in his Will that any who tried to thwart his intentions should 'forever lose all and everie such legacie' sought.[186] Compromise was the order of the day. By 8 December Hay was reporting to the Council that the Crerars had ratified the Will and had accepted 4000 merks Scots for doing so.[187]

At a meeting on 23 August the town council had confidently agreed to follow the advice of Heriot's Executors that the payments to George Heriot's mother and three half-sisters should include interest backdated to the date of the Will.[188] With the realisation of Scottish legacies underway it then dispatched Hay again to London on 15 November 'to crave compt reckoning and payment' from the executors of money still owed to it.[189] In particular, Hay was to press for payment from His Majesty, the Duke of Buckingham and Sir Anthony Thomas.[190] This was to prove extremely difficult, and early in the New Year on 3 January Hay wrote to the town council for advice on how to proceed. It replied on 19 January 1626, pressing him to insist on repayment and urging him to be diligent in selling off jewels. If he was able to collect any surplus revenue, it was to be used to pay off any existing debts.[191]

Hay did not have his problems to seek. He had arrived in London on 13 December 1625 and seen Johnstone three days later. He did have an audience with Charles I on 20 December, but there was to be no discussion of private matters until after his Coronation. Not surprisingly, Hay became increasingly frustrated and exasperated by the continual delays. As he awaited the forthcoming Coronation, Hay spent his time going through the huge Inventory of unsold jewels in the hope of expediting large sales. Unfortunately what seemed an ideal opportunity proved a great disappointment, for corslets rather than jewels were in great demand. However, although he did make some headway with the Executors after spending a morning with all three,[192] he was forced to turn to the King's jeweller, William

Ward, and sold him a large part of the disposal stock in February 1626 for £5,250 sterling before returning to Edinburgh.[193]

Hay was sent south again in September in an attempt to finalise matters.[194] He reported that the debts had 'not been gathered in so diligentlie by the Executors as was expected'.[195] De Laune had been ill, Terrie had broken a rib in his side, while Heriot's niece, Franchischetta, continued to cause problems:[196] only Balcanquall appeared to have been doing all he could to assist. The town council's patience was running out: there was a growing feeling that the executors were dragging their feet, and on 19 January 1627 Hay was told to put an 'end to that business the best he can'.[197] Hay must have been pleased with such instructions, for he had already made five separate journeys to London on Heriot business, and to keep his enthusiasm kindled in May 1627 he was paid 3,200 merks for his 'pains and trouble'.[198] He rapidly concluded matters with the executors. The final sum paid over to him was £23,625 10s 3½d. sterling, less than at one time had been expected but more than the original estimates, and seemingly adequate to bring to fruition Heriot's wishes.[199] (See Appendix 7.)

The settlement prompted Balcanquall to make his long-promised visit to Edinburgh. He arrived in June 1627 ready to fulfil his obligations. On 6 June the town council, in its turn, determined to confer with him on 'the frame of the Hospital to be foundit'.[200] It had already been preparing itself by ensuring that when discussing Heriot business as 'Governors', its meetings were conducted in a set, ordered fashion, with the senior minister present opening the meeting with a prayer and the youngest minister closing it. About twenty-five representatives, consisting of baillies, treasurer, councillors, merchants and deacons of crafts, attended the average meeting, chaired by the Lord Provost.

At an important gathering of the Governors on 22 June 1627 chaired by Provost David Aikinheid, it was reported that Balcanquall, now Dean of Rochester, had, with the Council members, 'viewed . . . the tenementis' specified by Heriot in his will for the proposed Hospital. They had been unimpressed: following examination these were deemed 'uncapable of so great a work' envisaged, which would include orchards, gardens and walks. [201] Perhaps this implies that Balcanquall brought with him a grandiose plan which reflected the extent of the bequest now available, or perhaps it reflected a new realisation that Heriot's original site did not do real justice to the Hospital now being planned. Certainly the town council was 'all in ane voyce'[202] that the ruinous buildings were unsuitable as they stood, and that their complete replacement would be more expensive than building afresh elsewhere in a more spacious and healthy site. As the latter option was preferred the more elevated and open field of eight and a half acres of the Hie Riggs, recently bought by the City from Sir George Touris of Inverleith, outwith the City Wall and adjoining Greyfriars' Churchyard, was considered more suitable. The governors of the Hospital bought the land for 7,600 merks for the project,[203] expecting that the work would go ahead 'with all expedition'.[204] On 22 June 1627 Nicoll Udwart was elected third treasurer of the Hospital for the building work, and following Heriot's prudent financial practices it was agreed that the Hospital would be built from the rents of the monies, lands and tenements, leaving the original capital intact. Although this made sound financial sense it was to prolong significantly the period taken to build the Hospital.[205]

The Hospital building was expected to start on 15 March 1628 and 'all to be done conforme to the paterne and prescript maid be the said Dean of Rochester with adyvse of the saids provost, baillies, Ministers and Counsell.'[206] According to Sir John Summerson,[207] Balcanquall 'determined the general lines of the plan – a hollow square with corner pavilions, and staircase turrets in the inner angles, the main entrance in the centre of one side, the chapel immediately opposite. This plan plainly derives from a house illustrated by Serlio in his seventh book'.[208] It appears, then, that Balcanquall's pattern was based on a plan for a Mediterranean villa known as 'Il Rosmarino' in Provence.[209]

It seems probable that Balcanquall placed this plan before the governors in June 1627, and this was confirmed in Chapter 1 of his 'Statutes' which pressed for the Hospital to be completed as soon as possible and 'that conforme to the paterne given be him to thaime to that effect'. His plan included internal as well as external arrangements, and the Statutes, written before the Hospital was founded, refer to the various apartments, suggesting that Balcanquall had detailed proposals before him at that time.

The 'Statutis' of the Hospital, which Balcanquall presented to the Governors on 4 July 1627, were a decisive contribution to the history of the Hospital. He left nothing to the imagination: every detail was prescribed. Each page was signed by Balcanquall and they were contained in a leather embossed case.[210] In return he received a gratuity 'for his paines'[211] and expenses, and he was also paid his outstanding legacy. At a meeting on the morning of 13 July the town council sanctioned Nicoll Udwart 'to fraught ane ship to bring home jeasting and other commodious tymber for their wark.'[212] In the afternoon

OVERLEAF.
These plans of ground and first floors show Heriot's Hospital to be the first completely regular design in Scotland with four equal ranges of buildings disposed round a central quadrangle.

HERIOT'S HOSPITAL, EDINBURGH.

GROUND PLAN

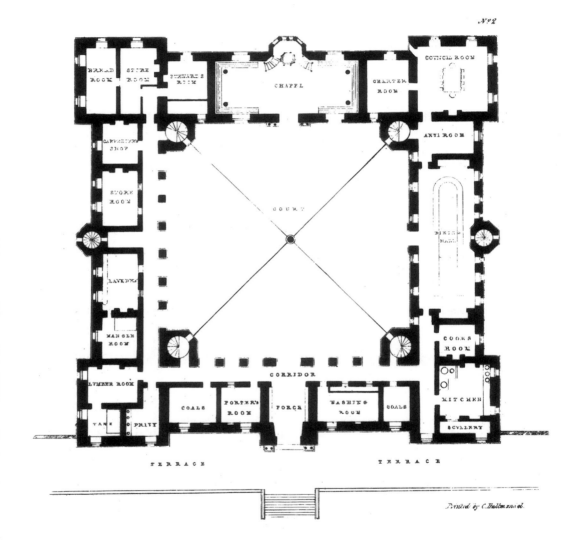

BREAD ROOM

STORE ROOM

STEWART'S ROOM

CHAPEL

CHARTER ROOM

COUNCIL ROOM

CARPENTER'S SHOP

ANTI ROOM

STORE ROOM

COURT

DINING HALL

LAUNDRY

MANGLE ROOM

COOK'S ROOM

LUMBER ROOM

CORRIDOR

KITCHEN

TANK

PRIVY

COALS

PORTER'S ROOM

FORGE

WASHING ROOM

COALS

SCULLERY

TERRACE

TERRACE

Printed by C. Hullmandel.

HERIOT'S HOSPITAL EDINBVRGH

FIRST FLOOR PLAN

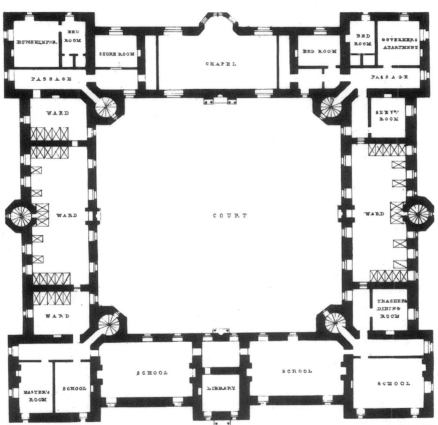

HOVSEKEEPER · BED ROOM · STORE ROOM · CHAPEL · BED ROOM · BED ROOM · GOVERNERS APARTMENT

PASSAGE · PASSAGE

WARD · SERVTS ROOM

WARD · COURT · WARD

WARD · TEACHERS DINING ROOM

MASTER'S ROOM · SCHOOL · SCHOOL · LIBRARY · SCHOOL · SCHOOL

Printed by C. Hullmandel.

of the same day the same individuals convened as 'Guiders and Governors of the Hospital' and accepted Balcanquall's 'buik of Statuttis underwritten subscribit with his hand and seallit with his seale'.[213] The Governors considered their content but following Heriot's instructions accepted the Statutes without amendment 'for them and their successors in all time'.[214]

The twenty-three chapters of the Statutes were then detailed in the Records.[215] They set the tone and the ethos for the Hospital. Prayers were to be said morning and evening, with a service every morning between 7 and 8 a.m. (Chapter XXI): the Chapel was to be central in Hospital life. The first Monday in June every year was to be kept for a 'solemn celebration and thanksgiving' for George Heriot (Chapter II) with a sermon on charitable maintenance to be given by Edinburgh ministers in Greyfriars' Church (the Church also being used every Sunday). The treasurer was to have a pivotal role : he was to be an 'able man' elected annually (Chapter V), with four auditors certifying his accounts every three months (Chapter VI). The Clerk or Registrar, elected for life, was to deal with legal and administrative matters (Chapter VII). The Master was to have a single vote and voice in the governing body: he was to be an unmarried God-fearing man who had led an honest life, and it was his duty to instruct the scholars three times a week in their catechism and to control the other Hospital staff. He was not to meddle in points of divinity, and was to read only the prayers delivered to him and not give his own (Chapter IX). Under the Master would be a Schoolmaster who would teach the scholars to read and write Scots distinctly, to cypher and cast all manner of accounts and also Latin rudiments 'but no further'.[216] Then at the age of ten or eleven they would have no further Hospital instruction, but would be sent out to the Grammar School.[217] The scholars of the Hospital would be the poor children of 'Burgesses and friemen'[218] of Edinburgh and the object of the Hospital was to relieve the poor: significantly, Balcanquall appears to have deliberately omitted Heriot's emphasis on 'fatherless' boys.[219] They would be between seven and sixteen years of age.[220] At the latter age it was expected that they would be apprenticed to a trade, but a few 'hopeful scholars' would go on to College for a further four years' study (Chapter XIII).[221] The scholars were to be elected twice a year – in April and October. Detailed job descriptions of butler, cook, caterer, porter, gardener and six unmarried women for domestic duties were included in Chapters XIV to XIX respectively. Provision was also made for a doctor of physick to deal with the sick and an apothecary for the supply of drugs (Chapter XX). An oath specified in Chapter III of the document was being taken by the governors within a month of their being handed over. Any controversy in interpretation of the Statutes was to be settled by recourse to those specified in Heriot's will, viz., any three of the Lord Chancellor, the two Archbishops of the Episcopalian Church, the Lord President of the College of Justice and the Lord Advocate (Chapter XXII).

The Statutes were comprehensive in their content and were to be the yardstick for the workings of the Hospital for over two and a half centuries. That they were to last so long, and be referred to so much, was a testimony to their common sense. Significantly, although Chapter 1 of the Statutes implied that the 'paterne' had already been given over, Balcanquall did not explicitly claim to have created it. Given that at the beginning of the Statutes, in Chapter IV, again twice in Chapter XXII, in Chapter XXIII and in signing and putting his seal on the Statutes, he reiterated that he was their 'compiler', it seems likely that if Balcanquall had been the architect of the Hospital he would have boasted of the fact. This he never did. In fact, his legacy is not the building, but the Statutes themselves for, being the first in Scotland, he had no precedents to follow. Although Heriot had seen Christ's Hospital as the model for his own Hospital in Edinburgh, Balcanquall used sparingly the former's ordinances and rules which had been laid down in 1557. The 'faint resemblances'[222] in the constitutions could owe something to a connection that both Balcanquall and Christ's had with the Savoy. Allowing that they were similar in intention one is impressed more by the differences than by the similarities with the Statutes produced by Balcanquall.[223] Unlike Heriot's, Christ's tended to admit its boys from the clergy and lesser professions. Heriot scholars were to be dressed in 'sad, russet cloathe doublettis breikis, and stockingsis or hose and gowns of the same colour, with black hattis and stringis' (Chapter XIII). Balcanquall did not follow the blue and yellow of Christ's, and allowed Heriot boys a hat (with strings) because of the inclement weather.

It can be assumed that the example of George Heriot as a 'prototype'[224] encouraged the Hutcheson brothers in their venture in Glasgow. George Hutcheson's 'Draft Contract' and Thomas Hutcheson's Mortification indicated a wish to found a Hospital for the fatherless and motherless poor and to bind it to Glasgow. In their case the close link between Hospital and City led to the bankruptcy of the former by the latter in 1654, but it was also responsible for preserving the Hospital's existence, ensuring that it began to take in boys again in 1661. Perhaps the opening of Heriot's for business in 1659 was an important stimulus to this revival of schooling in the west. Certainly Glasgow did not wish to be left behind Edinburgh in this respect as the new notion of civic pride developed. An important demonstration of this was the ruling by Glasgow City Fathers in 1667 that the Master at Hutchesons' Hospital be paid more than his equivalent at Heriot's – in this case £20 sterling per annum as opposed to the £17 sterling being paid in Edinburgh.[225]

As in the Heriot case, there were times at Hutchesons' Hospital when the duties of the municipal dignitaries controlling the bequest conflicted with their duties as trustees and the interests of the Hospital were seemingly of secondary importance. Nonetheless in both cases the funds of the Hospitals greatly increased. Between 1641 – when the Hutcheson brothers left £4,000 sterling for their Hospital – and 1880, the original capital had grown to £373,000 with an annual revenue of £18,000. To the credit of Hutchesons' their Preceptor – the manager of its trust – performed his duties gratuitously from 1641 until 1709, when James Sloss, with nine years' service, was given 200 pounds Scots for his 'extraordinary services'. It only became a paid office in 1789. Such control of finances compares most favourably with the almost extravagant expenditure of the Heriot Governors on high wages, salaries and pensions.

The Governors of both Heriot's and Hutchesons' Hospitals were successful in their policies of buying land as an investment for the future. In the case of Heriot's, as early as 5 July 1625 John Hay and three other commissioners bought an estate in Broughton from Thomas Flyming and the lands at Lochflatt from John Maxwell for the Heriot's Trust.[226] Yet there were other ways in which, in a country like Scotland, just rising into increased commercial and agricultural activity, trust funds could be laid out to advantage. The funds of John Watson's Institution were increased from the £4,000 left by the founder in 1759 to more than £120,000 in 1824. The management of this fund by the Commissioners of the Signet ranks comparison with both Heriot and Hutcheson administration. Credit then must be given to the trustees of all such legacies, but in the case of Heriot's the impression is one of governors conscious of their inheritance but also aware that the interests of the Town, and occasionally their own interests, were as important.

Indeed, one of the early decisions of the town council was to have lasting consequences for Heriot's Hospital. It determined that its own treasurer, George Suttie, should be elected treasurer of the Hospital to ensure that a proper record of all transactions was kept and audited. This guaranteed no financial independence for Heriot's and, although natural at the time, was to have far-reaching results – usually detrimental – for the Hospital.

Given the legacy of Heriot it was not surprising that he was chosen by Sir Walter Scott as a hero for *The Fortunes of Nigel*. As 'worth of character,

goodness of heart, and rectitude of principle' were the qualities he desired most to emphasise, Scott 'made free with the name of a person who has left the most magnificent proofs of his benevolence and charity that the capital has to display'.[227] It was Scott who, in the early nineteenth century, popularised Heriot as 'Jingling Geordie '[228] both north and south of the border. He viewed him as representing the new age of trade and commerce, while at the same time respecting and valuing the manners of the feudal past. The novel succeeded precisely because Heriot was properly deemed to personify traditional virtues while simultaneously being in tune with the needs of a changing Scotland.[229] It was another Scott triumph: by 10 a.m. on its morning of publication in May 1822, the publisher, Archibald Constable, had sold 7,000 copies from his London outlet in Cheapside.[230] As a historical novelist Scott raised the profile of George Heriot, and it seemed only proper that when the Scott monument was erected in April 1854 a miniature statue of Heriot, with a model of the 'Wark' in his left hand, was placed conspicuously at its south-west corner.[231]

The Dick Sheppard Memorial Chapel is on the south side of the Crypt of St Martin-in-the-Fields, London. Over the altar hangs a lamp which burns perpetually in memory of George Heriot, whose burial place lies nearby. Every Founder's Day a short memorial service is held in the Chapel.

If Scott raised awareness of Heriot in the nineteenth century it was Nigel Tranter (1909–2000) who added to his reputation more recently. Tranter had attended Heriot's School as a pupil between 1917 and 1927, and throughout his life he retained 'the liveliest affection' for his old school.[232] His prolific writings contain myriad references to George Heriot, but the major tributes are to be found in the humorous and affectionate characterisation of Jinglin' Geordie and his relations with James VI and I in *The Wisest Fool* (1974) and *Poetic Justice* (1996). In these works Heriot's standing and character were enhanced[233] and he and his legacy continued to be admired just as they had been in previous centuries.

CHAPTER TWO

The 'Wark'[1]

Following the orders of the town council the Hospital treasurer, Nicoll Udwart, on 14 July 1627 commissioned the Leith shipowners, David Robertson and James Bannatyne the younger, to transport a shipload of large timber from 'Norroway'. In the event, the ship was so packed that it had to leave behind some of its cargo but the remainder was stored on arrival in Leith until it was needed at the site (in 1629). The Account was tendered and Udwart paid £756 13s. 4d. on 7 September. One assumes that Bannatyne, in particular, ensured the completion of the order, for in January 1628 he was paid 100 merks 'for his painis taken in bringing home the timber from Gottenberrie'.[2]

The governors rightly saw the building of the Hospital as a prestigious project, and they determined to employ a man of experience and standing as designer and contractor. By 14 September 1627 they had chosen William Wallace, who had been appointed principal master-mason to all the King's works in Scotland in April 1617,[3] just before his production of moulds for the ornamental plaster ceilings in Edinburgh Castle. He had also carried out carving work in the Great Hall in Stirling Castle, and although primarily responsible for the general supervision of the building operations for the north wing of Linlithgow Palace (1618–20) he personally involved himself in work on the stone firepaces and window pediments.[4] Such elaborate strapwork ornament was developed further by him at Heriot's. He was known also for his involvement at Winton House, East Lothian,[5] whose richly fluted chimneys were to be copied at Heriot's by Wallace's successors, and at Moray House in the Canongate.[6]

Udwart's Accounts give a clear picture of the progress made with the fabric of the Hospital. Wallace was mentioned for the first time on 22 January 1628[7] when he was paid for measuring the ground and for filling in the ditch at the Town Wall (which had to be extended to accommodate the Hospital) and he was given his first week's payment on 8 March.[8] Andrew Davidson was appointed overseer of the work on 19 May at £3 (Scots) weekly. Given that Wallace was at this time being paid exactly double that amount (as for

‡   29

example on 5 April and again on 31 May), he occupied a predominant position. On 3 June the governors were present as the final preparations of the ground were begun and the first sod turned, and throughout the month Wallace appears to have been on site continuously. All was made ready for the foundation ceremony, and on 1 July 1628 'In ye name of God, We begane to lay the ground-stane on ane Tyisday eftir ye Sermone, and I gaive in drink-silver to the Maister-Maissone [Wallace] and his Companiones at the founding ye Wark, tua rosnobillis, is £21 6s. 8d.'[9] As a later writer commented: 'If they did not pray for Heriot's soul, we may readily believe they drank his health.'[10]

During July 1628, Wallace was supported by Robert Short and James Gilbert[11] and eight other masons, each being paid £3 12s. (Scots) a week.[12] Stone was brought in during August from Ravelstone.[13] On 16 August 'given to the Deacone [Wallace] and maissones to drink, at the laying of the Soll of the grait Entrie, and the cruikis imputting to it . . . 30s.'[14] On 20 September and again on 15 October Wallace appears to have been employing twelve other masons (again at £3 12s. Scots each per week).[15] However, Wallace was in demand elsewhere and this led to frequent absences from the 'wark' which led the governors on 1 January 1629 to pay him £6 13s. 4d. (Scots) 'at his entrie to the work agane',[16] perhaps as an incentive to keep him on site. He certainly appeared to have taken the hint and was on hand during January, when he took delivery of a vast quantity of Ravelstone stone.[17] He progressed the building;[18] the 'Eist Quarter' was begun at the end of March

The Foundation Stone of Heriot's Hospital, dated 1 July 1628, was laid after a special ceremony at the north-west corner of 'the Wark'.

1629,[19] with the first 'irone wyndowis' put up on 23 May.[20] Work on the kitchen was completed during the summer, and the 'Wester Quarter' was begun on 1 August.[21]

Looking at the period from October 1628 to March 1629 Wallace was paid for usually three, sometimes four, days per week, and this despite an illness in early February.[22] He then, according to the sums being paid out, appears to have been more regular in his attendance and in appreciation on 3 August 1629 Udwart was ordered to pay to Wallace 'Maister Maisone and Maister of Wark to the Hospital . . . for his bygone painis and extraordinarie service done in the frame and building of the said wark this year bygone the sum of ane hundreth pund.'[23] It does seem that the governors saw Wallace as indispensable in executing Balcanquall's general plan from Serlio's design, with the many other masons involved seen, with one exception, as mere assistants. The exception – William Aytoun, maisone – was named in the accounts for the first time in 1629 and assumed prominence as Wallace's right-hand man.[24]

Wallace acquired a boy apprentice and his wage was increased to £7 10s. a week to cover this.[25] On 11 June 1630 'for the key aill, quhen the grait Oger pend of the Foir Entrie was put over . . . 58s.'.[26] On 27 September Wallace was paid 100 merks for his work of the previous year, with Aytoun named as 'his extraordinar'.[27] Wallace probably needed to remind the governors that he had been given a gratuity of £100 the previous year, for on 11 October he was given another 50 merks.[28] On 28 March 1631 James Macmath was appointed an overseer and maister of wark at £4 a week. The following month saw work being done on the chapel doorway, and by May some 23 masons were being employed.[29] The well in the centre of the pend was being dug by September. Meantime on 1 August Wallace was paid his annual 100 punds for his bygone pains and to ensure his continued attendance on site. The final weekly payment was made to him on 29 October 1631, as it would appear that he died suddenly shortly afterwards.[30] Treasurer Robert Halieburton appears to have visited Wallace on his sick bed and was 'directit be the counsell to get the modell of the work'.[31] On 21 November his widow, Agnes Blackhall,[32] left with young children to support, handed over his 'haill mouldis and drauchtis' to the governors in exchange for a gratuity of 200 merks, which symbolised their regard for Wallace and the 'extraordinarie painis and great care' he had taken of the 'wark' through his advice and in its building.[33]

Wallace's mason mark – a saltire cross with a heart at the top right arm – is found only on the ground floor of the Hospital courtyard, especially on the pilastered north arcade.[34] With the bulk of the building still to complete it was natural for the governors to choose as Wallace's successor the man on the site

already, William Aytoun, whose portrait still remains in the Hospital.[35] A stringent contract, dated 5 December 1631 and signed on 13 February 1632, spelled out his role.[36] It committed Aytoun to carve himself and direct the work of others; to take forward 'the modell' already begun and significantly 'to doe and performe all and quhatsumevier ungle William Wallace last Maister Maissone at the said work ather did or intendit to be done at the same'. Although Aytoun seems to have accepted the pattern set down, there is a difference between the style of the ground floor of the Hospital completed by Wallace and the 'more daring style of ornament on the upper storey, where many of the pediments are broken' and bolder.[37] Aytoun specialised more in fine ornamental detail and his more varied and elaborate work is in contrast to that of Wallace.[38] By May 1632 Aytoun was leading a team of at least forty masons working on the site.

Although recent historiography has emphasised the predominant role of Wallace in the design and building of the Hospital, previous generations had a different view. In the later eighteenth century, beginning with Hugo Arnot,[39] the belief grew up that Inigo Jones was the architect, although older authorities had made no mention of him. Arnott's book was well received and his view was soon adopted by others. In 1845, in the standard authoritative history, the Revd Dr William Steven claimed that 'the reputed architect was Inigo Jones' despite the 'remarkable' fact that the name of Jones appeared nowhere in the extensive records or other documents of the Hospital.[40] However, such an omission was most

William Wallace, the King's master-mason, was on site from March 1628 and was instrumental in taking forward the general plan provided. His mason's mark is found only on the ground floor of the building.

damaging to the claims of Jones. Given the meticulousness of George Heriot and the pride of the town council in their City, if the celebrated Jones had been involved then it seems extremely likely that it would have been documented.

Steven was, however, probably more accurate when stressing the similarity between Frederiksborg in Denmark with the Hospital (although Steven thought that too was a work of Jones!).[41] The marriage of James VI and Anna, beloved sister of the great Danish builder, Christian IV, led to links with architectural consequences. Kronborg Slot had just been completed and its north wing housed the Scottish couple during their 1590 visit. The royal entourage, which included William Schaw, Master of Work, must have been impressed, and it is perhaps no coincidence that the positioning and architecture of the chapel at Heriot's follows the Kronborg style of triumphal arch entrance and oriel window.[42] Frederiksborg was begun in 1602 and Rosenborg Palace around 1613–15 and these provided the 'closest parallel'[43] to Scottish developments. Significantly Christian IV relied heavily on his Netherlandish masons.[44]

Inadvertently, Steven had begun a controversy. The issue was taken up by David Laing, treasurer to the Society of Antiquaries of Scotland,[45] who examined all the available primary evidence and concluded that Wallace was 'no ordinary builder', but was the architect. The governors were concerned that this conclusion, produced within a very few years of the official History, contradicted Steven's version. One of their number, Councillor Robert Ritchie, pressed for an inquiry,[46] and on 28 October 1853 the governors decided that a house committee should examine the Statutes and other documentary evidence. It reported on 7 September 1854 in a 32-page booklet which was printed and circulated.[47] Surprisingly, it added little to previous knowledge and so unsurprisingly it came to no definitive conclusion. As the 'official' version it resurrected the claims of Jones and Balcanquall and played down the role of Wallace, stressing the presumptive evidence for the 'traditional' view.

Such an unsatisfactory conclusion meant that the issue remained alive. On 23 July 1856 it erupted again at a meeting of the Archaeological Institute in Edinburgh, when Laing was overwhelmingly supported in his contention that Wallace was the architect. The governors did not welcome such intrusions into their domain, and Councillor Ritchie issued a riposte in a sequel report of another 32 pages in late 1856. He still contended that a plan of the Hospital was in existence before Wallace was employed as master-mason, which meant that Jones and Balcanquall, who were contemporaries,

had stronger claims to be the architects of the Hospital. Given this scenario it was more likely that the architect (Jones) rather than the divine (Balcanquall) would have been the author of so great a work.[48]

However, the classic architectural treatises of the nineteenth century remained unconvinced. R.W. Billings[49] contrasted the building's symmetry with its seemingly 'piecemeal' design. He saw Wallace and Aytoun as the original architects, with Andrew Davidson also important as a master-mason in daily decision-making. MacGibbon and Ross,[50] too, stressed the great freedom Wallace had in the construction of the Hospital, finding that he was more than a 'mere ordinary builder'. Contemporaneously Hippolyte J. Blanc[51] dismissed Balcanquall as not having the energy or the expertise to have been the architect and discounted Jones too. As Wallace was being paid comparatively large sums to encourage him to spend more time at Heriot's and less on other Crown business, he was the clear architect. By the time of Blanc's address at the fourth annual meeting of the Old Edinburgh Club[52] he was suggesting that Wallace was probably from Tranent before he was made a burgess of Edinburgh on 21 November 1621.[53] As Wallace had been employed locally he would have been recommended by his clerical brother at Tranent to Dr Balcanquall, whose brother was also a minister at Tranent. With the architectural features of the neighbourhood resembling each other markedly and matching the details of the Hospital[54] it was Blanc's conclusion that they were all by the same architect. As the term 'master-mason' was used until the later seventeenth century when the term 'architect' was substituted, Wallace's claim to be the architect was 'incontestable'.

Clement Gunn, writing probably in 1902, followed Laing and Blanc and placed Wallace in his historical context. Given Wallace's residence in Edinburgh from November 1621, when he was elected a burgess, and his position as 'Deacon'[55] by September 1624, it can be assumed that Wallace 'was both a well-known and esteemed citizen' as well as one 'capable of occupying responsible office'. Gunn also stressed Wallace's previous works at Edinburgh and Linlithgow[56] with octagonal staircase turrets, enriched pedimented windows and embattled parapets. As royal master-mason from 1617, Wallace was a 'devizer' of buildings and the sums of money he received from the governors proved his services were of a professional character. His importance explained the determination of the governors to win him back from his independent practice and their dependence upon his personal attention. For Gunn, Heriot's Hospital was Wallace's *magnum opus*.[57]

William Aytoun was Wallace's successor as master-mason of the Hospital building. He was responsible for the varied and elaborate ornamental detail on the upper floors.

There is much evidence to support these interpretations. Balcanquall had given over a general plan to the governors, but as an amateur in building he seems to have been more interested in getting the Hospital completed rather than in the details of the 'wark' itself. Certainly his correspondence with the governors suggested such an interpretation, for he only twice had contact with them again.[58] It was William Wallace who was in charge of the project and it was he who produced the templates and working drawings from Balcanquall's 'paterne', almost certainly a version of Serlio's ground-plan. On Wallace's death the Governors were scrupulous in ensuring that these designs were their property, and they were given over to Aytoun, who was obliged in his contract with treasurer Halieburtoun[59] 'to devyse, plott and sett down quhat he sall think meittest for the decorment of the said wark and paterne thairof alreddie begun, quhere defect beis fund.'[60] It is true that in the early seventeenth century 'none of the agents involved in the organisation of architectural projects precisely corresponded to the present-day architect',[61] but Wallace and Aytoun were the nearest to that position. They played the creative role provided they kept the governors informed of their intentions. They used the pattern books of the period, having knowledge of du Cerceau, de l'Orme, Palladio and Serlio. Later, with the Duke of Alva's persecution of the Protestant Flemings in 1566, a flood of refugees from the Netherlands meant that they became familiar with the work of de Vries and, later, Dietterlin. 'It seems likely that many Scottish buildings of the time were designed in this way.'[62]

The plan of the building was the first completely regular design in Scotland – four equal ranges of buildings deployed round a central quadrangle, with four square towers at each corner rising a storey higher. Originally these were to have giant bell-cast lead roofs, but in the event only two were executed and then dismantled for structural reasons. It was a massive structure and the rooms were through-going in the traditional Scottish manner. Six spiral staircases were incorporated, one in each internal angle of the courtyard and one in each of the two external lateral façades on the east and west sides. The Serlio plan was followed closely in the beginning and arcades were built on the north and east sides. However, the later south and west sides were modified with chapel and refectory introduced at the lower level.

A notable feature of the building was the strong definition of the successive storeys by prominent string courses. This followed traditional Scottish fashion and has a parallel in Wallace's earlier work at Winton House. Other features were the tidy Mannerist corner designs: the 'fantastic' Heriot's

Hospital being the 'best known example' of a building with buckle quoins.[63] Perhaps these were an addition by John Mylne, who followed Aytoun as master-mason.[64] They were a decorative way of turning corners on a harled building and seem to have derived from the northern treatises of de Vries and Dietterlin.

The four corner towers have flat roofs with protecting parapets ornamented and pierced at intervals. At each external angle of the corner towers a small circular bartizan on the corbelling breaks the abrupt skyline of the flat roof. The chimneys are tall separate stacks, English in origin. Originally the grouped octagonal chimneys rose from gablet bases, with two plain astragals near the top, between which the rose and star from the Heriot family crest were placed. On the north front the wallhead has been raised to mask these gablets, but towards the quadrangle the original arrangement has been retained. The roofs on the east, south and west sides are sloping, while that on the north side is flat.

The Hospital is designed to be approached from the town of Edinburgh, with its 'show front' towards the town. The original entrance was from the north-west by a piece of ground situated near the West Port, which had been gifted to the governors by Charles I on 9 March 1629. Then they purchased land under the Castle Wall from John Ormiston on 22 April 1644 for 1200 merks, to produce a 'more commodious entrie' by demolishing part of the Town Wall and making an entrance from Heriot Bridge.[65] Robert Mylne was contracted on 25 March 1661 to build an entry from the Cowgate 'straight up to ye town-wall, and from ye town-wall to the entrie of the outer-court, with a pair of large stairs entering up thereto, and a way for conveying of provisions to the House by ane entrie upon the east side of ye court.' A porter's lodge was also to be created on the west side of the Entry. In time, however, this became increasingly inconvenient. The governors determined to make the ascent from the Grassmarket more accessible for transport. They bought up the property in the area, demolished the houses and created Heriot Bridge, a street linking the Hospital by an arch projecting into the Grassmarket. The Telfer extension to the Flodden Wall (1628–36) ensured that the building was inside the City boundaries.

The impressive main wooden door in the north face leads into a vaulted entrance known as the Pend. It is part of the frontispiece which owed much to the Chapel Royal's antique classical doorway at Stirling Castle designed by William Schaw in 1593.[66] The windows are alternately surmounted with triangular and circular pediments – closed on the ground floor, while open on the upper floors. The imposts of the highest line of windows are Doric pilasters, mostly panelled, although in some cases fluted, while the two lines of windows below are plain with foliated brackets under the pediments. The pediments of these contain the arms of George Heriot, supporting alternatively a rose or a star, and symbols of his profession.

Undoubtedly the grandest moment in the architecture of the exterior is supplied by the two-storey classical entrance which Wallace contrived to mark the main door of the Hospital. On either side of the Pend door are two Doric columns, standing on massive pedestals and supporting an entablature, the cornice of which is sixteen feet above the ground. The frieze, containing four panels, is enriched with ornament carvings in the metopes to illustrate the origins and the purposes of the Hospital. The first compartment (on the left) represents George Heriot as a goldsmith at his forge in the act of blowing bellows, with an antique seat and table. Over his work bench, with its fixed leather aprons to catch the filings of the precious metal, are the tools of his craft, arranged in orderly fashion on a rack. There is also the motto FUNDENDO FUNDAVI.[67] The second compartment shows an altar with a heart on it, and above, the name of God in Hebrew, surrounded by a halo. On the right stands a female figure (a widow) with a baby in her arms and two naked children clinging to her. On the left side of the altar is another figure (representing Charity). The motto in this compartment is HIS COR INCALUIT.[68] The third compartment contains five boys dressed in the uniform of Heriot's Hospital with two of their governors. Above them a hand, with the founder's initials, points from the clouds, with the motto SIC VOS DEUS, UT VOS EOS.[69] The right compartment shows several pupils and their master at lessons with the motto DEUS NOBIS HAEC OTIA FECIT.[70] These small, intricately carved mouldings exquisitely and succinctly unfold the Heriot bequest.

Four small and richly carved obelisks surmount the cornice above the Doric columns. Over the door is an aedicule with an arched recess between the windows of the first floor. It contains the armorial bearings of George Heriot with the motto, IMPENDO.[71] Below the Arms is inscribed INSIGNIA GEORGII HERIOTI FUNDATORIS PIETAS LIGAT ASTRA TERRIS.[72] The recess is flanked by Corinthian columns with spiral flutings. The cornice is surmounted by a tablet with the initials G.H.; on it are seated two cherubs supporting a pedestal crowned with the figure of a boy working on an anvil. This Corinthian order rests on the more massive Doric below it. In the centre of the Doric frieze is a monogram containing the name of George Heriot. The soffit is decorated with a laurel branch, charged with three roses and a star, again referring to the arms of Heriot.

The Pend opens out into a quadrangle which conveys a sense of amplitude and yet one of real enclosure. It is a handsome architectural space bounded by polygonal towers in each corner and featuring bizarre chapel windows – the only Gothic contrast to the otherwise classical framework. The turret oriel, above the chapel door, which dominates the south front, is a dummy window which lights into nothing. Heriot's Hospital courtyard is grand, heroic architecture.

The quadrangle is bounded on the north and east by a classical arcade with rounded arches supported on broad piers,[73] which results in a Renaissance 'feel'. Over the archway within the quadrangle on the north side is an aedicule and a decorated niche containing a statue of George Heriot, 5ft 10 in. in height, standing on a richly carved corbel. This figure was completed by Robert Mylne and the likeness was taken from Heriot's portrait.[74] The shafts of the columns are ornamented completely with diamond facets. On the frieze is inscribed CORPORIS HAEC, ANIMI EST HOC OPUS EFFIGIES.[75] A group of cherubs above the entablature point to various emblems around them. Higher up is seen one of the numerous sundials skilfully turned to decorative advantage, matching two others placed in the centres of the east and west sides; the remainder are set out on the outer faces of the towers.[76] A view of this north range from within the courtyard has been justly described as 'one of the finest architectural ensembles in the whole of Scotland'.[77]

Over the upper range of windows in the quadrangle on the north side a series of medallion portraits, in high relief, symbolises the loyalty of the masons to the Crown. They include (from left to right) Henrietta Maria, Charles I, Anna of Denmark, James VI, Princess Elizabeth, the Elector Palatine and young Prince Henry Frederick (who had died in 1612). On the corresponding lower range are the family of Heriot himself and his armorial bearings. On the east side of the quadrangle the four Evangelists are represented over the central upper windows. King David of Israel, with his harp, appears over the north window of this row, and King Solomon over the south. The Tree of Life, with two babes watering it, is carved on the lower storey. On the north corner of the row are mermaids with scorpions on the south corner. On the middle of the east side is a stone tablet with the inscription 'Honour the Lord with thy riches and with the first of all thine increase, so shall thy barnes be filled with abundance. To doe good and to distribute, forget not, for with such sacrifices God is pleased.' On the west side, above the windows of the top storey, allegorical figures of the four continents then known are carved – Europe, Asia, Africa and America. Of the remaining two windows, one represents Death, with the hand on the skull, and the other, Adam and Eve.[78] The entrance to the refectory is on this side.

Above the door were the arms of the founder, within a square tablet, in a carved frame of raised stone, with the motto, 'I distribute chearfullie' and underneath 'George Heriot Jeweller'. The doorcase is based on a famous design by the Italian Mannerist architect, G.B. Vignola, for the main portal of the Palazzo Farnese at Caprarola, north of Rome. Vignola had included an illustration of this doorcase in his *Rules of the Five Orders* published in 1562.[79]

Altogether there are 202 sculptured single-light aedicular windows in the Hospital,[80] and 18 finely carved initials of the founder. Only two of the decorations above the windows are the same, those in the ground-floor windows on either side of the midway external turret on the west side.[81] On the south side of the courtyard beautifully decorated oriel windows fill three sides of an octagonal tower, and although appearing as three separate windows they are in fact divided by six mullions and crossed by five trefoiled arches. There was from 1649 a stone-carved well in the middle of the quadrangle and the latter's surface was laid with pavement later that century.[82]

The two finest historical rooms in the Hospital are the Old Refectory, or Wester Laigh Hall, and the Council Room or Chamber. The former is a long, low room entered immediately from the quadrangle with cavernous Renaissance fireplaces at either end spanned by remarkable flat arches and ornamented with massive decorations. One bears Heriot's coat of arms and the other an elaborate monogram consisting of all the letters in the name of George Heriot ingeniously interwoven. The refectory[83] is 60 feet long, 20 feet wide and 13 feet high and was traditionally furnished with six oaken tables in three rows extending the entire length. Its walls were soon to be hung with framed boards which detailed in gold letters the benefactions given to the Hospital. The fireplaces are remarkable for not containing fires, even in the depth of winter when the cold was keenly felt.

The solid austerity of the refectory is in marked contrast to the warmth of the council chamber, 27 feet square by 13 feet high, which in April 1690 was entirely wainscoted with fine old oak panels.[84] The room, as the meeting place of the governors, received special attention at an early stage, and is impressive with its low ceiling and precise crisp mouldings in finely polished oak. It includes an entablature of the Corinthian order, perhaps by Alexander Eizat, whose carving for a number of Sir William Bruce's commissions was of a similar character. An ornamental breaking formed on the north side of the room, with the pilasters of the same order, frames a moulded Bolection fireplace, with a finely carved mantelpiece and a highly relieved wreath and festoon of fruits, flowers and grain, surrounding the founder's arms.[85] Originally this space contained a painting by Bonar representing a tradition in the Hospital that three boys in the mid-eighteenth century, while playing on the banks of the Water of Leith, discovered the mineral spring where St Bernard's Well was later erected.[86] The fireplace is tiled inside with Dutch tiles. The room also contains an unusually large seventeenth-century oak gate-leg council table[87], and in a later era a special oak stand was introduced to house copies of important documents relating to the history of the Hospital,[88] and a Jacobean settle which appears to have belonged to Heriot, having his name on the back and containing his coat of arms.[89] A tunnel-vaulted, fireproof charter room, to house documents, was built in stone adjacent to the council room on the east[90]

The chapel, on the south side of the quadrangle, is built in a Gothic style quite different from the rest of the building.[91] It was an imitation of the perpendicular early English style and its design may have been influenced by Archbishop Laud, who liked Gothic churches and who visited the Hospital in 1633 for the coronation of Charles I. The National Covenant of 1638 was also influential in a return to Gothic as an overt protest against the classical bent of the Court and its English episcopalian associations.[92] Certainly the chapel, in accordance with high church ideas then prevalent, with the communion table at the east end, was designed to lie east and west in the traditional manner. The great oriel window opposite the entrance door was designed to house the pulpit. The windows of the chapel were the nearest parallel in Scotland to Oxford Gothic and, in the style of late Scottish flamboyant, have been hailed as 'the finest examples in Scotland of the last phase of this style'.[93] The outside decorations of the doorway are more classical in concept. The doorway is placed centrally, flanked on each side by paired Corinthian columns raised on panelled pedestals and surmounted by an entablature. The design was taken from the most up-to-date source of Alexandre Francini's *Book of Architecture* published in Paris in 1631,[94] either an addition to the original design or, more likely, a tribute to the flexibility which the master-masons on the spot had for improvisation. On the centre of the frieze is a clasped Bible on a reading desk, with the words VERBUM DOMINI MANET IN AETERNUM.[95] The soffit of the doorway is decorated with alternate roses and stars; the keystone enriched with a console and spandrels with large foliations in triangular panels. At each end of the entablature, over the coupled figures, are segmental pediments surmounted by cherubs' heads; and over the whole order is a second open segmental pediment. Within this pediment an aedicule supported by two caryatids encloses a tablet with the inscription AURIFICI DEDERAT MIHI VIS DIVINA PERENNEM ET FACERE IN TERRIS IN CAELO ET FERRE [CORONOM] — inferred from a crown carved in relief at the foot.[96] Above are the armorial bearings of the Incorporation of Goldsmiths. The large windows lighting the chapel on each side of the doorway contain fine examples of decorated tracery in jewel colours. The tracery of the circular windows above is arranged on the east in the form of a rose and on the west in the form of a star.

The chapel is 60 feet long, 22 feet wide and 40 feet high, but it remained relatively unfinished for some time. It was repaired in 1673 from old and poor materials, with its walls remaining bare and the roof left with little ornament, although its floor was in better condition: in 1745 being 'elegantly paved with black and white marble'.[97] The chapel was refitted again in 1787, when an Adamesque ceiling and other ornaments were introduced,[98] but needed to be redone for safety reasons in the mid-1830s, with Gillespie Graham, Augustus Pugin and Edinburgh's leading cabinetmaker and upholsterer, William Trotter, co-operating to produce the chapel we largely see today.[99] The ceiling is a very fine example of enriched Neo-Gothic, and is embossed, painted and gilded. It is divided into compartments, with massive moulded arched ribs, supported by corbels of angels bearing scrolls with illuminated mottoes. This was a significant switch from the somewhat tame Neo-Classical to grandiose, confident pre-Victorian Gothic Revival work, and as such was dictated by taste rather than structure. The new pulpit, placed in the recess formed by the oriel window facing the door, consisted of an elaborate oak carving with a pinnacled canopy tapering to the ceiling, some 35 feet from the floor, with a precentor's box recessed in front, and was regarded as 'something exceptional and a sight-of-the-moment' in the later 1830s.[100] Later in the century the pulpit was horizontally bisected, with one half allocated to each end of the chapel to provide additional floor space. Above the inside entrance door, cut in oak, in raised antique characters, GLORIA IN EXCELSIS DEO[101] is inscribed. On the south side a pair of Gothic windows flank a fine mullioned bay window, crowned externally by an ogee lead dome and filled with the crests and escutcheons of noble Scottish families and the arms of the Incorporated Trades of Edinburgh. (See Appendix 5.)

The north elevation of the Hospital formerly had a roof similar to those on the other sides and was "the show front" facing the Grassmarket. The south elevation is dominated by the Chapel.

Although it has been argued that Heriot's Hospital was 'as thoroughly Scottish a building as anything could be'[102] one is impressed by the range of design books consulted by the master-masons, and it depended 'in a sophisticated way on a range of foreign sources.'[103] The result was a courtyard palace in the North European idiom,[104] a remarkable building criticised by many contemporaries as a 'pauper palace', and as such deemed too splendid for its intended purpose. However, altogether it is a superb memorial to George Heriot and was

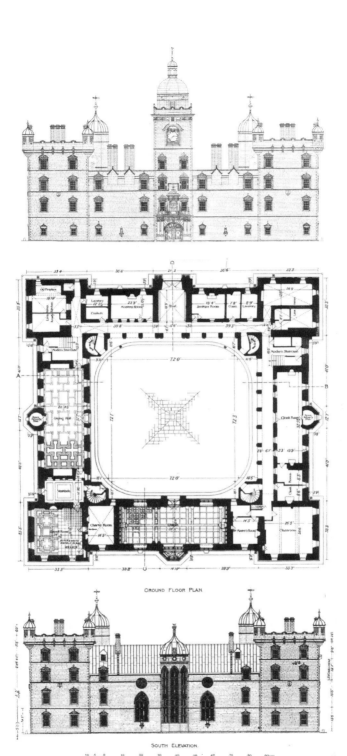

GROUND FLOOR PLAN

SOUTH ELEVATION

magnificently completed by the addition of its central tower in the 1690s.[105]

The Heriot's Hospital building was also to be influential in later building style. Its tradition of a massive quadrangular, symmetrical form with bartizaned corner towers was continued in Drumlanrig Castle, rebuilt for the Duke of Queensberry in the 1680s. In fact, the Duke was following fairly closely a scheme prepared for his grandfather, the first Earl of Queensberry in 1618. It is possible that Wallace was the provider of the original plans which he later used as the basis for the Hospital.[106]

The Adam brothers appear to have been inspired by the Hospital.[107] James Adam regarded it 'as an outstanding example of architectural composition.' The designs of James and John Adam for a new castle for the Duke of Douglas in 1757 (in the event only one side was built and it was demolished in 1951) were freely based on Heriot's Hospital, as the polygonal towers, set midway on each side, had the same position and much the same form. Robert Adam's brother-in-law, John Clerk of Eldin, was stressing the grandeur and influence of the Hospital building in the 1790s.[108] Overall, it is clear that the 'Wark' was 'a rich treasury for the Adam brethren and for many others'[109] in the eighteenth century and beyond. David Hamilton revived the Scots Renaissance style with bartizan towers and strapwork for Dunlop House in 1832–4, and when Floors Castle, Kelso, was being remodelled by William Playfair between 1837 and 1847 he also drew inspiration from Heriot's, particularly from its dramatic roofline of cupolas, turrets and pinnacles.

Many later commentators have stressed the importance of the building. Its 'monumentally symmetrical arrangement'[110] influenced the design of large educational buildings in the nineteenth century, including Madras College, Marischal College, Donaldson's Hospital, Stewart's College and Fettes College.[111] Later in the same century MacGibbon and Ross held it to be 'the finest and most important public building erected in Scotland during the seventeenth century'[112] following the demolition of Glasgow College; this influenced Charles Rennie Mackintosh who, in 1892, agreed with this assessment. Mackintosh was particularly impressed with the chapel and admired its Anglo–Flemish strapwork which, following Fergusson,[113] he saw as 'a rich complicated piece of blind tracery' (instead of the usual straight-lined or curved pediments as in England).[114] More recently terminology might differ but the sentiments remain the same. 'Here for the first time is a building in Scotland where the stranglehold of Gothic traditions has been loosened by the influence of the Renaissance'.[115] It is still seen as a prodigy in Scottish terms and the 'largest and most perfect early seventeenth-century structure in Scotland.'[116] Generations of staff and boys would heartily agree with such verdicts on their home. The governors might later be criticised for the large sums spent on the 'wark' but the unique results would be forever a fitting tribute to Edinburgh's generous benefactor.

CHAPTER THREE

The Hospital Opens

The building of the 'Wark' took considerable time. As early as 14 April 1628 Balcanquall was writing from the Savoy urging that the work of construction be carried out speedily and that trees be planted immediately so that 'they may come to some forwardness by that tyme the building is like to be inhabited'.[1] On 5 October 1629 he wrote again – this time from Rochester – to the town council, hoping that its members would 'incourage and spurre on your threasorer and all other officers' working on the hospital so that good progress will have been made on the building in time for the planned visit of Charles I. This would 'give testimonie to the many strangers who will look upon it, that wee of oure nation can dischairge the traist for pious uses committed to us, as of well as they use to doe it in this countrey'.[2] He would only have been partly reassured by Christopher Lowther's comment that the wark had begun when he saw it on 9 November 1629.[3]

Much of the 1630s was taken up with the recovery of debts, which proved a slow and protracted process. Given the reliance of the Hospital treasurer on interest it was a top priority to pressurise the debtors, and John Hay, in particular, continued to press the King for repayment.[4] Failing to make progress led him to use the good offices of others, and Robert Johnstone's petition to Charles I on 6 April 1631[5] was referred to the Lord Treasurer who was instructed to pay up, and so enable the pious work to proceed. However, there appears to have been no cash available, so the embarrassing issue remained unresolved.

On 3 October 1631 Hay detailed, for the governors, the extent of the debts still outstanding and this resulted in renewed efforts to collect them. At last, on 18 December 1632, the Duke of Buckingham paid part of his debt on the advice of de Laune, one of the executors, and this led to a review downwards of his outstanding debt. When Buckingham paid another £1,000 sterling via Johnstone the rest of the money owed by him was written off on 26 August 1633.[6]

The governors then concentrated their attention on the King's debt. Archbishop Laud had visited the Hospital, and on 25 October 1633 wrote to the town council expressing his pleasure that the 'worthy worke' was 'in good forwardness'.[7] Meantime, Johnstone contacted him in the hope he would intercede with the King on the governors' behalf. Although Laud appears to have 'mooved his Majestie effectualie'[8] and Charles wanted the debt settled, the Lord Treasurer advised that there was unlikely to be progress on the matter simply because there was no money available.

On the retiral of Hay from the Clerkship of the Hospital, in January 1634, his successor, Alexander Guthrie[9], corresponded with the Lord Register about the debt. It seemed that some progress had been made when, in October 1634, a letter from Charles I to the governors was received: he urged them to proceed with the 'wark' as he had given orders for his debt to be paid.[10] However, the money still did not appear, and by February 1636 Guthrie was being instructed to settle as soon as possible, accepting not less than £5,000 from the King.[11] Although the bargain with the King was struck the money still was not forthcoming so the governors told him to secure help from Laud and settle for anything he could get. The matter was discussed by the governors at meetings in July and August 1636 and again in December 1636 and January 1637.

Finally, realising that there was no likelihood that either the King's or the Earl of Roxburgh's debts would be paid, the governors decided to do another deal over land. They had already bought some of the Broughton estate.[12] They bought another eighteen acres for £4,120 16s. 8d. (Scots) in February 1634, and in July 1636 decided to go further.[13] The Barony of Broughton had been bought by Robert, Earl of Roxburgh,[14] who in turn sold the property to Charles I, but the money was not paid and the King reassigned the land to the Earl in the nature of a mortgage. The governors bought the Barony, which encompassed land in the three Lothians, Stirlingshire and Peeblesshire, for £38,733 6s. 8d. (Scots) and for only £14,606 13s. 4d. (Scots) the town council shared in the purchase.[15] The debts of the King and Roxburgh were cancelled; the Hospital took Broughton and Canon Mills, while the Town took the Canongate, North Leith, the Pleasance and parts of South Leith.[16] From 1636 the Barony of Broughton was governed by a baillie elected annually by the governors of the Hospital who 'possessed to the full the baronial powers of pit and gallows over their tenants therein.'[17] For the town council a formidable rival in the Canongate had been taken over at remarkably little cost,[18] and Leith subordinated – an old policy come to fruition.

The acquisition of land was to be very significant in the future history of the Hospital, and there were to be real and important benefits as a result. However, the mechanics of this particular deal suggests that the town council used the Hospital for its own financial ends. This was unsurprising given the composition of the governing body and the constant muddle the council finances always seemed to be in. Nonetheless, it remains a serious charge. The Hospital seems to have suffered the same fate as the College did in this period at the hands of the town council.[19] One can but speculate how the worth and wealth of the Hospital would have developed if it had been in the forefront of the Council's thinking instead of taking second place. Certainly the funds of the Hospital were a source of annual loans as early as 1633, when £12,000 was borrowed and the Heriot revenues were to prove of particular help to the Town in November 1638 when the latter was faced with paying the King's tax and the building of Parliament House.[20]

Given the financial circumstances of the 1630s, work on the Hospital continued gradually and intermittently. Hardened female prisoners were used to help with the clearing and transport of stone, as there were no houses of correction for them.[21] They were chained and shackled to carts transporting materials to prevent escape. On 2 June 1632 the treasurer paid 'For 6 shakells to the wemeinis hands . . . 14 loks for thair waistis and thair hands.'[22] On 16 February 1633 payment was made to John Ronald for 'two grait stones to the chappell zet heid, and for two grait stones for the housing the inner zet heid for George Heriott's pictour'. Aytoun was paid on 6 July 1633 'for hewing ye bybill above the entrie of the chapell.' In December 1633 the governors agreed 'to theak the Chapell [roof] with lead' and the treasurer was to buy the materials at 'the cheapest price and the best he can'.[23] The work was contracted out to John Bland, an English plumber from Newcastle, who appeared to have done an acceptable job on the chapel roof, for he was employed to do further roofing work on the Hospital. His detailed contract of 2 November 1635 stipulated that if he proved negligent he would be removed and punished.[24] He did not disappoint, however, and was used extensively in the later 1630s.

By 1633–6 work was concentrated on the chapel windows,[25] the council room[26] and the hall entry.[27] The Hospital was a hive of activity with 10–19 masons and 9–15 labourers working during the winter months of 1635 and some 29–40 masons and 15–17 labourers in the summer of 1636. Lime was brought from Kirkliston and Westhouses[28] and the Dutchman, Peter Cornelisone, brought 207 'grait treis' from Norway to Leith which the carter, William Barron, delivered to the Hospital.[29] Most of the iron work was handled by Thomas Brown of Leith, Deacon of the Blacksmiths' craft, and of particular interest was the supply of heavy painted gratings to protect ground-floor windows.[30] Clearly, much progress was being made, and although there were signs that the building was being well progressed, on his visit on 26 June

1635 Sir William Brereton commented: 'Here is a dainty hospital erecting, not yet finished.'[31] As early as September 1634 work was being done on chimney heads,[32] while Aytoun and two other masons were dressing the stone for Heriot's statue in April 1637. However, in early 1637 the governors temporarily ran out of money. On 3 January of that year Bland was given £5 sterling to take himself and his family back to Newcastle 'till he sould be written for be the counsell quhen they would have adoe to cast mair lead'.[33] The treasurer, Edward Edgar, reported on 10 April that in order to advance the building further money needed to be borrowed.[34] This was done and during the summer of 1637 some 23–32 masons and 13–16 labourers worked on the 'wark' and the following winter there was no need to cut back with on average 28 masons, 10 barrowmen and 5 wrights on site at any one time. There was also the beginnings of the real timbering of the building under the wright, John Scott. The books of treasurer, Thomas Charteris,[35] remained in credit balance and £9,898 16s. 6d. was spent on the fabric.[36]

The situation worsened, however, during the treasurership of Patrick Baxter,[37] and the building of the Hospital was interrupted by the Bishops' Wars, national events which resulted in many of the tenants on Heriot land being ruined. 'For causses and consideratiounes moveing thame, and in respect of the dangerous tyme; and in regaird that the thesaurer can get nane of the annuels payit, ordanes the wark to cease for a space, and the maisones and workmen to be dismist for a

Sir Walter Scott's publication of *The Fortunes of Nigel* in 1822 stimulated public interest in George Heriot and his Hospital. This view of the Hospital from the Castle Hill dates from the reign of George IV (1820-1830).

tyme.'[38] Revenues from rents fell by 25 per cent, and the work was abandoned on 6 April 1639, and not resumed until 10 August when fourteen masons were re-employed. The governors themselves did not meet during this time, and when they did so in August they had little business to conduct.[39] Ominously, the figure of unpaid debts rose markedly, and in his accounts for 1639–40 Baxter faced the first deficit in the accounts (of some £796 15s.).[40] During 1640 fortifications were raised at the wark[41] and work on the building slowed right down again between 16 May and mid-November.[42] With the Civil War continuing to cause havoc John Edgar, tenth treasurer between 1640–3, found annual rents plummeting in 1641 to £8,635 4s., a mere one-third of the previous year's already diminished revenues. In such circumstances work on the Hospital was cut right back, and from 4 September 1641 only Aytoun remained on site at the south-west tower.[43] A limited amount of other work continued in the form of plastering of the rooms above the hall. However, although the overall situation improved in April 1642 when eight masons were re-employed,[44] the death of John Watt in March 1642, after twelve years' service as a master-mason, was a blow to the governors, who clearly valued his contribution to the work done. Consequently they gave his widow, Isobel Merschell, 100 merks as a consideration and gratuity for his 'bygone pains'.[45]

Another factor hindering the building was the onerous financial demands which the governors faced. They continued to fulfil their obligations and paid out numerous legacies and demands for expenses: on 31 August 1635 the governors agreed to pay an annuity of 200 merks to Christian Heriot, sister of the founder, and wife of Archibald Lindsay, doctor of medicine.[46] In February 1637 Christian Blaw, the founder's stepmother, contacted the governors[47] to inform them that her grandson, John Ahanna,[48] was destitute. Conscious of the relationship of the boy to George Heriot, and that if the Hospital had been finished his claim to admission would have been undeniable, the governors decided that he should have £200 Scots every year till the 'wark be perfytit'.[49]

The generosity of the governors to relatives of the founder was again in evidence in November 1643. Elizabeth Band, the elder of Heriot's natural daughters, had lost her husband, James Jossie, and the governors unanimously voted her an annual pension of 1000 merks Scots 'for bringing upe and intertyineing of the said tua childreine in meatt, clothes, learning, and uthris necessaris; and this to indure aye and til the saids bairnes be past the aige of learning of gramar and uther authours.'[50] Again in May 1648 George Scott, nephew of the founder,[51] received a gratuity of 600 merks 'for the love, favour, and affectione the Counsell has to George Scott, merchant, sister's son to the founder of the Hospitall; and for the respect they have to the said George, and for his better encouragement to attend upone the first vacant place within the Wark'.[52]

Despite such costs the governors took every opportunity to buy any land which came on the market in the Edinburgh area. Between 1636 and 1649 the governors were involved in thirteen such transactions, which involved in total the best part of 200 acres and cost 180,000 merks. Given the financial background the governors showed much foresight in buying land with any and all unemployed capital. Scarcely an opportunity went by without the governors snapping up property and land, especially in Broughton and Restalrig, which was acquired in perpetuity for the Heriot Trust. A mid-nineteenth century plan of the Hospital lands gives some indication of the results of such accummulations.[53] Indeed, as late as 1872, Heriot's Hospital was the largest landowner in Edinburgh, with 180 acres ownership (excluding Crown property).[54]

The death in London in October 1639 of one of the executors of Heriot's will, the lawyer, Robert Johnstone of Blackfriars, proved significant for the Hospital. He, like Balcanquall, had played an important role in its first days, but, unlike Balcanquall, who immersed himself in national affairs, he continued to be of service to the governors in the 1630s. He assiduously pursued debtors for the governors and constantly berated those who he felt were not as persistent as himself. As late as 22 May 1637 he attacked de Laune who never 'used diligence, caire or concurrance for the getting of anie part of the poore estate'.[55] Johnstone was in correspondence with the governors on 22 February and 20 August 1639[56] on outstanding financial matters. Johnstone pressed 'for piety, conscience and creditt's cause' that some poor orphans should be placed immediately in the Hospital.[57] Given that he remained in touch his plea implied that the building was well advanced and was evidence that the governors were slow to place pupils in the institution. He also understood that the agenda for the town council was different from that for the Hospital and as an encouragement to them to press ahead, his will provided £1,000 sterling 'to be put out for profit, to buy gowns, stockings, shirts and clothes, unto the poor children of Mr Heriot's Hospital' and the interest of £100 sterling to maintain an able schoolmaster there. He also endowed eight poor students to attend the University of Edinburgh and, failing applications in the name of Johnstone from the High School of Edinburgh and Moffat Grammar School, the town council were to choose able scholars from Heriot's.[58] Such generosity set a precedent for other benefactors to follow.[59]

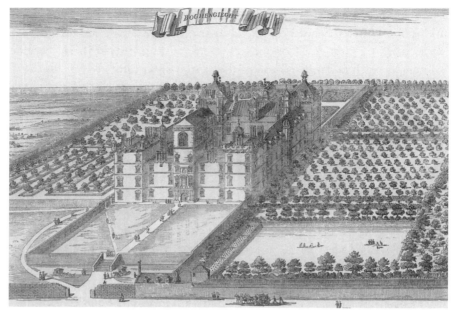

It seems likely that the original plan for the Hospital, following Serlio, had included high pavilion roofs at every corner, but Aytoun was instructed by the governors on 28 March 1642 that when the work resumed he was to platform each of the towers on the north front with a bartizan at the corner marks. This entailed dismantling the spectacular but troublesome lead ogee roofs on the two north towers, and the attic between them was built up, incorporating the existing dormers.[60] Perhaps this led to more work for the masons, as more were employed throughout 1643 and 1644.[61] The resulting flat roofs on the north side and the remaining pavilion roofs on the south side gave the Hospital a lop-sided look, and this is captured in the Revd James Gordon of Rothiemay's view of 1647.[62] It also shows the 'wark' complete and enclosed by the crenellated ramparts of the city on the west and south sides, with a wall separating it from Greyfriars Churchyard.[63] However, given that the prospect also exhibits a lofty Gothic crown on the gateway tower that it never possessed 'the evidence of his drawing must be suspect'.[64] In fact, the governors had determined to add 22 feet to the tower, with two great windows on each side, and Aytoun accepted their instructions in December 1644. In the event, the contract was not completed, as Aytoun died, probably in July 1645, of the 'seiknes'[65] but he left a more or less completed Hospital building, otherwise the governors would not have contemplated adding an expensive and comparatively useless tower.

James Gordon, minister of Rothiemay, produced a view of 'Herioti Orphanotrophium' in 1647. However, he shows 'the Wark' as complete and gives it a Gothic crown it never possessed.

Aytoun's successor, John Mylne younger,[66] had replaced his father as royal master-mason on 1 February 1636,[67] and had been involved in work on the Tron Kirk (1637–42) and Cowane's Hospital, Stirling (1637–48). He became prominent as a leading master-mason at the wark as early as 9 April 1642.[68] However, there is no trace of him being employed at the Hospital after 14 December 1644, and he does not appear in the 1645 accounts.[69] Indeed, no masons or workers worked at all in this period, except James Pettigrew, despite the demands of Mylne for payment. In the event, the governors, appreciating his importance with the loss of Aytoun, paid Mylne £252 (Scots) on 20 August 1646.[70] However, this did not result in increased activity, for little work was done during 1646–7 nor under the new treasurer, William Simpson, in 1647–8 when only £1,900 was spent, and most of that on wages for Mylne, Scott and the gardener, as well as on timber and nails.[71]

On 26 January 1648 Mylne and John Scott, master wright,[72] reported to the governors their belief that 'for the weilfaire' of the Hospital the pavilion roof of the south-west tower should be dismantled. Scott held that 'it was never his oponione that the said southwest torret sould be built in the way that now it standis'.[73] Presumably it had been constructed this way over a decade previously and now looked out of place, as well as being less functional than the north roofs. The governors seemed more interested in architectural niceties than opening the hospital and took the advice proffered. They ordered the south-west tower to be rebuilt in the same style as those on the north side.

Another early alteration, probably done before 1647, was carried out on the front north face with the removal of the high slate roof along the north front and its replacement by flat leads. Originally, all four sides had matching steep sloping roofs rising from half dormers at the eaves level. Again such work was done mainly for appearances' sake and the wall-head or parapet was raised to the top of the gablets, thus hiding the lower parts of the octagonal chimneys. The change can still be traced in the break from ashlar to rubble that follows the line of a high gable along the side of the towers, and in the built-up parapet on the north front.

The governors intervened, again, on 23 July 1649, ordering treasurer George Wauchop 'to tak down the stone wark of the south-east towr, and to make the same as the north-west and north east towrs ar, And to cause theik the said south-east towr as they ar, And this to be done with all diligence and to make the samen wattertight.'[74] However, after visiting the building on 14 November 1649 it was found that this had not been done properly, and the governors demanded that the previous orders be implemented immediately.

There was also concern that the flooring needed work and the windows needed to be made watertight. Despite this, it seems that the orders of 1649 were not finally carried out until after an inspection on 6 June 1692 when the governors again determined to regularise the building. The south-east quarter was completed in the style of the turrets on the north-side, and the pavilion turret on the south-west was replaced with a platform tower in the style of the turret.

National events continued to affect the Hospital during the Civil War. The tenants of the Hospital complained of the serious losses they had sustained at the hands of the West Country army of Charles II which had eaten and destroyed much of their 1649 crop. The governors resolved to give a specific deduction to tenants, depending upon the level of destruction they experienced.[75] However, the situation did not improve, and on 4 November 1653 the governors agreed to accept merks instead of pounds for the rents for 1648–50 inclusive, provided the tenants involved paid promptly.[76]

Worse was to follow. The building was more or less complete[77] when Cromwell invaded Scotland with 16,000 men in July 1650. The yards were used for gun placements and the entrance barricaded with stone and lime. However, in early September, having defeated the Scots at the battle of Dunbar, Cromwell occupied Edinburgh. He immediately laid siege to Edinburgh Castle and the proximity of the unoccupied Hospital ensured its take-over by Cromwell to quarter his sick and wounded soldiers.

By October of the following year a more serious threat seemed to be emerging when Cromwell claimed the right to the Hospital and its income on the grounds that Heriot was a naturalised Englishman who had acquired the bulk of his fortune in England. It was also suggested that the governors had subverted Heriot's intentions and applied the Hospital rents for purposes outwith his instructions. The governors sent George Wauchop to Leith with legal documentation to give over to General Lambert. When this seemed to have little effect, on 7 November 1653, the city ministers 'rose up and went their way from the council, and would not be accessory to the actings or doings of any thing, till they advised with the rest of the brethren.'[78] Fortunately, Cromwell was too busy elsewhere to pursue this plan, and after the payment of £300 sterling in September 1654 Hospital privileges seemed safe.[79] Nonetheless the ministers continued to boycott governors' meetings[80] and only returned in August 1658 when the national situation changed and Cromwell had departed.[81]

Generally the 1650s was a period of inactivity for the governors as they awaited a change in national circumstances and there is evidence that town council officials did not attend carefully to Heriot affairs.[82] Given Cromwell's comments on the Hospital, the governors felt it prudent to lie low and busied themselves with minor and extraneous matters. When the Protector supported the claims of the founder's natural daughter, Elizabeth, widow of James Jossie, who had married William Don in England in March 1655, the governors agreed to award her an annual pension of £55 sterling 'in equal halfs . . . during all the Days of her Lifetime',[83] which they paid in September of that year.[84]

The change the governors awaited finally arrived, and on 15 March 1658 Baillie Robert Sandilands, William Thomson[85] and the Revd John Stirling were appointed to meet with General Monck, commander of the English troops, and 'to deal for the Removeal of the Sick sodgers out of the Hospital House To some other Lodging and yards In and about Edinburgh'.[86] Although Monck saw the advantages in gaining popular support by restoring the 'Wark' to its legitimate use he drove a hard bargain. The governors were obliged to rent a large building in the Canongate from Robert Murray for 600 merks a year and began its reparation to house Monck's sick. They also provided a physician, apothecary, surgeon's mate and gardener, as necessary attendants on the infirmary before Monck finally agreed to vacate the Hospital on 22 July 1658.[87] Altogether it cost the governors £3,111 18s. 6d. to remove the sick 'bag and baguage' out of the wark.[88]

Having had no maintenance for a decade the governors set about preparing the 'wark' for habitation. A committee visited 'the fabrick' to decide on the 'necessary reperations.'[89] It was found that the roof had to be made watertight and in particular the south-west turret needed immediate attention,[90] aggravated by the 'great Spaits and Innundations of rains, which unexpectedly has fallen in so great aboundance both in spring and Harvest this year the like . . . has not been usually seen in many ages bypast'.[91] Many windows were broken and were to be attended to immediately; the beds also were to be built as quickly as possible.[92] Treasurer John Meine was instructed to repair the 'Great Entry'.

A committee of twelve under Lord Provost Sir James Stewart ascertained the income coming in from rents, the number of persons to be employed in the Hospital and the number of children it could reasonably support. The momentum continued. On 8 November 1658 it was agreed to go ahead and appoint a 'fitt Schoolmaster' at £11 sterling along with Johnstone's legacy (which added another £6 sterling per annum). Twenty-four boys were to be accepted into four rooms with three beds in each and a separate room set aside for the schoolmaster. Provision was to be made for a caterer for buying meat and keeping accounts, an unmarried porter, and three single 'ancient grave women'[93] for domestic chores.

Appreciating that the opening of the Hospital would result in a flood of applications for entry the governors set up a committee of seven to decide on which boys to select. On 19 January 1659 the governors accepted the first two scholars – brothers, George and Robert Bell, aged eleven and seven respectively – who fulfilled the clauses of the Statutes as they were 'Poor Fatherless orphans Burgeses Bairns of Honest decent and their Mother unable to maintain them being in a weak condition'.[94] The burgess and guild tickets of their deceased father, Patrick, were also produced. The same circumstances applied to James Rae, who was accepted on 14 March. The same day the fourth scholar elected – James Hardie – was a motherless bairn whose father, Gilbert – a vintner – was in such a poor condition that he was unable to maintain his children. By 11 April some thirty boys had been accepted. Of these, twenty were fatherless, three were motherless, while the other seven qualified because of the 'mean' or 'sad' condition of a usually large family.[95] The total number in the Hospital was increased to thirty-five on 14 June, to forty on 8 August, and finally to forty-three on 26 September 1659, when the governors decided not to admit any more boys until the books had been audited, fearing that the burden already undertaken was already greater than what could be sustained. It was agreed that the treasurer's books would be audited monthly – more often than stipulated by the Statutes – and four governors were given this task. John Mylne[96] was one of this group, and his expertise was used following the rainstorms of early June, which returned again at the beginning of August and September, when he examined and repaired the damage done to Heriot property.[97]

A committee of governors was appointed to examine the qualifications of prospective schoolmasters.[98] They interviewed James Scot, the son of George Scot, merchant, and a relative of the founder, but found him to be a 'weak professor'[99] of grammar and arithmetic. William Hamilton, Robert Purdie and James Adamson, the latter two both students, were also examined. The governors found Hamilton and Purdie equal in these areas and in handwriting, but preferred the former as a burgess bairn 'whom they are to prefer to strangers'[100]. So Hamilton was elected the first schoolmaster of Heriot's Hospital on 11 April 1659.[101]

Other appointments on the large staff were made around the same time.[102] Marion Jameson, a widow of 58 and of good report, was placed in charge of washing, making beds, sweeping rooms, attending the sick and making meals. To support her, Margaret Hutcheson (aged 45) and Lelias Houston were chosen. Gilbert Hardie was the first porter, and was expected by the Statutes to be 'of guid strength able to keip out all sturdie beggeris and vagrant persones', while Patrick Campbell became cook, baker and brewer. Most importantly the governors appointed, on 18 April 1659, James Lawson, tailor, to be 'Master-Governor' of the Hospital,[103] with a yearly salary of 500 merks. Although not a teacher, the master was charged with ensuring that the scholars were brought up in the fear of Almighty God[104] and that all under him diligently attended to their respective occupations. He was resident in the Hospital and was not to sleep out without the express permission of the Lord Provost or one of the ministers. He was entitled to a new gown every year, and was expected to wear it. The master was responsible for the discipline of the boys, staff and servants, and for collating all accounts for submission to the treasurer.

All seemed ready for opening, and the governors visited the 'wark' for a final inspection. They chose the senior Edinburgh minister, the Revd Robert Douglas,[105] to preach the anniversary sermon on Monday 27 June 1659 in Greyfriars' Church, and the Hospital 'wes dedicat in a very soleme maner'.[106] The scholars were described as being 'weel arrayit in purpour clothes and cassocks', all with new hats and shoes. A contemporary account held that 'This Hospitall wes not ane ordinary hospitall, bot a hospitall very famous with hallis, chalmeris, kitchingis, brewhousis, yairdis, orcherdis, a chappell, and all uther necessaries'.[107]

At a meeting of governors after the dedication it was decided that in future the annual anniversary ceremony would take place on the first Monday of June to conform with the Statutes.[108] The governors were impressed with Douglas's sermon, for that very afternoon they ordered the treasurer to pay 100 merks Scots 'for the extraordinary pains' taken by him.[109] Such an extravagant gesture was an early example of the governors being 'good to their own' and this expensive tradition was to continue throughout the days of the Hospital.[110] Later, on 5 March 1660, the governors began another tradition, having the sermon printed in commemoration of the founder.[111] In 1660 the Revd Robert Laurie of the Tron Church was the chosen preacher, and the change to Episcopacy was seen when he returned to take the service in 1668 as Dean of Edinburgh. After debates and differences as to which ministers should preach upon the Anniversary Day it was finally confirmed in 1677 that the ministers would preach according to their seniority. This was 'to be a perpetual Rule in all time coming'.[112]

By July 1659 the governors were turning their attention to the moral and physical welfare of the scholars. Prayers were organised by the governors before dinner and supper, and their

OVERLEAF.
John Slezer's engraving of 'Edinburgh: Southside of the Castle' was included in the 1693 edition of *Theatrum Scotiae*. On the extreme right it shows Heriot's Hospital before the completion of its clock tower.

Facies Arcis EDENBURGEENÆ

Southside of the Castle of EDINBURGH.

'catechisms'[113] were to be taught every Thursday and Sunday afternoon. These perhaps were not carried out effectively, for on three separate occasions the ministers were asked to organise a set form of prayers and service.[114] The diet of the scholars was to alternate between meat and fish: the former on Monday, Tuesday, Thursday and Sunday, the latter on the other three days.[115] Despite original intentions the scholars were still sleeping four or five to a bed in dormitories on the first floor of the west side of the quadrangle over the refectory. As the classrooms were on the first floor above the pend entrance there was an abundance of unused rooms in the Hospital. The governors determined to provide 'fit rooms' for themselves, a dining room above the kitchen and a chamber for the master.[116]

One issue which concerned the governors was the age of the scholars. Under the Statutes boys were expected to be in the Hospital from seven to sixteen years of age. However, in 1659 the average age at entry was eight years and eight months, with a number of boys in their teens. When, on 5 March 1660, two boys were the first to be apprenticed (William Walker and Michael Moffat) to the skinner trade, both had only been in the Hospital since the previous August and September respectively. The governors felt that taking in older boys was not what had been originally envisaged, and entry to the Hospital was therefore restricted to boys aged between seven and ten.[117] A contributory factor to this change was the cost of apprenticeships, which totalled 300 merks each, including outfits and other necessities for the outside world.[118] The governors also felt that boys should not leave the Hospital early, and on 10 December 1667 it was decided that any parents removing their children before their sixteenth birthday should forfeit their Hospital benefits. These issues remained contentious, and on 8 June 1676 the governors felt obliged to reiterate the policy that no boy over the age of ten would be taken into the Hospital,[119] while decreasing to 200 merks the maximum received by boys leaving the Hospital. Apprenticeships remained the goal of the governors for the vast majority of the pupils, but they still made provision at this time for some boys, on reaching 16 years, to go on to the Grammar School 'for their further education', with their fees being paid by the Hospital funds.[120]

On 21 March 1659 the Principal of the College of Edinburgh, Robert Leighton,[121] petitioned the governors to provide for the ten bursaries[122] simultaneous with the opening of the Hospital.[123] A committee of five met with their College counterparts and took legal advice from two eminent advocates, Sir John Gilmour and John Nisbet. At their meeting on 16 January 1660 the governors found themselves divided. Some held that the codicil of Heriot's Will stipulated his desire to provide for ten bursaries and therefore there could be no amendment or even delay in fulfilling his 'orders': others believed that the bursaries could only be established when the main purposes of the Hospital were achieved and the rents were adequate to maintain them. The latter group argued that Heriot's prime intention was to maintain poor and distressed burgess bairns and the provision for bursaries was secondary to this. Given this division among the twenty-four governors present it was agreed that the issue be remitted to a committee of ten under Lord Provost Sir James Stewart. However, the committee suffered from the same divisions, and on 13 February the matter was referred back to the whole governing body. The first vote in its history was then taken, but the deadlock continued when the votes for each side were equal in number.[124] The only way forward was to submit the case to Lord Hoptoun, a leading legal authority, which the governors did on 5 March. Finally, on 7 May a compromise was accepted by the governors. In the difficult financial climate five bursars were to be maintained meantime at the College at £5 sterling each per annum, with priority being given to Hospital scholars. This reduced number of bursars was immediately elected at the next meeting of the governors on 21 May 1660,[125] although in fact none of them came from the Hospital.

After years of delay the Hospital had finally opened and set to work to turn Heriot's bequest into a reality. Whether the governors would always be able to live up to his high ideals was another question. Already there were some worrying signs. Of the nine boys enrolled in the Hospital in 1660 only three were fatherless, and two of these were the children of a relative of the founder. The governors were taking full advantage of Balcanquall's decision to drop the criterion of 'fatherless', and it seemed that Heriot's Hospital would never emulate Christ's in the way that Heriot had originally desired. Moreover, one of the earliest boys was the son of a town councillor, which laid the governors open to the charge of favouring their own. Other issues involved money. At one level there was expenditure on themselves, which took the form of 'ane denner' for Lord Provost and town council on 28 November 1648 costing £50 18s.,[126] or just the monies authorised by themselves, as on 28 May 1649, when £14 10s. 8d. was 'spent that day the Counsell sat in Heriottis hospitall'.[127] There were also the controversial financial deals. Lendings to the 'guid towne' were regular and substantial. During 1646 alone 17,000 merks (£11,333 6s. 8d.) were lent. In addition there was the way the Council benefited from the Hospital's land deals. Only time would tell whether these were aberrations or the tip of a more extensive problem. Heriot's bequest had taken its concrete form but had not got off to a very auspicious start.

CHAPTER FOUR

The Early Years of the Hospital

With the Hospital open the governors returned to inactivity. Certainly they continued to meet regularly, but on 9 August 1661, 15 December 1662 and again on 10 August 1663 there were 'no transactions' despite full attendances.[1] At other meetings, maintenance of the Hospital was the constant theme, although early visitors were impressed with what they found. The Frenchman, Jorevin de Rocheford, visiting in 1661, talked of the 'great edifice' which looked more like a palace than a hospital,[2] while the widely travelled Englishman, John Ray, arrived on 19 August 1662 and believed the building 'would make a very handsome college, comparable to the best in our universities'.[3] However, a different and more critical view was expressed by the Revd James Brome, a Kentish clergyman who visited in 1669. He saw it as falling into a 'ruinous and desolate condition'[4] and this was confirmed by an internal report of 16 May 1670 that the south-west of the building was 'ruinous' with lead missing from the roof.

Another area of concern to the governors was the incomplete nature of the chapel. On 7 April 1673 they determined to make use of the materials from the dismantled kirk of Cromwell's Citadel in Leith; its timber seats, steeple, stone and glass work were taken for the chapel's repair. Such economy was commendable but necessitated further remedial work within a short time.[5] It is also explains why Thomas Kirke of Cookridge, Yorkshire, described the Hospital on 1 June 1677 as 'a very fine building, though not finished'. It partly explains the comment from Ralph Thoresby, of Leeds, after his visit on 14 September 1681: 'A most stately structure, but sadly perverted as to the design of the founder, many of his vast donations being lost or misemployed'.[6] By March 1682 the treasurer was being pressed to replace speedily the glass windows in the chapel and to install more comfortable seats for both staff and boys.[7] It was not until 14 August 1683 that he was finally able to report that the Hospital chapel was 'fully repaired' and fit for morning and evening services. All boys were then to attend the chapel after the ringing of the bell and the shutting of the gates, while absentees were to be reported to the treasurer.

Perhaps stimulated by the preceding terrible winter and spring it was decided on 3 May 1675 that the steeple of the Hospital 'be finished and a top put there upon'.[8] A group of governors met with Robert Mylne and commissioned him 'to think on a drawing' to complete the tower for their next meeting. It is not exactly clear why Mylne did not complete this commission, as Sir William Bruce, the eminent Scottish architect, supplied the design, and Deacon Sandilands was instructed to go ahead 'with all possible diligence'[9] with the work. Once begun, however, there were problems, and although the treasurer tried to encourage Sandiland's men to work assiduously by giving them twelve pennies Scots daily for their morning drink,[10] the undertaking was not completed.

It was a constant struggle to keep the building in good order. The southeast quarter of the 'wark' was repaired in 1684 but seems to have remained unfinished. In 1687 an inspection of the fabric of the building found many of the glass windows broken and defects in the lead roof of the south-west quarter. In the unused rooms poorly fitting windows let the rain in, resulting in rotting of the floors and other damage. It was recommended that after the repairs were complete the master should inspect the building weekly and report any defects. Meantime, on 5 November 1689, the treasurer had been instructed 'to lay the great hall in the Hospital and the piazza with plain stones and the court with square casway stones with all convenient dilligence'.[11]

After the work in 1693, which resulted in a 'regular and uniform' Hospital,[12] all that was left to complete was the steeple, and Robert Mylne presented his drawings for this work on 6 March 1693, being paid 3,100 merks for the contract.[13] Two bells were ultimately placed in the clock-tower: the larger bell, 2 ft. 1 in. in height and 2 ft 8½ in. in diameter, was enriched with seven annular bands and a floriated crown with a three-lined inscription:

> George Heriots Hospital
> By order of Thomas Fisher Thezaurer
> John Meikle Fecit Edinburgh 1701.

The smaller bell was 1 ft 4½ in. high and 1 ft 8 in. in diameter, had two annular bands and was inscribed:

> For George Heriots Hospital 1755 Edr. Tho Henderson fecit.[14]

From then, the octagonal cupola with shell niches and a stone dome dominated the north face of the 'wark'. The dome with balastrude featured an open lantern and was capped with a star. Thus the work envisaged some half a century earlier was finally completed in magnificent style, and the great shaft of stone of the central tower was to preside ever afterwards over the whole courtyard.

The use of the Hospital building was another issue, given its surplus capacity. The governors offered Andrew Anderson, the king's printer in Scotland, three or four rooms in the Hospital on 18 March 1672.[15] Anderson had been given the exclusive right to print, *inter alia*, books of the common and civil law[16] and although he died in 1676 his widow carried on using the premises until the printing presses were ordered to be removed in June 1680.[17] This probably resulted in the petition in August 1680 of Sir Thomas Murray of Glendoick, Clerk Register, who could not find 'any convenient place in the city for his presses and drying of the Acts [of Parliament] when printed'.[18] Given that there were 'several rooms useless in the Hospital which might accommodate him', the governors leased him the Wester Laigh Hall for the presses and several rooms above it for drying the Acts.

On 8 August 1684 the Chancellor, James Drummond, 4th Earl of Perth, and the Lord Advocate, Sir George Mackenzie of Rosehaugh, attended a meeting at the Hospital in their role as supervisors appointed by the founder to be involved in cases involving the interpretation of the Statutes. They considered whether the east corner of the building could be let for rent for indwellers but decided that this went against Heriot's intention, which had been to allow only poor boys and no others to use the Hospital. This does not, however, seem to have prevented the renting out of rooms for business purposes.[19] After all there was much to be said for using the spare rooms for profit, especially as the Hospital seemed immune from fire in a way which the town of Edinburgh was not. Perhaps this was the result of the strict regulations for users: they were not allowed access to the building at night, and were never at any time allowed to use lights indoors.

The Heriot gardens encompassing the Hospital were a major preoccupation of the governors, particularly when they had no control over the remainder of the building in the 1650s, which perhaps explains their 'progressive outlook' in developing a physical garden.[20] When the Hospital opened, the gardener, James Cuthbertson, was to furnish beets, leek, cabbage, parsnips, turnips, onions, carrots and salads. Furthermore, he was to ensure 'that the Easter yeard, the south part thereof, be planted with all sort of Phisical, Medicinal, and all sort of other herbs, such as the country can afford, conform to the fullest catalogue that can be that such who intend to studie Herbs may have full access there, they not wronging or molesting the samen,

and that the remainant of that yard, which is called the wilderness or maise that the walks be kept clean'.[21] As the botanical class in the University had not yet been established this was the first public garden in Edinburgh devoted to that purpose.

On 4 April 1670 the governors found Cuthbertson 'deficient in his performance', although he promised to do better in the future. However, on 5 August 1672, the governors complained that the yards were again in an unacceptable condition. Cuthbertson argued that the disorder was a result of the misuse of the keys to the gardens which the governors and treasurer possessed, as all sorts of people were able to come in and spoil the precincts. It was then agreed to limit the numbers of keys in use to see what difference this made, and there was some improvement in the situation. It was nevertheless reported on 2 June 1673 that although Cuthbertson provided herbs and kail he seldom delivered roots. The yards remained 'in very great disorder' and were 'all overgrown with weeds'. Cuthbertson was accused of allowing his family to use the gardens and of uncivil treatment of the governors, whose patience was exhausted. He was dismissed, and the master was to ensure that he stayed away from the gardens.[22] The following year great improvements in

The Old Refectory (Wester Laigh Hall) has cavernous Renaissance fireplaces at each end spanned by flat arches and ornamented with massive decorations. The fireplaces were not used for fires even in the depths of winter.

the layout and state of the gardens were undertaken by a large workforce under the supervision of Deacon Sandilands. The new gardener, Thomas Borthwick, was a much more successful employee. The Heriot gardens flourished under him and James Stevenson, gardener from 1696, who rebuilt walks,[23] brought in new flowers from abroad, and enabled the governors to extend the cultivated area to feed the growing numbers in the Hospital.[24]

Such were the concerns of the governors rather than the activities of the masters of the Hospital in this period, confirming the secondary role which education took. The first master, James Lawson, was in charge for five and a half years without ever coming to the attention of the governors. Perhaps he did his job well. On his death on 12 December 1664 the governors appointed Robert Davidson as his successor on the same contract. However, by the time of the fourth master, William Smieton, the governors had settled the induction procedures. On 19 December 1670 Smieton took the requisite oath of allegiance, and in a formal ceremony the keys of the Hospital were delivered to him and 'the whole servants being conveen'd were commanded to give him all due obedience which they promised to do'.[25]

On 25 March 1673 Smieton was accused by both treasurers of Heriot Hospital and the Town of committing many 'miscarridges (and) misbehaviors'.[26] To avoid the seemingly inevitable result Smieton resigned immediately, and his office was declared vacant on 30 March. A week later the Council proceeded to select the new master from a short-leet of three, and elected Harry Morrison, advocate, 'be plurality of voices'.[27]

On 7 November 1681 the auditors reported that the master of the Hospital, Morrison, 'was very unfit for his charge insofar as he was negligent and remiss in his dutie whereby the Hospital was at a great Loss'.[28] Morrison survived an investigation. On 1 July 1689 he was found negligent in his duty of overseeing the children and was given 'a reproof' and exhorted to observe his duties more conscientiously. He must have gained in favour for treasurer Fisher argued on 5 September 1692 that the master's salary of 100 merks was 'too mean and not becoming the quality of the masters of the House'[29] and the governors decided to award him £200 Scots per annum. Morrison, however, was the subject of another complaint on 15 April 1695 when he was accused of not ensuring that the scholars' clothes were neat and clean. His public rebuke was inserted in the minute book as a 'second admonition'.[30] On 9 November 1696 he was deemed to have failed to visit the children's chambers for a long time to see if they had been swept and cleaned. As a result he was publicly warned and this was recorded as his third and final admonition. Despite these difficulties Morrison was to retain office until

August 1699. His successor, James Buchan, was soon in difficulties with the governors. He was publicly rebuked by them on 5 May 1701 when he admitted allowing the schoolmaster, Thomas Heriot, to use the keys of the building to entertain outsiders in the Hospital at unreasonable hours.[31] The governors were even more annoyed with Heriot, judging his actions as an 'ill example to the children committed to his charge and a great scandal to the good order that ought to be observed within the Hospital'.[32] He was warned by the Lord Provost that this offence warranted three rebukes in one, and another misdemeanour would result in instant dismissal.

Some staff, however, were dismissed. On 8 September 1684 James Cairns, steward of the Hospital, was warned about his future conduct after behaving irreverently towards the treasurer and master, disobeying their commands and being frequently drunk. He was finally dismissed on 8 December 1685 for repeating these offences.[33] Thomas Ballantine, steward to the treasurer, turned Quaker in January 1686. A Committee of ministers held him unfit for his employment unless he 'quitte his oppinion'. When all their 'endeavours proved ineffectual' the governors declared his position vacant and replaced him immediately.[34] One of the schoolmasters, Henry Kinnear, who had been appointed in August 1681 dismissed himself by marrying and so contravening the Statutes. The governors declared his post vacant on 20 April 1696.

Sir James Rocheid of Inverleith, the Clerk of the Hospital, was 'turned off' on 5 January 1685 for a number of 'misdemeanours'.[35] It was alleged that he had procured an unwarranted lease of Canonmills, that he had encroached on the Hospital's grounds by building a little wash-house near Inverleith, and that he had not attended the meetings of the governors.[36] He was immediately dismissed without investigation, only one governor – the Revd James Trotter – suggesting delay.[37] However, Rocheid was able to produce evidence that he was not guilty of at least the first two charges and he was reinstated on 4 October 1686.[38]

David Pringle, surgeon and barber to the Hospital from 1660, was summoned to cut the hair of sixty boys on the day of the anniversary sermon in June 1671. He employed a barber, William Wood, who was only licensed to practise in the nearby suburb of Portsburgh. This contravened the rules of the city corporation, and Pringle was called before the Deacon of Barber-Surgeons, Archibald Temple. Wood was imprisoned in the Tolbooth and a warrant was obtained to apprehend Pringle. As a result Pringle 'necessitat for some time to keep his house, and durst not come abroad, they having officers both at the head and foot of the close to watch and catch him'.[39] He was finally taken and he too was jailed and deprived of the benefits of membership of his

incorporation. Pringle refused to accept the judgment, arguing that he had made a genuine mistake and would guarantee that it would not happen again. The trivial affair had escalated beyond all reasonable bounds, as both sides would not give way. In the event the matter reached the Privy Council, which employed the Earls of Argyll and Linlithgow to settle matters. On 11 January 1672 Pringle apologised and the corporation restored his privileges.[40]

Pringle attended to the Covenanting prisoners on 1 July 1679, when they were being held in Greyfriars' Churchyard.[41] He died in 1687 after twenty-six years of service. His son, David, being of the same profession as his father and a great-nephew of the founder, asked the governors to keep the post open for him while he went to France 'to get further insight in the Art of Surgeoncy and pharmacy'. The governors unanimously agreed,[42] and Pringle remained in office until his early death in 1694. He in turn was succeeded by Archibald Fisher,[43] his brother-in-law.

The scholars themselves interested the governors only periodically, and usually only when they caused problems. On 26 September 1666 the treasurer and master were to keep excluded any scholars who deserted the Hospital. They were to be allowed back after eight days only after petitioning the governors, and in the 1690s it was decided that deserters would not be readmitted.[44] Thereafter this regulation was read annually to the scholars and was affixed to the Hospital door to ensure that the boys could not plead ignorance in mitigation.

However, at times standards of learning achieved by the scholars and the role of the High School in this process were issues of concern. A committee of four consulted the Statutes and recommended on 26 June 1665 that scholars could be taught their grammar in the Hospital, but twenty-three continued to go to the High School in April 1666.[45] This practice of scholars going on to the High School continued, for on 21 October 1678 the school-master explained that thirty-six Hospital boys went three times a day to classes in the High School, some by way of the Cowgate and some by way of the High Street. He suspected that some did not arrive at the school. Formerly the boys went through Greyfriars' Churchyard, Potterow, the College and entered the High School from the back, so bypassing the High Street, but this route was now blocked, as the churchyard was now locked. To overcome this problem the governors agreed that a key be made for the use of the scholars, and the door was to be opened and locked for them three times daily. From then

Above the main entrance on the north face of the Hospital is a frieze which contains four panels illustrating in superb detail the origins and purposes of the Hospital. From top: George Heriot the goldsmith at his forge with bellows; Charity is to the left of the altar, and a widow with children to the right; five boys with two guardians (governors); pupils and their teacher at lessons.

on, if a scholar was absent an example was to be made of him.[46] When, on 1 December 1690, a number of Hospital scholars were involved in breaking windows in the College, the governors insisted that the scholars go two-by-two in gowns to the High School, and the master was to appoint censors among the boys to supervise and watch them.[47]

The governors, on 4 November 1678, instructed the ministers to test the ability of the scholars, who were only to go to the High School if their proficiency warranted it. On 6 June 1681 the boys were deemed 'not proficient in their learning'[48] and the schoolmaster was 'to take more pains'. It became standard routine for the ministers, in rotation, to inspect the scholars monthly and to judge their proficiency[49] and the master of the High School, William Skene, petitioned the governors, requesting them to allow the twenty-three boys, withdrawn for 'alleged' lack of proficiency in writing, to be sent back to the High School, and the relevant chapters of the Statutes to be observed.[50]

Treasurer Thomas Fisher, however, did not the let the matter rest, and again questioned the practice of sending boys to the High School. In 1695 a committee found forty-two attending. Tests found that a few could not write well nor had they the arithmetic standards needed to become a merchant. As this was contrary to the twelfth chapter of the Statutes,[51] the governors decided on 9 September 1695 that the boys would return from the High School to the Hospital every morning at 11 a.m. to be taught writing and the rules of arithmetic, until perfected. At the same time, given the increased number of boys, it was decided that a second doctor (assistant) be appointed to teach writing, arithmetic and 'musick'.[52] The schoolmaster remained in charge of teaching Latin rudiments. The use of censors amongst the scholars was approved and a system of punishments was spelled out. Those who contravened rules on one occasion were to be given a sharp rebuke; a second contravention was to result in a whipping and a third in suspension.

These measures did not solve the intractable problem of poor academic standards. On 21 December 1696[53] and again on 11 October 1697 the governors agreed that the boys were imperfect in Latin rudiments and could not read or write Scots distinctly as the Statutes required. They reiterated the need for boys to accomplish this by the age of eleven, before going on to attend the High School for five years.[54] Most extraordinarily, in their endeavours to raise standards, the holidays were abandoned on 5 September 1698 because of the 'many inconveniences that have and may happen to fall out thro' granting and allowing a vacance to the children'.[55] The governors believed that all the good work being done in the Hospital was being undone when the boys were open to outside influences.

A contemporary account from Lord Fountainhall[56] gave a glimpse of how national events affected the scholars. In 1681–2 the Earl of Argyll was tried and convicted of high treason for refusing the Test Oath, which had to be taken by all holding public office. Fountainhall disapproved of these proceedings and narrated with glee how the 'children of Heriot's Hospitall, finding that the dog which keiped the yairds of that Hospitall had a publick charge and office, they ordained him to take the Test, and offered him the paper; but he, loving a bone rather than it, absolutely refused it; then they rubbed it over with butter (which they called an Explication of the Test, in imitation of Argyll), and he licked off the butter, but did spit out the paper, for which they held a jurie on him, and, in derision of the sentence against Argyll, they found the dog guilty of treason, and actually hanged him'.[57] The whole episode caused considerable mirth in the capital, but one source held that the governors were so horrified with the result that 'some of the young wags are said to have smarted for it afterwards'.[58]

Despite recurrent financial difficulties the governors frequently exhibited generosity in their dealings with those connected with the founder or his Hospital. On 14 March 1670 they gave a gratuity of £60 Scots to the widow of the ex-steward Somerville. On 7 November 1692 they increased the allowance given to the scholars at the College for four years

The Chapel, on the south side of the Quad, was built in an earlier Gothic manner different from the rest of the building. It is an imitation of the perpendicular early English style.

from £84 Scots to £100 Scots per annum 'for their more comfortable sustenance'. They also decided to insist on 300 merks being given over as apprentice fees to masters.[59] They would continue to ensure that all leaving the Hospital be given a new suit of clothes, with hat, shoes, stockings, linens and other necessities, and expected all masters to do the same when the boys completed their apprenticeships. On occasion the governors had their generosity repaid. On 10 June 1695 Robert Sandilands, a prominent and successful Edinburgh merchant and erstwhile British Consul to the Court of Brandenburg, gifted the Hospital 2,000 punds Scots[60] and in return he and his representatives in perpetuity gained the right to appoint two boys to the Hospital.[61] In an effort to encourage others to follow this example the governors ordained on 20 October 1696 that Sandilands' name and bequest be written on a board in gold letters and hung up in the Hospital.[62]

In June 1695 the governors of the Hospital 'on behalf of the poor thereof' applied to Parliament to be exempted from the excise duty on beer and ale. They suggested that the Hospital had become 'an ornament to the nation' and an exemption would be an encouragement to 'such pious works'. Although it was a 'small matter', the sum involved being not more than £10 sterling per annum, it would nonetheless be a 'singular advantage . . . to the poor of Heriot's Hospital'. The argument was accepted, and on 15 July the Estates of Parliament in Edinburgh gave the exemption.[63]

The century ended with the governors improving the inside as well as the outside of the Hospital. They were conscious of the loss of the original portrait of George Heriot by Van Somer,[64] and in June 1694 they attempted to have a portrait of him completed for the council room. With no immediate progress on the issue on 4 April 1698 treasurer Fisher was instructed to commission a full-sized portrait. George Scougall, the Scottish painter, was employed, and the result of his labour was exhibited in the council room, where it remains today.[65]

The example of Heriot's Hospital was the role-model for others to follow. Mary Erskine, widow of James Hair, Edinburgh apothecary, decided to open a Hospital for the daughters of merchant burgesses. She approached the Merchant Company of Edinburgh in 1694 with the offer of money to help in founding such a Hospital. The Company agreed, and raised a 'fund for the lasses' to supplement the bequest of 10,000 merks set aside by Mary Erskine. She was also to help found a parallel Hospital under the Incorporation of Trades, opened in 1704 – the Trades Maiden Hospital, for 'the needy children of the town's tradesmen, deceased or in difficult circumstances'.[66] As early as 1702–3 treasurer Fisher of Heriot's was being billed for seventy-three pairs of boys' stockings at twelve shillings per pair, which the girls of The Merchant Maiden Hospital had knitted.[67] By 1725 the girls were joining in the anniversary service in Greyfriars' Church on June Day – the birthday of George Heriot.[68]

By the end of its first half-century of existence Heriot's Hospital was in a position to take in more boys. The worsening economic situation in the country in the 1690s led the governors to increase the roll to 114 in November 1693 and then to 130 by July 1695. Such a dramatic increase at the end of the century reflected the diminishing fortunes of the merchant and craft classes in Edinburgh. With the other institutions Heriot's Hospital 'without doubt prevented the early death of many children'[69] and this important contribution certainly was much more significant than the negligible role it played in educational terms.

However, the governors must have been pleased that the Hospital 'arrested the attention of all visitors to Edinburgh'.[70] The Revd Thomas Morer wrote about the 'beautiful front of a large Hospital' after his 1689 visit,[71] while the 1695 edition of Camden's *Britannia* described it as 'a stately Fabrick like a Palace'.[72] Even Joseph Taylor, a barrister of the Inner Temple, who was somewhat contemptuous of the Scots, talked of 'the citizens having much reason to commend the Hospital' following his 1705 visit.[73] They must also have been especially satisfied by the lack of public criticism during this period of their administration; yet the evidence of the use of Hospital funds for Town purposes was accumulating. On 7 November 1677 the Town debt to Heriot's was recorded as £15,866 13s. 4d.,[74] while on 11 February 1704 the town chamberlain put twopence on the price of a pint of ale to pay off a Heriot bond. Indeed, it seems likely that Thomas Fisher was appointed as Heriot treasurer with the future of the Town as much in mind as the future of the Hospital. Throughout his time constant use was made by the Town of Heriot money,[75] and the returns to the Hospital, such as permission to use water from the Town's supply, suggest that the balance of advantage remained very much in the Town's favour.

CHAPTER FIVE

The Hospital in the First Half of the Eighteenth Century

During the first half of the eighteenth century the dominant issues affecting the Hospital were internal rather than external, domestic rather than national. The comings and goings over the Union of the Parliaments came and went without disturbing life in the institution. The outbreak of Rebellion in 1715, however, led to great activity in the City. The wall, near the Hospital, was guarded nightly, its fortifications repaired, and the level of the Nor' Loch was raised in expectation of the arrival of the rebels. 'Considering the eminent danger the good town of Edinburgh is threatened with by enemies both to his Majesty and present Government' and the fact that the 'peace of the City thereby to be disturbed'[1] ensured the cancellation of the governors' meeting of 10 October. They appointed Baillie William Neilson, the Dean of Guild Robert Craig, and the Deacon of Goldsmiths David Mitchell, to decide when it was safe to meet again. The three met at the Hospital on 17 October and again on 31 October, before bringing together, on 14 November, all thirty-two governors, along with the Hospital master, John Watson, and Hospital treasurer, James Young of Killicanty, in attendance.

The explosion which damaged the west gable end of Greyfriars' Church and destroyed its steeple on 7 May 1718 surprised and alarmed the inhabitants of the Hospital.[2] However, the hurricane of 14 January 1739, and the resulting widespread damage to Heriot property, hit home more, as the governors found themselves liable for the repairs of their tenants from such acts of providence.[3] They were also affected by the events of 1745–6, for their meeting of 12 August 1745 was to be their last until 19 January 1747 – the longest gap between meetings in the whole history of the Hospital. At the latter meeting the treasurer, David Flint, was thanked for managing Hospital affairs during 'the late times of disturbance and confusion'. This acknowledgement of his good work certainly headed off any criticism that he had not been re-elected properly because of the 'confusions of the times and the want of Magistrates and Councellors in the City'.[4] The boys, too, had reacted to the exciting situation and there was a suggestion that a number of older ones had enlisted with the Jacobites.[5]

The period was a quiet one in building terms. Treasurer Young reported on 25 September 1727 that the 'whole Easter Side' of the Hospital had fallen into disrepair, especially the roof,[6] and the governors embarked upon £200 sterling worth of repair. Internally, on 19 April 1730, it was decided to improve the furnishings of the council room and thirty chairs at nine shillings each were ordered, including a special chair for the Lord Provost at the same rate. Such piecemeal improvements would always be a feature of Hospital history, but there was also a realisation of the need to be more systematic in the inspection of the fabric of the 'wark'. This led in October 1734 to the setting up of a committee with the sole function of keeping the building under constant review, and from October 1740 onwards this committee was elected annually. Its first action was to draw attention to the poor state of the well in the middle of the court, which was cleaned, and a pump fitted to supply water for the Hospital.

Visitors to Edinburgh continued to comment favourably on the Hospital building. Macky, writing in 1724, held that 'the building exceeds anything of the kind in Europe. He (Balcanquall) hath done more like a pricely Palace than a Habitation for necessitous children . . . Its Entry . . . looks more like an Avenue to a royal Palace than a Hospital.'[7] Daniel Defoe, writing around the same time, described the Hospital as 'a large and stately building, the most magnificent of its kind in the world'.[8] The *Gentleman's Magazine* of 1745 had an article on the Hospital and its architecture – the first detailed description of the building. The author believed that 'the magnificence of this building is not suitable to the charitable purpose for which it was designed' and related that it had been observed by a foreigner, before Holyrood Palace was built by Charles II, that 'there was at Edinburgh a palace for beggars, and a dungeon for kings'.[9] James Ray of Whitehaven, a volunteer with Cumberland's army, wrote on 30 January 1746 a description of the 'wark' as 'a large stately building, adorned with a consecrated Chapel, and pleasant Gardens'.[10]

The use of the building by outsiders continued. Its reputation as a safe and significant repository is clear from the number of citizens placing their personal papers there during the major rebellions,[11] as well as the proposal to use it as a convenient storage place for the public records in December 1723.[12] A petition from James Blair and John Nairn, who had had the use of a room in the Hospital for some time to keep the papers and books of their considerable printing business, was discussed by the governors on 28 August 1732.

The governors agreed rental terms for a limited period, with strict instructions that access would only be permitted during daylight, and on no account were lighted candles to be used. A survey done in March 1743 found that ten rooms in the Hospital were in the possession of others.[13] It was proposed to charge a rent of thirty shillings annually for each room. This was probably the highest number of rooms being let, for the governors were soon pressing via the Court of Session for the vacating of Anderson's rooms. However, Lord Selskrig was to apply for, and was successful in being granted, an apartment for keeping his estate and other papers on 20 April 1747.

The governors turned their attention periodically to the gardens, especially when they were 'in disrepair'[14] in summer 1729.[15] It took, however, until 20 May 1734 for William Butcher to present a plan for forming the flower garden in 'ane handsome modern manner'.[16] There was an immediate reaction from some governors who feared the cost implications, and a less ambitious plan was adopted. Part of the Wester garden was to be cleared of all trees and bushes, and employed to produce herbs and roots for the kitchen. This, however, does not seem to have solved the problem of providing sufficiently for the Hospital's needs, as in August 1737 the steward was having to buy extra roots and herbs from market stalls. On 9 January 1738 a committee visited the gardens and found a plentiful supply of kail and leeks but few other roots or herbs. Its members decided to take advice from the physician and surgeon of the requirements of the scholars, and in June 1739 the gardener, Robert Reid, was instructed to give over £10 sterling to the steward to buy roots and herbs for the kitchen, thereby solving the problem provisionally at least.

The governors were also concerned at the use of the gardens for meetings and events. Following a public meeting on 12 June 1747 a committee was set up to investigate a number of complaints and the 'offence' caused to some people.[17] More problems surfaced in 1751. David Waddel, tacksman of Heriot Gardens, and John Frederick Lampe[18] had publicly advertised a concert of vocal and instrumental music to be held in the gardens on Tuesday, 4 June. Lampe had arrived in Edinburgh the previous November with a small opera company, and during the summer of 1751 he put on the first-ever season of English opera in Scotland and started open-air concerts.[19]

At a meeting on 3 June the Lord Provost argued that such an event 'would be hurtful to the City in general and greatly prejudicial to the Hospital in particular'. All twenty-three governors, voting unanimously their 'aversion to such a

Over the archway, within the Quad on the north side, stands the statue of George Heriot, 5 feet 10 inches in height. Completed by Robert Mylne, the likeness was taken from Heriot's portrait.

practice',[20] resolved to take all proper and legal methods to stop the concert. By their next meeting on 26 September the treasurer reported that he had consulted with the advocate, Robert Craigie. Waddel had been called before the City Baillies and a warrant obtained, prohibiting a concert in Heriot Gardens. The Baillies ordered Waddel to take down the theatre erected for the musicians and instantly to deliver the key of the inner garden to the treasurer to ensure that the order was obeyed. Waddel had appealed to the Lords of Session but this had been rejected on 21 June.[21]

One of the most recurrent themes of this time was staff difficulties. Robert Innes, student in the College of Edinburgh, was appointed one of the doctors in October 1719, but within two months a 'misunderstanding' had arisen between him and the other doctor, Hardie.[22] This was taken as an excuse to set up a wide-ranging investigation into the running of the Hospital, as a number of governors clearly felt that standards were declining and irregularities creeping in. The committee under Baillie Wightman carried out extensive interviews with all staff, and in February 1720 held that the master, John Watson, was too aged and infirm to continue in office; the schoolmaster, Thomas Herriot, had frequently failed to perform public worship in the chapel, had not instructed the doctors to visit the boys' chambers or oversee their rising or going to bed, and his social life was also criticised; the butler, William Mitchelson, had sold ale outside the Hospital and had run short in his accounts. Watson and Mitchelson were instantly dismissed, while Herriot was publicly rebuked. In the meantime the original issue resulted in Wightman's committee deciding to replace both Hardie and Innes. Such incidents between doctors occurred regularly.

Relationships between masters and schoolmasters and their assistants, the doctors, could also be fragile. The 'misunderstanding' between David Christie (master) and William Dyce (doctor) reached such a pitch in October 1721 that the master called Dyce 'opprobrous and scurulous names'[23] and Dyce retaliated by threatening the master with his fist in front of all the boys in the chapel. Christie was given an official warning, while Dyce was dismissed.

On 28 August 1732, at a meeting of the governors, the Lord Provost read out a letter complaining of negligence by the teachers in the Hospital. No lessons had been taught for three days, and the scholars had behaved indecently and in a disorderly fashion in church. The staff were warned to improve in these areas 'upon their peril if they failed so to do'.[24]

Given the restrictive conditions of the Hospital it is perhaps not surprising that relationships often broke down. As the Statutes had not mentioned 'doctors', on 12 November 1711, the governors spelled out their duties. It was a demanding role which involved teaching large classes of boys, looking after large numbers from 7 a.m. to 10.30 p.m., taking prayers mornings and evenings, supervising all meals and exercises, visiting chambers morning and night, inspecting the proficiency of High School boys, and even on Sundays checking that 'none of the boys lurk from Chapel' by accompanying them[25] and catechising the boys and servants. Not surprisingly, these extensive duties took their toll on the doctors. The work of the schoolmasters was not so demanding, and a committee investigating their hours on 1 September 1735 decided that they should attend the same hours as the High School staff.[26]

In January 1735 the new master, William Mathieson, complained that schoolmaster David Doig had broken the regulations regarding good order and had 'emitted some disrespectful expressions'[27] to him. Doig was called before the governors and given his first admonition. A committee of eight governors was appointed to meet Mathieson and Doig in the Laigh Coffee House in an effort to bring them together, but this failed, and Mathieson offered to resign. The governors tried to dissuade him, but he proved 'inflexible'.[28] Doig left soon after, but *his* resignation was accepted 'instantly'.[29] The governors advertised for replacements, looking for a master 'of respect and prudence', 'unmarried' and 'between 40 and 60'. In a schoolmaster the governors were looking for someone of 'good repute, unmarried, of the age of 40 or thereby, that will undergo a comparative trial'. As an incentive 'his entertainment in the Hospital is handsome'.[30]

In January 1737 the governors gave Mathieson's successor as master, John Hunter, his first warning for having used rash and indecent language, and for his irregular visiting of the boys in their rooms. However, in February 1740, a great number of boys complained of being harshly treated by Hunter, and a committee was set up to inquire into these complaints and other suggestions of unacceptable practices occurring in the Hospital. Within six weeks the committee had reported that Hunter had frequently been seen beating the boys cruelly and unmercifully, dragging some by the ear or hair; punching others in the ears, resulting in bleeding; nine boys mentioned having suffered similar treatment, mostly in chapel, 'for no faults or for very slender misdemeanours'.[31] Hunter, it was also alleged, had also forced reluctant schoolmasters to whip the boys. On one occasion a boy was forced to go without shoes for a whole weekend: when one of the doctors protested on the Monday that the boy had been punished enough, Hunter insisted he be whipped by him, and when the doctor protested, he was accused of disobedience.

Hunter did little to prevent disorder and noise in the chapel or at meals, and he did not explain to the household what was expected, only that he should be obeyed without question. He often ordered staff to punish boys without explanation. During October and November 1739 Hunter had been seen the worse of drink, and in particular was seen staggering in and out of chapel: he was not understood during catechism, and the servants and boys smirked and laughed. Hunter demanded the right to examine the witnesses, and six meetings of the governors in 1740[32] were taken up with the issue, with the evidence left lying on the table of the council room for the perusal of the governors. Finally, on 17 June the governors concluded that the case against Hunter was 'sufficiently proven',[33] and he was dismissed immediately. On 19 June the *Caledonian Mercury* held that if a well-qualified person came forward the governors 'have resolved not to be confined to the present arrangement (which is £25, bed, board and washing) but to have a regard to the merit of the person'.[34]

Problems with other staff were also a recurrent theme of this period. In August 1703 the governors demanded that the steward should stop selling ale to the servants, and in an attempt to cut down the traffic in ale the allowance to women servants was cut.[35] They also demanded that the steward, mistress, cook and servants should no longer keep back the best meat. Given the scale of the problem the governors determined to dispense with the services of the whole household, but as it would have been impossible to replace all at once it was decided that the master and treasurer would begin by dismissing the most guilty first. Later, on 24 February 1729, some servants were dismissed for taking money from the boys in return for food – a practice which remained prevalent in the Hospital despite all attempts to end it.

Acquiring women servants of the proper quality proved a major difficulty. The six on the staff in the seventeenth century were joined by four others in 1704. Each of them was placed in charge of one room of boys[36] and their main occupation was to keep the chambers clean and wash the boys' clothes. In June 1708 the master, John Watson, complained about the women servants, their carriage and their behaviour toward him. After investigation three of them were dismissed. From then onwards new servants were interviewed in the hope of ensuring that they were fit for the work.

Dr George Mackenzie[37] was appointed physician of the Hospital at £10 sterling per annum on 4 June 1705. The governors were reluctant to elect him because of his episcopalian persuasion but accepted him on the prompting of his

The North Doorway is the grandest of architecture and is the classical entrance which William Wallace contrived to mark the main door of the Hospital.

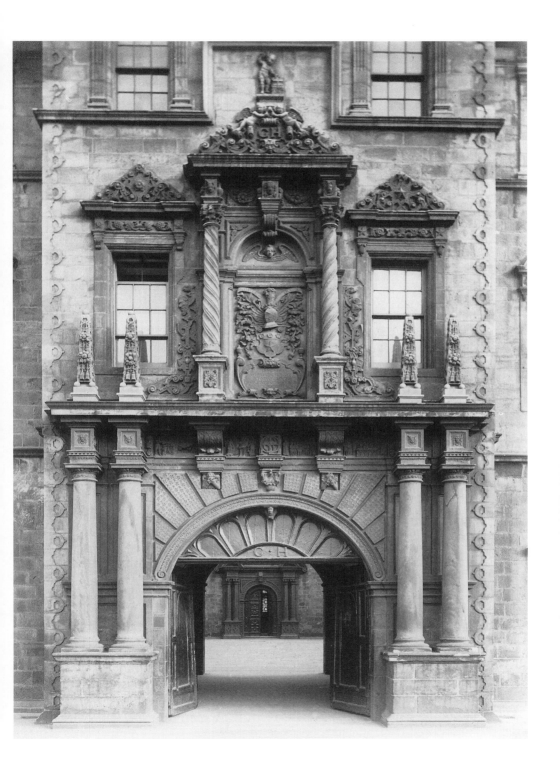

immediate predecessor, Sir Archibald Stevenson, physician since August 1666, who had agreed to cancel a claim against the Hospital for £200 sterling if they did so. As soon as he took office he pressed for two well-aired rooms for sick boys, but it took until May 1711 for one room to be prepared 'for the tender and sickly children'.[38] On 2 July 1711 the governors dismissed Mackenzie, rescinding the Act electing him which they declared was 'void and null in all tyme coming'[39] and he was replaced by the Presbyterian Dr Gilbert Rule. Given the usual prudence of the governors, one can assume that they had good reason for their action: Mackenzie's extreme Jacobite views were probably the cause.[40] However, Mackenzie objected that the action was contrary to the Statutes which did not allow the dismissal of an officer (except the gardener) without charges. His sixteen-page letter to the governors was a complete defence of his position[41] and he put forward his case in person in the council room on 6 August 1711. In particular he held that the Hospital had been more flourishing under episcopalian rule rather than under the regime of their Presbyterian successors. He was scathing in his personal attack on the master and his failings, especially with regard to his teaching of the catechism and the failure to commemmorate the founder other than on Founder's Day.[42] Despite this the governors reinstated Mackenzie, providing he withdraw his accusations. However, Mackenzie stood his ground and refused to retract his letter. The governors allowed the case to lie for over a year, until, on 27 December 1714, they finally dismissed him as he 'had not retracted the printed letter',[43] and confirmed Rule as the Hospital physician.[44]

It was not always possible for the governors to obtain their first choice for appointments. On 2 April 1711, following the death of treasurer Thomas Fisher,[45] the governors elected George Watson (1654–1723), merchant burgess of Edinburgh, as his successor. He had already been treasurer of the Merchant Maiden Hospital between 1702–04 and had been one of its nine governors since 1700. As one successful in business, banking and finance who had not invested in the Darien Scheme[46] the governors pressed him to accept. However, 'after using all means with him [Watson] to accept of the said office they could not prevail with him to accept thereof'.[47] However, Watson did not forget Heriot's in his will. As well as leaving 8,300 merks to the Merchant Maiden he left 5,000 merks to Heriot's[48] and stipulated that his own Hospital[49] constitution should be 'as near to the rules of the foundation and management of Heriot's Hospital and the Merchant Maiden Hospital, as the nature of the thing will allow of'.[50] This explained why the Statutes of Watson's Hospital were similar in many respects to those set out almost exactly a century before by Balcanquall, in particular in Chapters VIII and IX on the election of the headmaster and schoolmaster.[51]

The original site for Watson's Hospital at Thomson's Yards at the south-east corner of the town was deemed, at only one acre and a quarter, as too small. Moreover, as it lay between the University and the High School it was believed that the building of a hospital there would result in insults from both students and pupils, and open the Hospital boys to their vices. The committee, investigating an alternative, also observed that 'the vices of the Boys of Heriot's Hospital have been owing to their being situate so near the Grass Mercate, who being despised by the better sort as Charity Boys, ly under too great a temptation of taking up with mean and wicked boys'.[52] This led to the selling of Thomson's Yards and the acquiring of the site of seven and a half acres opposite Heriot's.[53] The first foundationers entered Watson's Hospital in 1741.

When Robert Gordon, merchant in Aberdeen, determined, in his 'Deed of Mortification and Disposition' registered in Edinburgh on 24 May 1731, to found a Hospital, he also followed closely Heriot's example.[54] Gordon left £10,000 sterling for the 'maintenance, aliment, entertainment, and education of young boys, whose parents are poor and indigent, and not able to maintain them at schools, and put them to trades and employments'.[55] His plans were also to be effected by the provost, baillies, members of the town council and the four ministers of 'the Old and New Churches' of Aberdeen. His Hospital was to take indigent male children and grandchildren of 'decayed merchants and brethren of guild' of the town. He chose the Black-Fryars ground on the north-side of School-hill as its site, but perhaps learning from the Heriot experience, Gordon limited expenditure on the building of his Hospital to 30,000 merks Scots. The pivotal role of the treasurer, the four auditors elected annually, and the office and work of the clerk followed the Heriot pattern. The detailed arrangements for other officers, the ages of those elected to the foundation and the apprentice fee system also owed much to the Heriot Statutes. Indeed, the only completely novel idea was Gordon's provision for any ex-Hospital boys who were successful in life to pay back what had been laid out and expended on them, during the time they were in the Hospital.[56] Although Gordon never mentioned Heriot's Hospital in his deed (or appendix) it, too, was strikingly similar to that produced by Balcanquall, another testimony to the importance and influence of the Heriot precedent.

There were an increasing number of references to problems with the Heriot boys in this period. On 16 April 1716 the governors were informed that the Hospital children 'were taken up very oft with feghting and bickaring with other children and prentice boys'.[57] On 16 October 1727 the master,

David Christie, reported that one of the boys, Alexander Mitchell, was guilty of many misdemeanours and theft. A committee of governors was set up to decide his future and it resolved on 19 February 1728 to exclude him 'to the Terrour of the other boys educated therein not to be guilty of the like practises'.[58] It was not successful: within the year Robert Dickson was excluded from the Hospital for some time for 'vicious' practices such as pick-pocketing and thieving.

Another problem manifesting itself was that of boys absenting themselves overnight without permission. Accordingly, the governors decided on 2 June 1729 that absentees would not be taken in again until their case had been reviewed. It was reported on 25 July of the same year that eleven boys had absented themselves, three of them for several nights. Although they were all taken back into the Hospital a notice was put up in the chapel[59] warning that any overnight absentees would in future be excluded. All the boys of the institution were then called together in the chapel by the Lord Provost and lectured by the Revd William Millar. The governors pressed forward on this issue, and at their next meeting on 15 September it was decided that the master and schoolmaster would take a register of the boys every evening after chapel prayers in order to ensure that none were out at 'unreasonable' hours.

After the significant desertions of July 1729 some governors expressed a desire for some clarification of procedures, and a committee recommended a new set of rules on 20 April 1730. Any boy absenting himself from the Hospital overnight was to be publicly rebuked by the governors, whipped in front of all boys in the chapel with the governors present, and this was to be recorded. On a second transgression the same punishment was to be meted out, but for several hours each day for eight days the transgressor(s) was to be detained in stocks (which were to be made specially for the Hospital) and this, in turn, was to be recorded. For a third offence exclusion from the Hospital and loss of its benefits was to be automatic, although the governors still retained the right to exclude boys on a first or second offence if other crimes were involved. This Act was to be read publicly to the boys and their parent(s) on their admission. The governors agreed to these changes and instantly rebuked John Dalgleish and John Cumming, who had absented themselves a first time, and who were 'carried to the chapel and there whipped in the presence of two members of the Council and of the whole Boys in the Hospital'.[60]

In December 1730 Thomas Spence was excluded for the theft of a piece of leather; he denied it but 'the leather was taken out of his chest by one of the members of the Council' and he was excluded; his father's appeal for readmission was subsequently rejected. Another boy, Robert Anderson, stayed out overnight and was whipped. Although some governors were clearly unhappy at the violence involved in these new arrangements, after further discussion it was decided to retain them. In April 1731 another boy was excluded for 'notorious theft'[61] and three others were whipped for staying out all night. A year later, on 17 April 1732, the stocks were used for the first time for three boys, with three others being excluded later that year.

The governors endeavoured to close one of the loopholes used by the boys to subvert their new rules. The annual June Day ceremony had become a time for decorating the statue of the founder in the quadrangle, but there were complaints against boys leaving the Hospital, claiming 'to purchase flowers for busking the Statue'.[62] The governors insisted on 22 February 1731 that this should cease: the master would not allow them such liberty, and the gardener was to provide flowers in future for the decoration. This, however, seems to have had little effect: the June Day ceremony of 1738 was followed by complaints by neighbours of the Hospital that boys had plundered flowers from their gardens. The rule was then reiterated and the gardener instructed 'to provide a flower and put it in the hand of the statue on the first Monday of June yearly'.[63] This led to a reaction the following year, for the boys 'took it so ill, that when the psalm was raised, they would not so much as open a lip, but hanged their heads'.[64]

Although there were fewer incidents recorded in the later 1730s there were still complaints from the governors of the boys exhibiting 'habits of vice and idleness'.[65] Outsiders, too, seemed to have a low opinion of the boys at this time. On Tuesday, 27 October 1741, the celebrated George Whitefield preached in the chapel and the diary of a 'very worthy Christian in Edinburgh' held that as a result 'a great change is wrought upon many of the boys; for there . . . Fellowship meetings are set up, which is quite new there; for the boys of that hospital were noted for being the wickedest boys about town'.[66]

More significant, however, in the long term were the problems which seem to have been widespread around the middle of the century. In April 1748 the first recorded case of bullying was reported, but as usual the governors dealt leniently with the culprit. A more serious incident occurred in October 1751. After an investigation involving the interview of a number of staff, two boys were to be confined in a 'sure part' of the Hospital and fed on a 'spare dyet'.[67] Yet, despite reports from the Hospital physician and surgeon on the victim's condition, the governors were lenient again, exhorting the boys to follow their example of goodness. More worrying was their belief that all boys entering the Hospital 'come under engagements to one another in no case whatever to reveal or discover to the masters or others belonging to the Hospital any injury they themselves should receive or which they may have been accessory to'.[68] The governors rightly believed that this practice was contrary to, and inconsistent with, the proper government of the Hospital, and resolved that any boy found guilty of attempting such 'engagement' was to be excluded. Exclusion was also to be the punishment for any who were involved in the practice of bullying, and those victims who refused to reveal who had bullied them. Unfortunately, other than such general strictures, the governors failed to deal with the insidious and endemic condition which was developing in the institution and the 'Garring Law',[69] which developed in the Hospital, was to cause great concern and suffering for many as time went on.

During this period Statute XIII and its regulation on uniform began to be enforced, as the governors decided that from 7 June 1703 all children were to be clothed on their entry to the Hospital in 'sad russet cloath'.[70] The public liked to see the Hospital uniform, and staff probably favoured it as an aid to discipline and a help in identifying wrongdoers or runaways.[71] In 1704 all boys were to have two pair of breeches and three shirts. However, by February 1736 a committee was reporting on the poor conditions of the boys' clothes; their dirty shoes of a tan colour were torn, and in many cases the boys had their feet right through them. Little time was spent by the governors on discussing the leisure time of the boys, but it is clear that the boys were constantly playing ball in the chapel in bad weather, and the consequent damage, particularly to the windows, resulted in an order to the master in 1750 to stamp out the practice.

Not surprisingly the governors seem to have taken increasingly seriously the problems regarding standards of learning in the Hospital. In September 1708 they instituted an improved inspection of the education of the pupils. They decided to reintroduce the former system of the seventeenth century, but on a more formal basis.[72] Immediately after the new council had been elected, every October, it was to be divided into six committees with three members (including a minister) on each, which would take over the role of inspection of the boys for two months on a rotational basis. In fact, the interest of the ministers ensured that the committees concentrated their attention on religious teaching, but this more rigorous appraisal of the staff of the Hospital remained in existence throughout the remainder of its history. The first committee report held that the children 'did answer very distinctly to ilk question put to them and gave an very good account thereof and approved of the method the Schoolmasters and doctors had begun with for instructing'.[73] Usually this was the style and tenor of such reports, but on 6 October 1712 it was reported that the children 'had come farr short of their knowledge in the said principals of Religion by what they were the last year'.[74] This resulted in the schoolmaster and doctors being called in before the governors and being instructed 'to be more carefull' in their teaching. At the same time it was agreed that the Hospital boys attending College should be examined four times a year by its principal, and he was to ascertain their proficiency, or lack of it, and report to the governors.

At times the governors made suggestions regarding the curriculum. In October 1721 they stressed the great benefit of children being taught to write and account in the best manner, and also being taught the idiom and orthography of the English language by means of Sir Richard Steill's *English Gramer* in the same manner as the Latin language was taught, no matter whatever employment the boys might follow later. By April 1722 the governors were encouraged by the progress the boys were making in both writing and arithmetic, and in their understanding of the many Latin words which were adapted into and used in the English language.

It had been decided in February 1730 that the master should teach book-keeping to all who might benefit from it,[75] but the proposal was reviewed by the governors, and on 19 April 1731 they held that 'writing and arithmetic are the finishing accomplishments for all the boys in the Hospital whether they design for merchants or tradesmen; and therefore that the teaching of booking be set aside and discontinued in time coming'.[76] This decision, however, owed much to the lack of expertise and enthusiasm for the subject by those working in the institution (Hepburn and Hunter) at the time. When the Hospital did have a schoolmaster capable of teaching the subject, book-keeping became an accepted part of the curriculum again.[77]

Concern about the standards of those Hospital boys who were attending the High School re-emerged in October 1709, and the governors reiterated their policy of September 1695 in order to ensure that the boys returned every forenoon to the Hospital at 11 a.m. to be taught their writing and the rules of arithmetic. When it was claimed in October 1728 that those going to the High School gained 'little or no education thereby'[78] a committee under Baillie Duncan Campbell was set up, which, on examining the boys, found them 'not qualified in the terms of the Statutes'. On its recommendation the governors decided that the boys would stay in the Hospital an extra year and only attend the High School when considered qualified by the master and schoolmaster. Further consideration of the measures needed to encourage and further the education of Hospital boys 'whose Genius leads them to prosecute their Studies' either in the Hospital or the High School was begun. Such worries about the High School led to two boys being taken away from there to spend all their time in Hospital, and the porter was sent to the High School every Saturday morning to bring back a certificate of the weekly attendance of Hospital boys there. Some governors contrasted progress in the Hospital with progress in the High School, and in June 1736 they were stressing the deficiency of the High School boys in Latin. Even the boys themselves were sometimes reluctant to attend, four of them (out of seven attending) having their petition to stay in the Hospital rejected by the governors in October 1738. The growing confidence in the Hospital and the decrease in confidence in the High School led to the decision to withdraw boys completely from the latter in April 1739, confirmed by the governors in 1742. Traditionally this was seen as the beginning of the monastic period of the Hospital, but there is evidence that the Hospital was not as isolated as previously suggested.[79]

The governors did not forget their responsibility to the vast majority of Hospital boys who were apprenticed after their time in the 'wark'. In November 1707 the governors were interviewing employers to see how proficient the apprentices were, and to see whether either masters or apprentices had any complaints. Of real concern for the governors was how to ensure that all apprentices kept their commitment to return to the Hospital every year on Commemoration Day to celebrate the founder's birth. On rare occasions when a boy was totally unfit for employment, as in a case of blindness recorded in June 1725, the governors paid towards his upkeep after his departure. From time to time they debated whether boys should be allowed to be apprenticed while remaining resident in the Hospital, but this was not accepted. It was conceded on 16 April 1739, however, that boys could be apprenticed before they were sixteen, could live out, and be granted an allowance in lieu of board and lodging until they reached the age of sixteen.[80]

It became increasingly common in this period for benefactors to show generosity to the Hospital. On 2 February 1708 Sir James Gray gifted £100 sterling,[81] while in March 1711 the ex-treasurer, Thomas Fisher, left some property to the Trust on his death. On 27 September 1718 Captain Dougal Campbell, grandson of Archibald Campbell of Inverawe, in Argyllshire, bequeathed £100 sterling to the Hospital: he had no particular connection with Heriot's, but wished to support the concept of charity schools. When the money was finally received in June 1720 it was agreed that his name be put up in gold letters on a board in the Hospital.[82] The legacy of 5,000 merks which George Watson had bequeathed to Heriot's for maintaining two boys there – 'the children or grandchildren of decayed merchants in Edinburgh of the name of Watson or Davidson, preferring always the name of Watson' – was accepted by the governors at their meeting on 20 April 1724.[83]

The first former boy of the Hospital to gift money was Thomas Aitken, periwig-maker in London, whose legacy of £58 15s. was received in September 1736. When, around the same time, the Revd John Glen returned the traditional fee of 100 merks for preaching the anniversary sermon, the governors decided to put up a board to commemorate the gifts of both Aitken and Glen.[84] The practice of acknowledging the debt owed to the Hospital by former boys became increasingly popular. On 26 September 1751 the governors received from the trustee of the will of Thomas Heriot, Dean of Guild, the sum of £100 sterling and the annual rent thereof: the terms stipulated that a half of the annual rent be paid equally to two boys in the Hospital who excelled at writing, the other half to go to two boys who excelled in arithmetic. Another board was prepared.[85]

Long-lasting arrangements for the operation of the Hospital were instituted at this time.[86] The rules were comprehensively updated on 2 October 1752. Every meal, its content and its timing, was itemised. Each aspect of the curriculum was spelled out; arithmetic and English standards were determined; the free time of the boys was set at one afternoon a fortnight as well as every Saturday afternoon; the boys were allowed out only by permission of the master, and if they were going farther than two miles the permission of the governors was needed. They were not to be allowed out in rainy or stormy weather except in cases of absolute necessity, and in all events any boy outside the Hospital was to wear a badge on his breast; following earlier problems 'any boy found guilty of imposing or executing oaths of secrecy . . . [to be] excluded'. As well as previous rules, mention was now made of not allowing illumination of the windows or cock-fighting. Censors were to help in wards, and all the boys who could do so were obliged to make a fair and clean copy of these rules, so that all staff and governors had a copy to hand.

The governors, still committed to, and appreciating, the importance of land acquisition, decided in 1704 to buy the estate of Coates, immediately to the west of the Town. The total sum agreed with its owner, Archibald, Earl of Rosebery, was £59,655 Scots, and treasurer Fisher informed the governors on 4 February 1706 that the final payment had been made to the Bank of Scotland to complete the purchase.[87] When Fisher reported on 3 June 1706 that he had agreed with Robert Gray to buy his estate of Warriston on the north side of the Town for 50,600 merks the governors unanimously agreed and the sale went through, recording the event on a board still extant in the

Old Refectory.[88] Such dealings, by the treasurer and governors, consolidated and built on previous land acquisitions, but in the short-term they diminished revenue, and it is significant that 1707 was the first year when no boys were taken into the Hospital since 1679.

The next financial crisis for the Hospital seems to have been in 1717. On 15 April of that year only one boy was elected. He was only taken in as a result of his being a relative of the founder and to replace a desertion, the treasurer also claiming that the reserves had almost disappeared and would do so completely by 1720.[89] He argued that there were too many boys in the Hospital given the price of corn (which determined the income from rents) and the level of sums being spent on apprentice fees. On 11 February 1717 the governors accepted his suggestions that, until reserves recovered, the number of boys be reduced to 120 and the apprentice fee be reduced from £200 sterling to 200 merks, although the latter sum would be paid when boys took up their apprenticeship instead of being delayed a year.

The financial situation improved with prudent management and strict control. The number of boys entering the Hospital returned to normal levels. By June 1742 numbers were back up to 136.[90] They were to drop again in 1733 and 1734, partly for financial reasons, although the fact that the governors were able to raise apprentice fees to 300 merks in the latter year to persuade employers to take them on perhaps suggests that other factors, such as the epidemics of 'fevers of the cold' which affected Edinburgh then, may have been important. Normality returned until 1746 when no meetings meant no entrants. In October 1748 it was reported that the annual revenue of each of the previous six years under treasurer David Flint had been found to be in the red and 'that if this method was persisted in it might prove dangerous to the Hospital'.[91]

It was this situation which led William Maitland, a well-known English antiquary, to make a blistering attack on the Hospital's administration. In *The History of Edinburgh from its Foundation to the Present Time*,[92] published in 1753, he was critical of many aspects of the Hospital and its operation, claiming that Heriot had bequeathed some £43,608 11s. 3d. sterling.[93] Maitland held that it was 'piteous' to be admitting only thirty boys to 'so magnificent and spacious an edifice, which is sufficient for the reception of many Hundreds, as was the Fund likewise for their maintenance'. He suggested the Hospital could maintain over 316 boys, and so 'does not reflect much Honour on the governors of that Time; for by their imprudent and unjustifiable Conduct, they erected a fabrick so

The design of the Chapel interior was probably influenced by Archbishop Laud, who liked Gothic churches and visited the Hospital in 1633. It was re-fitted in the 1830s.

sumptuous, at the Expense of Twenty Years labour, and above twenty seven thousand Pounds Sterling Charge, that it is probably excelled every Structure of its Kind then upon Earth . . . more proper for the Residence of a great King than the habitation of a few and needy Orphans. For, till this Time, the Vanity of Man was not got to such a Height of Extravagance as to erect Palaces for Beggars.' He further attacked the tradition of giving 100 merks for a sermon, which he deemed to be an 'enormous sum', the equivalent of a small yearly stipend in England, which was a grievance calling out for redress. This was evidence of Heriot's property being 'squandered' by the indiscretions of a few inconsiderate governors. He also criticised Balcanquall for the unalterable oath at the end of the Statutes, believing such arrangements to be 'insolent, daring and iniquitous', predating the arguments against such 'dead hand' legalities common in the nineteenth century.

Maitland's comments were seized upon by the critics of the Hospital. They led to Alexander Brown's lawsuit in the Court of Session, which was only successfully defeated by the governors in July 1765 when they produced the original seventeenth-century vouchers.[94] Although Maitland's own criticisms have not stood the test of time, other commentators however made more telling attacks. Certainly there would appear to be some substance in the charge that the governors did not find sufficient time to attend properly to the state of education and morals in the Hospital.[95] In this period, perhaps, more than any other, they were preoccupied with the details of numerous business transactions relating to the feuing of Heriot property and other such concerns.

Furthermore, there seems to be growing evidence of an increase in the number of examples of the town council favouring its own members in dubious deals which resulted in the Hospital suffering a loss of land and income. In March 1730 the governors feued the town council five acres of land at the head of Broughton Loan for an annual duty of £10 8s. 5d. sterling.[96] The councillors in turn sub-feued to Picard emigrants[97] who tried to introduce silk manufacture and planted their mulberry trees on the slopes of Moutrie's Hill.[98] These were blasted by the east wind and the land soon came back onto the market. It was acquired by the Board of Trustees for Manufactures and subfeued at great profit for streets and buildings in 1809. Here was one example of the governors giving up Heriot land of considerable value without adequate compensation.

Another example occurred when, in 1737, Heriot's Croft and St Leonards were granted in feu to the City by the governors and these valuable lands (from Lauriston Place south-eastwards to the Queen's Park and to Rosehall on the Dalkeith Road) were soon enriching others. Councillor Thomas Hope of Rankeillour, in particular, gained the feu on Clerk Street, Rankeillor Street and Montague Street for a mere 3s. 4d. per annum! Non-town councillors on the governing body, such as the Revd Robert Wallace and the then treasurer of the Hospital, Thomas Heriot, protested strongly but in vain.[99]

Another important charge directed against the governors at this time was that of 'jobbing'. Perhaps it was inevitable that the deacons of the Incorporated trades would use their seats on the governing body to take up all the contracts on offer. However, there are examples of this going beyond all reasonable bounds. In 1731, the treasurer contracted with the deacon of bakers to furnish bread to the Hospital for thirteen years.[100] Such arrangements brought those running the institution into disrepute. The most unfortunate feature was that it took until April 1846 before the governing body agreed that no governor could give estimates for Hospital work or furnishings, or be employed, when he had a pecuniary interest. Till then the reputation of Heriot's Hospital continued to be stained by the recurrent excesses of its supposed guardians.

CHAPTER SIX

The Hospital in the Later Eighteenth Century

During the later eighteenth century the Hospital was even more involved in Town affairs than before and not always to its advantage. As chairman of governors in early 1759 Lord Provost George Drummond acquainted his fellow governors with his intended improvements for Edinburgh which also involved property owned by the Hospital. A very large committee of eighteen persons was set up to advise on the interests of Heriot's on 16 April, and after a long discussion the governors agreed that if the scheme could be 'so contrived as that it may be executed without lessening the revenue or hurting the interest of the hospital, it is the duty of the Governors thereof heartily to concur in every measure which may promote the welfare of the City'.[1]

It took until 26 November 1759 for Drummond to present to a full meeting of thirty-four governors an act of the town council applying for a feu of between thirty and forty acres of the Heriot lands of Broughton.[2] Technically such a petition could not be remitted, but the governors decided to waive their own rules to do so. This resulted in a storm of protest from the Revd John Glen, supported by the Revds Wallace, Walker, Lundie, Dick and Erskine, who as ministers saw themselves as the bulwark of Heriot's interests against those of the town. They had already signalled their alarm at a pamphlet issued earlier in the year which suggested that the Hospital was too rich, while the town council's finances needed repair, and that an extension of the royalty of the town would enable the feuing of land at existing rents from the Hospital. To them such manoeuvring was a way for the town to solve its financial problems using lands belonging to the Hospital. However, the numerical domination of the governing body by the councillors guaranteed a safe majority to press forward.[3]

On 10 December the committee reported that granting the proposed feu would benefit Heriot's Hospital, and prove of public utility. It proposed an early commencement of the feu and detailed the intended financial settlement. Before the vote was taken Glen again protested against the 'indefensible' alienation of Heriot lands. Others supported his stance on the grounds that the true value was not being given for the lands.[4] Glen further protested that the town councillors as petitioners in the feu should be regarded as parties in the issue and therefore they should not be allowed to vote. The facts, that the Hospital was to receive the relatively low price of five bolls of barley per acre at the expiration of the forty-five-year tack and that the Merchant and Incorporated Trades offered £3,700 more than the town council for the land, were both powerful and convincing arguments supporting Glen's case.

On 14 December Baillie David Flint produced 'answers' to Glen's protest and was supported by the Lord Provost and other councillors who held that it was contrary to the Statutes of the Hospital to debar members from voting on any issue, given the oath they had taken.[5] The Revd Wallace moved that the Hospital feu out parcels of land to the highest bidders, who would be bound to lay out their houses in a way which would conform with the town council's plan. This was rejected by the governors, other than the seven ministers, on the grounds that they could not bind their successors to grant feus. The councillors doubted whether the Trust had the right to involve itself in paving streets, bringing in water and providing for the other needs of the inhabitants. Moreover, even if this could be done, compensation would be needed for those giving up their tack, otherwise there would be no progress for a generation. After this heated discussion a report, granting the City over thirty-seven acres, was approved on 14 December by 29–8.

The Revd Wallace immediately protested that this was unnecessary and detrimental to the interest and revenue of the Hospital. He argued that this action was null and void as the 'majority of legal and unexceptionable voters voted against'.[6] He received the support of six others. Support also came from a powerful source: Gilbert Clerk, clerk of the Hospital since 1734, held that the feu meant that the Hospital would be 'for ever deprived of what he always reckoned up to be the most valuable and promising article belonging to his office'.[7] The ministers felt so strongly that they had published a 28-page booklet to explain their dissent and protest.[8] It was a convincing statement, but in simple terms the councillors believed that the Hospital was too rich and the Town too poor. The fact that the legal expenses of the dispute were paid with Hospital money only added insult to injury.

The warm reception given to their arguments led the opposers of the feu to take their case to the Court of Session, but their Bill of Suspension was refused by Lord Edgefield. However, public opinion was now aroused, and the Merchant Company joined forces with the fourteen Incorporated Trades of Edinburgh in pursuing a lawsuit against the governors. Various pamphlets appeared blaming the governors for feuing land to favourites, being inattentive to the financial interests of the Hospital, and for tacitly tolerating the perfunctory discharge of duty on the part of certain officials.[9] The final decision of the Court of Session accepted the majority of governors' 'Answer'[10] and on 20 November 1766 Lord Auchinleck held that the feu to the Town 'was a lawful act of administration'. The competency of the governors to feu the lands of the Hospital also legitimised their actions in 1737.

Years later, in 1826, the town council was to be defended by Sir Walter Scott from the charge of being guilty of sacrificing the interests of the Hospital to those of the city. He argued that 'to execute such a speculation as the erection of a New Town, was a task far beyond the duties and powers of the trustees of the Hospital . . .. The transaction, thus considered, seems to have been fair and beneficial, – as much to the Hospital, who obtained a price for their property much above what corresponded with any revenue they could themselves derive from it; – to the magistrates, as administrators for the city, who acquired the means of carrying through a most important train of improvements, and at the same time augmented the common good, or municipal property; – and to the public, because the acquisition of that property by the magistrates, and its being included in the extended royalty, were indispensably necessary to the very existence of those splendid improvements, which have elevated Edinburgh into one of the most magnificent cities in Europe.'[11] With the benefit of hindsight Scott's view has something to commend it, but his need to defend the actions of the town councillors over sixty years after the event suggests that the results of the transaction for the Hospital were not nearly as beneficial as those accruing to the Town.[12]

Another matter of concern was the loss accrued because of the neglect, sometimes culpable and designed, of the governors to enforce the payment of rents.[13] On another occasion, the treasurer of the Hospital arrested the revenues of the Town for a large debt due to the charity: but the town council, in their capacity as governors, discharged the treasurer from insisting on the arrestment. Another allegation was that in 1758 Lord Provost Drummond, knowing Baillie Rochead was a candidate for his office, offered him the treasurership of the Hospital 'as a bait, to keep him away from the Provostship',[14] despite the existing incumbent being very efficient and highly esteemed. Although the case, supported by the Merchant Company, was not proved, appointments in the Hospital were automatically linked with local politics and there was always the possibility of fraud.

Charges of maladministration came to the surface again in 1773 when 'An Address to the Citizens of Edinburgh relative to the Management of George Heriot's Hospital by a Free Burgess of Edinburgh' appeared. It held that 'ever since the foundation of the charity, the governors have made its funds subservient to the interest of the town, or themselves.' The 'Free Burgess' claimed that the governors evaded the instruction of Heriot that the lands which he directed his trustees to purchase should be held 'in perpetuity'. They feued out parcels of ground to their favourites 'at shameful under-rates'. They then allowed the feuars, in their charters, to purchase outright a part of their feu-duties (usually between one-third and one-fifth). The sub-feuing often occurred at a much higher rate: in Broughton, Bailie Stewart paid the Hospital £2 10s. an acre, while he collected £16 an acre from the sub-feuars. In another case, the magistrates purchased from the governors (mainly themselves) five acres of land adjoining the City at twenty years' purchase and sold it a few days later to 'the trustees for the improvement of fisheries and manufactures' at twenty-five years' purchase for higher sums, the Town pocketing the difference.[15]

A further attack on the financial dealings of the governors appeared in the *Edinburgh Gazetteer* of 7 December 1792 in a letter signed 'A.B.' addressed to the previous Lord Provost, Sir James Stirling. It claimed that the governors had sold superiorities at a lower price than had been offered for them. At their meeting six days later the governors maintained that those allegations contained 'very injurious reflections on the conduct of the Governors'.[16] Although they felt that it would be improper to answer an anonymous publication they decided to place a copy of their minute in all local newspapers, asking A.B. to come forward so that they could refute his insinuations.

The Hospital also found itself embroiled in national affairs when, on 29 April 1773, the Lord Advocate sent the governors a copy of the Mortmain Bill which was before Parliament. The measure's purpose was to empower trustees of charities to invest their funds in government securities. It was felt in Edinburgh that such a bill would discourage future benefactors and that the income of the trusts would be lower than that from their previous investments. Also there was a strong national feeling in Scotland that Scottish resources should not be diverted to England. At its meeting on 7 May the governors set up a committee of seven to meet with representatives of other charitable institutions and different corporations and co-ordinate a petition to oppose the bill. Within a month the town council, the Society for Propagating Christian Knowledge and the Trinity and Trades Maiden Hospitals had all joined with Heriot's in this action. Meantime, the Merchant Company, the governors of Watson's Hospital, and the councils of Glasgow, Stirling and Aberdeen, had also petitioned the House of Commons for leave to be heard against the bill.[17] Robert Fergusson,[18] in a poetic dialogue between the spirits of George Heriot and George Watson, made his own feelings on the bill clear (in the words of Watson):

> The council winna lack sae meikle grace
> As lat our heritage at wanworth gang,
> Or the succeeding generations wrang
> O' braw bien maintenance an' walth o' lear,
> Whilk else had drappit to their children's skair;
> For mony a deep, and mony a rare engyne
> Ha'e sprung frae Herriot's wark, and sprung frae mine.[19]

He deprecated the possibility of change in his own Hospital and that of Heriot's, and his views won the day when the government, facing such opposition, abandoned the bill.

Within a short period the Hospital was again involved nationally, this time with the aerial voyages of the Tuscan, Vincenzo Lunardi,[20] the first 'aerial traveller' in England.[21] Following successful ascents in London and Liverpool he arrived in Edinburgh in September 1785, but when he was denied the use of George Square for his proposed ascent the Lord Provost suggested the Hospital gardens. Lunardi had Sir William Forbes write a letter to the governors 'who having heard my story, and read the advertisement, immediately complied with my request'.[22] Another version suggested he had to indulge in a 'little string-pulling'[23] to ensure their agreement. This seems more likely, given the opposition of governors before and after this time to any use of the Hospital grounds for such activities. Perhaps the international reputation of Lunardi was a factor in persuading them.

On 5 October at 12 noon a flag was displayed from the Castle and a gun (brought from Leith Fort) was fired on Heriot Green to signify the beginning of the process of filling up the balloon. By 2.20 p.m. this was complete, and when the ballast had been organised Lunardi ordered the machine to be carried to the eastern part of the grounds so that the ladies present could get a better view of the ascent. At 2.50 p.m. the balloon ascended, and according to one account[24] Lunardi went up 'in the most grand and magnificent manner'; an eye-witness said it resembled a sky-rocket. After an hour and a half in the air he landed some forty-six miles away just east of Ceres in Fife. He was to make a number of ascents in Scotland[25] before undertaking another trip from Heriot's Green on 20

Vincenzo Lunardi (1759-1806), the famous Tuscan balloonist, ascended from Heriot Green in front of great crowds in 1785 and 1786.

December: on that day Lunardi ascended just before 1 p.m. with a flag hoisted on the 'wark' and dressed in the uniform of the Scots Archers (of which he was an honorary member), but he came down in the sea off East Lothian. He also ascended from Heriot's Green for his last Scottish venture, on 31 July 1786, when he used his refurbished and enlarged balloon. This may have been the 'transparent balloon' which, under Lunardi's direction, the girls of the Merchant Maiden Hospital constructed for him, and which was on view in Parliament House.[26] With little wind he came down only a few miles away, near Musselburgh.

Lunardi's Scottish flights were to be his greatest successes, despite a later career which involved displays in Italy, Spain and Portugal. While in Scotland he proved an attractive figure, loved in particular by fashionable ladies.[27] Heriot's Hospital and grounds were remarkable sights on the days of the ascents, particularly on the first occasion when an estimated crowd of 80,000 turned up. All business stopped and most of the town's shops closed. Unfortunately pick-pocketing spoiled the spectacle for several hundred people and a gang of eight men and women were run to earth in Aberdeen and stood trial.[28] However, despite Lunardi's showmanship public interest waned, his last flight attracted only 'polite interest'[29] and within a week he had left Scotland never to return.

Since its opening the principal approach to the Hospital had been from the north, by a narrow street, Heriot's Bridge, rising from the Grassmarket, with an arch which carried across the footpath of the street to render communication easier by a more gentle ascent. The inhabitants, however, found it an undesirable obstruction, as it projected into the middle of the Grassmarket, and they petitioned the governors for its removal in April 1759. As nothing was done, and as Edinburgh was witnessing a number of street improvements, they again resorted to a petition on 13 September 1762 for the removal of the bridge so that 'it might no longer prevent an uninterrupted view in one of the best streets within the city'. The filth and stench of the street was renowned, and it was deemed necessary to deal with the eyesore and nuisance. Carriages were now using the street, which had been intended as a footpath, and some Hospital boys had been hurt when walking into town. Recognising the benefits of improvement to the Hospital and Town, the governors agreed to pay one-third of the expense up to £33 6s. 8d. and to ask the town council and petitioners to pay the other two-thirds. The bridge was removed immediately and a barrier was placed at the north end of the entry to prevent its use by carriages.[30]

Having inspected the area and discussed various suggested improvements the governors decided to consult the architect, John Adam, 'as to the properest manner of levelling the Avenue to the Hospital.'[31] His written report was discussed on 2 November 1762. He suggested that the avenue should begin from the Grassmarket without any steps and gradually rise to the Old City Wall, where a broad flight of steps would lead to a gateway and a porter's lodge. The governors agreed to his scheme, and on its completion Adam's account was presented in February 1765. [32]

As early as June 1786 the Lord Provost proposed that the stone wall on the south side of Heriot gardens, part of the Old Town Wall, be removed and replaced by an iron rail. When this took place the following summer it left other gardens exposed and resulted in a petition from Archibald Keddie, under-gardener of the Hospital, claiming compensation for the loss of much of his fruit and garden produce.[33] When some of the iron spikes from the railing were stolen the treasurer was authorised to advertise in the newspapers offering a reward of ten guineas for information on who stole the iron, to be paid on conviction of the offenders. However, whatever the problems, the Hospital was now open to public view on the south side, a marked improvement on the previous enclosed monastery-like building.

Further discussions took place with town officials in early 1791 over the possible enclosure of land at the north front of the Hospital and it was proposed to build a porter's lodge there at the gate to prevent those who had no business with the Hospital from being admitted and to prevent boys from going out without permission. This seems to have been completed quickly, following a plan of the Town's superintendent of public works, William Sibbald Snr, and the building was then enclosed by a wall on the north side.

Suggestions were made to improve the interior courtyard. With improved water supplies to the Hospital it was proposed for the first time to remove the well in the middle of the court in February 1773, but this was not carried out. On 7 October 1793 the treasurer presented an estimate of £352 17s. for the expense of 'paving the Court of the Hospital with free stone'.[34] The governors agreed that either the pavement should be repaired or completely relaid, and an appropriate advert for further estimates was placed in local newspapers. On 11 November an estimate of £238 11s. sterling from William Sibbald Jnr for paving with droved (Estler) stone was accepted. As the work was completed that winter 'much to the satisfaction of the governors'[35] Sibbald was contracted to pave the common hall, kitchen, washing house and the area of the piazzas and the passages for £120.

In November 1800 Count Rumford, the German name of Sir Benjamin Thomson, was thanked for 'a most essential improvement'[36] to the kitchen, washing house, wards and dining hall of the Hospital, and it was expected that his work would result in great savings.[37]

The building and its immediate grounds were still subject to much external use in this period. On 7 June 1762 a great many rooms in the Hospital were reported as occupied by booksellers, filled with stationery and title deeds,[38] and Alexander Gray, Keeper of the Signet, relating that warrands and records in the Signet Office 'had swelled to such a bulk',[39] requested the rent of a secure apartment in the Hospital. It was Heriot's central position which led to a memorial from the Earl of Morton, Lord Clerk Register of Scotland and Robert Ord, Lord Chief Baron of the Exchequer, who had been appointed by George III and financed by him to build a proper repository for the Records of Scotland. Their request of 26 August 1765 suggested the north-west part of the Hospital gardens as a good site for the building, which would not affect the 'wark'. Although an initial deal was struck with an acre feued out, it fell through, much to the delight of Bailie Thomas Hogg, the only objecting governor.[40] Nonetheless, further rooms were rented out in 1775 for the storage of furniture[41] and for storing boxes of papers.[42] Others followed suit and accepted similar arrangements.[43] Despite these a number of rooms remained empty and the whole of the third floor uninhabited.[44]

It was at this period that the governors showed their willingness to support the patriotic measures being taken to defend the country. On 8 October 1781 the Edinburgh Defensive Band petitioned the governors, asking that it be given the use of any sufficient dry spare room in the Hospital for holding their arms and an area in the grounds for exercise. The governors agreed.[45] When the newly formed Caledonian Band under the Earl of Buchan asked for similar arrangements in September 1782 these were immediately granted under the same conditions. For some years, and particularly during the French Wars, the bands were to use the Heriot Green on the south side of the Hospital regularly for drill. The Edinburgh (later Royal) Volunteers mustered there on 26 September 1794 under Colonel Maxwell to receive their colours. A second troop, raised in 1797 to prevent the threatened French invasion of Ireland, also mustered on Heriot Green. With the Peace of Amiens in May 1802 the Volunteers dispersed at the Hospital and remustered there in September 1803, then augmented to 1,000, with the outbreak of the Napoleonic Wars.[46]

To those using the Hospital as a storage and the presence of these bands can be added the Gentlemen Bowlers in Edinburgh who in January 1768 had petitioned the governors asking for a 21-year lease of the green to form two greens on the south side and the garden to the east commonly called the

Wilderness. On 6 June the governors agreed, believing that the exercise involved would be beneficial: the conditions were a rent of £28 per annum, the area to be well kept and no entertainments allowed. Although the green was to fall into disuse after 1786, when the area was exposed to 'every evil disposed person'[47] it was restored by the governors at a cost of £80 18s. 9d. in October 1792, and a revived Bowling Society agreed to pay a yearly rent of £5 under a 19-year lease.[48]

Problems with boys intensified at this time. One incident led the governors to advertise: 'There are two boys in Heriot's hospital cloathing, wandering about in the country these fifteen days, one of them has red hair, of nine years old. N.B. They are not to be trusted to, if they say they will, go home themselves.'[49] The treasurer informed council on 17 September 1764 that some Hospital boys had got into a garden near the 'wark' and had stolen three pocket napkins and two pairs of stockings, while others stole pigeons.[50]

However, in late July 1775, the first major disturbance in the history of the Hospital took place. When the boys had asked for permission to play on a Wednesday afternoon and were refused, some seventy left the Hospital without permission. The resulting governors' inquiry excluded two boys, but following a petition[51] from the Hospital boys, both Robert Ballantyne and Alves Morison, in front of all the boys in the chapel on 16 October 1775, admitted their evil nature and their concealment and lying. They agreed not to form any pact, but would tell the truth and answer questions. It was accepted that if censors[52] among the boys were appointed they would promote a 'general reformation among their comrades'.[53] The boys were allowed back but were kept apart from others at mealtimes for some time. The Lord Provost warned that any boys found forming a pact or disobeying the master would be excluded.

In April 1777 a committee reported that 'two boys had been decoyed away by a girl to a house of bad fame'. Brydon Fyfe and Alexander Duff admitted this and more as 'each of them had commerce with that girl'.[54] This was deemed a major misdemeanour and the boys were excluded to ensure that no others followed their example. The governors looked into the background of the problem, and in a report of 13 December 1779 blamed the 'relaxation of discipline' and recommended the end of the 'freedom' of the boys. The tightening up of regulations was deemed crucial in order to isolate Heriot boys from the corrupting influence of the 'idle and unprincipled boys of the town'. Treasurer Carmichael and Baillie Wordie were instrumental in pressing for a more rigorous curriculum. They were responsible for the appointment of a committee under Baillie William Thomson, which produced a plan of education – the most complete and comprehensive to date – consisting of twenty articles, adopted almost in entirety by the governors on 19 April 1780. From then on Heriot boys would only be able to leave the Hospital on Saturday afternoons and every second Wednesday evening, and large bounds for exercise were introduced. A proper place was 'fitted up for the confinement of such boys as are obnoxious to punishment' and they were kept in solitary. A numerical list of all the pupils was made, and all were to have their number on the inside of their cap so that any who were guilty of an offence might be more easily discovered.[55]

The changes seem to have made little immediate impact, for another major disturbance was reported in August 1780, twenty-two boys staying out of the Hospital for varying lengths of time. An allegation of stealing compounded the matter, and the unwillingness of the boys to answer questions made the situation even more serious. The governors were clear on the need for action or 'there will be an end of all order in the Hospital'.[56] Eight of the offenders were confined and fed on bread and water while the inquiry progressed. In the end the governors excluded four, stripping off their Hospital clothes; two others were solitarily confined for four days and two others for two days. The governors hoped their firm action would lead to improved discipline, but they were to be disappointed. On 11 March 1782 five boys had to be 'severely whipped publicly in the Hall'[57] after admitting eloping for some time, and more were punished in similar fashion for similar crimes the following month.

Problems escalated further, and on 28 October 1782 the governor of Watson's Hospital, James Richardson, wrote giving details of Heriot boys who had that afternoon gone to Watson's Hospital, beaten some boys, cursed the servants and insulted Richardson and his staff. Windows were broken and a Watson's boy badly hurt. Richardson complained that he had drawn the attention of the master of Heriot's to a number of previous incidents, but given this serious disturbance, he now asked the treasurer for action, which followed immediately. The boys concerned were chastised and promised not to reoffend. However, four days later Heriot boys attacked Watson's Hospital again, and the porter was asked to quell resistance. Fearing for his life the porter refused and was dismissed. The boys were again chastised but the next morning refused to take their breakfast and threw their dishes onto the floor. They marched out in a body and went out to their recreation area making a terrible noise. The master and staff could not get them to return. By the time the Lord Provost had called out the Town Guard the boys had retreated indoors. This example of 'totall Rebellion'[58] led the governors to confine all the boys for two days in the Hospital. The boys petitioned the governors, admitting their 'great crime', but the governors could not ignore the seriousness of the happenings: they expelled the eight 'most guilty' and confined another eight boys for eight days. All the other Hospital boys were deprived of their recreation until the master decided that their good behaviour warranted the end of their punishment.

These events were to colour all later thinking so that, for example, in April 1790 in order to avoid a repeat of 1782[59] Thomson, still master, was recommending strict reaction to a boy who had deserted. When, in December 1791, the governors could not decide the degrees of guilt of those involved in stealing, when the boys refused to implicate each other, they responded by expelling all four involved. In October 1792 four boys broke into a garden in Fountainbridge and destroyed fruit trees. They were publicly whipped in the hall in front of the assembled school, were confined for fourteen days and for the same period had a resticted diet and ate separately.

Such general severity did not solve the constant bickering[60] with the boys of Watson's Hospital. Things came to a head again in November 1792. After two particular incidents twenty-two boys stayed out all night, and when they were confined in the Hospital they proved 'quite unruly and abused their teachers'.[61] Having interviewed a number of boys and having got nowhere the governors believed that the 'Garring Law', outlawed in 1751,[62] was still in existence.[63] Eventually two boys were expelled and ten others signed a paper obliging them to keep the rules in the future.

The survival of the 'Garring Law' was not surprising given the monastic nature of the Hospital, which had developed its own rules and customs. The 'garrers' ruled over all younger Herioters except those who had entered the Hospital six months after them. When boys joined the Hospital they were 'tamed into the garring law' to ensure that they would never disclose any secrets of the fraternity or how boys were ill-treated. Any breaking of the secrecy meant being called before the garrers, sentenced and punished. Parents of young boys gave them money to use in an attempt to curry favour and avoid the worst excesses of the system.[64] At their peak the 'garrers' also controlled some members of the household, thereby evading many regulations.

The closeness and secrecy of the boys was exhibited when, in 1783, James Hay, an 18-year-old 'Auld Callant',[65] escaped with the help of his father, a stabler in the Grassmarket, from the Tolbooth Prison while waiting execution after being found guilty of a charge of petty theft from a 'dram-shop' in the Canongate. As he was hunted by the whole of the Town he hid in 'Bluidy'

Mackenzie's tomb (of Covenanting fame) in Greyfriars' Churchyard and was supplied with food by the boys from the Hospital. The boys were not even tempted to give him away, and when the hue and cry died down after nearly six weeks Hay was able to escape abroad.[66]

The situation was not helped by the appointment and background of a number of those who held the office of master. For the most part they were decayed tradesmen who, never having had a liberal education themselves, were completely ignorant of how to go about managing and training youths. A number were cavalier in their attitude and left the schooling to others, without any supervision. Neglect led to abuse, and the conditions were rife for such abuse to fester and grow. As a later commentator suggested, 'Wherever the head was unsound the whole organisation speedily became deranged; and the depraving influence even of one ill-judged appointment, may probably have extended its unhappy consequences, not only over the duration of a single incumbency, but over every succeeding period.'[67] Blame, therefore, for the widespread nature of bullying lies with staff as well as boys. The laxity of discipline and the lack of warm personal relationships endemic in a hospital environment when boys were cut off from the civilising influence of home life contributed to the strength and durability of the Garring system. Although masters could to some extent arrest its evils with a strong hand it needed fundamental changes in the Hospital structure itself before it was finally eradicated. This was not to begin to happen until the middle of the nineteenth century.[68]

Certainly the masters of this period were not up to their task. From September 1741 until March 1795 the Hospital was poorly led, before a master of potential was appointed in the person of George Irvine. The poor standing of the top post in the Hospital was seen when he resigned in August 1805 to become one of the masters in the High School. This was not to be the last time that the Hospital, to its detriment, was to lose one of its most promising staff.

Complaints levelled against staff were common at this time. The vocal music master, Cornforth Gilson,[69] was accused of being remiss and negligent in his attendance in October 1762, and was warned when he employed someone in his place in April 1764. Further problems arose in April and October 1776. As Gilson had been appointed by the town council to organise the teaching of church music in the city churches, he had probably been given the Heriot post as an extra inducement. However, although he perhaps treated the Hospital accordingly, he was a man of some ability, being an author and composer, and he took a choir from Heriot's to the Musical

Society of Edinburgh to perform in their oratorios three times a year in St Cecilia's Hall.[70]

As far as the curriculum was concerned the later eighteenth century saw not just an emphasis on traditional subjects, but also a widening of the curriculum in the Hospital. Indeed when the town council brought Franks from England to improve church music in Edinburgh he was appointed to the Hospital, 'as this was a most necessary branch of education for the boys'.[71] However, music was to be kept in its 'proper' place and was fitted in between lessons so as not to interfere with school hours.

In May 1766 the governors authorised the purchase of a pair of globes and proper books for giving boys some skill in geography and navigation. When in April 1767 the College was keen to obtain a quality drawing master it was suggested that Heriot's contribute, as the boys would benefit from attending such classes. Drawing was to form part of the Hospital syllabus shortly afterwards, but no specialist teacher joined the staff until 1836.[72]

Despite previous decisions, the governors were still clearly in two minds as time went on regarding boys going on to the High School to further their education. By 1758 Heriot boys were again going there, but it was insisted that they only did so having being examined and after the governors were convinced that it was in the boy's interest. Even when they did go on there the boys had to be repeatedly examined by a committee of the governors. In the regulations of 1780 it was stipulated that only those boys who 'show an uncommon genius for learning'.[73] were to enter the High School. Heriot boys who did attend were allowed to forego the normal class registration fee (normally £1 1s. in the later eighteenth century), and it was normal for the High School masters to leave a tactful blank beside the names of these 'free pupils' in the class registers. However, Willie Nichol, a master between 1776 and 1795,[74] took a perverse pleasure in drawing attention to them, and always commented on his lists, 'does not pay', 'refuses to pay' or 'will not pay'. In his register of 1779 and again in 1782 he grouped the seven and five boys respectively as 'Herioters' as if this was a collective unpleasant noun. In 1781 Nichol noted at the bottom of his class list: 'David Ferrier, a Herioter, seized with the moral contagion common to that Hospital, has lapsed in company with another boy as wicked as himself'.[75]

The problems involved with June Day continued in this period. In June 1763 it proved impossible to collect all the boys together for their exams, because a number were 'employed in the country preparing flowers for ornamenting George Heriot's Statue'.[76] Three years later an unsigned letter was produced at a governors' meeting, alleging that people were being charged to view the statue, and further complaining that the Heriot gardeners, according to their usual custom, 'have pillaged and destroyed all the flower gardens in the neighbourhood in order to dress a statue'.[77] Usually the boys, rather than the gardeners, were accused, and perhaps this explains the 1780 regulation which held that the dressing of the statue was to be taken out of the hands of the boys entirely and put under the care of a gardener who was to furnish the flowers necessary at an agreed price.[78] He was not to receive any fee if he accepted one flower from a Heriot boy![79]

By this time June Day was an important day in the Edinburgh calendar for locals and visitors alike. Alexander Belsches, an Edinburgh advocate, attended the church, 'where was the whole world'[80] and was impressed with the singing in June 1768, while Sylas Neville, originally from London, studied medicine at Edinburgh University and attended the 1773 celebrations.[81] He witnessed the boys adorning Heriot's statue with flowers in the morning and went back to see the statue in the evening.

Meanwhile, grave financial problems had resurfaced. In December 1762 the treasurer, Rochead, was not able to produce his accounts, as his 'affairs were in disorder'.[82] Within three weeks he had resigned and his furniture was being valued for auction. A new treasurer, John Carmichael, was elected immediately, and by April 1763 was reporting on the financial crisis facing the Hospital. For at least ten years expenses had outstripped income and the number of boys in the Hospital had increased from 100 to 140.[83] The urgent need, he argued, was to reduce the number of boys until the debts of the Hospital, estimated at over £2,000, were cleared. This explains why no boys were elected in April or October 1763 and again none in April and October 1764. Only one boy was to be elected in April 1765, and that was Henry Raeburn.[84] However the governors decided to take in another five boys, so over-ruling the committee's recommendations. In October 1765 they again restricted entrance – this time to one boy. Fortunately within a few years the governors, through the financial prudence of Carmichael, were able to return to the normal intake levels. The total number of boys in the Hospital fell back, but rose again in the 1790s to 116. In April 1802 it was announced that from October of that year the total number would be 120.[85]

In April 1779, with finances flourishing, the governors decided to mark Carmichael's success by having a full-length portrait of him completed 'by one of the best portrait painters that can be found'. It was placed in the Hospital as 'a lasting Memorial of Mr Carmichael's good and faithfull services'.[86]

James Jackson proved a considerable success as Treasurer of the Hospital between 1793 and 1805. The Governors had Sir Henry Raeburn paint his portrait.

Carmichael was to retire soon afterwards, but on his death in 1785 the governors unanimously determined to show their public gratitude for his extricating the Hospital from its financial difficulties and for exhibiting a 'steadiness and integrity scarcely to be paralleled'.[87] They erected a stone monument in Greyfriars' Churchyard on the outer north wall of the Church near his burial place, with an inscription to incite others to follow his example.[88]

The Hospital was fortunate to appoint another treasurer in James Jackson, who took office in July 1793. He was aware of criticisms that the Hospital had not been discriminating enough when reviewing the circumstances of those applying for election, and to overcome these he brought forward comprehensive new regulations in October 1796. Jackson's success in the internal management of the institution and his financial expertise resulted in Lord Provost Elder praising his term of office in April 1798 as a 'most flourishing' time, and the governors decided to express their thanks by asking him 'to sit to Mr Raeburn to have his picture drawn'.[89] It was unanimously agreed that this be done, the resulting portrait being hung up in the council room, where it remains to this day. Jackson finally resigned in March 1805.[90]

The generosity of benefactors to the Hospital intensified in this period. In 1757 its late surgeon, George Cunningham,[91] left £25 sterling to the institution and his donation was put up in gold letters on a board.[92] In December 1758 Miss Eupham Murray, daughter of an Edinburgh baker, left £50 sterling of life-rent and £240 sterling to the governors.[93] In April 1759 they received £100 sterling from Jean Gilchrist, formerly of Lombard Street, London, to be placed in trust for the interest to benefit a child (preferring the name Gilchrist).[94] In June 1760, the treasurer heard from Carolina that £200 sterling of merchant Alexander Robertson's legacy[95] had been received. In October 1769 the treasurer received £50 from the trustees of George Seaman of Charleston, South Carolina. As a result of a legacy in 1774 from Janet Callander, daughter of the deceased Patrick, skinner and glover in Edinburgh, the Corporation and Society of Skinners in Edinburgh agreed to nominate and maintain a boy in the Hospital. In the same year the property left by Daniel Robertson, a tailor and former pupil, of London, yielded £50 sterling.[96] In October 1791, the widow of William Abercrombie, 'Doctor of Physick' of York,[97] intimated to the treasurer that on her death all his bankstock was to be equally divided between the Hospital and the Royal Infirmary.[98] It seems no coincidence that the benefactors were Auld Callants who had been successful in their careers at a distance from Edinburgh.

On 29 May 1792 Alexander Cunningham, W.S., wrote to the Lord Provost as chairman of governors: 'I have the honour to send . . . a Cup which beyond a doubt belonged to the worthy Founder. The Cup by accident came into the possession of Mr. John Stewart a friend of mine and he has desired me to convey it to the Honourable governors of the Hospital.'[99] The 'Heriot Loving Cup' was an antique cup formed of a nautilus shell with silver mounts, set on a slender stem spreading into a stepped chased foot.[100] For long enough it was thought to have been the work of George Heriot himself, but its markings show that it was made by Robert Denniestoun between 1611 and 1613.[101] The Cup traditionally was produced at the anniversary dinner of the governors every June Day evening when the health of George Heriot is celebrated.

After a century and a half since the opening of the Hospital the governors had much to be proud of. With difficulty they had weathered a storm of criticisms over their conduct of business, particularly between 1759 and 1773, and had gained legal backing for their position. Influential visitors, too, were impressed, and the Hospital became an integral part of most eighteenth-century works containing prints and drawings of Edinburgh. Sir William Burrell, M.P, on his tour in October 1758, stressed the 'magnificent building' of the Hospital[102] and these precise words were used by the Bishop of Meath on 15 September 1760[103] with Alexander Kincaid,[104] a generation later, believing that it 'was justly esteemed one of the finest pieces of architecture in Edinburgh'. Sir Roger Newdigate described the wark in August 1766 as 'very handsome and as shewy a building as any in the city',[105] while Thomas Newte also believed it to be a 'magnificent fabric' on his 1785 tour.[106]

However, Maitland's criticisms of 1753 also had an impact, and his figures were taken up by others. Thomas Pennant believed that the fine building was 'much too magnificent for the end proposed, that of educating poor children'[107] and followed Maitland in believing that Heriot had left almost £44,000 to build the wark. Edward Topham, a captain in the Guards living in Edinburgh in 1774–5, also viewed the building as 'a large and magnificent edifice' which 'has infinitely more the look of a palace than Holyroodhouse'. However, he too made reference to Maitland's figures of £27,000 to build and £43,600 left by Heriot.[108] More significantly, Alexander Kincaid suggested that Heriot's executors did not have the benevolent intention of the founder much at heart, for they spent too much on the building instead of on the education of poor boys. In fact, Heriot's money had been 'thrown away on this pile of building'. Others, too, followed Maitland,[109] but added little new to his charges.

Fortunately, Maitland did not have things all his own way, for Hugo Arnot published an impressive work which included a defence of the Hospital and its governors.[110] He blamed Maitland for getting his sums wrong, accusing him of having been responsible for the 'unjust murmurings . . . and even of having been the means of spiriting up lawsuits' against the governors. However, according to Arnot, 'nothing can be more groundless and calumnious than that charge of mismanagement and embezzlement of the hospital's revenues, so frequently thrown out against its managers; a charge suggested, partly by Maitland's blunder already mentioned, but chiefly made use of as a popular topick for scandalizing the magistrates of Edinburgh, when any political job makes it expedient to spread such calumnies.' This view was reinforced by Thomas Newte, who believed that 'the prosperous state, both of the boys and the funds belonging to the Hospital, is chiefly to be attributed to the truly paternal care and attention which are bestowed on its affairs by the governors'.

To their great credit the governors could claim to have made good appointments in Carmichael and Jackson, who laid the foundations for financial stability for succeeding generations. More than anything else, it was Jackson's 1796 regulations which in the short-term silenced critics of the governors and their admission policy, and longer term enabled the governors to stave off attacks on their regime for over half a century, and allowed them to turn their attention to the educational aspects of the Hospital. Jackson had learned the lessons of the past and understood the potential difficulties of being Dean of Guild of the Town (1799–1801), while being treasurer of the Hospital. He was determined that Heriot's would not lose out financially and he kept a firm control on Heriot's property and money. At long last Heriot's bequest could flourish as never before.

CHAPTER SEVEN

The Hospital in the Early Nineteenth Century

Confirmation of Heriot's importance as a building of national significance was seen in 1818 when J.M.W. Turner and Sir Walter Scott collaborated on *The Provincial and Picturesque Scenery of Scotland*. Although only the first volume was produced, one of Turner's eight pictures was devoted to a 'charming'[1] view of 'Heriot's Hospital' from the Grassmarket.[2] Turner juxtaposed the poor of the area with the 'magnificent hospital', and in so doing alluded to the institution's 'long and venerable history of philanthrophy'.[3]

However, given the great stretches of land owned by the governors, the Hospital remained even more deeply involved in municipal affairs. On 4 June 1823 the governors discussed a petition from the directors of Edinburgh Academy, signed, amongst others, by 'Leonard Horner, Walter Scott, Robert Dundas, H.[enry] Cockburn and Tho. Kinnear', who argued that many 'individuals of great respectability in this City'[4] had experienced much inconvenience because of the crowded nature of the High School[5] and its distance from the New Town. This led the Heriot governors to agree on 10 June 1823 to give a feu of three acres of Canonmills Park[6] to the directors.[7] The foundation stone of Edinburgh Academy was laid within three weeks[8] and the new school, designed by William Burn, was opened on 1 October 1824 with 372 boys in attendance.[9]

Such a development had repercussions for the Town, and by 10 June 1825 the governors were involved in discussions on moving the High School from Infirmary Street to a piece of ground on the Calton Hill situated at Miller's Knowe on the north side of Regent Road. Within a week a joint committee of governors and town council had visited the proposed site for a new High School and agreed on the way forward. The foundation stone of this building, designed by Thomas Hamilton, was laid on 28 July 1825 and opened formally on 23 June 1829.

A third group – the Trustees of James Donaldson's Hospital – approached the governors on 4 June 1832, proposing to build 'a large and splendid' building[10] on the most elevated part of Coates for the education of deaf and dumb children. The trustees wished no houses nearby to encroach on their building and spoil its appearance, and they accepted the feu terms offered by the governors on 18 June. William H. Playfair was called in by the trustees and between 1841 and 1851 he produced a massive 'palatial quadrangular complex ranged round a courtyard with an array of towers and turrets'.[11]

If the positive reaction of the governors to these requests was to change the face of Edinburgh education, even more significant was their own unique contribution to educational provision, made long before the Scottish Education Act of 1872. The healthy financial situation of the Hospital, the foundations of which had been laid by Carmichael, was becoming almost an embarrassment in this period. In October 1818 the funds showed a surplus of £3,320, and the governors decided on 26 November that in accordance with the will and codicil of the founder they should increase the five bursaries given to the University of Edinburgh to ten.[12] Despite this, the annual surplus in April 1820 had risen to £4,239 6s. and the governors responded, on 9 April 1821, by increasing the numbers of boys in the Hospital to its maximum of 180 (from 175).

Large annual surpluses continued: in April 1825 it was £4,158 7s. 8d. and part was used to improve the appearance of the boys; they were to have two suits of clothes per annum (instead of three over two years) and the quality of the cloth was improved. An additional teacher could be afforded by the Hospital in May 1825 to deal with new boys. William Muir was appointed, and much of the building work of this time was a direct result of this improved financial strength. However, the most dramatic and far-reaching proposal was put forward by Duncan McLaren[13] on 13 May 1835. He suggested applying part of the surplus revenue of the Hospital to 'the erection of one or more schools for the education of sons of such burgesses as cannot be admitted into the Hospital'.[14] Showing a distrust of the hospital system, before most of his contemporaries, McLaren believed that '£800 a year spent on out-schools was better than £8,000 in the Hospital'. He hoped to develop a complete system of free elementary education with schools built and run by Heriot money in each of the thirteen of Edinburgh's parishes in a radical plan to educate all of the poorer classes.[15] At a full meeting of thirty-seven governors and the house-governor on 12 October 1835 McLaren's imaginative proposals were accepted[16] and those present 'approved generally of the object contemplated'.

On 18 February 1836 the governors petitioned Parliament to extend their powers 'to enable them to found and erect schools within Edinburgh for the education of children of burgesses and others, and the more effectually to enable them to apply the revenue of the said Hospital in accordance with the true spirit of the pious donation'.[17] A Bill was brought forward by the Attorney-General on 14 March and the clerk of the governors, Isaac Bayley, was asked to hold himself ready to go to London, as the agent of the Hospital, to carry it through Parliament.

McLaren's innovative scheme was supported by the *Scotsman* and the *Edinburgh Patriot* newspapers. Local MPs were sympathetic; Sir George Clerk of Penicuik (Conservative, Edinburghshire) saw it as 'not inconsistent with his [Heriot's] benevolent intention', while city Liberal MP Sir James Campbell viewed it as 'in conformity with the intentions of the founder'[18] and strenuously supported the bill. It was also backed by the Company of Merchants on 22 April. Opposition came in the form of petitions from the Incorporated Trades (22 March), Incorporation of Waulkers (23 March), of Tailors (11 April), of Hammermen (12 April), of Cordiners (15 April), and finally of Bakers (2 May) contending that their children had preferable rights which should have been included in the proposed Act. Despite this, the weight of opinion was firmly on the governors' side and on 14 July the bill received royal assent from William IV.[19]

At a meeting of the governors on 28 July the 'Act to explain and extend the powers of the governors of the Hospital in Edinburgh'[20] was presented. The surplus revenue could now be put toward founding and erecting schools in Edinburgh for educating not only the children of burgesses and freemen, but also the the poor. Furthermore, the more obsolete of Balcanquall's Statutes could now be updated and revised, provided such amendments were accepted at two special governors' meetings held at least three months apart, and by two-thirds of the governors present at the second meeting, and then by two of the President of Court of Session, Lord Advocate and Dean of the Faculty of Advocates. Pleased with this outcome the governors expressed unanimously 'their approbation of the eminent services of Councillor McLaren in having originated and greatly aided in bringing to a successful issue this important measure'.[21] Two years later Solicitor-General Rutherford paid warm tribute to McLaren for his actions in promoting 'the cause of education', and diffusing its benefits more extensively over the community.[22]

A small group of governors, however, were unhappy with the Hospital Act.[23] Three governors – Councillors Jameson and Johnston, and the Revd Wilkie – protested against the lack of sufficient notice about the meetings when decisions had been taken. Three other governors – Councillors Dick,

Banks and Laing – also opposed the principles behind the Act which diverted funds from the original purposes of the founder,[24] as the Hospital already was contributing much to the relief of the poor beyond its obligations. However, a solid group of thirty-seven governors, on 17 October 1836, having calculated an annual surplus of £3,000, decided to erect the first out-school 'on the waste area at the entrance to the Heriot grounds leading from the Grassmarket opposite the porter's lodge'.[25]

The governors were anxious to ensure that the first of their out-schools was fitted out to the highest specifications of the time. Their superintendent of works,[26] Alexander Black, visited various schools throughout the country before laying five different designs on the council room table. At a meeting on 14 December plan 4, which accommodated 400 children and was based on Madras College,[27] was deemed the most appropriate. On the afternoon of Monday 17 April 1837, before the usual meeting the governors, treasurer, clerk, teachers and boys walked in procession from the Hospital to the site of the new school at Heriot Bridge to witness the foundation ceremony.[28] The boys were accommodated on a raised platform, extending along three sides of the square, with the Revd Daniel Wilkie of New Greyfriars leading the service.

By June 1838 McLaren's committee of eleven governors[29] had agreed that the sessional school[30] in Market Street should be taken as the model for the new school in curriculum and books; that girls would be taught sewing;[31] that teaching staff would be appointed by the governors and could be removed on three months' notice, but would have increased salaries provided their attendance was satisfactory; and that the school would run evening classes for which those enrolling would pay the teacher one shilling and sixpence per month.[32] The scholars were to be elected by the governors who would give priority to the children of burgesses and freemen in poor circumstances, and then to the children of poor citizens who had been resident for at least a year in Edinburgh. All these decisions[33] were accepted without controversy, but the committee members 'on the question whether the school should be absolutely and strictly a Free school . . . were equally divided'.[34] The committee could only recommend that if the governors decided to charge fees then they should be small – a penny a week – and the funds raised should be applied exclusively to the maintenance of a library for the use of the scholars. This important issue – free or fee – delayed the opening of the Heriot Bridge School which had been expected in September.

This, however, did not dampen the enthusiasm of the governors for expanding the Hospital outdoor-school network. Plans were pushed ahead for

more schools in High School Yards, at Cowgate Port and Old Assembly Close – the most densely populated parts of the Old Town. After further discussion it was McLaren's influence which led, on 6 September 1838, to the decision of the governors 'that the Schools should be free schools and that no fees should be exacted for the education of the children attending them'.[35] Even the classbooks and stationery were to be supplied free, which meant that the Heriot schools were out of line with sessional and other elementary schools where small fees were charged. Such a momentous decision – understandable in the circumstances – was to be important within a short time for creating much opposition to the schools and the Hospital.[36]

A fortnight after the opening of the first school was advertised, there were more than 700 applications, and so, on 15 October 1838 the Hospital out-school at Heriot Bridge opened at 10 a.m. 'when almost all the children who had been admitted had attended in a most respectable manner'.[37] It immediately reached its capacity of 318 juveniles with a waiting list and an experienced headmaster George Anderson was elected as the master.

McLaren and his school committee pressed ahead with the building and equipping of four juvenile and two infant schools.[38] Proud of their achievements the governors welcomed a government inspection, which was carried out by HMI John Gibson, whose report was published in the minutes of the Council on Education in 1842–3. It held that 'the superinten-

Alexander Black, Superintendent of Works at the Hospital between 1833 and 1858, ensured that the architecture of the outdoor schools followed a common, distinctive character. The Cowgate Port School is an example of an unmistakably modern version of the Hospital.

dence of these Schools is of the most complete and stringent kind. They are frequently visited by those interested in the elevation and amelioration of the condition of the poorer classes. Strangers are attracted towards them by the accounts which they hear of the immense good they are accomplishing, and the wonderful change which they promise to effect upon our poor population. Every one projecting the institution of Schools for the poor, in Edinburgh, and the surrounding country, looks to them as the best models.' He approved of the weekly inspections of the house-governor of the Hospital and the fortnightly visits of the governors. Gibson went further and praised the Heriot schools as forming 'by far the most valuable elementary educational machinery existing in this country. The course of instruction is extensive, and based upon the soundest principles. The teachers are thoroughly qualified to conduct it with efficiency, and are admirably supported by the instrumentality of apprentice teachers.'[39] They were paid well above normal teaching salaries which ensured competition for jobs and ensured high-quality staff. Gordon judged their regimes constant and effective, without recourse to severity. He stressed the interesting and useful knowledge which was communicated in the infant schools and the good training they were for the juvenile schools. McLaren and the governors must have taken much encouragement from this respected external judgment.

Although McLaren, who attended his first meeting on 18 November 1833, was only on the governing body until 1839, and as Lord Provost he was chairman of the governors between 1851–4, serving again in 1860–1, he dominated 'Heriot' thinking right up to 1886. He insisted that the governors spread the benefits of the Hospital to the widest possible number. Believing strongly in different classes being educated together to encourage social cohesion, he defeated an attempt in 1839 to create separate schools for burgesses' children.[40] He placed a strong emphasis on moral and religious education in the new schools, which all had an hour of religious instruction, with no child being exempted. He also ended the religious test for teaching staff, a generation before Parliament did so. As teachers in Heriot schools did not need to make a declaration of religious belief, in time, Congregationalists, United Presbyterians and Free Churchmen, as well as members of the Established Church, became Heriot teachers. In a real sense McLaren and the Heriot outdoor schools pioneered educational reform and set an example not followed elsewhere in Scotland until the passage of the Scottish Education Act of 1872.[41]

Meantime, the governors had not neglected their first priority of the Hospital. On 10 July 1815 they agreed to the plan of the superintendent of

works, Thomas Bonnar, aimed at developing the area in front of the Hospital. At a cost of £110 the gravel surface was restored and thickened to ensure it would be 'firm and handsome'[42] and a pavement was added. With the north front improved, treasurer Denholm produced a plan on 16 October 1815 'for ornamenting the ground upon the south side of the Hospital with trees, shrubs, and gravel walks'[43] but this was not followed through. When Playfair introduced a plan on 20 November 1823 to open up the south side of the Hospital, it was agreed that it 'should be carried into execution with as little delay as possible'.[44] But still the governors delayed.

However, other changes were made. On 5 December 1822 the new treasurer, Kincaid Mackenzie, reported that the well in the centre of the quadrangle was in a 'state of decay'[45] and in need of repair. Believing that its construction ill accorded with the beautiful harmony of the buildings, he suggested removing the well and substituting a pedestal with a gas lantern on it to illuminate the square. The governors consulted 'professional people of taste'[46] and found them of the opinion that no erection whatsoever should be made in the centre of the

James Denholm, an Auld Callant, was Treasurer of the Hospital from 1813-1822 and introduced a new level of profession-alism into the financial affairs of the Trust. His memorial is W.H. Playfair's elegant cenotaph of white marble.

square, which should be lit with gas lamps in each corner. The well was thus removed. Mackenzie continued in his efforts to improve the building and suggested the removal of the iron gratings on the lower windows on the north-side, which he believed gave the Hospital the appearance of a prison or a place of confinement. On 11 August 1823 the governors accepted that the gratings were not needed for security and had them removed.

In July 1825 Bonnar put forward detailed plans of the Hospital edifice ,showing the different apartments in each storey and reported upon the state of the building and the repairs and alterations required. The drawings showed the new sick room which had been fitted out in 1819,[47] the wash house designed by Playfair and erected by John Inglis in 1820[48] and the rooms which had been set aside in September 1824 in the north-east corner for the purpose of punishing boys by placing them in solitary confinement. However, it also highlighted defects in other parts of the building and led to a massive programme of repair.[49] Furthermore, on 31 October 1826 the visiting committee recommended that the projecting spouts on the north side of the courtyard should be removed 'as inconvenient and hurtful to the building'[50] and that the eaves should be led down into the drain in the same way as on the other sides. The governors put out to estimate a year later.

At last, on 27 January 1827 the governors gave approval for work to be done to improve the approach to the Hospital from the south via the Vennel, which by now was in a serious state of disrepair, and also the approach from the west gate to the Hospital. Such work revived interest in Playfair's 1823 plan, and in November 1827 Bonnar pressed for its review. When the governors agreed, Playfair was asked to submit an updated proposal. This was completed in January 1828 and was very different from his original designs. The governors rationalised the situation by suggesting that 'in point of beauty and effect much has been gained by delay'.[51] It was decided, however, to go ahead with a phased development, which Playfair agreed would not prejudice the general features. In late 1828, the overdue improvements to the grounds encompassing the Hospital on the south side were begun.

Previously the Hospital had been surrounded by a grass field, divided by a plain stone wall. Under Playfair's direction the grounds were tastefully laid out, a larger space of playground was assigned to the boys, and the splendid approach from the south was gradually completed. From this time on, visitors to the Hospital, whether travelling by carriage or on foot, entered from Lauriston Place, by a grand lodge in the same style as the 'wark'. The Hospital was approached from the south by a spacious terrace walk, fenced by an ornamental parapet formed by an open balustrade on an elegant basement of hewn stone. From this terrace were flights of steps leading to the lawns. Playfair's Account 'for the Porter's Lodge, Terrace and laying out the ground' from 1829 to April 1832 for £626 10s. 10d. was submitted to the governors in May 1832.[52] When all the work on the south side was complete the governors in November 1838 accepted Playfair's plan for a new entrance to the Hospital from the Grassmarket.

Significantly, in February 1833, Dr Brunton moved 'a Committee be appointed to consider the steps that ought to be taken for the repair of the exterior of the Hospital'.[53] A committee of seven under Brunton was set up and it reported on 26 April 1833, arguing that work should be extensive and immediate. Its members believed that it was the duty of the governors not only to preserve, but also, so far as necessary, to adorn the structure of which they were the guardians. Their predecessors had built the 'wark' and used ornaments lavishly 'upon every part of the building that was likely to catch the eye', but those parts enclosed 'in the privacy of the garden were comparatively unadorned'.[54] Now that a new grand approach to the Hospital was being created from the south it was deemed important to finish the other sides of the building to the same high standard as that of the north front. This involved renewing the walls in ashlar,[55] but additional expense[56] was incurred by renewing the window frames which were all in a parlous state. Because of the delicate nature of the task, which was to take several years to complete, and the fact that local builders had little experience of such work, it was decided to experiment with the receding part of the south front between the south-east and south-west turrets. When this was successfully completed in October 1833 the governors authorised the newly appointed superintendent of works, Alexander Black, to go ahead with the rest of the building.[57]

The work was commenced in the presence of the governors, officials and the boys of the Hospital. In the foundations were placed a bottle containing several documents, and a silver plate, on which was engraved the names of the governors and functionaries, and also an inscription in Latin by Dr Brunton.[58] The alterations were executed in a most satisfactory manner, six inches being removed from the walls of the three sides and replaced by hewn stone,[59] although future generations noticed that the north front was of a lighter colour than those of the other three sides, contrasting the 'cold hue' of Craigleith stone used with the golden colour of the original Ravelstone stone.[60]

The governors at this point turned their attention to the roof of the chapel. On 30 December 1833, the ordinary committee reported that it considered the 'lathing of the whole ceiling to be insufficient, that the plaster which is overloaded with ornament is unsafe and consequently that both lath and plaster ought to be immediately taken down'. It held that although the interior had only been completed just over forty years previously[61] the 'ceiling has been slightly and injudiciously executed, and the decorations also executed in a style unworthy of, and incompatible with, the architectural character of the Edifice'.[62] So the committee ordered 'the centre compartment which is the most dangerous part to be immediately taken down' and suggested that the 'whole plaster-work and ornaments which encumber and overload the other compartments should be pulled down also and replaced in the meantime with good lath and plain plaster'.[63] It was suggested that not too much should be spent on these repairs because when funds permitted 'the interior of this Chapel should be renovated in a style worthy of the building of which it forms so conspicuous and interesting a portion. It has unques-tionably been intended by the Architect of the Edifice that this apartment should present the most imposing and attractive features of internal decoration, and that it should in every respect harmonize with the exterior in those ornamental details'.[64] The report went further: 'so long as the Chapel is allowed to remain as it now stands it cannot but be deemed discreditable to the governors in the eye of every enlightened stranger or visitor. By properly repairing it therefore according to the principles of design which characterize the Architecture of the Elizabethan period, the stigma will be removed and the whole Edifice completed in accordance with the intention of its Architect, and rendered in every respect worthy of its benevolent Founder.'[65] The committee recommended that the chapel be fitted up, with the roof being done first, and the governors accepted James Gillespie Graham's offer to prepare a design gratuitously as there was no official architect to the Hospital.

Graham[66] was 'already something of a celebrity in the production of Gothic artefacts'[67] and he submitted his designs for the restoration of the chapel on 31 October 1834.[68] These were prepared by Augustus Pugin[69] or were copied from Pugin's plates in *Specimens of Gothic Architecture of 1821*.[70] The governors had them carried out by the late summer of the following year and the committee of superintendence reported on 12 October 1835 its satisfaction 'that the work in all its details has been executed in a manner highly creditable to the Contractor'.[71] It held that 'Heriot's Hospital presents externally one of the best and most imposing specimens (of which the modern Athens can boast) of what may be termed our national style of architecture, and consequently attracts much attention from visitors'.[72] The committee pressed the governors to push forward with the work on the chapel without delay – finishing the plastering of the walls; painting the ceiling in imitation of oak; completing the entrance door and pulpit and stalls, and thus 'the Chapel would then be ready for occupation'.[73] It argued that the 'present marble pavement having been improperly laid on the ground renders the Chapel damp and uncomfortable; the new oak floor, which would be raised one step above the level of the Court would not only remedy this evil but save a considerable annual outlay for matting which from the dampness of the present floor is found indispensable'.[74] It realised the expense involved but reminded the governors 'that the interior of the Chapel is the only part of the original edifice now left incomplete'.[75]

Superintendent Black calculated that the refurbished chapel would hold 288 boys[76] with the stalls at either end accommodating thirty-four masters and governors. Despite the arguments of the committee that it must have been the intention to complete the interior in line with the exterior the governors voted thirty to three against the proposals. Dr Brunton held that the alterations were too expensive and his motion to ask Graham to prepare a modified plan costing no more than £1,000 was carried by nineteen to fifteen. Even then the Calvinist views of the Revd Dr John Lee[77] and five other governors led them to protest against such a level of expenditure. They believed that the chapel should only be fitted for two hundred; that much waste had been seen in three Edinburgh churches in the previous twenty-five years; they disapproved of the ornaments and appendages and believed the introduction of stalls compared unfavourably with the plainness of the other places of worship used by the boys. Not only did Presbyterian practice oppose showy ceremonial and graded structures but Lee also argued that seventeenth-century tradition would rule out seating, and the chapel of Christ's Hospital – the model for Heriot's – did not have oak benches. Heriot himself had had limited ambitions for his building and had not envisaged an ambitious chapel. Even the episcopalian times of Heriot and Balcanquall had not produced a will or statutes which emphasised hierarchy. Thus 'the costly operations now meditated have no such tendency' and 'are at variance with the spirit and professions which provide both the Will and the Statutes'.[78] Despite these protests the governors considered amended proposals from Graham on 7 April 1836 and accepted the lowest estimate proferred by cabinetmakers Messrs Trotter for £935. The governors thanked Gillespie Graham for modifying his plans to meet their views as to cost[79] and gave him £40 for his expenses.

On 12 November 1836 Gillespie Graham, who had attended his last meeting as a governor the previous month, wrote to the governors reporting that the work on the chapel 'has been executed to my entire satisfaction, and when completed I hope it will prove a specimen of Gothic Architecture not unworthy of the artizans of this or of any former period'.[80] He offered his services to the governors in any future projects.[81] He was to be called in again on 27 November for discussions on some additional work to complete the chapel. As the total expenditure for the refit stood at £1,524 8s. 5d. it was estimated that another £260 would pay for Graham's recommendations for stained glass, the new oak door, gas-light fittings and varnishing of the oak.[82] The governors agreed to go ahead with the further work but on the most competitive of terms. Graham was asked to provide a second full design for the stained glass of plainer description than his previous design.[83]

The issue of seating had not been finally resolved. The superintendent was asked on 7 June 1838 to prepare a plan, and it was suggested that the seats within the screen at each end of the chapel should be raised to allow those using them to see over the railing in front of them. Gillespie Graham furnished designs for the bench seats of massive oak with richly carved ends.[84] The beginning of the following year saw the chapel being used again for morning and evening worship as formerly.[85]

Although the chapel was the centre of attention the governors improved other parts of the interior of the Hospital during this period. On 30 November 1827 the visiting committee considered the state of the council room and recommended the restoration of the oak to its original colour. The governors agreed on the importance of ensuring that 'the original character of the apartment should be restored'.[86] With that complete the governors asked Gillespie Graham to furnish designs for chairs, thirty-six of which were supplied by William Trotter at £2 2s. in late 1836 'besides a handsome arm chair to correspond for the Lord Provost or Preses'.[87] It seemed appropriate that the governors pressed the house committee 'to get a proper table for the Council Room for the use of the governors at general meetings'.[88]

In the early part of the century the greens around the Hospital continued to cause concern. When the treasurer represented on 24 November 1806 that they had been much cut up by officers drilling volunteer corps riding on horseback and the exercise of artillery the governors banned horses and artillery from entering the walled area of the Hospital. However, problems remained. The volunteers continued to cause damage, the attending crowds of boys and dogs greatly disturbed the sheep, and the windows of the Hospital were constantly broken. On 15 June 1807 the governors withdrew the privilege of exercising within the grounds, but following a request in late August from Lt-Col. Rt Hon. Charles Hope of the 1st Regiment Royal Edinburgh Volunteers they agreed that recruits without rifles or drums could drill on the back green.

It appears that a club for Auld Callants had been in existence by 1716, perhaps even 1712.[89] Significantly, this period was one which saw the growth of social gatherings centred in a number of Edinburgh's taverns.[90] In the case of Heriot's the earliest group took the form of a Decorating Club whose main function was to organise the decorating of Heriot's statue on the anniversary of the founder's birthday.[91] Officials wore elaborate regalia and the club invested in medals, bells and caps[92] which were handed down to its successors.[93] As the century progressed its rules were formalised, and in 1802 they stipulated a maximum membership of eighteen members who had attended the Hospital[94] and were at least four years out of it (establishing the minimum age of eighteen)[95]: members could remain in the club only for four years, suggesting a youthful organisation of active members all fully involved in the decoration of the statue. Clearly the club was popular, for in the rules of 1804 it proved necessary to end the limit on the size of membership. The club met quarterly and at its May meeting decisions about who was responsible for decorating which part of the 'Wark' were made and the ornaments for the decoration – horns, shield, vases – were distributed amongst the members Any in need of repair were attended to, and usually representatives of the club would meet with the treasurer of the Hospital to discuss the arrangements for the decoration.

The actual anniversary day was a day of celebration as the minutes of the club prove: 'Baxter's Tavern,[96] June 4, 1804. This being the Anniversary of the Birth of our Worthy Patron the club met at the Hospital and after playing at the ball according to custom proceeded to Mr. Baxters, to Dinner. After Dinner the club were honoured with the Company of Mr. Jackson, treasurer, Mr. Finlay and Mr. Little, Teachers of George Heriot's Hospital and we all spent the evening with chearfulness and good humour and parted quite sober.'[97]

In 1805 when the office-bearers found that there were not enough flowers for the decoration they went to Musselburgh to forage. At midnight on the Sunday evening (2 June 1805) the club met and proceeded to the decoration which was complete by 9 a.m. 'in a manner that did honour to themselves and satisfactory to all who beheld it'.[98] That evening on anniversary day the club met at Baxter's Tavern at 6 p.m., when seventeen members sat down to dinner, after which treasurer Henderson and late-treasurer Jackson honoured the meeting with a visit. Unfortunately by 10 p.m. 'a shameful disturbance took place owing to some of the members getting beastly drunk to their great disgrace'.[99] The situation deteriorated further and the club 'insensibly dispersed', a number having 'to carry those who could not walk'.[100] Such behaviour was deemed intolerable, and when the club met again according to custom two days later in the Hospital to take down the decorations, new rules were agreed. From then on as soon as any member of the club appeared tipsy he was to be expelled from the meeting; also if any member of the club wounded or bruised another he was to be fined 2s. 6d. These rules were read over before dinner on every anniversary day.

The popularity of the club grew and its numbers reached forty-three by 1806. In May of that year the club invited eight Old Herioters to dinner on anniversary day. On 1 June the club took its usual nine hours overnight to decorate the statue, and on the following anniversary day the Decorating Club reciprocated a visit from the Social Club – the official celebration group.[101]

Some idea of the scale of the operation can be seen in the 1807 arrangements. The club found that they only had forty-five dozen narcissus instead of the desired 350 dozen![102] The anniversary celebrations took their usual form – church, 'some games at the Ball', toasts and songs, with the night spent 'with all the Jolity and Chearfulness such an occasion could inspire'. However, a footnote in the minutes of the club gives a hint of some difficulties. 'There having been some misunderstanding between some Old Herioters and the Governor [house-governor Somerville] of the Hospital a complaint was made by him to the Magistrates or Governors and by that means there was no deputation from the Social Club.' Seemingly on the last Sunday in May the house-governor returned from church to find the Hospital 'filled with persons of various descriptions'.[103] The porter reported that a number of old Herioters, including one William Reid, using very abusive language against the house-governor, had burst open the gate and forced their way in. The house-governor remonstrated with them about their behaviour and the example being set to the boys, and announced that they would be admitted at the proper time for decorating the statue. Reid advanced from the crowd, insulted the house-governor and threatened to kick him. As Reid had done this before the treasurer was instructed to take legal measures against Reid who was confirmed as one of those 'who denominate themselves the Decorating Club'.[104]

Later that same Sunday, club members broke into the Hospital and forced some 'garrers' to absent themselves from evening prayers. When the boys went into supper a number of the club followed, despite the attempts of the house-governor and masters to stop them, obliged the boys to strip, toss their jugs in the air and run naked through the courtyard. In the riot some younger boys were hurt. The club then forced a number of garrers to help them all night with the decoration. On the following day, Monday 1 June 1807, the crowd in the Hospital became riotous, broke windows and doors, insulted the masters and maltreated the servants.

These incidents led the governors to set up an inquiry into the activities of the Decorating Club. On 3 July it reported that the existence of the club and its contact with the boys was 'utterly incompatible with the subordination which is so indispensable for the maintenance of good order and that respect and obedience which children owe to those who have the superintendence of their morals and education'.[105] The governors believed that while the club existed the Garring Law would never be finally ended. Boys when punished warned masters that they would receive a visit from the club. The club claimed a right of access to the Hospital and of interfering with the management of the boys. To deal with this state of affairs the governors insisted that former members of the Hospital would no longer be allowed access without special permission, while on commemoration day the statue 'shall in future be decorated solely by gardeners employed for that purpose at the expense of the Hospital'.[106] The boys in the Hospital were to be furnished with flowers for the decoration at the expense of the Hospital and were forbidden to steal flowers from gardens in the vicinity. The Hospital gates would be locked at 7 p.m. after the ceremony.[107]

A letter from the Hospital treasurer, giving the details of these decisions, was read at a meeting of the Decorating Club on 16 March 1808. However, its members decided to continue with their usual meetings, and on anniversary day[108] it met in Murray's Tavern and had a convivial evening. The decoration was done according to the instructions of the governors, but according to club members 'it was done in such a stile which brought complaints from everyone: the public were so enraged at the behaviour of the Governors to the Club and the manner of the decoration . . . that a general throwing of Sticks, Stones, Turfs took place which brought the Properties down a good dail sooner then they were put up'.

The hostility between the Decorating Club and the governors continued unabated. On 4 June 1810 the club minutes made their point with force: 'The decorating remains still as it was, in the hands of the gardeners, who shamefully and disgustful to every beholder, place round the statue a few flowers, unnaturally and irregularly, which gives but little honour to the present governors, and makes Somerville be despised by every well-wisher.'

Some Auld Callants came together to form a Friendly and Relief Society, and the 'Articles of the Society of the Sons of Heriot, consisting of those interested in George Heriot's Hospital' were drawn up. Heriot's Benefit Society was instituted on Monday 5 June 1815.[109] Entry was by recommendation from two members and restricted to men under 40 years of age of 'sober and good character, and free from any maim or bruise, or any secret bodily disease'.[110] All paid an entry fee of ten shillings, and two shillings a quarter, and meetings were held every three months. Any member who had contributed for two years 'disabled from work by sickness or other evident misfortune' would receive benefit eight days after application.[111] Anyone seen intoxicated or out of their home or lodging after 10 p.m. would immediately lose any benefits being received.[112] The scheme also made provision for death expenses.[113] It proved a most successful venture.[114]

Despite no longer having a *raison d'être* the Decorating Club remained in existence and even attempted to restrict membership to those whose characters were deemed acceptable to its members. It continued to meet on anniversary day and toasts to 'The Immortal Memory of George Heriot', 'All Old Herioters throughout the Globe' and 'Teachers of George Heriot's Hospital' were the order of the day.

In May 1816 arrangements were made 'to commemorate that festival meeting as was considered as far as was traced back to be the Hundered year of that Laborious and well deserving the Name of H.D. Club'. Although the members felt that their work had not been appreciated it was deemed their duty 'for the benefit we have hitherto received from that place'. Despite its union with a similar group, the Brotherly Club (probably begun in 1815), in May 1820, which led to a temporary increase in support – thirty-two attending the anniversary dinner that year – the Decorating Club fell into abeyance in September 1823. It was revived on 16 June 1828 when new office-bearers decided to petition the Duke of Hamilton 'for a renewal of the two standards of colours which was presented to the herioters on 22 of June 1724'.[115] It was also agreed to have a Jubilee Supper on Tuesday 1 July to celebrate 200 years of the Hospital. This took place in Barry's Hotel and involved the governors and the Lord Provost, who took the chair, and members of the Decorating Club also attended.

Traditionally the anniversary day was a joyous occasion for Edinburgh. The 'busking' ceremony[116] was done by the Auld Callants, who 'bulged the properties'. This involved the use of flowers as the shields, thistles, cornucopias, and crown, with other devices emblematic of the name and character of Heriot. The whole was encompassed with a massive wreath of flowers – the festoon. The girls of the Trades Maiden Hospital prepared a bouquet which was placed in the hands of the founder. A church service was held and a sermon preached in Greyfriars' Church by the Edinburgh ministers in rotation. Not only Herioters but the boys of George Watson's

Hospital and the Girls of the Merchant and Trades Maiden Hospitals also assembled, accompanied by their officials and governors, as well as their relatives. When the out-schools opened, their pupils also joined the celebrations and all assembled on the green in front of the Hospital making it a special day for many in Edinburgh. The out-school children were provided with refreshment while the Hospital boys were served with a special dinner and toasted the memory of the pious founder.

With building work going on in 1828 the governors decided to avoid decorating the statue on anniversary day, as the ceremony 'never fails to attract a vast concourse of people and many of them rather of a tumultuous character'.[117] This was unfortunate for it was the 200th anniversary of the Hospital's foundation. However, a special ceremony took place in the chapel with prizes being distributed by the Lord Provost and an address given by the Revd Dr Gordon. All adjourned to the refectory, where the governors and visitors drank to the memory of the pious founder from the 'Founder's Cup', the boys joining in the toast. The governors, teachers and leading officers of the Hospital dined together as part of a memorable occasion. Only limited celebrations were held after 1828, but in 1832, the house-governor was allowed to provide fireworks 'as formerly'.[118] The governors also continued to hold their annual dinner, although in the 1830s a small group began to question whether such 'entertainments' were a legitimate cost in the treasurer's accounts. By 1853 the guest list was being scrutinised by a special committee.

As early as February 1773 the governors were considering the need for a special anthem. By the 1790s they were being composed annually and an Old Herioters' Anthem Club grew up.[119] Two anthems were used annually: one was written especially for the celebrations, although it was sometimes repeated and sometimes adapted, while the other anthem was standard.[120] R.A. Smith and W.D. Kenward composed anthems in the 1820s and 1830s.[121] Every May the education committee decided on the anthem to be sung and usually employed a band to play it. When on the grounds of expense Councillor Russell tried to end the practice in May 1837 there was little support for his motion, although some governors wished to restrict the size of the band.[122] Opposition came from a different source on 3 February 1842 when the governors of Watson's Hospital held that they had 'been desirous for sometime to make a change' in reforming the anthem which the boys of both Hospitals sang every June.[123] The Heriot governors were displeased with such interference but agreed to a joint committee of both governing bodies, which was deadlocked at its meeting on 14 March. With the Heriot governors blocking change the anthem was kept.[124]

With the 'busking' ceremony in abeyance the Decorating Club became less significant. In January 1834 an Auld Callants Club was formed 'to venerate the memory of the Founder and to perpetuate the recollections, the intimacies and the attachments of their boyhood'.[125] Its founder, and until 1864 secretary, was Robert Morham, and it remained in existence as a commemoration club until the 1880s.[126] More ephemeral was the Old Herioters' Association, which held its first meeting in the religious instruction room of the Hospital on 7 October 1848 to promote 'the moral and intellectual improvement of young men, who had been educated in George Heriot's Hospital'.[127] Although it attracted thirty-eight members to its first meeting it soon was struggling and was re-constituted as the Old Herioters' Mutual Improvement Association in 1853 with an emphasis on essay-writing and criticism, debate, conversation and recitation. It held eighteen meetings a year under its president, James Currie, but was dissolved in 1857.

The calibre of house-governors seems to have improved in the early nineteenth century. From his appointment in March 1795 until he demitted office George Irvine had an unblemished record. On 23 August 1805 the governors thanked him for his 'exemplary conduct and faithful discharge'[128] of his duties on his appointment to a classical mastership at the High School. He was to remain there until his retirement in August 1829 and 'was much respected and beloved by his pupils'.[129] The governors promoted the Revd John Somerville,[130] one of the masters in the Hospital, to the position of house-governor. He also was an improvement on many of his predecessors, although he did not always keep good health. His doctor had recommended that he take up horse-riding, and he purchased a pony which the governors allowed him to graze in the greens adjoining the Hospital.[131] After the events of 1807 he did a great deal to combat the 'Garring Law' and although he was never able to stamp it out he exposed its worst features when he could and vigorously prosecuted those involved.

Somerville's efforts were not appreciated by certain parents who complained of his flogging 'to a degree never before known, at least in any seminary of learning in a civilised nation such as ours'.[132] Eleven parents sent a letter to the governors complaining that his cruelty, rather than the commission of crimes, had resulted in the desertions. The governors went to great lengths to investigate their claims. The ordinary committee had the boys concerned strip to see what marks of violence they had on their bodies; they found none. It contended that all punishments had been meted out for good reason and all in front of all the Hospital boys. The committee unanimously agreed that Somerville had 'done no more than his duty'[133]and, if anything, had perhaps erred on the side of leniency. He had to be supported, otherwise the discipline and order of the Hospital would be destroyed. It condemned the conduct of the parents, some of whom had encouraged the boys in their disobedience.

In the event one garrer was expelled while another fifteen had to promise to desist from garring on threat of expulsion if they did not comply. A circular notice was sent to all boys' guardians, who were expected to impress upon the boys the need to desist from garring. It also assured parents that boys who disclosed the machinations and conduct of others would be afforded all possible protection. The governors determined to stamp out the Garring Law by whatever 'means of watchfulness and severity shall be found necessary'[134] and Somerville was thanked for his efforts.

When Walter Nichol, first teacher of mathematics in the Hospital, resigned in August 1813 he suggested that 'in the boys too, since the departure of those who were trained under the Garring law . . . it has been my fortune to witness a progress in propriety of manner and docility of disposition, which has left very little of what is really painful in a teacher's situation and duties and which has converted the heavy drudgery of forcing a barren soil into the recreation of watching over spontaneous fertility'.[135] The governors felt that this improvement had much to do with Somerville and he was profusely thanked for his efforts when he resigned in 1816 to become minister of Currie Parish Church.[136]

Somerville's successor, John Christison, had been headmaster of George Watson's Hospital and came to Heriot's in August 1816, aged 58, with a reputation as a fine mathematician. He was in post barely two years when on Monday 28 September 1818 'almost the whole boys' of the Hospital had left it 'in a body' giving as their reason that 'some of them had been severely punished without sufficient cause'.[137]

The importance of the issue and the report of the special committee on the desertions resulted in eight separate governors' meetings within a month in November–December 1818. There was ample evidence that garring continued, but the governors disagreed on the severity and extent of punishments to be meted out. After much debate one boy was expelled, some were flogged and others confined. It was also decided that the 'indulgence of a vacation'[138] in summer 1819 would only be given to those who had not deserted on 28 September. However, on Christmas Eve five boys deserted, and after considerable discussion a majority of the governors determined to expel them.

The special committee recommended that the character of parents should be vouched for by their minister or elder before their boys were elected to the

Hospital. It claimed that the long vacation was 'productive of material injury to all the boys'[139]and recommended that it be restricted to two weeks, that the governors check that the boys stayed with proper persons and how their time would be spent. A hierarchy of punishments was established to prevent desertions which involved whipping, confinement and expulsion with loss of rights. The committee pressed for the final extinction of the pernicious system of garring by expelling the garrers, protecting younger boys, rewarding older boys who rejected garring and introducing a system of rewards for good behaviour.

Christison had more problems to deal with when, on Thursday 25 March, 1819, fourteen boys deserted and remained out all night, and on the following morning another ninety deserted – all to return during that day. Christison could give no reason for the insurbordination. All 104 boys were confined on Saturday 27 March, deprived of their play and warned about the consequences of any repetition of such actions. This seemed to quieten things for a while. However, on 7 June, 110 boys deserted for a time in the course of the day, followed by some 80 later on the same day. Although punishment was meted out to the ringleaders on the last of these desertions the governors agreed to look into preventative measures for the future. A special committee met twice and interviewed both staff and boys but was unable to discover any particular cause for the desertions. It was 'disposed to trace them in general to the evil influence of a few boys by whom the others and the younger were misled'.[140] No additional punishments were deemed necessary but the committee recommended that the boys and their parents should be warned about their future action. This was the situation when on 27 September it was reported that twenty-four boys had deserted, eight of whom had run away on two previous occasions, but no cause could be put forward for these developments. The committee responded by recommending the immediate expulsion of three boys and the strong admonition of the other five. Yet four days later, on 11 October, six boys 'leaped over the walls'[141] resulting in the special committee deciding to meet urgently to review the position. Before it could do so, on the evening of 12 October four more boys had deserted. The committee responded to these events by expelling three boys, who in front of the others in the chapel 'had their coats taken off by the House Porter'.[142] The three other boys (who received favourable reports from the house-governor) were taken back but were put in solitary confinement for a week and fed on bread and water. The latter punishment was also meted out to the four boys who had deserted the following day.

The special committee met a number of times and determined 'that very material changes are necessary both in the management and in the education of the boys'.[143] In particular, it stressed the need for the entire separation of the new entrants from the rest of the boys for a year after their admission to the Hospital. This would require an additional English master who would devote himself exclusively to the younger boys. Given the ill-health of Christison the committee pressed for his immediate resignation and in compensation he was to be offered his salary during his lifetime. When the governors offered this to the house-governor he accepted, agreeing, however, to stay on until his successor was appointed.

Christison's final days as house-governor were marked by more trouble. On 19 January 1825 it was reported that the store-cellar of the housekeeper had been broken into and three dozen wine-bottles taken. After an investigation it was discovered that a regular system of plunder had been going on, continuing for at least two months. Boys had false keys and other housebreaking equipment: they had even taken the steward's keys during the night from his room to steal meal and potatoes from his stores. They had let themselves down by ropes and sheets from their sleeping quarters into Heriot Green and had sold some of the wine in town. The governors claimed that most of the boys who slept in the low east ward were involved and 'the Garring Law is practised in that ward to the fullest extent'.[144] The special committee recommended the expulsion of three boys, the inspection of all locks, doors and windows, and that the porter sleep in the low east ward. Following their suggestion that the privilege of boys visiting town be rescinded, the governing body responded by restricting them to only one visit a fortnight, the older boys one Saturday, the younger boys the other. Moreover, the boys were to be allowed out only if a parent or near relation collected and returned them. Six boys reacted to these restrictions by breaking into the room where William Douglas was being confined. Their parents were told to remove them from the Hospital immediately, otherwise they would be expelled: five decided to go before expulsion to ensure they retained their allowances.

The governors set up a committee in March 1825 to examine the credentials of the twenty candidates for the vacant house-governorship. 'By a great majority'[145] it recommended the Revd James Boyd for the post.[146] He took the oath and was installed as house-governor on 6 June 1825 and immediately inherited a new set of regulations. These emphasised the lessons of recent years: the character of the parents of boys elected would be investigated and emphasis placed on the attention they paid to educate their family and the proficiency already achieved by the boys. New boys would be separated from the others for eighteen months. They were to have separate teachers, separate hours for meals, exercise and visits, separate places in chapel and church, separate sleeping wards, and they would be cared for by female servants. The education of the boys was to be accommodated as far as possible to the capacity and prospects of each individual and 'hopeful scholars' were to be encouraged. However, boys who were unfitted to study languages were to be taught more useful things. Yet all were to have a fair trial of Latin. After a year, if a boy was in the bottom third of the class then he was to be given another year at the subject: only after this second year, if he remained in the lowest group, was he to give up Latin and study something more useful. Degrading punishments were to be used sparingly and then in public by the house-governor only for moral blame and not literary negligence: gentle treatment was to be used whenever possible. Relatives were not to be welcome in the Hospital unless called by the governors or visiting boys when sick. Boys could only leave the Hospital if collected and returned by trustworthy parents. They were only to be allowed out once every three weeks. The governors were to decide if a boy deserved an annual summer vacation of maximum two weeks taken from the beginning of August, but only if he had behaved in the course of the year.[147]

The new regulations detailed the job specification of the house-governor: he was to be the 'head of the family'.[148] He was to teach no more than three hours a day, teaching the more advanced boys topics of general interest to them whatever their destination in life, e.g., general outlines of history and geography, first principles of natural history and of mechanical philosophy, the elements of English composition and the higher branches of religious instruction. He was to visit the other classes every week and examine them on their work, keeping appropriate records of the places of the boys. The specific jobs of teachers (four of them resident in the Hospital), mistress, steward, nine female servants, two porters (in charge of gates and showing visitors round the buildings) and wardsmen (two steady men who patrolled the playground and slept in the senior wards), were also detailed.

Boyd seems to have been popular and successful. The governors reported their satisfaction in June 1826, and in particular the essays of the highest class merited 'much commendation'.[149] They applauded the internal discipline of the Hospital which they deemed steady and without severity, stressing their belief that kindly treatment and due vigilance have the happiest of effects. Boyd had instituted an annual examination at the end of May and prizes were introduced and distributed to those boys who had distinguished themselves during the year in exemplary conduct, ability and diligence. As well as prizes in books, silver medals were presented for the first time to 'the most meritorious of the youths'.[150]

Boyd contributed in other ways to the development of the Hospital. He persuaded the governors on 17 October 1825 that £400 should be spent immediately for books for the library and £30 annually from then on. He also helped develop the curriculum. He was present at the meeting in July 1826 when the governors discussed the possible introduction of gymnastic exercises, of the type practised in military academies, into the Hospital. They took medical advice and visited the Military and Naval Academy to witness their activities, which greatly impressed those who attended. The governors were persuaded that Sergeant-Major Lawson of the Military Academy could instruct 150 boys daily between 5 and 7 p.m. Gymnastic exercises soon became an established part of Hospital life, although they were performed privately (not for display) and the apparatus introduced was only used during instruction to avoid accidents.[151] Unfortunately for the Hospital Dr Boyd resigned to become one of the classical masters in the High School in August 1829.[152] He was a great loss to the Hospital for he had 'such ability and integrity that his character was well known to the citizens of Edinburgh'.[153] At their meeting on 21 August the Heriot governors recorded their strong sense of the value of his services to the Hospital.[154]

A sub-committee of eleven governors examined the testimonials of the six candidates for the vacant post and favoured the Revd Hector Holme, who had been one of the English masters in Heriot's Hospital since 1825 over house-governor Cunningham of Watson's Hospital. Holme was appointed house-governor on 14 September 1829, but his was not to be an altogether happy appointment. He proved a good teacher and his tenure was relatively peaceful, but on 6 June 1837, at a governors' meeting he went beserk.[155] Dr Abercrombie was sent for and he gave Holme a sedative. Three days later he was removed out of the Hospital to lodgings in Hill Square and placed under the charge of two men 'properly qualified for the superintendence of one in his unfortunate situation'.[156] As his condition deteriorated Holme was placed in Saughton Asylum on 3 July and John Oswald, the senior resident master, took over the house-governor's duties temporarily.

The incapacity of the house-governor was new territory for the Hospital and the governors decided that although they wished to act 'with tenderness towards Mr Holme' they 'had a paramount duty to discharge to the Institution'.[157] This led to a discussion on 7 September when it was reported that 'there has long existed – even further back than any one now living can remember – a want of harmony between the Head Master and the other masters such as greatly to mar their efficiency and seriously to interfere with the usefulness of the Institution and the administration of its affairs by the governors'.[158] To remove these evils a committee suggested that the clause in Balcanquall's Statutes which conferred a suffrage and voice to the house-governor should be ended to ensure that he would win respect through strength of character rather than official privilege. It was pointed out that in no other Edinburgh Hospital was the house-governor a voting member of a governing body and in none of them 'has the same want of harmony been known to exist as in Heriot's Hospital'.[159]

By 30 October Holme's condition was improving, but a group of governors was determined to press forward with the reforms and get rid of him. When Holme's lawyer suggested that an annuity of 100 guineas for life would enable Holme to resign, the governors unanimously agreed to his terms and accepted his resignation on 4 January 1838.[160]

The way was now clear for a more considered review of the position and status of the house-governor.[161] By March the governors voted 24 to 5 to accept a married man as house-governor. With Holme gone they even decided by 18 to 10 to raise the status of the house-governor rather than lower it, and decided to increase the salary to £300.[162] On the motion of Councillor Macaulay it was agreed by a two-thirds majority (14–5 of those voting, 14–7 of those present on 26 April) that the house-governor should hold office only during the governors' pleasure, and he could be removed by a two-thirds majority. The governors also agreed to Macaulay's proposal that the right of the house-governor to a vote on the governing body should be removed.

On 2 November 1838 the Lord President of the Court of Session, Charles Hope, the Lord Advocate Murray, and the Dean of the Faculty of Advocates, John Hope, approved these changes, ensuring that they came into force immediately.[163] After over two centuries Heriot's fell into line with the other Hospitals and the house-governor no longer had the right to a voice in the business nor a seat on the governing body. Further, the house-governor would no longer be in post for life, as he could now be dismissed by two-thirds of governors present voting at a special meeting. Finally, exhibiting a more enlightened approach and suggesting an increasingly critical view of monasticism, the house-governor could now be a married man.

A special committee of eleven on candidates for the office of house-governor chaired by the Lord Provost produced a short-leet of candidates over the age of thirty for the job. Four were interviewed, including Dr James Boyd.[164] On 11 April 1839 in the final vote it was decided by 24–19 to appoint the Revd Dr William Steven (over James Cumming) to the post of house-governor (and Inspector of the New Schools) at a salary of £315 (which included an allowance of £15 for coal and gas) and the promise of suitable accommodation in the Hospital for him and his family. A new and important era in the Hospital was about to begin.

The Hospital was fortunate in some of its other staff at this time. Dr James Hamilton[165] was elected physician of the Hospital in 1773 and was joined as co-physician by Dr Buchan in 1795. On 11 April 1806 the governors decided to increase the salary of the physician to £60 per annum and that of the surgeon to £50.[166] This increase was a direct result of Hamilton's work during the scarlatina epidemic in 1804. He later published an authoritative textbook which gave a very favourable description of Hospital conditions. 'Great attention to the cleanliness of every part of the Hospital, is added to the advantages of situation. The diet of the children is well regulated:[167] there is an abundant supply of spring-well water from the city's reservoir, which adjoins the House: and the medical gentlemen attached to the Hospital, and acting under the regulations of the governors, put a negative on the admission of any child who appears to them to labour under scrofula. These circumstances are so favourable to the health of the inmates of this Foundation, that I have the satisfaction to say, that, during thirty-two years that I have had the medical superintendence of it, I have seldom known any serious illness prevailing among them.'[168] Hamilton remained in the service of the Hospital until his death.[169]

During this period the Wood family continued to hold the position of surgeon. In 1829 the governors turned to one of their number, Councillor William Wood,[170] as surgeon, for he 'had given frequent and inestimable proof of his zeal and ability in promoting the welfare of this Hospital'.[171] His reputation was such that when Hamilton died in 1835 it was decided to employ a consulting physician, Dr John Abercrombie, who was to be paid one guinea for each visit when called in, while Wood's duties were extended to superintendence of all medical duties at an increased salary of £80 per annum. This was not only a vote of confidence in Wood but was also a reflection of his belief that 'for a considerable time past the boys have been in the enjoyment of perfect health'.[172]

Wood's assertion had much to commend it. Since the outbreak of scarlet fever in the Hospital between September and December 1804 when of the total population of 140 (120 boys and 20 adults) in the Hospital, over 50 boys contracted the disease and three had died,[173] epidemics had not affected the Hospital again until 23 October 1832. Immediately before then 179 boys, 17 female and 10 male adults were in very good health except for several boys affected with chronic scrofulous sores. The cholera epidemic earlier in 1832 had resulted in the enforcement of strict quarantine regulations and the inmates had not been affected.[174] However, scarlet fever was introduced by a male servant living outside the Hospital's precincts, whose son had contracted the disease. Hamilton had called in Wood and the epidemic had proved mild: 44 boys contracted the disease but only one death occured due to the 'favourable circumstances in which the sick were placed'.[175] No further cases were found after January 1833. The governors followed Wood's advice and fitted up an additional sick-room. The two rooms now available were large and ventilated, and each of them was capable of taking twelve boys in separate beds. A well-constructed bath in the room adjoining the sick-rooms with constantly boiling water available whenever needed was also available. The governors also provided another room with six beds, which was to be used to ascertain illness, and also a recovery room. Perhaps the history of epidemics in the Hospital and these improvements explain Wood's optimism that Heriot's was well equipped to deal with future epidemics. However, he had underestimated the nature and virulence of disease and his optimism was shattered by the different type and character of the outbreak of 1836.

Scarlet fever had broken out again in Edinburgh in July 1835 and reached the Hospital the following January. It was to last for three months and was to kill three boys directly.[176] It seems to have been the cause of house-governor Holme's illness, for he was to die later of its secondary effects. Of the 207 in the Hospital,[177] some 45 were affected. Clearly worried about this impact Wood investigated the situation elsewhere.[178] Wood would not be optimistic again during his appointment which lasted until 1858 (when he was succeeded by his son, Andrew). He constantly warned the governors of the need to keep the boys in the Hospital during periods of illness in Edinburgh, although they did not always follow his cautious advice.[179]

Occasionally an event occurred which was out of the ordinary. On 2 May 1822 one of the boys fell out of a window, and the treasurer was given the job of securing the windows to avoid a recurrence. On 18 April 1836 it was reported that Peter Russell had been struck behind the ear by the cane wielded by Sergeant-Major Lawson. This incident led to the introduction of a medical book to record the visits of the doctor and cases of importance. Russell's condition worsened and within a week he was dead. The governors called in the Edinburgh University Professor of Medical Jurisprudence to examine the body, along with Dr Wood. Fortunately for Lawson and the Hospital the detailed medical report found diseased tuberculosis and that (conveniently) Russell's death was not the result of the blow. It seems more than coincidence that the curriculum was changed later in 1836 and Lawson's services were dispensed with; his action did not fit in well with the ethos which the governors were trying to develop in the Hospital.[180]

The governors seem to have been satisfied with the standards of learning being achieved in the Hospital. On 30 October 1809 they decided that 'considering the advantage which the Hospital now has, and may at all times enjoy, of a skilful and approved teacher of the Latin language it is not necessary that any of the boys connected with this Institution should be educated at the High School'.[181] Moreover, the most 'hopeful scholars' were to stay on until sixteen years of age and then four of them at any one time would go on to the College of Edinburgh for four years and be maintained at £30 annually. Shortly thereafter the education committee reported on 9 August 1810 that they were 'gratified and delighted. Indeed we do not recollect to have seen any seminary better taught or in a more flourishing condition'.[182] They praised progress in Latin, English, writing and arithmetic and were agreeably surprised to see what was being done in Greek, geometry and algebra. The governors responded by increasing the salaries of the staff – £20 extra for the house-governor and £10 extra for teachers. It was suggested that the improvement was the result of the separation of the teaching of English from the classical department (which included the teaching of French) which had occured in January 1809, and it was argued that further 'division of labour' should occur. By November the teaching of writing and book-keeping was separated from that of mathematics and geography and an additional teacher employed. Walter Nichol remained as the mathematics teacher and his teaching included geometry, algebra, arithmetics, mensuration, navigation, fortification and geography. He was a gifted teacher who emphasised understanding and reasoning processes rather than rote learning, and he seems to have been very successful in teaching, despite the class size of 40![183]

The governors were always being requested to broaden the curriculum and so improve the education offered in the Hospital. They were often sympathetic to innovations and could be proud of their efforts to keep up to date with new developments.[184] D.B. Reid gave a series of lectures in chemistry in the Hospital in July 1836, but the lack of a co-ordinated course of physics and chemistry remained a real weakness.[185] The governors decided to employ François Espinasse, a native French speaker, to teach the language to the older boys in December 1835[186] and also introduced mechanical drawing for three hours a week, which was deemed useful for professionals needing a knowledge of the principles of mechanics, architecture and other arts.

Conditions in the sleeping wards remained basic.[187] The four large wards were situated on the east and west sides of the quad, while the four small wards lay on the second storey of each of the towers (except the south-west) and on the north front below the bartizan between the steeple and the north-east tower. Three wardsmen supervised the boys and slept in cubicles in three of the large wards, while the fourth large ward was visited by the steward. The gatekeeper visited some wards, while the ward with new boys had a maid in attendance. All the wards had a monitor. In December 1805 it was decided that instead of every boy having a separate chamber-pot under each bed there should be a large tub for the whole ward. This was to decrease the offensive spilling of urine on the floor, which also rotted the floorboards. The governors also introduced a contrivance by which urine, as soon as it was discharged, was taken by pipe outwith the building. In April 1836 the house committee considered the expediency and practicability of each boy having a bed to himself in place of sharing with another. Within a month it had reported that it was inexpedient[188] but recommended stricter superintendence in the sleeping wards as a poor substitute.

Again during this period there is little attention given to apprenticeships. On 30 November 1810 the governors agreed to Convener Denholm's motion that a special committee be appointed to consider the levels of apprenticeship fees. It met on 28 December and recommended that each apprentice be given £10 sterling annually during his apprenticeship for a period not exceeding five years for a maximum total of £50, excluding the £5 paid to each boy at the expiry of his indentures to purchase clothes. The governors agreed to this on 14 January 1811 and thus the ancient fee paid to masters was replaced by the modern allowance paid to apprentices. The change was justified on the grounds that, although the premium for masters was falling into disuse, the payment of adequate wages for apprentices had not become an established custom.

During this period the Hospital became more professional in its approach to its affairs. The ordinary committee had reported on 1 July 1809 that given the great increase in the revenue of the Hospital it would contribute to the business of the treasurer and auditors if quarterly and annual accounts were regularly prepared for the inspection of the auditors by a professional accountant. The governors accepted this recommendation and unanimously nominated and immediately appointed William Scott Moncrieff to the new post at a salary of £25 per annum. The appointment of James Denholm as treasurer in August 1813 also proved successful,[189] for he took over at a time of increasing debts. Within three months of his appointment as treasurer it was decided to end the customary benefits the treasurer received by way of discounts on articles purchased for the Hospital, and instead the salary was increased from £200 to £500 per annum to reflect the importance of the post. The superintendent of works was to be directly responsible to Denholm and contracts were to be agreed on exact specifications and costing. Other non-building contracts were to be entered into for not longer than a year at a time and sealed tenders were to be transmitted to the treasurer who was to open them in the presence of the governors, who in turn were to direct him to accept the most competitive tender. All other officers in the Hospital were to be accountable to the treasurer who was to have an office in a central position in town with rent paid. Clearly it was expected that this new professional approach would increase financial efficiency, and the surpluses apparent from 1818 onwards were partially a result of such measures. The governors believed so, and on 6 April 1820 thanked Denholm for his 'unremitting attention and faithful discharge of his duty in all respects'.[190] On his death in September 1822 as a mark of respect the governors directed the house-governor, masters and boys to attend his funeral and to accompany the body when it was removed from the hearse at the west end of Princes Street to the place of interment in St Cuthbert's Churchyard. A committee of five was set up to decide on what mark of respect should be paid by the governors to Denholm given 'his meritorious and zealous services as treasurer'.[191] This resulted in W.H. Playfair producing an elegant design for a monument in July 1824.[192] It was a cenotaph of white marble with an inscription composed by the Revd Dr Brunton which stressed 'the intelligence, and kindliness, and heartful zeal, with which, during nine years, he managed the affairs of the Hospital as its treasurer'. Originally it was placed at the west end of the chapel but in 1840 it was moved to the vestibule area outside the council room.

The governing body themselves attempted to be more professional too. On 11 December 1810 the Lord Provost laid down that no longer could verbal motions be discussed but only written motions which had to be lodged with the Clerk to be entered in the minutes. From August 1829 agendas for meetings were delivered by Hospital messenger forty-eight hours before meetings. The position of the chairman was clarified after counsel's opinion was taken in July 1830: as the Statutes made no mention of a chairman there could be no casting vote in the event of a tie. In November 1834 a new ten-committee structure was introduced, with each electing their own conveners.[193] In May 1835 it was decided to have regularised meetings of the governing body on the first Thursday of each month at 11 a.m. Later that year, in November 1835, when Parliament allowed the substitution of affirmation for oath the governors took legal advice from Thomas Thomson and Andrew Rutherford and decided to introduce a declaration in place of Balcanquall's oath.[194] Then in September 1839 the governors opened up their meetings to the press in the hope that unfounded allegations of 'jobbing' would be dispelled.[195]

The governors were usually strict in their admission policy for boys entering the Hospital. When it was believed in October 1814 that burgess tickets were being bought for no other purpose than to gain entitlement to education in the Hospital the governors tried to prevent such abuse.[196] Again in December 1821 when William, son of Peter McNiven, the messenger of the Hospital, was elected, seventeen governors protested that although McNiven had a burgess ticket he did not need it for his occupation and had bought it only to have his children educated in the Hospital. When it was found that the circumstances of James Alison, tailor, in January 1824, were 'such as not to entitle him to any benefit from the funds of the Hospital'[197] the governors insisted he repay £8 3s. 6d., which he did. Another such case occurred in April 1835 when it was found that the financial circumstances of William Hume, plumber, were such that when his son left the Hospital he was by no means poor. Interesting was the governors' consideration of what constituted the most deserving cases for election. This issue erupted in April 1835 when the governors rejected the claim of the fatherless William Ross for election on the grounds that he was over ten years of age and unable to read. The Revd Lee protested that a fatherless boy had priority even if his reading was poor and there was no provision for rejection on such grounds in the original Statutes. As the boy concerned was only three weeks past his tenth birthday and the Statutes mentioned that boys had to be between seven and sixteen years of age, Lee held that if Ross was not elected they would be frustrating the intentions of the founder. Mrs Ann Ross put her son, William, forward for election again in October 1836 but he was again rejected by 18–11. Five governors, including Dr Lee, continued their protest and this encouraged widow Ross to go to the Court of Session in December 1836. It was not until 4 June 1840 that the clerk was able to read Lord Moncrieff's decision of 20 May of that year. He held Ross eligible for entry but argued that the Court of Session was not competent to intervene as the governors had the absolute and sole power of electing boys. However, Moncrieff also held that the Statutes stipulated boys between seven and sixteen years of age, and the governors did not have the power to declare any boy over ten years of age ineligible. He also believed that the regulations of 21 December 1829 requiring the house-governor to give a preliminary examination before accepting him into the

Hospital was an innovation 'contrary to the whole spirit and object of George Heriot's foundation'.[198] His Will evidently stated the nature of teaching to be elementary and the boys' poverty and orphan condition pointed to this, as did Heriot's intention to relieve the poor. Moncrieff contended that George Heriot had meant his foundation to serve precisely those who were now being rejected. It might, in other words, be convenient not to have elementary education, but it was the original purpose and should be provided. Although there was a preference for accepting fatherless boys the Court could not take over the governors' function and compel acceptance of them. Moncrieff suggested that there were 'abuses' in the management of the Hospital[199] but the Court of Session could not redress such abuses or errors. To improve the situation and to avoid future disputes Moncrieff suggested that the governors produce a 'Code of Laws'.[200] The case of the 'Boy Ross' did not end there. The governors wished to overturn the decision that Ross was qualified to enter the Hospital, and the law committee of the governing body decided on 7 August 1843 to appeal to the House of Lords.[201] The governors were ultimately vindicated in their position when the Lords decided on 19 March 1846 that the governors had the sole power of election of boys and there was no case to answer.[202]

The success in this case for the governors ensured a continuation of their practices for entry and exit from the Hospital. On 11 December 1809 the governors had agreed that boys arriving in the Hospital should not have developed habits of idleness and vice otherwise the usefulness and good order of the institution would be diminished. It was agreed that every application for admittance would henceforth be accompanied by a certificate to ensure that boys had been instructed in the principles of religion and had from the age of six attended English classes. By July 1828 the governors had agreed that boys would only be allowed into the Hospital not only if they passed a medical and were physically fit, but also if they were free from any speech impediment. When in December 1829 one of the boys elected was found not to have an elementary education the parents involved were reprimanded. The governors were also able to maintain their policy of boys leaving at the age of fourteen, other than those going on to College.

The governors also found themselves the recipients of generosity on the part of others. Dr Fleming was given the task in January 1811 of preparing the letter of thanks to the Earl of Buchan for his present of an original painting of the pious founder of the Hospital and another painting of the founder's father.[203] Various legacies were left to the Hospital. On 30 October 1804 John Gilchrist LLD, Professor of Hindustani in the College of Fort-William,

Bengal, gave £100 sterling as a gift, rather 'as a act of justice than bounty', for 'that excellent institution'[204] where he was educated. On 11 March 1805 the governors were informed of a legacy of £200 in the will of David Arbuthnot, a London tailor, who had been brought up in the Hospital. The treasurer was instructed to include the donations on a board to be hung in the council room.[205] These were commented on by Robert Southey, the Poet Laureate, when he visited on Wednesday, 18 August 1819.[206] On 20 April 1829 the governors were informed that George Gray, late of Baltimore in Maryland, had left money to the Hospital and on 19 April 1830 £2,504 was received.[207] At its meeting on 8 February 1838 the governors heard of the will of the Revd Robert Blair, DD, of Norfolk, who had died on 1 December 1837, leaving a legacy to the Hospital for a bursary to pay the education of a student of divinity at Edinburgh University for four years.[208] However, as the century wore on and the very existence of the Hospital seemed to be in doubt, such legacies dried up.[209]

Travellers continued to visit the Hospital as a principal building in the town. Significantly in this period it became the centre of European and American attention. On 4 December 1815 the governors' monthly meeting was interrupted by the arrival of the Archdukes John and Lewis of Austria who 'were conducted by the governors through the different apartments of the house'.[210] Dr S.H. Spiker, Librarian to the King of Prussia, visited the following year and suggested the building was more like an ancient feudal castle than a charitable institution. John Griscom, Professor of Chemistry and Natural Philosophy at the New York Institute, also visited the Hospital in 1819 and believed the building made 'a handsome appearance' though 'erected in the antiquated style of turrets at the corners, and a square court within'. In the classes he found 'the pronounciation of the reading master was strongly Scottish' and gave a detailed example of what he experienced.[211]

Most importantly the first educational commentary on the Hospital was made by Alex. Dallas Bache, who was sent by the Board of Trustees for Girard College of Orphans in Philadelphia to obtain information and report back on good practice abroad. He visited Europe between September 1836 and October 1838 and examined schools in Ireland, Scotland, England, France, Switzerland, Holland, Belgium, and the chief states of Germany and Italy. His 666 page report was produced on 1 May 1839, and contained nineteen valuable pages on Heriot's Hospital.[212] He was the first to make critical comments on its accommodation, government and curriculum.

Bache saw it as a defect that the four resident masters in the Hospital had no regular meetings together and were not directly consulted on matters such as discipline and instruction.[213] He criticised the separation of new boys from the other inmates for twelve months: 'By this regulation it seems to me that the force of good example is made ineffective, and that each new set of boys require a new training.'[214] On the other hand he praised the arrangements for leaving the Hospital as 'highly judicious'.[215]

Bache made some penetrating remarks on the curriculum. He criticised mathematical teaching while praising the mode of instructing drawing which followed the Prussian system. His most fulsome praise was for the religious and moral instruction which led to the production of young men who were a credit to the Hospital. He suggested that the novelty of gymnastics had worn off and the boys grew weary of the exercises and preferred their ordinary sports. Three hours of play per day was deemed too little, especially for younger boys, and the length of school sessions was criticised. Furthermore, 'the amount of time which these boys are employed in the class-room, frequently reaching for the elder ones to eight hours a day, and the variety of subjects brought before them in their short course, at the longest but seven years, appears from observation to be highly detrimental to intellectual development. It is, indeed, said to diminish the amount of repressive discipline necessary in the institution, by taming the spirit by over intellectual work, but a saving of this sort is a real loss. It is probable that the diet, and limited amount of exercise at Heriot's, may also have something to do with the absence of youthful buoyancy and activity which I noticed among the pupils.'[216]

The long hours also had their effect on the staff. He commented that the masters were overburdened – teaching six or seven hours a day, supervising studies for an hour, and in rotation being involved in taking charge of the boys rising and going to bed, and at meals – and 'the compensation which they receive for this devotion is not such as to attach them permanently to the institution'.[217] With his strong views on discipline Bache recommended the masters adopt a gentle approach, as continental schools which had developed a spirit of kindness between master and pupil compared favourably with British schools which still practised a harsher regime. He wanted Heriot masters to become involved in playground supervision and believed that such increased intimacy with the boys outside the classroom would reap benefits.

Interestingly Bache mentioned that the boys did not do any menial work as they were attended by servants. This was no training for their position once they left the Hospital and a number of employers commented on the lack of social graces, aggravated by ignorance of normal family life. He also examined the class boys were coming from and the occupations they were placed in. He found that over a three-year period (1833–5) the fathers of 67 out of 73 boys were tradesmen or shopkeepers and found that 66 boys remained in that class. The Hospital could not claim to be increasing the professional classes. What of the criticism, widespread even in the 1830s, that from its foundation the Hospital had not produced a single great man? This Bache rejected, for the Hospital infused into the industrial classes a great number of sober, steady citizens, and some distinguished citizens as well.

On the whole Bache seems to have been impressed by the Hospital more than the Hospital seems to have been impressed by Bache. No mention of his report is to be found in the records and the official histories of Steven and Bedford also made no mention of it. This is somewhat surprising, given the extent of the co-operation which house-governor Holme and treasurer Bayley clearly gave Bache. He also had access to printed documents, made 'repeated visits to the institution at various hours' and had a number of conversations with governors and masters.[218] As a result Bache was well informed about the Hospital and it seems unfortunate that his suggestions for improvement were not taken on board.

It seems likely that Horace Mann, the Secretary of the Board of Education in Massachussetts, visited the Hospital during his European tour of 1843. Although he was not to mention Heriot's specifically in his detailed report,[219] later commentators have related how impressed Mann was with the education provided in the Hospital.[220] Certainly he approved of the thorough-ness of the Scottish teaching of reading, believing it furnished 'a model worthy of being copied by the world'. He was aware of the 'superior education' of the Scots which he put down to their good teacher-training. He also commented on the 'prodigious energy and vivacity' of the Scots which Mann felt should be tempered by a more gentle approach. He was surprised that the severe discipline of Scottish schools did not detract more from relationships between teacher and pupil which he thought were good. He was critical, however, of the monitor system, and the poor ventilation and feather beds which he claimed impaired vigour and energy.[221]

The significance and importance of Heriot's is clear from its inclusion in all these educational itineraries of the period. It even featured in an early French tourist guide to Scotland.[222] It was increasingly of interest not just for being a model for seminaries elsewhere, but also because the Hospital was now at the centre stage of a development of a network of outdoor schools which within a relatively short time were to become of crucial importance to the educational system in Edinburgh and Scotland. It was also popular with the overwhelming majority of the people of Edinburgh,[223] who believed, with much justification, that the governors were going a long way toward realising Heriot's vision in the early nineteenth century. Their critics had been temporarily quietened, if not completely put to rest.[224]

CHAPTER EIGHT

The Hospital under Steven and Fairbairn

The election of the Revd Dr William Steven under the new regulations was an important event in the development of the Hospital. It is significant that he was called Head-Master.[1] Steven arrived from the National Scottish Church in Rotterdam to take the oath of allegiance on 6 June 1839.[2] The south-west turret rooms were converted into a house for him and his family,[3] as it was expected that the enhanced salary would ensure a permanent and long-lasting tenure of office.[4] Given this new arrangement the governors agreed that the senior resident master, John Oswald, could now live outside the Hospital with a salary increased from £90 to £160 per annum to pay for accommodation and meals.[5] Within a month William Dunnett, the classical master, who had been on the staff only a year, also was allowed to be non-resident and had his salary increased to £150 to give 'adequate encouragement to a well qualified and energetic teacher'.[6] The resident teachers, George Panton (English) and William Marr (arithmetic and mathematics), were soon complaining about the onerous nature of looking after the boys at prayers and meals, formerly shared by four staff but now being done by two. They claimed that their duties occupied eleven hours a day and they had no time for self-improvement or lesson preparation. On 12 March 1840 they petitioned the governors to 'ensure their permanent usefulness was not impaired'. By June, Steven had persuaded the governors that Panton[7] and Marr should also reside out of the Hospital for a trial period, with salaries increased to £150. All the staff were expected to take their turn of a weekly rota of duty and all four were to attend church with the boys and walk with them on a Sunday evening.

Steven quickly assessed the strengths and weaknesses of the Hospital and he soon gave two detailed reports of recommendations – the first to the house committee on 26 September 1839 and the second to the education committee on 31 October. The governors belatedly responded at their meeting on 7 May 1840 by accepting and putting many of them into effect. High on Steven's list of priorities was the task of cutting down the seclusion of the Hospital, ensuring the boys had more contact with each other and the outside world. Senior and junior boys were to dine together, and boys who conducted themselves properly were to be allowed more frequent contact with their relations. Steven also ended the practice of searching the boys at the gate on their return to the Hospital. He pressed for the annual sum of £30 for the library, which had not been spent during Holme's illness, to be spent immediately, and a catalogue of books be printed. He would then appoint librarians 'from among the steadiest and best behaved of the boys'.[8] Steven also pressed for a museum for the articles which were scattered around the Hospital, and which included minerals and rock specimens, and planned that the boys themselves would supervise the new enterprise.

Steven's curriculum reforms were also symptomatic of a changed regime. He prepared a scheme of progressive religious instruction which avoided the 'irksomeness' resulting from covering the same ground over and over again and cut the number of hours of instruction on a Sunday evening. Targets were to be set for each year which were aimed at increasing interest and improving standards. He believed in developing a variety of teaching strategies to improve the effectiveness of learning. He supported the recent introduction in October 1839 of the class in practical mechanics for one hour three times a week to senior boys which he deemed 'a measure of much importance and which is succeeding admirably'.[9] Disappointed that, despite good teaching, the boys 'do not sing in church' he pressed the music master, William Kenward, 'to devise some remedy'.[10] He insisted that the English department, which also taught history and geography, concentrate on teaching English to the advanced classes as it was 'of paramount importance to the boys'.[11] Whether he had read Bache's report is not clear[12] but he certainly agreed that the teaching of classics had too high a priority. Steven argued that 109 boys (of the total of 180 in the Hospital) studying Latin was too many, 'considering the situation in life that many of the boys afterwards fill'.[13] He recommended that all boys be thoroughly drilled in Latin grammar as a means of developing principles of grammar, but only those with classical ability should continue thereafter, with the others concentrating on those branches of learning which had a direct bearing on their future occupations in life. Only 'hopeful scholars' would study Greek to help them with the first Greek class at the University, while he understood that acquaintance with the French language was highly important for those who showed an aptitude for studying languages. His detailed plan of the hours of instruction for the boys was accepted by the governors who also agreed to come more often to the Hospital to inspect progress.[14]

Steven also posed fundamental questions about the very character of the Hospital for the governors to consider. 'There always have been certain boys in the Hospital nearly incapable of receiving education and whose benefit from the Institution amounts to very little more than their maintenance. Such boys are found to be a great drag on the rest.'[15] Steven suggested that boys, after a full and fair trial in language and other classes, who were deemed incapable of receiving the benefits of education, should be removed.[16] Such a radical proposal was to have far-reaching consequences.

Steven also reorganised the exam system on a more rational basis. Exams were now to take place just before the summer vacation at the very end of July, and boys would now be admitted to the Hospital in September (instead of June) and February (instead of December). The result was to ensure a full eleven months of teaching for the Hospital, whereas before boys elected in April arrived in June and then had their classes interrupted by the vacation, which meant all the work covered in June had to be revised in September.[17] Steven also spent considerable time improving the manners of the boys and was also keen to give further responsibility to senior boys by involving them in a more developed monitorial system. Such policies impressed the governors who had never experienced such a comprehensive internal appraisal of the Hospital system and Steven was widely praised for his reforms.

Steven was also involved in supervising the work of the outdoor schools. He visited a school at least once a week and reported to the governors on the schools four times a year. He kept the stock of available textbooks in the Hospital and distributed them as and when needed. The end result was an increased, and indeed increasing, workload but he was expected to agree willingly to this as the outdoor schools were liable to supply the future inmates of the Hospital, and it was thus helpful to know the youngsters and evaluate their early instruction. Steven, however, must have been surprised at the pace of McLaren's reforms as the school committee pressed ahead with the building and equipping of four juvenile and two infant schools, which were all up and running by January 1841.

It was a disappointment for the governors when, on 4 December 1843, Steven wrote to them resigning his position. Although he had accepted the ministry of Trinity College Church[18] in the city, he would always 'cherish' his connection 'with this venerable and most interesting Establishment' and he pledged that he would always be ready to help advance its best interests.[19] He was as good as his word, for on 8 January 1844 he attended, as was his right as a city minister, and took the declaration as a governor of the Hospital. At this meeting the Lord Provost praised his tenureship as house-governor when 'internal peace and prosperity had been maintained during the five years of Dr Steven's incumbency not more by his intelligence and good management than by the kindliness of his disposition which instead of leading either the Masters or scholars to regard him with dread or apprehension induced them to look up to him with affection and confidence'.[20] Steven's contribution to the Hospital was to continue for some years. On 28 July he wrote from his home in Meadow Lodge and presented a copy of his *Memoir of George Heriot* to the governors as it was 'on the eve of being published'.[21] The governors accepted and thanked Steven for dedicating the book to them. The treasurer was instructed to purchase a hundred copies, having them bound and given to each of the governors and teachers. Steven continued to be a loyal and hard-working governor, attending his final meeting on 18 August 1856.

The governors moved quickly to draw up a short-leet for the house-governor vacancy. Both internal candidates, Oswald and Dunnett, had some support, but were dropped after the first ballot, and in a straight vote James Fairbairn, the Rector of Bathgate Academy, won by 24–14 over the Revd Dr John Forbes, headmaster of John Watson's Institution. Fairbairn was inducted on Monday 18 March 1844. He took the usual oath in front of all the governors, scholars, officers and servants in the hall and an address was given by the Revd Dr Brunton. All in the Hospital were expected to yield respectful obedience to Fairbairn on pain of expulsion. Steven had set a high standard and had bequeathed a peaceful and progressive regime. It was hoped that Fairbairn would be able to build on these foundations.[22]

Within a few months of taking up his post, Fairbairn was faced with a crucial debate on the future of the Hospital, initiated by research done by Councillor William Johnston, who on 12 December 1844 announced that only 52 of the boys in the Hospital (of 180) were fatherless. As the 1836 Act had resulted in new schools for poor citizens, and with the now extensive provision of other Hospitals in the town,[23] Johnston believed that it was proper to limit the entry to Heriot's to poor, fatherless boys, freemen's sons of Edinburgh, some boarding with their own families. (He suggested opening more foundation schools to give a liberal education to children of burgesses and freemen who were alive and wished aid.) This challenge to the existing system – advocating a complete return to Heriot's original Will – led the governors to set up a special committee of fifteen, which included Lord Provost Black and the dominant governors of the period – Brunton, Lee and Steven. It took evidence from nine separate individuals, with testimony ranging back to 1809, and reported on 17 April 1845.

The central theme of its report was a devastating critique of the hospital system which it characterised as 'a system by which a large number of young persons are educated in a state of comparative isolation from the world under

a nearly total privation of the proper home influences and of the cultivation and exercise of domestic and social affection'.[24] The result was that the Hospital boys were 'sullen and reserved',[25] lacked self-dependence, were ignorant of the outside world, were awkward in manner and had an inferiority complex. 'Bad principles and conduct'[26] appeared to be growing and this was aggravated by the lack of knowledge the governors had of applicants, resulting in the election of many with a poor disposition. Boys still protected offenders by a preconcerted system of falsehood and this was encouraged by the size of the dormitories, the lack of adequate supervision and the low level of religious feeling, despite the good religious training in the Hospital,[27] which was a hot-bed of pernicious and degrading practices.

The report proposed certain remedies: it recommended the subdivision of dormitories into rooms for 10–12 boys with separate beds and their own space under the constant charge of well principled, intelligent and elderly females; boys should be allowed more contact with the outside world; there should be a room provided for entertaining groups of boys in an effort to increase respect by combining entertainment with education. After due considera-tion,[28] the governors agreed, in October, to order 118 single beds (allowing the 62 younger boys to continue to sleep double), and to execute the substantial structural alterations involved.

Meantime, moves to open up the Hospital more to outside influence gathered pace. The Revd Dr Robert Lee, Minister of Old Greyfriars, took the opportunity of the anniversary day sermon, in June 1846, to mount a defence of the family, and in so doing attacked parents who used the hospital system. In the preface to the printed version in August he went further, claiming it was 'impossible to communicate to a youth secluded in an hospital, any thing deserving the name of a good education'.[29] For Lee, the system was 'radically vicious', and 'productive of deleterious influences, both intellectual and moral, on the minds of those who are subjected to this training'.[30] He pointed out that 98 boys had been left in the Hospital on 22 July 1845 at the beginning of the annual summer holiday and some 68 of them remained there at its end on 12 August, although only five of them were orphans.[31] The Hospital was, for Lee, a mere monastery, which alienated boys from their parents by a system of tyranny and terrorism which kept down the 'smouldering embers of disaffection'.[32] The solution was to strengthen family ties by ensuring that only orphans stayed in the Hospital, while all those with a parent should live at home.

With 200 years of history behind the system, however, it

Collaboration between James Gillespie Graham and Augustus Pugin resulted in a complete refurbishment of the Chapel interior in 1835-36. The Chapel was then used for morning and evening worship as formerly.

was unlikely to fold without a struggle. Lee was faced with an immediate and bitter reaction. An 'Auld Callant' produced a comprehensive defence of the Hospital[33] based on his own experience of six years' residence. During his whole time there had been no insubordination and only two desertions. Families, he contended, were proud of their Hospital connection, which was a ray of hope for a decaying family. In fact, for the boys the greatest punishment was to deprive them of the opportunity of joining their family and meeting their friends. The Hospital admitted youths only 'after the fireside feelings have been fully matured'[34] and the intervals of a Herioter's separation from his parents were too short to have an adverse effect. The 'Auld Callant' explained that the number of boys left in the Hospital over the summer was a result of Hospital rules, which required boys to be taken instantly to the country after departure. For him boarding out would mean the end of the advantages of early rising, and the regularity of diet and attendance. The boys were happy for indeed 'the Herioter is no monk'.[35]

The April 1845 report had perhaps been too critical and probably ahead of its time. The Hospital system at Heriot's still had its defenders and it survived, in the short term at least, the criticisms of the 1840s. However, the threats were not over and were to surface again twenty years later. Meantime the governors found themselves preoccupied with another crisis, for despite their hopes Fairbairn's tenure of office was soon to degenerate into the most turbulent in the history of the Hospital.

Early in November 1846, Fairbairn reported serious and extensive acts of insubordination. On the evening of 8 November seven boys had deserted and the governors set up a special committee of five, under the Lord Provost, to inquire into the reasons behind the desertions and suggest ways to avoid such a recurrence. It proved too late. Before the committee could meet, further acts of insubordination had taken place. Fairbairn reported to the governors, on 11 November, that, although he could not point to major problems, for some time the boys had been quarrelsome and reluctant to attend to their studies.

Lord Provost Black questioned the boys but found their statements to be of 'the most trifling and frivolous nature, such as receiving some slight correction from the wardsman – occasional confinement by one boy, that one of the men would not give his brother more blankets when he was unwell – and by another, that he could not get his hands warmed in the morning for want of pockets in his trousers'.[36] Lord Provost Black told the boys what he thought of their grievances and packed them off to bed about 11 p.m. Next morning there was more trouble. The governors deliberated 'at great length'[37] and unanimously removed 42 boys from the Hospital from 2 p.m on 14

November. It was also decided that another ten boys involved in the desertions were not to be allowed to return, at least meantime. The special committee set about interviewing all the boys to determine their final fate but within a fortnight the press criticism of the Hospital and its officers led to an extension of the committee's remit to include an examination of the internal management of the Hospital. On 7 December 1846 the special committee reported that 23 boys had made out mitigating circumstances, told all they knew and were contrite for their actions. The governors accepted the committee's recommendation and allowed these boys to return to the Hospital. The committee was also empowered to readmit other boys if after investigation it found that they should be taken back.[38]

The special committee's final report[39] was a firm effort to give a detailed explanation to clear up misunderstandings in the public mind that the boys had been unjustly treated by being punished before the full investigation of the disturbances had been completed. All 52 boys had been guilty of insubordination by openly violating the rules of the Hospital. Ten had deserted, 35 had been caught in the green at night defying the house-governor, and seven had admitted destroying furniture or insulting teachers. Only after the examination of some boys and staff, when no real cause of the incidents had been found, did the governors act to exclude the 52 to vindicate their authority, but left open the possibility of their eventual return. This was deemed to have been the best possible action, as the boys would not have told their stories if they had been allowed back into the Hospital as the ringleaders would have prevented them from doing so. In the event, many boys admitted their guilt and were allowed to return, while the governors undertook a more searching inquiry.[40]

The special committee held that the acts of insubordination originated with a few, while the great majority of boys had joined the 'rebellion' through thoughtlessness. However, there existed 'as there appears always to have existed in the Hospital'[41] a domination of younger boys by older boys, and even well-behaved boys were drawn into acts otherwise out of character. Fairbairn came in for his share of criticism, for the committee regretted that the house-governor himself had not dealt with the matter, as calling for the Lord Provost gave the appearance of lack of control, which aggravated the situation. The governors could not complain about the limited play-time allowed the boys and their confinement on Saturdays had been their own decision. However, Fairbairn's use of confinement, although following the letter of the regulations, was felt in need of revision. The porters, too, especially George Scott, were ordered to act reasonably and kindly and report any misconduct to the house-governor.

Specific proposals were soon introduced to improve the situation in the Hospital. Firstly, the house-governor was to be relieved of all outdoor duties and spend all his time on Hospital affairs: in particular Fairbairn was to spend more time with the older boys and check improper language. Secondly, boys were to leave the Hospital immediately when their time was up in April and October (not waiting till August and February respectively)[42] even if they had not reached fourteen years of age. Boys would be taken before the age of ten to avoid them being in classes with younger boys (a result of their neglected education). Thirdly, older boys would spend less time in lessons, especially in those subjects for which they had no aptitude. When their talents and desires were known (and the wishes of their parents) they would concentrate on suitable aspects of the curriculum. Fourthly, staffing in the Hospital was to be improved – the house-governor was to receive the help of another master throughout the day. Lastly, the servants were to remain all night in the wards with their charges.

Such changes were real and tangible improvements, but it was significant that Lord Provost Black believed that the disturbances were the manifestations of internal evils inherent in the Hospital and the corrective measures decided upon would only repress the problems temporarily. He called for a 'radical change'[43] and, believing that the cause of disorder was the attempt to train up so large a number of boys en masse, held that there was a need to break them into smaller units. Black argued that it would be best to limit the Hospital to the forty to fifty fatherless boys and others who could not properly be boarded with their parents. This would allow the benefits to be extended to another 200 to 250 others. Under his proposals the boys would only meet at class hours (as in the High School), and only the fatherless would live in the Hospital. Black envisaged greater competition and the raising of intellectual and moral standards, which would root out insubordination.[44]

The matter was not yet closed. A number of governors expressed disapproval at the expulsion of the five boys and it was agreed by 24 to 12 to rescind the expulsions and look at other punishments. On 11 February 1847 all the boys involved in the disturbances were reprimanded and all restored to their privileges in the Hospital. By late March the governors had accepted the thrust of the special committee's comments that too much time was spent in classes and too many branches of education were covered and a new timetable was published.[45] Singing and dancing were cut down and 'turning as a branch of education' was done away with completely. Further, on 19 April 1847, following Black's comments, the governors agreed by 18 to 14 to set up a committee of eight to inquire into and report on the state of Hospital discipline at periods of outbreaks of insubordination. This clearly encouraged one parent to complain about the corporal punishment meted out by Fairbairn but, in May 1847, the governors supported the house-governor's right to maintain proper discipline.

The 'foolish insurrection'[46] resulted in a great deal of bad publicity for the Hospital and the Hospital system. The *Scottish Guardian*[47] attacked the moral training which resulted in setting loose on society 'rebels, destroyers of property and liars'. The system of boarding and lodging in Heriot's Hospital was attacked as producing the worst effects, as it removed home influence and kept boys continually together, breeding an espirit de corps which rendered them unmanageable. The issue was even taken up by the *London Times* which made a devastating attack on the mismanagement of the affair by the governors.[48]

By April 1848 the house-governor was reporting more misconduct, this time of twenty-two boys. Six were involved in 'borrowing' the steward's keys while he was asleep and stealing food and money from the storeroom; two boys had deserted the Hospital; fourteen others knew of the misconduct and had received part of the spoils. The governors set up a sub-committee of four, which proceeded immediately to the Hospital to investigate and report. This time the boys admitted everything: the actions had been planned beforehand and indulged in over three months. There appeared no mitigating circumstances, as the food was not needed. Given their leniency eighteen months earlier, the governors decided to expel twelve, who were turned out with the buttons cut from their coats, while the other ten were privately whipped and confined for three months.[49] Nonetheless, they were conscious of the need to blend punishment with justice. Following a petition from Janet Davidson, on behalf of her expelled son, Alexander, the governors accepted that the boy's youth and his being fatherless were factors which should have been taken into account along with his single improper act. After 'much hesitation'[50] and determination not to set a precedent, it was agreed that the boy be sent to an outdoor school before being apprenticed. This encouraged other parents to petition. Henry Lumsden held that the expulsions had been made without a full and impartial inquiry, but his charges were ultimately rejected as 'frivolous, vexatious and unfounded'.[51] On 25 September 1848 the house-governor reported that the three months' confinement of the boys involved in the misbehaviour had expired and satisfaction was expressed that their conduct had been good and that 'punishment had been attended with good effects'.[52] Although the governors gave a vote of confidence to Fairbairn,

stressing his anxiety to promote the welfare of the boys and the 'very satisfactory'[53] state of the Hospital, they asked their house committee 'to consider and
revise and bring up such a Code of regulations for the internal management
of the House as they would recommend to be adopted'.[54]

Appreciating that the issue of the future of the hospital system would have
to be faced sooner or later, the governors, meantime, busied themselves with
routine business. Although there were no major building developments in
progress they pressed ahead with improvements. It was at this time that the
stained-glass windows were replaced. Working drawings were produced by
Messrs Ballantine and Allan for the seventy-two coats of arms for the great
oriel window, and work on the chapel was complete by 23 October 1843.[55]
(Appendix 5.)

Councillor Robert Ritchie made suggestions to improve the quality of life
for the Hospital inmates. In April 1849 he pressed the governors to erect urinals
in the dormitories in order to discontinue the unpleasant practice of having a
slop pail in the middle of each dormitory; having viewed other institutions he
wished to have sheds erected for the boys in wet weather; for comfort he
suggested the use of cotton or woollen underclothing in place of cotton lining
in the boys' trousers, and he also desired the removal of the remaining double
beds and their replacement with single beds.[56] The governors accepted the least
expensive of his proposals: underclothing was introduced and one dormitory
was fitted out with urinals. Ritchie continued his campaign to improve
cleanliness, comfort and decorum. He accepted that it was impossible
meantime to increase the provision of single beds, but he was able to gain more
bed space, giving more air, more room for the wardsmen and better lavatory
provision. In June 1851 he again raised the issue of covered sheds, and superintendent Black was instructed to submit plans for a covered playground in the
space at the south side of the garden near the Vennel gate. These were
submitted and the sheds were erected during the following year.[57]

In July 1854 the governors determined to improve the comfort of the boys
by creating a suite of four apartments, immediately opposite the dining hall,
for private reading and conversation. When they opened on 4 October 1855
two rooms were devoted to silent reading, with newspapers and periodicals
provided and the other two were for conversation and quiet games.

Despite the overcrowded curriculum the governors tried to raise the boys'
awareness of things scientific. In March 1845 a private collection of minerals
had been gifted to the Hospital on the 'understanding that it is in contem-
plation to form a museum for the use of the pupils'[58] but the governors,
realising their educational potential but not wishing to be beholden to

anyone, purchased the minerals for £100.[59] In December 1847 they pressed the house-governor to arrange the minerals and fossils in the Hospital as soon as possible. Fairbairn responded by asking for the help of a competent person for arranging, numbering and cataloguing mineral specimens, and this was accomplished within six months. In July 1850 Fairbairn was asked what use was being made of the collection: he declared that as the higher sections had 8 hours 25 minutes of study (25 minutes more than the education committee recommended) they were only given an introduction: the younger boys were given an hour a week on the minerals. On 3 February 1853 the governors accepted a box of fifty-two specimens from Elba from John Nimmo, former Heriot bursar then resident in Genoa, to add to the 'Hospital museum now forming'.[60]

In September 1849 the education committee recommended the teaching of another hour of French each day by Monsieur Chaumont (to come from preparation time) because so little time was being spent on the subject. The following month, Fairbairn recommended an increase in the hours of drawing to two hours a week for the fourth class (as well as the fifth class) as the subject was very useful for a number of boys in their later employment. The governors agreed, despite the resulting increase in the hours of work. However, the attempts by Councillor Ritchie to introduce German in 1852 fell on deaf ears.

The return of Duncan McLaren to the governing body in October 1851 was a turning point in the history of the Hospital. In the influential role of Lord Provost and chairman of the governors he determined to confront and deal with what he deemed to be the major issues facing Heriot's and its outdoor schools. Within a year he was proposing that as the Hospital was 'inadequate to contain with the necessary comforts and advantages' its total complement of 180 boys, the governors should reduce the number of boys to 150 over a number of years.[61] He argued that the money saved could go to extending the number attending outdoor schools. Such views were contentious, but the governors did agree that the Hospital funds could sustain another outdoor school immediately.[62] Steven (who in the next two years was to oppose McLaren on every issue of substance) took up the challenge, opposing McLaren's proposed reduction in the number of scholars. However, on 3 February 1853 McLaren's proposals were carried by 18 to 10 with Steven dissenting.[63] To ensure there was no undue hardship over applications it was agreed that there would be a reduction of 25 per cent in elections of boys until the figure of 150 was reached. Steven continued his forceful opposition, and on 18 April 1853 gave a powerful defence of his position.[64]

By the time of the governors' meeting on 17 October 1853 Steven's position had been strengthened. He gained a powerful ally in the Revd Dr Nisbet, who argued that the governors should admit as many boys as could 'adequately and with such comfort and consideration for their health be maintained there'.[65] Nisbet persuaded the governors to appoint two eminent medical men, Dr W.P. Alison and Dr James Duncan, to investigate this matter. This they did and, having examined military and infirmary situations and having used the most modern of physiological tests, produced an impressive range of statistics in their report of 1 December 1853.[66] The death rate in the Hospital between 1840 and 1853 at 1 in 270 annually was 'very satisfactory'[67] and they found low levels of scrofulous disease. Indeed, the health of the pupils seemed to improve once they entered the Hospital and evidence from the masters of apprentices suggested a high level of good health. To give a broader perspective Alison and Duncan looked in some depth at other charity institutions[68] and concluded that the Heriot dormitories were 'extremely well fitted for accommodating the present number of boys with due regard to their health and comfort'.[69] There was no need to reduce to 150,[70] for as small children huddle together to maintain their temperatures, a cautious approach was advisable when considering any change in the present practice for boys under ten years of age.[71] With such powerful evidence, Steven's position was vindicated and he was able to reverse the previous decision. The proposal to reduce the Hospital population was defeated by 19 to 5 with McLaren now registering his dissent.

McLaren was not one to give up easily, especially given his strong views on the issue. On 2 February 1854 he suggested that the real question was whether in wards 7 and 8 with 38 and 22 boys in double beds there should be a reduction to 19 and 11 respectively. The other wards were adequate, while the medical report emphasised the general question and the average size of all wards, with no mention of wards 7 and 8.[72] McLaren held that when institutions increased space they reduced mortality[73] and the high mortality rate in Watson's (1 in 114) was a result of overcrowding. He was also struck by what he considered a high mortality rate in Heriot's compared with similar institutions.[74] However, McLaren was only supported by three other governors and this upset Drs Alison and Duncan who, aggrieved at the publicity McLaren's arguments had obtained, within a month had produced a detailed response of their own. They held that they had been asked to report on the total situation and felt McLaren had

Duncan McLaren (1800-1886) became a member of the Governing Body in 1833 and later Lord Provost of Edinburgh and Radical MP for the city. He dominated Heriot thinking right up until his death and ensured that the Governors spread the benefit of the Hospital widely. *Scottish National Portrait Gallery.*

ignored the evidence of the Trades Maiden, the change in the mortality rate in the Orphan Hospital before leaving its old premises in 1833[75] and had been misleading on Watson's.[76] Steven, now the spokesman for the majority of the governors, argued that the issue involved all the dormitories and that the mere shifting of a few beds did not necessitate medical advice. Having changed their decision once when given overwhelming medical advice, there was no possibility that they would do so again.[77]

In fact, much more was at stake than the numbers in the Hospital, and McLaren's reforming agenda resulted in specific and detailed proposals[78] for change being put forward for discussion at a special general meeting held on 7 August 1854. The leading spokesman for reform, the Revd Dr Robert Lee, who had kept his powder dry since 1846, believed that this was an ideal time and opportunity to introduce changes. As the great majority of Hospital boys went on to trades it did not appear 'expedient to preserve in the attempt to make them all classical scholars'[79] especially as the attempts were unsuccessful and interfered with the attainment of a useful English education. Lee pressed for the introduction of a more suitable education and McLaren supported the plea. The vote was won 17 to 10, despite Steven's efforts to defeat the motion. Lee pressed on to recommend that boys should receive two years of English education and should study the Latin language only in the third year. At the end of their third year, after taking the views of the boys themselves into account, they would be separated into those going on to manual work and those who were able to become hopeful scholars. McLaren again supported this, but Steven argued that all boys should have a two years' trial of Latin, and Steven carried his amendment by 18 to 10. Both sides then combined and agreed that at the end of their fourth year those boys going on to trades would be instructed in English, geography, arithmetic, mathematics and drawing to fit them for employment. Only those with the aptitude or desire to study French would do so. It was agreed that more stress than before would be placed on teaching common things, that the boys should receive more elementary teaching in botany, mineralogy, and in the knowledge of what Britain produced, and that music should be a recreation rather than a task. Even the two hours devoted daily by older boys to the study of Latin and Greek could be more usefully and pleasantly employed, it was argued. The final recommendation which Lee proposed was again contentious. He recommended that boys likely to make good progress in learning should be sent to the High School at the end of their fourth year at the Hospital for their classical education, leaving the classical teacher at Heriot's to help with exercises. The Hospital would specialise in other areas, especially mathematics. McLaren pressed for this, but Steven was able to rally enough support to defeat the proposal by 15 to 13.

McLaren's struggle with Steven continued. On 2 October 1854 McLaren moved that after the appointment of a new house-governor a group of boys, numbering no more than ten, should be kept at the High School annually for the completion of their education. Steven was able to defeat the motion 19 to 14.[80] However, at McLaren's last meeting on 16 October before he gave up office, he had one final victory. Dr Steven moved that boys convicted of absconding from the Hospital should forfeit £5 from their apprentice fee for a first offence, £10 for a second offence, and be deprived of their whole fee for a third offence. Steven saw this problem as most injurious to the Hospital and financial penalties as a good way of punishing boys and their parents. McLaren mustered 17 votes, while Steven's motion gained only five votes. With his retirement from the Lord Provostship McLaren left the governing body and was unanimously thanked for his 'great talent, tact and discretion'.[81] His influence, however, was not over, and he was to continue to be involved with Heriot's for another thirty years. His immediate opponent, Steven, failed to have his nominee appointed as the new house-governor, and increasingly took a back-seat.[55]

The debate on the Hospital and its curriculum temporarily obscured the disharmony which centred round the poor relationship between the governors and the house-governor. Many of the former had been disillusioned by Fairbairn since the 1846 'rebellion' and matters had not been helped by his frequent absences. Indeed, in August 1850 it was reported that Fairbairn's health was so poor, following three years of heart trouble, that it was unlikely he would work again.[83] The governors were in a quandary: a number pressed for Fairbairn's immediate resignation but others saw this as too premature. When Steven offered to cover as many of the house-governor's duties as he could, it was agreed to accept this offer and delay a final decision. By early 1851 Fairbairn confirmed that he expected to be back shortly, and he resumed work after an absence of nearly five months. He became unwell again in the summer of 1853 and Dunnett, as senior master, took charge for two weeks. As Fairbairn was still not fit enough for work after two weeks it was agreed that the masters – Dunnett, Marr and Redpath[56] – would each take charge of the Hospital in rotation for two weeks at a time. After nine months' leave of absence in Moffat, Fairbairn returned to work in May 1854, but experienced further health problems in late June as a result of an overdose of digitalis. He returned again to work after an absence of three weeks, just in time to deal with the sudden death, on 11 July, of Dunnett, who had been classical master for 16 years, and organised the highest three sections of boys to attend the funeral two days later.

Facing growing disquiet about his position and effectiveness in this new situation Fairbairn tried to take the steam out of a move to replace him. He produced a report for 'an improved course of study for the boys in the Hospital'.[85] He also brought forward his suggestions on the Hospital library and produced a catalogue detailing and numbering the 3,042 volumes which had 'occupied most of my leisure time during the last ten years'.[86] Fairbairn stressed that when he had revived the library[87] it had no catalogue, the books were in a sorry state and volumes were missing or scattered. As a result of his work the books had been bound, the missing volumes had been replaced and additions were made. The books had been arranged in library presses with numbers inscribed on them corresponding to those in his catalogue. Although the governors were impressed with his work and went ahead and printed the catalogue they were not to be diverted from their intention.

At the governors' meeting on 3 August 1854 the debate was not about whether Fairbairn should remain, but instead about the terms of his pension. In the event they preferred Steven's more generous motion and its terms were enough to persuade Fairbairn to tender his immediate resignation. He went, praising the governors for their fairness and liberality.[88] He also praised the good conduct of the boys of the Hospital wherein 'a happiness and quiet order prevail which render the charge of them a pleasure'.[89]

As a result of some rearrangement of teaching responsibilities in August 1854, the new house-governor when appointed was to take over the English teaching and also instruct the boys in general knowledge and natural history. He was to remain in charge of the internal management of the Hospital but it was agreed to redistribute some of his duties among the other teachers. The governors then determined to advertise for the new house-governor, aged between 30 and 45.

To outsiders, however, Heriot's Hospital remained a model for other institutions to admire and copy. It was reported at the governors' meeting on 6 October 1842 that the Bishop of London had visited both the Hospital and certain of the outdoor schools and 'had expressed himself highly pleased with what he had seen and the progress of the children'.[90] In November 1849 one of the governors of Christ Church Hospital held that Heriot's 'was considerably in advance of that great Institution'.[91] The son of Sir James McGrigor, Director General of the Army Medical Department, was enchanted with the Hospital and reported that he 'had never witnessed an Institution in which there was so much attention paid to education, health and comfort'.[92]

However, the most famous visitor was Hans Christian Andersen, who signed the visitors' book on 16 August 1847. Having paid his first visit to England and received a good reception he travelled north at the end of the London season as the guest of Baron Charles J.T. Hambro to Lixmount House, Trinity. He was entranced with Scotland, as he idealised Walter Scott and was delirious to hear that he was much read in Scotland and was regarded as the 'Danish Walter Scott'. Sir James Young Simpson, who had just discovered chloroform, was his guide round Edinburgh.[93] He was introduced to Holyrood (with which he was not impressed) and Heriot's Hospital, where the writer was greatly touched by the reverence shown towards him by a porter. 'What, so young as that! Why, I've read him often and often, and got my lads to read him too. It is a remarkable thing to live to see such men; as a rule they are either old or dead before anyone hears anything about them.'[94] Such wide reading says much for the education of the Hospital, given that his first books were only translated into English in 1845.[95]

European educationalists visited the Hospital to make their own, usually favourable, judgements. Andersen's account probably persuaded the Norwegian schoolmaster, Hartvig Nissen,[96] to make an official visit in 1852, when investigating good practice abroad in the continuing development of the Norwegian elementary school system. His report[97] gave an accurate historical account of the Hospital and the then ten outdoor schools. It discussed the 'varied' curriculum of the Hospital which depended upon 'the children's different future plans'. He was impressed that 'when a child reaches the age of 12, a discussion between the headmaster and the boy's relatives will decide the pupil's future, and in the final two years in the Hospital his education will be directed towards this end'.[98] He reported in more detail on the outdoor schools and particularly was impressed by the headmasters' contracts which ensured high salaries but also stipulated dismissal when it was of benefit to the school. Nissen noted that the schools were not only inspected by the Hospital governors but also by an employed inspector, whose duty it was to visit every one of the schools at least twice weekly. He also mentioned that unlike other schools the outdoor schools were free, 'which seemed within the spirit of Mr. Heriot's Will'.[99] He believed that 90 per cent of the pupils were the children of working-class or very poor parents. Bad behaviour resulted in discussion with parents, and if this continued pupils were excluded. This also happened if a pupil failed to attend three times without explanation.[100] Altogether the Heriot educational experiment had much to teach even a country with an advanced educational system such as Norway, and his Scottish experience was held to have 'radicalised' his educational views.[101]

Nissen's somewhat glowing report, however, was at odds with that given by Dr Edward Woodford, the Government Inspector for the eastern division, who had been invited into the Hospital by the governors.[102] He spent three days at Heriot's in July 1854[103] and reported his findings on 5 August. They must have made disappointing reading for the governors. In English, writing and mechanics the attainment of the boys was behind that of boys of similar age elsewhere. In vocal music the preparation of pieces for public occasions interfered with progress. In Latin the shortcomings in grammar were considerable, while in French more work was required in writing, dictation and conversation. Only arithmetic and mathematics came out with a very good report. His general conclusion that 'there was a general deficiency, according to the average standard in ordinary schools, in which the same subjects are taught'.[104] He also commented on the existence of secret societies which frustrated the objectives of the teaching staff and resulted in cunning or unnecessary reserve in later life. Clearly there was much for the new house-governor to do.[105]

CHAPTER NINE

The Hospital under Bedford and Lowe

The increase in the status and renown of the Hospital was apparent when the governors advertised for a new house-governor in September 1854. Eight candidates from Scotland were joined by three from England. At their meeting on 2 October Lord Provost McLaren, seconded by the Revd Dr Lee, proposed Frederick William Bedford, aged 31, headmaster of the Higher and Lower Schools associated with the Mechanics Institution and Literary Society, Leeds. The Revd Dr Steven proposed, with the Revd Smith seconding, Adam Smith, aged 38, the rector of the Academy of Arbroath. Bedford was elected by 29–15 as house-governor or 'Head Teacher of the Hospital'.[1]

McLaren had proposed Bedford, believing that the governors were not looking so much for a teacher but a leader to contribute to the general good of the Hospital. He viewed Bedford as a man of strong good sense, of conciliatory manners, of gentlemanly bearing and deportment, and of such winning ways as would enable him to be popular with the boys, be respected by staff and have the confidence of the parents. Bedford was elected, therefore, with great hopes but his background and education led to a difficult first few months before he won over his Scottish colleagues. Fortunately he seemed to appreciate his delicate situation and did not put a foot wrong.[2] His competence and caring attitude led to better relationships among the staff, and the general ethos of the Hospital improved noticeably in a short time.

At a special meeting on 1 November 1854 Bedford took the oath of office and Lord Provost McLaren addressed all in terms of the Statutes.[3] Following Woodford's disappointing findings in August the governors had set in motion an inquiry to investigate his conclusions. A sub-committee agreed that the 'average standard of education in all the sections is far from satisfactory'.[4] In particular, the English department was in an 'inefficient state' with no history being taught by it at all.[5] The governors wished to ensure that boys entering the Hospital should sit a stricter entry exam, should have a more rigorous private study regime while in the Hospital, and should have a new timetable introduced which would leave French until later in school life and give more prominence to the basic subjects. Significantly the governors saw the role of

the new house-governor as critical. They, for the first time, suggested their willingness to limit their role to deciding on general principles while leaving the day-to-day business to the judgement and discretion of Bedford. Although this was never to be properly achieved, it is symptomatic of the increased status and power of Bedford, who could expect more support and autonomy, certainly as long as he was sucessful and his educational ideas did not conflict with those of the governors.

Bedford himself reported on 22 December on how he found the Hospital and made some initial suggestions for improvement. He stressed the primacy of English teaching and the immediate need to introduce a 'progressive course of geographical and historical information'. He wanted to devote more time to these at the expense of 'subsidiary studies' – French, drawing, vocal music and dancing – especially given his view that the standards of the English department were 'below average'.[6] He, however, intended to give lectures in natural philosophy interlinked with a course on practical mechanics. Bedford believed that the want of intellectual tone in the Hospital was due to the emphasis on teaching rooms rather than study rooms and there existed few opportunities for the development of the mind by individual exertion. 'A stringent bracing up of the English studies, joined with a judicious use of the Hospital Library, will do much towards the improvement of the general tone.'[7]

In a supplementary report Bedford recommended the introduction of an elementary department to improve early training to compensate for the loss of parental influence, the use of a reading room between 7 and 8 a.m. to give the boys time and place to prepare their lessons, the introduction of desks for the boys,[8] and the attendance of junior masters during recreation time in place of wardsmen. Bedford from the very beginning of his time in office stressed the need to humanise the Hospital: periodicals were to be introduced into the new reading rooms;[9] he instituted weekly tea-parties to bring the boys into contact with his family, and given his English experience he resolved to use more extensively the monitorial system with senior boys on duty in the chapel, in the dining hall, at church and on all special occasions.[10]

Staffing in the Hospital was crucial for Bedford. He strongly condemned the use of wardsmen during recreational periods, as he believed that they could not feel empathy for his plans for the intellectual and moral improvement of the boys.[11] To counteract this he persuaded the governors to appoint a resident master, who was to be responsible for discipline after

Frederick William Bedford (1824-1880) was appointed 'Head Teacher' of the Hospital in 1854. He raised the stature of the post and unlike his predecessors was allowed to run the Hospital day-to-day without Governor interference.

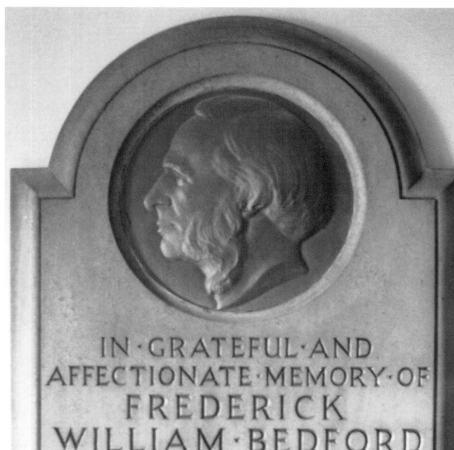

IN·GRATEFUL·AND·
AFFECTIONATE·MEMORY·OF
FREDERICK
WILLIAM·BEDFORD
D·C·L: LL·D: Ph·D·
HOUSE·GOVERNOR
AND·HEADMASTER
GEORGE·HERIOT'S·HOSPITAL
1854 ~ 1880
THE·GIFT·OF·HIS·SON·LT·COL·
SIR·CHARLES·H·BEDFORD
D·C·L: LL·D: D·Sc: M·D: I·M·S·

class hours, to take his share with some of the other masters in helping in the preparation of the next day's lessons and mixing with the boys.

The number of teaching staff had to be increased to get the best results. Despite the number of masters being deceptively large, a number being part-time, Bedford pressed for extra additional masters to be appointed, and the cutting of class size in the Hospital from 45 to 30. Unfortunately Bedford had no power to appoint or dismiss masters under the Statutes, although later in his evidence to the Endowed Schools (Scotland) Commission he argued for just such a power.[12] At a special general meeting of the governors on 15 March 1855 Bedford's initial staffing recommendations were accepted.[13] James Scholfield was appointed principal English master on 1 May:[14] he was only twenty-eight but had been Bedford's principal assistant master for five years in Leeds. He clearly had been greatly influenced by his mentor, and not only was he in sympathy with Bedford's educational views but he could follow instructions and had precisely the necessary experience. He took the post in an effort to assist Bedford 'in raising the educational character of the Hospital'.[15] The partnership and friendship of Bedford and Scholfield[16] and their success helped overcome any prejudices remaining amongst the staff and governors, against the only English house-governor the Hospital had known.[17]

By July 1855 the governors approved further changes. In the writing department a system of daily marking was introduced: these marks were to be added up to determine prizes, which were to be awarded in a more equitable manner. The boys were to send a quarterly letter to their relatives and this was to be accompanied by a report from Bedford on their conduct, and specimen writing books were to be used regularly. Bedford spent some time with Dalgleish, the writing master, before the new session began to ensure he appreciated why such changes were worthwhile advances.[18] He then amalgamated the duties of the English and classical masters in an attempt to make classical studies contribute more to the English education of the boys, even introducing Greek as a means of doing so.[19] Bedford himself took only English composition under his wing. He then increased the length of exams for the outgoing boys from two to four hours in length. Papers were to be printed and a marking scheme worked out to ensure consistency of marking throughout the curriculum. The boy who gained the highest mark was to gain a silver medal to mark his proficiency. The answers would be kept from year to year to compare answers and measure standards. Significantly, the dux medal was to go to the best behaved boy in the senior class, for Bedford considered praiseworthy conduct more

Bedford wore himself out leading the Hospital and died prematurely in office in 1880. He has been viewed as the 'Dr Arnold of Scotland'.

important than academic achievement for that honoured position.

In April 1856 Bedford arranged for boys, after a year's unsuccessful pursuit of classical studies, to drop Latin to enable them to concentrate on subjects which were more relevant to their future occupations.[20] He initiated technical instruction of a very practical kind, which in the mid-nineteenth century was a radical educational development; in particular he introduced physiology and health lectures for seniors. Conscious of the need to prepare those seeking university scholarships Bedford began a special course of training. Importantly, he stressed the necessity of teaching the boys to think.

On 25 March 1858 Bedford pressed for the boys to have more frequent contact with their friends. He suggested that time could be found in the late afternoon or evenings of certain weekdays for such meetings, which, he argued, should be part of a gradual preparation for the world at large. He did away with the practice of public caning and put forward the idea of doing away with corporal punishment altogether. He nevertheless appreciated that any changes would have to be experimental and would be ended if abused. Such views were ahead of their time. Very seldom did Bedford resort to such punishments, and when he did so he used a cane but never commented on the obvious folded towels used by the boys to reduce the impact. There is evidence, however, to suggest that a number of other masters administered beatings regularly.

Bedford held that many truants were docile and well-behaved when in the Hospital. If they truanted as a result of thoughtlessness no severe punishment was needed; if however they truanted in a desire to resist authority or to influence others then ordinary punishment was inadequate. He suggested that many boys who had truanted in the history of the Hospital afterwards became exemplary and well-behaved pupils. Each case, he argued, should be judged on its merits.[21]

The humanity of Bedford was also seen in his approach to the servants of the Hospital. John Robertson, house steward since 1847, applied to the governors to allow him to retain his post after his forthcoming marriage. Bedford immediately set out a forceful case supporting Robertson's request. A junior master, who was already with the boys between 7 and 8 a.m. and every other week until 8.30 p.m., could take over the role of sleeping in the ward and have the steward's two rooms in the Hospital as his home. As Robertson had served the Hospital conscientiously for twelve years he deserved special consideration: the quality of the man was more significant than an old convention.[22] Bedford also held that making the stewardship a married man's post and filling it with the most deserving wardsmen would improve the quality of the wardsmen. The governors accepted his arguments and from April 1859 the steward was allowed to marry and the junior master was required to live in the Hospital. Bedford, the humanitarian, had, at the same time, established that his policies would now be enforced 24 hours a day.

The governors prided themselves on the quality of the food served in the Hospital and were pleased with Voigt's view that it was 'unbelievely good'[23] and his comments on the impressive amounts spent on maintaining good quantity and quality.[24] However, by the diet table in the regulations, at 5 p.m. the boys were allowed bread and milk as an intermediate meal between dinner (at 1 p.m.) and supper (at 8 p.m.). Bedford believed it was not enough to satisfy the hunger of the boys and had experimented with an amalgamated meal at 5.50 p.m.: the usual porridge, with milk and bread, with extra porridge if needed. The governors agreed to make this permanent. Moreover, on Sundays rice was available but, as this was not popular, Bedford persuaded the governors to introduce in its place a rotation of boiled eggs, cheese and rhubarb.

In July 1859 Bedford stressed the need to provide a course of regular systematic instruction in gymnastics for senior boys, as MacGlashan only taught dancing and calisthenics which, argued Bedford, was a glaring omission, particularly as other institutions, such as George Watson's and John Watson's Hospitals, employed both a dancing master and a drill sergeant. The governors agreed to introduce a course of gymnastic lessons for four months as an experiment.[25] Throughout his time Bedford accepted the need for curricular innovation. His recommendation that Alexander McIvor of the chemistry department of Edinburgh University be asked to give a series of lectures to senior boys on experimental science was accepted by the governors on 8 January 1863.[26] He wholeheartedly supported the suggestion of Lord Provost Chambers that boys would be allowed to visit manufacturing and industrial works 'as calculated to be a source both of amusement and profit to them'.[27] He accordingly took the senior section to Chambers' large printing works.[28]

On 1 December 1859 Bedford reported to the governors that there were in the Hospital several boys 'whose intellects are so low that he despairs of being able to do much with them in the way of education',[29] although they were receiving extra attention. The governors agreed that they should guard against the admission of such boys to the Hospital, and left it up to Bedford to find out more about future applicants in order to prevent the admission of such cases.[30] A report of 23 July 1861 on the twenty-five outgoing boys also made for depressing reading. Sixteen of them had given up classical studies because of their inability to cope intellectually.[31] Such evidence led to discussions on the election of boys, and a special committee of nineteen was set up, in October, to deal with this issue.[32]

Bedford's tenure saw a number of controversies, some of which were outwith his remit or control. As Duncan McLaren had become more advanced in his politics his good relationship with *The Scotsman* newspaper broke down[33] and by the 1850s both parties exhibited hostility and animosity towards each other. In 1856 McLaren took the paper to court and, after a two-day trial, won £400 damages from the proprietor (John Ritchie) and editor (Alexander Russel).[34] In a letter to the governors, dated 8 January 1857, McLaren gifted the whole sum for their use. He wanted the money invested and the interest gained to be used in the Heriot outdoor schools to reward two boys and two girls in each school who exhibited 'general good conduct'.[35] Children could only win the prize once and each conduct prize was to include pocket bibles and money.[18] At first the governors were enthusiastic about the offer, but at their meeting on 5 March 1857 Dean of Guild Wemyss opposed its acceptance as it would perpetuate acrimony, resulting as it did from a private feud. Town clerk Marwick wondered what the governors' reaction would be if *The Scotsman* offered to purchase psalm books to be presented along with McLaren bibles.[37] However, Lord Provost Melville argued that acceptance was in the best interests of the Hospital and the governors backed him 27 to 17.[38]

The editor of *The Scotsman* immediately took up Marwick's idea. He and his proprietor wrote to the governors asking them to accept £100, the interest from which would provide psalm books as prizes in the outdoor schools. The money was the surplus from the sums given by the public, who disapproved of McLaren's prosecution and verdict, after the payment of £1,200 on damages and expenses. The newspapermen argued that if the governors accepted a donation commemorating one side of the case then they were bound to accept a donation commemorating the other side. Despite the Lord Provost's desire to accept both donations Marwick led the opposition, which carried the day by twenty-five votes to fifteen.[39] Editor Russel had achieved his objective of making all parties look ridiculous, and in so doing had exacerbated his bad relationship with McLaren.

Another controversy of the time reflected the growth of the Scottish temperance movement. At the governors' meeting on 6 May 1858 the newly elected Councillor Hope pressed for an end to the use of drink in the Hospital[40] or, failing that, the organisation of founder's day in such a way as not to 'lead or tempt any of the members of the British League of Juvenile

Abstainers in the Hospital to violate their principles and abstinence practice'.[41] Hope's aim was to make abstinence respectable in the Hospital, and the governors agreed 'that all drinking usages in connection with the Boys on George Heriot's Day and on other occasions under the control of the Governors as well within the house as within the grounds of Heriot's Hospital be abolished'.[42] However, it became an issue again the following year, on 5 May 1859, as the governors planned special celebrations in the Hospital's bicentenary year. Councillor Greig proposed that boys should have a glass of ginger wine to toast the founder on June Day, believing that its abolition the previous year had been a miserable economy, particularly as the governors themselves had a dinner on the same day with claret, champagne and liquors being served.[43] Greig argued that such a small drop of wine could do no harm and trained the boys in customs which in later life they would be expected to conform to. For Hope it was not an issue of quantity but one of principle and he set out his case in a pamphlet.[44]

Even the ministers on the governing body were split on the issue. The Revd Robertson, though not a total abstainer himself, believed that the June Day glass tended to produce the sinister effect of associating enjoyment with drinking in the minds of the Heriot boys, which was to be deprecated.[45] He was opposed by the the Revd Dr Robert Lee, who quoted biblical authority: 'Thou shalt eat and drink, and rejoice before the Lord.' For him a glass of weak wine would not result in a love of drinking. The Revd Dr Smith felt it was miserly to deprive the boys of wine, especially as the governors gave their own sons wine and brought them up as gentlemen. The Revd Dr Murray believed Hope's alternative of sucking an orange to celebrate the founder would be monstrous: boys could be brought up too aesthetically and too devoutly. On the other hand Councillor Ford supported abstinence, having heard from the staff that several junior boys had been the worse for drink the previous June Day. Bailie Blackadder testified that given the abolition of the practice it would be wrong to put the clock back. Lord Provost Melville, too, was not keen to bring back wine.

At the end of the debate, Councillor Greig moved 'that the Boys in the Hospital be allowed a glass of weak wine on Heriot's day as formerly'. This was carried nineteen to twelve. As this was voluntary, Hope was given permission to ask the boys individually whether they wished to take wine or not. Fifty-eight declared they would not. Hope celebrated by inviting them to a soirée.

The details of the actual June Day ceremony were commented on at length by the temperance press. 'When the three recognised toasts in the programme had been concluded, it was observed that a great many of the glasses had not been touched, and that the majority of them were still half full. Whether this arose from the fact that the pupils had an inward suspicion that the wine was not so very 'weak' as it seemed, or that the juvenile abstainers, who are said to constitute a goodly proportion of the boys, had resolved to adhere religiously to their pledge, more especially as Councillor Hope's watchful eye was upon them, we cannot tell; but the circumstance above noticed was too patent to be overlooked, and was, indeed, the theme of general comment'.[46] House-governor Bedford proposed a further toast: to the governors. The Lord Provost responded with a toast to Bedford and the teaching staff. Finally Bailie Blackadder toasted treasurer Dick and matron McDonald. When the Lord Provost called for three hearty cheers to the founder the boys and governors responded vigorously. Councillor Hope had kept his seat while the toasts were being drunk (even during the loyal toast) but asked for one more cheer for George Heriot, which resulted in a deafening noise. Although Bedford had remained aloof from the controversy he was criticised by the temperance press for his actions on June Day. 'It was not until he invited, nay, almost commanded the boys to drain their glasses, that the "weak wine" was finally consumed.'[47]

At the following June Day celebrations in June 1860 the majority of Heriot boys kept the pledge. Councillor Hope proposed at the governors' meeting on 5 July that the 97 abstaining boys of the Hospital be allowed to accept his invitation[48] to accompany the British League Boys on an excursion to Dirleton. It was opposed by Bailie Grieve and defeated thirteen to four,[49] but Hope went ahead and held a further soirée. When in 1861 only 52 boys took wine, Bedford, after consultation with the Lord Provost and convener of the house committee, decided not to place wine on the table in future but to give each a plate of dry fruit in addition to the orange and fruit pie usually given. Hope, who remained a town councillor until 1889, enquired for a year or two about whether wine would be supplied, but as the answer was always negative the issue died.

The issue of Temperance split the Governing Body in 1858-59 when Councillor John Hope tried to abolish alcohol from the Hospital. In 1859 he was supported by 'the gallant fifty-eight' Hospital boys (out of one hundred and eighty).

Throughout such controversies the governors attended to the routine work of maintaining the fabric of the 'wark'. Bedford had persuaded them to restore the two rooms on the upper floor of the south-west turret to the house-governor's private use, which was agreed to, as he had 'too little accommodation'.[50] This was one of the last jobs of Alexander Black,[51] while the first of his successor, Chesser, was the cleaning of Heriot's statue. In 1858 the decayed corbel work on

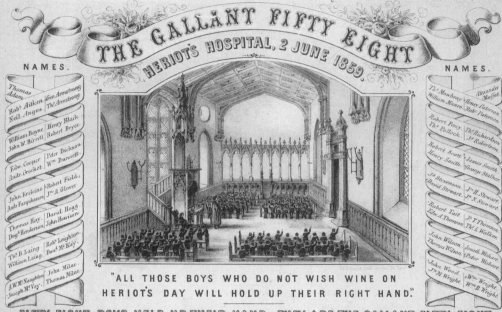

THE GALLANT FIFTY EIGHT

HERIOT'S HOSPITAL, 2 JUNE 1859.

"ALL THOSE BOYS WHO DO NOT WISH WINE ON HERIOT'S DAY WILL HOLD UP THEIR RIGHT HAND."

FIFTY EIGHT BOYS HELD UP THEIR HAND. THEY ARE THE GALLANT FIFTY EIGHT.

THE above drawing is designed to commemorate the noble avowal of Abstinence principle made by fifty-eight boys of Heriot's Hospital on June 2, 1859.

The practice, previous to June 1858, at the Boys' Annual Dinner on Heriot's day (the first Monday of June) had been, for the Lord Provost or presiding Magistrate, in the presence of the Governors and the Public, to invite the boys to drink six or more toasts suited to the occasion, and for that purpose each boy was provided with one glass of wine, without regard to whether they were abstainers or not.

The custom had been objected to on many grounds ; *by some*, as a most objectionable initiation of the boys into the drinking usages—the curse of society ; *by others*, as a positive temptation and injury to those boys, who, having entered the Hospital as Abstainers, were now to be corrupted and seduced from, or at all events tempted to abandon, their Abstinence principles, under the special influence of an ordinance carried out in the presence of the whole Governors ; *by others*, from it being reported that several of the junior boys had afterwards become rather the worse of it ; *by others*, from the partaking boys drinking, in addition to their own allowance, the wine provided for the abstaining boys. It was therefore proposed in 1858 by COUNCILLOR HOPE, one of the Governors, that either the wine should be discontinued entirely, or that a separate provision be made for the abstaining boys, so that none of them be led or tempted to violate their Abstinence principles, or appear to hold an inferior position from adhering to their principles, and the Governors *unanimously* decided in favour of the former alternative, AND ABOLISHED THE WINE ENTIRELY.

BAILIE BLACKADDER presided at the celebration and Boys' dinner on June-day 1858, and while the boys received oranges, etc., in place of the wine, the Bailie substituted sentiments for toasts, and thus everything passed off admirably, while loyalty to the Sovereign, and the memory of the Founder, and other kindred subjects, were duly inculcated, and with hearty cheers responded to by the boys.

On June 2, 1859, on the motion of COUNCILLOR GREIG, the Governors, by a majority, rescinded the resolution of the previous year, and restored the wine, but in carrying out the resolution it was needful to ascertain which were the partaking boys, for whom wine was to be provided, and which were the abstaining boys for whom no wine was to be provided. This was done by intimating that

"All those Boys who do not wish Wine on Heriot's Day will hold up their right hand."

The result was that fifty-eight boys boldly avowed their principles on that occasion, by holding up their hands, and it is this event which the above picture is designed to commemorate—

They are the Gallant Fifty-Eight.

It is known there are many other abstaining boys in the Hospital *who did not take the wine on June-day* 1859, but who lacked the presence of mind to avow their Abstinence principles when the question was put. It is hoped, when the question is put, with reference to June-day 1860, they, being better prepared, will hold up their right hand, and that many others will join the Gallant Band. May the Lord preserve the Gallant Fifty-eight and give them the needful fortitude to continue in their Abstinence course, and as they have begun, so may they, by His grace through Christ, be enabled to say "*No*" to all sin, and to all temptation to sin ; and may their example exercise a healthy influence on their comrades, and lead to the virtual abandonment of all the drinking usages in the Hospital. Happy the boys who may be privileged to share in accomplishing this Grand Reformation !

the north-west tower was repaired. Success with this gave Chesser the confidence to inspect the exterior fabric of the whole building, and he presented the governors with an extensive catalogue of work to be done which they agreed he should tackle systematically.[52] He was constantly to return to his theme of the decayed fabric of the building, and most summers he employed extra help, often in unsettled weather, to repair and preserve the unique features of the 'wark'.

National events continued to impinge on life in the Hospital. Bedford suspended classes on 2 May 1856 for the signing of the Peace Proclamation by the Powers in Paris to end formally the Crimean War, and closed for the day at 11 a.m. on Monday, 25 January 1858, for the royal wedding of Princess Victoria to Frederick of Hohenzollern. In January 1863, the governors asked Chesser to consider what decorations or illuminations would be most suitable in the Hospital to celebrate the forthcoming marriage of the Prince of Wales to Alexandra of Denmark on 10 March. Chesser held an experimental illumination with a number of governors present and they were so impressed that he was instructed to proceed with plans to illuminate the north front on the evening of the marriage day up to a cost of £60. He was also asked to repeat his experiment for the committee of Citizens who had charge of illuminating the Town.[53] The event was such a success that they deemed the money well spent. So much so that the governors repeated the illumination a decade later, in 1874, on the marriage of Alfred, Duke of Edinburgh, to the Grand Duchess Maria of Russia,[54] while the pupils had a holiday and a better than usual dinner.[55]

During 1863 Bedford was complaining about the damage to desks and forms in the classrooms as the boys did not have enough playground space.[56] However, space was at a premium, and Bedford was forced to return to the issue in October 1866. He stressed again the vital need to provide additional accommodation for recreation, as there were only two classrooms, partly occupied by desks, in which the boys were allowed to play according to the regulations. The property committee believed that the existing playshed could be extended and the existing turning house could be converted into a classroom. Bedford pressed for these changes to be implemented, for during inclement weather the confinement of the boys in the Hospital 'is little better than a kind of imprisonment'.[57] He believed that the few boys doing turning could choose drawing instead, or have lessons in turning from the Hospital wright. In April 1867 his request was granted and the additional recreation room was created.

Following a recommendation from Bedford, Superintendent Chesser was instructed on 1 October 1863 to cut numbers in the paving of the quad at suitable intervals to mark the position of each of the 180 boys.[58] In August 1866, Chesser submitted a report on the state of the chapel, whose extremely dirty condition had been noticed by the Lord Provost. His suggestions of replaning over and waxing the oak floor and repainting the walls and roof were accepted. He then turned his attention to the council room and his work there was praised by the Lord Provost at a meeting on 9 April 1868 when he drew the attentions of the other governors to the 'very handsome manner in which the Council Room had been decorated'.[59] It was suggested that the room would be enhanced by a clock, and after a model was exhibited and approved it was agreed on 7 May 1868 that Chesser install the clock on the wall facing the chairman.[60] Having looked into the problems of the tower clock in 1866, Bedford had been directed 'not to allow the Great Bell to be rung in the future'[61] but the work was unfinished. Chesser instructed Robert Bryson to complete the improvements in August 1871.[62]

On 5 December 1867 Councillor Ford moved that 'whereas the Hospital grounds next Lauriston exhibit a mass of black earth and tangled brushwood, offensive to the eye and discreditable to the institution . . . [suggest] said ground being laid out in a style more in accordance with the enduring beauty of the Structure inside'.[63] This was remitted to the property committee which visited the area and agreed. It was decided to preserve the old trees and a limited number of the smaller ones, while the rest of the trees and the bushes were removed, the ground smoothed down and sown out in grass. Chesser was proud of the improvements and the 'new' front took on the appearance it has today.

Bedford was generally pleased with the quality of staff, and Voigt, after observation, agreed with his assessment that they were 'superior teachers', and praised them for their teaching strategies and the opportunities given the weakest boys to reach the standards of the best.[19] However, Bedford was unhappy with the singing master, Kenward, who had defective hearing which resulted in many discordant notes, but he persevered with him because of his long service.[65] Wardsmen came and went, as they had always done, with remarkable regularity. One exception to this was Magnus Manson, who, after 18 years in the post, resigned in November 1864 and was awarded a gratuity of ten guineas by the governors for his loyal service. To improve standards Bedford prepared a job description of the work of each of the wardsmen and female servants. The role of steward and matron in the supervision of these workers was crucial. The finance and property committee recommended that matters would improve if the steward lived on site, and Chesser suggested the use of the building adjoining the Vennel. This structure had formerly been used as a drying house when the washing had been done in the Hospital, and he believed it could be converted into a suitable dwelling house with private access to it from the Vennel. As there were clear advantages in regulating the Vennel entrance, especially with the steward deputising for the house-governor during the latter's annual vacation, by the summer of 1868 the conversion and redecoration had taken place.[66]

There was a fair amount of stability with other staff. Drum-major John Levick had been appointed gatekeeper and drill instructor in February 1863, but his role expanded after the treasurer successfully applied to the Secretary of War for carbines for the boys in May 1865. A rack was set up in the Hospital by Chesser and Levick taught the boys the use of carbines and saw they were kept clean and in good order. In April 1868 they were praising Levick's 'great fidelity and satisfaction' as gatekeeper, warder and drill instructor and raised his salary by £8 per annum.[67]

Debate raged on amongst the governors about the commemoration of June Day and the expenses involved. Councillor Russell, now treasurer of the Town, returned to his theme of earlier days. He pressed in April 1857 for an audit of the expenses involved in 'entertainments and incidentals' and urged the governors to look at ways of curtailing them in future. However, the house committee decided 7–3 to continue the anniversary dinner for governors, teachers and other officials, including those who rendered gratuitious services during the year, deciding also, however, to limit expenditure to fifteen shillings each. It did, however, recommend a series of proposals to save money: the ending of lunch to governors and committees on days of examination; changing the annual excursion[68] of boys and governors to a picnic taken from the Hospital; the ending of the annual anthem, not only on grounds of expense, but also because it disrupted the other studies of the boys; and abandoning the newly instituted tea party for apprentices.[69] Finally, the committee argued for the end of the practice of assembling all the pupils of the Hospital and outdoor schools on June Day on the Hospital Green, not just because it interfered with their studies for a couple of days beforehand, but also because 'it is found now not to answer the original purpose intended from the great increase in the Schools and the impossibility of the Pupils hearing the address which it has been customary to give them'.[70] Instead it was suggested that the children of the outdoor schools should on June Day get an entire holiday 'which the committee believe will be considered by them a greater boon than having to assemble as heretofore and getting a small bun'.[71]

However, the governing body thought the proposals went too far. In the event the children in the outdoor schools did get their 'poke' with threepenny bun (currant loaf or 'brick') and an orange as usual for June Day; female and apprentice teachers received their usual cake; the governors had their usual dinner at Barry's, although they did not partake of their usual claret; and the boys and governors went on the last Friday in July 1857 to Selkirk. In 1858 the governors approved of having their annual dinner with only Councillor Hope dissenting and all Hospital and outdoor children were to meet as usual on the Green on June Day with their bun and orange as formerly. In 1859, Bedford asked the governors to consider special arrangements for the 200th anniversary of the opening of the Hospital. The 'Auld Callants' were determined not to be left out, and the governors agreed that, as in the years before 1827, they would be allowed to decorate the courtyard of the Hospital.

The 1859 celebrations were held on Monday 6 June 'with much festive ceremony'.[72] The traditional 'busking the Statue' was revived and 'fulfilled with a degree of taste and elegant effect probably never surpassed'.[73] The design was partly supplied from the recollections of auld callants and partly copied from a sketch in the possession of an aged callant, who was present in 1859 at his 72nd anniversary celebration. The north front of the quad was externally decorated. The woodwork over the folding doors of the porch was covered with crimson drapery. Extending across the porch was a festoon of flowers with pendants, and above was a bust of George Heriot, crowned with laurel. The arch leading into the quad was turned into a sylvan bower. Flowers in wire baskets hung from every available point, while the Trades Maidens exercised their prerogative of arranging the bouquet in the founder's hand.

About 11 a.m. the children of the eight juvenile and four infant outdoor schools were brought up to the Hospital under their respective teachers, and shown the various decorations before the public arrived. Detachments of thirty boys and girls from each of the juvenile schools were selected to accompany the Hospital boys to the New Greyfriars' Church, where the service was also attended, as usual, by the pupils and staff of George Watson's and the Merchant Maiden and Trades' Maiden Hospitals. The Lord Provost, magistrates and council attended in their official finery, along with most of the clerical governors. Every available space in the church, as well as in the passages, lobbies and stairs, was crowded. The Revd Smith of Trinity College Church, delivering the sermon, concluded: 'No man can deny that an institution which, during 200 years, has fed, clothed, and educated more than 4,000 of the sons of our burgesses – which in the course of the last fifty years has turned out, to my knowledge, upwards of fifty members of the College of Justice, fifty medical practitioners, thirty clergymen, and forty teachers and professors, many of them bearing names of the highest note in their several professions – which, moreover, day by day provides an excellent education for the children of our working classes in thousands in all quarters of the city – no man can deny that an institution which has done all this, and far more, has fulfilled the pious intention of its founder, and proved itself not undeserving the good wishes and the gratitude of the public.'[74]

After the service, the governors, along with the City officials, proceeded to the Greens in front of the Hospital, where the children were arranged as usual in a great circle, of which the Hospital boys (knaps) formed the centre, and the pupils of the outdoor schools, 3,200 in number, constituted the radii.[75] Lord Provost Melville, surrounded by the other magistrates and governors, ascended the platform and 'The Merry Month of June', written by an Auld Callant, W. Scott Douglas, was sung for the first time by the assembled juveniles.[76] Then the Lord Provost addressed the children.[77] After the singing of the national anthem, the children of the outdoor schools dispersed, while the Hospital boys proceeded to the crowded dining hall to partake of the good cheer provided for them. The 'loving cup' was produced and the Lord Provost proposed a series of loyal and complimentary toasts.

The afternoon was given over to games on the Greens around 'Geordie's bush' and 'scuddin' in the quad by the Auld Callants.[78] It involved the stotting of a ball of their own manufacture on the ground and then, as it rose, propelling it with the closed fist forcibly upward.[20] The boys became very proficient in their aim to 'douf' [perch] it upon the lead roof and the game was particularly exciting when several boys struggled after the same ball. At 4 p.m. the celebrations proper ended, though games and frolics continued in the Meadows till much later.

In the evening the governors and Hospital officials attended the usual dinner in a city hotel. As honorary guests on this occasion the Lord Provost and magistrates of Glasgow were invited, as well as a committee of twelve Auld Callants who had done such a splendid job in organising the special decorations. June Day had gained a new lease of life and became again the great celebration of the Hospital.

Although the general celebrations of 1859 were a great success the usual excursion was marred by tragedy. Given the extra expense of June Day[80] it was decided to restrict the excursion to a picnic near Edinburgh, Hopetoun being selected. While on the final part of the journey there James Harvey was killed under the wheels of a loaded cart.[81] However, the excursions continued: Kinross, North Berwick, Peebles, Melrose, Kelso and Lanark were all venues. Boys saved up for the occasion, which took place annually on the last Friday of June. They were woken at 5 a.m. and had breakfast of bread milk. After hurried prayers in the hall (instead of chapel) the boys fell in, not according to seniority as usual, but friends and brothers together. After marching down to Waverley Station led by the Heriot Band and journey by special train, the boys were given another breakfast of baps and milk in a park or local hall, depending on the weather. For dinner there was cold roast and for supper bread and milk again. The day involved a cricket match and other games which led to the presenting of prizes provided by the governors. Afterwards the three most senior classes wrote essays on the details of the excursion with money prizes awarded for the best.

Bedford and his staff had to contend with periodic epidemics. During December 1862 all boys were re-examined and a number revaccinated by Dr Wood.[82] In October 1867 John Allan died of scarlet fever, with another thirteen boys affected. Between 24 December 1870 and 3 April 1871 an epidemic of typhoid fever occurred in the Hospital and thirty-eight boys and the sick-nurse were treated. Of the cases seven were deemed dangerous but all were restored to perfect health. Bedford issued a circular on 16 January to the parents of all the boys, following advice from Wood, informing them that on application boys would be allowed out of the Hospital every evening from 5 p.m. to 9 a.m. This relieved the problem of space and enabled the sick boys to be isolated in one wing of the Hospital. Dr Stevenson Macadam was called in to investigate the water supply of the Hospital on 21 January 1871 and reported that, although the cisterns required immediate cleaning out, the water was not unwholesome.[83] Wood suggested that the typhoid was probably the result of a recent protracted drought which had prevented the drains from being flushed out by rain, resulting in the accumulation of sewage matter. When the rains did come they stirred up the sewage and the resulting miasmata had generated the typhoid.[84] He doubted whether the deficient water supply to the Hospital was a threat to health. On 11 December 1876 Dr Wood informed the governors that the Hospital had seventeen cases of typhoid. This time it was the milk that was found to be of poor quality and unfit for use. After one death[85] the governors increased the number of water closets and urinals available to the boys.[86]

A more important issue, even controversy, however, arose which was to have significant repercussions, as it was provoked by Bedford himself. From his earliest days it was clear that the house-governor was committed to Heriot's. He already had shown this when he edited Steven's *Memoirs of George Heriot*.[87] He confirmed this again when he asked the governors on 15 November 1861 to allow his own son to attend classes in the Hospital so that

he would benefit from his father's educational views. The governors agreed on
5 December provided it was judiciously carried out.[88] What was not so clear
was Bedford's commitment to the system of which Heriot's was a part!

At the seventh meeting of the National Association for the Promotion of
Social Sciences held in Edinburgh in October 1863 Bedford gave a paper
entitled 'The Hospital System of Scotland'.[89] His remarks attracted public
attention and 'gave birth to the agitation'[90] which led the governors to propose
changes to the system of education offered in Heriot's. Bedford held that the
funds of the the fourteen hospitals in Scotland were administered 'with
exemplary discretion and fidelity' while 'the very best possible kind of
education is given to both boys and girls'.[91] He suggested that 'no hospital is
good or bad in its influence simply because it is an hospital'[92] and all systems
had advantages and evils. The problem of the system pertained only to
Edinburgh where the hospitals were concentrated with 860 pupils attending
for an annual outlay of between £40,000 and £50,000.

In his address Bedford stated that many deserving and destitute families
gained much from the foundations and the officials did much for them. Yet
it was claimed that hospital-trained children lacked ordinary intelligence,
were less smart and more docile, and exhibited less affection for their home
and relatives. However, as the famous English public schools were monastic
institutions like the Scottish hospitals why were the former praised and the
latter criticised? Perhaps the supposed 'evils' could be explained by the
differences between the systems: the hospitals were free, their admission age
was usually earlier (at eight) and the period of residence usually longer (six
years). According to Bedford, young children arrived at the hospitals often
scarcely able to utter an intelligible sentence. They sought information and
help from others a little older in the system who in turn had obtained their
views from a similarly unsatisfactory source. With children cut off from home
influence between the ages of eight and fourteen they missed out on parental
discipline, with its tenderness and responsibility, which could not be
adequately substituted. This helped explain why discipline was not so
effective in hospitals where the numbers were too large to control and the
wardsmen were involved in domestic and playground supervision. During
holidays, some children preferred to stay in the hospitals because of the better
food and greater domestic comfort, which bred alienation from parents. This
was the very opposite of English public schools where comforts were poorer,
the parental home had established a hold and the school had to wean the boys
away from domestic indulgences.[93]

Bedford did not stress the credit side of hospitals, which were remarkable

George Heriot (1563-1624) left the bulk of his considerable fortune for the founding of a Hospital
for the upbringing and education of 'poor fatherless boys, friemen's sons' of Edinburgh. This portrait
was painted by George or John Scougall about 1698 from an original now lost.

ANNA·D·G·REG
SCOTORVM
ÆTA·19
1595

Gordg beriatt I ernestlie dissyr youe present to send
us tua hundrethe pundes with all expidition becaus
I man best me away present lie

Anna R

TOP.

Anna of Denmark, sister of Christian IV and from 1589 Consort of James VI of Scotland, proved a compulsive spender. She used George Heriot as an extensive supplier of jewels from 1593 until her death in 1619.

BOTTOM.

A Royal I.O.U. from Anna to George Heriot asking for urgent financial help. Although undated, it seems to have been written quickly, perhaps in 1594 when Anna was still working on her written Scots.

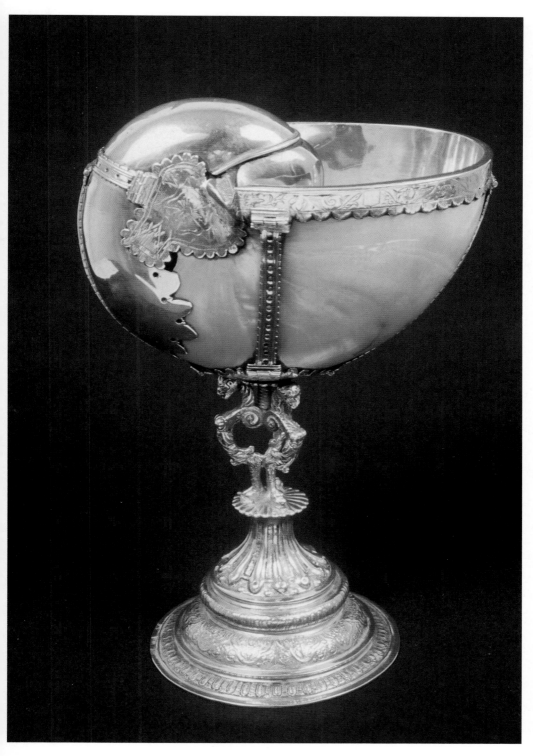

This Loving Cup was presented to the Heriot Governors in 1792 in the belief that it was the work of Heriot himself. It was made, however, by Robert Denniestoun between 1611-33 but owned by Heriot and included in the inventory of his estate.

Sir Henry Raeburn (1756-1823) attended Heriot's Hospital between 1765 and 1772, having lost both his parents at the age of six. He went on to become the leading portrait painter of his generation. *National Gallery of Scotland.*

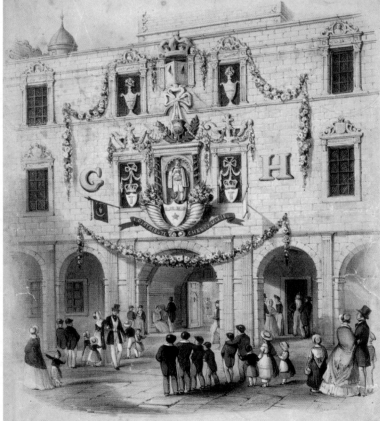

TOP.

Following collaboration with Sir Walter Scott, J.M.W. Turner painted this famous view of
'Heriot's Hospital from the Grassmarket'. He juxtaposes the poor of the immediate area with the
dominant Hospital, alluding to its charitable purposes. *National Gallery of Scotland.*

BOTTOM.

The Busking of Heriot's statue on Founder's Day was revived in
spectacular fashion in 1859 for the Bicentennial Celebrations.

The New Science Block was opened by the Secretary of State for Scotland in October 1912. It signified the special importance of science subjects in the Heriot curriculum and ensured that the School led the country in science facilities.

The New School was opened in 1934 and enabled Heriot's to take in pupils from the age of five. Art, Technical and Gymnastics facilities were upgraded and this reinforced Heriot's claim to be a modern and well-equipped School.

The Council Room was the meeting place of the Governors from the opening of the Hospital. It was entirely wainscoted with oak panels in 1690 and contains a large seventeenth-century oak gate-leg table. The Jacobean settle in the background appears to have belonged to George Heriot.

The Old Refectory of the Hospital was converted in the 1970s into a large comfortable New Staff Room.

TOP.
The heritage of cricket – past and present players celebrate the opening of the KJF Scotland
pavilion in August 2002. Ken Scotland is seated second from the right.

BOTTOM.
Since 1926 the School has boasted some of the finest playing fields in Scotland at Goldenacre.
With the advent of co-education in 1979 excellent hockey facilities have been added.

TOP.

Heriot's FP rugby teams have been consistently among the strongest in the first flight of Scottish rugby.
Having won a number of championships, most recently the FP 1st XV won the title again in 1999-2000.

BOTTOM.

A club for Auld Callants (former pupils of the Hospital) was formed early in the eighteenth century.
The School's Heriot Club celebrated its Centenary in 1991 under its President, Michael Gilbert,
now Chairman of the Governors. Here, unusually, we see eight Presidents.

TOP.

Since its revival in 1923 the garlanding of George Heriot every June at Founder's Day has followed traditional lines. Garlands of flowers adorn Heriot's statue and a bouquet is placed in his right hand.

BOTTOM.

The Officers' Training Corps (OTC) was introduced by Headmaster Clark in 1909. The Pipe Band has become an increasingly important part of its successor, the Combined Cadet Force, and plays on all major School occasions.

The Chapel has played a significant part in Heriot's history, and in recent years Former Pupils have used it for family services. Here the School's Senior Strings practise for just such an occasion.

The new Junior School was created in two major stages and in total twelve
modern classrooms were built on the east end of the playground.

for their healthiness, exhibiting as they did low sickness and mortality rates, partly as a result of the strict medical examinations given to the children prior to election and partly the regular, sound and sufficient diet children received once admitted. They also had the advantage of being able to introduce a progressive course of education which could be planned over a number of years. However, a number of hospitals, like Heriot's Hospital, had seen recent improvements. Bedford wished to go further. To bring the outside world more into the lives of children he wanted the introduction of non-resident pupils into all hospitals. He called for resident teachers to replace wardsmen in the supervision of the children in playground, playroom and sleeping areas. For him hospitals were for the children of destitute widows and unfortunate tradesmen of the burgess (middle) class, while the children of fully employed parents did not belong there. To send children there weakened a parent's self-esteem and resulted in the loss of the privilege of responsibility and the expense of educating the child according to the requirements of the appropriate station in life.[94]

Bedford's comments were controversial and influential. A number of Heriot governors resented not only their content but also the manner in which they were delivered. They had had no experience of an employee speaking so candidly and found it difficult to accept. Moreover, Bedford's assertion that Heriot had meant to benefit the lower middle classes – the class represented by the burgess class in Heriot's time – was resented by some councillors, who considered the working classes – to whose votes many of them looked for election to the town council – the rightful beneficiaries of Heriot's charity. It was not surprising then that from 1863 Bedford was at loggerheads with a number of the governors.

Having raised some fundamental issues on the future of the hospital system Bedford hoped others would take up his cause, but it was not until 4 April 1867 that the governors remitted the Revd Dr Nisbet's motion to the education committee 'to take into consideration the state of Education in the Hospital and to report whether any suggestions occur to be made by them for its improvement'.[95] Six months later, on 3 October, they also agreed to remit to the education and law committees Councillor Stott's motion 'to consider and report as to the expediency and practicability of limiting the numbers of boys boarded and lodged in the Hospital to the fatherless, motherless and really clamant cases and instead thereof to extend the benefit of a first class education to outdoor scholars the sons of burgesses'.[96] A sub-committee of seven under the Revd Dr Gray examined a great deal of evidence going back some considerable time, and, on account of the importance of the matters involved, all submissions were printed for all the governors to examine.

Councillor Stott, whose experience as a governor of Watson's gave him a unique perspective, argued that reform of Heriot's was overdue. He compared its 'dingy, low-roofed dormitories' with the modern buildings of Watson's, Donaldson's and Stewart's, and believed the good results at Watson's showed what could be achieved when outdoor pupils were introduced.[97] He attacked the hospital system as vicious, cramping the intellectual power of boys and leading to a lower standard of morality than normally prevailed because of an ignorance of family life. He proposed reducing the number of resident boys to 100 (or at most 120), and introducing 80 (or 60) outdoor boys, sons of burgesses, who would attend and dine daily, while resident boys would stay with their families all Saturday, after church in the morning and afternoon of Sunday and on Sunday evenings.

Isaac Bayley, the clerk, held that only the fatherless, the descendants of Heriot and really clamant cases, were entitled to admission to Heriot's Hospital. However, 'clamant', according to the Statutes, referred to boys 'whose parents are not sufficiently able to maintain them, as the intention of the Founder is only to relieve the poor'. According to Bayley's interpretation, a burgess and freeman who lived in comparative affluence and then fell on hard times was 'poor' and his case 'clamant', but someone who had never occupied a good position and was actually poorer than the former case was not to be held eligible because such parents never had a right or expectation for their children to have an education other than that provided in the outdoor schools, which had been established to cater for the lower orders with less income. Yet if the governors followed such a line they would not fill the Hospital, as there were not enough clamant cases given the ever-decreasing number of burgesses. Indeed, for some years the main reason for claiming burgess-ship had been to gain admission to Heriot's and other hospitals. Moreover, at the last election to Heriot's, twenty-four applicants had filled twenty-four vacancies, although it was believed that a number were not clamant cases.

Having started the whole process house-governor Bedford felt it proper to make his contribution to the debate, which he did in his letter to the governors dated 11 November 1867. He held that the number of boys in the Hospital was 'much too large' and the present system of supervision was 'very faulty'. He strongly believed in 'the home system' and wanted boys to board and lodge at home, but as this required parliamentary sanction he suggested other improvements. All boys should have single beds and there needed to be more room between beds, more ventilation, the supervision of three resident

masters (in place of the present one) who would require more room than the wardsmen. All this would require more accommodation and hence a reduction in the number of boys to 100 or at most 120. As dining facilities were adequate for 180 it was possible to add non-resident boys at the expense of resident boys. Given the need for greater space those boys who could not be accommodated in the Hospital should be boarded with their parents, receive the same education as inmates, be furnished with the same uniform,[96] and have an allowance instead of victuals. Bedford wished the numbers of resident and non-resident boys to number not fewer than 180 in total, with both having the same advantages on leaving the Hospital.

The Revd Dr Nisbet believed the Statutes stipulated that Heriot had wished boys to have a liberal education. However, the regulations were modified from time to time to meet standards requisite for entering College and Nisbet held that this was just such a time. Boys left the Hospital at the age of fourteen, after four or five years' education, and even 'hopeful scholars' staying a little longer could not reach the appropriate standard for College entry. To combat this, Nisbet advocated returning to the previous practice of taking boys earlier and keeping them longer. He also believed that Heriot's would gain from the inclusion of day scholars: Watson's had benefited from them and Fettes intended to include them.

John Chesser, superintendent of works, gave details on the space available in various hospitals:

During the nineteenth century all Hospital boys had their own number in the Quad (1-180) which was used for roll call, and placed on their possessions.

| | Average Space per Boy | |
	Domitory (cubic feet)	Classroom (cubic feet)
Heriot's (180 inmates)	407	268
Watson's (86 + 25 day)	560	508
J. Watson's (90)	670	406
Stewart's (72)	600	724

No government statistics were available, but in the *Manual of School Management* by Thomas Morrison the space given for a classroom was 637 cubic feet. By any standard Heriot's Hospital was overcrowded. This information was supplemented by a medical report of December 1853 on the numbers of boys which the dormitories could accommodate.

Important also was the legal opinion of Lord Advocate Rutherfurd and John Inglis,[99] on whether the governors had the right to allow boys to go home every evening and lodge in their parents' home.[100] In Rutherfurd's opinion, Heriot intended to benefit only fatherless boys. However, since 1659, boys with parents were also admitted provided they were poor. Perhaps the governors believed that there was not a sufficient number of poor fatherless boys to fill the Hospital. The Statutes'[101] reference to 'parents' suggested the eligibility of boys who were not fatherless. Yet Rutherfurd had held that 'parents' could only mean mothers, as the sentence in which it is found referred specifically to the class Heriot intended to relieve, namely poor fatherless boys.[102] For Balcanquall 'parents' had not been intended to sanction the admission of boys whose fathers were alive, but only to prevent the admission of those boys who, though fatherless, were not poor, but had mothers or other friends able to maintain them. Rutherfurd then suggested that as boys with fathers had been admitted on the authority of the governors then the governors could allow them to sleep in their parents' houses as nothing in the Statutes forbade it. Balcanquall, however, had believed the objects of the charity would reside within the Hospital. Although there was no obligation on the governors to maintain 180 boys in the Hospital or to keep the establishment precisely as it was, they had a clear duty to maintain and educate as many poor burgess children as the building could adequately house. Having done this, the governors could then give education and food to others who could live at home. What they could not do was to make room in the Hospital for such youths by reducing the accommodation being presently provided. Furthermore they could not resolve that only fatherless boys would be eligible in future, and with room in the Hospital then set up a school for non-residents.

Rutherfurd believed that regard should always be given to Heriot's design: the religious and virtuous education of the youths of the Hospital. It might be necessary to set aside and overrule particular clauses to achieve this. Thus if the governors believed that the separation of boys from their parents was resulting in evil then they could and should be able to change the arrangements, even if the Statutes stated otherwise. The design of Heriot was more important than the particular method by which he proposed to achieve that design. Naturally the 1836 Act had to be construed with reference to the Statutes and this ensured that the governors were bound to admit the numbers the revenue could maintain before spending any surplus on outdoor education.

The other contentious issue touched on by Rutherfurd was Heriot's reference in his will to 'freemen's sons' and Balcanqual's reference in the Statutes to 'burgesses and freemen'. Some governors had contended that Heriot intended his Hospital for the sons of decayed burgesses only, and not those who through poverty became burgesses to get their children into the Hospital. Others contended that following seventeenth-century practice only burgesses who resided within Edinburgh and carried on business there were residents paying 'scot and lot' (city taxes) and so eligible to have their children enter the Hospital. Although the town council required evidence of residence before admitting to burgess-ship the governors had found many applicants for admission admitting that they had never resided or carried on business within the city. For Rutherfurd, however, burgess-ship and poverty were sufficient qualifications. The governors could not reject sons of burgesses who had never lived or carried on business within the royalty.

The opinion of John Inglis was similar. It was not lawful for the governors to change the qualifications for admission, nor to change the nature of benefits, e.g., ending education or ending maintenance. The governors needed parliamentary sanction to convert the Hospital into a school. They had no right to inquire into the qualifications for becoming a burgess, which was the responsibility of the town council. He declared that it was not uncommon for the class, for whose benefit a charity was originally created, to change so markedly that had the founder foreseen changes he would not have destined his property in perpetuity for the benefit of such persons. However, the rule of law dictated that when a bequest was clear then it must receive effect unless it was held to be against good morals or public policy.

The final document to be examined was the report by Drs Robert Christison, Andrew Wood and Henry D. Littlejohn dated 2 January 1868 on the sufficiency of the dormitories and classrooms from a sanitary and moral viewpoint. They reported that the boys were remarkably healthy; there were few in the sick-room, not much incidence of epidemic disease had been experienced, and deaths had numbered five in fourteen years.[103] The 180 boys were in eight wards, 154 of them in single beds, but the report suggested that the beds were too close together, that double-beds should be done away with, and beds should be moved away from the windows for safety and health reasons. It suggested that play areas were needed, for the boys only had classrooms which were full of furniture and dust. However, all classrooms except the museum were suitable in size, light and ventilation. The dining hall was suitable for 180. The reading room and conversation room were too dark, gloomy and small. The chapel was too cold in wintry weather, especially since it was used early in the morning and late in the evening.

Such was the evidence which the joint committee of the education and law committees had before it. In its deliberations much emphasis was placed on medical advice, and it was decided that the dormitories were not adequate to contain 180 beds or provide proper sleeping accommodation for them. As there was no room in the Hospital for increasing the number of dormitories without converting classrooms it was agreed that only a reduction in the number of boys would solve the problem. Medical opinion favoured a reduction to 120, and three members of the committee concurred. Bailie Tawse, however, preferred 150. Whatever the reduction, the joint committee recommended that the governors admit an equal number of non-resident sons of burgesses as day scholars, following the Watson's example. The committee also approved of taking applicants early and keeping hopeful scholars until they were aged sixteen. On 27 July 1868, the governors accepted the joint report by 13 to 2, and a special committee under the Lord Provost was set up to carry it forward.

This new committee under Lord Provost Chambers met for the first of a number of meetings on 24 September and put forward its radical plans to the governors on 12 November. The main change for resident boys was that they should enter the Hospital as soon after their seventh birthday as possible, having been tested in their general level of attainment, and that they should be allowed by the house-governor to remain out of the Hospital from Saturday until Monday morning. Significantly a new class of non-resident boys was to be introduced. These day scholars too would enter as soon after seven as possible and were to come from respectable families and exhibit good conduct and fair scholarship. They would arrive at the Hospital at 8 a.m. for chapel, receive breakfast, lunch and dinner with the residents, and leave immediately after classes were over. On Sundays they would arrive for 10.40

a.m. to attend church and religious instruction before leaving after dinner (although parents could gain exemptions for their children from these requirements). They would be entitled to compete for open prizes, and they were to receive a pair of shoes and cap annually and wear clothes of a different colour. The non-resident boys would leave after their fourteenth birthday but would stay on if they became hopeful scholars. Parents of resident boys could transfer to non-resident status and the ten vacancies would be filled by both resident and non-resident boys. Showing how far opinion had progressed and how few defenders the hospital system had, without much discussion the governors accepted the report.[104] The proposed changes were advertised once in all Edinburgh newspapers to burgesses and introduced without further fuss or discussion.

In February 1869, eleven of the seventeen boys elected were non-resident and shortly Bedford reported that the new arrangements had been 'on the whole very satisfactory'.[105] Unfortunately, however, most parents could not afford to keep their children in the Hospital until the age of sixteen, and tended to remove some of the most promising scholars and put them into an apprenticeship or trade. Bedford also complained of the occasional irregularity in attendance of some non-resident boys and those who spent weekends at home. This was partly due to the fact that boys taken sick at home did not receive such prompt and skilful attention as that enjoyed by the resident boys, and thus were kept longer away from their classes; and partly due to the indulgence of parents who listened to the excuses of their children and kept them at home. However, on the credit side, Bedford believed that discipline was better and 'the old corporate feeling, with its secret policy, seems to have been greatly modified by the action of the recent regulations; and the little irritations of feeling caused by the necessary exercise of discipline, which occasionally in past years used to grow into troublesome dimensions, seem now soothed down, either by a more frequent association with out-door friends, or by a daily interruption of intercourse with companions in class or play'.[106]

While such important changes in the Hospital were being introduced, Bedford's management and his educational system were subjected to a succession of independent inspections. Daniel Fearnon, an assistant commissioner sent by the Schools Enquiry Commissioners to examine certain schools and compare them with the English grammar schools, visited the Hospital in 1868 and tested the boys both orally and in writing, in arithmetic, Euclid, geography, history, French, Latin and the Greek Testament. He was critical of standards except in English subjects 'which were very creditable'.[107] In other areas the boys 'seemed inferior to the general average of boys of a similar age in a good burgh day-school', this despite his belief that the amount of work required of boys, particularly in their senior years, was heavy. Particularly unsatisfactory was their knowledge of French, which he believed was begun too late and was not good while it lasted. He praised the thorough system of class places and marking for lessons and the great care taken to make the boys diligent and stimulate interest in their studies, as well as the quarterly reports on conduct and progress which were sent home by Bedford. He criticised two masters but praised Bedford's efforts with the boys, who he found 'extremely docile, remarkably well-behaved and well-mannered, but less full of life and vigour in their studies than the scholars of a good burgh school'.[108]

Fearnon also mentioned the change from the 'antiquated dress' of the Statutes to 'one more suitable for modern customs'. He praised the library and its contents – books, periodicals, newspapers – which the boys used as a quiet place out of school hours; the good day room where the boys could talk and play at quiet games and the fact that the boys were allowed to play cricket on the grass on the Hospital courts. 'The greatest care appears to be taken for the comfort and well-being of the boys in every respect.' This led him to conclude that 'it would be difficult to find a more favourable example than this, by which to judge of the results of hospital education. Everything that the system will permit appears to be done by the governors and head master, not only to make the boys happy and comfortable, but also to stimulate them to mental exertion and intellectual vigour. And the liberality of many of the regulations in this hospital is worthy of imitation by most of our similar institutions in England.'[109]

The weaknesses which he saw he put down to lack of fees, which he believed would stimulate the masters and their teaching; the lack of competition and the monastic life which prevented the stimulation of the boys; and the ambitious and extensive curriculum, which resulted in quality being sacrificed for quantity. However, by the time he reported, the governors had determined on changes which they believed would meet Fearnon's criticisms. In particular, the lengthened course of study and the greater freedom offered to the boys, the sending of boys to compete with others at the University local-examinations and having the Hospital education inspected by professional examiners, were all seen as countering his comments.[110]

A few months after Fearnon's visit all the classes in the Hospital were subjected to an examination of four days' duration by Simon S. Laurie, who, as Inspector of the Dick Bequest Schools and Secretary of the Education committee of the Church of Scotland, had, in April 1868, been asked to report on the state of education at the Hospitals under the charge of the Merchant Company.[111] On 7 May 1868 Heriot's education committee pressed the governors to invite Laurie[112] to inspect the Hospital in June or July and hoped he would be able to visit annually.[113] His report was presented to the governors on 17 August. In summary he reported that 'when regard is had to the age at which the boys leave the Hospital, and to the time devoted to each branch of instruction, the results are of a very satisfactory kind. Every teacher works with zeal; and if defects are to be found anywhere, they are to be traced to other causes than the want of either capacity or conscientiousness. Such defects as I found were of a kind easily remedied.'[114]

In the summer of the following year HMI Gordon was prevailed upon to do an unofficial inspection of the Hospital classes. He began by examining the boys in reading, writing and arithmetic, and measuring their attainment in terms of the Revised Code.[115] He commented on the 'highly satisfactory' results, the boys reaching 98 per cent overall. He mentioned the 'very articulate and correct style of reading' and the 'round, open, well-formed penmanship' in writing. He suggested that the good results owed everything to 'careful and efficient teaching' and 'good discipline'.[116] He even contradicted Fearnon's conclusion and saw the boys as cheerful and obedient, although the changed disposition of the boys could have been the result of the new regulations which had been in effect in the intervening year. Fortunately, all external inspections commended Bedford's leadership and Gordon, in particular, paid tribute to the 'great zeal evinced by Dr Bedford in the discharge of his duties'.[117]

Such commendations kept Bedford's critics at bay. His lecture in 1863 was still resented in a number of circles and he was regarded with suspicion. When in April 1866 it was suggested that the house-governor again attend governors' meetings, after some discussion the motion was withdrawn.[118] Another example of lack of confidence was apparent in Bedford's position with regard to the outdoor schools. In March 1861 he had been unanimously appointed as their inspector and annually the position was confirmed. By July 1869, however, deliberations on the reappointment led to further discussion and a vote, although in the event Bedford survived comfortably by thirty votes to four.[119]

Bedford's last years as house-governor were quieter, although his critics still took opportunities when they arose. He had time to update the *History of the Hospital*, producing a third edition in February 1878. 'With the prospect of legislation on the Endowed Institutions . . . it occurred to me that the

History of the Hospital should be brought up to the latest date so as to embody the very important changes made during the last years'. Although he perhaps overestimated the changes made, the governors appreciated his work and ordered copies of the History. The Royal Commission Report of 1880 claimed to have been influenced by Bedford's testimony that the hospital system was unsatisfactory and unsuccessful and this gave added ammunition to his critics.

Bedford's failing health was aggravated by the stress brought on by the constant sniping at his decisions, and he suffered a stroke on 6 September 1880, dying prematurely ten days later, after the longest tenure as house-governor in Heriot's history. His body was buried in the Grange Cemetery five days later. All along the route there the streets were thronged and the traffic was interrupted. A special service was then held in Heriot's chapel, where he had been inducted and where his daughters had been married. He left a wife, two sons and two daughters.[120]

One governor, Councillor Thomas Murray, spoke for a significant number of them when he held[121] that under Bedford the Hospital was 'in a very efficient state of education' and bore 'a favourable comparison . . . with the character of any other similar Institution'.[122] However, Bedford did provoke further criticism in 1873 when his educational views for remodelling the Hospital were placed before the Royal Commission on Endowed Schools. His view that the foundation should benefit the lower middle class of the burgess class and his opposition to free education 'got him into trouble with the majority of governors'.[123] From then on Bedford had to be increasingly careful and was the victim of intrigue and dubious tactics. According to one source, many of the problems were engendered 'merely to sap his position and often with no further object than to annoy one who appeared to threaten the patronage which, as Municipal governors, or as permanent officials of the Hospital, they then enjoyed'.[124] Although this view was not disinterested, the 'rough and ready ways of municipal committees led to his discomforture'[125] and there were numerous examples of the more 'objective' ministers supporting Bedford and his policies against the vested interests of a number of councillors.

Bedford has been viewed as 'the Dr Arnold of Scotland'.[126] He stressed character before education as the determining factor in success or failure, and for him the Hospital aimed to form boys who viewed indolence as unmanly and contemptible. He tolerated and indeed tried to get the best out of 'fagging', believing it afforded an effective and natural safeguard against lawless tyranny. 'By frequent meetings and conversations with the senior boys, and by using their best endeavours to develop in them high principles, a sense of responsibility, and by showing trust in them, there was always a majority on the side of virtue and true manliness who were effective in maintaining a tone in which bullying was minimised as far as it ever will be in a boyish community.'[127] At their meeting on 7 October 1880 the governors unanimously agreed that Bedford was 'honoured in the community for his scholarly attainments and his uprightness and amiability of character' and that 'the interest he at all times desired to take in the welfare of the boys, while under his care and after they left the Hospital, marked his fitness for the position of house-governor, and made its impression on those who had been under the charge'.[128] As one commentator claimed, he took the 'educational and domestic condition of the Hospital to the high-water mark of perfection which was obtainable from an institution based on an obsolete monasticism'.[129]

The changed status in the post of house-governor was seen in the number and quality of the field of applicants.[130] Of the twenty-nine who applied only seven came from Scotland – the remainder, except for one Welshman, from England. The two strongest proved to be Nathaniel Leask of Abbey Park, St Andrews, aged 39, and David F. Lowe, a former master at the Hospital, who was Rector at Bathgate Academy, aged 37. The governors, still immensely proud of the unique character of Heriot's, chose Lowe by twenty-six to twenty-one, and he was inducted into his new post in early January 1881.[131] Lowe was a graduate of Edinburgh University and had spent his first five years teaching English, then French, in the Hospital, before his seven years in charge of Bathgate. According to the testimony of Sir Alexander Grant, Lowe was an excellent teacher and a most efficient administrator.

Lowe inherited a Hospital under attack and he was preoccupied from his earliest days with the struggle to reform the Hospital, although there was little he could do to influence events. He had little opportunity to innovate and was restricted in what he was able to do. Like Bedford he was keen to maintain a modern curriculum. He was successful in expanding chemistry and in introducing physiology and botany in 1883. He extended the teaching of French to more boys, developed lecture courses in mechanics and natural history, and gave more prominence to shorthand.[132] However, like his predecessor, Lowe was unable to persuade the governors to build swimming baths for the Hospital boys.[133] The experiment of taking them to Pitt Street Baths on a Saturday morning was continued.[134] Lowe found the governors to be content with the Scottish tradition, reported by the Argyll Commission in 1868, of a work ethic which had little time or desire for sport or recreation.[135]

Nonetheless, bolstered by a petition from the Old Herioters for more sporting facilities, Lowe persevered, and the governors agreed in October 1884 that one of the parlours on the east side be converted into a gymnasium for gymnastic and drill instruction.[136]

If Lowe was restricted in what he achieved as the last house-governor of the Hospital then it was a reflection of the role he was expected to play. He certainly was a worthy successor to Bedford, and he was a strong candidate for the post of headmaster in the new Heriot's when the Hospital was reconstituted as a School in 1886.

CHAPTER TEN

The End of the Hospital

As we saw in the previous chapter fundamental changes in the Hospital system were unleashed by the Lawrie report. By October 1868 his proposals were advanced as the Merchant Company used its powerful political influence to persuade the Lord Advocate to bring forward the Endowed Hospitals (Scotland) bill to allow hospitals to be turned into day schools.

On 8 April 1869 Lord Provost Chambers instructed the clerk of the Heriot trust to procure copies of the bill, and he called a special general meeting of the governors for 3 May which twenty-seven attended. Clause by clause they examined the bill, which was due to have its third reading in the Commons on 6 May, and resolved to put forward some amendments. The Revd Dr Robertson, Baillie Fyfe and Clerk of Trust Bayley were sent as a deputation to London to effect their resolution. They persuaded Duncan McLaren, MP for Edinburgh, to put forward a motion in Parliament to carry the governors' amendments into effect and decided to meet with the representatives of other hospitals to co-ordinate tactics.[1] This resulted in an agreement with the merchant committee on changes in the bill to make it more workable. Chambers forwarded a copy of these changes to the Lord Advocate Moncrieff, urging their adoption.[2]

At its third reading on 17 June 1869 Dr Lyon Playfair[3] attacked the narrowness of the proposed bill, comparing it unfavourably with the recent English Endowed Schools' Act.[4] The Scottish bill allowed endowed institutions to apply to the Home Secretary for approval of their reform schemes, but did not stipulate any framework on the nature of reforms or set up a commission to supervise the process.[5] Playfair went further, making a devastating attack on the wealthy hospital schools for their 'miserable' number of scholars. They were responsible for destroying individuality and for pauperising both morally and intellectually: a distinguished hospital boy was unheard of in Scotland. He went on to attack specifically the Heriot outdoor schools, which allowed parents to shirk their responsibilities. They were not feeders by merit to the Hospital, having no connection with the

Hospital except their name, and ensuring that the old system of patronage remained unchallenged.[6] Playfair had his own solution for the hospitals: they should not ignore the middle class who could pay for education, but should concentrate on an elite of the poorer classes, and give them education suitable for their future occupations; they should also link up with the universities and establish themselves as distinctive, special schools – in trade, commerce, and science. Playfair pressed the Lord Advocate to postpone the bill and place hospitals under a Scottish National Board with a short time scale to reform themselves.

Although supported by James A. Campbell (Conservative) the other speakers in the debate, McLaren, W.E. Forster[7] and the introducer of the bill, Charles S. Parker (Liberal), pressed for the bill.[8] Parker believed it gave the managers of hospitals a chance to reform and did not prevent a future comprehensive review. The Lord Advocate felt that Playfair had misunderstood the bill: it was not a measure designed to help trustees to tackle faults. Reform of hospitals was for the future.[9]

The Heriot governors appreciated that as the bill would become law it was important to ensure that enough time would be available under the legislation to allow the Hospitals to work out and complete their own alterations. They determined to work with the Merchant Company to extend the duration of the Act by a further year. On 27 June the clerk, the Lord Provost and certain governors went with the master of the Merchant Company and met the Lord Advocate and other government members in London. They succeeded in their aim: despite some misgivings Moncrieff agreed to their proposals. The way was clear for the passage of the bill, which gained royal assent on 26 July.[10]

The Merchant Company was far ahead of Heriot's in its thinking, and went forward immediately with its radical reforms without opposition.[11] Five large, fee-paying schools were formed from their hospitals in 1870.[12] Although the Act was permissive it was only to operate until 31 December 1871 with the possibility of an extension until 31 July 1872. The governors were aware that if they did not reform Heriot's Hospital there was good reason to believe that a compulsory Act would be introduced, as in England, to force reform on them.[13] A committee of thirteen was set up under the Lord Provost to carry this forward.

Unfortunately for Heriot's its scheme for reform was laid down at the very time when the complaints of private school teachers,[14] and the surprise at the radical nature of the Merchant Company's reforms, were leading the Liberal government to have second thoughts about the 1869 Act. The special committee had decided to 'increase the usefulness and efficiency' of the Hospital by introducing a scheme which would allow the governors to limit the number of foundationers to between forty and sixty fatherless or motherless boys (not just the sons of burgesses, who would still have preference, but also embracing the sons of persons who had carried on business in Edinburgh), while simultaneously admitting fee-paying boys. It also wished to maintain the boys within or without the Hospital. The committee favoured the creation of more outdoor schools, but also intended to ask for the power to erect industrial schools for destitute children. Having agreed on the main principles to be included in a provisional order, the committee decided to ask for a number of other powers: these would allow the governors to develop a commercial and scientific curriculum in the Hospital, to restrict entry to boys who had already reached a certain academic level, to regulate the age and attainments of non-residents, and to open the non-resident ranks to boys who were neither fatherless nor the sons of burgesses. As for the outdoor schools, the governors wished to charge fees and build a secondary outdoor school for classical and commercial instruction. Further, the governors were keen to establish evening classes, and to devote an additional £940 a year to the support of university bursaries (including £240 for non-foundationers), while extending them for more than four years, and pay the fees of boys on leaving the Hospital if they attended the Watt Institution.

On 2 June 1870, following the unanimous acceptance of Councillor Tawse's motion to approve its report, it was also unanimously agreed to petition the Secretary of State.[15] In just over a month the proposed provisional order had been drafted and discussed clause by clause 'at very great length' by the governors.[16] Having been laid on the table for ten days the governors unanimously followed Tawse in accepting the order on 14 July. But the unanimity of the governors on the issue of introducing fees into both the Hospital and outdoor schools was not to last long, and this perhaps explains McLaren's comment that the order 'went too far on some points'.[17] However, they pressed on with their proposed reform.

To begin with all went according to plan. A deputation of Tawse, house-governor Bedford (a significant inclusion), Bayley and three other governors, travelled to London on 4 August, meeting subsequently with the Lord Advocate and Home Secretary Bruce. The deputation came home, reassured that their order would be dealt with quickly and the governors thanked the Edinburgh MPs for their help.[18] However, nothing happened. All involved were genuinely surprised and disappointed when the government dragged its feet on the issue, and early in 1871 the governors determined to ask McLaren to press Bruce for a decision.

When it eventually came, it emanated, not from Bruce himself, but from one of the under-secretaries in his department, who, on 22 March 1871, intimated that the home secretary declined to grant the order as the Crown law officers held it to be unlawful. They believed that it would 'effect a radical change in the constitution and purposes of the trust, as authorising the governors to reduce the number of boys to be admitted to the Hospital, empowering them to convert the Hospital into a Day-School and to establish a system of Schools for all Classes'.[19] The law officers argued that the 1869 Act did not allow such a change, as the governors could not abolish or reduce the benefits of the Hospital but only provide for its better government.

On 28 March the Heriot special committee reconvened and expressed 'much surprise and disappointment'[20] at Bruce's decision, especially given the nine months' delay before it had been announced. What was understandably difficult for the Heriot governors to understand was the seeming volte-face of government ministers. In spring 1869, when the bill was being discussed, it had been the governors who had objected to its apparently sweeping nature and had proposed to the Lord Advocate an amendment that powers granted should not be inconsistent with the spirit of foundation grants and mortifications. The response of the government had been to stress the great object of the bill – to bring about changes in foundations as it was strongly felt that the congregating of large numbers of boys for bed and board was an evil and tended to pauperise parents, and that it was for education alone that Hospital funds should in future be deployed. The governors had understood that if they did not voluntarily propose large reforms, and in particular break up the 'monastic system' of the Hospitals, reforms would be imposed upon the governors. The bill went ahead without the limitation the governors desired, but they still proceeded with the order. No hint had ever been given that the powers the governors now sought were beyond that allowed in the 1869 Act. And even if Bruce believed that they went too far why had he not modified or altered the order to bring it into line with his views rather than simply rejecting it?

The governors appeared to have an unanswerable case. As the committee held, 'when the history of the Act is considered, with the provisional order granted to the Merchant Company, it is not a little startling to be now told that the Act did not contemplate and does not confer power for the reduction of the number of Boys in the Hospital, and for the conversion of the Hospital itself partially into an educational establishment, in place of retaining it for a residential house'.[21] Indeed, specifically to avoid objection, the Heriot governors had followed the Merchant Company example. As Bruce had insisted that the Company should change their proposal to reduce the number of residents in their hospitals to specify a certain number with the power to reduce them further, so the Heriot governors thus altered their order for permissive power to reduce their residents to sixty with the power to reduce further if they saw fit. In other areas they did not ask for such extensive powers as the Merchant Company had received the previous year. It seemed extraordinary that Heriot's was being denied what the Merchant Company had gained, especially on the grounds that the Act did not confer power to the Secretary of State to grant in one case what he had granted in another.

The special committee asked Bruce to reconsider his decision and if need be issue an order with the modifications and alterations he deemed necessary. The governing body, at its meeting on 13 April 1871, was determined to continue the struggle and all twenty-five present unanimously agreed on the content of the appeal to Bruce.[22] Trying to salvage what they felt undoubtedly fell within the Act, an amended order dated 15 April was produced. The governors proposed extending the class of boys in the Hospital in an effort to provide secondary education to the industrious poor, providing evening classes and additional bursaries and grants to help boys and girls obtain a university education.

Tawse continued his leadership of the governors by travelling again to London and, after discussions with a number of Scottish MPs, he met with the Home Secretary on 12 May. Bruce was reported as being receptive to accepting an amended order which excluded the power to reduce foundationers in the Hospital which his law officers deemed beyond his powers notwithstanding the decision on the Merchant Company's scheme. Tawse immediately modified the order on these lines and resubmitted it to Bruce on the following day. Despite repeated communications Bruce refused to respond until the Cabinet had discussed the matter. At last, on 29 June, a circular was issued by the Home Office to the trustees of all endowed institutions, which set out the government's intentions. It envisaged passing a new Act which would not merely extend the period for carrying out the 1869 Act but would also confer additional powers on the Home Secretary or commissioners appointed by him. Furthermore the governors also were informed that Sir Edward Colebrooke was proposing an amendment to the bill to allow an enquiry into endowed schools. The Heriot governors immediately discerned a threat, and when the special committee met again on 4 July it determined that any attempt to divert the funds from the objectives for which George

Heriot left them 'should be most strenuously resisted'.[23]

Bruce wrote to the governors also on 29 June informing them that 'his present information as to the educational requirements of Edinburgh would not justify him in sanctioning either of the Schemes submitted to him'.[24] As the 1869 Act was not well adapted to furnish the requisite information Bruce said he was willing to co-operate with the governing bodies of institutions coming within its scope by continuing the Act, and at the same time providing for an enquiry which would command the confidence of all interested parties and allow the government to perform its part with greater certainty and fuller knowledge. However, in the event, the government decided not to continue the Act, but to alter its provision. This was the background to the bill introduced into the House of Commons by the Lord Advocate and read for the first time on 14 July.

At a poorly attended special general meeting four days later – only 11 governors attended – it was unanimously agreed to petition against an enquiry by the Lords of the Committee of the Privy Council on Education rather than the Home Office, which was deemed more sympathetic to and more understanding of the Scottish experience, and the right of the former to amend the standing orders of hospitals and to change governing bodies unless specifically agreed to by the bodies involved. The governors also objected to the funds of the Hospital being made liable for expenses, especially those involved in defeating the order. These objections were transmitted to the Edinburgh MPs, McLaren and John Miller, to present to the Commons.

It was no surprise when the government finally rejected the amended provisional order, but there was some good news. Given the opposition to the bill and the lateness of the parliamentary session the government decided not to proceed with it. However, this was only a temporary respite as the government announced its intention to reintroduce its bill in the forthcoming session. The governors, in turn, determined that they would use every consti-tutional means to defeat attempts to have reform forced upon them. At their meeting on 5 October 1871 the twenty-seven governors present unanimously agreed to make the citizens of Edinburgh aware of the government's objectives, which they believed were to divert the revenue of the Hospital from the industrious poor of Edinburgh, for whose benefit they were bequeathed, to other parties or objects. Moreover, they initiated steps to apply for a private Act of Parliament to carry out their own reforms and improve-ments[25] following legal opinions which held that the governors were justified in promoting the bill.[26] However, when the Court of Session affirmed that public trustees were personally liable for the expenses of the unsuccessful attempt to obtain parliamentary process, the governors reluctantly decided not to proceed with the private Act.

The governors found themselves under attack from another quarter at this time. The Principal of Edinburgh University, Sir Alexander Grant, with a background of Harrow and Balliol, was an Angliciser, supportive of the reform of English endowments. Appreciating that Parliament would not approve the public funding of secondary education, he was anxious that endowment funds be unlocked, and he launched particular attacks on Heriot's Hospital and schools both in print[27] and in his opening address to the students in 1871. His original suggestion was that the 'wark' would make a good building for accommodating university students. He saw the hospitals generally as 'splendid mausoleums', and by including all costs in his figures suggested that the Edinburgh hospitals educated 1,100 at the enormous annual cost of £41 each. He argued that 'it is no light thing to acquiesce in the waste and squandering of £50,000 per annum set apart for educational purposes'. Grant felt that the experiment of the out-schools had failed, as they had not been used as feeders to send boys of promise to the Hospital and thence to the university. Instead hospitals demoralised and pauperised parents and produced dull and undistinguished scholars. His argument struck a chord, for McLaren felt it necessary to rally support and spell out the counter-arguments in some detail.[28]

Lord Advocate, George Young, dissatisfied with progress on endowments, decided to withdraw his proposed bill, continuing and amending the 1869 Act, and accepted instead Colebrooke's motion for a Royal Commission to enquire into all endowed institutions in Scotland and the changes needed to increase their usefulness and efficiency. The Heriot governors immediately responded by setting up a new special committee to monitor developments, and when the commission secretary, Simon S. Laurie, asked Dr Gray and Baillie Tawse to give evidence, the governors asked Baillie Lewis to do so as well.[29] Duncan McLaren protested at the lack of an Edinburgh[30] or Hospital voice on the Commission and its dominance by Whigs[31] and refused, perhaps unwisely, to give evidence.[32] Instead he conducted a vigorous press campaign, culminating in his presentation to each governor and official of the trust a copy of his Address on 'Heriot's Hospital trust and its proper management' on 30 December.

The Colebrooke Commission began to take oral evidence on Heriot's on Monday 25 November 1872 with HMI John Gordon giving a detailed account of the standards of education being achieved in the Hospital and in the outdoor schools. His was generally a sympathetic account, from firsthand

experience in the Hospital in 1869, although he stressed that it needed to go further into higher education.[33] House-governor Bedford followed the next day. Because of the recent introduction of day-scholars he had modified the views he had expressed in 1863.[34] However, Bedford remained critical of the bulk of Heriot parents who he believed shifted care from themselves to a public charity and expected education as of right. He also criticised the taking of boys at age seven which he deemed too young, preferring age nine. He wanted to introduce a competitive entry exam to prevent boys being held back by weaker brethren. He also believed that an increasing number of parents were unwilling to send their boys to Heriot's, as the hospital system had been 'considerably discredited'[35] and public opinion branded them. Bedford proposed that the Hospital become a day-school of 300 with the orphans (forty-six in total) boarded out. The out-schools would be feeders to the hospital, with nearby Heriot's Bridge a preparatory school of two hundred boys for Heriot's.[36] He envisaged a separate school for girls. Bedford proposed limiting the foundation to the class Heriot intended to benefit, but non-residents would be expected to pay a small fee.[37] He also wanted more freedom to hire and fire staff (as in England), which he believed would raise educational standards in the Hospital. Given Bedford's experience and position his evidence, especially his devastating criticism of the effect of the hospital system on children and teachers, had a powerful, even decisive impact.[38]

Having heard evidence from other educational 'experts'[39] the Revd James Currie, rector of Trinity College and Principal of the Church of Scotland Training College in Edinburgh, a former pupil of, and master in, Heriot's,[40] gave an unfavourable and unsympathetic account of hospital life, describing how narrow, monotonous, stifling and stagnant it was. Although his information was dated the commissioners were impressed by his arguments. He emphasised that the teaching at Heriot's was the same as elsewhere, but less effective because of the hospital system. With no agency to counteract degeneration the moral tone always declined, and the longer boys were there the worse they became. Currie's remedy followed Bedford's suggestions. Heriot's should become a secondary school, open to those of merit, with those benefiting from Heriot's Will being boarded out. Currie wished to see Heriot's as a technical school on the German model specialising in the theoretical and practical teaching of science.[41]

The financial and administrative structure of the Hospital

From 1866 John Tawse played a prominent part within the Governing Body. He was the chief spokesman for Heriot's before both the Colebrooke and Moncrieff Commissions. He was Clerk and Law Agent of the Trust until his death in 1892.

was examined when on 5 December 1872 first William Forrester and then Isaac Bayley gave evidence. Forrester, a governor between 1852 and 1860, and since 3 January 1861 Heriot's treasurer, explained that the land in possession of the Hospital was practically the same as it had been two centuries before, while remarkably only £230 had been lost in irrecoverable debt out of £210,533 in the past decade.[42] There could no criticism of the financial management of the Hospital.[43] Bayley, as clerk and agent of the Hospital since 6 July 1830, was able to give firsthand information on the changes affecting the institution. In particular he explained that before the 1846 Burgess Act abolished trading restrictions in the Scottish burghs only members of the Incorporated Trades were able to purchase a burgess ticket, and that this was the class Heriot intended to benefit when they fell on hard times. This lower middle-class group – shopkeepers, builders, masons, wrights, those carrying on business – were the burgesses of Heriot's day, and should remain the beneficiaries of Heriot's Hospital, rather than the working class in general.[44] The governors wished to continue to restrict entry to the class Heriot intended to benefit. Bayley, too, supported the introduction of fees in the out-schools. He held that governors could not increase the number of bursaries in Heriot's Will from ten, despite their desire to do so. However, they had increased their value to £20 and opened them to outsiders, believing this to be Heriot's intention. They wanted to offer additional university bursaries for pupils in other Edinburgh schools to compete for.

The next to give evidence was Dr James Donaldson, Rector of Edinburgh High School, who believed that it was the duty of the state to support middle-class education: he had already given such advice to the Argyll Commission.[45] He wanted to tempt back the upper class from their boarding schools to mix with other classes, especially to his 'national' school – a public classical school with up to 1,000 pupils and 60 teachers, as in Paris and Berlin – which would meet the secondary needs of the city. Donaldson was frustrated in this with the Merchant Company opening their day-schools to the middle class. However, this development meant that there was no role left for Heriot's other than to send their pupils elsewhere and give over some of their funds to the School Board, especially as the middle class did not want to send their children to schools where hospital boys had been.[46] He criticised the 'absurdity of private individuals managing public education'[47]and, as Germany proved, the only way to run education was publicly. Therefore, the new School Boards must have control of all educational endowments.

The first of the Heriot 'heavyweights', the Revd Dr Gray, minister of Lady Yester's parish, and a governor since 1850, gave evidence next, on 7 December.

He suggested that although Heriot had expected his legacy to be used for orphans he also wished his Hospital to be based on Christ's, which did not confine its benefits to them. Heriot's priority was to relieve the very poor who should receive free education, but Gray supported the introduction of small fees (1d. or 2d. per week) in the outdoor schools to give cheap education to the less needy. He saw Heriot's trust as 'the patrimony of the poor . . . and . . . they have a right to it'.[48] He argued that the evils of monasticism had been greatly reduced and he wanted to keep the Hospital as a home for fatherless boys. Even opening bursaries to competition would be unfair to the poor. Gray was determined to defend Heriot's against spoilation and wished to establish four more schools for the poor to meet the demand.

Gray was followed by Bailie Tawse, a member of the town council since 1866, and the 'chief spokesman' for Heriot's.[49] He believed that the class applying for Hospital education were of a lower class than that which Heriot intended to benefit, and he supported restricting it to fatherless bairns. The outdoor schools should be open to the poor if too few burgesses applied, and fees should be introduced. He defended the rejected provisional order which had proposed the extension of the Hospital benefits to include decayed persons of Heriot's own class (all those in business) to a maximum of sixty (Tawse thought this figure was too low), and the inclusion of a maximum 200 to 250 fee-paying pupils in the Hospital. He too opposed full open competition for bursaries because it penalised the poor. Tawse defended the opening of evening classes which were being attended by 811 people in four of the out-schools. For him McLaren's 1836 Act was an addition to Heriot's Will: he favoured educating boys in the Hospital rather than sending them on to the High School. Like Gray he thought the Heriot governors should take on the whole education of the working classes of Edinburgh. He disagreed with Donaldson: Heriot's should offer a classical, commercial and technical education for the working classes at a moderate fee,[50] while the Merchant Company was charging significantly more.[51] Heriot's would not be underselling but catering for different classes.

Tawse was followed by Bailie David Lewis,[52] a shoemaker and independent Liberal town councillor since 1863, who had supported the extension of admission to the Hospital to other classes as it was increasingly difficult to find suitable candidates to admit. Indeed Lewis argued that numbers in the Hospital should be limited and boarding ended with the surplus funds being spent on the outdoor schools, which he believed did more good. Unlike the majority of governors, Lewis opposed the introduction of fees in the outdoor schools, believing that working class people did not have the funds available, as recent wage rises had been swallowed up by increases in the cost of living. Lewis strongly defended Heriot's bequest as local, aimed at meeting the needs of the poor in Edinburgh. Like Tawse, he believed Heriot's catered for a class below the Merchant Company schools. Although Lewis recognised that Heriot had in mind a class higher than the poorest, with the changes in society and Merchant Company provision he argued that it should now be for the poorest.[53]

Dr Lyon Playfair gave evidence as an opponent of the hospital system and its evils, believing it rarely produced 'a man above mediocrity'.[54] He believed that Edinburgh had gained endowments from being Scotland's capital and should share its educational benefits with the rest of the country. Playfair held that elementary schools should be paid for by ratepayers and Heriot schools should begin where elementary schools ended. They in turn would be feeders for higher schools into which the Hospital should be converted. In particular Heriot's should be a technical school, teaching children up to seventeen years of age the science for trade and industry on the continental model[55] and not a technological school teaching the trade and industries themselves. Playfair believed that 'no man has a right to state what is to be the destination of his endowment for all time'.[56] When Heriot left his bequest for orphans and fatherless children there was no state provision for them, but now the situation had changed. Playfair opposed free education for its effects on parents and children, but bursaries through exertion were to be commended.

If Playfair was an opponent of Heriot's, Sir Alexander Grant was an outright enemy. He had already demanded radical reform of hospitals and their conversion into day schools. They would form technical[57] or large trades[58] schools rather than the classical form of the High School or Merchant Company schools. He bemoaned the lack of good secondary schools, which meant that there was no entry exam for universities. Hospital funds needed to be diverted into improving secondary education. No Heriot boys had gone to university in the previous year despite the existence of bursaries, and in an exceptionally good year only a half of the 80 to 83 students going up to university had good enough standards to complete their degree in three, as opposed to four years. Grant had opposed the provisional order because it was 'mere repetition of the Merchant Company's scheme and therefore uncalled for'.[59] It was true that extending primary education saved ratepayers' money but the true objective of Heriot had been to give Edinburgh something it would not have had without his endowment. Grant claimed he did not wish to eliminate Heriot funds which he agreed could not be used for university purposes, but if the governors boarded out pupils then the Hospital building could be turned into a residence hall for poor students going to university: this would be in keeping with the spirit of Heriot's foundation, would cost under £3,000 per annum and could be under the governors' control.

A number of others who gave evidence criticised the hospital system. William Jolly, an inspector of schools who had been a master in Watson's Hospital, gave a devastating critique of its educational, intellectual and, above all, moral evils. He advised everyone not to send boys to hospitals.[60] Dr Findlater, headmaster at Gordon's Hospital between 1842 and 1849, added his condemnation of the system, especially 'its want of reponsiveness'.[61] Finally, on 21 January 1873, Professor Fleeming Jenkin, of the engineering department of Edinburgh University, argued that primary education should be restricted to literary subjects, and that Heriot's could be turned into a scientific school as an experiment, following the model of the Ecole Chaptal in Paris, with charging of fees to secure the employment of very able staff.

By the 1870s the overwhelming weight of opinion in Scotland was heavily against the hospital system. The advantages of hospitals – unbroken regularity of attendance, regular and wholesome meals, and healthy children – were no longer deemed sufficient to justify the retention of 'monasticism'. The fate of the Fettes bequest showed just how they were viewed. Sir William Fettes had died in 1836 leaving the residue of his estates 'for the maintenance, education and outfit of young people, whose parents have either died without leaving sufficient funds for that purpose, or who, from innocent misfortune during their own lives, are unable to give suitable education to their children'. Although it seems probable that Fettes was thinking along the lines of a hospital, the trustees under Lord-Justice-General John Inglis were given 'most ample and unlimited powers' for making regulations. Inglis was not keen to add another hospital to an already crowded and criticised system and did not believe poverty alone should be a qualification for participating in the benefits of an educational endowment. He decided to provide a school on the English public school model with fifty foundationers from the professional classes who had fallen on difficult times. A substantial building was begun in 1863, and the school opened in 1870, with a headmaster and staff from England. Needless to say the Colebrooke Commission approved of this development which they saw as a direct result of the failed hospital system.

McLaren's fears that the Commission's domination by representatives of the secondary education party would result in unsympathetic treatment seem to have been borne out. Tawse and Lewis faced close questioning, and the members of the Edinburgh Trades Council also had to deal with hostile cross-examination.[62] The latter gave evidence on 25 October 1873 and Secretary

Cubie's claims that Heriot wished not to 'turn out the great but artisans and citizens'[63] fell on stony ground. Cubie argued that fees were contrary to Heriot's Will, would cause division between paying and non-paying scholars, and would relieve the burden on rich as well as poor. He opposed the extension of bursaries, for, as the University of Edinburgh had 'cut its connection with Edinburgh' (taking students from all over the country), it 'must bear the cost'.[64] The commissioners did not take kindly to Reekie's warning that given the feeling in the working class it would be 'very dangerous' to touch Heriot's bequest,[65] nor to Cubie's assertion that even changes by the governors themselves would cause excitement for 'since the time of the Provisional order, at the municipal elections steps have been taken to educate our town councillors to a better state of mind'.[66] On fees, too, the Edinburgh Trades Council representatives had a hard time. Even they had to admit that when one pays for something it is valued!

Colebrooke's recommendations, published in March 1875, were seen as a crushing blow to the remaining hospitals, and Heriot's in particular. As expected, the report dwelt on the negative influence of the system on children and exposed hospitals as costly, even extravagant. In the year ending 31 December 1873 Heriot's was by far the most expensive of the nineteen endowment hospitals: it spent £54 18s. on each Hospital boy and a total of £9,883 on strictly Hospital purposes.[67] Average hospital expenditure was somewhat lower at £34 per head per annum – still remarkably high, especially when cheap, elementary education was now within easy reach and parents of about 80 per cent of hospital children in Scotland came from families where annual wages were under £80 per annum. It also criticised Heriot's for setting aside the original purpose of the bequest – 'a remarkable example of disregard of the founder's will'[68] – with never more than 34 per cent of foundationers being fatherless,[69] this despite the fact that Scotland had 1,510 foundationers in 25 schools and 950 were fatherless. Heriot governors had not met this greater need. Moreover, George Heriot wished to afford the highest education to boys of merit (sending boys to college and bursaries to universities) but the full number of bursaries had not been taken up since 1818 and they had not been increased in number or value.[70] The governors had failed to realise Heriot's ambitions in this regard[71] and they had also failed to emulate Christ's Hospital, for on average only two boys left Heriot's annually to go to University. Even when the Court of Session had held in 1843 that fatherless boys had a 'legal right of preference' the governors had failed to act on this opinion. They continued to take in the children of those who paid £5 for the burgess ticket which was not the class Heriot intended to benefit. Even Bailie

Lewis had admitted that the outdoor schools were not authorised by the founder being 'totally foreign to the Will', which made it difficult to disapprove of other proposed changes to the original arrangements. Given this catalogue of criticisms the recommendations were not a surprise.

Fundamentally, Colebrooke was totally out of sympathy with the free education offered by Heriot's Hospital and out-schools.[72] Orthodox opinion, which Colebrook followed, held that parents benefiting from free education, when they did not need it, lost self-respect. Parents who can work and earn wages should maintain and educate their own children. Charities which take over a parent's role pauperise the community. Even in cases of need relatives should contribute. As the cost of educating a child was estimated at about £3 per year, and maintenance at around £6 per year, an artisan receiving an average wage of £78 per annum with a family of five children could afford to pay a small fee for education. For orthodox Liberals gratuitous education when indiscriminate was pernicious. Moreover, Colebrooke regarded better education as the reward of merit, sincerely wishing to benefit all classes of society and, despite claims to the contrary, had no calculated plan to deprive the poor of endowments.

Having satisfied itself that Heriot had intended his endowment to benefit the lower-middle rather than the working classes the Colebrooke Commission endorsed the Merchant Company model of reform. Specifically for Heriot's it recommended an increase in the number of bursaries, with some attached to St Andrews University given its mention in the Will, which should bear the same proportion to the existing revenue as the amount specified by Heriot bore to the original bequest. Heriot's trust should end apprentice allowances because they were not tied to merit; indeed they were a form of charity or dole,[73] but there should be available small sums to use for special needy cases.[74] The outdoor schools should not be expanded in number following the passage of the 1872 Education Act and they should be opened to fee-paying pupils. The commissioners believed that Heriot's should become a purely secondary school with charitable foundationers attending the outdoor schools until the age of thirteen, when an open competitive exam would determine who would gain scholarships to it.[75] The school would be open to everyone paying a moderate fee, with entry by exam to keep standards up. Following the evidence of Playfair[76] and Jenkin it was argued that Heriot's should follow the German *Realschule* and be 'specially adapted to the wants of the industrial and commercial classes' with a mathematical, scientific and practical curriculum.[77] Indeed to ensure that classics did not take over, it was to be specifically excluded from the timetable, and classical scholars were to be sent to the High School!'[78] Finally, Colebrooke sought to limit the number of boys boarded and educated at the expense of the Hospital to 60 orphans:[79] with only 21 applicants for 27 vacancies in 1872 there was a need to restrict the foundation numbers.[80] However, the commissioners wanted the foundation to be opened to boys seeking secondary instruction from any part of Scotland, which was perhaps the most unacceptable recommendation for the Heriot governors who strenuously argued that Heriot's bequest was exclusively for Edinburgh. The commissioners took the modern view that all endowments need to take account of changed circumstances, while improved communications and mobility made restrictions of locality less meaningful. In any case they did not believe that Heriot was concerned with restricting his endowment to Edinburgh.[81] However, it was difficult to refute the claim that 'we have been influenced by a desire to return to what we believe to have been the purposes of the testator, modifying the interpretation of these only in so far as the altered circumstances of the country and the increase in the fund demand'.

Fortunately for the Heriot governors the Colebrooke Commission had no executive powers, but with Heriot's the largest and richest of the unreformed endowments, reform was inevitable. Yet the governors still believed that they could reform themselves and stave off the 'worst' aspects of Colebrooke. The return to power of the Conservatives in the spring of 1874 helped them in this, yet nothing could be taken for granted. On 1 April 1875 the treasurer laid a copy of the Colebrooke Report on the council room table, while Bailie Tawse explained its implications for the Hospital. The governors set up another special committee of eleven under Tawse, with full powers to take all steps it considered necessary or desirable.[82] It also produced a printed statement of their views, which was forwarded to the Home Secretary and the Lord Advocate. It then organised a deputation under Bailie Tawse, including the treasurer, to go to London when M.E. Grant Duff[83] was introducing his pro-Colebrooke motion in the Commons on 9 July 1875.

In the ensuing debate, Duff praised the commission's suggestion that Heriot's become a *Realschule* and pressed for endowments to be used to improve secondary education. John Ramsay,[84] a commission member, drew attention to the great similarities between the recommendations being put forward now and the governors' own proposals of 1870. James W. Barclay[85] was keen to liberalise and modernise endowments and suggested that as founders wished to do the maximum amount of good, the funds should be used to do precisely that, taking changed circumstances into account. Colebrook[86] was pleased with the reception his report had received in

Scotland, but he understood that some governors were unwilling to part with power. He held that the time for indiscriminate gratuitous education was over and that competition would improve the quality of education. As far as possible the wishes of original founders should be considered, but Parliament had to ensure that institutions conferred the greatest benefit on the greatest number. At this time, given that Scotland was well endowed with elementary schools and universities, but behind all other European countries in secondary schools, there was no doubt how the government could produce the greatest benefit. Playfair wanted the Edinburgh endowments to be spread throughout Scotland, arguing that Heriot's bequest had been altered in the past to suit contemporary requirements in order to do good, and it needed to be altered again.

As expected, McLaren led the defence of the Hospital. The commission had not included anyone acquainted with the management of the Edinburgh institutions, had resisted the inclusion of the President of the Chamber of Commerce, and had included only one Conservative in its total of seven members. Its report had been unanimously rejected by all fifty-four members of the governing body. Moreover 'during the last three yearly elections to the town council of Edinburgh, the candidates were asked whether they would approve of such an appropriation as this of the funds of Heriot's Hospital, and without one exception in each of the wards of the city not a man came forward and said he would approve of this proposition'.[87] The reason for this unanimity of feeling was because of the good management of the Trust over two and a half centuries. Now the yearly income was almost equal to the original sum left. 'The governors have not only done all that Heriot desired, but they have so administered the trust as to produce results conferring an incalculably greater benefit on the community.'[88] Moreover, the outdoor schools gave free education to more than 4,500 children and had been praised as the best conducted schools in Europe.[89] Even the commissioners admitted that they were the best schools in Edinburgh! Each child's education cost thirty shillings, so each poor mechanic's son in effect received a bursary of thirty shillings. Attendance was 89 per cent while Edinburgh board schools' attendance was only 73 per cent, and the only compulsion was moral, as teachers ejected pupils who were absent without good cause on three occasions. Few boys went on from Heriot's to university because they preferred to learn trades, and this seemed appropriate since Scotland already had a good percentage going on to university. The commissioners' suggestion of a *Realschule* for Edinburgh with a small population engaged in trades and manufactures seemed more appropriate for Glasgow. McLaren believed that the commissioners overvalued a university education, and suggested that poor boys did not wish to spend years at university and should not be disparaged for that. Why also did the commissioners think that free education pauperised, while those with bursaries at universities were not deemed pauperised? For McLaren such thinking suggested different standards between the poor and richer classes. Indeed open competition for bursaries would be unfair to the former, who could not compete on equal terms with the latter and was certainly not what George Heriot envisaged.

McLaren was supported by John Maitland,[90] Ernest Noel[91] and the MP for Stafford, Macdonald. Maitland[92] believed the commission had misrepresented the hospital system: 'an hospital was really nothing more than a public school for the poorer classes'.[93] He believed the commission sought to prejudice the public against hospitals by talking of a 'monastic system', yet the children therein saw more of their parents than children in public schools. The founding of Fettes showed how highly Scots thought of the system: it was an hospital for the better-off classes. Noel did not believe that the government should interfere with the will of founders of charities as long as they were not detrimental to public interest. He believed that recent changes in Heriot's Hospital improved the institution, and it was doing 'great good',[94] and he criticised the commission for recommending a change in the size of the governing body from 54 to 15.[95] Macdonald opposed the spoilation of funds of any institution, particularly in the case of Heriot's, where the governors were carrying out the founder's intention to educate the poor. If spoilation were to take place endowments would dry up.

The Conservative Lord Advocate Gordon believed that 'the question is not quite as clear as the Commissioners . . . appear to think . . . and . . . there are difficulties connected with the subject'.[96] He asked for more time to consider the matter with the Home Secretary, conscious as he was of the need to promote secondary education while at the same time protecting the rights of particular endowments. The governors were heartened by this statement but appreciated that the threat was far from over. Indeed *The Scotsman* took up the attack against McLaren and Heriot's on 12 July 1875.[97] It suggested that Noel had let the cat out of the bag when he mentioned changing the composition of the governing body. The loss of patronage was the real issue. Normal meetings, it claimed, were poorly attended, however, when a mistress in an outdoor school was to be appointed forty-eight turned up! When a treasurer had been elected all fifteen clerical members attended, while at the immediately preceding meeting no minister had been present to say prayers. In the previous four years an average of two ministers attended per meeting (indeed two ministers had not attended at all during that period).[98] Clearly the governing body had to be pruned to become more responsible and more in line with the size of other educational bodies.[99] On the same day *The Daily Review* contained an editorial on the 'preliminary skirmish' which had taken place in the Commons. It praised the Heriot governors for their long and efficient management of the trust but, with the provision of national education, suggested the time had come for change. The governors, instead of educating the poor to the low level of artisans and small tradesmen, should give them the chance to aim higher, because the 'University is the birthright of the poorest in a sense which is true of no other country in the world'. It was left to the Conservative *Courant* on 20 July to support the working men of Edinburgh who 'were beginning to take action to save the revenues from being diverted'.

Meantime a Heriot's trust defence committee (HTDC) was formed[100] and at a meeting on 24 July, chaired by its secretary, John C. Burn,[101] plans were made for a large public meeting. A committee was appointed to prepare a statement of their case to be submitted to the citizens, and a deputation was organised to meet with the trades council, which resulted in a very favourable reception. The appeal statement was ready by mid-August. It explained how the High School had raised its fees from £4 to £12 per annum while the subsidy from the burgh funds had been raised from £200 to £900. Thus poor citizens were deprived of this benefit while still contributing towards the education of children of those who were capable of educating them themselves. It further explained how the poor had also been set aside in Gillespie's, Stewart's, Watson's and Fettes'. It asked in the words of Duncan McLaren: 'When is this system of transfer from the poor to the rich to stop?' It called on the citizens to defend their own endowment and 'defeat this latest unscrupulous and illegal attempt to defraud us, the industrial and poorer classes of this city'.[102] Twenty-five thousand copies of the four-page statement were to be produced and distributed in time for the forthcoming municipal elections.

The HTDC held its public meeting, chaired by Bailie Tawse, in the Music Hall on Thursday, 14 October 1875. A line of speakers gave their wholehearted support to Heriot's. McLaren, who got a rousing reception, held that if the Heriot schools were taken over the rates would go up by three pence in the pound.[103] He put forward recent absentee figures: Gillespie's 12 per cent; School Board schools 37 per cent and Heriot schools 8 per cent:[104] if a child is absent on a Monday then he is often kept off the rest of the week to save money when fees are paid. He then rejected the claim that free schools pauperised: you could not be pauperised by using your own property. The Scottish tradition of John Knox had been free schools, and it was not until 1803 that fees were introduced. Free education remained in the USA, Canada, Switzerland, Australia, Norway and Denmark. Of the fifteen subjects the commissioners detailed as being taught in continental schools[105] fourteen of these were taught in Watson's and Stewart's.[106] Watson's in fact taught six subjects not taught in foreign schools![107] The pet scheme of the commissioners based on the German curriculum was merely 'clap-trap and humbug'. Maitland then spoke to contrast the 'openness of decisions made by the Heriot governors and the private decisions taken over Fettes'. The meeting also had contributions from a blacksmith, joiner and tailor before a resolution was accepted unanimously.[108]

Following the public meeting the correspondence columns of local newspapers were full of contributions to the debate. Grant and Maitland traded insults, with McLaren weighing in on Maitland's side. Dickson took on Lewis and was supported by a number who had personal experience of parents with children attending free schools but who could afford to pay fees.[109] One suggestion made was that fees would help to ensure that in poor families more than two children would be able to gain entry to the outdoor schools. However, it was *The Scotsman* newspaper which took every opportunity to attack McLaren and the Heriot's party.[110] McLaren was pressing for the abolition of boarding in the Hospital which was central to Heriot's Will,[111] while opposing the establishment of an industrial school which was not contemplated by Heriot's Will.[112] This resulted in McLaren being accused not only of inconsistency but of producing a new proposal not included in his address of December 1872. Moreover, when he suggested that the Hospital should be converted into a great civic secondary which would be attended by the poor boys and girls of the outdoor schools who desired the benefits of a higher education, *The Scotsman* accused him of adopting the arguments of Principal Grant for a 'ladder' scheme.

On Thursday 2 December 1875 a deputation from the HTDC, led by J.C. Burn, was admitted to the council room to lay a memorial before the governors at their monthly meeting. Burn presented the resolutions passed at the public meeting in October, strongly condemning the Colebrooke Report.[113] Heartened by the reaction the HTDC sent a deputation of seven to meet with the Lord Advocate, which it did for over an hour on 23 December. The committee then turned its attention to the Association for the Promotion of Secondary Education in Scotland, which it attacked for promoting education theories at the expense of endowments such as Heriot's, which had been left for a special and distinctive purpose. The HTDC was concerned by the deputation from the association received by Home Secretary Cross on 11 May 1876.[114] However, it became apparent that Cross had no immediate plans for endowments, which gave the Heriot's party the initiative meantime, and on 1 June the governors agreed that the special committee contact other hospitals with a view to taking joint action to enable them to extend the benefits of their institutions to those classes in the community for whom they were primarily designed.[115]

Despite pressure from the special committee the governors delayed making final decisions, instead enlarging the special committee to fifteen (from twelve) and instructing it to consider the adequacy of the existing accommodation in the Hospital, and to report on what measures could be taken under existing powers to extend the benefit of the Hospital. At a further general meeting, on 6 July, Bailie Tawse persuaded the governors to resurrect their plans of 1845–6, when four new classrooms were planned on the north-west portion of the Hospital grounds. Although they did not commit themselves to erecting these classrooms the governors agreed to examine the proposals in view of their need for more accommodation to teach higher education to the sons of burgesses attending the outdoor schools.[116] Tawse pressed on, and at a meeting on 2 August the governors accepted the motion that the Hospital begin competitive exams to elect sons of burgesses from the outdoor schools who would receive £5 annually in lieu of clothing and attend Hospital classes.[117]

During the summer the special committee met on 17 July and asked superintendent of works Chesser to report on the Hospital classrooms and the usage of other rooms, on how the Hospital could be altered to improve classrooms (assuming 120 residents), on how it could be changed for wholly educational purposes, with buildings in the grounds for boarding, and how it could be developed for wholly boarding with buildings in the grounds for educating the boys. It met again on 25 and 31 July and inquired from Dr Wood, architect Robert Anderson and Chesser what arrangements were needed to make the Hospital suitable for the accommodation of 120 residents and 60 non-residents.

All this information was available at the next meeting on 10 November, when house-governor Bedford was asked to give his educational opinion on the various proposals.[118] Treasurer Lewis updated the governors on the activities of the Association for Promoting Secondary Education: at a meeting in Edinburgh the week previously there had been talk of the resistance offered by 'local jealousy or vested interests' being overcome by a government initiative, and there was also an expectation that a select committee would be appointed which would result within a year of an executive commission dealing with the question. Lewis argued that the Hospital was in 'imminent peril'[119] and pressed for action.[120] The special committee recommended that the governors apply to Parliament for a private Act to extend the powers of the governors. Given the importance of the decisions to be taken, the meeting was, according to one report, 'stormy'[121] as some governors complained of the limited time they were being given to make up their minds. It was agreed that in the first instance the Lord Advocate and Home Secretary should be consulted to see if they were willing to introduce a bill empowering the governors to prepare a provisional order, and they should meet again within the week.

The governors reassembled on Thursday 16 November in private. A sub-committee had met with the Lord Advocate, who was unable to give any information on the government's intentions. The governors were divided on the issue, but after a prolonged discussion Councillor Anderson's view, in favour of a provisional order, prevailed over Bailie Cranston's,[122] by 22–8.[123]

The annual general meeting in mid-November of the Association for Promoting Secondary Education in Edinburgh resulted in the reactivation of the HTDC, which dispatched the usual deputation to the Lord Advocate. However, there was a growing feeling and realisation that matters were coming to a head. House-governor Bedford brought up to date his 'History of the Hospital' embodying the important changes of the last six years, as he expected imminent legislation on endowed institutions.[124] When the Queen's speech announced that a government measure would be brought forward, McLaren, supported by Maitland and Cameron, tried to forestall it by introducing his Hospitals [Scotland] Bill into the House of Commons in mid-February 1878. It was almost exactly a replica of Moncrieff's Act of 1869, which had expired in 1871, being a permissive measure for facilitating the operation of self-reform. No institution would be touched until its own governors or trustees became convinced that it needed reform. Given the history of the 1870s which had entailed the failure of the provisional order route and the five bulky blue books of evidence which had overwhelmingly put the case for change, McLaren was whistling in the wind. When on 29 March the Duke of Richmond published the government bill on endowed schools and hospitals, McLaren withdrew his. Richmond's bill was as expected: it included a commission, mainly from parties hostile to existing institutions, with wide powers to amend existing endowments and the right of the Secretary of State to override governing bodies.[125] The special committee met on 8 April and immediately sent a deputation of nine to London to lobby

Richmond and the Lord Advocate, and put their case in a series of meetings from 10–12 April. On their return a special general meeting of the governing body was called for 22 April to review the situation.

At the meeting a group from the HTDC, with George Stephen as chief spokesman, was heard, and he pressed the governors to call a public meeting on the bill, which, having passed through the Lords, had been given over to the Commons six days earlier. After the deputation left, the governors discussed the progress of the bill. Their supporters had gained some concessions in committee but the governors still objected strongly to the threat to disfranchise governors and give power to the Secretary of State to divert the institutions from the purposes contemplated by founders. The governors gave the special committee a watching brief as the bill entered its second reading in the Commons. Meantime, the committee met with representatives from the Edinburgh School Board, which supported the governors in their fight and encouraged them to inform the citizens of Edinburgh of the threat. Fortified by such support the governors issued a 'statement' to stir the hearts and minds of the Edinburgh populace on 4 May. Another deputation led by Bailie Tawse went to London, this time to lobby members of the Commons, while separate delegations of the town council and the Edinburgh School Board did likewise. The HTD Association held a public meeting in the Music Hall, Edinburgh, which in turn led to the organisation of a further deputation to go to London. Given such pressure and agitation the parliamentary correspondent of *The Daily Review* on 9 May related that 'there is a very decided feeling among certain Liberal members, which also extends to the Conservative ranks, against the passing of the bill in its present form'. The deputations joined up with sympathetic MPs and had meetings with Home Secretary Cross and the Lord Advocate which, according to press accounts, seem to have gone well.[126] The governors were hopeful of alterations being made in the bill to meet some of their objections.

The counter-attack was not long in coming. In the columns of *The Scotsman*[127] Alexander Craig Sellar asked whether it was 'fair to the people of Scotland that the multitude of educational trusts and endowments which are scattered up and down the country, and which, collectively, are of something like eight times the value of the Heriot Foundation, considerable though that Foundation is, should be retained in a state of comparative uselessness because the managers of the Heriot Foundation see, or imagine that they see, some indefinite danger which may in some indefinite way affect their interest if the bill becomes law'. A powerful group led by Colebrooke met with Cross and Lord Advocate Watson and pressed for a limited period of fifteen months to be given to trustees to bring forward reforms, after which, failing action, the commissioners should acquire certain initiating powers. Lyon Playfair felt that the opposition to reform had been exaggerated, and Scottish trusts should be reformed in the same way as English trusts.

During the various meetings Cross appears to have exhibited his disapproval of the Colebrooke Report and in particular supported the retention of Heriot's as an Edinburgh trust and agreed that there should be no arrangement to grant bursaries to be competed for from all parts of Scotland and all classes. Cross also accepted the need for amendments to ensure that any revision of a provisional order would not include any radical alteration without the approval of the governing body. He also conceded that the Trust representation should continue to be localised. These concessions seemed to be a complete victory for the Heriot party, but given the Home Secretary's previous championing of the local administration of local trusts they should not have been a real surprise. Cross appreciated that an unamended bill would have given him such extensive powers as to ensure tremendous pressure on him from all sides, although he did retain the right to veto proposals. He therefore resisted attempts to 'strengthen' the bill and retained its permissive character, withholding from the commissioners the power of initiating reform. However, Cross conceded that if trustees did not take advantage of the period of grace then the government would move toward compulsory legislation.

The bill, as amended, became the Endowed Institutions (Scotland) Act on 8 August, 1878. Like its predecessor of 1869, it set up an executive commission to end in December 1880. It gave Heriot's a breathing space but the governors appreciated that they had only a limited time to settle the long-running issue. They procured copies of it immediately and began to discuss what powers they should apply for in a new provisional order.[128]

Following a number of meetings of the special committee a draft of a proposed provisional order was ready by the end of January 1879.[129] After further tinkering three special meetings of governors were held on 12, 17 and 21 March to finalise the order. It was decided by 20–7 not to include the Revd Giffen's motion for power to reduce the present number of foundationers, nor clause 7 of the 1870 order, by 17–5, which sanctioned the boarding out of resident foundationers. After letters from McLaren and discussions with Lord Shand and Thomas Knox [President and treasurer of the Schools of Arts respectively] an amendment was carried on clause 20 concerning proposals for the Watt Institute. The governors approved the new order and petitioned the Secretary of State.[130]

The Heriot provisional order of 1879 was a more radical document than that of 1870. The governors appear to have been determined to ram home their seeming advantage. Firstly, the position of the outdoor schools was to be maintained and no longer to be dependent upon surplus revenue but to have as great a claim on the trust as the Hospital itself. No longer was there any intention to charge fees; despite all the pressure on this issue the governors were in no mood to compromise.[131] Secondly, the Hospital was to retain the 120 resident foundationers – the 'evils' of monasticism being conveniently forgotten – but was also to have the same number of day scholars,[132] 'sons of burgesses of Edinburgh whose parents may not be sufficiently able to maintain them'.[133] Its instruction was to be not only a liberal English, but also an advanced classical, commercial and scientific education. The governors would be allowed to reject unsuitable applicants on character or educational grounds. Significantly, as well as the free education on offer, day scholars were to receive £7 per annum for clothing. This extension was aimed at encouraging poor parents to apply to the Hospital, but it was a considerable challenge to Colebrooke's emphasis on merit and open examination. Thirdly, and a new inclusion, the governors asked 'to erect, found, and carry on a higher or secondary school or schools'[134] with priority for children of deceased burgesses of Edinburgh who might be in poor circumstances, then children of burgesses of Edinburgh who were unable to maintain them, and finally children of poor persons of Edinburgh. As entry was to be by competitive examination, rivalry with existing institutions would be intensified. Fourthly, the work of the Heriot Foundation was to be extended in a number of ways: girls 'of promise and merit'[135] were to be given bursaries of £15 per annum for three years to gain higher education and the governors might establish girls' schools in the future; evening classes were included, with provision for secondary education with fees, and the transfer of the Watt Institute and School of Arts to the Heriot Trust was to take place with an assurance that it would be maintained, improved and extended as 'a college for providing technical and general education for the industrial classes of both sexes'.[136] Finally, an extension of bursaries was envisaged: bursaries would be given to resident foundationers who became apprentices, and sixteen bursaries of £30 per annum for four years were open to day scholars who became 'hopeful' scholars at the University of Edinburgh.[137] Allowances of £5 per annum were to be available to any Hospital day scholar or any pupils at the new Higher schools to continue education, but were to be granted annually and after examination.[138]

The governors were pleased with their labours. They had produced a comprehensive scheme which was aimed at strengthening the provision of education in Edinburgh. It was a 'ladder' system which was designed to carry deserving scholars, the children of the poor, by easy gradations from the elementary schools to the end of their university course, making provision at the same time for the new requirements in education. It was commended for being devised in a 'wise, liberal and comprehensive spirit,'[139]and it was expected that it would be supported enthusiastically by the citizens of Edinburgh.[140]

On 1 April a meeting of the subscribers to the Watt Institute, with Lord Shand presiding, was held in Chambers Street to consider the proposal that its buildings and other property should be given over to the Heriot governors for an industrial college.[141] Given its critical condition Shand and Knox had negotiated an arrangement with the Heriot governors for which they now sought approval. In return for their building, worth £11,000, they received a guarantee of representation for the existing Board in the continued adminis- tration and management of the institution.[142] Overwhelmingly the meeting agreed with the proposals. Another hurdle had been overcome.

Home Secretary Cross forwarded the Heriot petition and proposed provisional order to the commissioners on 19 April 1879. Following the usual procedure the commissioners, chaired by Lord Moncrieff,[143] took oral evidence, beginning their work on Heriot's in Dowell's Rooms, George Street, Edinburgh, on Monday 26 May. The chief spokesman for the Heriot party was Bailie Tawse, who immediately had to explain why the composition of the governing body was not to be changed.[144] He also had to explain why the governors would not charge fees and contended that there were sufficient poor burgesses[145] in Edinburgh to fill a secondary school.[146] Each of the commissioners returned to this issue of fees.[147] Tawse argued that Heriot's had no money to extend bursaries beyond Edinburgh, and when pressed he argued that such bursaries were not needed, as the University was well endowed with one bursary for every five or six students in the Faculty of Arts.[148] In reply to Ramsay's questioning Tawse explained the numbers and difference between the beneficiaries of Heriot's trust: 4,939 attending outdoor schools with free education, books and stationery; 213 in the Hospital, made up of 120 resident foundationers, sixty non-residents who received education, clothing, dinner in the evenings and apprentice fee, and thirty-three day- scholars as a 'trial'[149] who received education and £5 allowance for clothing. The Order would end the class of non-residents who would become day scholars receiving education and £7 for clothing. Answering Donaldson's questions, Tawse admitted that the governors did not wish to accept a government grant, because it would mean interference in areas like religious education. He also had to defend the retention of 120 boarders in the Hospital, suggesting that privately some governors did not support the decision.

Two days later the commissioners reconvened in Messrs Lyon and Turnbull's rooms, and took evidence firstly from Sir Alexander Grant of Edinburgh University. He claimed that his university had only seven open bursaries for 2,600 students[150] and would be content if Heriot bursaries were increased from ten to twenty in number and from £20 to £30 in value.[151] He argued that it would be impossible to overestimate the value of competitive bursaries in the Faculty of Arts as an incentive to the schools to send up their pupils to the University in an advanced state of preparation. Then David Lewis, treasurer of the trust, gave evidence. He tried to explain the change in opinion of the governing body on charging fees since 1870.[152] He attributed this to two factors: firstly, because the governors were fully aware of the difficulties that prevailed on the part of many applicants to educate their children; and secondly, because public opinion was against the proposal to charge fees. On the ability of parents to pay fees Lewis had no hesitation in saying that generally they were not in a position to educate their children. He had done a random survey of 100 schedules and found the average income was just over £1 per week.[153] It was Lewis's impression that they did not apply unless they were really in somewhat struggling circumstances, knowing that the governors were exceedingly strict. He thought that the citizens of Edinburgh desired to adhere to the Will of the founder and did not wish to depart from the principle of free education.

The next session was in the same venue on Saturday 7 June when Duncan McLaren gave evidence for most of the afternoon. He strongly defended the Heriot Trust as an Edinburgh trust with St Andrews University having no legitimate claim. He argued that the passage of the 1876 Burgess Act[154] removed the grounds for some of the recommendations of the Colebrooke Commission. Although he did not favour the hospital system he had changed his mind on it and no longer wanted it to be abolished entirely. He defended its retention given that the Hospital was open to so many in Edinburgh and that the boys included so many poor and fatherless children of drunken and improvident parents. He defended gratuitous education and advocated the abolition of school fees throughout the country. Overall his contribution was an able defence of Heriot's, but hardly a demolition of the University party, as McLaren's biographer claimed.[155]

On Monday 9 June the commissioners interviewed George Stephen,

chairman of the HTDC, and concentrated their questioning on the 1870 order. Stephen claimed that the citizens had not been aware of its contents until it was rejected. 'But no sooner did we find what the clauses in the Order were than at the next election we dismissed from the Council those who were in favour of the clauses. We only left those in the Council who confessed contrition.' He gave over to Moncrieff at the close of his examination a copy of the resolutions that had been passed at the public meetings in Edinburgh. This evidence was counter-productive, suggesting as it did that the governors were not free agents but were controlled by the HTDC. This explained why the order of 1879 was so much more radical than that of 1870. Such developments were bound to be influential in the thinking of the commissioners, whose wish to reform the composition of the governing body was greatly strengthened.[156]

The commissioners took further evidence on 20 June when Dr James Taylor, late secretary of the Board of Education of Scotland, discussed the free education offered by the Heriot outdoor schools. Given the success of the latter in achieving a high attendance of pupils, Taylor recommended 'an experiment to be made in free education in some Board schools in different parts of the country'.[157] He was followed by Professor Calderwood, who had been chairman of the first school board in Edinburgh for three years.[158] His experience was that a large proportion of the better working men did not wish their children to be sent to a free school, and that the children attending the Heriot schools were somewhat lower in class terms than those of the board schools. However, the latter also contained a class decidedly lower than those who attended the Heriot schools. He believed it would be a real gain if a uniform scale of fees were charged in all schools. The Heriot trust would confer greater advantage on the City if fees were introduced and grants taken up, for this would allow trust funds to pay the fees of the really needy. Calderwood did not believe that free schools improved attendance, for they removed the incentive from parents who wished to get their money's worth from education.

Calderwood was followed by house-governor Bedford who gave his views on the hospital system.[159] Originally he had been a great critic, but since the boys had been allowed to mix more freely with the boys of the town it had improved and 'the Hospital [i.e. Heriot's] was in as favourable condition as any of the kind in the country'. He objected, however, to the boarding-out system, and believed the Hospital had to be retained, as Heriot had established it for fatherless boys. He

Robert Lawson Tait (1845-1899), an Auld Callant, qualified in medicine and became assistant to Sir James Simpson. He was one of Scotland's greatest surgeons and a famous gynaecologist.

hoped that it might be converted into a large day-school, and that the 50 orphans[160] might be educated there, and maintained in a home either in the hospital or outside, thereby having an opportunity of mixing with other boys. Asked by Moncrieff about free education, Bedford opposed it. He did not think Hospital funds should be used for the purpose of subsidising education.

On the following day the commissioners took evidence firstly from W.W. Waddell, a schools inspector. He traced the history of outdoor inspection[161] and from the results Moncrieff agreed that Heriot schools 'were reasonably well managed'. Waddell gave detailed statistical evidence showing that overall Heriot schools had better examination results than board schools. According to HMI Gibson this could be explained in terms of the teachers having higher salaries, the masters being assisted by apprentice teachers and the school buildings being of a superior kind.[162] The Heriot schools also had other advantages: the children attended more regularly; they did not need to comply with government regulations and could put backward scholars into the infant schools no matter what their age. However, there were disadvantages: firstly, the class of children attending. A teacher had classified children as those with parents who were in fairly comfortable circumstances and attentive to the interests of their children, those with parents who were somewhat negligent and poor, and those whose parents were extremely negligent and poor. The Heriot schools admitted the second group, and left the first and third groups to the board schools. Other disadvantages included the staffing, which was at the government minimum, much below the board schools' levels,[163] and the lack of desk accommodation, which had been a complaint for ten years. Significantly in 1877 only fourteen pupils had been presented in the sixth standard,[164] which did not bring credit upon the Heriot schools, and the higher number of successful presentations at higher standards in the board schools reflected the better class of children attending the latter.

The commissioners then re-examined treasurer Lewis.[165] He admitted that for some years children as old as ten years of age remained in the infant department because they did not know their alphabet, but this practice had now ceased. When pressed on why the governors had changed their minds on fees since 1870 he suggested that they now appreciated the needy circumstances of many parents and the public had shown itself decidedly opposed to charging fees. In the outdoor schools, in 1878, 2,314 schedules were issued and 1,634 accepted, the average wage of the latter being 17s. 4d. per week.[166] The governors had also changed their position on the reduction of resident foundationers since the passage of the 1876 Burgess Act, which had greatly increased the number of orphan children eligible for election. As for the university bursaries which Heriot stipulated, Lewis held that Heriot was interested in the boys and not the University. He favoured retaining apprentice allowances because they guided and controlled the apprentices, turning them into good useful citizens.

The commissioners quickly determined their views and reported back to the Home Secretary in a letter dated 21 July 1879. They accepted that the proposal to take over the Watt Institute deserved the approval of the Secretary of State, incorporating the recent arrangement by which the directors were to be represented on the new board. This was of sufficient importance 'to justify its being the subject of a Provisional order'. However, the other proposals of the Heriot governors were 'imperfect and unsatisfactory in themselves' and were not suitable as the foundation of a permanent settlement of the affairs of the Hospital. Given the evidence about the unsatisfactory hospital system the commissioners were surprised not to find a clause reducing the number of resident foundationers (as in 1870). Given the agreement in 1870 about the need to use Heriot funds more extensively they were also surprised that the governors did not intend to increase the bursaries to the University nor to exact fees in the outdoor schools. Without dealing with these matters the commissioners did not think it possible 'to place the administration of the Hospital on a right or satisfactory footing'. The commissioners felt that the evidence regarding the injurious nature of the hospital system was clear; the governors in 1870 wished to benefit the University and charge fees. No good explanation had been given as to why these areas were omitted from the order of 1879.[167] The changed circumstances of the period demanded that these issues be tackled; the conflicting views on the results of free education in the Heriot schools proved a need to deal with the matter. These omissions alone influenced the commissioners in rejecting the scheme. However, the evidence of George Stephen relating the control and pressure on the governors was incompatible with good administration. For this reason there had to be 'a thorough revision of the governing body', which was manifestly 'too large for efficient administration'.

The commission report was given over to the Heriot governors on 4 December 1879 and the special committee of the governors met on 6 and 7 January 1880 in the treasurer's chambers,[168] and finalised a statement which was unanimously approved by the governors.[169] It was a lengthy defence of their position. In particular it stressed the new situation following the 1876 Act, which would ensure within a short time that the 'hospital will consist almost exclusively of boys who have been deprived of one or both parents'. It defended the boys turned out by the hospital system: they had extensive playgrounds, library and reading room; they mixed with non-residents and day scholars, and spent annually 140 days out of the hospital: why was it different from Fettes? It believed its expenditure of £9,000 on the Watt Institute and sixteen additional bursaries for Edinburgh[170] was fair. Charging fees had been suggested in 1874 to increase revenue and give more poor persons the benefit of the education provided, but the governors now held it to be against the wishes of the founder and opposed by the Town. The altering of the composition of the governing body was ruled out as 'too extravagant and revolutionary to be seriously entertained'. Moreover, it was subversive of the constitution of the trust and unsupported by claims of maladministration. The governors themselves challenged the damaging evidence of Stephen. The public had known of the 1870 order which had been widely published, and at the November municipal elections not a single question was put to candidates on its content – issues such as the City water supply taking priority.[171] The provisional order of 1879 (like that of 1870) was aimed at providing secondary education to the class which needed it, and on these grounds the governors appealed to the Home Secretary to accept their order.

In a real sense the contest was now a class struggle based on different views as to the rightful beneficiaries of Heriot's bequest. It can be argued that the governors in 1870 had been persuaded to endow secondary education and the trust was benefiting primarily the same social class as that to which the resident foundationers belonged. By 1879 the governors had been persuaded to develop primary and secondary education and benefit a lower class of the community. If the 1870 scheme recognised the trust as a middle-class trust, the scheme of 1879 sought to treat it as an artisan-class trust. The omission of a number of features of the 1870 order made it more expressly one for the benefit of the other classes. It was this move toward a working-class trust, in harmony with the principles, or in obedience to the orders, of the HTDC which made it objectionable to the commissioners. Was the change justified? Unfortunately for the order's supporters Tawse himself in 1872 had admitted that the then foundationers were often from a lower class than Heriot intended. He believed the beneficiaries should be those of Heriot's own class who had carried on business but who had fallen back in their circumstances. This was indeed the original qualification, as Heriot stated in his Disposition, and despite all the arguments of McLaren and the governors it still seemed the most plausible explanation.

The victory of Gladstone in the general election of April 1880 meant a change in the personalities of government if not its policies. The re-election victories of McLaren and Cowan in Edinburgh[172] certainly strengthened the hands of the governors, who pressed their claims again. In early June 1880 deputations from the governors and the HTDC had interviews with the Home Secretary, Sir William Harcourt, the former accompanied by the new Lord Advocate McLaren (son of Duncan McLaren). A deal seems to have been struck, and the governors left London with high hopes.[173] Within a week the Home Secretary produced a revised provisional order, which was discussed by the governors at a special meeting on 11 June, when they went over the order clause by clause. No change in the governing body was to be made and free education was to continue. These 'victories' for the governors were to some extent balanced by the provision for a reduction in the number of resident foundationers to sixty, an increase in the number of open bursaries by ten (each worth £30 per annum) and the prohibition of any additional free school. The motion of the Lord Provost expressing the governors' 'acquiescence' with the changes was agreed unanimously.[174] The special committee was instructed to have the order placed before Parliament as soon as possible.[175] The HTDC also fell into line behind the order. Meantime uproar broke out at Harcourt's decision and he faced 'prodigious efforts – so terribly prodigious as to border on the ridiculous'[176] to intensify opposition to the order in Parliament.[177] Colebrooke led the attack in the Commons on 17 June, but although Harcourt held that the matter was not finally concluded, he defended the compromise as a step forward. He committed himself to giving the order over to the commissioners, which he did immediately. They responded with a memorandum dated 26 June, which confirmed their previous view that there should be no sanctioning of the order unless it was accompanied by 'a thorough inquiry into the constitution of the governing body'. Other questions which needed to be dealt with included the financing of the additional bursaries,[178] a complete examination of the accounts, [179] the position and number of resident foundationers and the whole area of the expediency of continuing the free schools on present lines. Only the take-over of the Watt Institute gained their support.

The Lord Advocate immediately wrote to the governors asking whether a change in the governing body could be arranged.[180] The special committee met on 28 June and rejected this out of hand but the governors were increasingly worried at the course events were taking when the government published Earl Spencer's bill.[181] The governors persuaded the Duke of Buccleuch to petition against the 'despotic powers of the Commission which were subversive' of popular government[182] during the second reading in the Lords on 9 July.[183] Lord President Spencer expressed the government's intention to reform endowments as only 2 per cent of them had taken advantage of the permissive legislation.[184] He proposed a commission of five which would lay schemes before Parliament (similar to the earlier English legislation).[185]

The special committee met again on 12 July and decided that 'considering the objectionable nature of its provisions' the bill should be 'opposed in every possible way'.[186] In particular, the committee stressed the need to ensure endowments were retained for use in the localities for which they were granted; that institutions whose provisional orders were under consideration of the commissioners or Home Secretary should be exempted from the operation of the bill; and that the institutions which were managed by Governing Bodies wholly or to a large extent popularly elected and whose proceedings are regularly reported through the press should be exempted from the bill or at least not have their governing body changed.[187] A deputation of six, including the Lord Provost, clerk and treasurer, was dispatched to London to press their case.[188]

The special committee met again the following day to finalise the contents of a letter to Harcourt. In it the governors answered the point in the commissioners' memorandum of 26 June. As the governors had deleted the proposal to build additional secondary schools and the number of foundationers was to be halved the money saved would pay for the bursaries. The composition of the governing body was not raised in the petition and was outwith the remit of the commissioners. The governors felt that they had already answered the charge of undue public opinion being brought to bear. The committee ended its letter by asking Harcourt to help them obtain the order.

In committee in the Lords the government's bill remained unscathed and none of the Heriot objections were accepted.[189] It had its third and final reading on 26 July.[190] The dissenting voice of Lord Denman was overcome and the bill moved on to the Commons.[191] The special committee had separate meetings on 26, 27 and 28 July, and prepared a statement for MPs explaining why the Hospital should be exempted from the bill. It was a document of eight articles which ended by warning MPs of the power commissioners would have under the bill to change existing endowments, and their fear of 'arbitrary proposals'.[192] In particular, certain parties desired to abolish the present governing body and appropriate the funds of the Hospital to provide 'secondary education for all classes, without regard to either locality, circumstances or necessity'. The governors believed that if passed the bill would allow the dispossession of the poor of Edinburgh of their inheritance and its appropriation for the benefit of a class for whom it was never intended by George Heriot.[193]

The bill was introduced into the Commons on 27 July, with its second reading set for 2 August. The special committee had a second meeting on 28 July and organised a deputation of eight led by the Lord Provost and including the clerk and treasurer to proceed to London and take all measures necessary to oppose the bill.[194] It found the vice-president of the Education Department, Mundella, sympathetic to their efforts to keep funds in the locality and for the class to whom they were left.[195] It also met with Lord Advocate McLaren and protested that the bill was being hurried through at the end of a parliamentary session. Both Mundella and McLaren seemed willing to accept amendments but were unwilling to agree to the exclusion of the Hospital from the bill. At a meeting of Scottish MPs on 9 August a majority favoured going ahead with the bill, but a strong minority intimated their determination to continue opposing the measure.[196] The government, faced with this situation, began to waver, and the treasurer remained in London to monitor the situation, reporting on 17 August that the bill had been withdrawn, as there was not enough time available to proceed with it. Relief, however, again was to be short-lived, for the government announced that it would bring forward a bill with similar objectives in the next parliamentary session.

The special committee met on 30 August and had before them various letters from Lord Advocate McLaren, and Harcourt's letter of 27 July, in which he stated that he felt he could go no further with the Heriot scheme, except the section dealing with the Watt Institute. He believed that the only course open to the governors, if they were unwilling to come under a general Act, was an application to Parliament. Meantime, on 13 September, Lord Spencer visited the Fountainbridge Board School then toured the Hospital, being shown round by Ridpath, as Bedford was indisposed, and ending his fact-finding mission by visiting the school in High School Yards. Such events, however, were but side-issues to the main event. With Bailie Cranston holding that the preservation of the Heriot funds in the hands of the present governors was 'the Alpha and Omega of the Council's work at present,'[197] the special committee met on 27 October, 3 and 9 November, and took soundings as to future tactics.

Having in December 1880 prolonged the Endowment Institutions (Scotland) Act for another seven months until 31 July 1881, on Friday 14 January 1881 Vice-President of the Council Mundella introduced the Endowed Schools and Hospitals (Scotland) Bill into the Commons.[198] Although substantially on the same lines as the 1880 bill he believed it was an improvement on the bill abandoned the previous August. It was not the government's intention to delocalise endowments. Secondary education would not be indiscriminate. The number of commissioners would be increased from five to seven. The municipal representation was to be maintained. In order to appease its critics the government was taking on policies of 'an undoubted Heriot ring'.[199] However, given the powers of the commissioners and the sweep of the bill the Heriot governors retained their suspicions.

Duncan McLaren had been the leading supporter of the Heriot cause in Parliament since his election as an Edinburgh MP in 1865. Certainly his work in 1880 had much to do with the failure of the proposed government bill.[200] With business unfinished he had been persuaded to stand again for election in April 1880, despite his advanced years. However, his son John, when appointed Lord Advocate, lost his seat in the consequent by-election (May 1880) and failed again at Berwick-on-Tweed. Duncan decided to stand down in Edinburgh to make way for John at a by-election in January 1881.[201] This was a great blow to Heriot's, but retaining a McLaren in an influential position in a Liberal government seemed a source of some compensation. Indeed during the election campaign the citizens of Edinburgh naturally took advantage of the situation and pressed John McLaren for guarantees for the defence of the Hospital. At a packed meeting in the Music Hall on 22 January, McLaren explained how he had impressed on the education department the desirability of maintaining popular election to governing bodies, and he believed Mundella was sympathetic to this plea. He committed himself to supporting bodies like the Heriot's board and opposed the usurping of functions by cliques. Such a stance and his commitment towards continuing the work of his father were instrumental in ensuring a victory of 11,390 votes to 3,940 over his Liberal opponent (the Conservatives did not stand).

The special committee of the governors met on 3 and 4 February and reviewed Mundella's bill clause by clause. It produced a memorial to be forwarded to the Lord Advocate, objecting to the proposed change in the composition of representative governing bodies, the proposed discontinuing of apprentice allowances and the denial of an appeal to the Court of Session against a decision of the commissioners. It was finalised at another meeting on 8 February and forwarded to McLaren, who acknowledged receipt and promised their comments would be considered by the education department before the bill went any further.

By mid-May it was increasingly clear that the government was struggling to get through its programme, particularly given the serious Irish crisis and its dominance of parliamentary time. Lord Advocate McLaren, however, was still working behind the scenes, and in a letter dated 14 May to the Lord Provost he told of his efforts to persuade Mundella that a popularly elected governing body should only be replaced by one with three-quarters of its members elected.[202] However, Mundella remained unconvinced, and deadlock resulted as the Heriot governors insisted on the representative principle.[203] It was the decision of McLaren to support the government and the education department which broke the impasse. He was immediately accused of a breach of trust, and the HTDC was reactivated; another deputation set off for London on 14 June.

Matters turned again when the Scottish members sought a meeting with the Home Secretary and Lord Advocate, and a number of the former held it inexpedient to progress further with the bill that session. They argued that there was no chance of such an important measure receiving adequate consideration and proper treatment if it were pressed forward so late in the parliamentary year. By early August it was being reported that 24 Scottish Liberal MPs had requested Gladstone to drop the bill, and seven of them actively blocked its further passage, complaining bitterly over Mundella's 'bullying tactics'.[204] The government reluctantly decided to withdraw the bill meantime,[205] but to show he meant business Mundella had a motion approved by the Commons on 17 August ordering completion of a questionnaire on educational endowments with specific information on governing bodies. Such action was a marker for another attempt by the government to deal with the issue in the following session.[206]

The elevation of Lord Advocate McLaren and his replacement by J.B. Balfour led to an electoral campaign in Edinburgh in August 1881. At his Music Hall meeting on 19 August one of the candidates, Buchanan, spoke of the 'burning question' in Edinburgh – the future government of Heriot's Hospital – and felt that any changes to its constitution had to retain two-thirds directly elected by the people of the Town.[207] His 'soundness' on this issue was a prerequisite for election, and he included specific support in his election address.[208] The matter was discussed at the Educational Institute of Scotland's general meeting in Edinburgh on the same day and was debated in September at the Trade Union Congress in London.

On 20 February 1882 Councillor Doig moved that as the government was about to introduce a bill to regulate endowments and promote secondary education the governors remit their 1870 provisional order to the special committee to remodel and amend.[209] In fact, Mundella did not introduce the new Educational Endowments (Scotland) bill into the Commons until 1 May,[210] claiming that its necessity had been 'admitted on all hands'.[211] The new measure had been 'altered . . . both in form and substance', and particularly on the disputed issue of governing bodies the bill provided a preponderance of popular representation where it already existed.[212] The forty-five clauses of the bill were published in full in *The Scotsman* on 3 May, and having digested its contents the special committee met three days later to discuss it. As the second reading of the bill was to take place on 16 May the Lord Provost and Bailie Anderson were sent to London to discuss the timing with Mundella, who agreed to postpone the reading for no more than six days. The special committee met again on 15 and 16 May and objected to clause 6 which ensured in the Heriot case that the majority of the new governing body would be popularly elected but would give the commissioners some control over what form this representation might take. A special meeting of the governors was held on 18 May and they insisted that no changes should be made in governing bodies unless these were 'clearly shown to be absolutely necessary'.[213] The governors refused to compromise on the issue: they were a stable and representative group combining local administration and popular government and they would not give way to an irresponsible body. They unanimously supported the detailed amendments which were then proposed.[214]

Following precedent and past success the governors sent a deputation of five, including the treasurer, to London. Accompanied by Edinburgh MPs Cowan and Buchanan it met Mundella, Lord Rosebery[215] and the Lord Advocate on 21 May. Although reassurances were given that the intention was not to reduce representative elements already existing, but to infuse new vigour into the administration of trusts by the introduction of kindred elements, the government would not accept the governors' amendments. On the other issue the governors received 'the most clear and emphatic assurance'[216] that there was no intention to delocalise or divert funds from original purposes. The meeting, although changing no positions, led to a growing optimism in the governors' ranks[217] that the government might modify the bill to bring it more into harmony with their view, for it was felt that if it did not the measure was 'doomed'.[218] Eight MPs placed opposing motions on the table of the Commons.

The special committee prepared a statement on its position and gave details on why the proposed bill was objectionable.[219] It was circulated on 13 June to all Scottish MPs. Meantime the retired Duncan McLaren proposed detailed amendments to the bill in an attempt to break the deadlock. The HTDC met and decided to petition Parliament to amend the bill (23 June). The governors sent a deputation of three to watch over the progress of the bill, while a separate clerical representation went to London to meet Mundella to put the case for protecting the position of the clergy.[220] With time short and options limited the government decided to sit on a Saturday to complete its business, and when this was proposed the government won the vote 130 to 109.[221] The second reading, therefore, took place on Saturday 15 July, between 5 p.m. and 7.35 p.m. and Mundella proposed amendments to clause 6, raising popular representation to two-thirds and an amendment to clause 15 to ensure that endowments left to the poor should not be alienated from them.[222] He also deleted all reference to endorsement of the recommendations of the commissioners appointed in 1872 and 1878. Despite objections to the debate 'in the fag-end of a Saturday, at the fag-end of a session'[223] all MPs who had put down blocking motions were given the opportunity to speak, but none put forward an amendment, although there remained a deep resentment of the limited time allowed for the bill.

When the bill went into committee in the Commons Buchanan led the attack. He pressed for concessions from the government, in particular demanding three-quarters as the proportion for the popularly elected element in governing bodies. The governors issued another statement to all Scottish MPs dated 19 July 1882. It concentrated on insisting on no change in the proportion of municipal representatives and on the free schools of the 1836 Act. The government pressed for another Saturday sitting and won easily by 130 to 36 on Thursday 20 July.[224] The marathon session began at 12.15 p.m. with Dr Charles Cameron defending free primary education.[225] He lost his amendment by 89 to 19.[226] The House then went into committee on the bill. Barclay led the defence of popularly elected governing bodies. He lost his amendment 95 to 12.[227] After nearly eleven hours the government succeeded in pushing forward, exposing the Heriot free schools to abolition. This now became the central issue and the battleground changed.[228]

A petition from 150 citizens to Lord Provost Boyd led to a public meeting on 27 July to 'protest against the action of the government in threatening to suppress the Free Out-Door Schools, and to misappropriate the Funds to other than the rightful Beneficiaries'. The special committee of the governors met again and determined to appeal to Premier Gladstone, explaining the dangers of alienating Edinburgh and the 'people of Scotland'. This approach did have its advantages, particularly as there was some evidence that the senior ranks of the government were genuinely surprised at the strength of feeling aroused in Edinburgh. Meantime, a petition on the issue was issued by the town council. Bad feeling erupted, however, when it was leaked that Lord Balfour of Burleigh was to be the chairman of the new commission.

Government thinking was clear: the appointment of the Tory Balfour would conciliate the House of Lords and keep the peers in check. Scottish Liberals were incensed. Separate deputations from the governors, the town council, the HTDC and a new citizens' committee all set off for London in early August. They met Lord Carlingford at the Education Office but gained nothing concrete from the interviews. The Hospital deputation prepared a statement for distribution to the peers and persuaded the Duke of Buccleuch to put forward various Heriot amendments. Meantime, the government announced the other members of the commission at the beginning of the Commons' debate on 2 August. In so doing Mundella took the wind from many sails: the five Liberals and two Conservatives included representatives of Edinburgh and Glasgow, and the mercantile and legal sections were also represented.[229] The group was seen as balanced and fair. The debate was good-humoured and the opponents of the bill gave the impression of wishing to bury the hatchet. The bill passed its third reading without major amendment.

Lord Carlingford moved the second reading in the Lords on 8 August, and although Buccleuch did his duty by Heriot's it came to nothing. *The Times* of that date typified the coolness of the establishment to the Heriot position. 'The circle of palatial buildings which girdles Edinburgh, and which are known as hospitals, have never been such valuable factors in the educational influences of Scotland as, considering their wealth, they might have been, and it was often hard to say whether they did more good than harm. While the real working educational institutions of Scotland suffer from chilling, benumbing poverty, they were smitten by the vices incident to opulence. Not having availed themselves of an opportunity to reform themselves, they have been taken in hand by parliament.' The Lords went into committee on the bill on 10 August, but Buccleuch's amendments and petition were rejected and the bill was passed for the third time on 14 August and received a royal assent four days later. It seemed as if the long battle was nearly over, with the Heriot 'Ring' in full retreat. However, the governors still had a few shots left in their locker.

With the Act taking effect on 1 November 1882 the governors had a brief respite until 24 November when the special committee met and authorised the clerk to draw up another draft scheme. This was presented to them on 20 December and after two further meetings on 2 and 12 January the governors thought that they were near to finalising their scheme. However, on 22 January the clerk tabled a circular just received from the commissioners regarding the preparation of schemes and a memorandum of suggestions. These required their draft scheme to be rewritten, which the governors decided to do despite the delay, in order to keep in with the commissioners.[230] The committee went over the scheme clause by clause, on 8 and 9 February and, after a discussion about the costs involved, on 14 February it was agreed that 'in the course of five or six years the governors would be able to carry out all the proposed Scheme'.[231] The whole governing body went over the proposals: the first twenty-nine clauses on 19 February[232] and the other twenty-one clauses two days later.[233]

The special committee met on 29 March to be informed that the governors' scheme[234] had been lodged with the commissioners and acknowledged. The clerk had also forwarded a copy to Edinburgh MPs Cowan and Buchanan, and also to Duncan McLaren. As usual the commissioners were not to be hurried and their reply was not forthcoming until late September, when the governors were informed that an inquiry on Heriot's Hospital would be held. The governors agreed that the Lord Provost would make a general statement on the objectives of the proposed scheme, and the committee conveners and trust officials would be on hand to give further information if required.[235]

The Balfour Commission met the Heriot party in the Merchants' Hall, Hanover Street, Edinburgh, at 11 a.m. on Wednesday 3 October. Lord Provost George Harrison, Bailie Anderson, the Revd C. Giffen, Bailie Hall, the Revd J. Webster,[236] Councillor Turnbull and treasurer David Lewis all gave evidence. The governors still stood by a governing body of fifty-four, which with committee work could mean as many as forty-seven meetings a year for some governors. They asked to provide for 120 foundationers who would be given £25 each to board out: they would sit a qualifying test and be given a general commercial and classical education. Between two and five hopeful scholars a year would still come from the foundationers.[237]

The issues which the commissioners returned to were not new territory: the size and composition of the governing body, the relationship between the clerical and municipal governors, and the poor attendance of some governors. Why not hand over the Hospital to the school board? Why the need for apprentice fees? Were there not many children at the Heriot schools who could pay fees? The cost of 'incidentals' and the accounts of the trust? Having answered these questions and having heard the evidence given by representatives of the school board and the High School to the commissioners, the Revd Giffen, Bailie Anderson and treasurer Lewis replied on 10 October 1883.[238]

So the matter rested until 11 July 1884 when the commissioners' Draft Scheme for the administration of the Hospital endowment and the Watt Institute and School of Arts was published.[239] Three days later it was examined by the special committee and the clerk completed a report on the proposed scheme on 6 August. It was immediately apparent that there was a 'wide divergence'[240] between the governors' scheme of February 1883 and the commissioners' proposals. The latter gave 'a greater prominence to technical education than the Act of 1882 appears to warrant',[241] and in so doing subordinated the hospital and emphasised the educational merits rather than the necessitous circumstances of the pupils. In particular, the governors objected to the proposal to change the governing body, the discontinuance of the outdoor schools, as they interfered with the board schools, the proposed revolution in the character and the history of the Hospital by excluding Greek from the curriculum,[242] the omission of the provision of apprentice allowances and bursaries to hopeful scholars, the transfer of the outdoor school buildings to the school board and the proposals envisaged for the Watt Heriot College which were far more extensive than the governors had intended. Given these great differences a large number of objections were produced.[243] On 29 September the special committee went over the draft of objections produced by the clerk and it accepted them unanimously.[244]

The secretary of the commissioners informed the governors that they would meet on Monday 20 October 1884 at 11.30am to hear parties on the objections to the draft scheme on Heriot's. Given the experience of other hospitals before the commissioners the governors determined not to be caught unawares and decided to have Counsel present. In fact, on the day, the Heriot Advocate, Gloag, took up about half of the total time for objections. He held that the governing body enjoyed 'the confidence of the public of Edinburgh and the poor of Edinburgh' which he deemed to be 'considerations outweighing almost anything', given that it had been subjected to three public inquiries and nothing untoward had been exposed.[245] He objected to the commission's proposals for the town council to nominate eleven of the new governing body of twenty-one as they deviated 'from its want of resemblance to what was proposed by the founder, from the want of certainty that there will be publicity of its proceedings, and from its want of responsibility to the public'.[246] He rejected university representation, as Heriot had excluded it. Gloag further contested that the Heriot schools should be discontinued, as they interfered with board schools, and no complaint had been received from the latter,[247] and if scholars had their fees paid there would be a 'great danger that they would be identified with the pauper-paid scholars, and that they would be subjected amongst their neighbours in the school to the stigma of pauperism'.[248] The bursaries suggested had 'too little regard to the necessities of the children and too much regard to the question of merit'.

Gloag thought Heriot was anxious to help destitute boys regardless of merit, which was related to previous advantage and previous effort.[249] Further the bursaries planned, of £5 and £10 (to a total sum of £2,000 per annum and awarded after competitive examination from state schools, with up to one-third reserved to Heriot's pupils) were not enough of an incentive for poor parents.[250] In its place Gloag wished to give foundationers £10 per annum for five years to find their way in life. Necessity should be placed before merit.[251]

Another area of contention for Gloag was the development of a modern commercial curriculum (as in France, or similar to Allan Glen's) which for the commissioners meant the end of classical training at Heriot's, and the necessity for prospective university students to proceed from Heriot's to the High School first. For Gloag this put a stigma of second class education on Heriot's.[252] He questioned the sums to be expended on the Watt Institution, suggesting that less should be spent on the 'somewhat dazzling and far-reaching scheme' proposed.[253] Generally the governors wished to preserve the links between the Hospital and the University, which the exclusion of Greek from the curriculum would break, and the provision of the poorer classes to have a classical education. The commissioners argued that allowing Gordon's to teach Greek since 1881 had led to 'a considerable amount of harm', weakening the High School of Aberdeen.[254] The governors, however, claimed that Heriot boys going to the High School had been abandoned as 'the boys were marked' and not well received due to their espirit de corps.[255] The commissioners continued to argue for a strengthening of the ladder through the High School, while the governors believed that poor boys would be competing on unequal conditions for university bursaries.[256]

Although the governors obtained a fair hearing, the commissioners were unimpressed by their objections. If the main issue was the existence of the free schools it was clearly expedient that the whole education of Edinburgh should be under one board, and the Heriot schools, although good in themselves, harmed the rest of the system. Moreover, the criticism remained that the poorest children were not always the recipients of free education and the Heriot schools, in accommodation terms at least, were not up to the government Code requirements. Certainly the commissioners did not take long over their deliberations. They submitted their scheme to the Scottish Education Department and it was laid on the table by the Heriot's clerk on 18 December and given over to the special committee, which met on 7 January 1885.

The commissioners had accepted the governors' contention that the governing body could not add to committees persons who were non-governors. They had also compromised, and instead of forcing Heriot's to hand over their outdoor school buildings to the school board, a clause allowed the governors to sell or lease them. However, in most other areas their objections had been dismissed. As was their right they determined to object again, and prepared another draft of objections, which were approved on 2 February by the committee, and two weeks later by the whole governing body.

The new 'Objectives' (1885) were similar in thrust, and indeed content, to the 1884 objections. They held that the scheme proposed paid too much attention to educational merits and too little to the necessitous circumstances of the beneficiaries.[257] They objected to competitive examinations being used for even the most elementary type of education. As ever, they vigorously opposed the 'unnecessary and violent change in the Governing Body' and the subordination of 'the great and original idea of the Founder and the School for which the funds were left to a new object of a magnitude quite unwarranted by any evidence placed before the Commissioners or required in such a City as Edinburgh'.[258] They complained bitterly that the Hospital Day School was to be limited to a higher commercial and elementary technical school,[259] while the foundationers would not be able to follow a learned profession unless they showed a marked predilection for classical learning at a prematurely early age.[260] Further the governors held that the proposed scheme unnecessarily restricted the class from which the foundationers were to come, and found it extraordinary that the free schools were to be abolished.[261]

To add insult to injury the governors felt that in their own proposals they had made ample provision for university and higher education. They had intended to establish twenty-four new bursaries and three fellowships in addition to the ten bursaries provided under Heriot's Codicil, which were to be increased to an annual value of £25 each. However, the commissioners proposed to give fifty bursaries to the University with a value of £1,320 per annum and three fellowships of £100 each; forty further bursaries were to go to the High School (at least £1,050); £1,000 was to be set aside for bursaries for girls and one-sixth of any surplus was to go to technological and training college bursaries. The total sum involved would be at least £3,820 per annum, which the governors deemed 'excessive', especially since the recipients would not be necessitous, but would accrue as the result of a competitive examination. They also objected to the principle of open competition for the bursaries, which they saw in terms of the governors providing the funds but having no voice in the selection of the bursars.

The governors unanimously agreed to their objections on 16 February 1885, and when they lodged them with the Scottish Education Department they requested that an opportunity be afforded them of being heard.[262] This was agreed, and on 23 March at 2.30 p.m. the Lord Provost, Bailies Anderson and Turnbull, the Revd Giffen, and the treasurer and law agent met with the education officials in London. They made no progress. Four days later the SED approved the commissioners' scheme. The governors were running out of options.

When the scheme was laid before both Houses of Parliament the governors determined to ask the City members[263] to make the necessary motion, asking that Her Majesty's consent should be refused.[264] The clerk was further asked to prepare a memorandum of information for the City members and also to prepare a short statement of the main grounds of objection to be circulated among MPs. This was sent in mid-July to every member of the House of Commons and Lords by post. By this time public opinion in Edinburgh had been aroused again, and the citizens had been asked to sign a petition: 'To prevent the poor of the City from being robbed, and the free schools closed, for the purpose of providing scholarships and bursaries for the children of the middle and upper classes.' A total of 42,000 did so!

City MP Buchanan had put his motion down along the lines suggested by the governors. It was down for 23 July, but was not taken until 2 a.m. and consequently the discussion was necessarily short. McLaren seconded the motion: the scheme went against the wishes of the founder; it was opposed by the town council unanimously, by the Free Presbytery and by the trades council; it needed to be delayed and improved.

J.A. Campbell spoke for the commissioners, explaining that the change in the composition of the governing body was not being introduced because the previous governors had not done their best, but from a conviction that a smaller body, composed of persons elected with special reference to the work they had to do, would be more efficient. He detailed the proposed new body: of the total of twenty-one governors, eleven were to be elected by the town council and three by the school board, so that the public bodies of the City had a two-thirds' majority on the board. It was, according to Campbell, a 'carefully-constructed Board'[265] and was near the number which Heriot envisaged in his arrangements for the Hospital. It would also be less likely to be dominated by the wishes of the community and would take more account of what was best in the interests of education. Campbell also defended the abolition of the outdoor schools. Their educational results had been 'very good' but he claimed that 'better work might have been done at less expense'.[266] In their place the scheme would spend £3,500 per annum on free education for poor children at public and state-aided schools, £250 on maintenance and clothing, and £2,150 on bursaries. The new school to replace the Hospital was not to be a low status establishment, but a 'very different kind of school and in some respects would be placed in an altogether higher position'.[267] He refuted the claim that the scholarships and bursaries were for the middle and upper classes: only £1,170 out of a total net income of £21,000 was not restricted to the poor. In conclusion, Campbell believed that 'no scheme had received more careful consideration'.[268]

Campbell was followed in the debate by another of the commissioners – Ramsay, who clearly thought that the poor of Edinburgh had much to be grateful for in the scheme. Vice-president of the council, Stanhope, although not responsible for the proposals, believed they were an honest attempt to carry out as far as possible the original intentions of the founder, and he supported them. Sir Edward Colebrooke, as chairman of a previous commission, also put his weight behind the scheme, which he believed was not very different from that which his own commission had proposed. He had suggested the introduction of fees into the outdoor schools but accepted the need to abolish the schools completely. Free schools were, contrary to the view of some,[269] a deviation from the intentions of the founder. They were for the poor of Edinburgh and not the poor orphans, the children of destitute burgesses. Perhaps this was fair in 1836 when there was no public provision for education, but no parliament in 1885 would agree to such a development. His commission had strongly supported the absolute necessity for changing the governing body. 'After the long controversy that had gone on for 20 years it was high time that they should arrive at a settlement of the question on a fair and liberal interpretation of the terms of the trust.'[270] It was left to Mundella on the Liberal side to put the finishing touches to the Heriot party. He stressed that even Sir George Harrison, the Lord Provost of Edinburgh, had admitted that the new scheme was preferable to the present one. It was not being imposed from outside Scotland: the education department made no recommendations but handed it over to the Scottish committee. Even a change of government did not mean a change in policy, for there was a unanimous desire on both sides to accept the scheme. It was good for Edinburgh, and although he never suggested a line of it he believed 'a nobler scheme had never been brought before that House'.[271] He believed that the provision for the poor would result in an increase in free education from the 4,500 pupils educated in the outdoor schools to 7,000 in better equipped schools. Furthermore, the poor children would not face the taunt of being charity children. The absurdity of Heriot's money taking the place of a government grant or relieving the rich ratepayers of Edinburgh would end. Given the strength of argument it was not surprising that Buchanan's motion was defeated 49 to 15. What was perhaps surprising was the loyalty of the Heriot Ring, which continued to defend Heriot's to the very end!

The special committee met again on 31 July, when it discussed a letter from the citizens' committee of the Heriot Defence Association which pressed the governors to 'take urgent and immediate steps for the purpose of opposing the scheme of HM commissioners in the House of Lords'.[272] It was decided to contact Prime Minister Salisbury and ask him to receive a deputation from the governors. He was telegraphed immediately, and the Lord Advocate, who was at the volunteer camp at Aberlady, was also contacted. Unfortunately, Salisbury's diary on the day suggested was full, but the Lord Advocate promised that he would 'do what I can to further governors' wishes'.[273] At a further special committee meeting the following day a written representation was drafted and copies sent to Salisbury and the Lord Advocate. In fact a group of governors were able to meet the latter late that Saturday evening (1 August) and again he expressed his willingness to do his best to help. This he did, and he arranged a meeting between a deputation of governors and Salisbury on Wednesday 5 August at 2.30 p.m. Bailies Anderson, Cranston and Turnbull, the Revd Giffen and the treasurer and law agent attended. Thanks to the continued good offices of the Lord Advocate the deputation was then able to meet with the President of the Council, Lord Cranbrook. The governors were determined that no stone would be left unturned in their endeavours to 'save' Heriot's. However, there was little left to do.

The scheme was approved by order in council on 12 August and forwarded to the clerk of the trust for implementation. Lord Provost Harrison announced that the first meeting of the new governing body would take place on Thursday 8 October, and the special committee was asked to settle outstanding matters.[274] When this took place the new body asked the governors of the Hospital to continue to exercise all necessary acts of administration relative to the endowment until 31 December. They agreed, and the last meeting of twenty-four Hospital governors, which dealt with routine business, was held on 3 December 1885,[275] and without ceremony Heriot's Hospital lost its struggle for survival.

CHAPTER ELEVEN

The School under Lowe and Clark

Although the new governing body of the school[1] was different in composition from that of the Hospital the organisation of standing committees followed the Hospital pattern and trust officials remained in place,[2] with the non-teaching staff, although fewer in number, also being retained. Significantly it was decided at a special meeting on 8 March 1886 by 17 to 2 to appoint David Lowe, house-governor of the Hospital, as headmaster of the enlarged Day School,[3] over F. Grant Ogilvie of Gordon's College.[4]

As an insider Lowe's appointment made sense to the cautious governors who wished to control the major changes afoot as much as possible. In the summer of 1886 Lowe appointed thirteen teaching staff – seven from the Hospital and six outsiders – to cope with the increased numbers of pupils presenting themselves at the new school. He had, however, other urgent matters to contend with. The change to a day school also meant the boarding out of the boys, although in the event most of them stayed with their own parents. Assessing the suitability of the Hospital buildings for the new curricular emphasis on science and technical subjects led him, and John Chesser, as early as April 1886, to begin visiting technical schools in Aberdeen, Glasgow and Manchester. It was left to the governors to end the Heriot free schools, which they did, while unanimously recording 'their sense of the unspeakable benefit' which they had conferred on the people of Edinburgh.[5] The Heriot Bridge school was retained for accommodation while the buildings at Abbeyhill, Stockbridge and Davie Street were bought immediately by the school board.[6] The money brought in enabled the trust to purchase premises at 20 York Place for £3,300 in January 1889.[7]

It was, however, June Day 1886 which brought home the different regime now operating. The governors determined to continue celebrating Heriot's birthday, but with no outdoor scholars and the general public not present it proved a dismal occasion with only about 200 attending. The Auld Callants showed their distaste for the changes by refusing to decorate Heriot's statue, and did not attend, while local newspapers

David F. Lowe followed Bedford as Head of the Hospital in 1880 and became the first Headmaster of the School in 1886. He retired in 1908.

expressed their regret at the loss of a cherished local festival.[8] Those who did return to the 'wark' felt 'let down' by the experience[9] and as late as 1913 an 'Old Boy' was lamenting the loss of the Hospital customs.[10]

The accommodation arrangements which had been made in 1886 for the tranche of new boys proved inadequate when some 700 enrolled in October 1887. All available space was utilised, and even, despite concerns, the chapel's pulpit was removed and the governors agonised over whether to use the chapel as a classroom or an examination hall. The closing exhibition in July 1887 had been held at Oddfellows Hall, and this was changed to Watson's Hall in Archibald Place in 1888, and kept there for succeeding years.[11] The restrictions on altering the external aspect of the old building meant that separate new buildings would have to be created or developed. Chesser's original plans for a new technical building in the north-west of the grounds[12] were substituted by modifications of Heriot Bridge School. The governors accepted a tender for this work,[13] and on 3 February 1888 Lord Balfour of Burleigh opened the new and badly needed accommodation.[14] Along the north side of the playground at right angles to Heriot's Bridge a lecture room and laboratory were created for physics, similar space was constructed for chemistry, and two workshops – one for wood and one for iron – and a gymnasium were also included.[15] Balfour, as chairman of the Educational Endowments Commission, had been the 'creator' of the 1885 Heriot Trust Scheme, and as such was a somewhat contentious guest. Although he delivered an 'interesting address'[16] on technical education and the work of the Endowments Commission, less than half the governors were present to hear it.

Lowe, in his Hospital days, had supported the development of physical education and swimming,[17] and he was acutely aware that other institutions had already furthered their sport and sporting facilities. Traditionally, the Hospital games were informal and limited and took place on the cramped facilities of the Heriot greens or the crowded Meadows. Lowe understood the desirability of a more organised approach to games, which would lead to healthy physical development and further team spirit. It would also be a good way of occupying large numbers of boys all at once. He appointed David Lowe Turnbull to the staff in 1887, and as a rugby player and cricketer he was put in charge of games. Turnbull's version of events suggests that the 'wholesale destruction of window glass'[18] resulted in the governors' decision to lay out a school field.[19] Whatever the correct version, and Turnbull perhaps dramatises events, a triangular piece of ground in Warriston Road, opposite the entrance to Warriston Cemetery ('Puddocky') on the Logie Green estate, was purchased in November 1887 and equipped[20] with a small pavilion, really a shed, containing lockers and scorer desks at its windows.

However, the new ground proved soft[21] and it was not until the winter of 1888–9 that it was in proper condition to play football (both rugby and soccer) and, the following summer, cricket. This was to result in the creation of an FP Cricket Club in 1890 and an FP Rugby Club.[22] Although the provision of a playing field was a step forward it had room for only one cricket square, a rugby pitch and a football field, and contemporary reports are almost all highly critical of conditions and facilities.[23] The School did little to maintain the ground in its earliest years, although the appointment of a groundsman in 1894 and the first cricket professional, David Beaton, whose summer duties included maintenance of the ground in 1895, did improve matters.

The School persevered with both versions of football well into the 1890s,[24] but the provision of rugby seemed precarious, on account of the popularity of soccer. However, there were soon problems with the language of supporters of visiting football teams to Logie Green, and when the Scottish Football Association recognised professionalism 'turning [a] good game into a trade'[25] the governors discontinued the playing of soccer. Lowe, although a supporter of all sports and clubs, was probably pleased at this decision.[26]

As the School grew in size and prestige it was increasingly clear how inadequate the facilities for swimming and games remained. As early as 1875 plans had been prepared for swimming baths, and Lowe himself in 1882 had pressed the issue. The school board had opened baths at The High School, Sciennes Road School, and were building baths at Montpelier School, Bruntsfield, while the recently opened Fettes College boasted their own baths. The superintendent of works, Donald Gow,[27] suggested a site at the east end of the technical department, linking to the gymnasium. The governors accepted his plans in July 1894[28] and the estimate of £2,082 8s. 7d. in May of the following year.[29] The swimming baths when completed were deemed to be the most modern in the country.[30]

Lowe was then able to turn his attention to the fields, and following a report from him the governors set up a committee to consider sites for a new field. In November 1899 the eleven-acre site at Bangholm (Old Goldenacre) was purchased.[31] After some delay, partly due to the illness and subsequent death of Gow in February 1901,[32] the ground opened in October 1901, dominated by the Old 'red-bricked' Pavilion.[33] With three rugby pitches and a cricket square it proved a 'great improvement' on Warriston.[34] Moreover, the impact of these changes and the encouragement of D.L. Turnbull and 'Daddy' Cooper, who enthused pupils to take up rugby, secured the future of games.

Lowe made progress in other accommodation issues during his time as headmaster. He returned to the issue of a need for a hall and persuaded both the education and finance committee in February 1893 that it was vital for all the boys to be brought together for assembly and exams.[35] A plan for an examination hall was considered and accepted on 8 May,[36] with estimates of just under £8,000 approved on 12 June.[37] The tool house was removed to the north-west corner in order to enhance the appearance of the new hall, which cost in total £10,508 10s. 2d. to complete.[38]

The next areas requiring attention were the drawing classrooms, and Lowe proposed a site for a new drawing department. Having visited the former and agreeing that they were inadequate the superintendent of works, John Anderson, was asked on 13 November 1905 to prepare sketches.[39] In March 1907 Lowe was authorised to go to London to inspect the drawing departments of certain schools there.[40] The final building, costing £5,000, harmonised with the Hospital building, and was limited to one storey in height so as not to interfere with views. It had a square tower over the main doorway, and followed the 'wark' in terms of pediments, side-doors and lamp seats which broke up the plain walling. It included purpose-built facilities for art drawing, mechanical drawing, photography (dark room), clay modelling and a greenhouse for pupils to study plant form. A covered bridge gave easy access to the adjoining wood and engineering workshops. In art, Heriot's could now claim accommodation 'second-to-none'.[41]

The changed position of the governors was best illustrated in the years after 1886 by the interference of the Scottish Education Department (SED), especially in financial matters. Letters went back and forth from the governors and secretary Craik of the SED, as both attempted to assert their authority. The London auditors of the School seemed remote to Edinburgh sensibilities – perhaps the very reason that the SED refused to countenance Edinburgh auditors[42] – and their disallowance in 1891, backed by the SED, of the honorarium of £5 11s. 1d. traditionally given to the governor preacher of June Day[43] was symbolic of the gulf between local and central government representatives. The relationship appeared to reach an even lower point the following year, when there was deadlock over the governors' desire to pay a retiring allowance to cashier George Barclay.[44] Initially the governors refused to budge but had to back down when faced with legal opinion.[45] However, the honorarium itself was an altogether different and more difficult matter, pitting the second chapter of Balcanquall's Statutes against Section 94 of the 1885 scheme. A temporary truce was called by Craik in October 1892, when he accepted the honorarium, provided it was not given to a governor.[46]

Such issues and conflicts led the governors to believe that a review of the trust scheme was needed, and a special meeting was convened on 9 November 1896.[47] Although they made no headway on financial matters, at least the provision on Greek was relaxed. Most of the other changes introduced in December 1897[48] related to changes in the number, tenure and value of foundationer allowances, free scholarships and school bursaries. Foundationer numbers were to be increased to 150 boys, and 50 girls were added with an allowance of £20 per annum: the previous maximum of 60 free scholarships was now to become the minimum, with 100 the maximum; and the length of the ten school bursaries, worth £20 per annum each, was increased from three to four years (previously five in number). Under the new scheme pupils from state-aided schools were encouraged to sit for Heriot bursaries and by 1900 the numbers reached 222 boys and 310 girls[49] and peaked at 684 (237 boys and 447 girls) in 1902, before dropping markedly to 173 (74 boys and 99 girls) in 1903,[50] as a result of the 1901 Education Act which ensured that all stayed on at school until fourteen, the very age at which these Heriot bursaries became available.

In other ways, too, the Heriot governors contributed to wider education. They offered 25–30 university open bursaries at Edinburgh every year, continued to support boys during their apprenticeships, while the running and maintenance of the Heriot-Watt College in itself became a mammoth exercise, given the enrolment of 3,198 students in the 1891–2 session.[51] Yet it is the remarkable improvement in academic standards at Heriot's itself which is most noteworthy. Early SED inspections were promising: Professor Archibald Barr (of civil engineering and mechanics at the University of Edinburgh) and Alfred Daniell (advocate) visited on 6–9 June 1890 and were impressed with the adaptation of the new buildings. They were particularly struck with the leadership and teaching of J.B. Clark and John T. Morrison in physics and natural science.[52] Such 'local' views were confirmed by an unexpected source when Heriot's was given special mention in Marias Vachon's report for the 'Gray Book' published by the department of Public Instruction in France.[53] The governors were heartened by such praise, and that of Dr T.A. Stewart, who stressed the 'harmony that pervades all relationships from the Headmaster downwards' and the 'loyalty of the boys to their masters and the school' shown in good conduct, courtesy and politeness. Significantly, this October 1903 report saw J.B. Clark as 'a teacher of rare power and gifts',[54] and in October 1904 Physics again gained especial praise 'reflecting greatest credit on Mr Clark'.[55] The technical side, under the direction of T.A. Clark, was also of high standard, and Heriot's was represented at national exhibitions in Scotland, Europe, the USA and New Zealand.

Lowe must have been proud of his significant achievements. He had chosen a staff, with first-class qualifications, which was delivering quality teaching. Typical was the example of W. Leslie Thomson, who had been first prizewinner and medallist in mathematics for three years running at Edinburgh University before gaining a postgraduate scholarship to Cambridge, and then joining the staff of Heriot's in 1899.[56] Even non-teaching posts attracted men of calibre. William Duncan, appointed wardsman in 1882 and janitor in 1886, gained the 'respect and love of the staff and many generations of boys'.[57]

By the time of Lowe's retirement in 1908 only one governor from 1886 was still in office. So, in a real sense Lowe can take personal credit for many of the early achievements and successes of the school. At the Edinburgh University graduation in April 1907 Heriotors gained 81 first-class honours, including fifteen medals and ten prizes, and 62 second-class honours.[58] Lowe had proved 'a distinguished Rector',[59] and because of his kindness, patience and understanding had been 'a great and successful Headmaster'.[60] He knew every boy, although he was feared as 'a strict martinet',[61] for he was, first and foremost, a disciplinarian.

Lowe left a strong School of over one thousand pupils with improved accommodation. His contribution to education was acknowledged by the University of Edinburgh when it conferred on him the honorary degree of Doctor of Laws in 1899, and he was elected to the University Court in 1903 (remaining a member until 1917). In many small ways he moved the school forward: he introduced lunch of soup and meat in the old dining hall for the boys;[62] he divided the school year into three terms rather than four quarters;[63] he advanced the school curriculum, introducing separate geography (under Lee) and history (under Melville), and new subjects such as typewriting found a place.[64] He advanced the extracurricular life of the school by holding PE exhibitions and school concerts in the new examination hall, and a number of new clubs owed much to his encouragement,[65] especially the Literary Society, under Messrs Wood and Kunz, the Camera Club begun in 1903, and the Dramatic Club and Stamp Club. He also persuaded the governors that staff salaries should be paid monthly rather than quarterly.[66] It was thus due to Lowe that Heriot's earned a place 'in the first rank among kindred institutions'.[67]

The departure of Lowe coincided with the introduction of new SED regulations[68] which held that no secondary class could be over thirty in number and no practical class more

The Watt Institution and School of Art (founded in 1821) appealed for financial help and the Heriot Governors responded by negotiating an agreement in 1879 which involved them in running the Heriot-Watt College until 1927.

than twenty. As the School had 663 secondary pupils in fourteen classes it needed to extend to twenty-two classes, which meant eight extra classrooms and eleven extra new staff. Among the important appointments at this time was the promotion of William Gentle to head of physics, the appointment of A.M. Crawford to the mathematics department and the reappointment of John H. Melville to the chemistry and mathematics department.[69] The increase in classes meant the need to extend accommodation. The governors, therefore, decided to utilise the south-west turret rooms, which traditionally had been the home of heads, and turned them into classrooms.[70] This was seen as the last step in the destruction of the old regime, as after hours George Heriot, in the persona of his statue, would remain the sole inhabitant of the school until the next morning. The year 1909 would be the first since 1659 that the 'wark' was empty overnight. The superintendent of works also planned for new classrooms on the west side of the playground, while also sub-dividing larger classrooms in the old building.

J.B. Clark was the obvious and natural successor to Lowe. Even the pupils in their section of the magazine understood this and pledged their loyalty.[71] According to one source one felt greatness immediately one entered his laboratory because he exhibited 'the purest emanation of personality'.[72] Lowe, too, was a supporter: after all Clark was his protégé. At a special meeting of the governors on 9 March 1908 Clark was unanimously appointed as the next head of Heriot's at a salary of £700 per annum.[73]

Clark had served his apprenticeship at the School and was more than ready for the task of taking Heriot's forward.[74] He immediately rearranged class organisation for the 1908–09 session, replacing familiar middle and upper divisions with six-year sets of parallel classes (the lower school remained as before with nine classes),[75] and he brought in the class master system. He then introduced twelve prefects, elected by the masters and headed by a school captain with a distinctive badge. It was their duty 'to look after the discipline of the school outside the classrooms'.[76] He also added a house system which he knew was popular in public schools, and he believed that it could be used at Heriot's to develop athletics in an educational curriculum.

The houses – Castle, Greyfriars, Lauriston and Raeburn[77] – were soon involved in competition in seven-aside rugby matches, relay races and a water-polo championship. It did not take long for Clark's ambition to be fulfilled as the standard of sport, especially rugby,[78] improved markedly as a result of the new enthusiasm engendered.

J.B. Clark became Headmaster of Heriot's in 1908. Under his tenure Heriot's came to the forefront in scholarship and sport.

Although an insider Clark's reforms were comparable to

those of Steven in the 1840s in taking the school forward. He held a packed meeting in the physics lecture room to introduce his plan for an 'Officers' Training Corps' (OTC). The governors supported this initiative retrospectively,[79] probably because nearly a hundred boys over fourteen enrolled. Soon Heriot boys were wearing their uniform – the Glengarry bonnet, khaki service jacket and Gordon tartan kilt in their weekly drill with Sergeant-major Dalby. With the provision of rifles expected the headmaster then appealed for a miniature rifle range to be built.[80] The quality of the playing of the school band improved with the added numbers and more particularly with the added practice undertaken. Clark was also the promoter of the school boy scout troop – 57th North Edinburgh, with fifty enrolling at its first meeting.

In other areas too Clark was an innovator. He introduced an employment and information bureau in March 1910 based on his West Linton experience. Heriot's was the first school to organise a body aimed at giving careers advice to its pupils. The quality and variety of lunches improved with the development of better kitchen facilities. The curriculum expanded, in particular modern languages, with Russian, Spanish and Italian all being offered within a few years. The development of instrumental music tuition also appeared at this time. He also promoted the staff golf competition by gifting a rose bowl to be played for on their outing following founder's day: a tradition still observed. All in all, Clark had brought a new vigour to the school, and his professionalism set a standard for the rest of the staff. To cope with the new modern era a typist and shorthand writer was appointed.[81]

The long-standing issue of town councillors having divided loyalties reappeared in January 1907 when three governors determined to take further their opposition to the sale of Bellevue Park to Edinburgh Corporation for £3,500. They argued that the resolution to do so, which the governors had carried by 9 to 8, was incompetent, as the price accepted was below the market value and further vitiated by the fact that the majority included five town councillors. As both sellers and buyers in the transaction 'their interest was adverse'.[82] Whether such sales were in the interests of the Trust was debatable, but one way and another Heriot's land – the basis of earlier prosperity – was diminishing.

It was on grounds of national security and importance that the governors agreed, on 12 October 1908, to sell the Redford lands to the War Office as a site for cavalry barracks.[83] Secretary of State R.B. Haldane drove a hard bargain, and in January 1909 Heriot's land was sold for £16,500: the bargain included superiority rights, but excluded a pre-emption clause which the governors could have effected if the use of the land had been changed.[84]

In the shorter term, however, the availability of ready funds enabled headmaster Clark, early in 1910, to turn his attention to the modernisation of Heriot's science facilities. This priority was not just because the SED required all secondary pupils to receive science instruction, but more because of the fact that science was deemed the 'most important element in Heriot's curriculum'.[85] The education committee, under convener Professor Darroch, began a series of visitations, the most extensive and thorough ever undertaken by Heriot governors. In all, eight schools and colleges were investigated, and Darroch was soon convinced that if science teaching was to remain a special feature at Heriot's, additional facilities would have to be provided.[86]

Clark needed little prompting, and by May 1910 he was proposing a new building at the north-west corner of the grounds at a total cost of £12,000. To accommodate his plan it was decided to abolish the janitor's lodge and boys' shelter and incorporate these into the new building. Although significant in width, with a frontage of 174 feet, the new structure was planned without towers and turrets, to avoid any competition with the 'wark', and had the added attraction of acting as an effective screen to the high tenements overlooking the school on the west side.

Clark and the superintendent of works then visited science schools in England to view the latest scientific equipment for the new facilities, while the west end of the playground remained 'an unpleasant spectacle'[87] owing to the building work.

Eventually by summer 1912 the three-storeyed building was

In 1909 Headmaster J.B. Clark gifted a handsome Rose Bowl to be competed for by the staff at their golf outing following the Founder's Day Ceremony. This tradition still exists.

completed. The new science building was to be devoted to the teaching of physics, natural science and geography (with the chemistry department able to occupy what was formerly used for both physics and chemistry). It also included a new library, for which an initial stock of 1,000 volumes was acquired. The appeal of headmaster Clark for school leavers to donate a book also added to the collection, which stood at 1,400 at its opening. This valuable addition was formally opened by the Rt Hon T. Mackinnon Wood, Secretary of State for Scotland, on 4 October 1912.

The governors were proud of their new first-class facilities and an informed view claimed, with some justification, that Heriot's was in the vanguard of schools in Britain.[88] However, almost immediately there were concerns about cost. The new block had come in over budget at £16,000[89] and retrenchment was now the order of the day. Nothing seemed sacrosanct: even the foundationers' excursion, an annual feature since 1849, was discontinued.[90] A move to inclusiveness resulted in a decision that all boys should be involved in founder's day with the clergyman preaching a sermon to the whole school.[91] Lack of funds also resulted in Clark appealing to former pupils to help raise the £400 necessary to pay for the proposed new rifle range.

The outbreak of the First World War had an immediate impact on the school. Before the end of 1914 eight of the School staff were at the front with another half a dozen at camp preparing to go,[92] and more than a dozen boys who were still at school or had left in July 1914 found themselves in the same position. The popularity of the officers' training corps increased markedly overnight – from 108 to 166 – and in addition all boys in the senior school (over 700 in number) received military drill once a week on week days. However, the war was brought even closer after the governors' decision of November 1914 to allow the new battalion of Royal Scots, formed by Sir George McCrae, extensive use of school buildings and facilities (other than the 'wark'), although the death of Lieutenant James Miller, a member of the English/history staff, while serving with the Black Watch in France on 25 September 1915, came as a great blow to the Heriot community.

With an increasing number of male staff away[93] Clark turned to women for the first time to fill the vacancies. The appointments were expected to be temporary, but the first appointment, Miss Jenny K.B. Macpherson, set a different pattern. She taught geography until 1918, when she transferred to the junior school and remained at Heriot's for over thirty years. Miss Edith Dickson's appointment on 15 May 1915 was also to be long-lasting. By December 1916 some eighteen women had joined the staff.

Sympathy for Britain's ally, Russia, led to an interest in the Russian

language and from 1916 James Melville took Russian classes out of hours: the beginners' class comprised fifteen boys and the advanced class some twelve boys. Perhaps it was this initiative which persuaded Sir Edward Parrott, a local MP, to write to the governors in June 1916 enquiring whether they would consider giving free education to some Serbian boys.[94] Headmaster Clark was enthusiastic – his only son, George was at the front[95] – and ten Serbians arrived at the beginning of session 1916–17 to be followed by fifteen others a few weeks later.[96] They made an immediate impact on the Heriot community and showed their willingness to participate in school life, particularly in rugby, athletics and the OTC. They were accommodated in a hostel in Bright's Crescent, Newington, and were looked after by their class master, James E. Wood, of the classics department, who became very much their father figure. A number of the older Serbian boys were soon taking classes at Edinburgh University.

The newcomers settled into the routine of life at Heriot's and it was only on special occasions, such as the visit to the school of HRH Prince George of Serbia, on 28 May 1918, that their distinctiveness was recognised. When it was finally time to leave, even to go home to a restored and enlarged Serbia, the boys took a tearful farewell. At a special ceremony in the council chamber, immediately after founder's day on 2 June 1919, they asked permission to erect a brass tablet, which to this

During the First World War the Governors agreed to take in and educate some Serbian boys and ten arrived for the beginning of session 1916-17.

day is displayed in the old dining hall.[97]

The presence of the Serbian boys spurred others in their war efforts. An extensive programme of charity work was supported, by concerts, displays, bottle collections and sales of work, to provide for the Heriot beds in the Scottish Red Cross Hospital at Rouen, and also Christmas presents of shortbread and chocolate to all the old boys serving at the front on land or sea. Many of the older boys gave up their summer holidays to help: in 1916 sixty of them cut down 6,500 trees in Dumfriess-shire and the Heriot Timber Camp became an annual event.

The reduction of military age meant that even more pupils were called up, and by the end of hostilities in November 1918 some 2,657 Herioters (present and former pupils) were serving in HM Forces; of these 463 gave their lives.[98] At a meeting in the school hall on 29 January 1919, with the Lord Provost chairing, it was decided to inaugurate a movement to set up a memorial at the school. Included in the war honours was the Victoria Cross awarded posthumously to First Lieutenant David S. McGregor for his bravery near Hoogmolen on 22 October 1918.

In March 1922 the governors received a deputation from a memorial committee, with member of staff William Gentle prominent, which put forward plans for siting a memorial,

In total, some twenty-six Serbian boys were at Heriot's for three sessions. On their tearful departure they presented to the School a Brass Tablet, which is still displayed.

even producing a detailed design for consideration. James B. Dunn, a well-known architect and a former pupil, was the designer, and Alex Carrick agreed to do the sculpture work. On 10 April 1923 the weather cleared for the completed memorial to be formally dedicated and unveiled. It was positioned in the centre of the green slope to the east of the 'wark' and took the form of a mercat cross, the lower portion being octagonal in shape. On six of its sides were placed large panels bearing the names of the fallen. The central panel bore the Heriot crest, with the inscription 'To the glorious memory of the former pupils and staff of the School who fell in the Great War. The names of those who return not again are here inscribed to their honour for evermore – 1914–1919.'[99] Running round the upper portion of the octagon was a frieze bearing two quotations: Horace's 'dulce et decorum est pro patria mori' and Lawrence Binyon's 'at the going down of the sun and in the morning, we will remember them'. The upper monument consisted of an octagonal shaft surmounted by a sculptured device, symbolising self-sacrifice, of a pelican feeding her brood.

The moving ceremony was conducted partly in the school hall and partly at the memorial. After the service in the packed hall, all present, including Lord Provost Thomas Hutchison and headmaster Clark, marched behind the pipe band of the OTC playing a lament. The parents and relations of the fallen were joined by the boys of the school and the general public to see the Lord Provost unveil the memorial. Wreaths were laid by school staff, boys, Parent Heriot Club, the daughter clubs of London, Winnipeg and Vancouver, and the former pupil clubs of rugby, cricket, cross-country and golf.[100]

At the end of the war headmaster Clark led a staff of forty-seven.[101] The governors accepted the Craik Report on teachers' salaries of November 1918, on the grounds that Heriot's must match salaries elsewhere in order to attract 'the best teachers'. However, given the importance of English, mathematic, physics and chemistry, principal teachers of these subjects were paid more than the other heads of department.[102] Yet the staff remained unhappy, and in December 1919 a deputation led by William Gentle put the case to the governors for salaries above national scales to offset the limits on promotion. The argument was accepted, and by May 1920 this had been put into effect. From then on Heriot's staff could expect to be paid above the national scales, and such treatment was but one factor in ensuring staff loyalty. Certainly it was not uncommon for staff, once appointed, to remain at the school for much of their working life.

The immediate post-war period saw the departure of the first generation of Heriot's school staff, all appointed around the time of the change from

hospital to school in 1886. On the teaching staff, James Moonie (staff member 1886–1919), who revolutionised Heriot music, was the first to retire. He was followed by other teaching colleagues: Dr Samuel Walker, chemistry (1885–1921); Malcolm McKenzie, English (1886–1923); James E. Wood, classics (1887–1923); Robert Forrest, who had been with Dr Lowe at Bathgate, book-keeping (1881–1921); William Mackenzie, head of junior school (1884–1923); George A. Douglas, classics (1886–1925); D. Lowe Turnbull, German (1887–1925) and Murray Marr, who had joined in 1888 and died in service in December 1924. Service and trust staff also saw changes: David Ness, gatekeeper and janitor for twenty-six years, retired; Dr James Ritchie, medical officer since 1881, resigned in July 1920; George Lamb retired after a remarkable fifty-two years' service, seventeen as treasurer, and Peter Macnaughton also left, having been clerk and law agent between 1892 and 1923.

To replace this generation a galaxy of young talent was appointed to join the mainly pre-war generation of William Gentle (born 1877), William Carnon (b. 1883), William Hare (b. 1888), George A. Scott (b. 1888), James Ryrie (b. 1890) and Edith Dickson and Nan Gall (both born 1892). In 1919 Mary Couper (b. 1897) was appointed Spanish teacher[103] and the following year Joe Halliday (German) and James D. Westwood (English) arrived. The year 1921 saw the arrival of Kate Smyth (German) and D. Ritchie K. Middlemas (science and mathematics). In 1923–24 Bill Brow (chemistry), Willie Gould (history), Bill Inglis (classics) and Dougie Heath (commercial subjects) were new staff recruits; in 1925 Charles Broadwood (a former pupil), Norman Abercrombie (French) and Archie Campbell (mathematics) were Clark's final appointments. This impressive group was to dominate Heriot's for forty years, the last retiring in 1968.

On Monday 12 February 1923, at what was deemed to be the three-hundredth anniversary of the death of George Heriot, the governors held a special service in St Giles' Cathedral, and the Moderator of the General Assembly of the Church of Scotland, the Rt Revd John Smith, delivered the Commemoration Address. Along with the Order of Service, the Address was printed in pamphlet form, bearing the portrait of George Heriot on the front cover, and a copy was presented to each boy. The whole school, headed by the OTC and the boy scouts, who were to act as a guard of honour at the west door of the Cathedral, marched via Lauriston and George IV Bridge to St Giles'.

The former pupils of the Heriot Outdoor schools felt that they too would like to join in the special celebrations in 1923.

On 10 April 1923, the Heriot War Memorial was dedicated at a special ceremony at the School. Some 463 Herioters made the supreme sacrifice during the First World War.

The governors were sympathetic and agreed that a reunion could take place in the school playground and grounds from 5.30 p.m. to 8.00 p.m. on June Day. A total of 2,000 FPs turned up and celebrated with singing and dancing in accordance with earlier Hospital custom. Edinburgh had seen nothing like it since 1885.

Heriot's, however, was a very different institution in the 1920s from that of pre-1886. It was now part of a new Scottish day-school tradition, with impressive academic achievements and extensive extra-curricular opportunities. In sport, the name of Heriot's was increasingly synonymous with success and excellence. The former pupils, too, were successful, with the FP Rugby Club winning the Unofficial Scottish Rugby Championship in 1919–20, during an unbeaten season.[104] W.G. Dobson became the first Herioter to become a rugby internationalist in 1922.[105] Unfortunately the playing-fields were now too small for the needs of the school, and in February 1923 former pupils and headmaster Clark laid a plan before the governors to extend the boundary westward to Bangholm Terrace.[106] The governors agreed on the need for better facilities, including a grandstand, and the superintendent of works and Councillor Stark visited Dundee and Glasgow to view other developments. The work on the levelling and dressing of the grounds was estimated at well over £4,000 but it was the hefty £13,500 for grandstand, pavilion and dressing rooms which led the governors to ask the FP Rugby Club to contribute £6,000 to the final cost. The FPs agreed, having first obtained guarantees

Heriot's FP won the Unofficial Scottish Rugby Championship in 1919-20 for the first time in an unbeaten season. (Charles Broadwood, later significant in raising the standard of school rugby, is sitting on the front right.)

about usage and three representatives on the field committee of eighteen.[107] It was a proud day when the new recreation ground at New Goldenacre was opened by the Lord Provost, Sir William Sleigh, on 25 September 1926, the day of the FP rugby match against traditional rivals, Hawick. The grounds were now 'comparable with the best in the country'.[108]

Approaching the age of sixty-five, J.B. Clark gave notice to the governors of his impending retiral. His tenure had been outstanding by any standards, and the School was now firmly at the forefront in scholarship and sport. He had nursed the spirit of Heriot's and developed and moulded the staff into a formidable team. He was popular with all in the Heriot community and was affectionately called 'Jibs' by the boys. His service to education and to the University of Edinburgh was to be recognised by the conferment of the Degree of Doctor of Laws (1929) and later an OBE.[109]

The Heriot tradition of favouring insiders and the satisfaction of the governors of progress under Clark led the education committee on 30 December 1925 to decide not to advertise for a successor, but instead to recommend that the deputy head, William Gentle, be appointed headmaster. At a special meeting of the governors on 11 January 1926 it was unanimously agreed, in view of his qualifications and record, to offer the post to Gentle who accepted immediately.

CHAPTER TWELVE

The School under Gentle and Carnon

W illiam Gentle had been educated at Morgan Academy, Dundee, before becoming a pupil at Heriot's at the age of fourteen in 1891 and falling under the spell of Clark in mathematics and physics. He became a pupil teacher in October 1893, and having combined his university studies with teacher-training he was a fully qualified teacher by 1898. After a distinguished university career he worked as Clark's assistant before becoming head of a separate physics department in 1908, then deputy head (1923) before achieving the pinnacle of his career, following Clark as headmaster in 1926.[1]

Since 1886 Heriot's School had remained a somewhat 'closed community' but Gentle's appointment reaffirmed its exclusive nature. Although he was the obvious successor, Gentle was steeped in all things 'Heriot', becoming president of the Heriot Club in 1920 and being the driving force behind the war memorial. It was only in later years that this exclusive ethos was to create real problems which sapped and weakened the development of the School. However, this was not obvious when Gentle took over, and, following tradition, Heriot's continued to appoint insiders to senior posts. William Carnon became head of English in January 1925, Edward Hare was appointed in April 1926 as head of junior school, and then in the following year assistant to the head and deputy head, while Andrew Lee, who joined the staff in 1892, took up the post of deputy head along with his headship of geography in September 1926.[2]

Although Goldenacre could boast of its sports facilities[3] the same could not be said for accommodation at Lauriston Place. Gentle had inherited a total of thirty-six classrooms (which included nine used by the junior school) and a school just adequate for the demands of science, technical subjects, art and gymnastics, but certainly inadequate for all other disciplines. The shortage of decent-sized and appropriately designed rooms meant that, leaving aside the aforementioned subjects and staff, twenty-nine other teachers had only seventeen adequate classrooms to share. Gentle conservatively reported to the governors in February

William Gentle was Headmaster at Heriot's between 1926 and 1942. He was steeped in all things 'Heriot' and as a result strengthened the School and its traditions.

1928 that at least six additional classrooms were necessary.

By the beginning of the following session the governors had called in Sir George Washington Browne, president of the Royal Scottish Academy, to give advice on a proposed extension and requested the superintendent of works, John Anderson, to sketch alternative sites. Informed by them, a sub-committee of governors under Councillor Thomas Nelson produced a report which suggested beginning junior school at age five (instead of eight) but cutting numbers at intermediate level (twelve to fourteen), thus strengthening the junior school as a recruiting ground for the senior school, while keeping the overall school population at the same level. On this basis, Anderson produced alternative plans for the east end of the playground and the lawn to the north of the war memorial. The sub-committee favoured the former, which centred on a three-storeyed building of ten classrooms and a small hall, estimated to cost £35,000. On 16 July 1928 the education committee accepted unanimously the sub-committee's report providing the new building could be built without seriously affecting the appearance of the 'wark'. This was the crux of the argument which now raged. Browne's ideas were unacceptable to the governors who preferred a site between the examination hall and Lauriston Place, but the secretary of the SED, Sir George Macdonald, opposed increasing the size of the school and erecting a building of three storeys. By May 1929 the governors had agreed to both of these propositions and George Reid, architect, had produced a plan for a two-storey building of ten classrooms and a hall within the earlier agreed budget. Yet the precise site was still the subject of controversy. The Fine Art Commission held that the building along the eastern boundary, behind the war memorial and perfectly central with it, would cause least injury to Heriot's Hospital. Rather than accept this, the governors' education committee, on 29 November 1929, decided 7 to 4 to look outside the grounds for a site for a preparatory school. Reid submitted new plans for building between the Corn Exchange and Heriot's school buildings in May 1930, and the town council finally accepted these on 28 November 1930. But now that the national economic situation was deteriorating the governors determined to make extensive savings and introduced increased fees (although fees remained substantially below those of both the Merchant Company Schools and the Royal High School), Their plans and the means of financing them gained SED approval in July 1931. When tenders were accepted in December 1931 the total cost had spiralled, and, with the governors having second thoughts, Gentle had to spell out again in detail the reasons for the need for such accommodation. This he did to great effect, and his intervention was crucial in strengthening the governors'

resolve and convincing them to go forward with their plans.

The 'New School' was ready for the beginning of the 1934–35 session. The modern suite of buildings for the new preparatory department also catered for art and technical subjects as well as providing a new hall and extended gymnasium, and enabled Heriot's to claim to be 'one of the best organised and most modern and fully equipped schools in the country'.[4] The final cost of £55,702 9s. 6d. was a massive investment in the future and proved far-sighted. Immediately one hundred boys were taken in and three new staff – Miss McKenzie, Miss Brunton and Miss Redman – were recruited. Within two years the 'prep' reached its capacity of five classes.

It had been increasingly clear that the 1897 trust scheme needed revision. In particular, further development of the Heriot-Watt College was required and this would involve larger financial resources than the Heriot Trust could provide, while a separate governing body for the school would enable the Heriot governors to concentrate on a growing number of complex issues. A memo from the clerk and law agent, G. Malcolm Stuart, in November 1925, suggested cutting the governing body from 21 to 17 (omitting those specifically there to represent Heriot-Watt, and, following the Fettes example, including a Heriot FP), and introducing a Heriot-Watt governing body of 28 (including three from George Heriot Trust and ten from local industry). However,

On 11 July 1931 HM the Queen and HRH the Duchess of York were welcomed by Headmaster Gentle, and shown exhibits relating to the history of the School and Trust.

the governors determined to continue paying Heriot's annual contribution of £7,000 to Heriot-Watt stipulated under previous schemes; indeed in April 1927 this was increased to £8,000. In the event the new December 1927 scheme separated the institutions, and George J. Scott, treasurer of the Bank of Scotland, became the first FP representative on the Heriot governing body.[5] However, the subsequent successful history of Heriot-Watt College was built on the original rescue scheme of, and early support from, the Heriot Trust.

If Gentle presided over the ending of this close arrangement, the introduction of a former pupil onto the governing body was more than symbolic with distinguished former pupils contributing greatly to the governing body over the years.[6] Gentle was instrumental in cementing relationships within the Heriot community. In particular, he cultivated former pupils and persuaded Dr Bedford's son, Lieutenant-Colonel Sir Charles H. Bedford, of Woking, Surrey, to finance three school scholarships. A bronze plaque portrait of Dr Bedford, executed by Pilkington Jackson, was unveiled on 19 November 1928, above the fireplace in the entrance lobby to the council room.[7] It was Gentle, too, who convinced the governors that the School rather than St Giles' was the more appropriate venue for celebrating the tercentenary of the laying of the foundation stone on Friday 29 June 1928. Two services were held that day in the examination hall – juniors in the morning, and seniors in the afternoon. The following day a successful reunion was held in the grounds: it took the form of a garden party and included a gymnastic display by pupils and an exhibition of Heriot documents and memorabilia, including the Loving Cup.

For the most part, Gentle led a stable staff, numbering some fifty-seven teachers in 1926.[8] Whenever possible he continued the tradition of appointing former pupils or promoting next-in-line insiders. One exception to this stands out: W.A. McKerrow joined the staff in January 1927, three years after Bill Inglis, but the former was appointed head of Latin in July 1931. Inglis protested and sent a letter to the governors spelling out his qualifications for departmental leadership.[9] Gentle defended his decision, emphasising qualifications, although perhaps the personality and appearance of the flamboyant 'Algie' Inglis was a contributory factor.[10] Otherwise appointments followed a familiar pattern. With the retiral of deputy Andrew Lee in June 1928, James Melville, head of history, replaced him, while William Carnon of the English department had his salary increased 'in view of certain work undertaken by him for the headmaster'.[11] Melville was to be an outstanding success in his post and his 'abiding passion'[12] for Heriot's made him an ideal partner for Gentle. His death in the influenza epidemic on 19 January 1937 meant 'an almost irreparable loss'[13] for the School. After a brilliant school and university career he had changed from modern languages to history and when history became a separate department at Heriot's in 1908 he was made its first head of department. Under his leadership it became one of the strongest in Scotland, with Melville being acclaimed by a schools inspector as 'probably the best teacher (of History) he had ever known'.[14] Fortunately he was followed by another brilliant academic, William Gould, who proved a worthy successor.

Another significant appointment for the future seemed very unlikely at that time. David Morris, a foundationer, was allowed in September 1933 to remain at school beyond the leaving age because of his failure to gain employment as a result of a disability in his right arm.[15] In March 1934 Gentle decided to employ him on clerical work and so began an extraordinary career which was to have a profound effect on the history of the Trust.[16]

Gentle made other important appointments during his tenure as headmaster. E. Mercer ('Kipper') Heron joined English in September 1928, and in the following year J.G. ('Spud') Thomson was appointed to mathematics and Andrew Graham and Lindsay L. Mitchell to the junior school, to be joined by Gibby Galloway (former pupil) in April 1937 and another former pupil Roger J. Blamire in the chemistry department later that same year. Jules K. de D. Kunz died in December 1931 and was succeeded by William Bryce, who had joined the staff in 1895. In art, E.S. McFarlane retired in June 1933 after thirty-four years as head of department. His successor was James S. Ryrie, who had been at Heriot's since 1913. John H. Melville, another Heriot stalwart, who had served Dr Lowe as private secretary before moving to Alloa Academy, had returned to Heriot's in 1908 to join the chemistry department, which he took over in 1921, retiring in December 1937. He was replaced as head of chemistry by William T. Brow, who had joined the staff in 1923.

Gentle can also take credit for encouraging Heriot school journeys, which began with Edward Hare (and five other staff) taking 120 boys to London to visit the Wembley Exhibition in 1924. While in London one of the school's most successful former pupils, the Rt Hon. William Graham,[17] guided the group round the Houses of Parliament. John Wilson, second head of modern languages, led a camping tour of five weeks' duration to France and Northern Spain in 1926, taking advantage of the extremely favourable rate of exchange. The success of this trip in turn encouraged William Gould to take a group camping near Grenoble for a month the following year. Such trips, usually to western Europe, but occasionally further afield, became almost annual events, and after 1932 school cruises became popular to overcome the problems of currency and exchange. Such ventures were in great demand, and it has been estimated that between 1926 and 1935 some 240 pupils and staff embarked on tours while a similar number went on cruises.[18]

The headmastership of Gentle also saw the flowering of FPs in all walks of life. How the school laid to rest the criticisms made against the Hospital that no distinguished pupils were produced! In the Civil Service, William S. Douglas became Secretary to the Department of Health for Scotland; in academic life, Thomas Dalling succeeded to the Chair of Animal Pathology at Cambridge University in February 1937;[19] in medicine, Norman Dott became the doyen of brain surgeons;[20] while in sport Dan Drysdale captained the Scottish rugby team, beginning the marvellous tradition of Heriot's full-backs playing for their country, and was 'deemed the greatest ambassador the School ever had'.[21]

As the European situation deteriorated the governors began to make preparations for the impending national emergency. In April 1939 the school was shut for a week to enable evacuation procedures and arrangements to be worked out. Soon decisions were taken regarding protection of the pupils and buildings: the rocky nature of the subsoil meant that no trenches could be constructed in the grounds. Instead the governors thought of protecting ground floor windows of the 'wark' and the new technical block by use of heavy wooden beams, thus creating shelters. In fact, all early plans were based on the optimistic premise that there would be little direct threat or damage to the school: hence the stained-glass windows of the chapel remained in place, and the governors were reluctant to employ a nightwatchman for fire-fighting duties.

The Secretary of State announced on 25 September 1939 that schools could reopen if the neighbourhood was not especially vulnerable, although attendance of pupils would be left to the direction of parents. For Heriot's, this meant that the secondary department could open in relays, provided adequate shelters were provided.[22] Shelters subsequently appeared in the playground, play-shed area, south of the old examination hall, as well as a number in Lauriston Place and at Goldenacre. The SED gave half-funding for these structures. As far as the primary department was concerned it was decided that private homes would be used to keep in touch with pupils. With 1,245 on the roll (instead of the usual 1,490) education in the first months of the war was patchy. Gentle tried hard to conduct the School as normal, but although traditional teaching of poetry-reading could continue, it was very difficult to conduct chemistry experiments or cut up worms in makeshift conditions. After the second evacuation scheme in March 1940 some 610 pupils remained, but the ranks of the staff thinned too: George Scott, Hugh Gunn, P.B.S. Ireland, Arthur Blair, William Davie, Roger Blamire, T.G. Galloway, D.A.G. Heath, A. Graham, J.C. Neill and Douglas Hutton were all called up, followed shortly afterwards by A.T. Graves and Tony Welton in March 1943.[23] Given such gaps it was a remarkable feat of organisation for Gentle and Carnon to keep things going as well as they did. Teaching did continue. PE classes and swimming carried on, while rugby teams played home and away (thanks to Charlie Broadwood) and cricket and net practice also took place.[24]

Food was never actually scarce but it was bland and monotonous (sweets and fruit, apart from apples, were virtually unobtainable), but the mid-morning ritual of a third of a pint of milk continued as part of the health regime. Although for adults wartime was a stressful, grey, depressing time, on the whole it made surprisingly little difference to Heriot boys. The air-raid sirens occasionally sounded, usually because bombers were passing overhead on their way to Clydebank, but few bombs were dropped near Heriot's. So the boys felt no real sense of danger. Indeed the gas masks, which had to be carried everywhere, were used, in their cardboard boxes, as balls in rugby practice on the way to and from school. It was probably as well that they never had to be worn!

The senior boys were keen, however, to help with the war effort, and some seventy volunteers joined the thirty-six staff involved in the fire-watching teams organised by 'the capable kindly deputy headmaster.'[25] This activity consisted of sleeping for the night on camp beds in the council room,[26] complete with steel helmets, gas mask, buckets of sand, long shovels and stirrup pumps. With the addition of an Air Training Corps in early 1941[27] all boys at a certain age were expected to join one of the cadet forces, which trained everyone for war service. When not at cadet camp the rest of the Easter and summer 'holidays' were taken up with working at harvest or timber camps. Because of the lack of young fit men schoolboys were urgently needed on farms at harvest time. Usually this proved very hard work, and although paid was not usually as exciting or as much fun as timber camp.

With a school in good heart and full again – 1,459 enrolled in 1941–42 – William Gentle determined to resign, although the SED were willing to postpone his retiral in the special circumstances.[28] A sub-committee of seven governors under the Revd Dr C.W.G. Taylor interviewed nine of the forty-one applicants for the post of headmaster, including the three internal candidates – William Carnon, Edward Hare and George Scott.[29] Carnon,

Scott and David Collier, headmaster of Morgan Academy, Dundee, were short-leeted, and Carnon and Collier were interviewed by all the governors on 13 April 1942. By eleven votes to six William Carnon, deputy head, was appointed headmaster of Heriot's.[30] Although Carnon was in the twilight of his career and was seen in some quarters as a 'stop gap' he had certainly served his apprenticeship, having joined the staff in 1907, been appointed head of English in 1924, and deputy head in 1937. He was known as a good organiser and a gifted teacher and was seen as a quiet, firm and dignified gentleman of considerable charm, tact, sympathy and understanding.[31] In turn, he followed tradition, appointing insiders: Edward Hare was promoted to deputy, J.D. ('Chinky') Westwood to head of English and C.S. Broadwood as second head of English. Some governors protested that the deputy post should have been a governor decision and not a headmaster appointment, but in October 1942, the governors agreed that 'the whole organisation, discipline and management of the school' was the headmaster's responsibility and agreed to accept the tradition that this involved the appointment of all staff, including the deputy head.

The School roll for 1942–43 was 1,511[32] and Carnon was faced with the need to raise fees for the first time since 1929–30. Expenditure in 1941–42 was £41,415 with income of £10,323 (fees), £17,811 (endowments) and £13,281 (SED grant). With Heriot fees remaining comparatively cheap compared with 'competitors' – prep £6 to senior £12 per annum[33] – it was decided to raise them by thirty shillings per session.

The death of Robert Perkins of the mathematics department in December 1942 after thirty-three years' service at Heriot's[34] enabled Carnon to bring back Bill G.D. Brown to his old school, after spells at Pitlochry and in the Morgan at Dundee. Another significant appointment – long term – was that of Barbara Arneil, who joined the geography staff in 1943.[35] Two other staffing issues of this time warrant mention. On 13 March 1944 the clerk and treasurer reported 'with regret' to the governors that he had suspended the cashier, George D.S. Meikle, as a result of financial irregularity. Ultimately he was dismissed and replaced by James Barclay, with David Morris joining the permanent staff. Meantime in May 1945 headmaster Carnon suspended J.J. Rough of the art department as a result of aggressive behaviour towards other staff, and absenting himself from duty. Although reinstated, when Rough again transgressed in October Carnon called for his dismissal, and on 10 December 1945 the governors unanimously decided to fire him.[36] The Secretary of State authorised an enquiry into his

William Carnon became Headmaster of Heriot's in 1942, at the age of 59. He proved a good organiser, gifted teacher and charming gentleman and retired in 1947.

dismissal, but the report, by W.R. Milligan, KC, found there were no grounds to reconsider the governors' resolution. No doubt the staffing issues uncovered at this time revealed to the governors the danger of giving too much freedom to the teaching staff and the need for a strong headmaster, perhaps without the baggage of the insider, to take the School forward.

On a brighter note, Andrew Graham, who had joined Gentle's junior school staff in 1929 was made School chaplain by Carnon. This important post covered not just religious education but also entailed caring for the social and mental needs of the School, and as such was the forerunner of the School's commitment to the welfare of members of its community. Graham, an ordained Congregational church minister from 1937, visited, married and buried a generation of Herioters.[37]

The war made more demands on the School during Carnon's term. More of Goldenacre was ploughed up for food production, although HMI pressure for boys to have an extra physical instruction period enabled Carnon to prevent further encroachment on the playing fields. Moreover, the governors agreed to the railings being removed by the Ministry of Works, provided that the ornamental gate at Lauriston Place remained – although in the event not all were taken away – to ensure the safety of the general public among the air-raid shelters. However, during 1944–5, with the fortunes in war changing, the School gradually returned to normal. By that time over 200 Herioters had given their lives, including Lieutenant William Stott, one of the junior school staff, who was killed in December 1943.

Carnon had done most of his innovation as deputy and he, and others, appreciated that his tenure was but 'a bright and pleasant interlude'.[38] He revived the School Concert in the Usher Hall in July 1946, after a twenty-year gap, and he involved more seniors in the running of the School. In his final year he appointed twenty-three prefects, reduced by his immediate successor the following year to sixteen. The morning assembly, introduced by Gentle, became more prominent under Carnon. However, the pressure of the job soon made itself felt and led him to 'drag a leg'. He determined to resign[39] and enjoy his many interests outside School. He took with him into retirement William Forbes, who joined as second physics master in 1908, and who had been made head of physics in 1926; Andrew Hardie, who joined as assistant in technical subjects in 1907, and became head of department in 1919; William Goodall, who joined in 1919 and had been house master of Castle for 28 years, and Alexander M. Young, who had been a member of the biology department, also since 1919.[40]

The short-leet of four drawn up for Carnon's post in May 1947 marked a complete break with the past. All were external candidates. The three Scots and the head of modern languages at Winchester all made statements and answered the governors' questions. William McLachlan Dewar, Rector of Greenock Academy, was unanimously appointed headmaster.[41] A new era had begun.

CHAPTER THIRTEEN

The School under Dewar and McDonald

William McL. Dewar arrived at Heriot's with an impeccable pedigree. He had been an outstanding Classics student at Edinburgh University and achieved a first-class degree and the distinction of winning the Vans Dunlop and John Edward Baxter scholarships. He had proved himself in the classroom and in administration, first as assistant teacher at Aberdeen Grammar School (1929–32), then principal teacher of Classics at Dumfries Academy (1933–41) and finally as rector of Greenock Academy (1941–47). He had, however, two drawbacks as far as the Heriot's staff was concerned: he was an 'outsider' and he came with a determination to reform and modernise. A clash was inevitable – how deep and far-reaching that was to be would surprise everyone.

The strength of feeling against Dewar in some quarters was apparent from the first. Only three days after his appointment at Heriot's he received an anonymous letter written 'in particularly scurrilous and threatening terms'[1] at his home in Greenock. Some months later, in early 1948, the clerk and treasurer, E.F. Barron, also received an anonymous letter, this time 'casting reflections on the headmaster'.[2] This particular letter could only have been written by someone with an intimate knowledge of the School and the governors, and when they finally got round to enquiring into the details of the situation in November 1949 it was concluded 'that there was someone in the school seeking to undermine the authority of the headmaster'.[3] It was at this point that the Lord Provost asked the police to investigate the matter privately.

Given such a reception a less confident man might have lost his nerve. Bill Dewar, however, was not swayed from taking hard and difficult, even controversial, decisions.

To begin with he seemed on safe ground with staffing. Indeed, even before he arrived to be introduced to the school on Tuesday 16 September 1947 Dewar had a number of appointments to make. Significantly, a new post created by him was that of careers master, Alan Boyle being appointed to

William McL. Dewar was the first external appointment as Headmaster of Heriot's for almost a century. His efforts to modernise and take forward the School caused controversy. He retired in 1970 after twenty-three years in post.

a position then unique in Scotland: he promoted John Morrison (who joined the staff in 1922) to principal teacher of physics,[4] while Mercer Heron and Bill Inglis became second-in-charge of English and Classics respectively. David Stott (a former pupil – English), James Park (biology) and Alexander Weston (technical) joined the staff at this time.

However, two areas in particular were to prove especially contentious. For former pupils the 'burning question'[5] was how to satisfy the widespread desire to continue the family tradition of having been schooled at Heriot's. At the anniversary dinner in June 1948 a speech from J.C. Greenlees, the Loretto headmaster, stressing the family traditions of Heriot's, was welcomed enthusiastically by those present. Further, a special delegation of former pupils met with the governors to put their case,[6] implicitly criticising the policy of the new headmaster. This followed Dewar's seemingly hasty new arrangements for the Buskin Ceremony, which had restricted the attendance of former pupils. Naturally founder's day was not just symbolically important to the 'traditionalists', and it seemed particularly unwise that Dewar's 'improvements' were introduced without him ever having experienced the occasion himself.

Whether Dewar was given the nod to 'take on' a seemingly over-powerful staff resistant to change by the governors, or whether he was seen in some quarters as the strong leader needed to take Heriot's forward, or whether it was simply his very confident and decisive manner which put 'backs up', is not clear. What is clear, however, is that within a short time of his appointment relationships between Dewar and the staff, or at least a prominent section of older staff members, deteriorated and never fully recovered during his tenureship.

The editorial of *The Herioter* for July 1948 was a veiled attack on, and warning to, Dewar. Entitled 'Traditions' it held that: 'Good traditions are a factor of incomparable value in everything, and we firmly believe that they should not be overthrown without uncontestable reasons . . . The Heriot tradition is not something of a few years' growth . . .' And further that: 'Now, as possibly never before, all of us who are proud to be connected with the school are united in defence of our traditions . . .'[7] Clearly the new broom was sweeping clean more than expected, and some venerable cobwebs had been disturbed.

One of the issues, seen as crucial by a number of staff, was that of sport, especially rugby. Dewar believed that the practice of releasing some classes at 2.30 p.m. (instead of at 3.10 p.m.) to train at Goldenacre, was educationally unsound.[8] The loss of one period three times a week, Dewar argued, was not in the interests of the School. When the governors accepted Dewar's position[9] Charlie Broadwood submitted a letter on behalf of fifteen staff intimating their resignations from voluntary supervision and instruction in rugby from the beginning of session 1948–49. Dewar stood firm: rugby supervision should take place after hours until 4.30 p.m. The governors decided to have a special meeting on 16 July 1948, and Broadwood was invited to lead a small deputation party to put the case of the rugby masters: he argued that practice in winter would be impossible owing to early darkness.

In the governors' discussion that followed, an attempt to ask the headmaster to leave the meeting was heavily defeated (8 to 2).[10] Finally, with Councillor Williamson dissenting, the governors agreed that each class in the senior school be released at 2.30 p.m. one afternoon a week to go to Goldenacre for games, but that the school day be lengthened on Mondays by one period, closing at 3.50 p.m. While supporting the headmaster, the governors thanked the rugby masters for their past service and hoped 'that in the interests of the school and its pupils and the relations of the staff with the Headmaster' they would continue with their voluntary service in the future.[11] It took considerable correspondence between Broadwood and the trust officers, and a number of meetings between Dewar and the representatives of the rugby masters, before an 'amicable arrangement'[12] was finalised for the 1948–49 session.

An uneasy truce prevailed for a short time until Dewar unveiled his future curricular plans. A number were uncontentious: the accommodation for natural science seemed inadequate and Dewar pressed for the conversion of part of the pupils' cycle shed at the north-west corner of the science department into laboratories. The governors agreed to these changes and increased staffing, which resulted in a greater curricular emphasis on biology. However, it was his report on organised games which was to bring controversy. The governors agreed on their gradual introduction into the curriculum, with cricket for juniors in the summer of 1949, and then rugby for juniors in S1 the following session, with the progressive introduction of one period for games throughout the school. At the same time the extended Monday classes would end and 'normal hours' would be introduced.

Perhaps this arrangement was seen as the best 'long-term' solution to existing difficulties, but it was the governors' agreement to the appointment of a full-time games master – reputedly the first in Scotland – which was the stumbling block. The fact that the new games master, Donald M. Hastie,[13] came from Dewar's old school, Greenock Academy, in April 1949, aggravated the situation further.

By early in the session of 1949–50 Dewar was reporting to the governors on 'certain alleged grievances'[14] regarding the appointment of Hastie and the withdrawal from voluntary service of thirteen sports masters at Goldenacre. A special meeting of the governors discussed the issue on 24 October: the headmaster was instructed to try to solve the issue. However, Dewar's meeting the following day with the masters broke down as the 'two parties had no common ground'.[15]

The Lord Provost and chairman of the governors, Sir Andrew Murray, a Herioter himself, met with representatives of the sports masters – Messrs Broadwood, Blamire and Welton – while the Very Revd Dean R.J. Mackay met with the headmaster to try to find a working solution. As a result of these meetings the governors recommended that each sport would be controlled by a voluntary convener supported by a committee, with Hastie a member of the latter. The headmaster was 'instructed' to work out the details.

Neither Hastie nor Dewar accepted this development. Hastie sought legal advice, while Dewar announced to the governors on 21 November that the instructions given were 'incompatible with his authority as headmaster'[16] and outwith the terms of his contract. The governors backed down: the headmaster was recommended to ask Hastie to meet with representatives of the sports masters to find a way forward.

Negotiations between Hastie and Broadwood, now the spokesman of the masters, did find a modus operandi which was accepted by both parties.[17] The outstanding issues were left to the governors, who on 4 December, inevitably came down on the side of Hastie (and Dewar): Hastie would coach the 1st and 2nd rugby XVs and be convener of the committee in charge of school athletics.[18] It took a special meeting between Lord Provost Murray and the twelve sports masters (with Welton absent sick) to reach an agreement on the running of the annual school games, but this only ensured an uneasy truce. Criticism continued to be levied at any and all changes Hastie made. His first games on 4 June 1949 were held in front of the grandstand and not beside the cricket pavilion, which upset the traditionalists. By 1953 complaints were widespread that the games were becoming longer and longer and some FPs were concerned that a pleasant social gathering was being turned into a grand sports meeting.[19]

The battleground then moved to the long-established field committee, where Broadwood's influence still waxed strong and of which Hastie was not a member. By June 1951 the governors were questioning its constitution and functions.[20] In truth the field committee, which had been instituted in 1926 when the recreation field had been extended, had met infrequently after 1932 and indeed never met between 1938 and 1946. It was no surprise that the governors determined in May 1953 by 10 to 2 to end its existence. With his power base weakening Broadwood decided on a different tactic: he determined to withdraw from active involvement at Goldenacre, perhaps hoping that others would follow. The governors thanked him for his great contribution to Heriot sport,[21] for he had indeed been an outstanding coach and had produced six unbeaten rugby XVs during his coaching time: incredibly for seven successive years no school won a game against Heriot's at Goldenacre!

Although Broadwood remained a symbol for Dewar's critics until his retirement in 1962 he was more a thorn in the flesh rather than a real threat in his final years at the school. As Heriot's prospered, and particularly as Dewar proved himself an efficient and successful headmaster and appointed more and more staff who owed loyalty to him personally, Broadwood's position weakened, despite his clear popularity among sections of the Heriot's community. Perhaps Broadwood's finest hour was his going: Heriot boys saw him as a hero standing against the authoritarian Dewar. On 12 July 1962 after the presentation of gifts in the assembly hall, presided over by the school captain, James Cunningham, the boys lined the way from there, along the North Terrace, to cheer Broadwood into the quad, where the prefects had arranged a ceremony unique in the history of the school. On a platform facing Heriot's statue Cunningham presented Broadwood with a silver painted key and 'The Freedom of Heriot's'.[22]

Long before then Dewar had attempted to rebuild fences. For the 1949 founder's day two stands were erected in front of the chapel windows – one for FPs and one for staff and ex-staff. The established tradition of boys saluting the founder in the march past was restored – which greatly pleased former pupils in particular. Moreover, by May 1950 *The Herioter* magazine was applauding the continued rise in the proportion of former pupils' sons being admitted – reaching 50 per cent[23] – despite the welcome increase in competition for places.

Throughout Dewar's tenure there was a constant struggle to fill staffing vacancies, especially in science and modern languages. In an attempt to attract and retain quality teachers Dewar adopted the strategy of appointing young teachers coming out of teacher training college and treating them generously. The governors supported this successful tactic, but it was left to Dewar personally to appoint, and he responded by appointing a number who themselves were to become heads in their own right.[24]

All the staff knew where they stood with Dewar and he was a hard taskmaster. When John Westwood, the principal teacher of English, disregarded his instructions, Dewar did not hesitate to suspend him. At a special meeting of the governors on 22 November 1951 the governors supported the headmaster, but as it was suggested that Westwood's actions[25] were perhaps the result of ill-health he was asked to submit to a medical.[26] When a report was received from his own doctor the governors asked the specialist, Professor Sir David Henderson, for his opinion on Westwood's possible future behaviour. The governors set up a sub-committee to interview Westwood, but with his GP claiming that he was still 'mentally sick' this could not be carried out, and the suspension continued. However, following letters from Westwood the governors asked Professor Henderson for a further report. After some delay he examined Westwood on 11 April 1952 and recommended that he be retired on medical grounds. The governors pressed for this and offered an ex gratia payment of seven months' salary.[27] Westwood resigned on 31 May 1952. He had always been an eccentric and the parents of the more modern Heriot pupils were a driving force in his departure. Needless to say, however, *The Herioter* paid tribute to him in December 1952 for 'enriching Heriot's traditions'. The second in the department, Mercer Heron, took over Room 20 – the fifth principal teacher of English since 1886 to do so, following Malcolm Mackenzie, Murray Marr, William Carnon and Westwood.

The length of Dewar's tenure as headmaster meant that he was involved in a significant number of important staffing appointments. E.F. Barron, solicitor, clerk and treasurer of the trust, retired soon after Dewar's arrival, having been connected with Heriot's for over fifty years, and was replaced by another insider, Alexander Douglas.[28] The principal teachership of mathematics also changed hands when A.M. ('Circles') Crawford retired after forty-two years' service. Donald ('Trigger') Grant took over,[29] with Archie ('Pat') Campbell becoming second head.[30] Herbert Sowrey was the new principal teacher of physics, from Glasgow Academy, and the 1950s saw the appointment of a number of younger talented teachers whose careers were to blossom in due course.[31] When Hare retired as deputy head, Dewar decided to separate that post and that of head of the junior school. William A. McKerrow was appointed the new deputy head and T. Gibby Galloway made head of the junior School.[32] A new post of deputy head of the junior school was created and Ross Gall was appointed.

When John Mathieson, principal teacher of geography in 1939, died during the Easter holidays in 1955 he was succeeded by Ian Stone, while Alastair McCheyne became principal teacher of art when James Ryrie (principal teacher since 1933) retired, ensuring George Blamire's departure to Tranent. The year 1955 also saw the retiral after thirty years' teaching of Douglas A.G. Heath, who was replaced by John Hay as head of commercial subjects, while G.A. Scott eventually retired in 1958. He had joined the staff in October 1914, and had been head of natural science from 1919–54 and had written the standard textbook entitled *The Science of Living Things*.

The decade ended with the retiral of Joseph Halliday, principal teacher of German, in August 1959, after a lifetime of service. His replacement, from Fortrose Academy, Allan S. McDonald, was to play a significant role in the history of Heriot's. The early 1960s was to see further retirals: D.R.K ('The Mid') Middlemas who had arrived in September 1921 and in his final days had taught in the chemistry department; Edith Dickson and Nan Gall retired after forty-seven and forty-six years respectively in the junior school; Norman Abercrombie, principal teacher of French, who retired in 1925,[33] and Willie Gould, principal teacher of history, also left after thirty-nine splendid years. The trust office's Alexander Douglas was to retire in February 1963, and David Morris became clerk and treasurer with James Barclay as his assistant.[34]

From his earliest days in office Dewar was aware of the accommodation issues facing the school. He had inherited a roll of 1,531[35] and a dining hall which would only seat 130 at one time. From the first, therefore, there was a clear need for another building, which seemed best placed on a site south of the examination hall.[36] Plans were developed which included new lavatories and the demolition of the old ones, but their introduction was delayed, partly because of the high cost involved (the estimate in October 1948 was £71,240), and partly because of decreasing numbers: the roll fell to 1,361 in 1948–49 and fell further to 1,334 in 1950–51.[37] Dewar appreciated that he would have to be more modest in his accommodation ambitions and turned his attention to the need for a new natural science laboratory. It cost £4,240[38] and was completed in October 1950.

Although school numbers began to pick up again, particularly during the later 1950s, it was clear that the governors would need external financial help for any major building or refurbishment. When in 1956 Heriot's received a grant of £13,900 from the Industrial Fund for the Advancement of Scientific Education in Schools this enabled a refurbishment of the chemistry laboratories – the first since the 1880s – and ensured a modernised chemistry department of three elementary and two advanced labs, with two prep rooms and two balance rooms.[39]

By the early 1960s it was clear to Dewar that the inadequacies of the accommodation of the school could no longer be tolerated. Yet he knew that

any plans would have to preserve the 'wark' (and its view from the castle and its gardens.) Moreover, given the finances of the trust and the inability or unwillingness of the Scottish Education Department to help, Dewar determined to put forward for the first time an extensive scheme of modernisation and appeal for financial support directly to the Heriot community. His original development scheme envisaged a new block over several levels at the north-east corner of the playground on the swimming pool and play-shed site, containing an enlarged dining hall seating 300, two gymnasia and a new larger swimming pool (50 feet by 25 feet) and a conversion of the released seven classrooms to solve other accommodation issues.[40] The old refectory was to become a school museum, bringing together the memorabilia which had been accumulating haphazardly in the charter room over a significant period.[41]

Despite Dewar's claims in June 1964 that 'remarkable progress'[42] had been made in the scheme, this conveniently ignored a change of financial consultants. Hooker, Craigmyle & Company Limited were now engaged, and considerable

Founder's Day Celebrations continue on the first Monday of June (Heriot's birthday). All pupils, from the youngest to the oldest, participate in an impressive ceremony held, in reasonable weather, in the Quadrangle. The earlier, left-hand, picture is from 1968.

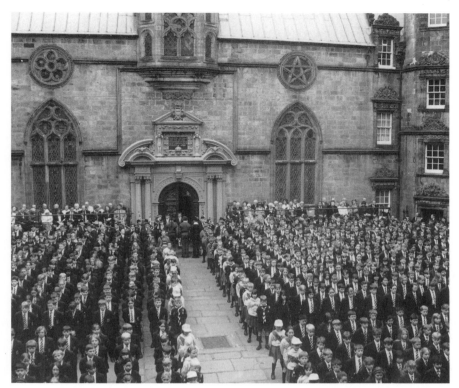

changes to the original plans by the architects (Ross-Smith and Jamieson) in order to achieve SED approval. However, the financial target of £45,000 from the parents was claimed to be the highest-ever appeal which the consultants had ever been associated with. Nonetheless, optimism was misplaced, for on 19 May 1964 representatives of the Royal Fine Arts Commission voiced concerns with the scheme, and then on 13 August the planning committee of Edinburgh Corporation objected to the application on the grounds that its height and bulk would detract from the setting and appearance of the existing school building. The governors, at their meeting on 12 October, agreed again to amend their plans, redrawing the central element, which was to be reduced by 30 feet (height) and 2 feet (bulk) respectively. However, when these amendments were not enough to persuade the corporation planning sub-committee to accept the scheme the governors, on 14 December, decided to appeal to the Secretary of State. The resulting public inquiry, with Sir Robert E. Russell as Reporter, began its deliberations on Monday 4 October 1965, but the outcome went against the School and the Secretary of State rejected the Heriot appeal in the summer of 1966.[43]

The School argued that it was committed by charter to its site, and now

spread over seven separate buildings.[44] The scheme it was putting forward was the only way to meet the educational needs of the School. Their case, however, was not helped by a widespread belief that given the state of sub-standard classrooms the governors would be interested in the long term in the Heriot Cross area for the Junior school. The City planners remained apprehensive that the governors would propose further building.

In putting forward their plans the governors placed priority on preservation of the southern aspect – the Playfair or modern landscape – as well as cost and convenience. The City view that the Castle Esplanade was the only public space from where to see the building completely[45] and a development on the north side would obscure part of the east lawn, was rejected by the governors on the grounds that the proposed Heriot-Watt development in the Grassmarket, already agreed by the Corporation, affected the appearance and setting of Heriot's Hospital even more.[46]

The School was further hampered in its plans by the reputation of the 'wark' as 'one of the supreme architectural

The School produced a line of distinguished rugby full-backs from Dan Drysdale to Kenneth Scotland, and most recently Andrew Irvine, one of the greats of the modern game.

treasures of Scotland'. The 'wark's' architectural quality was undoubtedly complemented by its setting. It was stressed that the confrontation of the two most conspicuous buildings in Edinburgh was deliberately designed.[47] Faced with the setback of rejection, in October 1966, Dewar persuaded the governors to concentrate on the immediate needs of the School – improved gymnasium, toilets, kitchen and dining facilities, and the governors set up a sub-committee which considered alternative schemes. On 8 May 1967, the governors agreed a new plan which involved:

1. Two gyms with changing formed from existing gym and adjoining science rooms
2. Alternative science rooms over the boiler house area to the south with part of the lavatories adjoining this room to the east
3. Refectory, kitchen and the remainder of the lavatory block to be formed on the shrubbery ground to the south of the existing hall.

They then approached the Royal Fine Art Commission and the Town on the planning issues. Eventually, following a written statement by the governors to the Secretary of State, in May 1969, he agreed in principle to building in the south-west grounds. Given the considerable delay the governors immediately agreed to a phased development: the new refectory to be in the first phase, followed by new classrooms and toilets, and finally the gymnasium development. Again, Dewar returned to his vision of preserving the old refectory to become the school's museum, and 'to house the many impressive relics and documents linked with its long history'.[48] The detailed Plan for Phase 1, with a cost limit of £100,000, was accepted by the governors on 25 August 1969.

The new plans were submitted as a matter of course to the Scottish Development Department, which in turn asked the Royal Fine Art Commission for comments. The latter suggested amendments, but the governors, tired at what they saw as the constant negative approach, rejected this and asked the Secretary of State for approval of the submitted plans, which was finally forthcoming in January 1970.

At long last, after an almost wasted decade, Heriot's took an important step forward. The dining hall estimate of £103.495 19s. 9d, from J.H. Russell & Company was accepted by the governors in April of that year. However, there was a sting in the tail. Given the financial constraints and the uncertainty for the future[49] it was decided that the time was not right for another appeal. Phase 2 – new classrooms, extended gymnasium and enlarged swimming-pool complex – was placed 'in abeyance meantime', and the new dining hall was a somewhat disappointing result after such high hopes.

If Dewar found the solution of accommodation problems elusive he was more successful in other areas. The tercentenary celebrations of the opening of the school, in 1959, were to prove a great personal success for him. On the Thursday before June Day (28 May) the school welcomed back a number of the Yugoslavs who had attended Heriot's during the First World War. The same day the headmaster and the president of the Heriot Club held a reception for twenty-five former school captains, including the first school captain of all, Major-General A.E. Potts.[50] The following morning a special commemoration service was conducted by the school chaplain, the Revd Andrew Graham, in the Assembly Halls, the Mound, and was addressed by the Rt Revd Dr Shepherd, Moderator of the General Assembly of the Church of Scotland. An exhibition, held in the art department, was opened later that day by W.F. Arbuckle, Secretary of the SED: it comprised more than 150 exhibits illustrating the vivid history of the school. That evening Dr Douglas Simpson gave a stimulating and important lecture on George Heriot's 'wark'.

On Saturday 30 May the school games were held with customary blue skies and bright sunshine. No fewer than fifteen former champions attended, including the doyen of them all, 'Billy' Grieve of 1903 fame. Other notable attendees included the ever-youthful, ever-popular figure of Mr Gentle and the Lord Provost, Sir Ian A. Johnson-Gilbert. Founder's day itself on Monday 1 June was the climax of the celebrations, with the dedication of the new memorial Greyfriars' Gates,[51] while the governors' dinner that evening proved a very special occasion.

The 'feel-good' factor towards the School which the celebrations created,[52] with Dewar as its leader, enjoying the limelight, and revelling in the attention, seemed to help change opinions. Dewar seemed more of a Heriot's man and his reputation grew in the 1960s, particularly as a result of his work on the 1966 trust scheme when he proved 'so alert to all the educational, sociological and political issues involved'.[53] Dewar's energy was also to prove crucial in taking the school development scheme forward, while he was indefatigable in promoting the appeal fund. Finally, in common with other grant-aided Scottish schools, Heriot's was invited in October 1968 to assist the Public Schools' 'Donnison' Commission. Dewar guaranteed confidentiality to parents, and this resulted in a remarkable return of 92 per cent (1,135 replied from 1,226 households for the 1,517 pupils). He also summarised the returns personally and prepared the report for the Commission.[54] In 1968 the analysis of parent occupations was: professional (degree and above) 38 per cent; professional (below degree) 29 per cent; service (retail, press, police, forces) 19 per cent; manual 11 per cent; housewife 3 per cent.

The views of the parents were a vote of total confidence in the School that Dewar had led and moulded. They valued the high academic standards and achievements; the traditions and spirit of the school and the esprit de corps engendered; the degree of concern shown by the school for the individual pupil; the all-round liberal education provided, with repeated particular reference to the variety of games and extracurricular activities available; the broad base of pupil recruitment; the positive effort directed to character building; and the closeness of the links between school and home. Dewar was particularly pleased personally with the references to the devotion of the teaching staff, not only in the classroom but also in the playing-fields and within the wide scope of extracurricular activity. Moreover, in the matter of fee increases parents made it clear that they would go to considerable lengths to keep their sons at Heriot's.

However, in the last years of headmastership, Dewar was faced firstly with a ceiling on the government grant to the school, and then the determination of the Labour government to reduce the grant from £101,000 in 1969 to £95,240 in 1970. Such pressure brought even more scrutiny to all forms of expenditure.

Although previous headmasters at Heriot's had played a part in education beyond the school, particularly Bedford in the nineteenth century, Dewar was the first to be much involved nationally. When the ordinary grade examination was mooted, with setting of papers and marking being taken over by the Scottish Examination Board, it was Dewar who used his wide knowledge of Scottish teachers to write inviting practitioners to take on the task of secretaries of the new subject panels. This established the 'central nervous system' of the SEB and Dewar himself proved a distinguished convener of its examination committee.[55] He was also appointed the chairman of the governors of Moray House, president of the Association of Headmasters of Scottish Senior Secondary schools (1958–9) and gained a number of distinctions.[56] In 1955 he was awarded an OBE, principally for his services to the Scottish Air Cadet Council; in 1958 he was elected a Fellow of the Royal Society of Edinburgh, and in 1962 he gained the Diploma de Chevalier des Palmes Académiques for services to French culture. Towards the end of his career, in 1970, he was awarded a Doctor of Letters from Heriot-Watt College.

On 13 October 1969 Dewar gave notice of his intention to retire, having reached the age of 65. A sub-committee of governors under vice-chairman Louden drew up a short-leet from the nineteen applicants.[57] The governors reverted to norm – probably even Dewar saw and supported the reasons for doing so – and Allan McDonald, deputy head and head of German, was appointed to take over as headmaster of the School.

Nobody who came into contact with Bill Dewar, whether pupil, staff, parent or governor, was neutral about him. Some of the staff who had opposed him in the beginning remained implacably opposed to him throughout his tenure. However, as time went on their numbers dwindled and Dewar himself mellowed and became increasingly accepted: the appreciation on his retiral about his 'loyal and devoted service' to Heriot's was sincere and deserved.

Dewar was one of the 'old school', remaining a disciplinarian all his life. He set high standards and was never afraid to do his job no matter how unpleasant it might be or how unpopular he might become. There were regular 'revolts' of pupils which led him to drastic measures: the cancellation of the mid-term holiday in February 1964 was one example. Nonetheless, he appreciated the need to move forward and there were many times when his innate common sense, allied to a warm sympathy and indeed compassion, kept him in touch with the young and the changing attitudes to all aspects of school life. Only later did schoolboys appreciate just how understanding and kind their headmaster had been! The modern Heriot's of today owes much to the leadership of William McL. Dewar.

His successor, Allan McDonald, had attended the Royal High School before returning to his native Glasgow as a pupil at Giffnock and at Eastwood schools. His time at the University of Glasgow, where he studied French and German, also coincided with service as a lieutenant in the 21st Army Group Signals. After postgraduate study at Glasgow and the Sorbonne he trained as a teacher and took up his first post at Johnstone High School in 1948. He moved to Eastwood and was also head of Department at Fortrose before being appointed principal teacher of German at Heriot's in 1959, succeeding Joe Halliday. He continued to hold this post, even after he succeeded William McKerrow as deputy head in September 1967. He proved the obvious but nonetheless inspired choice as headmaster: he worked hard and was meticulous over detail, and these assets allied to his sincerity and approachability were a powerful combination. As 'the perfect gentlemen' he was a successful headmaster as he had the confidence of Dr Dewar and 'insiders'. Having only arrived

Allan S. McDonald joined Heriot's in 1959 and following internal promotion became Headmaster in 1970. He led the School into co-education and played a leading part in keeping the School independent.

in 1959 he had little of the baggage of those who had been longer at Heriot's. Significantly, in one of his final decisions, Dr Dewar persuaded the governors to appoint David C. Mackenzie[58] depute head and John J. Roy[59] as second depute – a new post.

The 1970s were to prove a difficult time for the School. The surprise victory of the Tories under Edward Heath at the General Election of June 1970 at least took some immediate political pressure off grant-aided schools in the short term, with a new Secretary of State withdrawing Circular 600 and restoring grant-in-aid, but by calculations based on 40 per cent of expenditure, not the historic 60 per cent. However, there were other challenges pressing for decisions from the new headmaster.

McDonald inherited a full school of 1,544 pupils, despite the inexorable increase in fees.[60] The new regime was soon under pressure from the boys, who, perhaps rightly, felt that the new headmaster would be more sympathetic to their case, if put in the proper way, than the previous incumbent. The issue of hairstyle, in particular, was symbolic for the boys[61] and the regulations were challenged. On 14 February 1972 the governors, following representation from the headmaster, decided that given 'general social conditions prevailing throughout the City nowadays, hair may be long, provided it is kept clean and tidy: standards relating to hair to be at the discretion of the Headmaster'.[62] Unsurprisingly, the further request to have the school's attitude to smoking changed fell on deaf ears.[63]

The issue of staffing was also soon on the agenda. McDonald had been involved in appointing the new senior staff in infants, primary and secondary: Jean Redman, who had joined the school in 1934 and become infant mistress in 1945, retired, and was replaced by Nan Hastie (wife of games master, Donald); John Roy's and Gilbert Galloway's promotions were inspired decisions; both were loyal and well loved in the Heriot community. However, more fundamental changes followed when McDonald persuaded the governors to accept the implications of Circular 780 – the Green Paper on 'The Structure of Promoted Posts in Secondary Schools in Scotland'. On 12 April 1971 the governors agreed in principle to them and they were introduced for session 1972–73. Three faculties were set up – arts and humanities, sciences and technology, and guidance and leisure (both personal and careers). Again Heriot's proved it was not afraid to innovate, even before change had been introduced in the maintained sector.

The fees were again increased (by £10.50 per term) to cover

James Ross was a pupil of Heriot's (1929-1940) and, in his final year, School Captain, captain of rugby and athletics. A successful businessman, he was the powerful Chairman of Governors who fought off a determined State take-over of the School.

the new arrangements. As all appointments were internal, the result was an opportunity of promotion to principal teacher level for a younger generation of staff, which in turn led to innovation and enthusiasm both in and out of the classroom. The retiral of Herbert S. Sowrey[64] and William G.D. Brown[65] and the promotion of Alasdair Hogg[66] also helped in this regard.[67] The quality of both the staff and the pupils was clear, and this was borne out by the 1976 HMI visit which resulted in 'a very favourable report'.[68]

Another early issue was the role of parents who had been increasingly concerned about a possible threat to the school and naturally wished to be more involved, particularly as it seemed likely that the threat was liable to recur. Again it was Allan McDonald, personally convinced of the value of a new partnership, who steered the parents forward and persuaded the governors to agree to the setting up of a parents' association.[69] On 17 March the first meeting of the PA took place, and Ken Grimston was elected the first chairman. It was not long before the worth of the new body was being appreciated. Assistance was given to the school in material ways, and in its first days it provided another mini-bus and refurbished the junior hall. Most importantly, it proved a vital forum for representing parental opinion.

McDonald could feel very satisfied with his first few years as headmaster. By 1975 the roll had risen to 1,590.[70] Although this meant large classes and cramped accommodation, which did not help academic results, it reflected a confidence in the kind and quality of education available. The first open day of 21 June 1974, with the pageant on George Heriot as its centrepiece, confirmed such a view. However, financial stringency was having its effects. The number of girl foundationers (introduced in 1897) was reduced,[71] the anniversary dinner was only continued in modified and economical form, junior school boys were kept in school at lunchtime primarily to boost the popularity of school lunches and cut deficits, annual senior and university bursaries were discontinued, and in March 1975 the generous remission of fees to staff who brought their children to Heriot's was reviewed.[72] The situation was aggravated by the Houghton award for teachers' salaries, which, although overdue, ensured a substantial backdated rise for staff which forced the governors to increase fees immediately by £34 per term (and instituting a one-off surcharge of £35).

The advent of the Labour Government to power in 1974 led to an ultimatum to all grant-aided schools on their futures. On 17 February 1975 a special meeting of governors discussed the options. They decided 9 to 2 to issue a statement of intent, which was finally agreed on 10 March. The School would continue as long as possible under current arrangements, but if the government withdrew financial aid 'every endeavour would be made for the school to continue, even to the extent of going independent'.[73] The inevitable happened: within the month the government decided to end aid, but the block grant was to be phased out over six years from the beginning of the 1976 session, although large cuts in current and capital expenditure were demanded immediately. With grant-aided schools not making much of a fight in response, the Heriot governors flirted with the idea of joining in the Merchant Company scheme, which envisaged a 'consortium' of 'endowed independent schools,'[74] but there were worries that such a partnership was 'likely to mark the end of George Heriot's School as such'[75] and the talks collapsed. The only other option to continuing to independence was to integrate with the state system. Trust officials met with the SED and local education officials and politicians, but Councillor Foulkes, chairman of Lothian Region Education Committee, held that he could see no future for Heriot's in a comprehensive system, nor could he offer any reassurance on the future of the foundation. Given such a position it is unsurprising that the governors rejected a move towards the state system by 10 votes to 2 on 8 September 1975. Instead it was decided that Heriot's would continue under the existing arrangements as the grant was phased out, although it was appreciated that the resulting ever-increasing increase in fees was bound to affect numbers. Indeed already in 1975-76 the uncertainty over the future of the school had led to the role falling from 1,590 to 1,503. It is not surprising that the first governor discussion on the possible introduction of co-education occurred at this time, and in April 1976 a sub-committee of governors was formed to take the issue forward.

The composition of the governing body itself now became a matter of dispute. With the restructure of local government[76]and the introduction of a two-tier system a legal wrangle ensued between the new regional and district authorities. The governors decided not to invite any councillors to meetings until this was settled.[77] During the interregnum the vice-chairman the Revd Dr R. Stewart Louden, took over the chairmanship:[78] the first person other than the Lord Provost ever to have held the position. However, in December 1975 he retired and was succeeded by James Ross.[79] By March 1976 the governors had decided by 6 votes to 3 that the seven councillors should be shared between both authorities – three from the district and four from the region. However, on 21 May an undefended decree was pronounced in the Court of Session, declaring Lothian Regional Council entitled to all seven local authority governors on the George Heriot Trust Board.

With the composition of the governing body at least temporarily settled the usual issues surfaced. Fees had to be increased again as were the costs of school lunches. Gilbert Galloway, Ian Stone, Jean Stenhouse, [80] Jim Barclay from the trust, and Dr Alec Bateman[81] from the governing body all retired.[82] The old refectory was converted into a unique staff room much to the convenience, comfort and satisfaction of the vast majority of staff.[83] Yet, although there were financial issues about the phasing out of grant support, the advantage of growing independence for decision-making became increasingly apparent. The 1975 legislation for schools to complete 200 teaching days was not enforced at Heriot's, 197 being decided by the headmaster and governors for the working year, and from January 1977 the school no longer needed SED approval for salaries or fees. Unfortunately, numbers fell again in 1976 to 1,428, in 1977 to 1,358, and by 1978 they were down to 1,274.

Such a decline encouraged the governors' sub-committee on co-education, which reported favourably on the project, and on 2 December 1977 the governors authorised the architects, Reiach & Hall, to draw up detailed plans and estimates for the development scheme recommended in its report. During 1978 further progress on this move was made. There was envisaged a phased development and general introduction of girls in order to minimise disruption to the on-going school acitivities. The school was, therefore, in good heart during its 350th anniversary celebrations of the founding of the Hospital. All went well with these, and they climaxed with a visit from His Royal Highness the Duke of Edinburgh on 7 July.

Although it was of concern that in July 1978 when Lothian Regional Council appointed its eight governors it abandoned convention and insisted on them all being from the majority group (the Labour party), the final three governors' meetings of the year passed uneventfully. However, on 5 January 1979, unexpectedly, all the councillors turned up,[84] and James Ross found himself replaced as chairman by Duncan Milligan, following a 10 to 9 vote. An attempt to take Heriot's into the state system was now under way. In an article in *The Scotsman* newspaper on 12 January entitled 'Wind of change ruffles Heriot's' the new chairman appeared to reject the 8 September 1975 decision of the governors to go fully independent. At a special meeting of the governors on 22 January to clarify the position – not attended by the new chairman[85] – the 1975 decision was reaffirmed and the resulting press release held that all governors had a responsibility not to undermine the confidence of fee-paying parents, who now contributed 96 per cent of the income of the school.

The president of the Heriot Club, Iain Morrison, organised a meeting of various elements of the Heriot community, chaired by Sir Alan Hume, one of the club's representatives on the governing body. This co-ordinating committee began to meet regularly, and included representatives of governors, the Heriot Club, parents' association and staff. It met usually in Ken Grimston's offices and throughout was ably advised by James Mackay, soon to be Lord Advocate south of the border. The 'Heriot' governors – those committed to independence and opposed to state takeover – now began to operate a three-line-whip for governor meetings.

The school staff demanded a meeting with the new chairman, and on 7 February Chairman Milligan met with them in a hostile and uncomfortable confrontation. He was forced to accept that the governors' policy had not changed, but he maintained his contrary personal view. The staff, however, feared for their futures and that of the school. Where was the catchment area for Heriot's if taken into the state system? How could it continue to be recognisable as Heriot's? The staff set up their own staff association to defend themselves.

Meantime, following an extremely militant parents' association meeting of over 650 where Milligan was pressurised by vociferous poarents, PA chairman George Mann took legal advice on how to frustrate Labour plans.

With a 'hands off Heriot's' campaign building, at the Lothian Regional Council meeting on 20 February 1979 demonstrations of parents and former pupils took place with Ken Scotland and Andy Irvine, two famous Scottish rugby internationalists and former pupils, prominent. Deputations from the parents' association and Heriot Club were heard.

A vigorous correspondence now took place between the sides in the local press.[86] Dr Dewar, the most authoritative of sources, in a powerfully argued letter to *The Scotsman* contradicted Councillor Foulkes' assertion that George Heriot had intended to provide education for those who could not afford it, and his assertion that Heriot's had been moving inexorably towards being a private school. For Dewar the governors had closely observed the spirit of the founder's intention, and any recent increase in school fees was put firmly where it belonged, namely, at the door of the government for freezing and phasing out grant-in-aid.[87] (Appendix 8)

In early March, Lothian Regional Council's policy received unanimous backing at the Labour Party Scottish Conference at Perth, with Duncan Milligan arguing that a large private sector was a threat to comprehensives. By mid-month Foulkes had predicted that Heriot's would close within a decade if it did not join the state system.

The election result of May 1979 came to the rescue of Heriot's.[88] The victory of Mrs Thatcher meant that the immediate crisis was over, and indeed only one Labour regional councillor attended the June meeting of the governors. However, the threat was not entirely ended, for in November 1979 the Labour Party took an extra seat on the governing body when the education committee replaced Miss Mary Rose-Caden.[89] She was bitter about the decision: she was told only minutes before the beginning of the education meeting that she was to be replaced, despite having two years of her term of office to run. The Heriot Club asked opinion of counsel, and James McGhie's advice suggested that although the region could not change once an appointment was made, it really needed Miss Caden herself to object to its actions. When she did just this before the Court of Session, Lord Kincraig granted an interim interdict preventing Ian Christie, treasurer of the Edinburgh Labour Party, from taking up a seat on the governing body[90] and ensured continuation of Miss Caden on the board. The governors decided 8 to 6 to accept this decision and rejected the motion to seek further legal opinion.

At the crucial governors' meeting to elect office-bearers on 11 January 1980 all twenty-one governors were present. The 'Heriot' governors replaced Milligan as chairman with James Ross by 11 votes to 10, and Colonel Reid was elected vice-chairman (with Milligan standing) by the same vote. Lindsay Stewart was elected as finance convener. A masterstroke was the nomination of Miss Caden as education convener, although the Labour group proposed Milligan again against her. The Heriot 'party' stood together and Miss Caden was elected 11 to 10. In this way all the offices were won back and 'at this point convener Crighton, councillors Mrs Herriot, Lindsay, Mulvey, Taylor and Young left'.[91] The School was 'saved', at least for the present, and the position was further strengthened when in February 1980 the Regional Council decided to abandon its attempt to replace Miss Caden.

The Heriot community acted quickly to avoid further difficulties. After discussion with the Tory Secretary of State, George Younger, a new trust scheme was devised by the governors and accepted by 11 votes to 2.[92] Lothian regional representation was to be cut from eight to three; of the two educational representatives only one was to be appointed by the Region and the other by the governing body (ensuring Miss Caden could remain); three Heriot Club representatives were to have seats (an increase of one); three others were to be co-opted by the governing body and two parents' association members were to be introduced.[93] With the enactment of this scheme on 26 November 1980 the school would be free from further political interference or 'take-over'. The campaign of the 1970s to save the existence of the School had been successful, although the resulting increase of fees would certainly change its social mix: the comparisons with the 1870s and 1880s campaign to save the Hospital are obvious, despite the different result.

Given the furore and attention to the political issue the major educational change of co-education slipped in, almost surreptitiously. The lowest tender for building alterations – £59,118 from local firm Peter Walker & Son – was accepted and the first phase, begun in 1979, consisted of alterations to the toilets and cloakrooms in the new refectory and at the west end of the junior school, and alterations to the senior gymnasium changing-room accommodation, to provide facilities for girls. Similar work at Goldenacre was given to James Millar & Partners and cost £25,200.

The second phase followed in the summer of 1980 and William Black & Sons went ahead with around £100,000 of work.[94] The Old Physics Lecture Room (OPLR) was gutted and the space replanned to create new changing and toilet accommodation for girls and boys, with walk-through footbaths and showers leading to the swimming-pool. A new building was constructed in the narrow space between the junior school and the junior hall, two floors below playground level, and was designed to provide new separate club rooms for the scouts, guides, sub-aqua club and the sailing club. A new facility of a weight-training room was added.

Phase III in 1981 involved further modifications to form toilets, changing rooms and showers for girls, and a gym store at the east end of the junior hall and the conversion of a small classroom in the bridge link on the floor above, to give similar facilities for boys. These areas were designed to be used by the junior pupils during the day and the badminton club in the evenings, and also provided the necessary accommodation for licensing the use of the junior hall for public performances. It was, however, Phase IV, commencing in 1982, which was to prove the most far-reaching and costly. The plan was to demolish the old playsheds at the east end of the playground and erect a new junior school classroom block of eight classrooms for primary classes 1–4 at a cost of £313,000. The shape of the building was dictated by the area involved and the need to keep reduction of the playground area to a minimum. Its height had to be as low as possible as the planning department insisted on the requirement that it should not interrupt the view of the 'wark' and its podium from the Castle Esplanade. The form and materials used by John Monteith Limited were selected to be in keeping with the older surrounding buildings.

The 1979–80 session had opened with an increase in the total roll (1,274 to 1,390), but more significantly with 112 girls. Although normal routine quickly asserted itself there were immediate cultural changes. New clubs including cooking, sewing and Scottish country dancing appeared and the CCF benefited from the new female recruits. Gradually former pupils became accustomed to seeing girls in Heriot uniform, and in a relatively short time, like all good ideas, it was wondered why the decision had taken so long to be introduced. After all the Trust had supported girl foundationers in other local schools since 1897!

One of the strands of Conservative Party thinking had been how the government would support the grant-aided, soon to be independent, school sector. Their scheme involved assisted places introduced in place of grant-in-aid in 1981–82 and offered bursaries to 'lower income families'. Although the educational intention was admirable – to ensure that the social mix of the sector was as wide as possible and that a lack of money should be no barrier to entry – it was politically contentious. Moreover, by now Heriot governors feared that any government support, however well meant, would bring political strings. There were also practical issues: the scheme was only for secondary entrants and this might encourage parents to delay entry and hit at primary enrolment. The other major drawback – that the election of a government of a different political complexion would end the scheme[95] – could be overcome by the setting up of a specific bursary fund to deal with the results of that particular scenario. In October 1980, given the news from the Scottish Council for Independent schools that thirty-two schools had already decided to participate, McDonald advised cautiously that Heriot's should follow suit.

The financial pressures, especially those connected with the introduction of co-education, led the governors to investigate the savings that could be made by selling 20 York Place and accommodating the trust at Lauriston Place. By December 1979 Norman Gray & Partners had produced a plan utilising 1,000 square feet at the south end of the refectory at a cost of £42,000. This made good economic sense, especially given the £150,000 (less professional fees) brought in by the sale of York Place.[96] The Trust moved in September 1980, after ninety-one years in its previous location.

The condition of the stonework and roofs of the 'wark' were a real concern to the governors and a report from Historic Scotland, claiming the need for £270,000 worth of work, did not alleviate anxieties. Negotiations for grants took place, and a long-term remedial action plan was agreed. The tender for the first phase on the south-west tower and chimneys of £30,247 was accepted from D. Blake & Co Ltd.[97] And thus began the extensive and lengthy on-going work on the old building.

With the School safe and co-education introduced, Allan McDonald, although only approaching sixty, determined to retire. His tenure as headmaster had taken its toll but his constant good-naturedness and sincerity had won many admirers. In temperament he was very different from his predecessor, but like Dewar he believed in appointing good professionals and letting them get on with the job, although he had reverted to the Heriot tradition of promoting internally as the rule rather than the exception. There were fifty-three applicants for his post and four were interviewed on 24 and 25 March 1982. However, the governors failed to reach a decision. Following much discussion it was decided to readvertise the job. This time there were fifty-nine applicants and nine were interviewed. On 4 December after a run-off involving J.G. Carson, deputy head of Jordanhill School, Keith P. Pearson, deputy principal of George Watson's, was appointed to take over as headmaster of Heriot's with effect from 11 April 1983.

CHAPTER FOURTEEN

Into a New Era

Keith Pearson was born in Lancashire, attended Preston Grammar School and gained an exhibition to the University of Cambridge to read French and Spanish. After graduation he taught at Rossall School, before becoming head of modern languages at Watson's College, and in 1977 one of two deputy principals there under Sir Roger Young. Yet despite his pedigree he was, in a number of respects, a surprising appointment as headmaster of Heriot's. He was English; (and only Bedford before him had come from beyond Scotland); he was not a committed Christian (which was seen as a handicap by some); his only Scottish teaching experience had been at Watson's (still regarded as the 'traditional' rival) and although a keen sportsman he preferred soccer to rugby football. In the event it was perhaps because, like Dewar, he was an 'outsider' that he was able to make the hard decisions necessary to take Heriot's into a new era.

The school Pearson took over had survived the take-over bid of Lothian Region but in retrospect it had been a close-run thing, and Heriot's, in April 1983, was certainly not out of the woods. Its estimated deficit for 1982–83 was an enormous £148,000 which was translated into a need for a 20 per cent fee increase. The governors believed that parents would see this as excessive and feverishly resorted to drastic cost-cutting,[1] which led to a decrease in the deficit to £117,741 and an ultimate fee increase of 11 per cent.[2] More dramatically a number of governors, probably the majority, favoured postponing, even abandoning, the next phase of the co-educational programme. Pearson made a decisive contribution: he argued that without Phase V, which involved accommodation for food and nutrition, fabrics, audio-typing and secretarial studies, the curriculum would remain imbalanced and the demise of co-education was a distinct possibility. Chairman Ross backed his new appointment and a revised programme was scheduled. Heriot's could look forward to becoming a successful co-educational school, with boys and girls being equal partners.

Keith Pearson became Headmaster of Heriot's in 1983 following a period as Deputy Principal of traditional rivals, George Watson's College. He persuaded the Heriot Governors to move to full co-education and left the School in a strong position on his early retiral.

Financial problems had been a recurrent theme throughout the twentieth century, but three factors improved the situation markedly for Pearson and the school. Firstly, after years of dispute the long-awaited James Fraser Brown Bequest began to arrive in a series of payments. By September 1988 the money received totalled £1,319,240.50. Secondly, with the fear of take-over or closure ended, the roll of the school began to increase markedly. Pearson inherited a school of 1,276, but within a decade this had risen to 1,474, and important too was the increase in the take-up of junior school places.[3] Moreover, Pearson also saw the lack of a nursery as a weakness, particularly as practically all other Edinburgh fee-paying schools had instituted nurseries as a recruiting ground. In November 1983 Pearson persuaded the governors to introduce a nursery from the beginning of the following session,[4] with fifteen three-year-olds and fifteen four-year-olds.[5] Thirdly, Pearson was also fortunate in his advisers. The new secretary and treasurer, Craigie Dougan, was also an 'outsider' who had not been brought up with the traditional penny-pinching approach of the Trust. He was sympathetic to Pearson's ambitions and plans, as was George Sydserff, the member of staff given charge of marketing.

The stronger financial base persuaded Pearson and Dougan to take forward a plan to convert the assembly hall into a hall, library and music department. Despite the new library of 1968,

The New Junior School Block was opened by the Rt Hon Tom Morgan, Lord Provost of Edinburgh, in September 1983. His wife has a friendly chat with some of the pupils.

its facilities were woefully inadequate, and although Martin Rutherford, principal teacher of music until his departure for Australia, had progressed school music considerably, particularly concerts and tours, the instrumentalists had no accommodation. The governors considered the plan as expensive, as the cost per square foot seemed excessive compared with the real increase in accommodation achieved. However, Pearson argued that the development should be seen in the context of problems of school space and the ensuing improvements to be achieved in biology and home economics. The discussions with the various heritage and architectural groups took place, and in 1987–88 John Monteith Limited, with a budget of £1 million, created an upper level hall to accommodate the 1,000 pupils of the secondary department, and a ground floor of library, two large music rooms, four practice rooms, instrument stores and toilet facilities. The building was opened officially by the Lord Chancellor, Lord Mackay of Clashfern, on Friday 30 September 1988.[6]

The Gordian knot for Pearson to cut was the tradition of appointing teaching staff without advertisement or governor involvement. From the time of his own appointment Pearson determined to appoint the best in open competition, which caused anger and resentment. Further, a number of personal disappointments were aggravated by 'promises' which Pearson

The Greyfriars' extension, of four more classrooms for the Junior School, was opened by HRH The Princess Anne in June 1996.

was adamant should not have been given and would not be kept. Nonetheless, where internal candidates proved best at interview they were appointed. On the other hand, Pearson showed an appreciation of staff sensitivities and welfare by introducing a scheme for travelling scholarships, supporting salaries above national scales, promoting an early retirement scheme, introducing a management team,[7] and, most importantly, by persuading the governors to remain committed to a 'large' school. Pearson understood the effects downsizing would have on the morale of the staff, and he firmly opposed that option. Instead he worked hard to bring down the size of classes, rightly believing that optimum class sizes were important in delivering quality learning and teaching, and were also important in marketing terms for increasingly discriminating parents.

The year 1986 saw the celebration of the centenary of the School, and it was a time to ponder on how far Heriot's had progressed since its opening as a day school. Like similar schools with Hospital traditions it ranked well academically in the examination league tables, which were to be increasingly fashionable, and like them it now could be viewed as a national player as opposed to a local player in education. Its ethos, too, was comparable, although pupils, staff, governors and a considerable number of parents, probably saw Heriot's as unique, and certainly only a very few schools could match not just its traditions but the strong belief that numbers of the Heriot community have in them. In particular, there remained the appreciation of George Heriot and his historic bequest – the foundation still existing if not thriving – and the general desire to retain, even strengthen, a school with as wide a social mix in school population as possible.

This was also the year (1986) that the independent status of Heriot's was confirmed. In some respects this was a non-event, for the school had been set on its independent course in 1975, and with the failure of attempts to change this decision no other option was feasible. Yet it did mean a re-statement of school policy with Heriot's committing itself in the future to:

Alistair Hector became current Headmaster of Heriot's in 1997. With a Scottish education and varied teaching experience both north and south of the border, he is well placed to take the School forward in the future.

1. A broad-based curriculum leading to Scottish exams.
2. A wide range of extra-curricular activities.
3. Staff salaries and conditions of service to be at least the equal of those applicable for teachers in the maintained sector.
4. Headmaster and staff working together to ensure good discipline without corporal punishment.[8]

The contrast between the School of the later twentieth century

and the early Hospital is striking. In the seventeenth century Heriot's was a fragile experiment struggling to fulfil its founder's bequest. Some governors put themselves and Town before the Hospital, but fortunately they were but the few exceptions. In time, Heriot's became the model for educational establishments in Scotland and beyond. During the nineteenth century the governors made a significant contribution to education by instituting the impressive outdoor schools (Appendix 3) and the successful evening classes.[9] Even when forced to reform, the governors took over the running of the Heriot-Watt College and laid the foundations for its later university status.

One constant theme persists throughout: the June Day celebrations have continued uninterrupted since 1659 with the centrepiece being the anniversary sermon. As early as 1683 the Revd John Mackqueen eulogised George Heriot:

> I think his works may supersede any historical account of him. He has left a more lasting monument of his piety and charity to bear his name and perpetuate his fame, than all paper memorials whatsoever are capable to perform. So long as there will be any memory of this honourable city, his name shall be mentioned with honour and esteem. When all the flashes of sensual pleasure are quite extinct; when all the glances of temporal felicity and human excellency are quite forgot; when all the flowers of secular glory are withered away; when all earthly trophies are burned in their funeral ashes; when all the eulogies of conquerors engravened on brass, or those pompous inscriptions on marble undergo the fate of those drawn on the sand, or written in water; when all the stately monuments and sumptuous statues of the Roman heroes are levelled with the ground; when this world and all its parade shall be consumed; when the heavens shall be rolled together as a scroll, and the host thereof dissolved; when the elements shall melt, and the earth be burned up with fervent heat, the name of the renowned GEORGE HERIOT shall be blessed before the Lord, and his works shall be in everlasting remembrance.[10]

Such words were not overdrawn in the seventeenth century. The ensuing substantial fruits of George Heriot's Bequest, which have benefited thousands of children and adults in the last three and a half centuries, ensure that Mackqueen's views have stood the test of time.

Music and drama flourish in both Junior and Senior Schools. This collage shows scenes from the School play, about Jinglin' Geordie himself, in 2000. The play raised £12,000 for charity.

Appendices
—

APPENDIX I

Numbers entering Heriot's Hospital

1659	43
1660s	48
1670s	60
1680s	159
1690s	234 (total 1659 – 1699 = 544)
1700s	210
1710s	197
1720s	175
1730s	183
1740s	183 (total 1700 – 1749 = 948)
1750s	217
1760s	148
1770s	176
1780s	180
1790s	219 (total 1750 – 1799 = 940)
1800s	240
1810s	323
1820s	354
1830s	301
1840s	325 (total 1800 – 1849 = 1,543)
1850s	301
1860s	299 [+ 18 non-residents in 1869]
1870s	213 [+ 121 non-residents]
1880–5	136 (total 1850 – 1885 = 1,158) [+ 70 non-residents]
Total (1659 – 1885)	5,133

APPENDIX 2
Occupations of parents of Hospital boys (where known)

I. LATER I7TH CENTURY

	1659	1660s	1670s	1680s	1690s	TOTAL
Merchants	20	16	20	40	59	155
Hammermen[1]	–	2	3	12	32	49
Tailors	4	3	4	17	16	44
Wrights[2]	2	2	2	8	17	31
Skinners[3]	2	–	2	6	14	24
Cordiners[4]	–	1	5	10	7	23
Malters (Brewers)	2	–	2	10	8	22
Writers (Clerks)	1	4	2	4	9	20
Baxters (Bakers)	1	–	1	8	5	15
Ministers	1	2	–	7	6	16
Bonnetmakers[5]	–	–	–	4	9	13
Medical[6]	–	2	3	2	4	11
Websters (weavers)	–	–	1	–	10	11
Masons	3	–	3	3	2	11
Printers[7]	–	–	2	8	1	11
Soldiers/Sailors	–	1	1	1	7	10
Fleshers (Candlemakers)	–	–	1	–	7	8
TOTAL	43	48	60	159	234	544

1 Hammermen include metalworkers, blacksmiths, goldsmiths (jewellers), pewterers, armourers, locksmiths, founders, ironsmiths, tinsmiths.
2 Wrights include glaziers, boatwrights, painters, sawyers, slaterers, sievewrights.
3 Skinners include furriers, glovers.
4 Cordiners include leather workers, basketmakers, tanners, shoemakers, saddlers, upholsterers.
5 Bonnetmakers include dyers, litsters, waulkers, sheermen, hatters.
6 Medical include surgeons, barbers, apothecaries.
7 Printers include stationers, bookbinders, engravers, compositors, artists, map-makers.

2. FIRST HALF OF THE 18TH CENTURY

	1700S	1710S	1720S	1730S	1740S	TOTAL
Merchants	52	45	45	42	33	217
Hammermen	21	20	16	19	23	99
Wrights	9	14	14	21	17	75
Bakers	11	13	6	11	11	52
Skinners	9	9	6	16	11	51
Tailors	18	8	6	7	10	49
Bonnetmakers	11	11	14	6	5	47
Fleshers	5	3	3	12	17	40
Writers (Clerks)	21	9	3	3	4	40
Cordiners	7	13	6	4	6	36
Wigmakers	1	2	15	7	8	33
Malters	5	4	6	8	7	30
Medical	5	8	5	2	10	30
Ministers	5	11	–	–	1	17
Weavers	3	2	3	1	6	15
Masons	3	5	2	1	1	12
Printers	5	–	–	4	2	11
TOTAL	210	197	175	183	183	948

3. SECOND HALF OF THE 18TH CENTURY

	1750s	1760s	1770s	1780s	1790s	TOTAL
Hammermen	14	18	35	27	32	126
Merchants	29	21	21	25	22	118
Wrights	22	13	13	19	18	85
Cordiners	13	19	20	16	12	80
Fleshers	16	7	11	16	11	61
Medical	13	6	6	12	24	61
Skinners	20	7	15	11	7	60
Weavers	16	8	7	9	14	54
Bakers	18	4	8	5	15	50
Bonnetmakers	10	5	8	11	9	43
Tailors	4	6	10	10	9	39
Malters	11	4	4	2	9	30
Printers	–	5	4	4	6	19
Wigmakers	5	8	3	–	1	17
Grocers[8]	–	–	–	3	12	15
Coopers[9]	2	3	3	3	4	15
TOTAL	217	148	176	180	219	940

8 Grocers include shopmen.
9 Coopers include wood craftsmen, cabinet-makers, chair-makers, joiners

4. FIRST HALF OF THE 19TH CENTURY

	1800s	1810s	1820s	1830s	1840s	TOTAL
Hammermen	41	70	65	53	45	274
Wrights	30	66	65	51	37	249
Cordiners	18	23	32	28	30	131
Bonnetmakers	14	20	28	14	13	89
Masons	7	23	27	21	8	86
Fleshers	14	14	26	20	8	82
Tailors	13	14	13	13	24	77
Coopers	6	14	9	16	18	63
Printers	8	9	11	12	22	62
Grocers	10	5	10	10	26	61
Merchants	11	11	19	11	8	60
Bakers	6	10	13	11	8	48
Malters	12	2	6	11	16	47
Medical	15	9	3	5	1	33
Weavers	6	8	5	4	3	26
Writers (Clerks)	5	—	2	3	12	22
Hairdressers	2	1	—	2	13	18
Skinners	3	3	5	2	2	15
TOTAL	240	323	354	301	325	1543

5. 1850 – 1886

	1850s	1860s	1870s	1880-5	TOTAL
Hammermen	33	46	26	17	122
Coopers	17	34	34	17	102
Printers	22	26	36	12	96
Tailors	40	35	10	9	94
Wrights	29	28	27	10	94
Writers (Clerks)	15	12	28	18	73
Waiters[10]	17	15	30	5	67
Masons	9	15	14	24	62
Cordiners	16	18	17	8	59
Grocers	13	12	10	8	43
Malters	14	14	13	–	41
Bonnetmakers	19	5	4	3	31
Bakers	7	5	10	4	26
Fleshers	7	5	8	1	21
Merchants	3	6	3	1	13
TOTAL	301	317	334	206	1158

10 Waiters include butlers, caretakers, porters, footmen.

Status and Wages of Parents/Guardians of Heriot Hospital Children in March 1868

178 BOYS ON ROLL
8 fatherless and motherless
42 fatherless
17 motherless
111 both parents alive

Of the 138 parents or guardians, all of whom, with the exception of two, were tradesmen or operatives:

76 had incomes under £50 p.a.
48 had incomes between £50–£60 p.a.
7 had incomes between £60–£70 p.a.
3 had incomes between £70–£80 p.a.
4 had incomes between £80–£90 p.a.

Suggests that Heriot Hospital was serving a 'pauper' group who could not afford education.

Source: F.W. Bedford (1872), p. 194.

APPENDIX 3
The Heriot Outdoor Schools

SCHOOL	JUVENILE /INFANT	DATE OF OPENING	NUMBER OF PUPILS
1. Heriot Bridge	Juvenile	1838	318
2. High School Yards	Infant	1840	185
3. Cowgate Port	Juvenile	1840	336
4. Old Assembly Close	Juvenile	1840	315
5. Borthwick Close	Juvenile	1840	315
6. High School Yards	Juvenile	1840	336
7. Old Assembly Close	Infant	1841	185
8. Brown Square	Juvenile	1846	240
9. Rose Street	Juvenile	1848	326
10. Rose Street	Infant	1848	170
11. Broughton Street	Juvenile	1855	250
12. Broughton Street	Infant	1855	160
13. Victoria Street	Infant	1866	180
			+supplementary class[11]
14. Abbeyhill	Juvenile	1875	320
15. Abbeyhill	Infant	1875	180
16. Davie Street	Juvenile	1876	400
17. Davie Street	Infant	1876	200
18. Grindlay Street	Juvenile	1876	290[12]
19. Stockbridge	Juvenile	1877	400
20. Stockbridge	Infant	1877	200

In total 12 juvenile and 8 infant schools were erected.
(inc. supplementary class total capacity = 5,456)

According to Bedford (1878), p. 35 the accommodation was for 5,329. His arithmetic is suspect, and he omitted the infant Old Assembly Close school from his calculations.

11 The supplementary class was intended for neglected children of advanced years who were too old for admission to ordinary infant schools, and whose ignorance made them unfit for attendance at juvenile schools.
12 A temporary school for the Fountainbridge.

APPENDIX 4
Occupations and Wages of the Parents of Heriot Outdoor School Children

Table A. 1854–5: based on the report of David Dickson, City treasurer and Convener of the Sub-Committee of the Heriot governors on the Admission to the Schools between 1852–4.

950 children admitted, made up of 480 boys and 470 girls. Only 40 were the children of burgesses, who did not need to declare their income (some 4%). Of the other 910 families, the average weekly income was 13/7d.

Average age of children at admission (infant and juvenile): 7 years 2 months.

OCCUPATIONS OF PARENTS

Wrights[13]	95	Needlewomen	18
Porters[14]	91	Unemployed	17
Labourers	78	Hawkers	14
Coachmen[15]	61	Masons	14
Widows	61	Clerks	14
Tailors	60	Soldiers	13
Cordiners[16]	56	Grocers[19]	12
Printers[17]	53	Lodging Keepers	12
Hammermen[18]	50	Policemen	11
Bakers	45	41 Other trades	147
Washerwomen	28		

Children from families with income below 5/– per week	56
Children from families with income between 5/– and 10/– per week	141
Children from families with income between 10/– and 15/– per week	396
Children from families with income between 15/– and 20/– per week	270
Children from families with income between 20/– and 25/– per week	20
Children from families with income above 25/–	10
Unemployed	17
TOTAL	910

13 Wrights include upholsterers and painters
14 Porters include shop and street porters, footmen and waiters
15 Coachmen include cab drivers, grooms
16 Cordiners include shoemakers
17 Printers include bookbinders
18 Hammermen include smiths and brassfounders
19 Grocers include shopmen

Table B. January 1871 – March 1872 Figures when 1,688 Children were admitted to the Schools

Children from families with income below 5/– per week	17
Children from families with income between 5/– and 10/– per week	76
Children from families with income between 10/– and 15/– per week	201
Children from families with income between 15/– and 20/– per week	781
Children from families with income between 20/– and 25/– per week	223
Children from families with come above 25/–	48
No income or unemployed	342

The figures of 1871–2 suggest that one in five attending the outdoor schools could not have received education at all but for the free education provided. The average family income of 1871–2 was 13/9d, very similar to that of the 1850s. There had been no increase in children attending with a burgess background – only 22 of 1500 in 1871–2.

Source: Bedford (1872), pp. 272–7.

APPENDIX 5

Key to stain glass in the great oriel window in the chapel.
(Beginning at the left side of the upper row and reading towards the right.)

Row 1 *Emblems*	Rose	Shamrock	Mullet	Thistle	Portcullis	Fleur-de-Lys
			ARMS OF HOSPITAL OFFICE-BEARERS			
Row 2	Forrester	Hamilton	Douglas	Gordon	Fyffe	Logie
Row 3	Bruce	Hope	Gray	Keith	Ogilvie	Campbell
Row 4	Sutherland	Marjoribanks	Heriot	Primrose	Horne	McDonald
Row 5	Stewart	Drummond	Graham of Orchill	Oliphant of Gask	Ramsay	Hay
Row 6	Murray	Kerr	Morton	Athole	Scott	Lorn
Row 7	Arms of Isle of Man				Leslie	Somerville
Row 8 *Badges*	Thistle	St Andrew	Edinburgh City	Merchant Company	Order of Garter	Knights of Nova Scotia
Row 9 *Trades*	Surgeons	Goldsmiths	Skinners	Furriers	Hammermen	Wrights
Row 10	Masons	Tailors	Baxters	Fleshers	Cordiners	Websters
Row 11	Saddlers	Litsters and Bonnetmakers	Slaters	Glovers	Blacksmiths	Cutlers
Row 12	Hatters and Waulkers	Locksmiths	Sheersmiths	Lorimers	Armourers	Candlemakers

Source: Steven *et. al.* (1845), Appendix VIII, pp. 91–2.

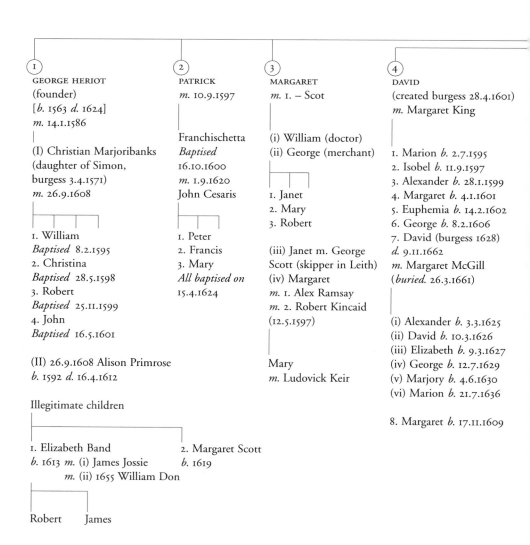

① GEORGE HERIOT
(founder)
[*b.* 1563 *d.* 1624]
m. 14.1.1586

(I) Christian Marjoribanks
(daughter of Simon,
burgess 3.4.1571)
m. 26.9.1608

1. William
Baptised 8.2.1595
2. Christina
Baptised 28.5.1598
3. Robert
Baptised 25.11.1599
4. John
Baptised 16.5.1601

(II) 26.9.1608 Alison Primrose
b. 1592 *d.* 16.4.1612

Illegitimate children

1. Elizabeth Band
b. 1613 *m.* (i) James Jossie
    m. (ii) 1655 William Don

2. Margaret Scott
b. 1619

Robert   James

② PATRICK
m. 10.9.1597

Franchischetta
Baptised
16.10.1600
m. 1.9.1620
John Cesaris

1. Peter
2. Francis
3. Mary
All baptised on
15.4.1624

③ MARGARET
m. 1. – Scot

(i) William (doctor)
(ii) George (merchant)

1. Janet
2. Mary
3. Robert

(iii) Janet m. George
Scott (skipper in Leith)
(iv) Margaret
m. 1. Alex Ramsay
m. 2. Robert Kincaid
(12.5.1597)

Mary
m. Ludovick Keir

④ DAVID
(created burgess 28.4.1601)
m. Margaret King

1. Marion *b.* 2.7.1595
2. Isobel *b.* 11.9.1597
3. Alexander *b.* 28.1.1599
4. Margaret *b.* 4.1.1601
5. Euphemia *b.* 14.2.1602
6. George *b.* 8.2.1606
7. David (burgess 1628)
d. 9.11.1662
m. Margaret McGill
(*buried.* 26.3.1661)

(i) Alexander *b.* 3.3.1625
(ii) David *b.* 10.3.1626
(iii) Elizabeth *b.* 9.3.1627
(iv) George *b.* 12.7.1629
(v) Marjory *b.* 4.6.1630
(vi) Marion *b.* 21.7.1636

8. Margaret *b.* 17.11.1609

The HERIOT family-tree

GEORGE HERIOT (*grandfather*) *m.* CHRISTIAN KYLE

GEORGE (*father*) [*b.* 1540 *d.* 1610]

m. 1. ELIZABETH BALDERSTONE – *m.* 2. CHRISTIAN BLAW (*died*: plague July/August 1645)

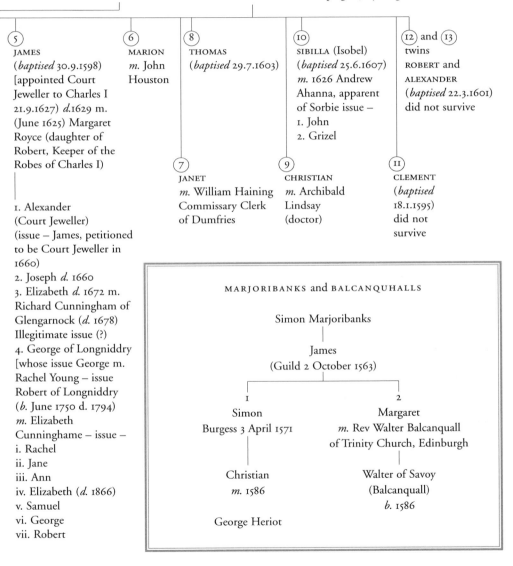

(5)
JAMES
(*baptised* 30.9.1598)
[appointed Court
Jeweller to Charles I
21.9.1627) *d.*1629 m.
(June 1625) Margaret
Royce (daughter of
Robert, Keeper of the
Robes of Charles I)

1. Alexander
(Court Jeweller)
(issue – James, petitioned
to be Court Jeweller in
1660)
2. Joseph *d.* 1660
3. Elizabeth *d.* 1672 m.
Richard Cunningham of
Glengarnock (*d.* 1678)
Illegitimate issue (?)
4. George of Longniddry
[whose issue George m.
Rachel Young – issue
Robert of Longniddry
(*b.* June 1750 *d.* 1794)
m. Elizabeth
Cunninghame – issue –
i. Rachel
ii. Jane
iii. Ann
iv. Elizabeth (*d.* 1866)
v. Samuel
vi. George
vii. Robert

(6)
MARION
m. John
Houston

(8)
THOMAS
(*baptised* 29.7.1603)

(7)
JANET
m. William Haining
Commissary Clerk
of Dumfries

(10)
SIBILLA (Isobel)
(*baptised* 25.6.1607)
m. 1626 Andrew
Ahanna, apparent
of Sorbie issue –
1. John
2. Grizel

(9)
CHRISTIAN
m. Archibald
Lindsay
(doctor)

(12) and (13)
twins
ROBERT and
ALEXANDER
(*baptised* 22.3.1601)
did not survive

(11)
CLEMENT
(*baptised*
18.1.1595)
did not
survive

MARJORIBANKS and BALCANQUHALLS

Simon Marjoribanks

James
(Guild 2 October 1563)

1
Simon
Burgess 3 April 1571

Christian
m. 1586

George Heriot

2
Margaret
m. Rev Walter Balcanquall
of Trinity Church, Edinburgh

Walter of Savoy
(Balcanquall)
b. 1586

APPENDIX 7

Account of Money Bequeathed by George Heriot for Founding the Hospital

	£	s.	d.
By *Disposition*, Heriot disposed debts owing to him in Scotland (sterling)	11,784	13	4
Deduct Annuities and Legacies	4,400	–	–
	= 7,384	13	4

Executors of Will and Testament gave as total charge to John Hay

				£	s.	d.
				40,123	3	7½
	£	s.	d.			
Deduct						
Funeral charges, servants' wages etc.	2,095	1	6			
Debts	5,427	8	2			
Legacies	5,938	6	8			
Jewels sold below appraised value	109	10	–			
Shortening of debts	1,308	5	2			
Clocks and watches given as presents	43	10	–			
Legacies in Testament unpaid by Executors	888	–	–	= 15,810	1	6
				24,313	2	1½
				+ 7,384	13	4
				= 31,697	15	5½

John Hay on 12 May 1627 took credit for:	£	s.	d.			
Lost on sale of jewels	3,338	7	4			
Lost on weight and telling	3	7	10			
Commissioners' expenses etc.	1,380	10	–			
Contract with HM and Earl of Roxburgh for £8,350 compounded to £5,000, therefore deduction of	3,350	–	–	= 8,072	5	2
				= £23,625	10	3½

Source: Steven (1845), pp. 53–4.
(*From Memorial for governors of George Heriot's Hospital and others, Defenders, against Alexander Brown and others, Pursuers, 23 July 1765, pp. 29–31*).

APPENDIX 8
Letter from W. McL. Dewar to The Scotsman *dated 5 February 1979*

Sir, Four years ago you permitted me to correct in your columns certain inaccurate and misleading references to the origins and development of George Heriot's endowment made in a Commons speech by the then Secretary of State for Scotland. I crave a like courtesy at this time to correct the same and similar inaccuracies occurring in recent statements by Lothian Region councillors and others on the subject of 'carrying out the intentions of pious founder, George Heriot,' particularly in respect of 'puire fatherless bairnes.'

A typical instance may be found in a statement by the chairman of Lothian Region Education Committee, who according to your report (February 1) told the committee that it was the belief of the Labour group that, in putting forward their proposals for a region majority on the trust, they had in mind the original intentions of George Heriot's will. 'He intended that education should be provided for those who could not afford it, but since then Heriot's has been moving inexorably towards becoming a private school.'

George Heriot's intentions were not and are not in doubt; copies of his will and his disposition of property – both lengthy documents – lie before me as I write.

1. Heriot's intention was to found not a school but a Hospital, i.e. a home, for boys: 'I intend . . . to found . . . ane publick pios and charitable worke within the saide Burghe of Edinburgh . . . in imitatione of the publict pios and religious work foundat within the Citie of London callit Chrystis Hospitall thair.'

2. Heriot did not leave his fortune for the benefit simpliciter of 'puire fatherless bairnes.' In his will that reference is followed immediately by the words 'friemens sones of that Towne of Edinburgh'; and elsewhere, in the disposition of his property, this was expanded into 'childrene of decayit Burgesses and freemen of the said Burgh.' In other words, Heriot had in mind the less fortunate members of his own merchant class in Edinburgh, and his purpose was so interpreted by his earliest trustees.

3. In terms again of Heriot's will, the endowment was from the outset private and independent. Its development, particularly in the extension

of its benefits more widely, became marked from 1836 onwards. In that year the governors, taking account of the shift in enlightened opinion in favour of the spread of elementary schooling, obtained – by promotion of a private Bill – parliamentary sanction to set up free schools in Edinburgh, to which would be admitted, first, burgesses' sons whom the hospital had not been able to accommodate, and then, if places were still available, 'the destitute children of all classes and of both sexes.' By 1845 the Heriot Schools (their official title, to distinguish them from the hospital) had enrolled 5444 Edinburgh children.

4. This private initiative, it should be observed, was taken almost 40 years before the national school system was established. Successive boards of governors have shown this same enlightenment in pursuing progressive policies, while at the same time adhering closely to the spirit and original purposes of the endowment. Thus, when the hospital system was ended in 1886 and the hospital became a day-school, the elaborate provision for 'fatherless bairnes' was continued and given an absolute priority in the endowment.

   At the same time a full secondary division was created complete with science laboratories and technical workshop; bursaries, both entrance and free-place, were provided on the basis of need, and were extended to include bursaries which could be held at schools other than Heriot's and at the universities and central institutions – all this at a time when authority, national and local, was lagging sadly behind in the field of education.

   The governors even found time – and the finances – to establish (in 1887) the first East of Scotland college of technology, the Heriot–Watt , and fully maintained it until 1928. Moreover, they continued for 38 years thereafter to contribute £8,000 annually to the college finances.

5. That the governors have loyally observed the spirit of the founder's intentions is attested in a large variety of ways: one illustration must suffice. Until very recently, in the endowment, i.e. through foundations and bursaries, one boy in every five at the top of the school was being educated free.

If today the school fees are increasingly beyond the means of a growing number of homes, this is in no way due to any change in policy on the part of the governors. It stems directly – and inexorably – from the action of the Government in 1975 in freezing and phasing out of the grant-in-aid.

W. MCL. DEWAR
35 Craiglockhart Grove
EDINBURGH
February 5, 1979

APPENDIX 9
George Heriot's Hospital and School: Office Bearers

TREASURERS			
George Suttie	1624	Kincaid Mackenzie	1822
James Rae	1626	Adam Luke	1830
Nicoll Uduart	1627	John Dick	1852
Robert Halieburton	1630	William Forrester	1861
William Cochrane	1632	David Lewis	1873
Robert Flemyng	1635	George Lamb	1905
Edward Edgar	1636	David Paton	1922
Thomas Charteris	1637		
Patrick Baxter	1638	CLERK AND TREASURER	
John Edgar	1640	Malcolm Stuart	1928
James Alison	1643	E.F. Barron	1935
William Sympson	1647	Alexander Douglas	1949
George Wauchope	1648	David Morris	1963
Andrew Ramsay	1652	Vivian Thomas	1979
Hew Hamyltoune	1654		
John Meine	1657	SECRETARY AND TREASURER	
Robert Gray	1659	Craigie Dougan	1983
James Abercrombie	1663	Fraser Simm	1994
Alexander Pitcairn	1669		
Hew Wallace	1675	CLERKS	
Richard Lothian	1678	Sir John Hay	1625
James Kirk	1681	Alexander Guthrie	1634
Thomas Fisher	1686	Sir William Thomson	1653
James Young of Killicanty	1711	James Rocheid	1668
Thomas Heriot	1732	James Hamilton	*joint* 1683
David Flint	1738	John Drummond	1685
Albert Munro of Coull	1748	John Richardson	*joint* 1685
James Rocheid of Inverleith	1758	Sir James Rocheid	*reponed* 1686
John Carmichael	1762	Aeneas McLeod	*joint* 1687
Archibald McDowal	1780	John Blair	1693
George Leslie	1788	Richard Strahan	1719
James Jackson	1793	Gilbert Clerk	1734
Thomas Henderson	*joint* 1804	Hugh Buchan	1761
Peter Hill	1809	William Buchan	1781
James Denholm	1813	John MacRitchie	1795
		Isaac Bayley	1830

George Bayley	1873	John Somerville	1805
John Tawse	1880	John Christison	1816
Peter Macnaughton	1893	James Boyd	1825
Malcolm Stuart	1924	Hector Holme	1829
		William Steven	1839
HEADMASTERS		James Fairbairn	1844
James Lawson	1659	Frederick W. Bedford	1865
David Davidsone	1664	David Lowe	1880
Robert Browne	1669	John Clark	1908
William Smeaton	1670	William Gentle	1926
Harry Moresone	1673	William Carnon	1942
James Buchan	1699	William Dewar	1947
John Watson	1702	Allan Macpherson	1970
David Chrystie	1720	Keith Pearson	1983
William Matheson	1734	Alistair Hector	1997
John Hunter	1735		
William Halieburton	1741	CHAIRMEN OF GOVERNORS	
John Henderson	1741	The Lord Provost of Edinburgh	
James Colvill	1757	1624-1975	
George Watson	1769	R. Stuart Louden	1975
William Hay	1773	James Ross	1976
Thomas Thomson	1782	Duncan Milligan	1979
David Cruickshanks	1792	James Ross	1980
James Maxwell Cockburn	1794	George Home	1989
George Irvine	1795	Michael Gilbert	1996

Notes

CHAPTER ONE

1 George Heriot's Disposition and Assignation of his Property to the Town of Edinburgh, dated 3 September 1623, in Dr William Steven: *Memoir of George Heriot with the History of the Hospital founded by him in Edinburgh* (Edinburgh 1845), Appendix V, p. 22; National Archives of Scotland (NAS): GD 421/ 1 vol. 1:(1).

2 G.W.B(allingall): *Selections from the Old Records (with notes) regarding the Heriots of Trabroun, Scotland* (printed for private collection) (Haddington 1894), pp. 9–13.

3 Gordon Donaldson: *All the Queen's Men. Power and politics in Mary Stewart's Scotland* (London 1983) p. 23.

4 *Ibid.,* p. 40 and p. 162.

5 *Ibid.,* pp. 140–1; Pauline Croft: *King James* (Basingstoke and New York 2003), pp. 16–18.

6 Robert Johnstone: *Historia Rerum Britannicarum . . . ab anno 1572, ad annum 1628* (Amsterdam 1655), p. 637; Steven (1845): *op. cit.,* pp. 1–2 and pp. 131–3; I.D. McFarlane: *Buchanan* (Bristol 1981), p. 21.

7 *Haddington Advertiser*, 8 November 1889.

8 David Mathew: *James I* (London 1967) suggests he was a first cousin to George Heriot (p. 66).

9 David M. Walker: *The Scottish Jurists* (Edinburgh 1985), pp. 54–66.

10 = Elphinstone.

11 Vol. I (Edinburgh 1871), p. 270 and p. 290.

12 Michael Lynch: *Edinburgh and the Reformation* (Edinburgh 1981), p. 334.

13 It is possible that a factor in Heriot's support of Mary was family loyalty as the Heriot Trabrouns were in the Marian camp (Gordon Donaldson, *op. cit.,* p. 114).

14 See the Tax Roll of June 1583: Michael Lynch, *op. cit.,* Appendix XII, p. 381.

15 James Colston: *The Incorporated Trades of Edinburgh* (Edinburgh 1891), p. 145.

16 In 1592, 1594, 1600, 1604 and 1605–6.

17 In 1585, 1594, 1596, 1597, 1598, 1599, 1602 and 1605.

18 Marguerite Wood (ed): *Extracts from the Records of the Burgh of Edinburgh, 1589–1603* (Edinburgh 1927), p. 31 and p. 45.

19 *Ibid.,* p. 311.

20 *Ibid.,* pp. 107–8, p. 207, p. 146 and p. 153.

21 *Ibid.,* p. 163, pp. 191–2 and p. 255.

22 *Ibid.,* p. 208.

23 David Masson (ed): *Register of the Privy Council of Scotland*, vol. VI, 1599–1604 (Edinburgh 1884), pp. 19–20.

24 *Extracts* (1927), *op. cit.,* p. 264 and p. 321.

25 M. Wood (ed): *Extracts from the Records of the Burgh of Edinburgh 1604–26* (Edinburgh 1931), p. 41.

26 Maurice Lee: *Great Britain's Solomon: James VI and I in His Three Kingdoms* (Urbana 1990), p. 79; Pauline Croft (2003): *op. cit.,* p. 29; Alan Stewart: *The Cradle King. A life of James VI and I* (London 2003), p. 144.

27 Black was charged with 'leasing-making', i.e. spreading a message likely to alienate the people from their King. See Alastair J. Mann: *The Scottish Book Trade 1500–1720. Print Commerce and Print Control in Early Modern Scotland* (East Linton 2000), p. 149 and p. 165.

28 M.S. Giuseppi (ed): *Calendar of State Papers (Scotland)*, vol. XII 1595–7 (Edinburgh 1952), p. viii and p. 395 ff.

29 Thomas McCrie: *Life of Andrew Melville* (Edinburgh 1899) plays down the event: p. 192. David Mathew: *op.cit.*, pp. 72–3: Julian Goodare: *State and Society in Early Modern Scotland* (Oxford 1999), p. 154.

30 M. Wood: *Extracts* (Edinburgh 1927), *op. cit.*, pp. xi–xii and p. 172; Alan R. MacDonald: 'James VI and the General Assembly, 1586–1618', p. 175, in Julian Goodare and Michael Lynch (eds): *The Reign of James VI* (East Linton 2000).

31 *Calendar of State Papers* (1952): *op. cit.*, p. xi.

32 *Inventory of Ancient and Historical Monuments of the City of Edinburgh* (Edinburgh 1951), pp. 53–4.

33 M. Wood: *Extracts* (1931): *op. cit.*, p. 68: 30 November 1610/1. A merk = 13½d. sterling, whilst a pound, or 20/- Scots, may be equated with 20d. sterling. One pound sterling was thus equivalent to 18 merks, or 12 pounds Scots.

34 John Gifford, Colin McWilliam and David Walker: *The Buildings of Scotland, Edinburgh* (London 1984), p. 157; Archibald Constable: *Memoirs of George Heriot, Jeweller to King James VI* (Edinburgh 1822), pp. 7–8. 'Viator, qui sapis, unde sies, quid sis, quidque futurus sis, hinc nosce. Vita mihi mortis, mors vitae, janua facta est ; Solaque mors mortis vivere posse dedit. Ergo quisquis adhuc mortali vesceris aura, Dum licet, ut possis vivere disce mori. G.H. 1610.' The tombstone was restored by the Governors of Heriot's School in 1913 (*The Scotsman*, 21 January 1913).

35 National Archives of Scotland (NAS): GD 421/1 vol. 5 [3]: Clement (baptised 18 January 1595) and twins Robert and Alexander (baptised 22 March 1601) do not seem to have survived. The Register of Baptisms and Marriages in Edinburgh parish begins in 1595 and all but one of the Heriot baptisms recorded appear there (the exception was Thomas, registered in the Canongate Register, which begins in 1564). Many pre-1595 events went unrecorded (*Edinburgh Register* 685(1)/1 and *Canongate* 685(3)/2).

36 See Appendix 6.

37 The original Statutes drawn up in 1627 laid aside the first Monday of June to celebrate George Heriot's birth. Robert Johnstone (*op. cit.*, 1655) held that Heriot was born in Edinburgh and died in his 60th year, making the year of his birth 1563.

38 Heriot was to repay the support of Inglis by taking Inglis' son, James, into apprentice-ship. One source suggested Heriot involved himself in marriage proposals for the young Inglis. When these were rejected by the latter on grounds of a prior attachment, Heriot discarded the young man in 1604. Up till then Inglis had been seen as Heriot's 'presumptive heir': *Historical and Genealogical Notices of the Family of Inglis of Milton-Bryant in Bedfordshire* (1874).

39 James Colston (1891): *op. cit.*, p. 27 and p. 31.

40 Dr William Steven (1845) *op. cit.*, p. 4 and his Appendix no. I, pp. 1–2; NAS: GD 421/1 vol. 2 [5].

41 NAS: GD 421/1 vol. 2 [2].

42 NAS: GD 421/2 [6].

43 One of the Luckenbooths, which may have been built as early as 1386 (Ian D. Whyte: *Scotland before the Industrial Revolution. An Economic and Social History c.1050–c.1750* (London 1995), p. 186). Early prints and drawings show the shops and booths: in particular Richard Gough, 'St Giles from the Parliament Square' (1771) and David Allan,

'The High Street before the removal of the Luckenbooths' (1793).

44 Robert Chambers: *Traditions of Edinburgh* (Edinburgh 1824; revised 1869), pp. 125–6. The shop and workshop of Heriot existed until 1809 when the extension to the Advocates' Library led to the destruction of the old closes to the west of St Giles. It was the centre one of three. The Luckenbooths were removed completely in 1817 (*Ibid.*, p. 116). This was confirmed by Lord Cockburn: *Memorials of his Time* (Edinburgh 1856), p. 95, who remembered seeing the name after 1805.

45 James Grant: *Cassell's Old and New Edinburgh. Its History, its People, and its Places* (London nd), vol. 1, p. 175.

46 = practice musters (Julian Goodare: *State and Society* (1999): *op. cit.*, pp. 150–158.); *Extracts* (1927): *op. cit.*, p. 17.

47 NAS: GD 421/1 vol. 2 [3].

48 NAS: GD 421/2: 34 – Receipts to George Heriot, 1593–1602 (16).

49 *Extracts* (1927): *op.cit.*, p. 64.

50 NAS: GD 421/1 vol. 3 [5] – including 'twa hingeris for lugis set with sevin dossane of rubyes'. Heriot's first attended the King in September 1593: *Extracts* (1927), p. 96.

51 *Extracts* (1927): *op. cit.*, p. 116 and p. 117. He failed conspicuously in the former, for Bailie John Macmoran was murdered by a scholar of the High School in September 1595, which led to sweeping changes there: *ibid.*, pp. 138–9: R. Chambers: *op. cit.*, pp. 89–90.

52 M. Lynch: *Scotland. A New History* (rev. ed. Edinburgh 2000), p. 176; Dr William Steven (1845): *op. cit.*, p. 23.

53 Dr William Steven: *ibid.*, Appendix no. III, p. 8.

54 Diary of Robert Birrel, burges of Edinburgh (from 1532 to 1605), p. 44, in G.B. Dalyell: *Fragments of Scottish History* (Edinburgh 1798); Grant, (1882): *op. cit.*, vol. II, p. 364.

55 NAS: GD 421/1 vol. 2 [35] dated 23 July 1597.

56 The collection of her mother-in-law, Mary Queen of Scots, had been largely dispersed by the Regent Moray in 1567–70: Julian Goodare: 'Thomas Foulis and the Scottish Fiscal Crisis of the 1590s', p. 174, in W.M. Ormrod, Margaret Bonney and Richard Bonney (eds): *Crises, Revolutions and Self-Sustained Growth. Essays in European Fiscal History, 1130–1830* (Stamford 1999).

57 Bruce P. Lenman: 'Jacobean Goldsmith-Jewellers as Credit-Creators: The Cases of James Mossman, James Cockie and George Heriot': *Scottish Historical Review*, LXXIV, 2, no. 198: October 1995, p. 169.

58 NAS: GD 421/1 vol. 3 [2]; G.P.V. Akrigg (ed.): *Letters of King James VI and I* (Berkeley 1984), p. 487. At times, James himself had to assign specific jewels. He did so on 22 March 1599 until Heriot was paid £6110 Scots and £610 interest. NAS: GD 421/2 [28]; D. Masson (ed.) (1884): *op. cit.*, pp. 128–9.

59 Jacob from Holland ran off in May 1594 but was arrested in North Shields and brought back to Scotland for execution (Maureen Meikle: 'Holde her at the Oeconomicke rule of the House': Anna of Denmark and Scottish Court Finances, 1589–1603', in Elizabeth Ewan and Maureen M. Meikle (eds): *Women in Scotland c.1100–c.1750* (East Linton 1999), p. 107; Annie I. Cameron (ed.): *Calendar of State Papers (Scotland) 1593–5* (Edinburgh 1936), vol. XI, pp. 339, 342–4, 356–7.

60 Lenman (1995): *op. cit.*, pp. 160–163; Gordon Donaldson: *op. cit.*, p. 125.

61 Julian Goodare: *State and Society* (1999): *op. cit.*, p. 123. See also Robert Chambers:

Domestic Annals of Scotland (from the Reformation to the Restoration) (Edinburgh 1858), 2 vols, vol. 1, p. 294.

62 On 6 December 1597.

63 J.D. Mackie (ed): *Calendar of State Papers (Scotland)*, vol. XIII (1) 1597–1603 (Edinburgh 1969), p. 373.

64 Steven (1845): *op. cit.*, Appendix IV, p. 9; Constable (1822): *op. cit.*, p. 13. Heriot had done work for James VI at Holyrood for 40 crowns for 'ane hatt string fourneist be him to our Dearest sone the prince'. NAS: GD421/1 vol. 3 [1].

65 NAS: GD 421/2 [11].

66 *Calendar of State Papers 1597–1603* (1969): *op. cit.*, p. 536.

67 Julian Goodare: 'James VI's English Subsidy', in Goodare and Lynch: *op. cit.*, p. 115; *Calendar of State Papers 1597–1603* (1969): *op. cit.*, p. x.

68 29 July 1601, NAS: GD421/1 vol. 3 [19]; Ethel Carleton Williams: *Anne of Denmark. Wife of James VI of Scotland. James I of England* (Chatham 1970), p. 68. Anna's finances were improved by the Octavians after 1593 but by 1598 the good work had been undone. The likely succession to the British throne was 'colouring the financial judgment' of both Anna and James (Maureen Meikle: *op. cit.*, pp. 108–9).

69 = a collet of a ring.

70 NAS, GD 421/2 – 29; Lenman (1995): *op. cit.*, p. 168

71 *Dictionary of National Biography* (*DNB*) (London 1891), vol. XXVI, p. 244. One historian, however, puts these sums in another perspective. He claims Anna was no more a spendthrift in Scotland than her consort or predecessors. Her expenditure of £12,000 in 1601–02 compares with that of £10,000 by James VI, and was similar to the expenditure of Margaret and James III in 1473–4 and Margaret and James IV in 1507–8: Thomas Riis: 'Scottish–Danish Relations in the 16th century', in T.C. Smout (ed.): *Scotland and Europe 1200–1850* (Edinburgh 1986), pp. 82–96.

72 Constable: *op. cit.* (1822), Appendix VII, p. 194 – from 1605–1615 Heriot supplied Anna with £40,000 sterling worth of jewels. This figure was also used by William McElwee: *The Wisest Fool in Christendom. The Reign of James I and VI* (London 1958), p. 172. D. Masson (ed.): (1884): *op. cit.*, pp. 314–316.

73 DNB (1891), pp. 244–5 ; NAS: GD 421/1 vol. 2 [23].

74 NAS: GD 421/1 vol. 3 [3].

75 Agnes Strickland: *Lives of the Queens of England*, 8 vols (London 1844), vol. 7, p. 364.

76 NAS: GD 421/1 vol. 3 [4]. Maureen Meikle (1999): *op. cit.*, p. 107 suggests that this was scribbled quickly and was probably written in 1594 when Anna was still perfecting her use of the Scots language in written form.

77 NAS: GD 421/1 vol. 3 [24].

78 NAS: GD 421/1 vol. 3 [25].

79 NAS :GD 421/1 vol. 3 [26]. Anna was the sister of Christian IV of Denmark.

80 Keith M. Brown: *Kingdom or Province? Scotland and the Regal Union 1603–1715* (London 1992), p. 11 Alan Stewart (2003): *op. cit.*, pp. 172–175.

81 NAS: GD 421/1 vol. 2 [12].

82 NAS: GD 421/1 vol. 2 [13].

83 *Ibid.*

84 Even Sir Walter Raleigh called upon his services on 30 July 1603 from the Tower of London: Mary A.E. Green (ed.); *Calendar of State Papers (Domestic) James I (1603–10)*

(London 1857), p. 25.

85 D. Scarisbrick: *Anne of Denmark's Jewellery Inventory* (Devonshire 1991).

86 Bruce P. Lenman (1995): *op. cit.*, p. 170.

87 In the mid-nineteenth century David Laing advised a Committee of Governors which classified and arranged the important documents of the Hospital. It produced 'An Inventory of Documents connected with the History of Heriot's Hospital' in November 1857. When these documents were handed over to the Scottish Record Office (now the National Archives of Scotland) in 1985, this Inventory formed the basis of the classification used. Volume 3 detailed the Accounts and Receipts for Jewels etc. from 1598 to 1623.

88 NAS: GD 421/2/32. The jewels received from Anna on 1 May 1609 'to be layed to pawn' at a value of £1305 sterling plus interest, with a further jewel received on 24 April 1613 'layed to pawn' for £700 sterling. plus interest until 24 April 1615: Bruce P. Lenman (1995): *op. cit.*, p. 171.

89 A natural history of Scotland of 1684: NAS – 33:3:22 p. 5.

90 *Edinburgh Register* 685(1)/1 confirms that a son, Robert, was baptised on 25 November 1599. See Appendix 6.

91 NAS: GD 421/1 vol. 2 [7].

92 *Edinburgh Register* 685(1)/43.

93 The inscription, translated from Latin, read – 'To his most pure and beloved wife, Alison Heriot, daughter of James Primrose, his Majesty's Clerk of Privy Council in the Kingdom of Scotland ; a woman richly endowed with all mental and personal gifts, and by pious education most accomplished, her sorrowful husband, George Heriot, Esquire, jeweller to the King, Queen, and the Princes Henry and Charles, dutifully, affectionately, and not without many a tear, erected this monument.' (*The Scotsman*, 10 February 1923.)

94 NAS: GD 421/1 vol. 3 [34]; Dr William Steven (1845): *op. cit.*, pp. 13–4.

95 Dr William Steven (1845): *op. cit.*, p. 14; Ethel Carleton Williams (1970*): op. cit.*, pp. 185–6.

96 Agnes Strickland (1844): *op. cit.*, p. 440; Dr William Steven (1845): *op. cit.*, p. 14.

97 Mary A.E. Green (1857): *op. cit.*, p. 574.

98 Mary A.E. Green (ed.): *Calendar of State Papers (Domestic) 1611–9* (London 1858), p. 91.

99 Details of the Heriot side of the correspondence are found in NAS: GD 421/1 vol. 4 [20–31].

100 Dr William Steven (1845): *op. cit.*, p. 17.

101 Primrose had nineteen children.

102 NAS: GD 421/2 – 33 [31]; Dr William Steven (1845): *op. cit.*, p. 20.

103 Dr William Steven (1845): *op. cit.*, pp. 26 –28.

104 NAS: GD 421/2 – 33 [10].

105 NAS: GD 421/2 – 33 [11]; Bruce P. Lenman (1995): *op. cit.*, p. 173.

106 NAS: GD 421/2 – 33 [12].

107 Frederick C. Dietz: *English Public Finance 1558–1641* (New York 1932), p. 164.

108 NAS: GD 421/1 vol. 3 [52].

109 Mary A.E. Green (ed.): *Calendar of State Papers (Domestic) James I of England. 1619–23* (London 1858), p. 193 – 18 November 1620; *DNB, op. cit.*, p. 245. The sugar farm was called in a year later by Lord Treasurer Middlesex.

110 Son and partner of Adam Lawtie.

111 In a letter of 7 May 1619. NAS: GD 421/1 vol. 4 [5].

112 Heriot also asked for details of the allowances he had paid to his sister and niece. NAS: GD 421/1 vol. 4 [8].

113 Heriot had another home in Gray's Close, which he instructed James Lawtie to sell on 12 January 1617. NAS: GD 421/1 vol. 4 [2].

114 The importance of Heriot to the Lawties is symbolised in the naming, in October 1619, of James Lawtie's new son, George, as 'an token of the duty and service' he owed Heriot. NAS: GD 421/1 vol. 4 [59].

115 Dr William Steven (1845): *op. cit.*, p. 29.

116 Ian D. Whyte (1995): *op. cit.*, pp. 280–1.

117 This was removed in 1843 when Messrs Nelson built an extensive publishing operation there. Heriot's initials, cut in wood, were to be seen in several parts of the house. Dr Steven presented a coloured drawing of the house to Messrs Nelson as 'the country residence of the founder of the Hospital'. It was destroyed in a fire in 1878. James Grant (1882): *op. cit.*, vol 2, pp. 354–5.

118 Bruce P. Lenman (1995): *op. cit.*, p. 174.

119 NAS, GD 421/2–33 [20]; Bruce P. Lenman (1995): *op. cit.*, p. 174.

120 *Calendar of State Papers 1619–23*: *op. cit.*, p. 507 and p. 525.

121 *Ibid.*, p. 530.

122 *Ibid.*, pp. 566 and 577.

123 NAS: GD 421/1 vol. 4 [55].

124 NAS: GD 421/1 vol. 4 [54].

125 NAS: GD 421/1 vol. 4 [9].

126 *Ibid.*, who 'had the care and keiping of me when I was a chyld'.

127 NAS: GD 421/1 vol. 4 [42].

128 The Disposition and Assignation was not registered until 2 January 1624, suggesting that it was viewed by Heriot as complementary to his Last Will and Testament.

129 Many of the Scots who followed James VI south left instructions for their corpses to be returned to Scotland, but clearly George Heriot had few close ties left there: see Keith M. Brown: 'The Vanishing Emperor. British Kingship at its Decline, 1603–1707', p. 17, in Roger A. Mason (ed.): *Scots and Britons. Scottish political thought and the Union of 1603* (Edinburgh 1994).

130 Robert Johnstone (1655): *op. cit.*, p. 638. Unfortunately the rebuilding of St Martin's in 1712 obliterated the monument. The treasurer of the Hospital in December 1866 was involved in correspondence when it was suggested that the remains of George Heriot were likely to be disturbed by the removal of St Martin's Workhouse in London to make way for the National Gallery. Although the governors were sceptical about Heriot's remains being there or being traced, the treasurer wrote requesting that if anything should appear to lead to the belief that Heriot's remains were there, he should be informed, and care should be taken of them, until the governors could give directions as to them. (*Record of Heriot's Hospital*, vol. 40, pp. 433–4). No remains were found.

131 £4.75m in 2003 prices.

132 Ian D. Whyte (1995): *op. cit.*, p. 281.

133 Although William H. Hill: *History of the Hospital and School Founded in Glasgow A.D. 1639–41 by George and Thomas Hutcheson of Lambhill* (Glasgow 1881), p. 23, claims that

Heriot was one of the very first to receive money on deposit, allowing interest thereon, and to honour cheques, on short notice, for customers.

134 Bruce P. Lenman (1995): *op. cit.*, p. 176.

135 *Record of Heriot's Hospital*, vol. 1 (March 1624–July 1662), p. 10.

136 *Ibid.* Among Heriot's executory papers was a paper on the operation of Christ's Hospital. NAS: GD 421/3 [11].

137 There was later some debate about the definition of 'orphan'. According to Dr Johnson, it meant a child without father or mother or without both father and mother.

138 *The Christ's Hospital Book* (London 1953), p. 7.

139 Edward C. Mack: *Public Schools and British Opinion, 1780–1860. An Examination of the Relationship between Contemporary Ideas and the Evolution of an English Institution* (London 1938), pp. 10–12.

140 *Record*, vol. I, p. 12.

141 Burgesses or freemen included all the incorporated trades and other householders who were burgesses. The system of 'watching and warding' was in force in Heriot's time, according to which every burgess had, in turn, to watch the city during the night and to turn out to fight as an armed civil soldier during any invasion or civil commotion. This led to the rule that every person carrying on any kind of business was compelled to become a burgess, for which a small fee was charged, to ensure that they shared in the obligations and labours connected with the defence of the city. Significantly, Heriot did not leave his funds to the more affluent class of 'burgess and guild brethren' to whom the revenues of Watson's Hospital and the Merchants' Maiden Hospital were destined. Moreover, in the 'Golden Charter' granted to the City by James VI in 1603, the inhabitants were distinguished as 'freemen and unfreemen' and customs were paid to burgesses by 'unfreemen and strangers', suggesting the existence below the burgess class of a considerable class of population.

142 *Record*, vol. 1, p. 10.

143 Isolation was not Heriot's object.

144 *Record*, vol. 1, p. 10. Some commentators suggest that by putting college before apprenticeship he expected the majority of boys to have a liberal (= secondary) education. If so, it strongly suggests that Heriot did not contemplate the poorest classes of society as those which were solely, or even chiefly, to benefit from his endowment.

145 *Record*, vol. 1, p. 10. In Heriot's time the ordinary town council numbered 25. It was increased by the Municipal Reform Act (1833) to 33, and when the Royalty was extended in 1856 it numbered 41, which it remained until the end of the Hospital.

146 *Ibid.* p. 11. Before 1625 there were six city ministers which were then increased to eight and in 1649 to ten. By the later nineteenth century there were 13.

147 *Ibid.*

148 *Ibid.*

149 Provision was made for his sister Margaret (£100 sterling annually) and her five children, William (£1,000 sterling); George (£800 sterling); Janet (£80 annually) and Margaret Scott (interest on £1,000), and Marie Kincaid (interest on £800).

150 *Record*, vol. 1, p. 19; NAS: GD 421/5/1.

151 Daughter of his deceased brother, Patrick, who had settled in Genoa. Patrick had married on 10 September 1597 and his daughter, Franchischetta, was baptised on 16 October 1600. She married John Cesaris 'de loco bordes' (from Bordeaux?) in France on

1 September 1620. Their three children – Peter, Francis and Mary – were baptised on 15 April 1624. NAS, GD 421/1 vol. 5 (21): certified entries from Genoese parish registers, 4–9 May 1624.

152 James received £2,000, a quarter in jewels; Thomas received £1,000 plus Indian stock to the same value at the age of twenty-five in 1627; Christian Blaw, Christian, Sibilla, Janet and Marion all received 500 merks life-rent.

153 Elizabeth inherited his property in Roehampton composed of three public rooms, two large bedrooms, kitchen, hall, four garret rooms, garden and stables; Margaret his property in St Martin-in-the-Fields, consisting of three public rooms, five bedrooms, kitchen, cellar, garret and garden. Both also received £200 sterling. Both were born after the death of Alison.

154 A relation, who received £30 sterling.

155 *Record*, vol. 1, p. 24.

156 Or Pirie.

157 *Record*, vol. 1, p. 25.

158 Balcanquall (1586–1645) was made Master of Savoy by James for a second time after his work as Scottish representative at the Synod of Dort in 1618 (W.B. Patterson: *King James VI and I and the Reunion of Christendom* (Cambridge 1997), pp. 233, 266 and 281).

159 *Record*, vol.1 p. 25.

160 *Ibid.*

161 *Ibid.* Again some significance can be attached to the order Heriot stipulated, especially given the lack of charitable or benevolent institutions at the time. Interestingly, Heriot no longer mentioned decayed burgesses or freemen. The interpretation of the significance of this is crucial for understanding all later debates about the Hospital. If Heriot had, on mature reflection, changed his mind and abandoned his previous intention, then it can be argued that the Hospital was for all those in poverty and qualifications such as fatherless and being children of burgesses were secondary. If, however, the Disposition and the Will were complementary documents, it meant that when he came to make his Will he decided that details for the Hospital would be organised by himself or Balcanquall later, so he did not repeat the previous arrangements he had made which were reserved for the Statutes. In this case the original intention to help the 'middle class' remained.

162 *Ibid.*, pp. 25–26.

163 Significantly, the ministers were now to be part of the governing body. Given the episcopalian nature of the church, Heriot probably expected them to be independent of the town councillors, but after the victory of Presbyterianism later in the century the ministers were appointed and paid by the town. Longer term, however, the ministers fiercely guarded their special position and often opposed the councillors who in turn criticised the ministers for pressing staff appointments in the Hospital to go to those aspiring to the ministry.

164 *Ibid.*, p. 27. This 'Scottish' dimension was later a cause of debate.

165 Still 1623 at the time, for under the old-style calendar the new year did not begin until 25 March.

166 A number of sources hold Balcanquall to have been a nephew of Heriot. Balcanquall was the son of Walter, minister of Trinity Church, Edinburgh and Margaret Marjoribanks, daughter of James, a merchant. Heriot married Christian Marjoribanks,

daughter of Simon, a merchant. James Marjoribanks became a guildbrother of Edinburgh on 2 October 1563 by right of his father, Simon, while Simon Marjoribanks became a burgess and guildbrother of Edinburgh on 3 April 1571 as eldest son of the deceased James Marjoribanks. Therefore, there could certainly have been a relationship between the Balcanqualls and the Heriots through the Marjoribanks. (See Appendix 6.) However, the term 'nephew' was used loosely in Old Scots. According to Sir William A. Craigie: *Dictionary of the Older Scottish Tongue* (Chicago 1937), 'nevoy' can mean the son of one's brother- or sister-in-law, as well as of one's brother or sister. It was used in some southern parts of the country for a grandson or great-grandson.

167 *Record,* vol. 1, p. 28.

168 *Ibid.,* with no reference to their previous schooling or training.

169 Wood (1931): *op. cit.,* p. 410; Frederick W. Bedford: *History of George Heriot's Hospital with a Memoir of the Founder* (3rd ed. Edinburgh 1872), pp. 34–5.

170 Wood: (1931): *op.cit.,* p. xxxii.

171 *Record,* vol. 1, p. 1; Wood (1931): *op. cit.,* pp. 250–1.

172 *Record,* vol. 1, p. 2; Wood (1931): *op. cit.,* p. 251.

173 Wood (1931): *op. cit.,* p. 411.

174 Wood (1931): *op. cit.,* pp. 411–2; Bedford (1872): *op. cit.,* pp. 38–9.

175 *Record,* vol. 1, p. 15; Wood (1931): *op. cit.,* pp. 251–2.

176 *Ibid.,* pp. 30–35 and NAS GD 421/1 vol. 1 (7); Wood (1931): *op. cit.,* p. 414.

177 *Record,* vol. 1, p. 37.

178 *Ibid.,* p. 38.

179 *Ibid.,* pp. 38–39.

180 NAS. GD 421/1 vol. 6 (3).

181 Wood (1931): *op. cit.,* pp. 414–5.

182 Although he himself was awarded £100 sterling providing he cooperated with Heriot's executors.

183 Wood (1931): *op. cit.,* p. 412.

184 Wood (1931): *op.cit.,* pp. 412–3, 415–6, 419; NAS: GD 421/1 vol. 6 [6]. Adamson claimed again in July 1627 because of the delay in his settlement and his resulting inability to escape the recent plague outbreak in London. NAS: GD 421/1 vol. 7 [18].

185 *Record,* vol. 1, p. 40. With such a reference the town council gave some credence to the rumour that Franchischetta was Heriot's natural daughter. Hay also wrote to the town council that she was 'exceeding lyke in visage to George Heriot her uncle' (3 May 1628). Wood (1931): *op. cit.,* p. 261.

186 *Record,* vol. 1, p. 27.

187 *Ibid.,* pp. 42 and 62. *Record,* vol. 1 (1931), p. 260; NAS: GD 421/3 [15]. In fact this was not the end of the matter as she resurrected har claims later – NAS, GD 421/1 vol. 5 (28–31), and her husband received another £30 sterling in October 1628.

188 *Record,* vol. 1, p. 58 – this had been recommended by the Executors in a letter of 30 June 1625 to end clamour. It was reasonable, it was argued, given their nearness in blood to Heriot (Marguerite Wood [1931]: *op. cit.,* pp. 417–8).

189 *Ibid.,* p. 64.

190 *Ibid.,* p. 67.

191 *Ibid.;* *Extracts* (1931), p. 295.

192 31 January 1626: NAS: GD 421/5/1. *Extracts* (1931), p. 421. Bedford, (1872) pp. 39–40.

193 NAS: GD421/1. vol.1 [8].

194 M. Wood (ed.) *Extracts from the Records of the Burgh of Edinburgh 1626–41* (Edinburgh 1936), pp. 9–10.

195 *Record*, vol. 1, p. 86.

196 *Extracts* (1936), pp. 258–9.

197 *Record*, vol. 1, p. 86. *Extracts* (1936), p. 19. Bedford (1872), p. 39.

198 *Record*, vol. 1, p. 137. *Extracts* (1936), pp. 25–6.

199 £2.25m in 2003 prices. *Record*, vol. 1, p. 137. *Extracts* (1936), *op. cit.*, pp. 25–7.

200 *Record*, vol. 1, p. 149; *Extracts* (1936), p. 27.

201 *Record*, vol. 1, p. 150; *Extracts* (1936), pp. 28–9.

202 *Record*, vol. 1, p. 150; *Extracts* (1936), pp. 28–9.

203 Again not to miss an opportunity the town council gained from the deal: it purchased ten acres for 5,800 merks. (Inventory (1951): *op.cit.*, p. 110). 21 January 1628.

204 *Record*, vol. 1, p. 151: Udwart's Accounts 1627–8 itemise the Hospital paying the town the sum of 4,966. 13/4 punds Scots on 24 March 1628: NAS: GD 421/5/1 vol I p. 19 item 1. *Extracts* (1936), p. 29 and p. 41. (Todrick's Wynd was sold to the Incorporation of Skinners for 2,300 merks on 28 May 1633 – *Record*, vol. 1, p. 241).

205 *Extracts* (1936), p. 29.

206 *Record*, vol. 1, p. 150. *Extracts* (1936), p. 29.

207 Sir John Summerson: *Architecture in Britain, 1530 to 1830* (7th edn, 1953. Frome, 1983), pp. 546–7.

208 Sebastiano Serlio (1475–1552), the famous Italian architect, whose seventh book, based on his collected papers, was published posthumously (1575) in Frankfurt.

209 Deborah Howard: *Scottish Architecture from the Reformation to the Restoration, 1560–1660* (Edinburgh 1995), p. 136.

210 NAS: GD 421/10 (1).

211 *Record*, vol. 1, p. 152; *Extracts* (1936), p. 30.

212 *Record*, vol. 1, p. 153; *Extracts* (1936), p. 30.

213 *Record*, vol. 1, pp. 161–2; *Extracts* (1936), pp. 30–1.

214 *Record*, vol. 1, p. 162; *Extracts* (1936), p. 31.

215 *Record*, vol. 1, pp. 162–180.

216 *Ibid.*, Chapter XII, p. 172.

217 Balcanquall had no thought of isolating the boys. The classical education which the boys would receive at the Grammar School prepared them for College. As Balcanquall knew Heriot's intentions here is another suggestion that Heriot endowed a middle-class institution.

218 Chapter XIII. 'Burgesses' had been mentioned in the Disposition but omitted from the Will. They reappeared here in the Statutes but the word 'decayed' did not reappear there. But the children were to be the 'children of burgesses and freemen of the said Burgh, and amongst these the kinsmen of the said George Heriot to be preferred'. This suggested that the poor burgesses of the Statutes were to be of the same class and kin to which George Heriot himself belonged; that they were the same as the 'decayed burgesses' of the Disposition, and as such were members of the 'middle class' fallen on hard times. See Chapter 9.

219 Presumably in the belief that there would not be a sufficient number of fatherless boys to fill the Hospital.

220 A year longer than Heriot had intended.

221 *Record*, vol. 1, p. 172. As these were different from the arrangements made for the 10 bursaries of the Codicil in Chapter XXII of the Statutes it explained the different classes of bursaries – out-bursars and house-bursars.

222 Alexander Law: *Education in Edinburgh in the Eighteenth Century* (London 1965), p. 107.

223 *32nd Report of the Charity Commissioners* [1840] for details of ordinances of Christ's Hospital.

224 William H. Hill: *op. cit.* (1881), p. 23.

225 A.D. Dunlop: *Hutchesons' Grammar: The History of a Glasgow School* (Glasgow 1992), p. 7 and p. 23.

226 The 86.5 acres in Broughton cost 33,600 merks and the 30 acres at Lochflatt 18,500 merks. *Record*, vol. 1, pp. 71, 79, 90. Bedford, *op. cit.* (1872), p. 41.

227 Waverley Novels: vol. XXVII, *The Fortunes of Nigel* (Edinburgh 1879), Introduction, p. 1. Written by Scott at Abbotsford on 1 July 1831.

228 Edgar Johnson: *Sir Walter Scott. The Great Unknown*, vol. II, 1821–32 (London 1970), p. 828 and Waverley Novels: vol. XXVII, *The Fortunes of Nigel* (Edinburgh 1879), vol. II, p. 289.

229 Robert C. Gordon: *Under Which King? A Study of the Scottish Waverley Novels* (Edinburgh 1969), pp. 129–38.

230 John Sutherland: *The Life of Walter Scott. A Critical Biography* (Oxford 1995), p. 252.

231 It was subscribed for among the former Herioters (called 'Auld Callants') and a special service of dedication took place on the anniversary of Heriot's birthday on 5 June 1854 (*The Scotsman*, 26 April 1854).

232 Ray Bradfield: *Nigel Tranter. Scotland's Storyteller* (Edinburgh 1999), p. 27.

233 *Ibid.*, pp. 233–4.

CHAPTER TWO

1 The 'Wark' was the affectionate name given to the Hospital by the Edinburgh populace.

2 *Record*, vol. 1, pp. 186, 188, 191. Presumably the timber came from Ryfylke (by Stavanger) in south-west Norway and was probably pinewood. (Arnvid Lillehammer: 'The Scottish-Norwegian Timber Trade in the Stavanger Area in the 16th and 17th Centuries', pp. 97–111 in T.C. Smout (ed.): *op. cit.*) Gothenburg in Sweden had been founded in 1621 and attracted much Scottish trade at this time due to the fifteen years of tax freedom granted to its burghers: Elsa-Britta Grage: *Scottish Merchants in Gothenburg, 1621–1850*, pp. 112–127, in T.C. Smout (ed.) (1986), *op. cit.*

3 John Imrie & John G. Dunbar (eds): *Accounts of The Master of Works*, vol II, 1616–49 (Edinburgh 1982), p. lx.

4 *Ibid.*, pp. lxxxi & 73; pp. xcii & 170; pp. xcviii & 127, p. 133.

5 Completed for George Seton, Earl of Winton, in 1620.

6 Imrie and Dunbar; *op. cit.*, p. lxx.

7 NAS: *Accounts*, GD 421/5/1, vol. 1, *Udwart's Accounts* 1627–8, p. 15, item 1.

8 *Udwart's Accounts, op. cit.*, p. 17, item 6.

9 *Udwart's Accounts, op. cit.*, p. 25, item 1.

10 Revd Robert Scott Mylne: *The Master Masons to the Crown of Scotland and their Works*

(Edinburgh 1893), p. 78.

11 Both earning £4 Scots weekly. *Udwart's Accounts, op.cit.*, p, 25, item 18.

12 *Ibid.*, p. 25, item 19.

13 *Ibid.*, p. 29, item 28. 15 August, 1628. Ravelston quarry was to be the source of most of the stone used in the building, although some was brought from Craigmillar in May 1636. David Laing, *op.cit.*, p. 24.

14 *Udwart's Accounts, op.cit.*, p. 31, items 15–17.

15 *Ibid.*, p. 34, item 11 and *Udwart's Accounts* (1628–9), p. 18, items 3–4.

16 *Ibid.* (1628–9), p. 25, item 20.

17 *Ibid.* (1628–9), 21 January, p. 28, item 7.

18 *Record*, vol. 1, p. 204.

19 *Udwart's Accounts* (1628–9), *op.cit.*, 28 March 1629, p. 35, item 12.

20 *Ibid.*, p. 41, item 15.

21 *Ibid.*, p. 51, item 8.

22 *Ibid.*, p. 25, item 25; p. 29, item 14.

23 *Ibid.*, p. 35 item 21 (April 7); *Record*, vol. 1, p. 207. NAS: GD 421/1, vol. 7 [31]. 'Frame' implying design or model.

24 *Udwart's Accounts* (1628–9), 10 March 1629, p. 32, item 28; 17 March, p. 33, item 27, and p. 34, item 8, and then no mention until August, when he was to be paid a bounty of £6 13s. 4d. Presumably he did not attend regularly enough, for in the event he was only paid £3 12s. (*Udwart's Accounts* 1629–30, p. 21, item 14: 1 January 1630, when Aytoun was paid a bounty of £6 13s. 4d.).

25 *Ibid.* (1629–30), p. 25, item 24.

26 *Ibid.* (1629–30), p. 37, item 8.

27 *Ibid.* (1629–30), p. 60, item 13.

28 *Record*, vol. 1, p. 217. SRO: GD 421/1, vol. 7 [32].

29 *Robert Halieburton's Accounts* (1630–1), p. 30, item 3. The work continued in June (*Ibid.*, p. 34, item 4) and in August (*Ibid.*, p. 38 item 16).

30 *Ibid.* (1630–1), p. 44, item 5.

31 *Robert Halieburton's Accounts* (1631–2), p. 64; although not mentioned in the Minutes, this suggests a 'modell' different from the 'moldis and drauchtis' restored later by Wallace's wife. See also James Melville: *Herioter*, April 1934, XXVIII, No. 1, p. 9.

32 Daughter of Andrew Blackhall, minister of Inveresk.

33 *Record*, vol. 1, p. 228. SRO: GD 421/1, vol. 7 [33].

34 Hippolyte J. Blanc: 'George Heriot's Hospital described from an Architectural Standpoint', in C.B. Gunn, H.J. Blanc and C.H. Bedford: *George Heriot's Hospital* [Edinburgh, nd (probably 1902)] described 40 different masons' marks on the ground floor, including that of Wallace, 58 on the first floor, 29 on the second floor and 19 on the towers and chimney heads (p. 175).

35 The picture of Aytoun and his wife was gifted by his great-granddaughter, Helen (daughter of Hector, mason in the Canongate and wife of William Dick, plasterer in Edinburgh) to the governors to be hung in Hospital on 10 October 1726. Aytoun came from Inchdernie, near Kirkcaldy.

36 NAS: GD 421/1, vol. 7 [34].

37 Deborah Howard: (1995) *op. cit.*, p. 137.

38 The ornamental detail of Argyll's Lodging, Stirling, is very similar to that at Heriot's,

suggesting Aytoun's involvement in the former. See Imrie and Dunbar, *op. cit.*, p. lxxi.

39 Hugo Arnot: *The History of Edinburgh from the Earliest Times* (Edinburgh 1788), p. 566.

40 Steven: (1845) *op. cit.*, p. 59.

41 Following A. Anderson Feldborg: *Denmark Delineated* (Edinburgh 1824), p. 88.

42 Thomas Riis: *Should Auld Acquaintance Be Forgot. Scottish-Danish Relations c.1450–1707* (Odense 1988), vol. 1.

43 Miles Glendinning, Ranald MacInnes & Aonghus MacKechnie: *A History of Scottish Architecture. From the Renaissance to the Present Day* (Edinburgh 1996), p. 39.

44 Henry-Russell Hitchcock: *Netherlandish Scrolled Gables of the Sixteenth and early Seventeenth Centuries* (New York 1978), p. 82; Jørgen Hein & Peter Kristianseni: *Rosenborg. Official Guide* (Copenhagen 1994), 3rd edn, pp. 5–7.

45 In a Paper entitled 'Who was the Architect of Heriot's Hospital?', read to a meeting of the Architectural Institute of Scotland on 27 November 1851 he examined the claims of Balcanquall, Jones and Wallace: *Transactions of the Architectural Institute of Scotland*, 2nd series, 1851–2, no. II, p. 12.

46 *Record*, vol. 35 (Feb. 1853 – Jan. 1855), pp. 168–9, 181.

47 *Ibid.*, pp. 442–3.

48 Frederick W. Bedford's *History of George Heriot's Hospital* (Edinburgh 1859), 2nd edn., p. 46.

49 *The Baronial and Ecclesiastical Antiquities of Scotland* (Edinburgh 1852), vol. 3.

50 David MacGibbon & Thomas Ross: *Castellated and Domestic Architecture* (Edinburgh 1887–92), vol. 4, p. 144.

51 In a Paper 'Heriot's Hospital and Contemporary Work' given to the Edinburgh Architectural Association on 28 January 1892, in *Transactions of the Edinburgh Architectural Association,* vol. II (Edinburgh 1892). Blanc was educated in the Hospital, was its Dux Medallist in 1859 and as a late Victorian architect brought a professional understanding to the debate. He had a real knowledge of medieval and early Renaissance architecture and was far removed from the earlier amateurs who wrote about the building. Jane K. Robinson: *An Insight into the Work of Hippolyte Jean Blanc. Architect. Edinburgh, 1844–1917.* (Dissertation, University of Edinburgh, June 1999).

52 On 30 January 1912 in the City Chambers.

53 Edinburgh Burgess Roll, 1406–1700, p. 510.

54 Prestonpans House, erected by the Hamilton family in 1628, with the same angular staircases and classic pediments, with tympanum of the Hamilton coat of arms similar to the ornate shields at the Hospital. Also the cross at Prestonpans has cannon gargoyles and niches similar to Heriot's.

55 Actually 'master of the masons of Edinburgh' between September 1624 and November 1626; signing the Lodge minute book as Deacon between January and October 1628, and in the minutes described as 'deacon' on 24 October 1631. See Imrie and Dunbar, *op. cit.*, p. lx.

56 In the extension to Linlithgow Palace (1618–21) Wallace was involved in turning a three-sided building into a square, including a courtyard, and Winton House (1620–7) was originally designed in the form of a square.

57 C.B. Gunn: *George Heriot's Hospital. Memories of a Modern Monk. Being Reminiscences of Life in the Hospital* (Edinburgh, nd. [probably 1902]), p. 173. Gunn had been educated in the Hospital between 1869 and 1875.

58 In October 1629 and in March 1630 when he was consulted over how he could help in the recovery of Buckingham's debt.

59 Treasurer of the Hospital between 13 November 1630 and 13 November 1632.

60 NAS: GD 421/1, vol. 7 [34]; David MacGibbon & Thomas Ross: *op.cit.,* vol. 5, p. 560.

61 Glendinning, MacInnes & MacKechnie (1996), *op.cit.,* pp. 38 & 65. The suggestion that the Hospital followed the pattern of royal projects, with the Master of Work – James Murray of Kilbaberton – having some general supervision, lacks documentary substantiation.

62 Deborah Howard (1995): *op. cit.,* p. 213.

63 Aonghus MacKechnie: 'Evidence of a post-1603 Court Architecture in Scotland?', *Architectural History,* vol. 31 (1988), pp. 107–121.

64 Probably in 1646 until the late 1650s.

65 Marguerite Wood (ed.): *Records of the Burgh of Edinburgh, 1642–1655* (Edinburgh 1938), p. 45. NAS: GD 421/5/1. *Treasurer's Accounts,* vol. 3 (1642–1652); 1647–8, p. 59. The sum of £866 13s. 4d. was not paid until the late 1650s (*Accounts,* 1657–8, p. 13). Dr William Steven (1845), p. 82; *Record,* vol. 1, pp. 323–4.

66 Deborah Howard: *op. cit.,* p. 33.

67 By founding (i.e., the metals) I have founded (i.e., the Hospital).

68 For these my heart has glowed.

69 So may God treat you, as you treat them.

70 God has given us these calm enjoyments.

71 Translated into 'I distribute chearfullie' or 'I spend on others'.

72 The Arms of George Heriot, the Founder, Piety binds Heaven to Earth.

73 Called the 'pillars' by the boys. This arcade was used by them as a shelter in bad weather.

74 Dr William Steven (1845): *op. cit.,* pp. 36–7. Heriot's portrait had been completed by Paul van Somer (1576–1621), who settled in London in 1616 and painted Queen Anna the following year. De Laune gifted Heriot's portrait to the town council in May 1637.

75 Of my body this statue, of my mind, this work is a representation.

76 Introduced as 'a manifestation of the Renaissance spirit of scientific enquiry'. Deborah Howard (1995): *op. cit.,* p. 104.

77 Alistair Rowan: 'George Heriot's Hospital, Edinburgh', *Country Life,* vol. CLVII, March 6, 1975, p. 556.

78 These windows represent the scope of existence from birth through the world to the grave. *RCAHMS* (1951), *op. cit.,* p. 113.

79 Peter Murray: *The Architecture of the Italian Renaissance* (London 1963), pp. 240–1. Bannister Fletcher: *A History of Architecture on the Comparative Method* 7th rev. edn. (London 1961), pp. 708–11.

80 Hippoltye J. Blanc in C.B. Gunn: (probably 1902), *op. cit.,* counted 209 which included pediments and strapwork heads (p. 155).

81 Mentioned first in the *Gentleman's Magazine* of 1745, *op. cit.,* p. 686.

82 Described in 1745 as 'a most magnificent stone structure' with a 'spacious square court, neatly paved, with an inclosed well of fine spray water in the middle'. *Ibid.,* p. 686.

83 The boys called it the Hall.

84 It was repainted again in June 1775 'to preserve the wainscot lining'. *Record,* vol. 11 (October 1774–June 1777), p. 31.

85 In the manner of Grinling Gibbons (1648–1720), the Anglo–Dutch wood-carver.

86 Still in place in 1827 according to Revd Thomas Thomson: *Historical and Descriptive Account of George Heriot's Hospital* (Edinburgh 1827).

87 And a 'good and sufficient Clock' (added in October 1759), *Record*, vol. 8 (Oct. 1744–Sept. 1761), p. 413.

88 Organised by F. Caird Inglis in 1937 (*The Scotsman*, 9 November 1937).

89 It was bought by the governors at Christie's in March 1936. Perhaps it was the settle mentioned in the Inventory of his property (*The Scotsman*, 10 and 18 March 1936).

90 The inner iron door was added in the Charter Room in 1773.

91 Richard Fawcett: *Scottish Architecture From the Accession of the Stewarts to the Reformation* (Edinburgh, 1994), pp. 334–5.

92 Deborah Howard (1995): *op. cit.*, 209.

93 *RCAHMS* (1951), *op. cit.*, p. 111.

94 John Cornforth:'Ornamentally Scottish', *Country Life*, 9 August 1990, pp. 60–1. Although Francini was not available in an English version until 1669. It also partially inspired the outer gate of Argyll's Lodging in Stirling, the similarity to Heriot's already having been noted. Richard Fawcett: *Argyll's Lodging, Stirling* (Edinburgh 1996): p. 17.

95 The Word of the Lord endureth forever. Made by William Aytoune for 4 punds, 17 shillings Scots.

96 Divine Providence has given to me, a goldsmith, not only to make an everlasting crown on earth but also to wear an everlasting crown in Heaven.

97 *Gentleman's Magazine, op.cit.*, p. 686.

98 On 16 October 1786 the governors agreed 'to get designs and estimates of the expense of finishing the Chapel of the Hospital in a proper manner' (*Record*, vol. 13 (June 1785–Oct. 1789)), p. 60. The repairs cost £92 16s.

99 See Chapter 7.

100 Thomas Frognall Dibdin, *A Bibliographical, Antiquarian and Picturesque Tour in the North Counties of England and Scotland*, two volumes (London 1838). Ian Gow: 'Pugin and Trotter', in *Caledonia Gothica. Pugin and the Gothic Revival in Scotland* (*Architectural Heritage*, VIII, Edinburgh 1997), p. 60.

101 Glory to God in the Highest.

102 W. Douglas Simpson, 'George Heriot's Hospital', *Old Edinburgh Club*, vol. 31 (1962), pp. 33–42.

103 Martin Kemp & Clare Farrow: 'Humanism in the Visual Arts *c.* 1530–*c.* 1630', pp. 32–47, in John MacQueen (ed.): *Humanism in Renaissance Scotland* (Edinburgh, 1990), p. 44.

104 Deborah Howard (1995), *op. cit.*, p. 136.

105 See Chapter 4.

106 Mark Girouard: 'Drumlanrig Castle, Dumfriesshire I', *Country Life*, 25 August 1960, p. 379.

107 James Macaulay: *The Gothic Revival, 1745–1845* (Glasgow 1975), p. 88.

108 Glendinning, MacInnes & MacKechnie (1996), *op. cit.*, p. 166.

109 James Macaulay: *op. cit.*, p. 151.

110 Glendinning *et. al.* (1996): *op. cit.*, p. 231.

111 William Burn (1832–34), Archibald Simpson (1837–42), W.H. Playfair (1842–51), David Rhind (1849–53), David Bryce (1863–70).

112 David MacGibbon & Thomas Ross: (1892), *op.cit.,* vol. IV, p. 145.

113 James Fergusson: *The History of Modern Styles of Architecture* (1873), 2nd edn, vol. 4, pp. 280–2. He was critical of the Hospital, believing it had no beauty nor was it worthy of admiration or imitation. He stressed its ungracefulness and its grotesque ornaments. However, what legitimised the building for Fergusson was its infinite variety of detail.

114 Pamela Robertson (ed.): *Charles Rennie Mackintosh. The Architectural Papers* (London 1990).

115 David McGill: *Heriot's Hospital* (dissertation of May 1974 to RIBA), p. 17.

116 Alistair Rowan (1975), *op. cit.,* p. 554.

CHAPTER THREE

1 NAS: GD 421/1, vol. 6 (8).

2 NAS: GD 421/1, vol. 6 (10).

3 Christopher Lowther: *Our Journall into Scotland Anno Domini 1629* (Edinburgh 1894), p. 36.

4 The town council had 'insisted' that Charles I should settle his debt as early as 1 November 1626 (*Extracts* (1936), p. 15).

5 For £8,369 12. 5d.; NAS: GD 421/1, vol. 6 [16]: Dr William Steven (1845): *op.cit.,* pp. 66–7.

6 *Record,* vol. 1, p. 243 (of £2,468 11s. 5d. owed). NAS: GD 421/1, vol. 6 [30].

7 NAS: GD 421/1, vol. 6 (33).

8 NAS: GD 421/1, vol. 6 (32).

9 Clerk until August 1653.

10 NAS: GD 421/1, vol. 6 [43]: Dr W. Steven (1845): *op. cit.,* p. 71.

11 NAS: GD 421/1, vol. 6 [57].

12 See Chapter I (1626 purchase).

13 *Record,* vol. 1, p. 251.

14 In 1627.

15 *Accounts* of Robert Flemyng (1635–36), p. 20. Following William Cochrane's treasurership (November 1632–November 1635) Flemyng became sixth treasurer.

16 NAS: GD 421/1, vol. 7 [7 (2)].

17 James Grant (1882), vol. 2, p. 182.

18 Marguerite Wood (ed.) (1936): *op. cit.,* p. xlvii. Wood believed that the 'docility' of the Town over the debt had brought about the 'bargain of Broughton' (*Ibid.,* p. xiii). Even Steven in his 'official' account stressed the good deal the town council gained 'for a comparatively small consideration': Steven (1845): *op. cit.,* p. 76.

19 D.B. Horn: *A Short History of the University of Edinburgh, 1556–1889* (Edinburgh 1967), p. 21.

20 *Extracts* (1636): pp. 130 & 211. In November 1634 the Town had borrowed £50,000 from Heriot's (*Ibid.,* p. 151). More borrowing took place in 1636 (*Extracts* (1638): p. 70). The Heriot governors also helped share in other costs, e.g., the repair bill of £120 for St Cuthbert's Church in July 1634 (*Extracts,* p. 146).

21 24 and 31 March 1631. Steven (1845): *op. cit.,* pp. 60–1.

22 *Accounts* (1631–2): p. 61. The prerogative of impressment was still exercised in time of

labour shortage, e.g., for Edinburgh Castle and Holyrood in 1633 for the king's visit (Imrie and Dunbar: *op. cit.*, p. lvi). There are numerous references to these 'undesirables' in the *Accounts*, which show no sympathy for them.

23 *Record*, vol. I, p. 248.

24 *Ibid.*, p. 267.

25 *Accounts* (1632–3): p. 48 (21 and 28 September 1633); *Accounts* (1633–4): p. 71 (26 April 1634).

26 *Accounts* (1633–4): p. 71 (16 August 1634).

27 *Ibid.*, p. 71 (11 October 1634) & *Accounts* (1634–5), p. 76 (19 September 1635), while the west side was the centre of attention in November 1636 (*Edgar's Accounts*, 1636–7: p. 77). Edward Edgar was seventh treasurer between November 1636 and November 1637.

28 Near Newbattle on 4 June 1636.

29 *Accounts* (1636–7): pp. 79 & 83.

30 All have now been removed except those over the Charter Room on the south front.

31 1844 edition of Chetham Society, p. 94ff; P. Hume Brown (ed.): *Early travellers in Scotland* (Edinburgh 1891): p. 141 wrongly gives the date as 1636.

32 *Accounts* (1633–4): p. 71 (13 September 1634).

33 *Accounts* (1637–8): p. 77.

34 *Record*, vol. I, p. 284.

35 Eighth treasurer between November 1637 and November 1638.

36 Although all the figures in this chapter are based on items in the Hospital *Accounts*, those detailing sums spent on the fabric are my own calculations and therefore should be used with caution.

37 Especially between November 1638 and November 1639. Baxter was ninth treasurer between 1638–40.

38 *Ibid.*, p. 299.

39 They continued to collect their expenses – fixed at 4s. per meeting in October 1634 – provided they arrived in time for prayers and roll-call. Despite the financial difficulties the governors increased their own attendance allowance to six shillings in November 1636. Even although practically all the meetings at this time were purely routine – electing officials and new governors, taking oaths, going over *Accounts* – the governors still met ten times in 1640.

40 *Accounts* (1639–40), p. 24.

41 John Spalding: *Memorials of the Troubles in Scotland and in England AD1624–AD1645* (Aberdeen 1850), 2 vols, vol. I, p. 259.

42 *Accounts* (1640–41), show 8–10 masons on site between 21 November 1640 and 13 March 1641, then only 2–4 masons working between 20 March and 4 September 1641.

43 However, the governors paid Clement Towers for glass for the south-west tower on 1 November 1641. NAS: GD 421/1, vol. 7 [46]. *Accounts* (1640–41), p. 74. Aytoun busied himself elsewhere, being employed 'for drawing the forme' of Innes House in Morayshire, which at that time 'was considered to be one of the largest and best planned country houses in all of Scotland'. Aytoun was paid £26 13s. 4d. on 4 September 1640 for this. (Joseph Innes: *Architectural History of Innes House* (nd), p. 6.)

44 *Accounts* (1641–2), show 10–14 masons working at the Hospital between April and November 1642.

45 NAS: GD 421/1, vol. 7 [48]. 28 March 1642 (*Accounts* 1641–42), pp. 27–8.

46 *Record*, vol. 1, p. 265.

47 NAS: GD 421/5 [377].

48 Son of her daughter Sybilla Heriot. NAS: GD 421/1, vol. 5 [44] wrongly calls him Richard.

49 Steven (1845), *op. cit.*, p. 76.

50 *Record*, vol. I, p. 321. NAS GD 421/1, vol. 5 [64]. She had two sons, Robert and James. She was given £10 sterling immediately to tide her over and was to receive regular quarterly payments until the boys reached 14 years of age. They attended the High School and the governors paid its Master, William Spence, directly for their education as they lived with him and his wife. *Accounts* (1642–43), p. 91. Termed the 'first foundationers' (*Edinburgh Evening News*, 17 December 1936).

51 Second son of Margaret, sister of the founder.

52 *Record*, vol. 1, p. 343.

53 Steven: *op. cit.*, between pp. 82 & 83.

54 Nicholas Morgan & Richard Trainor: 'The Dominant Classes', p. 119, in W. Hamish Fraser & R.J. Morris (eds.): *People and Society in Scotland, 1830–1914*. Richard Rodger: *The Transformation of Edinburgh. Land, Property and Trusts in the 19th Century* (Cambridge 2001), p. 117.

55 NAS: GD 421/1 vol. 6 [59].

56 NAS: GD 421/1 vol. 6 [66] and [71].

57 Alistair Rowan: article in *Country Life*, 13 March 1975, p. 635; Steven (1845), *op. cit.*, p. 77.

58 Johnstone's will was printed in Appendix VI to Constable (1822): *op. cit.*, pp. 161–192.

59 Extracts (1936), pp. 232–4.

60 *Record*, vol. I, pp. 323–4.

61 *Accounts* (1642–3) show 12–14 on site, while the *Accounts of James Alison* (1643–4) show 13–22 masons present from February to November 1644. Alison was eleventh treasurer between November 1643 and November 1647.

62 Gordon's drawing of 'Herioti Orphanotrophium'. The Bohemian Wenceslas Hollar's engraving, *The Citie of Edinburgh from the South*, although dated 1670, was probably made some years earlier. It shows the Hospital in stylised form but it is difficult to make out significant detail. However, Slezer's print of 1693, *Bogen-Gight*, follows Gordon in this lop-sided look.

63 *RCAHMS* [ED/2651].

64 Alistair Rowan: *Country Life*, 13 March 1975, p. 635. Although according to MacGibbon and Ross (1892): *op. cit.*, vol. 4, p. 140, following Laing (1851), p. 12, this perhaps had been the 'original intention'.

65 *Accounts* (1644–45) show 10–15 masons and 10–11 labourers working on site between 1 March and 21 June 1645 but work was abandoned completely in late July when a particularly virulent plague broke out – Edinburgh's last outbreak.

66 1611–1667. (Portrait in Scottish National Portrait Gallery, No. 1536.)

67 Imrie and Dunbar: *op. cit.*, p. lxi.

68 Indeed, significantly Mylne was placed ahead of Aytoun in the *Accounts* of John Edgar at this time and he received £6 a week, the same wage as Aytoun.

69 Mylne's appointment as master gunner in September 1646 and generally his contribution to the artillery during the Civil War may help explain his absence.

70 NAS: GD 421/1 vol. 7 [69]. *Accounts of James Alison* (1645–6), which also show that only £2,197 13s. 6d. was spent on the fabric that year (falling from £12,685 15s. 3d. the previous year) and £3,222 14s. 6d. the following year. Significantly, treasurer Alison presided over a rapid escalation in bad debts. They had reached £8,931 19s. 6d. in 1644–5 (*Accounts*, pp. 70–83), then rose to £12,158 11s. 11d. in 1645–6 (*Accounts*, pp. 55–71), and to £15,754 14s. 11d. in 1646–7 (*Accounts*, pp. 64–84). This led to the governors instituting an inquiry which was critical of Alison's methods and results, and in particular Argyll's defalcations.

71 Simpson reduced the bad debts to £14,362 13s. 5d. (*Accounts*, 1647–8, pp. 62–80) and ensured a 'recovery' to a credit balance of £1,561 16s. 1d. However, there seemed no mason work, or plaster work or iron work. Simpson was twelfh treasurer between November 1647 and November 1648.

72 Master wright to Edinburgh on 27 January 1637 and royal master wright on 9 June 1641. He worked on the Chapel Royal at Holyrood in 1642.

73 M. Wood: (1938), *op. cit.*, p. 142.

74 *Record*, vol. 1, p. 353. Wauchop was thirteenth treasurer between November 1648 and May 1652.

75 *Record*, vol. 1, p. 353.

76 *Ibid.*, p. 373.

77 And also habitable. William Anderson, who had been educated with Heriot and served him for sixteen years, asked for help from the governors in February 1647 (NAS: GD 421/1, vol. 7 [55]). He received a pension of £4 weekly (reduced to £3 in 1658) and accommodation and only left the Hospital for Trinity Hospital when the boys finally arrived in 1659. (NAS: GD 421/1 vol. 7 [64].)

78 *Record*, vol. I, p. 373.

79 John Nicoll: *A Diary of Public Transactions and other occurrences, chiefly in Scotland from January 1650 to June 1657* (Edinburgh 1836): p. 62.

80 Steven (1845): *op. cit.*, p. 86.

81 *Record*, vol. 1, p. 437.

82 The *Accounts* of the 1650s hardly mention work on the Hospital. Most money goes on wages and pensions. Treasurers were Andrew Ramsay (May 1652–November 1654); Hew Hamyltoune (November 1654–August 1657); John Meine (August 1657–August 1659). See also 11 April 1656: James Colston: *Trinity College and Trinity Hospital. A Historical Sketch* (Edinburgh 1896), p. 103.

83 *Ibid.*, pp. 398–9 & 407–8. The earlier financial support from the governors to Elizabeth had, by then, ended.

84 They also gave a yearly pension of £200 Scots to Mary Kincaid and Grizel Ahanna, nieces of the Founder, when in March 1657 they were reduced to poverty, suggesting that had the Hospital been operating, their eight children would have been educated and maintained there (*Record*, vol. 1, p. 415). They also gave further support to George Scott, Heriot's nephew, and his children, Janet, Mary and Robert, £24 Scots monthly. (*Ibid.*, pp. 430–1.)

85 Who had followed Guthrie as third Clerk in office in August 1653.

86 *Record*, vol. 1, p. 433.

87 NAS: GD 421/1, vol. 7 [66].

88 *Accounts* (1657–8), p. 13. The lasting legacy of Cromwell's troops is the legend that one of

his soldiers was left behind by his comrades and had fallen down, or been pushed down, the staircase of the north-west turret where he met his death. The 'drummer's step' was not used by the boys as it was bad luck and the level of this step was always less worn than the others.

89 *Record*, vol. 1, p. 438.

90 *Ibid.*, p. 440.

91 *Ibid.*, p. 443.

92 Mylne repaired 'Heriotes pictor' while John Telfer did the painter work which included the whole 'wark' and the 'laying of Mr Heriot's porterat over on oyle collir thruse over'. NAS: GD 421/1 vol. 7. [73] and [74].

93 *Record*, vol. 1, p. 455.

94 *Ibid.*, p. 456.

95 Of the occupations of the 26 fathers recorded, 15 were merchants, 4 were tailors, 3 were masons, 2 were vintners, one was a wright and another a skinner.

96 He had been appointed a governor when Deacon of Masons on 2 November 1653.

97 *Record*, vol. 1, p. 485. Especially after 7 September when a 'fearfull spaitt of wateor caused much damage'. M. Wood (ed.): *Extracts from the Records of the Burgh of Edinburgh, 1655–65* (Edinburgh 1940).

98 *Record*, vol. 1, p. 457.

99 *Ibid.*, p. 466.

100 *Ibid.*, p. 466.

101 Schoolmaster was an important post, next in authority to the master's, and both were to be resident and have meals together, separate from the boys and other staff. The schoolmaster's duties were to include supervision of the dormitories and of the boys' appearance. He was obliged to wear a gown, with a new one provided annually.

102 William Temple, first barber and surgeon, submitted his annual account in September 1660 for medicines for 'scabed heads' and 'marigold flowers' for nine boys with measles. NAS: GD 421/10 [42].

103 *Record*, vol. 1, p. 468.

104 This involved going over the Catechisms weekly with the boys.

105 Douglas had been a chaplain in the army of Gustavus Adolphus of Sweden, the preacher at the coronation of Charles II at Scone on New Year's Day 1651 and a leading figure in the Church of Scotland in the 1640s and 1650s.

106 John Nicoll (1836): *op.cit.*, p. 241.

107 *Ibid.*, p. 242.

108 However, as early as 1662 the governors broke this arrangement and the ceremony was not held until mid-June in that year for no obvious good reason.

109 *Accounts* (1658–9): p. 16.

110 Ended only by Scottish Education Department auditors in 1891.

111 Printed were the sermons of 1683, 1694, 1695, 1775, 1776, 1782 and 1841. (Dr W. Steven (1845): *op. cit.*, p. 94) as were those of 1846, 1848 and 1851)Frederick W. Bedford (1859): *op. cit.*, pp. 363-4).

112 *Record*, vol. 2 (August 1662–May 1688), p. 141.

113 The boys memorised the Shorter Catechism (of 1647). With 107 articles, this document was short only in comparison with the Larger Catechism (of 1648) which had 196 articles.

114 On 29 December 1662, 20 April 1674 and 3 January 1676.

115 *Record,* vol. 1, p. 477.

116 *Ibid.,* 495.

117 *Ibid.,* 506-7.

118 *Ibid.,* 510.

119 The governors must have ignored this as it was decided on 17 April 1727 that elections over 10 years of age had resulted 'in many inconveniences' and reiterated previous policy. (*Record,* vol. 5 (December 1718–March 1729), p. 256.)

120 *Record,* vol. 1, p. 495.

121 Wrongly designated Cleghorn in the *Records.* This is one of a number of mistakes suggesting that the transcript of the seventeenth-century minutes is somewhat unreliable. Certainly there are a number of blanks and at least one important section missing: see 8 August 1684.

122 Of £5 sterling each – mentioned in Heriot's Will.

123 *Record,* vol. 1, pp. 460–1.

124 *Ibid.,* 504.

125 *Ibid.,* 514.

126 *Accounts,* of George Wauchope (1648–9): p. 41.

127 *Accounts* (1648–49), p. 48. These expenditures were when bad debts were running at £14,743 9s. 5d. and only £2,682 6s. was being spent on the fabric.

CHAPTER FOUR

1 *Record,* vol. 1, pp. 525, 532.

2 P. Hume Brown (ed.): *op. cit.* (1891), p. 222.

3 *Ibid.,* pp. 234–5.

4 *Ibid.,* p. 246; James Brome: *Travels over England, Scotland and Wales* (London 1700), p. 200. He also complained that the use of the Hospital for storage was 'a very doleful spectacle', believing that it was a perversion of the founder's intentions.

5 The town council was determined to recover some of its expense as it had bought the Citadel for £6,000 in 1663, having already contributed £5,000 to its building following demands from Cromwell. *Inventory* (1951): p. 261. Another example of Heriot's coming second to the Council.

6 Thomas Kirke & Ralph Thoresby: *Tours in Scotland 1677 and 1681,* Hume Brown (ed.) (Edinburgh 1892).

7 *Record,* vol. 2 (August 1662–May 1688), p. 186.

8 *Ibid.,* p. 119.

9 *Ibid.,* p. 135 (10 July 1676).

10 David Pryde: *Heriot's Hospital. A Short History* (Edinburgh 1938), p. 11. Dr W. Steven (1845): *op. cit.,* p. 100.

11 *Record,* vol. 3 (June 1688–September 1701), p. 27.

12 *Ibid.,* p. 67.

13 *Ibid.,* p. 79.

14 Meikle had become a burgess in 1671, Henderson in 1724. The small bell now rings on the hour. The large bell is rung at the end of morning and lunch intervals to call the

boys back to classes.

15 He had already leased 'littell roumes' in the Hospital for four months in March 1667. NAS: GD 421/10 [64].

16 David M. Walker: *A Legal History of Scotland. vol. IV. The Seventeenth Century* (Edinburgh 1996), p. 132. Alastair J. Mann (2000): *op. cit.*, p. 16.

17 In fact nothing resulted from this order for on 2 September 1689 the treasurer was threatening Anderson's widow, Agnes Campbell, that unless she removed printing material padlocks would be put on the doors.

18 *Record*, vol. 2, p. 176.

19 Sir John Lauder of Fountainhall: *Historical Notices of Scottish Affairs,* vol. 2 [1683–88] (Edinburgh 1848), pp. 548–9.

20 Forbes W. Robertson: *Early Scottish Gardeners and their Plants, 1650–1750* (East Linton 2000), p. 129.

21 Steven (1845), *op. cit.*, p. 98.

22 When the governors found out that Cuthbertson had stolen lead roofing from the north side of the 'wark' they pressed charges and he was imprisoned.

23 The 'Heriot Promenade' is mentioned by Dr Archibald Pitcairne in his comedy 'The Assembly' of 1692. Duncan Fraser: *Edinburgh in Olden Times* (Montrose 1976), p. 116.

24 2 September 1700.

25 *Record*, vol. 2, p. 81. This tradition was followed for all later masters.

26 *Ibid.*, p. 96.

27 *Ibid.*, p. 98.

28 *Ibid.*, p. 188.

29 *Record*, vol. 3, p. 71.

30 *Ibid.*, p. 113.

31 They were playing cards after 10 p.m.

32 *Ibid.*, pp. 210–1.

33 Between March 1678 and December 1685 the post of steward (butler) was often mentioned. However, one has the impression that the transcript fails to mention many of the appointments and it can be assumed that a number came and went, most of them proving unworthy, many of them inefficient, perhaps immoral. As with all other positions in the Hospital the recipients owed their position to their friendship with governors and this explains the frequent attacks throughout the centuries, often accurate, on the corruption and depravity of a system of highly paid sinecures.

34 *Record*, vol. 2, pp. 230–1. Quakerism was viewed as a heresy from the mid-seventeenth century, but Ballantine was dismissed just as a new mood of toleration was spreading. Alaistair J. Mann (2000): *op. cit.*, pp. 56–7.

35 *Record*, vol. 2, p. 211.

36 Rocheid had already been indicted by the town council for, among other charges, 'persuading the Council of Heriot's Hospital to set a tack of their mills for 2,800 merks less than their value and 800 merks less than the offered price'. David Robertson and Marguerite Wood: *Castle and Town. Chapters in the History of the Royal Burgh of Edinburgh* (Edinburgh 1928), p. 140. He was reinstated by the Town in February 1686.

37 NAS: GD 421/9 [42].

38 *Record*, vol. 2, pp. 231, 236, 238–9.

39 Robert Chambers (1858): *op. cit.*, pp. 342–3.

40 Helen M. Dingwall: *Physicians, Surgeons and Apothecaries. Medicine in 17th Century Edinburgh* (East Linton 1995), pp. 58 & 216.

41 *Book of the Old Edinburgh Book Club*, vol. II, p. 92 and p. 109. After their defeat at Bothwell Brig 1,184 prisoners were left in an open field between June and November 1679 because no prison could take them in. Although not mentioned in the official *record* it appears that the wounded were treated in the Hospital. William Moir Bryce: *History of the Old Greyfriars' Church, Edinburgh* (Edinburgh 1912), p. 113.

42 *Record*, vol. 2, pp. 245–6.

43 Fisher's detailed account for £237 18s. for December 1694 to October 1695 is in NAS: GD 421/10 [48]. He obtained an extra payment of £100 because of the increasing amount of work dealing not only with sickness and child complaints but with accidents often amounting eight to ten a day! NAS: GD 421/10 [51].

44 On 4 April 1698.

45 *Record*, vol. 2, p. 47.

46 *Ibid.*, pp. 152–3.

47 *Record*, vol. 3, p. 48: the first use of senior pupils as censors to police the others.

48 *Ibid.*, p. 183.

49 The opposition to the sending of boys to the High School suggests a belief in the Hospital that it was offering the best liberal ('secondary') education possible at the time for burgesses' sons.

50 NAS: GD 421/10 [20].

51 Which held that boys would be taught to read Scots distinctly and write a good hand as well as learning Latin rudiments.

52 The introduction of 'musick' to the Hospital curriculum was significant at a time when there was a complete lack of music teaching in Scotland. The governors, however, had been approached by Lewis de France on his arrival in Edinburgh in September 1684. He suggested that psalm–singing should be begun and held himself 'readie and willing' to 'instruct the scholars in the grounds of musick' (John Maidment: *Analecta Scotica*, 2nd series (Edinburgh 1834–7), vol. 2, p. 263). Presumably he was not taken on for Fountainhall mentioned, on 9 September 1687, that the town council had placed a 'Popish Quirister' in the Hospital to teach music 'contrary to the Hospital's foundations.' (Sir John Lauder of Fountainhall: *op. cit.*, (1848), vol. 2, p. 818.) According to another source this was Jacques du Conton, who received 100 merks for teaching music in the Hospital. M. Wood and Helen Armit: *Extracts from the Records of the Burgh of Edinburgh, 1681–1689* (Edinburgh 1954), 24 August 1687.

53 NAS: GD 421/10 [21].

54 *Record*, vol. 3, pp. 118 & 162.

55 *Ibid.*, p. 172.

56 Sir John Lauder of Fountainhall: *Historical Observances . . . from October 1680 to April 1684* (Edinburgh 1840), pp. 55–6 and Appendix.

57 Donald Crawford (ed.): *Journals of Sir John Lauder, Lord Fountainhall* (Edinburgh 1900), p. xxxii. Unlike Argyll, who was executed in 1685, the dog did escape a similar fate and survived.

58 Revd T. Thomson: (1827), *op. cit.*, p. 21. Immediately after this 'a pasquinade, in the form of a letter from Scotland, was published in London, which, purporting to give an account of the trial of the said dog, contained a galling satire on the trial of Argyll.'

(*Ibid*, p. 20): *An Account of the Arraignment, Tryal, Escape, and Condemnation of the Dog of Heriot's Hospital in Scotland, that was supposed to have been hanged, but did at last slip the Halter.* London, 1682 (quoted in full by Thomson, pp. 20–24).

59 Believing the return to 200 merks had been 'too mean and inconsiderable', and accepting the complaints of tradesmen who had been increasingly unwilling to take Heriot apprentices. In fact, this decrease does not appear to have been put into effect.

60 £166 13s. 4d. sterling.

61 Steven (1845): *op. cit.*, pp. 108–9. Sandilands immediately presented two boys and after his death his descendants filled the vacancies when they occurred throughout the history of the Hospital. (Henry Raeburn, the famous portrait painter, was presented by Sarah Sandilands, eldest daughter of Robert, and accepted into the Hospital, in 1764.)

62 *Record*, vol. 3, p. 148.

63 Steven (1845): *op. cit.*, Appendix XIV, pp. 134–5.

64 This had been gifted to the governors by de Laune on 20 May 1637. 'It may pleasure them that never saw him. In me his remembrance can not die': NAS: GD 421/1 vol. 6 [58].

65 The governors of Hutchesons' Hospital seem to have followed this example for George Scougall was employed by them to paint portraits of both George and Thomas Hutcheson in 1717. William H. Hill (1881): *op. cit.*, p. 41.

66 Revd Edwin S. Towill: 'Minutes of the Trades Maiden Hospital', *Book of the Old Edinburgh Club*, vol. 28 (Edinburgh 1953), & Minutes of the Merchant Maiden Hospital, *Ibid.*, vol. 29 (Edinburgh 1956).

67 Margaret K.B. Sommerville: *The Merchant Maiden Hospital* (Oxford 1970), p. 13.

68 *Ibid.*, 22.

69 Helen M. Dingwall: *Late 17th Century Edinburgh: a demographic study* (Aldershot 1994), pp. 266–7. The actual numbers taken into the Hospital were: 1659, 43; 1660s, 48; 1670s, 60; 1680s, 159; 1690s, 234 (total, 544).

70 P. Hume Brown (1891): *op. cit.*, p. 222.

71 Thomas Morer: *A Short Account of Scotland* (London 1702), p. 77.

72 Stuart Piggott (1951), reprinted 1971, p. 903. The 1695 editor, Gibson, relied upon Sir Robert Sibbald for additional Scottish material.

73 Joseph Taylor: *1705. A Journey to Edenborough in Scotland* (Edinburgh 1903), pp. 107–8.

74 Marguerite Wood (ed.): *Extracts from the Records of the Burgh of Edinburgh, 1665–80* (Edinburgh 1950), p. 322.

75 Between 10 October 1688 and 4 March 1702 bonds of £58,403 10s. (Armit, *Extracts* (1689–1701), p. 86), £30,485 8s. (*Extracts, Ibid.*, p. 136) and £19,000 (Armit, *Extracts* 1701–18, p. 8) were taken.

CHAPTER FIVE

1 *Record*, vol. 4 (October 1701–October 1718), p. 297.

2 Since 1706 the town council had allowed the church tower to be used as a munitions store. Following the damage part of the congregation worshipped in Heriot's chapel while repairs were carried out.

3 *Record*, vol. 7 (October 1734–October 1744), pp. 130, 136, 140.

4 *Record*, vol. 8, p. 17.

5 *Ibid*, p. 27.

6 *Record*, vol. 5, p. 269.

7 John Macky: *A Journey through England. In familiar letters from a gentlemen here to a friend abroad.* The Second Edition, improved (London 1732), pp. 72–3.

8 Daniel Defoe: *A Tour thro' the Whole Island of Great Britain divided into circuits or journeys.* Three volumes (London 1727).

9 *Gentleman's Magazine, op. cit.,* p. 686.

10 James Ray : *Journal through Part of England and Scotland (along with army of HRH Duke of Cumberland) by a Volunteer,* 2nd edn (London 1747), Letter V, p. 90.

11 In some cases they remained until 1815 when they were consulted in a lawsuit. *Record*, vol. 20 (August 1813 – April 1816), pp. 384–5.

12 'Memorandum concerning the public records, at present lodged very inconveniently. Expounds the proposal to use Heriot's Hospital': Mar and Kellie Papers. 27 Dec. 1723. NAS – GD 124/10/511. This issue arose again in August 1765 when the Earl of Morton, Lord Clerk Register, requested the use of the north-west garden of the Hospital for the proposed record office but the plan fell through at a late stage (*Record*, vol. 9 (October 1761–October 1767) pp. 216, 218, 226; Steven (1845); *op. cit.,* pp. 158–9). Interestingly, as late as 1931 the first Librarian of the National Library of Scotland, Dr W.K. Dickson, suggested that it would have been worth waiting a generation (for a new National Library) if there had been a chance of getting the Heriot building.

13 Two by the Duke of Argyll, two by Dean of Guild Heriot, two by John Nairn (of Greenyeards), two by John Paton (bookseller) and two by the creditors of the deceased John Anderson, W.S.

14 *Record*, vol. 6 (March 1729–October 1734), p. 28.

15 They had been in a better condition in 1720 when a 'catalogue of flowers' existed to plant a border. Forbes W. Robertson (2000): *op. cit.,* pp. 94–95.

16 *Record*, vol. 7, p. 3.

17 *Record*, vol. 8, p. 30.

18 Lampe (1702–51) was a scholar, composer and performer, and a protégé of Handel, whose operas were highly popular in the eighteenth century. He attempted to introduce open-air concerts into Edinburgh following his success with them in London's pleasure gardens, Vauxhall and Ranelagh. Dennis R. Martin: *The Operas and Operatic Style of John Frederick Lampe* (Detroit 1985), p. 80.

19 D. Johnson: *Music and Society in Lowland Scotland in the 18th Century* (London 1972), p. 52.

20 *Record*, vol. 8, p. 111.

21 With the premature death of Lampe on 25 July 1751 the issue subsided, at least meantime. Lampe was buried in the Canongate Churchyard.

22 *Record,* vol. 5, p. 33.

23 *Record*, vol. 5, p. 96.

24 *Record*, vol. 6, p. 257.

25 One by leading and the other by taking up the rear.

26 In the mornings (Monday to Saturday inclusive) between 1 October and 1 March from 9 a.m. to 12 noon and from 1 March to 1 October from the time dismissed out of morning chapel to 9 a.m. and from 10 a.m. to 12 noon. In the afternoons on Mondays,

Wednesdays and Fridays between 2 p.m. and 5 p.m. and on Tuesdays and Thursdays 2 p.m. to 4 p.m. all year round. In April 1759 the governors, tired of staff difficulties caused partly by the inequality among the teachers, abolished the post of 'doctor' and instead determined to have three schoolmasters on the same footing teaching the three classes of boys. Dr W. Steven (1845), *op. cit.*, pp. 146–7.

27 *Record*, vol. 7, p. 11.

28 *Ibid.*, 12.

29 *Ibid.*, 18. Dr. David Doig later taught for half a century 'with great success and approbation' in the Grammar School of Stirling and was 'generally admitted to be one of the most eminent classical scholars in Scotland.' Revd Dr J. Lee: *Facts for the consideration of the Governors of Heriot's Hospital* (Edinburgh 1836), p. 22.

30 Adverts in the *Caledonian Mercury* on 8 May 1735 and in August 1733.

31 *Record*, vol. 7, p. 166.

32 On 28 April, 5 May, 6 May, 2 June, 6 June and 9 June.

33 *Record*, vol. 7, p. 182.

34 Steven (1845): *op. cit.*, p. 132.

35 From one pint daily to three mutchkins. (A mutchkin measured one quarter pint Scots or three quarters of an imperial pint.)

36 Each room had a maximum of 15 boys.

37 Author of *Lives and characters of the most eminent Writers of the Scots Nation* (Edinburgh 1708–22), 3 vols.

38 *Record*, vol. 4, p. 177.

39 *Ibid.*, p. 181.

40 Dr William Steven (1845): *op. cit.*, p. 112.

41 Dr George Mackenzie: *Letter on Heriot's Hospital* (Edinburgh 1711).

42 He claimed that this was due to Heriot's commitment to the Church of England.

43 Dr William Steven (1845): *op. cit.*, p. 113 ; *Record*, vol. 4, pp. 233–5, 284–6.

44 Rule remained physician until July 1730, and from June 1719 struggled to deal with outbreaks of scrofulous tumours in the Hospital. Boys affected were isolated and bathed regularly in the sulphurous mineral spring near Corstorphine. In 1741 David Foulis (1710–73) was appointed physician. By April 1747 with fewer cases of scrofula he persuaded the governors to end the trips and substituted regular consumption of tar water. Dr W. Steven (1845): *op. cit.*, p. 136.

45 Fisher left three dwelling-houses in a tenement in the Lawnmarket to the Hospital in his will (Steven (1845): *op. cit.*, pp. 119–20). As 23rd treasurer between October 1686 and April 1711 he was credited by Dr. Steven for his good financial management, especially between 1686 and 1694 when the number of boys in the Hospital doubled from 60 to 120.

46 Hector L. Waugh (ed.): *George Watson's College. History and Record, 1724–1970* (Edinburgh 1970), p. 10.

47 *Record*, vol. 4, p. 172. Watson was employed by several corporations and public societies. Perhaps his having just taken on the treasurership of the Society for the Propagation of Christian Knowledge in January 1711 explains his refusal to serve at Heriot's.

48 Hector L. Waugh (1970): *op. cit.*, p. 17. Board now hangs in the council room.

49 In the codicil to his will Watson left £144,000 Scots for his Hospital 'for entertaining and educating' the male children and grandchildren of decayed merchants in

Edinburgh. *Statutes and Rules of George Watson's Hospital* (Edinburgh 1842) p. xxviii.

50 Waugh (1970): *op. cit.*, p. 18; John Harrison: *The Company of Merchants of the City of Edinburgh and its Schools, 1694–1920* (Edinburgh 1920), p. 17; *Statutes* (1842): *op. cit.*, p. xxix.

51 *Statutes: Ibid.,* pp. 14-18.

52 John Gifford: *William Adam, 1689–1748. A Life and Times of Scotland's Universal Architect* (Edinburgh 1989), pp. 168-9.

53 That this was sold by the Heriot governors for about the same price as Thomson's Yards but was between five and six times larger again casts doubts on the financial practice of the governors. It was to be sold to the Royal Infirmary in 1869 for £43,000! Moreover, at the same time as the land was being transferred to Watson's the feu right of a much larger section to the east was sold to a builder for £1,200. Soon George Square, Buccleuch Place and Buccleuch Street were built and the feus became valuable. The town council soon offered to rebuy it for £1,600 but the builder refused to surrender it for less than £20,000.

54 Robert Anderson: *The History of Robert Gordon's Hospital, Aberdeen 1729 to 1881* (Aberdeen 1896), p. 6 and pp. 20–2; Alexander Walker: *Robert Gordon, His Hospital and His College* (Aberdeen 1886), p. 5.

55 'Deed of Mortification and Disposition of Robert Gordon. Merchant in Aberdeen – 1731', in *General Regulations* (Aberdeen 1850), p. 51.

56 Appendix to the Mortification and Disposition, in *General Regulations: op.cit.*, p. 83.

57 *Record,* vol. 4, p. 308.

58 *Record,* vol. 5, p. 278.

59 In capital letters!

60 *Record,* vol. 5, p. 108.

61 *Ibid.*, p. 185.

62 *Ibid.*, p. 175.

63 *Record,* vol. 7, p. 108.

64 *Caledonian Mercury,* 5 June 1739. Dr W. Steven (1845): *op. cit.*, p. 131.

65 *Record,* vol. 7, p. 144.

66 Quoted by Revd John Gillies: *Memoirs of the Life of the Reverend George Whitefield M.A.* (London 1772), p. 98.

67 *Record,* vol. 8, p. 132.

68 *Ibid.*, p. 135.

69 Garring comes from 'gaur' (Scots) = to force. A boy who had been in the Hospital for five years became a 'garrer'.

70 *Record,* vol. 4, p. 23.

71 The parts of the uniform found during building developments in 1952 appear to date from before 1740 and bear out the fact that the governors were then enforcing the Statute (*The Scotsman,* 14 October 1952; *The Evening Dispatch,* 10 June 1953).

72 See above, Chapter 4.

73 *Record,* vol. 4, p. 113.

74 *Ibid.*, p 213.

75 *Record,* vol. 6, p. 78.

76 *Record,* vol. 6, p. 180.

77 This was in November 1781 (if not before).

78 *Record*, vol. 5, p. 319.

79 See Chapter 6.

80 Interestingly, Watson's took a different view in its 1755 *Statutes*.

81 *Record*, vol. 4, p. 80.

82 *Record*, vol. 5, pp. 167–8.

83 *Ibid.*

84 *Record*, vol. 7, p. 162. In 1755, as the return of the fee became increasingly common, the governors determined to present a handsome, well-bound Bible when this happened.

85 Steven (1845): *op. cit.*, p. 139

86 *Record*, vol. 4, p. 191.

87 *Record*, vol. 4, pp. 33, 46, 48, 59.

88 *Ibid.*, pp. 61, 64, 66–7.

89 *Record*, vol. 4, p. 322.

90 Total number entering the Hospital between 1700 and 1750 was 948. Broken down as follows; 1700s, 210; 1710s, 197; 1720s, 175; 1730s, 183; 1740s, 183.

91 *Record*, vol. 8, p. 58. Interestingly, Flint, as 26th treasurer of the Hospital between October 1738 and October 1748, had in October 1741 been congratulated for his diligence, insight and knowledge. Dr W. Steven (1845): *op. cit.*, pp. 132–3.

92 Edinburgh 1753, p. 439, p. 440 and p. 450. Interestingly, Maitland was warm in his admiration for Watson's Hospital (Harrison (1920): *op. cit.*, p. 18) as a cause of civic pride only shortly after its opening (Maitland, *History of Edinburgh*, p. 483) and this comparison was even more galling for the Heriot governors.

93 This mistake was based on confusing Scottish money with sterling.

94 See Appendix 7.

95 Revd Dr John Lee (1836): *op. cit.*, p. 24.

96 Dr W Steven (1845): *op. cit.*, p. 123. *Record*, vol. 6, pp. 93, 101-3, 323.

97 After the revocation of the Edict of Nantes in 1685, which ended religious toleration in France, a colony of French Huguenot refugees came to Edinburgh. Picardy Place was named after them.

98 Where St James's Square was later built.

99 *Record*, vol. 7, pp. 75–77. Steven (1845): *op. cit.*, pp. 125–131, felt it necessary to vindicate the governors' decision, especially the turning down of a better offer, by quoting in full the legal opinions of Lord Advocate Charles Erskine and advocate James Graham of 17 August 1737. Bedford (1859) p. 101, when updating Steven, did not feel the need to do so.

100 Dr W. Steven (1845): *op. cit.*, p. 124.

CHAPTER SIX

1 *Record*, vol. 8, pp. 387–8.

2 Running eastward from about North Castle Street to the present St Andrew Square, comprising the west end of George Street and Queen Street, Young Street and North Charlotte Street.

3 *Record*, vol. 8, pp. 416–9.

4 Kitty Cruft and Andrew Fraser (ed.): *James Craig, 1744–1795* (Edinburgh 1995), p. 20.

5 *Record*, vol. 8, pp. 423–33.

6 *Ibid.*, p. 432.

7 *Ibid.*, p. 433.

8 *Reasons of Dissent and Protest by Mess, John Glen, Robert Wallace, George Kay, Robert Walker, Henry Lundie, John Erskine and Robert Dick, Ministers of Edinburgh and Administrators of George Heriot's Hospital. Against an Act of Council of the said Hospital of 14 Nov. 1759* (Edinburgh 1760).

9 *A Remonstrance . . . By the United Committees of the Merchant Company; the Incorporations of Goldsmiths, Skinners, Furriers, Hammermen, Wrights, Masons, Taylors, Baxters, Fleshers, Shoemakers, Weavers, Dyers, and Waukers; the Societies of Barbers and Candlemakers; and a Friendly Meeting of Persons bred in Heriot's Hospital, all Freemen Burgesses of Edinburgh* 1763. (Signed by Malcolm Brown.) *Memorial by a Considerable number of the Burgesses of the City of Edinburgh, relative to the Management of Mr George Heriot's Hospital* (Edinburgh 1763).

10 Of 19 November 1765.

11 Sir Walter Scott: *Provincial Antiquities and Picturesque Scenery of Scotland* (London 1826), vol. 1, pp. 102–3.

12 A recent work has suggested that the development of Edinburgh's Second New Town depended upon the 'mostly working in harmony' of town council and the Hospital. This 'required boldness, confidence and commitment which, considering the uncertainties of the times, was highly commendable'. (Connie Byrom: 'The Development of Edinburgh's Second New Town', in *Book of the Old Edinburgh Club*, New Series, vol. 3 (1994), p. 55.) However, this 'harmony' was mainly the result of the Town's superintendent of works producing the building plans for the Hospital, as William Sibbald did, in June 1792, for the ground north of Queen Street. A number of governors thought that their interests were not best served by such an arrangement. (13 December 1792: *Record*, vol. 14 (March 1790–November 1793), p. 196.)

13 In 1750 the tenants of Canonmills had fallen greatly in arrears and the governors, to save themselves trouble with the mills, agreed to alienate them altogether. The purchaser was an agent who exceeded his commission, and whose principal repudiated the transaction. The property was therefore thrown on the hands of the agent, who realised a handsome profit from the miscarriage.

14 Alexander Law (1965): *op. cit.*, p. 116. Rochead was treasurer of the Hospital from Oct. 1758 to Dec. 1762. He was given the salary of £40 for a clerk 'though he had no clerk, and kept no account at all'; in the end he was dismissed as a hopeless bankrupt, £1,000 in arrears to the trust on his own account, and over £2,000 on account of others (*The Scotsman*, 7 February 1881.)

15 Brutus, Lucius Junius (pseudonym): *Considerations on the Management of George Heriot's Hospital* (Edinburgh 1774).

16 *Record*, vol. 14, p. 198.

17 *Record*, vol. 10 (January 1768–October 1774), pp. 267–70, 273–6; *Cobbett's Parliamentary History of England*, vol. xvii, pp. 845–8.

18 1750–74.

19 'The Ghoists: A Kirk-Yard Eclogue', line 93ff. It appeared first in *The Weekly Magazine* on 13 May 1773. See F.W. Freeman: *Robert Fergusson and the Scots Humanist Compromise* (Edinburgh 1984).

20 1759–1806.

21 In 1783 Montgolfier had begun the craze for ballooning, and in Scotland James Tytler flew half a mile from Comely Gardens to Restalrig on 27 August 1784.

22 Alexander Law (ed.): *An Account of Five Aerial Voyages in Scotland by Vincent Lunardi – London 1786* (Edinburgh 1976), p. 16.

23 Leslie Gardiner: *Man in the Clouds. The Story of Vincenzo Lunardi* (Edinburgh 1963), p. 102.

24 John Kay: *A Series of Original Portraits and Caricature Etchings* (Edinburgh 1877), vol. I, p. 80.

25 Taking off from Kelso (on 22 October) and Glasgow (23 November and 5 December).

26 *Edinburgh Evening Courant*, 26 December 1785: admission sixpence.

27 Lunardi bonnets became the height of fashion: they were made of gauze or thin muslin and their upper part expanded on wire into the dimension of a miniature balloon. Mentioned in Robert Burns' poem of 1785, 'To a Louse'.

28 Leslie Gardiner (1963): *op. cit.*, p. 124.

29 *Ibid.*, p. 154.

30 Dr W. Steven (1845): *op. cit.*, pp. 157–8.

31 *Record*, vol. 9 (October 1761–October 1767), p. 41.

32 David King: *The Complete Works of Robert and James Adam* (Oxford 1991), Appendix C, p. 416: as it was a minor work John Adam was chosen, as he had a nearby town house in Edinburgh, rather than Robert or James, who were in London. The entrance was closed in the 1830s.

33 *Record*, vol. 13, p. 186. Dr Samuel Johnson mentioned in his Diary that he played bowls at Heriot's on Wednesday 31 August 1774. On 30 July he had promenaded through Heriot's Gardens 'which soothed and refreshed' him.

34 *Record*, vol. 14, p. 246.

35 *Record*, vol. 15 (April 1794–October 1800), p. 10. In his poem on 'The Wark' David Crawford praised the treasurer, James Jackson, for laying out the quad 'wi' hewen stanes' ('A Description of Heriot's Hospital', in *Poems, Chiefly in the Scottish Dialect, on various subjects* (Edinburgh 1798)). See also *The Herioter*, XIV, No. 1 (April 1920).

36 *Record*, vol. 16 (November 1800–April 1804), p. 2.

37 Rumford was known for his experiments on the nature and application of heat, and his service to the Hospital resulted in the presentation of an inscribed silver box from the governors.

38 Including those of the Duke of Argyll and Lord Selkirk (Dr W. Steven (1845): *op. cit.*, p. 157).

39 *Record*, vol. 9, p. 156 (17 September 1764).

40 Dr W. Steven (1845): *op. cit.*, pp. 158–9.

41 For John Balfour, Edinburgh merchant, on 15 April 1775.

42 For trustees of Charles Murray on 2 June 1777. They obtained a room on the third floor of the south-west turret for £10 sterling.

43 See 9 October 1786; *Record*, vol. 13, pp. 56–7.

44 Alexander Kincaid: *The History of Edinburgh from the Earliest Account to the Present Time* (Edinburgh 1787), p. 171.

45 The governors imposed strict safety conditions. The Edinburgh Defensive Band was witnessed by James Boswell on Monday 29 October 1781, Friday 30 November 1781 and

Saturday 13 July 1782, exercising on Heriot Green (Joseph W. Reed and Frederick Pottle (eds.): Boswell, *Laird of Auchinleck, 1778–82* (Edinburgh 1993), pp. 404–5, 410, 458).

46 Other companies were drilling on the green in 1804 and 1805 (W.T. Fyfe: *Edinburgh under Sir Walter Scott* (London 1906), p. 177).

47 *Record*, vol. 13, p. 186.

48 When this lease ended it seemed sensible to use the grounds more efficiently, especially given the high food prices during the Napoleonic Wars. On 19 October 1812 the governors decided to convert the bowling green into a kitchen garden for the boys.

49 *Caledonian Mercury*, 10 November 1762.

50 One of the boys involved was 'John' (James) Aitken. He was in October 1764 reprimanded for spending two nights out of the Hospital. He was apprenticed to John Bonnar, painter, in 1767. At the age of 24 he left Edinburgh to live in London, where he became a thief and highwayman. In 1776 he burned down part of Portsmouth dockyard and Bristol Town in an effort to disadvantage the British navy in the American War of Independence. He was hanged for his crimes on 10 March 1777 at Portsmouth Dockyard before an estimated crowd of 20,000. *DNB*, p. 205.

51 The petition said the boys would obey the rules if the offenders were allowed back, and they offered to report all cases of misdemeanours to the masters. It was as much a threat as an offer of help, but nonetheless was accepted. (*The Herioter*, December 1925, vol. xix, No. 3, pp. 11–12.)

52 Censors had been used sporadically in earlier periods but now became an accepted fact of Hospital life after 1791 and were officially recognised in the 1809 Rules. The master appointed older boys every week to be censors in the wards, classrooms and church, and they were accountable for any misbehaviour, and expected to inform on all who broke the rules.

53 *Record*, vol. 11, p. 50.

54 *Ibid.*, p. 111.

55 Steven (1845): *op. cit.*, pp. 166–71.

56 *Record*, vol. 12 (October 1777–April 1785), p. 86.

57 *Ibid.*, p. 200.

58 *Ibid.*, p. 245.

59 *Record*, vol. 14, p. 38.

60 'Bickers' were the pitched battles between Heriot and Watson boys involving stone-throwing. The proximity of the two Hospitals was the basis of the traditional rivalry between them. However, the esprit de corps of Heriot's meant that whenever one of their number was at the receiving end of a slight, however real or imaginary, it became an issue taken up by the whole Hospital. Bickering was to continue throughout the life of the Hospital, and there was a serious incident between the Heriot 'knaps' and the Watson 'neets' at Founder's Day in 1864. Given the contact between Heriot's and the High School, there are also examples of feuds between these two institutions, which were usually of a class nature.

61 *Record*, vol. 14, pp. 260–1.

62 See Chapter 5.

63 *Record*, vol. 14, p. 261.

64 The younger boys were forced to clean shoes, insult companions, buy or sell, lie, and steal. A woman servant said on 8 February 1793, 'If they are desired by these Garring

Boys to do the blackest action on earth, they must do it or hazard their lives.' Alexander Law (1965): *op. cit.*, p. 140.

65 = former pupil.

66 Francis Watt: *The Book of Edinburgh Anecdotes* (London 1913), pp. 278–9. One of the favourite games of the boys was to dare each other to approach Mackenzie's mausoleum and call through the key-hole 'Bluidy Mackenzie, come oot if ye daur, Lift the sneck a' draw the bar' before running away to safety.

67 Revd Dr John Lee: (1836): *op. cit.*, p. 3.

68 Not all governors showed a good example either. William Brodie, a wright and cabinet-maker in the Lawnmarket became a Deacon Councillor and member of the governing body in 1781. He was involved in gambling nightly at a club in Fleshmarket Close, and a series of robberies which culminated in his organisation of a raid on the Excise Office. He was caught, and with his accomplices executed at the west end of the Luckenbooths on 1 October 1788. (J. Kay (1877): *op. cit.*, vol. 1, pp. 256ff.)

69 Appointed 14 January 1757, from Durham.

70 Alexander Law (1965): *op. cit.*, p. 127.

71 *Record*, vol. 9, p. 317.

72 David Simson.

73 *Record*, vol. 12, p. 75.

74 Nichol was dismissed from his post at the High School after a violent attack upon the Rector, Alexander Adam. Walter Scott, a pupil there, was devastating in his criticism of Nichol. Paul H. Scott: 'Walter Scott at the High School', *Blackwood's Magazine*, Oct. 1980.

75 Edinburgh City Archives: SL137/15/4, Library subscription register, 1779–1805, pp. 21, 52, 67. There are no references to Heriot boys in the 1739–59 register (SL137/15/1) and only three references to Heriot boys in the 1760–78 register (SL137/15/2, pp. 191, 224, 258). The number of references increases to ten between 1779 and 1789 (SL 137/15/4, pp. 21, 32–3, 39, 46–7, 52, 67, 108, 153, 180, 220). There are no references between 1790 and 1805. These are the only evidence of Herioters in the High School records, which are incomplete. The governors expected 'hopeful scholars' going on to College to do so without paying fees (19 October 1772: *Record*, vol. 10, pp. 249–50). However, if Heriot bursars ever had free tickets of admission they seem to have been short-lived.

76 *Record*, vol. 9, p. 91.

77 *Ibid.*, p. 294. As relationships with neighbours deteriorated the governors excluded the public from access, which had been traditional. The gardens became less popular and the boys were allocated the west garden for recreation.

78 *Record*, vol. 12, p. 76.

79 David Crawford, Steward 1791–1810, published a volume of poems, one of which described the decoration of the statue (1798), *op. cit.*

80 Sir W. Fraser: *The Melvilles* (Edinburgh 1890), p. 266.

81 Basil Cozens-Hardy: *The Diary of Sylas Neville, 1767–88* (London 1950), pp. 202–3.

82 *Record*, vol. 9, p. 46.

83 Regarded then as the maximum.

84 The son of a proprietor of a textile-mill in Stockbridge, Henry Raeburn won one of the Dean of Guild's prizes for writing in June 1771. He left the Hospital in 1772 and was apprenticed for six years to James Gilliland, jeweller and craftsman. He chose to remain

in Edinburgh and became the leading portrait painter of his generation. Rose Harris: *Sir Henry Raeburn, 1756–1823* (Bristol 1966).

85 The total number of boys admitted between 1750 and 1800 was 940: 1750s, 217; 1760s, 148; 1770s, 176; 1780s, 180; 1790s, 219.

86 *Record*, vol. 12, p. 37. It was completed by David Martin (1737–97), principal Scottish assistant to Allan Ramsay (Revd Thomas Thomson, 1827, p. 43).

87 *Record*, vol. 13, p. 10; also letter in *Edinburgh Evening Courant*, 9 February 1780, which held that the Trust funds were embarrassed when Carmichael took over and he took them 'to affluence'.

88 Steven (1845): *op. cit.*, pp. 172–3. It has on its top a medallion portrait of Carmichael and an alto-relievo representation of the Hospital on the pedestal.

89 *Record*, vol. 15, p. 139.

90 *Record*, vol. 17, p. 11.

91 October 1737 to October 1755.

92 Steven (1845): *op. cit.*, p. 136.

93 *Ibid.*, p. 137.

94 *Record*, vol. 8, pp. 377–8.

95 A former pupil who left a legacy to the Hospital in February 1740 (*Record*, vol. 7, p. 162).

96 Revd Thomas Thomson (1827): *op. cit.*, p. 43. Dr W. Steven (1845): *op. cit.*, p. 136.

97 *Record*, vol. 14, p. 133.

98 According to the board which was hung in the old dining hall it yielded £800 sterling on her death in 1799.

99 *Record*, vol. 14, p. 178.

100 It was included in an inventory of his plate as 'a little love cupe in goldrine fashione'.

101 George Dalgleish and Stuart Maxwell: *The Loveable Craft, 1687–1987* (Edinburgh 1987), p. 23.

102 John G. Dunbar (ed.): *Sir William Burrell's Northern Tour, 1758* (East Linton 1997), p. 77.

103 Richard Pococke: *Tours in Scotland, 1747, 1750, 1760*, Daniel William Kemp (ed.) (Edinburgh 1887), p. 303.

104 Alexander Kincaid (1787): *op. cit.*, pp. 169–74.

105 Diary of Sir Roger Newdigate for 1766. CR136/A[563]. County Record Office, Warwick.

106 *A Tour in England and Scotland in 1785 by an English Gentleman* (London 1788), p. 312.

107 Thomas Pennant: *A Tour of Scotland* (Warrington 1774), p. 56.

108 Edward Topham: *Letters from Edinburgh written in the year 1774 and 1775* (Edinburgh 1776), 1971 edn, pp. 28, 31–2.

109 Francis Grose: *The Antiquities of Scotland*, vol. 1 (London 1789), pp. 34–7 and William Creech: *Letters addressed to Sir John Sinclair* (Edinburgh 1793), pp. 21–2, 24.

110 Hugo Arnot (1788): *op. cit.*, especially pp. 566–7.

CHAPTER SEVEN

1 Katrina Thomson: *Turner and Sir Walter Scott: The Provincial Antiquities and Picturesque Scenery of Scotland* (Edinburgh 1999), p. 7.

2 It can be viewed in the National Gallery of Scotland, which bought the picture in 1998.

3 Gerald Finley: *Landscapes of Memory: Turner as Illustrator to Scott* (London 1980), p. 90.

4 *Record*, vol. 23 (April 1822–March 1825), p. 210.

5 The High School Rector's class in session 1822–3 was 257! Magnus Magnusson: *The Clacken and the Slate: The Story of The Edinburgh Academy, 1824–1974* (London 1974), p. 27.

6 Or Distillery Park.

7 The town council had decided to stave off the threat of the new school by building its own new High School on this land, but reversed its decision.

8 Magnus Magnusson: *op. cit.*, p. 59.

9 The new school was aimed at a different clientèle from that of Heriot's, whose boys were held in high esteem by Sir Walter Scott. From his own youth he remembered them as 'bold, hardy and ingenious, beyond their years'. He admired their strong esprit de corps, and he believed that more of them carried into life 'the same firmness and intelligence of character' (Sir Walter Scott (1826): *op. cit.*, pp. 101–2).

10 *Record*, vol. 26 (April 1832–May 1835), p. 39.

11 Miles Glendinning *et al: op. cit.*, p. 231.

12 Since 1809 at £20 per annum.

13 Duncan McLaren, an Edinburgh draper, became a town councillor in 1833, later Lord Provost of Edinburgh and Radical M.P. from 1865–81.

14 *Record*, vol. 26, p. 566. J.B. Mackie: *The life and work of Duncan McLaren* (London 1888), vol. I, p. 134.

15 Mackie: *op.cit.,* I, pp. 135–6. After supplying the wants of burgesses' children McLaren wished to extend Heriot funds to give free education to the destitute children of all classes and of both sexes.

16 *Record*, vol. 27 (June 1835–June 1837), p. 82.

17 *House of Commons Journals*, vol. 91.

18 J.B. Mackie: *op. cit.*, p., I, p. 137.

19 In the Commons the Liberal MP for St Andrews Burghs, Andrew Johnston of Renniehill, contended that surplus revenue should go to the University of St Andrews as the erection of out-schools was a violation of Heriot's Will.

20 *Record*, vol. 27, pp. 322–38.

21 *Ibid.*, pp. 338–9.

22 Mackie: *op.cit.,* I, p. 139.

23 The Act is published in full by Dr W. Steven (1845): *op. cit.*, Appendix XV, pp. 135–45.

24 *Record*, vol. 27, p. 379.

25 *Ibid.*, p. 409.

26 Traditionally the Hospital had been under the supervision of 'overseers', the last being Alexander Peacock, elected on 9 October 1710. From then on the treasurer took over the role, and called in the aid of professionals when the occasion required. However, in June 1809, the governors appointed a superintendent of works, whose duties included being in charge of Hospital grounds, the feus and feuars, building plans, certificates and reports. John Paterson held office until July 1810, when Thomas Bonnar, also superintendent of works for the Town, took over. He retired in April 1832. The propriety of this was questioned by Dr John Inglis, who deemed it 'inexpedient' for one person to hold both positions 'on account of the intermixture of the respective properties of the

two bodies'. This seemed another example of Heriot's interests being too close to the Town's for comfort. (3 July 1810. *Records*, vol. 19 (July 1810–August 1813), p. 2.) McLaren persuaded the governors to employ an official who would devote the whole of his time to the business of the Hospital, and in March 1833 Alexander Black took office.

27 Built by William Burn in St Andrews between 1832 and 1834.

28 Dr Brunton had prepared an inscription for the foundation stone, and the plate and a copy of an engraving were deposited in the foundations along with (in a sealed bottle) a copy of George Heriot's Will, the *Statutes*, various acts, reports and minutes concerning the Schools, lists of governors and boys, accounts for 1836, copies of Edinburgh's newspapers for 17 April, coinage and details of the proposed school.

29 McLaren had been made convener of this committee on Hospital Schools on 5 January 1837.

30 Sessional schools developed after 1813 and were usually based on a single church and administered by its kirk session. R.D. Anderson: *Education and the Scottish People, 1750–1918* (Oxford 1995), p. 36.

31 There was no dissension in the taking-in of girls.

32 Three shillings per quarter.

33 Included in the regulations accepted by the governors on 19 September 1838 (Dr W. Steven (1845): *op. cit.*, pp. 256–8).

34 *Record*, vol. 28 (July 1837–August 1839), p. 354.

35 *Ibid.*, p. 390.

36 Proponents of orthodoxy persuaded the school committee on 6 July 1840 to recommend the introduction of a fee of a penny a week from scholars to secure 'more regular attendance' (*Record*, vol. 29 (April 1839–June 1841), p. 334) and to help build up a library. McLaren fought back: with daily attendance of 229 out of 250 he claimed attendance was as high as that of fee-paying schools with the same class of children. On 31 August 1840 the school committee voted 5 to 4 to continue the free school experiment. However, the issue resurfaced in December 1857, but again free education was retained by the governors 'without committing themselves on the subject of gratuitous education'. (*Record*, vol. 37 (July 1857–June 1860), p. 85.) Clearly, a number of governors felt uncomfortable about going against the political and educational orthodoxy of the time.

37 Baillie McLaren in *Record*, vol. 28, p. 425.

38 Infant schools were geared for children from two to six years, while juveniles were from five years upwards. They offered high quality elementary education. The curriculum of the juvenile schools included reading, writing, arithmetic, English grammar, geography, book-keeping, linear drawing and singing. They also had an 'industrial' department where all girls received daily an hour's instruction and practice in sewing, knitting and needlework. Infant schools were in High School Yards (opened 1840) with a roll of 65 boys and 80 girls (in July 1845) and Old Assembly Close (1841) with 113 boys and 82 girls. Juvenile schools were in Old Assembly Close (1840) with 161 boys and 179 girls; Borthwick Close (1840) with 161 boys and 176 girls; High School Yards (1840) with 175 boys and 165 girls; and Cowgate Port (1840) with 195 boys and 241 girls. (Dr W. Steven (1845): *op. cit.*, p. 260.)

39 Dr W. Steven (1845): *op. cit.*, pp. 265–9.

40 Mackie: *op. cit.*, I, p. 140.

41 At their height in 1878 the 20 Heriot free schools – 12 juvenile and 8 infant – accommodated 5,456 children. See Appendix 3 and F.W. Bedford: *Supplement to the Third Edition
of the History of George Heriot's Hospital* (Edinburgh, 1878), p. 35.

42 *Record*, vol. 20, p. 332.

43 *Ibid.*, p. 372.

44 *Record*, vol. 23, p. 289. Leonard B. Dean: 'William Henry Playfair and the Athens of the
North 1807 – 1857', Thesis, Edinburgh University, June 1999.

45 *Record*, vol. 23, p. 133.

46 *Ibid.*, p. 149.

47 NAS: GD 421/ vol. 5 (82) 24–5.

48 NAS: GD 421/ vol. 5 (101) 15.

49 Within a year £1,160 had been spent on carpentry work, £1,000 on masonry, £250 on
plumbing, and £152 on smith work.

50 *Record*, vol. 24 (April 1825–June 1828), pp. 334–5.

51 *Ibid.*, p. 517.

52 NAS: GD 421/ vol. 5 (286) 10. The governors were disappointed at the slow pace of
Playfair's work. His 'severe illness' delayed the design of the gate of the Hospital, which
was received on 30 July 1830. Playfair held that 'I have endeavoured to make it such as I
conceive it would have been, if it had been done at the time the Hospital was built'.

53 *Record*, vol. 26, p.149.

54 *Ibid.*, p. 172.

55 The work was estimated at £942.

56 Of over £400.

57 *Record*, vol. 26, p. 250.

58 'With the view of honouring the founder's memory, the governors caused the parts of
the building formerly less elegantly finished, to be faced with hewn stone, 1833.'

59 David Pryde (1938): *op. cit.*, p. 13.

60 *Inventory* (1951), p. 111.

61 In 1787.

62 *Record*, vol. 26, p. 311.

63 *Ibid.*

64 *Ibid.*, p. 312.

65 *Ibid.*

66 1776–1855.

67 James Macaulay: 'The architectural collaboration between J. Gillespie Graham and A.W.
Pugin', in *Architectural History*, vol. 27 (1984), p. 407.

68 *Record*, vol. 26, p. 480.

69 Macaulay (1984): *op. cit.*, p. 409, suggests that Pugin 'played a large part in the fitting-up
of the Chapel'. This is accepted by Paul Atterbury and Clive Wainwright: *Pugin. A
Gothic Passion* (Yale 1994), p. 220, and repeated in the former's article in *A. W.N. Pugin.
Master of Gothic Revival* (Yale 1995).

70 (London 1821), Plates XLII–XLIV, particularly Crosby Hall, London, of 1460, which has
the same cusped quatrefoil panels applied to the surface of the ceiling and had a central
oriel window very much like Heriot's, which is presumably why it was copied.

71 *Record*, vol. 27, p. 77.

72 *Ibid.*

73 *Ibid.*, p. 78. Alexander Black obtained estimates for the work – the entrance door and pulpit in carved oak, £300; carved oak stalls, £300; ornamental canopies, £938; and a new oak floor, £88.18s.

74 *Ibid.*, pp. 78–9. The black and white chequered marble was transferred to the council room.

75 *Ibid.*, p. 79.

76 Only 180 boys were in the Hospital.

77 Lee (1779–1859) took a charge in Edinburgh in 1823, and transferred to St Giles' Old in 1835 before resigning his pastorate, when he became Principal of Edinburgh University in 1840. He was probably the most distinguished divine left in the Church of Scotland after the Disruption of 1843.

78 *Record*, vol. 27, p. 95.

79 *Ibid.*, p. 230.

80 *Ibid.*, p. 427.

81 He wrote again from 4 Duke Street on 31 March 1837 stressing the need to finalise the heating system before laying down the oak floor. *Ibid.*, p. 513.

82 *Record*, vol. 28, p. 206.

83 In the event the governors accepted his first designs on 2 November and the estimate of William Copper & Company of £196 for the work (including glazing). Receipt for Gillespie Graham for the design fee in NAS: GD 421/5 [330] 21.

84 Twenty-eight, each 6 feet 6 inches long, were made by William Trotter and cost in total £98.

85 The chapel roof is similar to Gillespie Graham's enriched Neo-Gothic work at Duns Castle, Berwickshire, in 1818. Following completion of the chapel Gillespie Graham became involved, with Pugin, in the final embellishment of Taymouth Castle, Perthshire, where the library ceiling proved identical to that of Heriot's Chapel. Trotters of Edinburgh were also involved.

86 *Record*, vol. 24, p. 499.

87 *Record*, vol. 27, p. 344.

88 *Record*, vol. 28, p. 197. William Trotter had repaired the existing large table in August 1807.

89 'Early Heriot Clubs' by G.A.C. and J.W.D., in 'The Tercentenary of the Laying of the Foundation Stone of George Heriot's Hospital, 1628–1928', *Supplement to 'The Herioter'* (1928), p. 54.

90 Ian D. Whyte: *op.cit.*, p. 318.

91 As the skills of the Heriot decorators were valued they were involved annually in the decoration of Charles II's statue in Parliament Square for George III's birthday (4 June) up to 1805 (James Grant: vol. 2: *op. cit.*, p. 176) and the roof of Parliament House (Sir Walter Scott (1826): *op. cit.*, p. 102).

92 In 1792, 1793 and 1799.

93 The charter box of the club, its lid dated 1793, and its Rules and Regulations for 1792 and 1802 are still extant.

94 In fact the earliest surviving list numbers 13.

95 Three years, according to the 1792 Rules.

96 South Bridge Street.

97 *Minutes of Heriot's Decorating Club*, 1804, p. 3.

98 *Ibid.*, p. 24.

99 *Ibid.*, p. 25.

100 *Ibid.*, p. 26.

101 The Social Club existed between 1789 and 1808. It sent a deputation to the Decorating Club in 1789 and then annually from 1793. It reappeared in 1836 but failed in its efforts to combine with the Auld Callants in 1837. *Tercentenary Supplement* (1928), p. 55.

102 As well as 100 doz. ranunculus and 70 doz. tulips.

103 *Record*, vol. 17, p. 341 (31 May).

104 *Ibid.*, p. 343.

105 *Ibid.*, p. 350.

106 *Ibid.*, pp. 358–9.

107 William Reid 'expressed great contrition' (*Ibid.*, pp. 358–9) and offered an apology which was given before the whole Hospital, and the legal proceedings were dropped.

108 6 June 1808.

109 NAS: FS 1/17/82.

110 According to Article II of the constitution, published in 1820.

111 Six shillings a week for the first 13 weeks; four shillings for the next 13 weeks; three shillings for the next 13 weeks; and then 1s. 6d. a week for as long as distress continued.

112 Article XVI.

113 Highland Society: *Report on Friendly or Benefit Societies* (Edinburgh 1824).

114 At its centenary meeting on 20 June 1915 it was claimed that the 'Society had an unbroken record of success'. Its membership of 70 included seven annuitants, and it was in 'an exceptionally strong financial position'. *The Herioter*, vol. ix., no. 2 (July 1915).

115 By the Duchess of Hamilton.

116 Decorating the statue of George Heriot.

117 *Record*, vol. 24, p. 549. In fact, the statue was not to be decorated again until the 'special' celebrations of 1859.

118 *Record*, vol. 26, p. 30.

119 *Record*, vol. 15, p. 45.

120 Usually 'Who is the King of Glory?'

121 Smith in 1823, 1826, 1827 and 1828; Kedward in 1838, 1839 and 1840.

122 Revd Glover lost his motion to end the production of the anthem by 13 to 7 on 19 April 1842.

123 *Record*, vol. 30 (July 1841–December 1843), pp. 137–8. The issue was first discussed by the Watson's governors on 12 May 1840 and three days later its education committee disapproved of Watson's boys joining their Heriot counterparts 'in the public exhibition of their vocal powers' (Watson's Minutes, p. 242). It suggested that the service in Greyfriars should follow the normal sabbath pattern, with the whole congregation joining in, and with no prominent part for the boys (*Ibid.*, p. 243). Although not immediately followed up, the Watson's governors were soon pressing for a joint conference to discuss the anthem.

124 *Record*, vol. 30, p. 180. Faced with the intransigence of the Heriot governors, some of the Watson's party felt that their boys should not participate until the anthem was modified (rather than abandoned). They were defeated 6 to 4 at their governors' meeting on 12 May 1842, and Watson's boys continued to sing the anthem.

125 *Tercentenary Supplement* (1928), p. 57.

126 On 12 December 1849 house-governor Fairbairn accepted the post of an honorary member of the Auld Callants and declared himself happy 'at all times to promote the important objects of the Association'. Five days later Revd Dr Steven also accepted, and was 'much honoured by the distinction'. Such 'official' support guaranteed the success of the Former Pupil Association.

127 *Record*, vol. 33 (October 1847–April 1850), pp. 242–3.

128 *Record*, vol. 17, p. 122.

129 William Steven: *The History of the High School of Edinburgh* (Edinburgh 1849): Appendix VI, p. 108.

130 On 6 September 1805. Somerville declined to vote at the meeting of the governing body on 27 January 1812. This is the first indication of a house-governor voting.

131 *Record*, vol. 18 (February 1808–July 1810), p. 420.

132 *Ibid.*, p. 8.

133 *Ibid.*, p. 18.

134 *Ibid.*, p. 31.

135 *Record*, vol. 19, pp. 436–7.

136 After 1816 Currie became a popular destination for the annual excursion of boys. They did not return after June 1837, when Somerville either shot himself intentionally or accidentally with one of the air-guns which he was reported to have invented. (Diary of James Birrell, unpublished; written 1898–1901), p.48.)

137 *Record*, vol. 21 (April 1816–April 1819), p. 327.

138 *Ibid.*, p. 380.

139 *Ibid.*, p. 416.

140 *Record*, vol. 23, p. 376.

141 *Ibid.*, p. 423.

142 *Ibid.*, p. 451.

143 *Ibid.*, p. 459.

144 *Ibid.*, p. 484.

145 *Record*, vol. 24, p. 25.

146 He was a native of Paisley who had taken degrees (MA, LLD) at the Universities of Glasgow and Edinburgh, and had been licensed by the Presbytery of Dumbarton in May 1822.

147 Extended to three weeks' holiday in 1830.

148 *Record*, vol. 24, p. 79.

149 *Ibid.*, p. 244. *Selections from the Voluntary Exercises* of the senior boys were printed in 1827 and 1828 by the governors as a sign of their satisfaction with the standards Boyd was achieving. The exercises 'afforded proofs of proficiency in literature and maturity of mind most creditable to the pupils themselves, and to their teacher, Dr Boyd' (Steven (1845): *op. cit.*, p. 201). The relatives of the boys concerned presented Boyd with a gold watch 'for his zealous exertions in carrying into effect a salutary reformation in the internal government of the Institution, and in the moral and intellectual improvement of the Boys'. (*Ibid.*)

150 The silver medals had a profile of the founder, encircled with a quotation from the Roman poet, Lucan: 'Urbi pater est, urbique maritus' (He is to the City a Father, and to the City a husband). Both silver and gold medals are still distributed annually.

151 On medical advice gym was restricted to an hour a day in 1835 and calisthenic exercises

were introduced.

152 Succeeding George Irvine.

153 William Steven (1849): *op. cit.*, p. 229.

154 *Record*, vol. 25 (July 1828–March 1832), pp. 143–4.

155 The boys had already noticed a change in his behaviour, particularly outbursts in class (Birrell's Diary, pp. 20–1). The governors appreciated the problem for the first time when Holme unsuccessfully tried to persuade them to give a prize to his protégé ahead of those more deserving (*op. cit.*, pp. 42–3).

156 *Record*, vol. 28, p. 5.

157 *Ibid.*, pp. 40–1.

158 *Ibid.*, pp. 55–6. This, despite the success of Irvine and Boyd, who were seen as exceptions.

159 *Ibid.*, p. 57.

160 Holme died after a five days' illness on 16 September 1838, leaving a destitute blind mother of 85. The governors paid over the full 100 guineas to her.

161 Revd Dr J. Lee (1836): *op. cit.* had already set out what was at stake. 'During a very long period the benefits arising from this Institution have not been at all commensurate with the munificent means provided for the purposes of Education' (pp. 53–4). Here was the opportunity to change this. The governors had allowed evil to 'generally overbalance the good' (p. 3) and it was necessary to make a break from former practices which encouraged abuse and irregularity.

162 On 28 August 1837, with Holme still in office, the governors voted 18 to 9 to cut the house-governor's salary from £180 to £150 per annum.

163 *Record*, vol. 28, pp. 483–7.

164 His application in itself showed the increased status and rewards for the house-governor for it was the lack of these which had driven him away some years earlier.

165 1749–1835.

166 The salaries of these officers had been fixed on 10 September 1753, while the allowances for medicine and attendance had been agreed on 8 February 1725.

167 As early as 6 December 1742 the governors had agreed to introduce a lighter and more wholesome diet, including baked puddings of flour and rice on medical advice.

168 *Purgative Medicine* (written in March 1805), 5th edn (Edinburgh 1815), Appendix, pp. 57–62, 199–201.

169 Hamilton had inherited a system of regular medical visits which had been introduced in October 1737.

170 Wood was President of the Royal College of Surgeons between 1820–2 and 1828–30.

171 *Record*, vol. 25, p. 234.

172 *Record*, vol. 27, p. 138.

173 Hamilton had employed 'purgative medicines fully' (1815): *op. cit.*, Appendix, p. 59.

174 *Record*, vol. 25, p. 521 (16 December 1831): during the cholera epidemic in 1832 in Edinburgh 1,065 died and only 821 recovered, while in nearby Leith 267 died and only 164 recovered. (H.P. Tait: 'Two notable epidemics in Edinburgh and Leith' in *The Book of the Old Edinburgh Club*, XXXII (1966), p. 31.) Heriot's and Watson's were in 'seclusion' but the High School was closed.

175 Dr William Wood: article in *Edinburgh Medical and Surgical Journal*, vol. 43 (xliii) (1835), p. 35.

176 According to James Birrell the boys were unusually affected by the death of James Davidson because they had been teasing him before he took ill. The seventh section attended his burial at the Chapel of Ease in Buccleuch Street (Diary, pp. 13–4).

177 180 boys and 27 adults.

178 The Merchant Maiden, situated near Heriot's, had experienced 21 cases among its 104 inmates (93 girls) but no deaths; the Trades' Maiden in the Old Town had 7 cases among 53 (47 girls) and also no deaths; John Watson's had 22 cases among 132 (76 boys and 50 girls) and 1 death; George Watson's had 16 cases among 80 boys and 1 death; the Orphans' Hospital of 40 boys and 40 girls had 23 cases and no deaths. Dr William Wood: article in *Edinburgh Medical and Surgical Journal*, vol. 47 (xlvii) (1839), pp. 97–141.

179 *Record*, vol. 28, p. 228 (8 February 1838).

180 Gymnastic exercises were dropped and never restored (Birrell's Diary, p. 40).

181 *Record*, vol. 18, p. 267. This, at a time when the High School was advancing its classical teaching under the headships of Alexander Adam (1768–1809), James Pillans (1810–20) and A.R. Carson (1820–45) (M.L. Clarke: *Classical Education in Britain, 1500–1900* (Cambridge 1959), pp. 146–7). It was this excellence which ensured that house-bursars attended the rector's class at the High School for a year before going on to university. The arrangement, which was unpopular with Herioters, was ended in September 1856 (Bedford (1859): *op. cit.*, p. 175).

182 *Record*, vol. 19, p. 17.

183 Dr W. Steven (1845): *op. cit.*, p. 193.

184 Alex. Dallas Bache: *Report on Education in Europe (to the Trustees of Girard College for Orphans)* (Philadelphia 1839), p. 21.

185 *Ibid.*

186 Arnold had changed the status of modern languages at Rugby in 1830 (Michael McCrum: *Thomas Arnold. Head Master: A Reassessment* (Oxford 1989), pp. 61–2).

187 Although matresses had replaced chaff beds in June 1742.

188 Heriot's was not unusual in its unconcern over opportunities for homosexual temptations (J.R. de S. Honey: *Tom Brown's Universe* (London 1977), p. 168; Michael McCrum (1989): *op. cit.*, p. 79).

189 As an 'Auld Callant' he had been apprenticed to Hamden Pridie, a hat-maker, and in time had his own shop on the North Bridge. In 1793 he was elected Deacon of his Incorporation and was repeatedly elected Convener of Trades.

190 *Record*, vol. 22 (March 1819–February 1822), p. 185.

191 *Record*, vol. 23, p. 90.

192 It was a cenotaph of white marble with an inscription composed by the Revd Dr Brunton which stresses 'the intelligence, and kindliness, and heartful zeal, with which, during nine years, he managed the affairs of the Hospital as its treasurer'. Originally, it was placed at the west end of the chapel but was soon moved to the vestibule area outside the council room, where it still remains. Drawings in National Monuments Records of Scotland: EDD/iii/38 and EDD/iii/39.

193 This system appears not to have worked well, probably due to the small numbers involved, and the committees were joined together on 2 December 1841: Finance and Property; House and Apprentices; Education and New Schools; Law; and General Visiting Committee (5 in total).

194 It read: 'I hereby promise faithfully and diligently to perform the duties of my office as a Governor of George Heriot's Hospital so as to carry into effect the intentions of the Founder.' *Record*, vol. 27, p. 116. Before this, on 12 October 1778, Deacon William Miller, a Quaker, had affirmed instead of taking the oath (Dr W. Steven (1845): *op. cit.*, p. 165) and the oath itself had been unsuccessfully challenged on 13 October 1788 by the Revd Dr John Erskine (*Ibid.*, p. 174).

195 Steven (1845): *op. cit.*, pp. 216–7.

196 With the 1833 Burgh Reform Act the Deacons of the Incorporated Trades lost their place on the town council and becoming a burgess lost significance. It was not long before the town council and a number of the trades gave up compelling burgess-ship. In 1837 the town council reduced considerably the entry fee for burgess-ship to increase the number of entrants, and hence the revenue. When in 1846 the exclusive privileges of trading in burghs in Scotland were abolished it seemed that the main reason for becoming a burgess was to benefit from hospitals, especially Heriot's Hospital.

197 *Record*, vol. 23, p. 316.

198 *Record*, vol. 29, p. 286.

199 *Ibid.*, p. 290.

200 *Ibid.*, p. 292.

201 *Record*, vol. 30, p. 485.

202 Bedford (1859): *op. cit.*, pp. 157–60; *Record*, vol. 32 (February 1846–October 1847), pp. 39–45.

203 *Record*, vol. 17, p. 451. Both paintings are still to be found in the council room.

204 *Ibid.*, p. 70.

205 The plaque to Gilchrist and Arbuthnot now hangs in the lobby area beside the council room.

206 Robert Southey: *Journal of a Tour of Scotland in 1819* (Edinburgh 1972), pp. 10–12.

207 *Record*, vol. 25, p. 267.

208 On 2 November 1838 Blair's legacy was confirmed at £359 15s. 2d., which gave an annual bursary of £14 8s. for the divinity student.

209 The last major legacy was gifted by Dr James Abercrombie of Cape Town in 1864. He gave £500 'as a slight acknowledgment of my great obligations to that Seminary of Education' (*Record*, vol. 39 (December 1862–February 1865), p. 245).

210 *Record*, vol. 20, p. 391.

211 John Griscom: *A Year in Europe comprising a Journal of Observation in England, Scotland, Ireland, Germany, Switzerland, the north of Italy and Holland in 1818 and 1819*: 2 vols. (New York 1823), vol. II, pp. 367–8.

212 Alex. Dallas Bache (1839): *op. cit.*, pp. 13–32.

213 *Ibid.*, p. 17.

214 *Ibid.*, p. 18.

215 *Ibid.*, p. 19.

216 *Ibid.*, p. 30.

217 *Ibid.*, p. 21.

218 *Ibid.*, p 14.

219 *Report of an Educational Tour* (London 1846).

220 Duncan McLaren, on 16 December 1872, in his Address to the Literary Institute.

221 Ibid., pp. 46–59, 209–13.

222 *Guide Pittoresque du Voyageur en Ecosse* (Paris 1838).

223 The public increasingly flocked to visit an institution they were seemingly proud of. Numbers visiting increased from 575 in 1824 to 11,746 in 1844.

224 Surprisingly there was no questioning of the 1813 decision of the governors to support the Regent Bridge Scheme (carried out in 1818) perhaps because it was accepted by the Revd Dr John Inglis as chairman of the finance and property committee. Heriot's contributed £13,000, the Town £8,000 and Trinity Hospital £4,000. The Municipal Corporation Commissioners commented on the 'striking example of malversation' of Trinity House funds (General Report (London 1835), p. 38) given that the Hospital did not benefit from the transaction. On 19 March 1878 the First Division of the Court of Session ordered £4,000 to be restored to Trinity Hospital by the town council. (See Colston (1896): *op. cit.*, pp. 183–5, who believed that both Trinity and Heriot Hospitals did gain from transactions.) Another reason for lack of controversy may have been the collapse of building trades after 1822 which ended plans of the Heriot governors and Town for a great new surburb to the north-east of Edinburgh and halted expansion of the City for nearly half a century.

CHAPTER EIGHT

1 Steven himself gives the post this title in his *History* (*op. cit.*, 1845), p. 220.

2 Steven was born in Peebles on 22 November 1796 and attended the High School from October 1808. He entered College in 1814 and studied theology and qualified as a preacher in 1822. He became assistant to the Revd Dr Anderson, minister of the Scottish Church in Rotterdam in 1826. He was unanimously chosen as Anderson's successor in March 1829. He published a *History of the Scottish Church* (Rotterdam 1833). Given his small income, he applied for the house-governorship in 1839. By then he had gained an AM degree in 1822 and a DD from Leyden University in 1838. Once he had given up his post and returned to the ministry in 1843 he found the time to complete his *History of the Hospital* in 1845, and four years later he published the *History of the High School*.

3 Dining room, drawing room, business room, three bedrooms with fireplaces, dressing room, kitchen, servants' room, bathroom, two water closets. There were two other rooms on the upper floor which Steven used as well (these were taken back for other uses in 1854) and he had a private garden. Steven was married to Margaret Gibson, daughter of an eminent Rotterdam merchant, and they had five children (two sons and three daughters).

4 *Record,* vol. 19, p. 32.

5 Oswald became involved extensively in railway speculation which affected his attendance at the Hospital. On 21 May 1845 he was dismissed. (*Record,* vol. 34 (April 1850–January 1853) pp. 400, 417–19.)

6 *Ibid.,* p. 41.

7 Panton was given three weeks' leave of absence in February 1841 to have an operation to help cure his lameness. As a follower of Thomas Chalmers he also left the established Church of Scotland in 1843 at the Disruption. The governors allowed him to miss church attendance occasionally on Sundays when he was not on duty.

8 *Record,* vol. 29, p. 259.

9 *Ibid.*, p. 258. In fact, it was dropped again relatively quickly.

10 *Ibid.*, p. 261.

11 *Ibid.*, p. 262.

12 Bache had been devastating in his critique of classical courses in the Hospital: *op. cit.*, p. 23.

13 *Record*, vol. 29, p. 263.

14 Steven's timetable was full and perhaps inhibited further curriculum development. The governors declined offers to add lectures in chemistry (in December 1846) and weekly classes in natural science (in November 1847) despite claims that elements of science had already been introduced into the High School and into the best schools on the Continent. The governors believed that 'the Boys have already enough to do' (*Record*, vol. 33, p. 36).

15 *Record*, vol. 29, p. 265.

16 James Birrell suggests that such boys were numerous in the Hospital. He remembered four from his time, and in particular mentioned Thomas Nimmo, who remained in the first section throughout his time at the Hospital.

17 The lengthy school year at Heriot's, and indeed in all Scottish schools, compares with thirty-seven weeks at Arnold's Rugby (McCrum (1989): *op. cit.*, p. 19). This reflected the emphasis in the former of a 'severely scholastic' education which contrasted, according to H.H. Almond, later headmaster of Loretto, with an emphasis on physical exercise and games south of the border (J.A. Mangan: *Athleticism in the Victorian and Edwardian Public School. The Emergence and Consolidation of an Educational Ideology* (Cambridge 1981), pp. 48-58).

18 During his ministry there the congregation numbered only between seventy and eighty (Colston (1896): *op. cit.*, p. 159).

19 *Record*, vol. 30, p. 551.

20 *Record*, vol. 31 (January 1844–January 1846), p. 4.

21 *Ibid.*, p. 457.

22 In the Census taken on 31 March 1851 Fairbairn was aged 46, his wife Elizabeth 39, and their children: Mary 20, William 18, Jemina 12, Martin 11, Georgina 9, Ellen 7, Laurence 4 and Edward 1. *Edinburgh 1851 Census vol. II. The Old Town,* compiled by N.R. and S. Carmichael (Edinburgh 1994), pp. 408–411.

23 Watson's 80; John Watson's 120; Merchant Maiden 96; Trades Maiden 48; Orphan 90; Cauvians 20; Fettes for a number of particular groups; Donaldson's, plans for 200.

24 *Record*, vol. 31, p. 358.

25 *Ibid.*, p. 359.

26 *Ibid.*, p. 362.

27 *Ibid.*, p. 363.

28 *Ibid.*, p. 374–6.

29 Robert Lee DD: *A Sermon* (Edinburgh 1846), p. 5.

30 *Ibid.*, p. 6.

31 *Ibid.*, pp. 6–7. Perhaps an exceptional year, for some 28 remained in 1852 (Report to education committee, 6 December 1852).

32 *Record*, vol. 32, pp. 189, 195. Lee (1804–68) had become minister of Old Greyfriars in 1843 and was to be an important innovator in the Church of Scotland.

33 (Davidson), *The Herioter No Monk, by an 'Auld Callant'* (Edinburgh 1846).

34 *Ibid.*, p. 8.

35 *Ibid.*, p.16.

36 *Record*, vol. 32, p. 263.

37 *Ibid.*, p.268.

38 *Ibid.*, p. 278. On 7 January 1847 fifteen boys were taken back, and another four on 28 January.

39 *Ibid.*, pp. 319–57.

40 Eventually only five boys remained expelled, and they all had poor discipline records already.

41 *Ibid.*, p. 326.

42 This was to last only a year. Fairbairn complained that he had had to put back the formal examination to April and this materially affected the progress of the boys. The governors returned to August and February: *Record,* vol. 33, p. 55.

43 *Record,* vol. 32, p. 354.

44 *Ibid.*, p. 357.

45 *Ibid.*, p. 401.

46 Bedford (1859): *op. cit.*, p. 166.

47 Tuesday, 24 November 1846, p. 4.

48 30 December 1846.

49 *Record,* vol. 33, pp. 114–128.

50 *Ibid.*, p. 145.

51 *Ibid.*, p. 273.

52 *Ibid.*, p. 210.

53 *Ibid.*, pp. 273–4.

54 *Ibid.*, p. 135. These were indeed adopted on 20 October 1851. Boys between 7 and 9 years were to be admitted provided their parents were of good character and had given the boy educational and moral training. Newly elected boys were to be kept apart from the others for six months. Stress was placed on rewards for good conduct such as time-off with friends, and tea with the house-governor, while all punishments were to be logged and corporal punishment restricted.

55 *Record,* vol. 30, pp. 516–7.

56 *Record,* vol. 33, pp. 354–5. It was still common in the 1850s for two or more boys to share a bed in public schools (McCrum (1989): *op. cit.*, p. 79).

57 *Record,* vol. 34, p. 315.

58 Letter from R. Fraser, 17 South St Andrew Street; *Record,* vol. 31, p. 351.

59 *Record,* vol. 33, p. 384.

60 *Record,* vol. 35, p. 17.

61 *Record,* vol. 34, p. 504. The number had been at 180 since April 1821 (*Record,* vol. 22, p. 374).

62 Shortly after, on 6 January 1853, the governors decided to set up Broughton Street School for 230 juvenile and 120 infant scholars.

63 *Record,* vol. 35, pp. 18–19.

64 *Ibid.*, pp. 59–64.

65 *Ibid.*, p. 168.

66 Space allocated in Hospital was 518 cubic feet for each boy in single wards, and 316 cubic feet where double. They argued that 472 and 279 cubic feet respectively were needed.

67 Eight deaths in this time of which only 2 were from impure air: *Record,* vol. 35, p. 232.

68 Trades Maiden Hospital: 44 girls, two to a bed in two wards (till age 17). 354 cubic feet for each girl. George Watson's Hospital: 86 boys, 6 deaths in the previous 8 years (1 in 114), 325 cubic feet. Orphan Hospital: 92 children, 3 deaths in previous 4 years (1 in 120), 518 cubic feet.

69 *Record,* vol. 35, p. 241.

70 *Ibid.,* p. 228.

71 *Ibid.,* p. 242: both Watson's and the Orphan's had only double beds.

72 Ward 7 offered 308 cubic feet and Ward 8 had 325 cubic feet, which compared unfavourably with the space in other wards, as well as the space in the Trades Maiden and Orphan Hospitals, for each child.

73 Orphan Hospital reduced mortality from 1 in 66 to 1 in 120 by adding 50 per cent more space.

74 Edinburgh Academy (over 3 years) 1 in 875; High School (over 6 years) 1 in 816; Manchester Blue Coat (over 26 years) 1 in 520; Warrington Blue Coat (over 12 years) 0 deaths. *Record,* vol. 35, pp. 256–263.

75 From 1 in 17 to 1 in 66.

76 Not 1 in 114 over the last four years but over the last eight years which included the scarlet fever epidemic; in the last three years no deaths: now 1 in 215. *Record,* vol. 35, pp. 278–286.

77 *Ibid.,* pp. 286-92.

78 *Ibid.,* pp. 395-407.

79 *Ibid.,* p. 397.

80 *Ibid.,* pp. 471–2.

81 *Ibid.,* p. 490.

82 Steven's health deteriorated in the latter half of 1856 and he died at home in Great King Street on 2 April 1857. Obituaries praised his important work in the Hospital which he had elevated until 'it ranked among the best-conducted establishments of the City' (*Edinburgh Evening Courant* Supplement, Saturday 4 April, 1857). Although his funeral was private, some thirty former pupils were allowed to join the family service. This was a measure of the esteem in which he was held by Auld Callants who saw him as a friend and counsellor.

83 *Record,* vol. 34, p. 59.

84 English master.

85 *Record,* vol. 35, p. 360.

86 *Ibid.*

87 In 1844.

88 Having resigned on 3 August 1854, Fairbairn petitioned for his son, Laurence, to be admitted to the Hospital, but the Governors refused the request on 16 October, because he could be maintained by his father. However, the following month Fairbairn died and the governors donated 100 guineas to his family. On 16 April 1855 Laurence L.S. Fairbairn was elected to the foundation.

89 *Record,* vol. 35, p. 390.

90 *Record,* vol. 30, p. 270.

91 *Record,* vol. 33, p. 465.

92 *Ibid.,* pp. 465-6.

93 E. Gaskell: 'Three Letters by Sir James Young Simpson', *British Medical Journal,* May 1970, 2, pp. 414-16.

94 W. M. Parker: 'The Amiable Dane: Hans Andersen's Visit to Scotland', *Evening Dispatch,* 8 September 1943.

95 Alison Prince: *Hans Christian Andersen. The Fan Dancer* (London 1998), p. 258, stresses how much Andersen enjoyed his visit to the Hospital.

96 1815–74.

97 *Beskrivelse over Skotlands Almueskolevaesen* (Christiana 1854), pp. 116–21.

98 *Ibid.,* p. 118.

99 *Ibid.,* p. 121.

100 Nissen appreciated that the Scottish system of dealing with truancy by permanent exclusion would not be appropriate in Norway, where compulsory education already existed.

101 Lawrence Stenhouse: 'Hartvig Nissen's impressions of the Scottish educational system in the mid-nineteenth century', in *British Journal of Educational Studies,* vol. 9, no. 2 (May 1961), p. 144.

102 The outdoor schools had already been inspected. On 7 January 1841 Steven had been authorised to invite the Government Inspector of Schools, Gibson, to visit, and Lord Provost McLaren had on 5 February 1852 invited the HMI for Schools (Dr Woodford) to inspect them.

103 10, 11 and 24 July 1854.

104 Special Report on Heriot's Hospital and Heriot's Hospital Schools, in *Minutes of Committee of Council on Education,* 1855–6, p. 557.

105 Although it did also comment on the numbers of Auld Callants rising to respectable positions, and how prosperous Herioters throughout the world met up to celebrate June Day. *Ibid.,* p. 558.

CHAPTER NINE

1 *Record,* vol. 35, p. 467. Bedford was born on 24 April 1824 in Leeds, where his father had a senior position in the Revenue Department, and educated at the Grammar School there. He became a teacher at Woodhouse Grove (in West Riding, for sons of Wesleyan Methodist ministers) and was promoted to second master (John Roach: *A History of Secondary Education in England, 1800–1870* (London 1986) p. 177). He took over a headship in Leeds in 1847 where he increased pupil numbers and remodelled the curriculum on more practical lines. At the same time he studied and successfully completed his BA from Trinity College, Dublin (1850), his MA and PhD from Heidelberg (1851), and his LLB from Dublin (1853). He later took a LLD from Dublin (1858) and DCL from Oxford (1859). He was a successful public lecturer, a keen poet and a writer of educational publications which included Greek, Latin, French and English grammar books.

2 Dr J.A. Voigt: *Mittheilungen über das Unterrichswesen Englands und Schottlands* (Halle 1857). Voigt, principal master in the Royal Gymnasium of Halle, spent an entire week in the Hospital, beginning on Monday, 3 October 1855. His *Record* devoted twenty-two pages to a detailed description of the Hospital (pp. 189–211). He praised the new house-

governor and the ethos which he believed Bedford was working hard to create (pp. 202–3). He saw Bedford teaching and approved of the way he treated boys, which he compared to the way a father would treat his grown sons. Voigt characterised Bedford as a young, fresh man of demanding character.

3 *Record*, vol. 35, pp. 493–5.

4 *Record*, vol. 36 (February 1855–May 1857), p. 24.

5 *Ibid.*, p. 24.

6 As Voigt stressed, the boys did not come from homes where good English was spoken, and this meant that it was a challenge for the staff to get rid of their broad accents and Scotticisms. Bedford believed the junior classes were 'entirely ignorant of the rudiments of English Grammar', and immediately introduced an elementary textbook to familiarise them with the essentials of etymology.

7 *Record*, vol. 36, p. 53.

8 RCAHMS: EDD/III/63 contains examples of desk designs.

9 Ibid., EDD/III/59. Deemed 'comfortable' by Voigt, *op. cit.*, p. 192. The suite of four apartments, opposite the dining hall, had been suggested before Bedford's arrival but he ensured that two rooms were devoted to reading and two to conversation and quiet games (Bedford (1859), *op. cit.*, p. 171).

10 He did so immediately, for Voigt was impresed by the ten monitors, with blue bands around their arms, who patrolled the dining room and the playground, keeping them tidy.

11 They also came and went with great frequency. Some went voluntarily to better paid employment, but a significant number were dismissed for failing in their duties.

12 This power was given to headmasters in England by the Endowed Schools Act of 1869, and under the English Public Schools Act (1868) every headmaster had the right to appoint his assistant masters.

13 Voigt praised the relatively small class sizes which he believed helped to explain the progress made by the boys, for standards (he thought) were higher, especially in Latin, than he expected.

14 Dougall resigned.

15 *Record*, vol. 36, p. 88.

16 Cut tragically short by Scholfield's untimely death from pulmonary disease in April 1860.

17 See Voigt (1857), *op. cit.*

18 Unsurprisingly he does not appear to have been completely successful with Dalgleish, who, after over 30 years' service as writing master, resigned on 11 February 1857. He joined with his son in opening an educational institution in Edinburgh. *Record*, vol. 36, p. 498. He was to be followed by William Marr, who had been mathematical master for twenty years, who in turn resigned on 9 January 1858 to take a similar post in the Glasgow Academy. *Record*, vol. 37, pp. 103–6. Interestingly, while there 'Billy' Marr 'did not find controlling the boys easy, perhaps because he was too kind-hearted and too easily imposed on'. Iain MacLeod: *The Glasgow Academy. 150 Years* (Glasgow 1997), p. 13.

19 Bedford (1859), *op. cit.*, p. 170.

20 Given the governors' stance only 18 months before, it is remarkable that Bedford was able to go ahead with this without interference.

21 *Record*, vol. 37, pp. 249–51.

22 Voigt had also been impressed with Robertson, who 'took a genuine interest in his empire'. Voigt: *op. cit.*, p. 195.

23 *Ibid.*, p. 194.

24 *Ibid.*, pp. 195–6. Voigt quoted £1,561. 8s. 3d. being spent on the food for the boys in 1854. The porridge 'tasted not bad at all' (*Ibid.*, p. 193), while at lunch each boy received a 'heartily-filled plate of excellent soup', bread and best beef or ham, so much 'that I would have been completely full'.

25 *Record*, vol. 37, pp. 371–5.

26 Again overturning a previous decision.

27 *Record*, vol. 40, pp. 144–5 (13 November 1865).

28 In March 1866.

29 *Record*, vol. 37, p. 434. Similar to Steven in 1839.

30 In August 1863 applications for August had to be in by 1 June to allow adequate investigation of the background of parents. *Record*, vol. 39, p. 148.

31 *Record*, vol. 38 (July 1860–November 1862), p. 250.

32 *Ibid.*, pp. 257–9, 277.

33 According to Mackie relations cooled in January 1838 when McLaren was offered financial recompense for his newspaper contributions. As McLaren had no desire to work for money he ended the close assocation (Mackie (1888): *op. cit.*, I. pp. 154–6). The breach was aggravated as McLaren's radicalism developed, and his support of the *Scottish Press* in 1847 as the dissenting organ was a warning to *The Scotsman* (the Whig paper) on its editorial policy. The appointment of Russel as editor in 1845 widened the breach further.

34 In the edition of 30 January 1856 and its subsequent issue *The Scotsman* condemned McLaren's vindictiveness and caprice, referring to him as venomous and reviving the nickname 'Snake the Draper'. In the trial the newspaper failed to sustain its claim that there was a difference between McLaren's public and private character.

35 *Record*, vol. 34, p. 484.

36 Since 26 March 1733 boys leaving the Hospital 'in all time coming' were to be provided with new bibles: they were embossed with the letters G.H. on the outer cover (*Record*, vol. 6, p. 329).

37 Sir James D. Marwick: *A Retrospect* (Glasgow 1905), p. 52.

38 *Record*, vol. 36, pp. 508–513.

39 *Ibid.*, pp. 516–9.

40 Hope had worked ceaselessly for temperance since 1839. He had tried unsuccessfully to have temperance books included in those presented as prizes in the High School. He had protested at whisky-toddy being given as a treat at Christmas and New Year to boys of John Watson's. He founded the British League of Juvenile Abstainers in 1847 (Revd David Jamie: *John Hope, Philanthropist and Reformer* (Edinburgh 1900), p. 202).

41 *Record*, vol. 37, p. 167.

42 *Ibid.*, p. 184.

43 A number of governors, including Hope and Lee, had tried to abolish this habit without success.

44 *Dialogue between a Son and his Governor and the Views of Cousin John on the Motion to be Considered by the governors of George Heriot's Hospital on Thursday 2nd June, 1859* (Edinburgh 1859). A governor wished his son to be trained as a gentleman, and thus

envisaged drink in moderation. Drinking once a year was not enough to establish an appetite for drink. Cousin John, however, held that it established a principle. The Hospital was a training for future life, and it was necessary to emphasise sobriety. If toasts became acceptable, then boys would conform to drinking habits. The bias of training must be toward sobriety, and it was evil to bring back drink once it had been abolished.

45 *Weekly Journal of the Scottish Temperance League*, 11 June 1859, p. 490.

46 *Ibid.*

47 *Ibid.*

48 To commemorate the event as an incident in the temperance movement, Hope had an engraving made and the print appeared in *The Band of Hope Review* in June 1861. The copy of the periodical containing the picture was circulated in Edinburgh among members of the British League, only 1,000 copies being produced (Jamie (1900): *op. cit.*, pp. 357–362).

49 *Record*, vol. 37, p. 528 & vol. 38, p. 27.

50 *Record*, vol. 37, p. 6.

51 Black died in February 1858. In his period as superintendent of works (1836–58) he had, as an architect, contributed much to the building style and design of the Heriot outdoor schools. He ensured that they followed a common, distinctive character, unmistakably modern versions of the original 'wark'. Further, when the owners of Bonnington House commissioned a significant rebuilding Black, as architect, copied the syle of the Hospital. On his death, the governors decided that they would have little need for another architect, and changed the job specification to more of a clerk of works. John Chesser, of Dalmeny Park, was appointed to this post in April 1858 at a reduced salary of £120 per annum. In fact, he impressed quickly, and an increased workload helped to raise his salary to £400 per annum in February 1873. *Record*, vol. 43 (October 1871–December 1873), p. 277.

52 *Ibid.*, pp. 294–5.

53 *Record*, vol. 39, pp. 65–6.

54 *Record*, vol. 43, p. 460 (23 January 1874).

55 *Record*, vol. 44 (January 1874–June 1876), p. 12 (*The Scotsman*, 9 January 1874).

56 Bache (1839), *op. cit.*, pp. 14–15 had referred to this. He noted how the boys were allowed to use the courtyard at certain times for play. This had necessitated wire-gratings over the lower-storey windows to avoid damage.

57 *Record*, vol. 40, p. 379.

58 *Record*, vol. 39, p. 164.

59 *Record*, vol. 41 (March 1867–December 1868), p. 304.

60 *Ibid.*, p. 349.

61 *Record*, vol. 40, pp. 265–6.

62 *Record*, vol. 42 (January 1869–August 1871), p. 437.

63 *Record*, vol. 41, p. 186.

64 Voigt (1857): *op. cit.*, p. 203.

65 He had been appointed in 1837. On his death in 1860 T.M. Hunter of Cecilia Hall was appointed. Although he had worked as singing teacher in the juvenile outdoor schools, Bedford was soon complaining about his poor discipline.

66 *Record*, vol. 41, p. 337.

67 *Ibid.*, p. 326. A. Jamieson Baillie: *Walter Crighton or Reminiscences of George Heriot's Hospital* (Edinburgh, nd), 2nd edn, p. 136. However, in December 1878 Levick was accused of 'insubordination' by Bedford (*Scotsman*, 6 December 1878, 31 December 1878 and 1 January 1879): it proved a storm in a teacup but was symptomatic of poor relations between the officious Levick and the sensitive Bedford. Levick finally resigned in May 1884 with a pension of £30 per annum.

68 The annual excursion began in 1848, with governors going from 1849. In 1853 when St Andrews was visited, the principals and professors of the universities, the civic dignitaries and clergy, joined the Heriot's party in recognition of the special significance of the town in Heriot's Will.

69 This had been instituted following a suggestion from Councillor Clark. The first had been held on Friday 20 June 1856. In fact it was resurrected in February 1868 when a successful soirée was held. By 1871 this annual soirée was seen as part of the 'usual' arrangements organised by the governors.

70 *Record*, vol. 36, p. 553.

71 *Ibid.*

72 Bedford (1872): *op. cit.*, p. 178.

73 *Ibid.*

74 Bedford (1859): *op. cit.*, p. 349.

75 The plan of arrangement for the outdoor children on the Green in 1855 is exhibited in RCAHMS: EDD/111/141.

76 The Heriot March – 'While Gratitude Fills Every Breast' – words written by James Smith, was used on this occasion, also for the first time. The music was imported by Dr Bedford from Heidelberg where the tune was sung as a drinking song by students.

77 Bedford (1859): *op. cit.*, pp. 352–3.

78 This game was much the same to the Herioter as the wall-game was to the Eton boy, and it was said that Herioters had a unique style which was handed down from generation to generation.

79 The origins of the Heriot games are unclear. There must have been regular contact with Gairdner's eighteenth-century yarn-building works in the Vennel. The apprentices of Gairdner's made their own 'West Port Ball' and played a form of football against the Grassmarket apprentices of Gilmore's 'roperie'. Hospital boys watched and often participated in these games (Charles J. Smith: *Historic South Edinburgh*, vol. 1 (Edinburgh 1978), p. 180). Sir Walter Scott mentions the peculiar skill of Herioters for making balls, rackets and clacking-boards ((1826): *op. cit.*, p. 102).

80 The House Committee estimated £50 extra expenditure.

81 *Record*, vol. 37, pp. 369–71.

82 *Record*, vol. 39, p. 8. All boys were given a comprehensive medical on admission. In the 1850s 44% had recovered from scarlet fever, 65% from whooping cough and 76% from measles; in the 1860s the respective figures were 40%, 69% and 84%; in the 1870s 34%, 61% and 77%; in the 1880s 29%, 64% and 80%. *Register of Diseases got over by resident Hospital boys* (October 1853–1885).

83 The quality of the water supply had not been a problem since 1785, when a portion of Hospital ground on the west side of the gardens had been given over to the town council for the erection of a water cistern to supply south Edinburgh. No feu was charged for the ground and the Hospital was supplied with water free from then on

(*Record*, vol. 13, p. 7; vol. 14, p. 106).

84 Bedford (1872): *op. cit.*, p. 204.

85 *Record*, vol. 45 (July 1876–March 1879), p. 113.

86 *Ibid.*, pp. 125–6.

87 A copy of the edition was given to each governor on 6 October 1859, as it contained 'much useful information in regard to the Hospital'. *Record*, vol. 37, p. 411.

88 *Record*, vol. 38, p. 302.

89 George Hastings (ed.): *Transactions of the National Association for the Promotion of Social Sciences – Edinburgh Meeting, 1863* (London 1864), esp. pp. 340–348.

90 Clement B. Gunn: *op. cit.*, p. 189.

91 George Hastings (1864): *op. cit.*, p. 341.

92 *Ibid.*, p. 342.

93 Despite these advantages Arnold of Rugby at times doubted the value of a boarding education, chiefly because of the removal of parental influence (McCrum (1989): *op. cit.*, p. 117).

94 Although Bedford did not emphasise the point, particularly in his lecture, it is nonetheless clear that he opposed free education.

95 *Record*, vol. 41, p. 67.

96 *Ibid.*, p. 185.

97 Introduced in 1852 and deemed a success.

98 Bedford opposed the wearing of uniform which he believed had 'a cramping influence on a boy, and prevents him from cultivating and exhibiting tastes which are exponents of character'.

99 By 1868 he had become Lord-Justice General. The opinion dated from October 1847.

100 *Record*, vol. 32, pp. 529ff. See Chapter 8.

101 Chapter 12.

102 Governors forbidden to elect 'any burgess children, if their parents be well and sufficiently able to maintain them, since the intention of the Founder is only to relieve the poor'.

103 One annually in 504.

104 *Record*, vol. 41, p. 445.

105 Bedford: (1872): *op. cit.*, p. 193.

106 *Ibid.*, p. 194.

107 Suggesting that Bedford's emphasis on English was proving successful, but possibly at the expense of other areas.

108 Daniel R. Fearnon: *Report on Secondary Education in Scotland* (1868), Appendix X (i), Educational Hospitals, p. 182.

109 *Ibid.*, pp. 179–82.

110 The governors were totally out of sympathy with his idea of introducing fees, which was not contemplated for the Hospital. However, the outdoor schools were a different matter. Councillor Tawse raised this issue in May 1868, and again on 6 July 1871.

111 Laurie's Report of July 1868 is an important source of material on hospitals. It was critical of the poor educational results of hospitals which Laurie blamed on lack of home or family influence and the regimental routine which weakened the faculties of children. It also attacked the high costs which he put down to the highly paid officials. In the case of Watson's, which had introduced day boys by Act of Parliament as early as 1852, he

recommended the relaxation of the severity of the regime, a shortening of the long day, the abandonment of uniform and the encouragement for boys to be sent home where possible to their families at weekends.

112 It had previously, in November 1865 and January 1866, hoped that HMI Gordon would examine the classes, but he had been precluded from undertaking this by Privy Council regulations.

113 *Record*, vol. 41, p. 343.

114 Bedford (1872): *op. cit.*, p. 196.

115 Only parts of this Code were introduced into Scotland before 1873.

116 John Gordon: *Report to the Education Committee of George Heriot's Hospital* (Edinburgh, August 1869), especially pp. 2–3.

117 *Record*, vol. 42, p. 140. Gordon reported 'A more conscientious, active, zealous, and vigilant manager of any such Institution I have not known' (*Report*, 1869, p. 8).

118 *Record*, vol. 40, p. 284.

119 *Record*, vol. 42, p. 97.

120 The plaque to Bedford in the school was the work of Pilkington Jackson and was unveiled by Lady Bedford (*The Scotsman*, 20 November 1928). Bedford's son, Sir Charles H. Bedford, left the residue of his estate (£9,800) to Heriot's on his death in 1931.

121 Of 15 February 1858.

122 *Record*, vol. 37, p. 121.

123 *Scotsman*, 17 September 1880.

124 In C.B. Gunn: *op. cit.*, p. 200.

125 *Scotsman*, 17 September 1880.

126 *Ibid.*, p. 186.

127 *Ibid.*, p. 187.

128 *Record*, vol. 46 (April 1879–October 1881), p. 253.

129 C.B. Gunn: *op. cit.*, p. 184.

130 The High School had received half this number of applicants for the recent vacant rectorship.

131 *Record*, vol. 46, pp. 321, 344.

132 Introduced experimentally by Bedford in 1876.

133 Bedford had Chesser prepare a plan as early as 1875.

134 *Record*, vol. 46, p. 231.

135 *Argyll Commission 3rd Report*, vol. 1, p. 87.

136 *Record*, vol. 48 (February 1884–December 1885), pp. 90, 93, 118.

CHAPTER TEN

1 Hutchesons were invited to this meeting.

2 *Record*, vol. 42, p. 86.

3 Since 1868 an MP for one of two newly created university seats – Edinburgh and St Andrews (until 1885), with Moncrieff, MP for Glasgow and Aberdeen.

4 For the genesis of the English Act, see P.H.J.H. Gosden: *The Development of Educational Administration in England and Wales* (Oxford 1966), pp. 62–82; Colin Shrosbee: *Public Schools and Private Education. The Clarendon Commission, 1861–64, and*

the *Public Schools Acts* (Manchester 1988), pp. 1–5, and F.E. Balls: 'The origins of the Endowed Schools Act and its operation in England from 1869 to 1895', Cambridge University thesis, 1964.

5 Interestingly, Gladstone thought the Act too radical for the Commons and it was 'almost smuggled through Parliament unawares'. Brian Simon: *The State and Educational Change. Essays in the History of Education and Pedagogy* (London 1994), p. 60.

6 For Liberals a central belief was that no free education should be given except as a reward of merit. The poor should benefit from endowments only by their own achievement and not by favour. Unfortunately this did not take any account of local circumstances nor help the poor who would be disadvantaged by the cost of education and competition from other classes (John Roach: *Secondary Education in England, 1870–1902. Public activity and private enterprise* (London 1991), especially pp. 3–13).

7 Vice-president of the committee of Council on Education.

8 At this stage McLaren was supportive, but 'his eyes were soon opened' (Mackie (1888): *op. cit.*, ii, p. 185).

9 *Hansard*, 3rd series, vol. 197, 17 June 1869, cols 153–6.

10 The Endowed Institutions Act of 1869 allowed governors at a special meeting held with a month's notice to agree a petition by simple majority to send to the Home Secretary outlining plans for better government and administration. The Home Secretary could remit the petition to a Sheriff to take evidence. The resulting provisional order would become law if unchallenged within forty days.

11 Thomas J. Boyd: *Educational Hospital Reform. The Scheme of the Edinburgh Merchant Company* (Edinburgh 1871). Paper read before The British Association, Edinburgh 1871. Perhaps the real reason was that the Merchant Company reform was based on a consensus of aim: their endowments had been for the merchant burgess class, and this 'middle class' was the beneficiary of their reformed schools.

12 Watson's for boys, with a new girls' equivalent; Stewart's for boys and a Young Ladies' Institution (formerly the Merchant Maiden) – all four to be middle-class schools taking pupils at eight years old and providing a full liberal education. The fifth – Gillespie's – was aimed at the upper working class and took some time to become a higher-grade school, being handed over to the Edinburgh School Board in 1908. R.D. Anderson: *Education and Opportunity in Victorian Scotland. Schools and Universities* (Oxford 1983), p. 179.

13 *Record*, vol. 42, p. 117. The Endowed Schools Act of 1869 in England provided for the appointment of commissioners with wide powers to apply the intentions of the Act to individual schools. They had the power to alter statutes and governing bodies. Brian Simon (1994): *op. cit.*, p. 60.

14 Voiced in *Sit Jus: On the scholastic position and results of the Merchant Company's schools* (Edinburgh, 1870). Three hundred Edinburgh teachers presented a memorial to the Home Secretary holding that the Merchant Company's provisional order had come into operation before their 'force and scope had been ascertained, in accordance with a provision of the Act, by preliminary inquiry before the Sheriff' and that of the 4,000 scholars who had joined the Company's schools, over 3,000 had done so because of low fees and restricted bursaries and scholarships, and had left other schools, decimating their numbers. The teachers were being deprived of their living without compensation.

They argued the case for no more provisional orders till public inquiries had defined their scope and results. Bedford (1872), pp. 202–3.

15 *Record*, vol. 42, pp. 234–5.

16 *Ibid.*, p. 238.

17 *Address on Heriot's Hospital* (Edinburgh 1872).

18 *Record*, vol. 42, p. 268.

19 *Ibid.*, p. 386.

20 *Ibid.*

21 *Ibid.*, pp. 389–90.

22 Unusually the strong feelings of the governors were reflected in the decision to have the memorial and representation stitched up in the *Record*, vol. 42, p. 391ff.

23 *Ibid.*, p. 422.

24 *Ibid.*

25 *Record*, vol. 43, pp. 9–10.

26 *Ibid.*, pp. 65–6.

27 Sir Alexander Grant (ed.): *Recess Studies* (Edinburgh 1870), pp. 117–150. He quoted an eminent authority who held that he 'never knew an hospital boy who had either gratitude or self-dependence' (126). The 'dullness of Heriot boys is proverbial' (127).

28 Address of McLaren on the history of Heriot's Hospital to the Literary Institute on 16 December 1872: *The Scotsman*, 17 December 1872.

29 *Ibid.*, p. 248.

30 Half the Scottish endowments were in Edinburgh.

31 Chaired by Sir Thomas (Edward) Colebrooke; the other members of the Commission were Lord Rosebery, Sir William Stirling-Maxwell, Messrs C.S. Parker, J. Ramsay MP, H.H. Lancaster and Professor A. Craig Sellar. According to one commentator the Whigs were 'the smallest and least influential of the three political parties in Scotland' after the 1868 election (Mackie (1888), vol. II, p. 186).

32 *The Scotsman*, 7 December 1872.

33 Gordon stressed high pass rates (98 per cent in reading, writing and arithmetic), good accommodation and resources, able staff, care of governors and public interest (pp. 1–24).

34 'The Hospital System' (1864): Address before the Social Science Congress.

35 Colebrooke Commission, 1st Report (1873): Oral evidence, p. 60.

36 Giving a maximum of 500 boys directly under the headmaster.

37 Sixpence per month, which Bedford held only 10 per cent of parents would be unable to pay.

38 *Ibid.*, pp. 49–70.

39 Dr Hodgson, Professor of Political Economy at Edinburgh University, previously Principal of Liverpool Institute which incorporated three day schools and evening schools and involved 1,500 pupils (1839–47) and in Manchester (1847–51) who believed Heriot's Hospital 'greatly improved' (1st Report p. 71), while George Ogilvie, ex-head of Stewart's Hospital, told of having to send boys out to acquire knowledge of ordinary life and ease the teaching situation (*Ibid.*, pp. 103–4).

40 Currie had been a pupil in the Hospital between 1835 and 1842 and a master between 1847 and 1852.

41 *Ibid.*, pp. 122–33. Currie also suggested using the porters as 'a sort of police' (*Ibid.*, p. 123).

42 *Ibid.*, p. 138.

43 This was contradicted by the evidence of T.J. Boyd, Master of the Merchant Company, who stressed the financial extravagance of the hospital system: few benefits were achieved at much expense.

44 *Ibid.*, p. 149.

45 1864–7: Report on Primary Education. It made only passing reference to hospitals.

46 Donaldson had himself experienced this in October 1868, when the senior hospital boys of Watson's had been sent to the High School when the educational side of Watson's Hospital had closed. Some High School masters and parents protested at the decline in social tone as boys tainted with the stigma of charity entered, and some boys were withdrawn. R.D. Anderson (1983): *op. cit.*, 178.

47 *Colebrooke* (1873): p. 189.

48 *Ibid.*, p. 217.

49 Anderson (1983): *op. cit.*, p. 182.

50 £1 to £2 per annum, including books.

51 £5 to £7 per annum, excluding books.

52 Lewis became treasurer of the Heriot Trust in 1873.

53 *Colebrooke* (1873): pp. 259–79.

54 *Colebrooke* (1873): *Ibid.*, p. 295.

55 Playfair, as early as 1853, had published an account of the chief technical schools on the Continent.

56 *Colebrooke* (1873): p. 292.

57 Maths and science.

58 Book-keeping, languages and geography.

59 *Ibid.*, p. 305.

60 *Ibid.*, pp. 307–22.

61 *Ibid.*, pp. 322–27, especially p. 323.

62 On 11 February the Trades Council had unanimously passed a motion protesting against the funds of the Hospital being diverted to uses different from those in Heriot's Will, and sent this to Colebrooke (MacDougall (1968): p. 350). At a special meeting two weeks later the Trades Council unanimously opposed Hospital funds being diverted to middle-class (secondary) education and a memorial was sent to the commissioners (*Ibid.*, pp. 352–3).

63 *Second Report* (1874), col. 6807.

64 *Ibid.*, col. 6913.

65 *Ibid.*, col. 6917.

66 *Ibid.*, col. 6919.

67 *Colebrooke*, 3rd Report (1875), Table p. 33, cf. John Watson's £40 4s.; Trades' Maiden £35 15s.

68 *Ibid.*, p. 69.

69 62 out of 180.

70 Actually the governors had already addressed this in their provisional order of 1870.

71 Colebrooke pointed out the mention by Heriot in his disposition of the University of Edinburgh and his reference to the provost, baillies and council as 'representing the whole body and university of the said burgh of Edinburgh'.

72 Although the provisional order of 1870 had supported the introduction of fees, there was

still much division in the governing body on the issue.

73 Colebrooke opposed this on principle but took no evidence on the matter.

74 Every boy leaving the Hospital received an outfit, £10 a year for 5 years and £5 at the end of that time. The Statutes stipulated paying a fee, not to apprentices, but to their masters, as in the seventeenth century apprentices lived and were maintained by them. This had been changed in 1811.

75 The governors in 1870 desired to introduce an entrance examination to raise the standard and tone. With 1,210 places open to general competition, and as the scholarships only involved education, it can be assumed that few would come from beyond Edinburgh, and only a limited number would be taken up at all.

76 Evidence 3416–3420.

77 Here were similarities with the 1870 governors' proposals. The latter contemplated the erection of 'middle schools' for modern and technical education, reserving the Hospital for classical and scientific instruction.

78 This would ensure the Hospital would not compete with existing establishments, and significantly would be a return to the express terms of Balcanquall's Statutes.

79 Colebrooke thus accepted the provisional order's return to the original 'fatherless' qualification of Heriot. The provisional order of 1870 had suggested 40–60 foundationers, but proposed they be orphans and 'the sons of persons who have carried on business in Edinburgh on their own account'. Strict burgess-ship as a qualification was retained by the order which gave preference to burgesses, but only for foundationers, but the commissioners rejected it, arguing that, except to gain admission to hospitals, it had been a dead letter for forty years.

80 Both Colebrooke and the provisional order accepted resident foundationers being boarded out (and supervised) in families approved by the governors. The commissioners added that those who could not be boarded out advantageously should be accommodated in a 'hospital house'.

81 In his Disposition Heriot specifically mentioned Edinburgh 33 times and Scotland 9 times; in his will Edinburgh 9 times and Scotland 5 times; in his Codicil Edinburgh is mentioned 4 times, while Scotland is not mentioned. However, in the Disposition Heriot had proposed that failing Edinburgh his charity might be bestowed 'in any other boundis and partis of the said realme of Scotland'.

82 *Record*, vol. 44, p. 240.

83 Liberal MP for Elgin Burghs.

84 Liberal MP for Falkirk Burghs.

85 Liberal MP for Forfarshire.

86 Liberal MP for Lanarkshire North.

87 *Hansard*, 3rd series, vol. 225, col. 1279 (9 July 1875).

88 *Ibid.*, col. 1282.

89 Referring to Horace Mann's assessment.

90 Liberal MP for Kirkcudbrightshire.

91 Liberal MP for Dumfries Burghs.

92 A surprising defender of hospitals, given his background. Educated at Edinburgh Academy, St Andrews and Edinburgh Universities and University College, Oxford. An advocate. *According to Dod's Parliamentary Companion* (London 1874), he was a 'moderate but decided Liberal'.

93 *Hansard,* 3rd series, vol. 225, col. 1295.

94 *Hansard, Ibid.,* col. 1302.

95 The report implied that a governing body of 54 was unwieldy, but it made no specific recommendation for Heriot's. Its general recommendation was that in institutions which provided maintenance as well education the number of governors should range from 7 to 15 and should have additional representatives from universities. However, Parliament increased in 1872 the Board of Hutcheson's Hospital from 60 to 72 (including 6 more ministers). One wonders if Sir James Watson, Lord Provost of Glasgow in 1872, found difficulty in signing the report!

96 *Hansard, Ibid.,* col. 1300.

97 *The Scotsman* had supported the 1836 Act and congratulated the City on an advance 'which is likely to do more to elevate the character of our poor population than all the churches built since John Knox' (30 April 1836). R.M.W. Cowan: *The Newspaper in Scotland. A Study of its First Expansion, 1815–1860* (Glasgow 1946), p. 262. It had, however, broken away from Duncan McLaren in 1838. The relationship had worsened in the 1850s. See Chapter 9. It had suggested on 15 May 1875 that the provisional order of 1870 had to 'a remarkable extent' anticipated the 1875 report. Of its nine recommendations six were 'wholly forecast' and significant parts of others anticipated.

98 During 1875, a year of unusual Heriot excitement, there were 13 board meetings and the average attendance was 29. The worst attendees were the clergy, averaging 2 or 3 per meeting: 3 of the clergy, Messrs Fraser, Scott and Dr Wallace, did not attend at all.

99 Eton, 7; Westminster, 9; Harrow and Rugby, 12; Edinburgh and Glasgow School Boards, 15.

100 It met, on 17 July 1875, in Buchanan's Hotel, High Street, every Thursday at 7.30 p.m.

101 Blacksmith.

102 'Heriot Trust Defence Appeal', Edinburgh, August 1875, p. 4.

103 Conveniently ignoring the fees which the Board would receive from the schools and an increased parliamentary grant.

104 A letter in *The Scotsman* (18 October 1875) from H. Calderwood, Chairman of School Board, explained that absentee figure was usually nearer 25 per cent. The board had to force some parents who did not wish to send their children to school, which Heriot governors could not do. The Heriot governors could dismiss children which the board could not. (In actuality only twelve formal dismissals annually, although a much larger number of parents would withdraw their children.)

105 German, English, French, Italian, Latin, history, geography, natural history, physics, chemistry, commercial arithmetic, geometry, singing, gymnastics and drawing.

106 The exception was Italian.

107 Greek, algebra, botany, book-keeping, writing and fencing.

108 The meeting brought home the problem of the fee issue. Burn even suggested that, as the governors only supported the introduction of fees to extend education further among the poor, it was likely that they would change their mind on the matter if Heriot funds were to be used for a different purpose. One of the main reasons for opposing fees was the argument put forward by the Revd Dr Begg at the meeting, viz., you would be asking people to pay for what is already their own.

109 Including one 'schoolmaster' who claimed that the 'very cream' of children, and not the poor, were chosen.

110 *The Scotsman*, 3 December 1875, for example.

111 Confirmed by the choice of the name 'Hospital' and by modelling on Christ's Hospital.

112 As the first industrial school was given parliamentary recognition in 1866, this was a disingenuous argument. Indeed, in Heriot's time industrial arts were taught during apprenticeship and he made express provision in his Will to cover that.

113 *Record*, vol. 44, pp. 348–50.

114 It consisted of Sir William Stirling-Maxwell, Sir James Ferguson, Lord Balfour of Burleigh, Sir George Douglas, Colonel Mure, Messrs Dalrymple, Ramsay, Sellar and Meiklejohn.

115 *Record*, vol. 44, pp. 447–8.

116 *Record*, vol. 45, p. 19.

117 *Ibid.*, p. 33. This was taken further on 7 December 1876, when it was agreed that in February 1877 six boys below 10 and six boys below 12 would be elected (*Ibid.*, pp. 88–90). In the event 12 were elected from 57 who sat the examination (*Ibid.*, pp. 135–6).

118 *Ibid.*, p. 74.

119 *Record*, vol. 45, p. 76.

120 The author of 'Secondary Education in Scotland', *Blackwood's Magazine*, CXIX, March 1876, pp. 283–96, compared the 2nd report (p. 98) figure of £16,550 per annum available for secondary education in Scotland with the £174,532 per annum available for educational endowment, with nearly half devoted to supporting hospitals (p. 292).

121 *The Scotsman*, 14 November 1876.

122 For a private Act of Parliament.

123 *Record*, vol. 45, pp. 79–83.

124 *Ibid.*, p. 306.

125 First Reading on 29 March 1878 in the House of Lords, *Hansard*, 3rd series, vol. 239, col. 192–200.

126 The *Courant* and *The Scotsman* editions of 14 May 1878.

127 23 May 1878.

128 *Record*, vol. 45, p. 385.

129 All twenty-five articles were published in full in *The Scotsman* on 31 January 1879. (They were later modified to 23.)

130 *Record*, vol. 45, pp. 460–9.

131 The traditional view had followed Adam Smith, who argued that free tuition would deprive teachers, parents and children of incentive. This remained the orthodoxy. 'Few people in 1870 paid even lip service to free education as an objective; there was both clearly articulated opposition to it and a general lack of interest in it as an issue' (Gillian Sutherland: *Policy-Making in Elementary Education 1870–95* (London 1973), p. 163). There was only a gradual shift in opinion from the late 1870s onward, and nationally free schools became an issue after 1885.

132 By April 1879 the Hospital had 120 resident foundationers, 60 non-resident and 33 day scholars.

133 Clause 5.

134 To be called 'George Heriot's Hospital Higher School'. Clause 10, with teaching in English, technical education, modern languages and classics.

135 Clause 12.

136 Clauses 20 and 21.

137 Such bursaries could be extended a further two years (i.e., 6 years in all).

138 In the original draft of the order (31 January 1879) clause 17 had made provision for £300 p.a. to be given over to the University of Edinburgh for bursaries. (Heriot had stipulated ten bursaries of £5 p.a. each: these were raised in 1818 to £20 p.a. each. Thus the order as it originally was was not overly generous.) However, on 17 March, Tawse argued that the new arrangements would result in more boys going to university, and there was no need to include further provision for Edinburgh, because governors already had the power to do so. It does seem that, having increased bursaries in 1818 to take account of increases in the value of money, the governors could do so again. More debatable was whether they could increase the number of bursaries from the ten stipulated in the Codicil of the Will. It does not seem good politics to have omitted this clause as it looked like animus, particularly as the governors also omitted the three £100 p.a. fellowships, tenable for three years, of the 1870 order.

139 *The Daily Review*, 15 March 1879.

140 Although another view was that these second thoughts were worse than their first (The *Courant*, 6 July 1880).

141 The Watt Institution and School of Arts had been founded in 1821 by Leonard Horner, Robert Bryson and James Milne 'for the purpose of providing for the better education of the mechanics in Edinburgh, in such branches of physical science as are of practical application in their several trades'. It had been sustained by voluntary subscriptions, had developed an experienced staff, and given the upsurge in interest in the mid-1870s in a general and technical education for the industrial classes, had seen its student numbers increase to 2,200. This increase strained accommodation (there was only room for 1,000), staffing and resources and problems were aggravated by the increasing unwilling-ness of people to subscribe to it now that they contributed to school-rates. There seemed no alternative to its directors but to appeal for help from the Heriot or Merchant Company governors. The former had taken up the challenge.

142 Seven out of twenty-one governors to be nominated by the Watt Institution.

143 The other commissioners were: Lord Balfour of Burleigh (Con.), John Ramsay MP (Lib.), Sir James Watson (ex-Lord Provost of Glasgow), Professor P.G. Tait (of Edinburgh University), Dr James Donaldson (Rector of the High School) and James A. Campbell. (Five of these gentlemen were supporters of the secondary school movement.) Its composition was seen by McLaren as a 'renewed declaration of war on the part of the Education Department at the bidding of the spoilers of the heritage of the poor'. Mackie (1888): *op. cit.*, II, p. 193.

144 He also admitted that attendance at meetings was higher when elections for posts were being held. *Moncrieff Commission*, 1st Report of 1879, published 1880. Evidence Qns. 188–9, 255–7 (pp. 22, 28).

145 In later cross-examination by Donaldson Tawse admitted that since the 1876 Burgess Act the burgess class now included a number who were not intended by George Heriot to be admitted. Moncrieff Evidence Qns. 262–5, p. 37.

146 Tawse did not know that in Glasgow, according to Watson, a secondary school for 200–300 had been set up for people not able to pay the usual fees, but only 9 enrolled! He also had to admit that although a schedule of circumstances was completed by all prospective parents for the outdoor schools, there were no follow-up inquiries to ensure they were correct. (A governor visited every applicant to the Hospital before entry.)

(*Ibid.*, Qn 282.)

147 Watson penetratingly asked why the fees of the Watt Institute were to be kept.

148 *Moncrieff Commission*, 1st Report (1880), Evidence Qn 288: 159 bursaries for 888 students in the Faculty of Arts.

149 Evidence 192.

150 Aberdeen University had 40 bursaries for 700 students. Evidence Qn 533.

151 Evidence Qn 641.

152 Evidence Qns 681–7 and 693–701.

153 Evidence Qns 922–1025.

154 The burgess numbers increased from 500 to 24,000 as a result of McLaren's Act.

155 Mackie (1888): *op.cit.*, II, p. 193.

156 Evidence Qns 1052–1094.

157 *Ibid.*, Qns 1104–1136.

158 *Ibid.*, Qns 1137–1172.

159 Evidence Qns 1173–1219.

160 Later corrected by Tawse to 87 fatherless children and increasing every year.

161 Evidence Qns 1220–1295.

162 He admitted that this had changed, and the Heriot schools had not advanced in the same proportion as board schools.

163 Cross-examined by Mr Campbell, Waddell believed that a very slight addition was being made to the assistant staff of the Heriot schools, and they were becoming better qualified.

164 In 1874, 673 were presented in the third standard; 414 in fourth; 203 in fifth; 103 in sixth; and 49 in seventh. The third standard required only five lines from a book brought by the Inspector to be written in dictation, slowly, a few words at a time, and an acquaintance with the basic rules of arithmetic. Contemporaries believed that pupils at this level could neither write with ease nor count with accuracy.

165 Evidence Qns 1296–1414.

166 Average of all 2,314 was 19s. 1d. per week, suggesting that those admitted could not afford to pay fees.

167 Of the 54 governors involved in accepting the 1870 order, only 16 remained in 1879, although Bailie Tawse was the prime mover of both.

168 7 Royal Exchange.

169 *Record*, vol. 46, pp. 137–8.

170 According to Tawse 'The Commissioners had been so diligent in looking for omissions that they had apparently never seen the clause in the order providing for sixteen bursaries'. The commissioners, in suggesting that the order did not intend to increase bursaries, were perhaps comparing it with the 1870 order.

171 Probably Stephen confused the 1870 order and the 1875 Colebrooke Report, for the HTDC was not formed until July 1875 after publication of the latter. Since then all candidates at election had supported the Heriot stance and the documents supplied by Stephen to the Commissioners referred to meetings in late 1875. On 20 February 1880 the HTDC added its weight to the debate by writing to the Home Secretary in an attempt to modify Stephen's damaging testimony.

172 Both ex-Lord Provosts. Michael Dyer: *Men of Property and Intelligence. The Scottish Electoral System prior to 1884* (Aberdeen 1996), pp. 147–8.

173 *Daily Review*, 10 June 1880.

174 *Record*, vol. 46, p. 214. One is surprised by the 'wonderful unanimity' of the governors, but perhaps Harcourt's agreement to the appointment of an executive and compulsory commission to do the work which the Permissive Commission later failed to do was a contributory factor. *The Scotsman*, 12 June 1880.

175 If sanctioned by the Home Secretary and laid for 40 days without an address being presented against it, the order became law.

176 London Correspondent of *Daily Review*, 17 June 1880.

177 *The Scotsman* (10 July 1880) held that the Home Secretary had been 'betrayed into approving in a moment of darkness'.

178 In evidence the governors held that there were no funds available for these.

179 The commissioners condemned the amalgamation of the schools' funding and Hospital funds (for the 1836 Act ensured that the schools would be financed with the surplus revenue).

180 Lord Advocate McLaren himself thought the governing body too large and wanted it to compromise on a delegate committee of twenty (speech of 22 January 1881).

181 Educational Endowments (Scotland) Bill, which was to be compulsory (imposed without consent) rather than permissive.

182 *Edinburgh Evening Courant*, 9 July 1880.

183 *Hansard*, 3rd series, vol. 254, cols. 2–20.

184 Richmond in proposing the 1878 Act had promised a more stringent measure in two years if reform was not forthcoming.

185 It was seen in some quarters as a measure 'which promises to work great good in Scotland' (*The Times*, 10 July 1880).

186 *Record*, vol. 46, p. 234.

187 *Record, Ibid.*

188 The number of deputations and their expense became matters of considerable comment in the press. The accounts for 1880 show £603 19s. spent on deputations that year alone, this following £818 16s. 1d. spent on deputations to try to overturn the 1878 bill (later held to be £409: *Daily Review*, 24 July 1882).

189 *Hansard*, 3rd series, vol. 254, cols. 615–629.

190 *Ibid.*, cols. 1321–1323.

191 According to the *Courant* (31 July 1880) the bill passed through the Lords with an 'indecent haste' which would have caused uproar if a Conservative government had been in charge. 'A crisis in the history of the siege of Heriot's Hospital' had been reached.

192 *Record*, vol. 46, p. 243.

193 By 13 July the Edinburgh United Liberal Association had opposed the measure (65–11) and the town council held a public meeting in the Music Hall on 4 August.

194 In the event only six went.

195 Mundella was becoming increasingly important as Harcourt tried to remove himself from the situation and leave matters to education ministers.

196 Fourteen for, 10 against and 1 abstained. McLaren, Peddie, Holms and Grant determined to continue their opposition.

197 *The Scotsman*, 29 October 1880.

198 *Hansard*, 3rd series, 257, cols. 807–8.

199 *Glasgow Herald*, 18 January 1881. A clever play on words, as the leading members of the

Hospital side had increasingly been termed 'the Heriot Ring' in the national press. Probably first used by *The Scotsman* on 12 July 1880.

200 According to Lord Hartington the failure of the 1880 bill was the result of McLaren's 'Parnellite prescription for preventing good business being done': *The Scotsman*, 17 August 1880.

201 J. B. Mackie (1888): *op. cit.*, II, pp. 224–6.

202 *Daily Review*, 19 May 1881.

203 Although *The Scotsman* of 30 May 1881 reported a split in the Heriot delegation down in London to lobby on the second reading of the bill, with some willing to accept one half of the governing body being popularly elected, with the clerical governors being kept. It was the decision of McLaren to support the government and the education department which broke the impasse.

204 *Daily Review*, 2 August 1881.

205 Harcourt announced in the Commons on 2 August 1881.

206 *Daily Review*, 19 August 1881.

207 *Ibid.*, 20 August 1881.

208 *Ibid.*, 20 August 1881.

209 *Record*, vol. 47 (November 1881–January 1884), pp. 84–5.

210 Despite assurances in the Commons on 2 March 1882 to Ramsay (*Hansard*, vol. 266, cols. 1927–8) and prompting of Buchanan on 3 April 1882 (*Ibid.*, vol. 268, col.544).

211 *Hansard*, vol. 268, cols. 1916–7.

212 The *Courant*, 2 May 1882.

213 *Ibid.*, p. 128.

214 *Ibid.*, pp. 130–4 (*Daily Review*, 19 May 1882).

215 Under Secretary of State for the Home Department.

216 *Ibid.*, p. 146.

217 *The Scotsman* of 29 May 1882 held, however, that it was 'perfectly well known that the deputation returned to town in a dismal and crest fallen state'.

218 *Daily Review*, 25 May 1882.

219 Detailed in *Daily Review*, 13 June 1882.

220 This was the first time in all the discussions that the governing body had 'split' (*Daily Review*, 15 July 1882).

221 Messrs Buchanan, Grant, Holms and Peddie (all Liberals) opposed the government, unhappy at the limited time being given on a Saturday for such an important measure (House of Commons, 13 July 1882).

222 *Hansard*, vol. 272, col. 632–673.

223 Colonel Alexander (Conservative), *Ibid.*, vol. 272, col. 643.

224 *Ibid.*, vol. 272, col. 1167.

225 *Ibid.*, vol. 272, cols. 1340–1479.

226 Cameron, Buchanan, Fraser-Mackintosh, Cowan, Peddie, Grant, Sir George Campbell, Henderson, Barclay (all Liberals) and 10 Irish and English radicals.

227 The last defence included Cameron, Buchanan, Mackintosh, Peddie and Grant.

228 James Cowan, senior Edinburgh MP, was criticised for deserting the cause. The *Daily Review* (24 July 1882) called for his resignation. *The Scotsman* crowed (25 July 1882): 'Heriot bubble has now been most effectively pricked, and has been reduced to its true dimension.'

229 Lord Balfour, Earl of Elgin, Lord Shand, John Ramsay MP, J.A. Campbell MP, Lord Provost Ure of Glasgow and Lord Provost Boyd of Edinburgh.

230 *Record*, vol. 47, p. 271.

231 *Ibid.*, p. 276.

232 The governors voted 36–4 (all four were ministers) not to change the governing body (*Ibid.*, p. 277).

233 *Ibid.*, p. 283.

234 The Third Scheme (1883).

235 *Record*, vol. 48, p. 105.

236 Who as a governor criticised the scheme.

237 *Balfour Commission*, 1st Report (1884), pp. 570–2.

238 *Ibid.*, pp. 799–809.

239 Seen by McLaren as 'the most gigantic scheme of legalised robbery' Mackie (1888), II, p. 209. He thought of appealing to the working classes, but with the Reform Act in trouble he judged they were tired of the fight.

240 *Record*, vol. 48, p. 108.

241 *Ibid.*, p. 109.

242 Headmaster Lowe reported 29 boys in senior class were being taught Greek (*Balfour Commission* (1884), para. 6538). The governors felt that this exclusion lowered the status of the school and prevented any connection between the Hospital and the University for classical education, so infringing the right to university bursaries for the foundationers.

243 *Record*, vol. 48, pp. 108–14.

244 *Ibid.*, p. 126.

245 *Balfour Commission*, 2nd Report (1885), Minutes of Evidence para. 5885.

246 *Ibid.*, 5908.

247 *Ibid.*, 5968.

248 *Ibid.*, 5978.

249 *Ibid.*, 6055, 6066, 6068.

250 *Ibid.*, 6084, 6089, 6090, 6094, 6098–6103.

251 *Ibid.*, 6143, 6147, 6151, 6152.

252 *Ibid.*, 6164, 6165, 6167–78.

253 *Ibid.*, 6202.

254 *Ibid.*, 6551.

255 *Ibid.*, 6557–63 (Bailie Anderson and Mr Giffen).

256 *Ibid.*, 6565–66 (Bailie Anderson).

257 Objections (February 1885): Educational Endowments (Scotland) Commission, No. 82, p. 3.

258 This referred to the development of the Heriot College: an institution catering for 'all and sundry from every part of the world', taking members of all classes and 'fitted up extravagantly' at the expense of the original foundation.

259 And saw as a 'vital mistake' the prohibition of admission of boys to the Hospital school under ten years of age.

260 In particular, the governors viewed 'with the greatest dissatisfaction the proposed exclusion of Greek' from the curriculum, which they claimed lowered the status of the school, as even in the common elementary public schools Greek should be taught.

261 They argued that there was sufficient demand, given the number of fatherless and

necessitous children in Edinburgh, and justified the schools 'on the score of economy and efficiency'.

262 *Record*, vol. 48, p. 199.

263 Messrs Buchanan and Waddy.

264 *Record*, vol. 48, p. 289.

265 House of Commons Debates, 23 July 1885, col. 1746.

266 *Ibid.*, col. 1748.

267 *Ibid.*, col. 1749.

268 *Ibid.*, col. 1750.

269 Macdonald, MP for Stafford, still held this view.

270 House of Commons Debates, 23 July 1885, col. 1754.

271 *Ibid.*, col. 1756.

272 *Record*, vol. 48, p. 291.

273 *Ibid.*, p. 292.

274 *Ibid.*, p. 311, and *Record of George Heriot's Trust*, vol. 1 (October 1885–October 1887), pp. 1–7.

275 *Record of Hospital*, vol. 48, pp. 320–7.

CHAPTER ELEVEN

1 Consisting of eleven town councillors, three from the Edinburgh School Board, three City ministers, with one non-Presbyterian, two from the University of Edinburgh, and one representative from the Royal Society of Edinburgh, and another from the Edinburgh Chamber of Commerce.

2 John Tawse as clerk and law agent until his death in October 1892; David Lewis as treasurer until his resignation owing to ill-health in January 1905 and John Chesser as superintendent of works, who continued in post until his seventieth birthday in March 1889 (but was retained as a consultant until his death in early 1892).

3 Trust Minutes, vol. 1, pp. 93–5. Lowe was a native of Leslie, Fife, born on 11 January 1843, and trained at the Established Church Training College and at the University of Edinburgh, then spending two years in Wales before beginning his long connection with Heriot's in 1868. His five successful years on the Hospital staff, as firstly resident English master and then French master, ensured early promotion to the post of Rector of Bathgate Academy, which he left after seven years to replace Bedford.

4 Ogilvie was appointed Principal of Heriot-Watt College by the same governors on 14 May 1886: Trust Minutes, vol. 1, pp. 162–4.

5 Trust Minutes, vol. 1, p. 34.

6 Abbeyhill was sold for £2,690 and was renamed Regent Road Public school. St Bernard's school (Stockbridge) was sold for £2,500 and Davie Street for £2,200 (Trust Minutes, vol. 1, pp. 231, 309); Cowgate Port and High School Yards were sold in November 1888 (Trust records, vol. 2, November 1887–July 1889, p. 294) and the disposal of Broughton Street, Rose Street, Borthwick Close and Assembly Close followed soon after (*Ibid.*, p. 334). The others were deemed inappropriate for schooling for the future and were 'sold off at successively lower prices to various non-educational purchasers'. Walter Stephen: *Fabric and Function. A Century of School Building in Edinburgh, 1872–1972* (Edinburgh

1996), p. 22.

7 *Ibid.*, pp. 330–331.

8 Compared with, e.g., the celebration of June 1878 when nearly 8,000 spectators attended: *The Courant*, 4 June 1878.

9 Walter Crighton, in A. Jamieson Baillie (1898): *op. cit.*, pp. 275–82, stresses the splitting of the pulpit into two parts as a matter of much concern to former pupils.

10 *Evening Dispatch*, 25 April 1913. As one commentator suggested in 1914, June Day before 1886 was an occasion of revelry, whereas after 1886 it was a day of ceremony.

11 The governors clearly found this arrangement distasteful, given the traditional pre-eminence of Heriot's over Watson's and this was a factor in the priority given to building a large hall.

12 Trust Minutes, vol. 1, p. 229.

13 £5,184 3s. 6d., vol. 1, p. 364.

14 During the alterations the foundation stone of 1837 and the glass bottle deposited at that time were uncovered (see above, p. 116). It was redeposited with another bottle with the corresponding 1887 details (vol. 1, p. 389).

15 This enabled the old gymnasium on the east-side ground floor of the old building to be converted into a cloakroom, and the writing room above to be enlarged. Trust Minutes, vol. 2 (November 1887–July 1889), p. 121.

16 Vol. 2, pp. 86–7.

17 See above, pp. 195–6.

18 *The Herioter*, July 1922, vol. XVI, No 2.

19 D.M. Clark: *Heriot Rugby: 50 Years* (Edinburgh 1948), p. 5, suggests a less colourful story.

20 Trust Minutes, vol. 2, pp. 2, 40.

21 Ibid., p. 233.

22 Both were formed before the 'Parent Club' in 1891.

23 Hector MacQueen: *Heriot's FP Cricket Centenary* (Edinburgh 1989), pp. 7–8.

24 D.M. Clark talks of rugby being a 'tender plant' with soccer being much more popular.

25 D.L. Turnbull in the 1922 *Herioter*.

26 D.M. Clark (1948): *op.cit.*, p. 6.

27 Successor to Chesser.

28 Trust Minutes, vol. 5 (October 1893–June 1896), pp. 159–61.

29 Ibid., p 279.

30 The fashion of building the school baths ended mainly due to their great expense. After the 1890s no state school in Edinburgh had baths installed until 1959 (Walter M. Stephen (1996), *op. cit.*).

31 Trust Minutes, vol. 7 (March 1899–May 1901), p 145.

32 His successor was Edinburgh merchant, John Anderson, who took office in April of that year. Trust Minutes, vol. 7, p. 361.

33 The building cost £2,634 19s. od. to build. Trust Minutes, vol. 8 (June 1901–September 1903), p. 110.

34 D.M. Clark, *op.cit.*, p. 14.

35 Trust Minutes, vol. 4 (October 1891– July 1893), pp. 353, 362.

36 Ibid., pp. 397, 416.

37 Ibid., pp. 440–1.

38 Trust Minutes, vol. 5, p. 350.

39 Trust Minutes, vol. 9 (October 1903–December 1905), p. 425.

40 Trust Minutes, vol. 10 (January 1906–December 1907), p. 294.

41 *The Herioter*, vol. 1, No. 2, June 1907. This building no longer exists, as it was demolished in the 1930s to make way for the Prep School and the more modern art department.

42 Trust Minutes, vol. 2, pp. 169–174, 177–178.

43 On the grounds that a governor could not profit from his position. Trust Minutes, vol. 4, pp. 151, 173.

44 Trust Minutes, vol. 4, pp. 105–10.

45 Ibid., pp. 128–30.

46 Ibid., pp. 225–6, 261–2, 270–1, 287.

47 Trust Minutes, vol. 6 (July 1896–February 1899), p. 64.

48 Ibid., pp. 260–1.

49 Trust Minutes, vol. 7.

50 Trust Minutes, vol. 8.

51 Trust Minutes, vol. 4, p. 219. The Heriot governors were relieved of Art responsibilities by the SED in 1908, but otherwise they continued to run the College by means of a sub-committee of the trust until 1927.

52 Trust Minutes, vol. 3 (September 1889–July 1891), pp. 285–307.

53 Trust Minutes, vol. 3, pp. 270–1. 'Cette ecole présente une grande originalité et peut être considérée comme un type d'institution d'enseignement technique. Aujourd'hui George Heriot's school est une des très remarquables écoles techniques du royaume.'

54 Trust Minutes, vol. 9 (October 1903–December 1905), pp. 19–20.

55 Ibid., p 204.

56 He was head of mathematics at the school between 1908 and 1928.

57 *The Herioter*, vol. 2, No. 1, April 1908, p. 21. On his death in January 1908 the school and former pupils set up the memorial which now stands in King Edward Parish Church, Aberdeenshire.

58 *The Herioter*, vol. 1, No. 2, June 1907.

59 SED report of Dr Dunn in October 1904 (Trust Minutes, vol. 9, p 119).

60 The Revd Dr McGregor, convener of the education committee of Heriot's, 9 December 1907. Trust Minutes (10 January 1906–December 1907), pp. 463–6.

61 William Taylor: 'Reminiscences, 1887–91'. *The Herioter*, vol. II, III, No. 2, July 1949.

62 Trust Minutes, vol. 1, p. 21, and vol. 10, p. 219.

63 Trust Minutes, vol. 9, p. 82.

64 Trust Minutes, vol. 5, p. 358.

65 However, there was no religious element at the school other than a minister's prayer at the end of term. With nowhere for an assembly, the chapel was used for the singing classes of James Moonie.

66 Trust Minutes, vol. 9, p. 168.

67 Report of Dr Alfred Daniell, vol. 6, p. 47.

68 Regulation of Day School Code.

69 Trust Minutes, vol. 11 (June 1908–June 1909), pp. 75–6. Melville had joined the school in 1903, and after five years at Alloa Academy returned to spend the rest of his teaching career at Heriot's. He was appointed principal teacher of chemistry in 1921 and retired in 1937. A.M. Crawford in turn became principal teacher of mathematics and retired in 1949.

70 Trust Minutes, ibid., p. 3.

71 'Culled from the Classes', *The Herioter*, vol. 2, No. 3, December 1908.

72 George Kitchen: 'Reminiscences, 1894–9'. *The Herioter*, vol. 14, No. 1, October 1950, p. 31.

73 Trust Minutes, vol. 11, pp. 315–6.

74 He was born of humble origins on 30 April 1861, and educated in a country school in West Linton, travelling nearly five miles every morning and evening to and from school. It was on such journeys that he developed his lifelong interest in natural history. At the University of Edinburgh he had won medals in the diverse subjects of natural philosophy and English and a scholarship for being the most distinguished student in a laboratory. Clark shared responsibilities with John T. Morrison on the departure of A.Y. Fraser to Allan Glen's in July 1889 (Trust Minutes, vol. 2, pp. 456–7). When Morrison resigned to become Professor of Mathematics and Natural Philosophy at Stellenbosch, Cape Colony in January 1892, Clark was promoted to Principal Mathematics and Science Master.

75 IA, IB, IC, ID, IE, IF, IIA, IIB, IIC, IID, IIE, IIF, IIIA, IIIB, IIIC, IIID, IVA, IVB, IVC, V, VI.

76 *The Herioter*, vol. 2, No. 3, December 1908, p. 134.

77 Named after the geography of the area, with the exception of Raeburn, named after Sir Henry Raeburn.

78 Even the decline in FP rugby was halted with the sensational last-minute victory against undefeated Hawick on New Year's Day 1909 in front of the largest crowd Heriot's had ever witnessed.

79 8 to 3 in April 1909 (vol. 11, p. 413).

80 Given the shortage of money, this was not formally opened until March 1915.

81 Trust Minutes, vol. 11, p. 175.

82 Trust Minutes, ibid., p. 96.

83 Ibid., p. 232.

84 Ibid., pp. 259–63, 266, 286.

85 Trust Minutes, vol. 13 (1910 Minutes), p. 100.

86 The governors visited Watson's; Royal Grammar School, Newcastle; St Paul's School, London; Emmanuel School, Wandsworth; Dulwich College; St Dunstan's College, Catford; University College School, Frognal; and East Ham Technical College.

87 *The Heriotor*, vol. 5, No. 2, July 1911.

88 *The Herioter*, vol. 6, No. 2, July 1912.

89 For comparison the SED annual grant to Heriot's for 1933 was only £2,126.

90 The governors voted 9–4 to do this on 10 February 1913 (Trust Minutes, vol. 13, p. 56). It was begun again in 1921.

91 In the event the sermon on June Day 1913 was given to the whole school at St Giles' Cathedral but, faced with opposition to this, the compromise of New Greyfriars was used for the whole school in June 1914. However, on the casting vote of the Lord Provost, the governors reverted to tradition, and the sermon was given to foundationers only in the Chapel in 1915.

92 As early as October 1914 Robert H. Pender was a prisoner of war, and by December Captain James A. Todd had been wounded in action and invalided home.

93 By December 1915, seventeen staff were in military service.

94 Serbia had been the flash-point for war in 1914, and Russia was her protector.

95 Sadly killed in action on 12 November 1917, aged 22.

96 Their ages were under-14, four; under-15, four; under-16, nine; under-17, four; and under-18, four.

97 Now the staff room. The Founder's Day ceremony of 1919 was also significant because it was the first such service taken by a former pupil, the Revd Thomas Porteous, and the School Captain of that year, Dan Drysdale, was Captain of School, Captain of 1st rugby XV and Captain Major of the OTC and was to become a famous Scottish rugby fullback.

98 Of the 27 staff who served, two were killed.

99 The record of names owes everything to Dr Samuel Walker of the school staff, who prepared the memorial volume published at this time.

100 The war memorial for World War II was designed by J.S. Ryrie and unveiled and dedicated on 20 April 1951. It consisted of the addition of a rear wall with five panels containing the 222 names of the fallen. *The Herioter*, vol. 14, No. 2, May 1951.

101 With 24 away at the War, and Pender of the French department still in prison, this number included 22 temporary staff, of whom 21 were women.

102 £500 compared with £450.

103 Mary Cooper wrote her autobiography, *Zest for Life*, in 1979. Following her graduation at Edinburgh she was appointed French teacher after an interview with 'a tall man, one of the great Heriot Headmasters' (p. 45) (J.B. Clark). She spent time in Madrid and took over Spanish teaching in 1924: she took Honours in Spanish in 1927 and her PhD in 1936. She taught part-time at Edinburgh University between 1943 and 1962.

104 Heriot's won the 'championship' again in 1922–23 (again undefeated), 1927–8 and 1928–9, and were runners-up in 1921–2, 1924–5, 1926–7, 1937–8 and 1938–9 (D.M. Clark: *op. cit.*, p. 48).

105 At the end of 1923–4 Dan Drysdale, R.M. Kinnear and K.G.P. Hendrie went to South Africa with the British team and all played in the Tests. In 1924–5 Dan Drysdale became the first Herioter to captain a Scottish team. D.S. Kerr was capped in 1926–7 and A.H. Brown the following season.

106 His alternative of younger teams using the lawns in front of the School was unattractive to the governors.

107 Cricket, cross-country and the Heriot Club had one representative each.

108 *The Herioter*, December 1926, vol. 20, No. 3, p. 59; D.M. Clark: *op. cit.*, pp. 14–16. With turf from Dalmahoy and more land from allotments this statement on the 26 acres became increasingly true.

109 He died on 19 July 1947.

CHAPTER TWELVE

1 William Gentle was born on 19 January 1877 and gained six medals, two second places and numerous class prizes, as well as four scholarships at Edinburgh University. He graduated with BSc Honours in mathematics and natural philosophy in April 1903. While in post he helped design the general outline and equipment of the new science laboratories and lecture rooms, opened in 1912. He joined HM Forces during World

War I but was wounded in June 1917 at Messines and invalided home. He dedicated his life to his old school, and married Jessie Ainslie of the junior school staff in 1924.

2 He had a science degree and treated geography as a science subject – hence its inclusion in the new science building in 1912.

3 The ground size had doubled and shortly Goldenacre became the venue for international lacrosse matches.

4 G.A. Carse, vice-chairman of governors, 1942 Minutes, p. 97.

5 The others were 9 from the town council, 3 from Edinburgh Education Authority, 2 from the Church of Scotland, 1 from the United Free Church and 1 from Edinburgh University.

6 Good examples of this are Dr George A. Carse (Dux in School from 1898), Dr F.S. Fiddes (Captain of School in 1926) and D.M. Clark.

7 Bedford remained a firm friend of the school. He died suddenly in July 1931 when in Edinburgh for the Founder's Day celebrations. Following the death of Lady Bedford in August 1933, the residue of her estate (£9,800) was given over for further scholarships to the school in July 1937.

8 Only seven of these were to leave to join another school.

9 Trust Minutes, 1931, p. 109. Inglis had first-class honours in Classics.

10 When he retired from Heriot's in 1966 Bill (Algie) Inglis had helped improve the status of languages. Although he remained a bachelor, his 'relationship' with Kate Smyth of German was the talk of generations of Herioters. On her death she left her estate to Algie.

11 1928 Minutes, p. 160.

12 April 1937, *The Herioter*, 31, No. 1, p. 3. James Melville achieved six First Medals at the University of Edinburgh, where he gained a first-class honours degree in French and German. He remained a brilliant linguist of Teutonic, Latin and Slav tongues.

13 Trust Minutes, 1937, p. 13.

14 9 April 1937, p. 4.

15 Trust Minutes, 1933, p. 113.

16 David Morris became senior official at the Trust between 1962 and 1979. Another great servant of the Trust was appointed in May 1936, Norman Smillie, who had attended the School between 1927 and 1934 and was administrative assistant in the Trust between 1935 and 1982.

17 After successful school and university careers William Graham became an Edinburgh councillor in 1913 and Labour MP for Central Leith in 1918. In the First Labour Government in 1924 he was made Financial Secretary to the Treasury, and between 1929 and 1931 was a member of the Cabinet as President of the Board of Trade. He died prematurely on 8 January 1932 at the age of 44.

18 *The Herioter*, June 1936, vol. 30, No. 2.

19 He was at school between 1904 and 1908, and was also elected President of the Royal College of Veterinary Surgeons.

20 Dott's achievements are too numerous to mention. See Rush, Christopher, and Shaw, John F: *With Sharp Compassion. Norman Dott. Freeman Surgeon of Edinburgh* (Aberdeen 1990).

21 *The Herioter*, July 1946, vol. 40.

22 The Secretary of State vetoed the proposal to use the building as a shelter.

23 Tony Welton is one of the legends of the Heriot's staff. He took over the PE department

in 1939 – the first to hold a diploma in physical education as opposed to being an army instructor. While at war his wife, Elizabeth, took over his post. He remained head of PE until his promotion to assistant head of guidance and leisure in 1974. He retired in 1976.

24 Charlie Broadwood was another significant figure in the history of Heriot's. He ran school sport with volunteer staff help. His record was remarkable, especially at rugby. In 1942–43 Heriot's 1st XV rugby team was the 'team of the year' in Scotland and completed an unbeaten season – the sixth since 1930 (played 18, won 17, drew 1).

25 Couper: *op.cit.,* p. 164.

26 Women in the staffroom in the new prep building.

27 The sea cadets were instituted by Carnon in January 1943.

28 'Billy' Gentle remained a well-known figure in Heriot circles. He cut a dapper figure when seen out and about near his home in the southside of Edinburgh until his death in March 1964.

29 All six external candidates interviewed were heads of schools: three from Scotland and three from England.

30 Carnon was born in 1883 and was educated at Moray House School before becoming a pupil master there. He went on to university at Edinburgh and gained medals and prizes in English. After graduation in October 1907 he joined the Heriot's staff and the English department of Malcolm McKenzie. David Collier was a former pupil of Heriot's (1905–14) who went on to become a somewhat dour headmaster at Robert Gordon's College, in Aberdeen, between 1943 and 1960.

31 Ronnie Cramond at the governors' dinner in 2001 spoke of his teaching as 'positively inspirational'.

32 602 in junior school and 909 in senior school with 150 foundationers, 65 bursars, 60 free scholars and 1,236 fee-paying pupils.

33 Watson's £9 9s. 0d.– £19 19s. 0d; Royal High School £6 6s. 0d.– £14 14s. 0d.; Gillespie's £4 4s. 0d.–£7 10s. 0d.; and Trinity £2 0s. 0d.– £4 0s. 0d.

34 He had proved a skilful teacher of weaker pupils and was a Commander of the OTC during the war.

35 She was promoted to special assistant in geography and retired in 1983.

36 Trust Minutes, 1946, pp. 4, 57. The governors voted 11–0 with one abstention.

37 He retired in 1966, became president elect of the Congregational Church of Scotland and school governor.

38 *The Herioter,* vol. 41, No. 2, July 1947, p. 86.

39 Trust Minutes, 1947, p. 10. 'Billy' Carnon died in 1953.

40 Hugh Gunn left at this time after twenty-four years of teaching history and English to become headmaster of Tomintoul in Banffshire.

41 Trust Minutes, 1947, p. 73. Dr David S.M. Imrie from Duns; Robert Macintyre from Kilmarnock; and Ian D. McIntosh from Winchester were the other contenders.

CHAPTER THIRTEEN

1 1949, Trust Minutes, p. 154.

2 Ibid., p. 155.

3 Ibid.

4 Unfortunately Morrison died suddenly as the result of a brain haemorrhage on 10 January 1948.

5 *The Herioter*, July 1948, vol. XLII, No. 2, p. 69.

6 The governors accepted that former pupils should have priority in admission (1948 Trust Minutes, p. 82).

7 *The Herioter*, July 1948, vol. 42, No. 2.

8 This had only been introduced the previous session.

9 Trust Minutes, 12 July 1948, p. 99.

10 Trust Minutes, 1948, p. 116.

11 Ibid., p. 117.

12 Trust Minutes, 1948, p. 129.

13 Hastie was games master at Heriot's between 1949 and 1979 and was brought to the school to make games compulsory for all pupils. He increased the number of teams playing regularly to thirty in the school, and this figure even reached thirty-six on one occasion.

14 Trust Minutes, 1949, p. 116.

15 Ibid., p. 123.

16 Ibid., p. 143.

17 The negotiations are detailed in an appendix to the governors' minutes, 1950, pp. 39–42, and affected rugby, cross-country running, cricket and athletics.

18 Trust Minutes, 1949, p. 152.

19 *The Herioter*, vol. 47, No. 1, December 1953, p. 21.

20 Trust Minutes, 1951, p. 76.

21 Trust Minutes, 1951, p. 96.

22 *The Herioter*, vol. 42, No. 1, December 1962, pp. 6–8.

23 *The Herioter*, vol. 44, No. 2, May 1950, p. 72.

24 Examples include Allan McDonald, George Heriot's; Bob Nimmo, Dundee High School; Alastair Johnston, Kelso High School; George Jack, Liberton; Iain Agnew, Perth High School; David Allan, Preston Lodge; Ian Elder, Kirriemuir; Brian Lockhart, Robert Gordon's College.

25 He had taken some pupils into the Greyfriars Bobby's public house.

26 1951 Minutes, pp. 129–130.

27 1952 Minutes, p. 53.

28 Barron had been a pupil under Lowe and in the Trust was involved in four amendments to the Trust Scheme of Administration, especially the Provisional Order of 1927, which severed the Heriot-Watt College from Heriot's Trust.

29 He in turn was to leave in 1954 to become headmaster of Miller Academy, Thurso.

30 He became principal teacher following Grant's departure.

31 Including P. O'Malley (English/history), A.G. McPhee (mathematics), J.T. Jardine (physics/mathematics), H.G. McCall (Classics), T.J.C. Dennis (Spanish/French), R. Malcolm Hunter (PE), Jim Barr (physics), J.J. Caw (English) and W.T. Waitt (PE).

32 T. Gibby Galloway (former pupil) joined the staff in 1937 and taught English, history and junior school classes. He was promoted from the head of the junior school to second depute before retiring in 1975. He is a significant figure in the history of the School, contributing greatly to rugby, athletics, the Scottish School Boys' Club and the Heriot's Club.

33 'Abers' had a reputation as a strict disciplinarian and was the one member of staff whose pupils, including reputedly sixth formers, ran to his class.

34 Jim Barclay had left School as a foundationer in 1927 and became a junior clerk in the Trust office. He retired as the much respected assistant clerk and treasurer in 1976.

35 Prep 125, junior 453 and senior 953.

36 Trust Minutes, 1946, pp. 136–7.

37 Prep 122, junior 404, secondary 808.

38 1949 Minutes, p. 106.

39 The total cost, including furniture, was £23,932 according to the estimates accepted at a special meeting of the governors on 25 March 1957.

40 He held twenty-three classrooms to be sub-standard.

41 Memo of Dewar dated December 1961, and Paper to the governors, 26 January 1962.

42 *The Herioter*, vol. 58, No. 2.

43 Hearings at the City Chambers 4–8 October, with visits on 9 and 11 October; inspection of plans on 12 October. The Trust produced seven witnesses and the Corporation four. Trust Minutes, 1966, p. 39.

44 Old Building, Senior Hall, Physics Building, Prep Building, Art Building, Chemistry and Pool.

45 The others were Victoria Terrace, Lauriston Place.

46 Perhaps emphasis should be on the view of the Castle from Heriot's Hospital, and for two months this was marred by Tattoo scaffolding and seating without the protection of the Commission.

47 The painting by Patrick Naismith (1786–1831) illustrated this contrast and hangs on the main staircase of the City Chambers. Playfair in the nineteenth century had maintained the freestanding character of the building and strengthened the additional quality of repose. Thus the RFAC centred its arguments on the importance of keeping the setting and the view of the old building intact.

48 *The Herioter*, vol. 63, No. 2, May 1969.

49 The Donnison Commission was in the midst of reporting.

50 School Captain in 1908.

51 Designed by J. Eversdon Henderson, a Herioter, and constructed by Robert McP. Hadden, also a Herioter.

52 Even the boys were given an extended Founder's holiday of a week.

53 Dr J. Stewart Louden, vice-chairman of the governors, *The Herioter*, December 1970, p. 7. The composition of the governing body was, in time, to prove very significant. The Lord Provost remained chair of governors, with seven councillors nominated by Edinburgh Corporation from among their own number, two educationalists (not councillors) nominated by the Corporation, one from Heriot-Watt University, one from Edinburgh University, three from Edinburgh Presbytery, one from the Royal College of Physicians, one from Edinburgh Chamber of Commerce, one from Edinburgh District Trades Council, two from the Heriot Club and one space for co-option. The headmaster was to appoint non-teaching and teaching staff. The governing body was to be allowed to pay retiring allowances provided the Secretary of State agreed in writing. The foundationers were to consist of not less than 150 boys and not more than 150 girls, being fatherless children, needing aid for education and maintenance, over eight years of age and resident for one year in Edinburgh. Founder's Day was to be celebrated in the way

that the 'governors think fit' and 'reasonable expenditure' could be incurred.

54 282 fathers were old boys; nine mothers were former foundationers. Donnison showed how the background of the Heriot pupils had changed since Hospital days.

55 Although criticisms of the O Grade examination spilled over into criticism of Dewar personally.

56 His presidential addresses to headmasters were made in Dunblane in May 1958 and May 1959. The organisation has evolved today into the Headteachers' Association of Scotland.

57 Deputy head Allan McDonald was joined by local candidates, Douglas C.J. McMahon and Ronald Paul, and Bernard J. Moody from Maidstone, Kent.

58 David Mackenzie had been hitherto principal teacher of chemistry. He had taught at the High School of Glasgow before taking on that post in October 1963. He was later appointed Rector of Falkirk High School in August 1971.

59 John Roy had been the outstanding student of his year at Moray House and joined the staff in 1948. He proved a most successful principal teacher of technical and an outstanding depute – a disciplinarian who gained the respect and admiration of staff and pupils.

60 Fees for 1971–72 were Primary £117; Secondary 1/2 £120; Secondary 3 and above £123.

61 Dewar had, in his time, sent boys home to get their hair cut and supposedly even sent some away from school until their hair grew!

62 Trust Minutes, 1972, p. 10.

63 Trust Minutes, 1972, pp. 19–20.

64 Principal teacher of physics since 1951.

65 An FP at Heriot's since 1943, and principal teacher since 1969.

66 Principal teacher of history to deputy head at Craigmount High School.

67 There were other retirals too which occurred at this time. L. Lindsay Mitchell – a pupil under J.B. Clark had rejoined the junior school staff in 1929 and will be permanently remembered for his contribution to school cricket (1938–71); Stewart H. Millar, a pupil in September 1914, had gained a first-class honours degree in chemistry and joined the staff in 1946, retiring from the position of second head of department in 1962.

68 1976 Minutes, p. 49.

69 It was decided it was too early to create a parent/teacher association.

70 572 in junior school and 1,018 in senior school.

71 In fact, despite strenuous efforts to encourage widows to apply for foundations for their children, the numbers fell. In the 1970s the highest number of boys was 118 (with a low of 72) and the highest number of girls was 88, but had declined markedly throughout the 1970s to reach an all-time low of 19 in 1978.

72 Trust Minutes, 1975, p. 15.

73 Ibid.

74 Trust Minutes, 1975, pp. 34–5. It seems likely that the Merchant Company saw Heriot's as the possible 'fall guy'. Its plan was to sell Heriot's, and from the money raised to enable foundationers to attend a Merchant Company school.

75 Ibid., p. 42.

76 Local Government (Scotland) Act 1973.

77 Trust Minutes, 1975, p. 91.

78 He had been a member of the governing body since 1952 and vice-chairman since 1956.

79 Jimmy Ross had been a pupil at Heriot's between 1929 and 1940, and had been School

Captain in his final year. At school he was also captain of rugby and athletics. After university he joined his family business.

80 Jean Stenhouse taught in the prep department (1942–62) and the lower junior school (1962–75).

81 An FP, Alec Bateman, had been appointed to the governing body in October 1944 as a representative of the Royal College of Physicians. He was convener of education from 1965 and 'father' of the governing body for a considerable time. His thirty-two years of service were unequalled in modern times.

82 On the retiral of David Morris, clerk and treasurer, it was decided that his successor need not be a lawyer but an accountant with legal work farmed out. Vivien Thomas took over this post too.

83 The old male staffroom on the immediate right as one entered the pend was likened to a Victorian railway station waiting-room. It had a unique charm and atmosphere which were missed by some.

84 Four had not attended before.

85 Milligan had for fourteen years represented the Edinburgh and District Trades Council on the board. It was generally felt that Councillor George Foulkes, chairman of the Region's Education committee, was behind the strategy of the 'take-over' of Heriot's. He argued (*Evening News*, 18 January 1979) that the trust had moved away from George Heriot's intention to provide education for poor, fatherless children. He thought the School would become 'a haven for the privileged'. Foulkes also questioned the 1975 decision to go independent, which he argued was taken while the Local Authority representation was disputed. He suggested that the dispute was manoeuvred to keep the Region out of the Trust. However, paragraph 11 of the 1966 Trust scheme held that even if there were arguments about governor representation, decisions remained valid provided seven governors were present and voting. Milligan perhaps did not attend because 22 January was 'Black Monday' – with industrial action being taken by NUPE and other unions. Milligan, as area organiser of NUPE, had issued strike instructions to two janitors at Heriot's and he refused to cross their picket-line.

86 See *Evening News* and *The Scotsman* for 8 February, 20 February, 21 February, 12 March, 14 March, 15 March, 25 March 1979.

87 Unfortunately this was one of the great man's last contributions to Heriot's: he died on 16 September 1979.

88 The 'anti-Heriot' campaign lost momentum with Foulkes becoming a Westminster MP.

89 Mary Rose-Caden, an educational representative and an EIS officer, saw her role as a supporter of staff interests and refused to follow the Labour line.

90 *The Scotsman*, 1 December 1979. Trust Minutes, 1979, p. 128.

91 Trust Minutes, 1980, p. 4.

92 Trust Minutes, 1980, p. 26.

93 This 'reward' to the parents was given grudgingly, and indeed the governors and Heriot Club were constantly criticising PA representatives for acting precipitately and without consultation. The staff had to make do with a governor/staff liaison committee, although the generous decision of the governors to give full remission of all fees to all trust employees who had been in service before 11 March 1975 (and 90 per cent to those who arrived after this date) in July 1979 probably was a significant perk (although financial pressure was soon to force its modification). Also McDonald reasonably

accepted that when the governors' agenda involved welfare of girls he would be accompanied by a senior staff lady, who in practice became the new assistant head teacher for girls, Mrs Esther Henderson.

94 Trust Minutes, 1980.

95 This was eventually to happen in the 1990s, but the worst effects of its withdrawal were mitigated by its phasing out over a number of years.

96 Trust Minutes, 1980.

97 Trust Minutes, 1980, p. 129.

CHAPTER FOURTEEN

1 Trust investments were sold off, Russian was no longer to be offered as an S1 curriculum option, the salary of the clerk and treasurer, Vivian Thomas, was not increased, and the issue of staff fee remission was reopened.

2 Trust Minutes, 1983, p. 29.

3 The junior school grew from 393 to 480, while the senior school rose from 904 to 994.

4 Trust Minutes, 1983, p. 73.

5 The nursery success led to the opening in September 1992 of new enlarged accommodation for forty children in the morning and twenty in the afternoon in the extensive gardens to the east. The architects, Reiach & Hall, spent £400,000.

6 Other accommodation improvements followed. Most significantly was the Greyfriars' extension of four more classrooms for the junior school, opened by Her Royal Highness the Princess Anne in June 1996. It was connected to the eight classrooms created in 1983.

7 John Roy retired in 1985 to be replaced by Hugh Maclennan, another successful choice as depute. A new structure was most appropriate, given the retiral of three assistant heads. Tom Dennis had joined Heriot's in 1954, been head of Spanish between 1965–74 and AHT 1975–87; Jim Caw joined in 1955, was head of English before AHT 1981–90; and Gordon McCall joined in 1953, was PT Classics between 1967–76 and AHT from 1976–91.

8 Trust Minutes, 1985, p. 34.

9 Between 1873–81, 9,217 adults enrolled in evening classes: some 7,947 men and 1,243 women in arithmetic, mathematics, English composition, French, German, writing and book-keeping, shorthand, architectural and freehand drawing.

10 Steven (1845): *op. cit.*, p. 40.

Selected Bibliography

The Heriot Trust gave over most of its material to the Scottish Record Office, now the National Archives of Scotland (NAS), in 1985, and has retained only the original minute books of governors' meetings (NAS has written and microfilm copies). However, the Charter Room at Heriot's stores a number of reports and letters, and an asterisk in the bibliography denotes these.

The NAS has followed the classification of documents suggested by David Laing ('Inventory of Original Documents in the Archives of Heriot's Hospital', Edinburgh, 1857), and most of the documents mentioned by Laing still survive in the GD 421 series of papers in West Register House.

A. PRIMARY SOURCES

Record (Minute Books) of Heriot's Hospital*

Vol. No.	Period
1	March 1624–July 1662
2	August 1662–May 1688
3	June 1688–September 1701
4	October 1701–October 1718
5	December 1718–March 1729
6	March 1729–October 1734
7	October 1734–October 1744
8	October 1744–September 1761
9	October 1761–October 1767
10	January 1768–October 1774
11	October 1774–June 1777
12	October 1777–April 1785
13	June 1785–October 1789
14	March 1790–November 1793
15	April 1794–October 1800
16	November 1800–April 1804
17	June 1804–January 1808
18	February 1808–July 1810
19	July 1810–August 1813
20	August 1813–April 1816
21	April 1816–April 1819
22	March 1819–February 1822
23	April 1822–March 1825
24	April 1825–June 1828
25	July 1828–March 1832
26	April 1832–May 1835
27	June 1835–June 1837

28	July 1837–April 1839
29	April 1839–June 1841
30	July 1841–December 1843
31	January 1844–January 1846
32	February 1846–October 1847
33	October 1847–April 1850
34	April 1850–January 1853
35	February 1853–January 1855
36	February 1855–May 1857
37	July 1857–June 1860
38	July 1860–November 1862
39	December 1862–February 1865
40	April 1865–February 1867
41	March 1867–December 1868
42	January 1869–August 1871
43	October 1871–December 1873
44	January 1874–July 1876
45	July 1876–March 1879
46	April 1879–October 1881
47	November 1881–January 1884
48	February 1884–December 1885

Record (Minute Books) of Heriot's Trust*

1	October 1885–October 1887
2	November 1887–July 1889
3	September 1889–July 1891
4	October 1891–July 1893
5	October 1893–June 1896
6	July 1896–February 1899
7	March 1899–May 1901
8	June 1901–September 1903
9	October 1903–December 1905
10	January 1906–December 1907
11	January 1908–June 1909
12	July 1909–December 1909

After this time the Trust Minutes are a volume to each year.

Consulted were volumes from 1910 to 1990.

The school magazine, *The Herioter*, was produced regularly from its first edition in 1907, and is a valuable source of information.

Consulted were *Herioters* from 1907 to 1990.

'George Heriot's Disposition and Assignation of his Property to the Town of Edinburgh', dated 3 September 1623, reponed 2 January 1624, is printed in Steven (1845), Appendix V; Bedford (1859), pp. 238–51; Bedford (1872), pp. 291-307. His Last Will and Testament, of 10 December 1623, is found in Maitland (1753), pp. 431–9; Constable (1822), pp. 67–102; Steven (1845), Appendix VI; Bedford (1859), pp. 252–70 and Bedford (1872), pp. 307–28. These documents are also to be found in the NAS series, at GD 421/1 vol. 1 [1].

The original Statutes of the Hospital of 13 July 1627 are in the NAS series – GD 421/10[1] – and have been signed on every page by Walter Balcanquall. They are enclosed in a full leather embossed case. Another copy is found in GD421/1, vol. 1, [17], with corrections and additions in the hand of Balcanquall, and yet another fair copy in GD 421/1 vol. 1, [18] with the signature of D. Aikinhead, provost, and the other governors. The governors had the Statutes reprinted in 1696, 1734, 1789, 1811 and 1818, and copies of these are in the charter room.

The accounts of the early treasurers are also to be found in the NAS series – GD 421/5/1:

Volume 1 (1626–1633) includes the following:
1. Oct. 1627–Oct. 1628: Nicoll Udwart, 45 pages
2. Oct. 1628–Oct. 1629: Nicoll Udwart, 71 pages
3. Oct. 1629–Nov. 1630: Nicoll Udwart, 65 pages
4. Nov. 1630–Nov. 1631: Robert Halieburtoun, 53 pages
5. Nov. 1631–Nov. 1632: Robert Halieburtoun, 67 pages
6. Nov. 1632–Nov. 1633: William Cochrane, 55 pages

Volume 2 (1633–1642) includes:
1. Nov. 1633–Nov. 1634: William Cochrane, 75 pages
2. Nov. 1634–Nov. 1635: William Cochrane, 84 pages
3. Nov. 1635–Nov. 1636: Robert Flemyng, 87 pages
4. Nov. 1636–Nov. 1637: Edward Edgar, 88 pages
5. Nov. 1637–Nov. 1638: Thomas Charteris, 80 pages
6. Nov. 1638–Nov. 1639: Patrick Baxter, 72 pages
7. Nov. 1639–Nov. 1640: Patrick Baxter, 80 pages
8. Nov. 1640–Nov. 1641: John Edgar, 95 pages
9. Nov. 1641–Nov. 1642: John Edgar, 113 pages

Volume 3 (1642–1652) includes:
1. Nov. 1642–Nov. 1643: John Edgar, 100 pages
2. Nov. 1643–Nov. 1644: James Alison, 89 pages
3. Nov. 1644–Nov. 1645: James Alison, 84 pages
4. Nov. 1645–Nov. 1646: James Alison, 72 pages
5. Nov. 1646–Nov. 1647: James Alison, 85 pages
6. Nov. 1647–Nov. 1648: William Simpson, 81 pages
7. Nov. 1648–Nov. 1649: George Wauchope, 63 pages
8. Nov. 1649–May 1652: George Wauchope, 58 pages

(Gap between Nov. 1650 and May 1652)

Volumes 4 and 5 continue the series, but are even more difficult to follow and are not so helpful as previous volumes.

The series GD/421 also contains the following:

Personal papers of George Heriot	GD/421/2
Executory papers	GD/421/3
Minute Books (as above)	GD/421/4
Vouchers for years not in Accounts	GD/421/5/2
Estate papers	GD/421/9
Various Hospital matters (Admissions etc)	GD/421/10
Legal papers	GD/421/1 vol. 2
Business papers	GD/421/1 vol. 3
More legal papers (inc. Lawtie letters)	GD/421/1 vol. 4

Anon: The Last Will and Testament, and Codicil thereto, of George Heriot: and the Original Statutes of the Hospital by Walter Balcanquall (Edinburgh 1835).

The governors introduced various regulations, the most important being:
Regulations for George Heriot's Hospital (Edinburgh 1795)
Regulations for George Heriot's Hospital (Edinburgh 1809)
Regulations for the Internal Management of George Heriot's Hospital (Edinburgh 1833)
Regulations . . . as to the Superintendence to be exercised over the Boys at their leaving the Institution, and afterwards (Edinburgh 1834)
Regulations in regard to the Bursars of George Heriot's Hospital (Edinburgh 1844)
Also printed in Steven (1845), Appendix XI; Bedford (1859), pp. 320–4; Bedford (1872) pp. 372–4.
Regulations for the Internal Management of George Heriot's Hospital (Edinburgh 1849)
Regulations for the Internal Management, and for the Offices of treasurer and Superintendent of Works, of George Heriot's Hospital (Edinburgh 1851)*

Of their many reports the most significant were:

Report . . . on Outdoor Schools (Edinburgh 1836).

Report . . . upon the Office of House governor (Edinburgh 1838).

Report . . . relative to the Duties of House governor or Headmaster (Edinburgh 1844).

Fairbairn, James: Report . . . on the Observations of the House governor on the [above 1844] Report (Edinburgh 1844).

Report on the proposed Superannuation Scheme Fund (Edinburgh 1850).*

Laing, David: Who was the Architect of Heriot's Hospital (Transactions of the Architectural Institute of Scotland, 2nd session 1851–2; given on 27 November 1851).*

Rhind, David: On the Respective Claims of Inigo Jones; Dr Balcanquall, Dean of Rochester; and William Wallace – to have been the Designer of Heriot's Hospital (Transactions . . . ibid . . . given on 26 February 1852).*

Minutes and Report on the Number of Boys which the present Dormitories can adequately, and with comfort and consideration for their health, contain (Edinburgh 1853).

Ritchie, Robert: Report as to who was the Architect of Heriot's Hospital (Edinburgh 1855).*

Ritchie, Robert: Additional Report as to who was the Architect of Heriot's Hospital (Edinburgh 1856).*

Register of Diseases got over by Hospital boys at the time of their Admission to the Hospital (October 1853–1885).*

B. EARLY PRINTED SOURCES (CLASSIFIED BY CHRONOLOGY)

Johnstone, Robert: Historia Rerum Britannicarum . . . ab anno 1572 ad annum 1628 (Amsterdam 1655).

D.M.: An Account of the Arraignment, Tryal, Escape, and Condemnation of the Dog of Heriot's Hospital in Scotland, that was supposed to have been hang'd, but did at last slip the Halter (London 1682).

Sibbald, Sir Robert: *Scotia Illustrata . . . a natural history of Scotland of 1684* (Edinburgh 1684). [NAS: 33.3.22].

Slezer, Captain John: *Threatrum Scotiae* (London 1693).

Two Sermons presented at the Meeting of the Council of George Heriot's Hospital at Edinburgh (Edinburgh 1695) – 3 December 1694 Gilbert Rule, minister and Principal of the College of Edinburgh; first Monday of June 1695 George Meldrum, minister.

Memorial humbly presented to His Grace his Majesties Commissioner, and the Right Honourable the Estates of Parliament. By the Administrators of Heriot's Hospital in behalf of the Poor thereof. (Edinburgh 1695).

Acta Parliamenti, 1695, 449. Reprinted in Constable (1822) pp. 157–9; Steven (1845) Appendix XIV; Bedford (1859) pp. 333–4; Bedford (1872) pp. 389–90.

Brome, James: *Travels over England, Scotland and Wales* (London 1700).

Morer, Revd Thomas: *A Short Account of Scotland* (London 1702).

Mackenzie, Dr George: *Lives and characters of the most eminent Writers of the Scots Nation*, 3 vols (Edinburgh 1708–22).

Mackenzie, Dr George: *Letter On Heriot's Hospital* (Edinburgh 1711).

Defoe, Daniel: *A Tour thro' the whole Island of Great Britain divided into circuits or journies*. 3 vols. (London 1727).

Macky, John.: *A Journey through England. In familiar letters from a gentleman here to a friend abroad*. The second edition improved (written 1724, published London 1732).

Ray, James: *Journal through Part of England and Scotland (along with army under HRH Duke of Cumberland) by a Volunteer*. Letter V. Edinburgh, 30 January 1746 (2nd ed London 1747).

Maitland, William: *The History of Edinburgh from its Foundation to the Present Time* (Edinburgh 1753).

Burt, Sir Edward: *Letters from a gentleman in the North of Scotland*, 2 vols (Edinburgh 1754).

Reasons of Dissent and Protest by Mess. John Glen, Robert Wallace, George Kay, Robert Walker, Henry Lundie, John Erskine and Robert Dick, Ministers of Edinburgh and Administrators of George Heriot's Hospital (Edinburgh 1760).*

Brown, Malcolm: A Remonstrance by the United Committees of the Merchant Company . . . and Memorial by a considerable Number of the Burgesses of the City of Edinburgh, relative to the Management of Mr. George Heriot's Hospital (Edinburgh 1763).

Information for the Magistrates, Ministers and Council of the City of Edinburgh, governors of George Heriot's Hospital, and others, Defenders ; against Alexander Brown and others, Pursuers. 7 November 1764. (Edinburgh 1764).

Answer for the Magistrates, Ministers, and Council of the City of Edinburgh, governors of George Heriot's Hospital, Edinburgh, Defenders: to the Petition of the Merchant Company and Trades of Edinburgh, Pursuers. 19 November 1765. (Edinburgh 1765).

Newdigate, Sir Roger: Diary for 1766 (CR136/A[563], County Record Office, Warwick).

Information for the Merchant Company and Trades of Edinburgh against the Magistrates, Ministers and Council of the City of Edinburgh, governors of Heriot's Hospital, 18 June 1766 (Alex. Wright).

Gillies, Revd John: *Memoirs of the Life of the Reverend George Whitefield M.A.* (London 1772).

An Address to the Citizens of Edinburgh, relative to the Management of George Heriot's Hospital. By a Free Burgess of Edinburgh (Edinburgh 1773).

Brutus, Lucius Junius (pseudonym): Considerations on the Management of George Heriot's Hospital. Dedicated to the most impudent man alive [probably Gilbert Laurie] (Edinburgh 1774).

Pennant, Thomas: *A Tour of Scotland*, 3rd edn (Warrington 1774).

To the Rt Hon. Lord Provost, Magistrates and Council with Revd Ministers of Edinburgh, governors of Heriot's Hospital. The Petition of the Boys of the Hospital (10 October 1775).

Topham, Edward: *Letters from Edinburgh written in the years 1774 and 1775* (Edinburgh 1776).

Arnot, Hugo: *The History of Edinburgh from the Earliest Accounts to the Year 1780* (Edinburgh 1788).

Newte, Thomas: *A Tour in England and Scotland in 1785 by an English gentleman* (London 1788).

Grose, Francis: The Antiquities of Scotland, vol. 1 (London 1789).

Minutes relating to Heriot's Decorating Club (commencing 4 March 1792 and ending 15 January 1798).*

Kincaid, Alexander: *The History of Edinburgh From the Earliest Account to the Present Time* (Edinburgh 1787).

Creech, William: *Letters Addressed to Sir John Sinclair respecting the Mode of Living, Arts, Commerce, Literature, Manners etc. of Edinburgh in 1763 and since that Period* (Edinburgh 1793).

Crawford, David: *Poems Chiefly in the Scottish Dialect*, 2nd edn (Edinburgh 1798).

Dalyell, G.B.: *Fragments of Scottish History* (Edinburgh 1798).

Birrel, Diarey of Robert, burges of Edinburgh (from 1532 to 1605) in Dalyell, G.B.: *Fragments of Scottish History* (Edinburgh 1798).

Rules and Regulations of Heriot's Decorating Club (in 1802).*

G.H.D. Club 1804.*

Names and Places of Residences of Heriot's Decorating Club, undated. (*c.* 1814).*

Hamilton, Dr James: *Purgative Medicine*, 5th edn (Edinburgh 1815).

Pugin, Augustus: *Specimens of Gothic Architecture* (London 1821).

Constable, Archibald: *Memoirs of George Heriot, Jeweller to King James VI* (Edinburgh 1822).*

Griscom, John: *A Year in Europe comprising a Journal of Observation in England, Scotland, Ireland, Germany, Switzerland, the North of Italy and Holland in 1818 and 1819*, 2 vols (New York 1823).

Highland Society: *Report on the Friendly Societies* (Edinburgh 1824).

Chambers, Robert: *Traditions of Edinburgh* (Edinburgh 1824).

Feldborg, A. Anderson*: Denmark Delineated* (Edinburgh 1824).

Goldicutt, John: *Heriots'* [sic] *Hospital* (London 1826).

Scott, Sir Walter: *Provincial Antiquities and Picturesque Scenery of Scotland*, 2 vols, vol. 1 (London 1826).

[An Old Governor]: *Observations in regard to the Description of Boys who appear agreeably to the Statutes entitled to be admitted into George Heriot's Hospital* (Edinburgh 1827).*

Thomson, Revd Thomas: *Historical and Descriptive Account of George Heriot's Hospital* (Edinburgh 1827).

Chambers, Robert: *Lives of Illustrious Scotsmen* (Edinburgh 1834).

Glover, Thomas Miller: *A Few Remarks (by an Old Citizen) on a pamphlet speech of Bailie John Macfarlane 11 April 1834* (Edinburgh 1834).

Maidment, John: *Analecta Scotia*, 2nd series, vol. 2 (Edinburgh 1834–37).

Lee, Revd Dr John: *Facts for the consideration of the governors of George Heriot's Hospital, in connection with the questions relating to the Statutes, Duties, Salaries and Terms of Appointment of the Master and other Officers* (Edinburgh 1836).

6 and 7 Will. 4, c 25 An Act to explain and extend the power of the governors of the Hospital in Edinburgh, founded by George Heriot, Jeweller to King James the Sixth (Private Act 1836).

Nicoll, John: D Laing (ed.): *A Diary of Public Transactions and other occurrences, chiefly in Scotland from January 1650 to June 1657* (Edinburgh 1836).

Dibdin, T.F.: *A bibliographical, antiquarian and picturesque tour in the northern counties of England and in Scotland*, 2 vols (London 1838).

Bache, Alex. Dallas: *Report on Education in Europe (to the Trustees of the Girard College for Orphans)* (Philadelphia 1839).

Lauder, Sir John (of Fountainhall): *Historical Observances . . . from October 1680 to April 1684* (Edinburgh 1840).

Statutes and Rules of George Watson's Hospital (Edinburgh 1842).

Strickland, Agnes: *Lives of the Queens of England (from the Norman Conquest)*, vol. 7 (London 1844).

Steven, Revd Dr William: *Memoir of George Heriot with the History of the Hospital founded by him in Edinburgh* (Edinburgh 1845).

Mann, Horace: *Report of an Educational Tour* (London 1846).

Lee, Robert, D.D.: *A Sermon (Monday June 1st, 1846) . . . being the Commemoration of George Heriot's Birth-Day* (Edinburgh 1846).*

Davidson: *The Herioter No Monk or Strictures on the Sermon delivered to the Parents, Children, and governors . . . by Revd Dr R. Lee . . . By an Auld Callant* (Edinburgh 1846).

Case for the Feofees of Trust and governors of George Heriot his Hospital, for Opinion of Counsel ; with Answers to Queries (Edinburgh 1847).

Lauder, Sir John (of Fountainhall): *Historical Notices of Scottish Affairs*, vol. 1 1661–83 (Edinburgh 1848); vol. 2 1683–88 (Edinburgh 1848).

Steven, Revd Dr William: *The History of the High School of Edinburgh* (Edinburgh 1849).

Library Roll Book. Old Herioters Association (8 January 1850).*

Spalding, John: *Memorials of the Troubles in Scotland and in England A.D.1625–A.D.1645*, 2 vols (Aberdeen 1850).

George Heriot's Hospital. Education Committee. House governor's Reports (1 December 1851 to 2 December 1885).*

Billings, R. W.: *The Baronial and Ecclesiastical Antiquities of Scotland*, vol. 3 (Edinburgh 1852).

Obituary and Register of Diseases got over by the Boys, vol. 2 (1853–83).*

Catalogue of the Library of George Heriot's Hospital (Edinburgh 1854).*

Supplement to Catalogue (nd).*

Testimonials in favour of Dr Bedford (Edinburgh 1854).*

Cockburn, Lord: *Memorials of his Time* (Edinburgh 1856).

Green, Mary A.E. (ed.): *Calendar of State Papers (Domestic) James I 1603–10* (London 1857).

Voigt, J.A.: *Mittheilungen über des Unterrichtswesen Englands und Schottlands* (Halle 1857).

Chambers, *Robert: Domestic Annals of Scotland (from the Reformation to the Revolution)*, 2 vols (Edinburgh 1858).

Green, Mary A.E. (ed.): *Calendar of State Papers 1611–19* (London 1858).

Green, Mary A.E. (ed.): *ibid.*, 1619–23 (London 1858).

Dialogue between A Son and his governor and the views of Cousin John on the Motion to be considered by the governors of George Heriot's Hospital on Thursday 2nd June 1859 'That the boys in the Hospital are allowed a glass of weak wine on Heriot's day as formerly' (Edinburgh 1859).

Bedford, Frederick. W.: *History of George Heriot's Hospital with a Memoir of the Founder* (Edinburgh 1859), 3rd edn (Edinburgh 1872); Supplement to 3rd edn (Edinburgh 1878).*

Protest by Councillor David Curor against the Resolution of the Thirteen governors on 26 February 1862 (Edinburgh 1862).

Bedford, Frederick W. *The Hospital System* (Edinburgh 1864).

Hastings, George (ed.): *Transactions of the National Association for the Promotion of Social Sciences – Edinburgh Meeting 1863* (London 1864).

Laurie, Simon S.: *Reports on the Hospitals under the administration of the Merchant Company and General Remarks on Hospital Training* (Edinburgh 1868).

Grant, Sir Alexander (ed.): *Recess Studies* (Edinburgh 1870).

Sit Jus: *On the Scholastic Position and Results of the Merchant Company's Schools* (Edinburgh 1870).

Boyd, Thomas J.: *Educational Hospital Reform. The Scheme of the Edinburgh Merchant Company* (Edinburgh 1871).

Burgh of Edinburgh Accounts, vol. 1 (Edinburgh 1871).

Guide to George Heriot's Hospital (Edinburgh 1872).*

Fergusson, James: *The History of Modern Styles of Architecture*, vol. 4, 2nd edn London 1873).

McLaren, Duncan: *Heriot's Hospital Trust and its Proper Administration. An Address* (Edinburgh 1872), revised 2nd edn (Edinburgh 1873).

Regulations of George Heriot's Hospital Schools (Edinburgh 1876).*

Kay, John: *A Series of Original Portrait and Caricature Etchings* (Edinburgh 1877).

Burton, J.H. and Masson, D.: *Register of the Privy Council of Scotland*, 14 vols (Edinburgh 1877–98).

Scott, Sir Walter: Waverley Novels, vol. XXVI. *Fortunes of Nigel* (Edinburgh 1879).

Hobhouse, Sir Arthur: *The Dead Hand. Addresses on Endowments and Settlement of Property* (London 1880).

Hill, William H.: *History of the Hospital and School in Glasgow founded by George and Thomas Hutcheson of Lambhill 1639–41* (Glasgow 1881).

Laurie, Simon S.: *On the Educational Wants of Scotland* (Edinburgh 1881).

Grant, James: *Cassell's Old and New Edinburgh. Its History, its People, and its Places*, vol.l (London nd); vol. II (London 1882); vol. III (London nd).

Moncrieff, Lord: *An Educational retrospect* (Glasgow 1885).

Walker, Alexander: *Robert Gordon, His Hospital and His College* (Aberdeen 1886).

Pococke, Richard (Bishop of Meath); *Tours in Scotland, 1747, 1750, 1760* (ed. Kemp, Daniel William) (Edinburgh 1887).

Mackie, J. B.: *The life and work of Duncan McLaren*, 2 vols (London 1888).

Fraser, Sir W.: *The Melvilles* (Edinburgh 1890).

Brown, P. Hume (ed.): *Early Travellers in Scotland* (Edinburgh 1891).

Colston, James: *The Incorporated Trades of Edinburgh* (Edinburgh 1891).

Dictionary of National Biography (London 1891).

Kirke, Thomas and Thoresby, Ralph: *Tours in Scotland 1677 and 1681* (ed. P. Hume Brown) (Edinburgh 1892).

MacGibbon, David and Ross, Thomas: *The Castellated and Domestic Architecture of Scotland*, vol 4 (Edinburgh 1892).

Mylne, Revd Robert Scott: *The Master Masons to the Crown of Scotland and their Works* (Edinburgh 1893).

Ballingall, G.W.: *Selections from the Old Records (with notes) regarding the Heriots of Trabroun, Scotland* (Haddington 1894).

Lowther, Christopher: *Our Journall into Scotland Anno Domini 1629* (Edinburgh 1894).

Colston, James: *Trinity College and Trinity Hospital. A Historical Sketch* (Edinburgh 1896).

'Memories of George Heriot's Hospital. An Old Boy's Reminiscences' (*Weekly Scotsman*, 7 May 1898).

Diary of James Birrell: handwritten between 14 September 1898 and 6 August 1901, on Hospital life between 2 June 1835 and January 1838.*

Baillie, A. Jamieson: *Walter Crighton or Reminiscences of George Heriot's Hospital* (Edinburgh n.d.) (1st edn, 1898; 2nd edn, 1901; 3rd edn, 1906).

The Tercentenary of the Laying of the Foundation Stone of George Heriot's School (Edinburgh 1928).

Government commissions are a useful source of material on the Hospitals generally and Heriot's Hospital in particular. *The Argyll Education Commission (Scotland) Third Report* (1868); *The Colebrooke Commission into the Endowed Schools and Hospitals (Scotland)* has a wealth of information; *First Report* (1873) esp. pp. 517–523, *Second Report* (1874), *Third Report* (1875), pp. 43–55, and *Appendix to Third Report*, 2 vols (1875), esp. vol. I, pp. 3–18; the *Moncrieff Commission on Endowed Institutions in Scotland* is also very helpful; *First Report* (1880) in particular, but also *Second Report* (1881), *Third Report* (1881) and the *Special Report* (1881); and the *Balfour Commission*, especially its *Second Report* (1885).

OTHER OFFICIAL REPORTS

Woodford, Edward: 'Special Report on Heriot's Hospital, and the Heriot Hospital Schools, *Minutes of the Committee of Council on Education*, 1855–6 (1856), pp. 556–60.

Fearnon, Daniel R.: 'Heriot's Hospital', *School Inquiry Commission Report* (1868), 6, part 5, pp. 179–83.

Gordon, John: *Report to the Education Committee of George Heriot's Hospital* (1869).*

Gordon, John: *General Report upon the Edinburgh Heriot Schools* (1869).*

SCOTLAND'S EARLY NEWSPAPERS

From 1718 *Edinburgh Evening Courant* – before 1860 political neutrality with Conservative leanings, but after 1860 decidedly Conservative

From 1720 till 1867 *Caledonian Mercury* – which became ultra-radical in the mid-nineteenth century

From 1739 *The Scots Magazine.*

Between 1764 and 1859 *Edinburgh Advertiser* – Conservative in the nineteenth century

The Scotsman appeared in 1816 as a result of claims that mismanagement of local institutions were not reported by the press. Originally then a supporter of reform but under the editorship of Alexander Russel (1849–76) it tended to conservative Whiggism and opposed the radicalism of Duncan MacLaren.

C. LATER PRINTED (ARRANGED ALPHABETICALLY)

Akrigg, G.P.V. (ed.): *Letters of King James VI and I* (Berkeley 1984).

Allsobrook, David Ian: *Schools for the Shires: The reform of middle-class education in mid-Victorian England* (Manchester 1986).

Anderson, Robert: *The History of Robert Gordon's Hospital, Aberdeen, 1729 to 1881* (Aberdeen 1896).

Anderson, R.D.: *Education and Opportunity in Victorian Scotland. Schools and Universities* (Oxford 1983).

Anderson, R.D.: *Education and the Scottish People 1750–1918* (Oxford 1995).

Anderson, R.D.: *Scottish Education since the Reformation* (Dundee 1997).

Armit, Helen (ed.): *Extracts from the Records of the Burgh of Edinburgh, 1689–1701* (Edinburgh 1962).

Armit, Helen (ed.): *Extracts from the Records of the Burgh of Edinburgh, 1701–1718* (Edinburgh 1967).

Atterbury, Paul and Wainwright, Clive: Pugin. *A Gothic Passion* (New Haven 1994).

Atterbury, Paul (ed.): A.W.N. Pugin. *Master of Gothic Revival* (New Haven 1995).

Barroll, Leeds: *Anna of Denmark, Queen of England. A Cultural Biography* (Philadelphia 2001).

Bishop, A.S.: *The Rise of a Central Authority for English Education* (Cambridge 1971).

Bradfield Ray: *Nigel Tranter. Scotland's Storeyteller* (Edinburgh 1999).

Brown, Keith M.: *Kingdom or Province? Scotland and the Regal Union 1603–1715* (London 1992).

Bryce, W. Moir: *History of the Old Greyfriars' Church, Edinburgh* (Edinburgh 1912).

Butchart, R.: *Prints and Drawings of Edinburgh* (Edinburgh 1955).

Cameron, Annie I. (ed.): *Calendar of State Papers (Scotland) 1593–5* (Edinburgh 1936) vol. XI.

Carmichael, N.R. & Carmichael, S: *Edinburgh 1851 Census, vol. II. The Old Town* (Edinburgh 1994).

Cavers, Keith: *A Vision of Scotland, the Nation Observed by John Slezer 1671 To 1717* (Edinburgh 1993).

The Christ's Hospital Book (London 1953).

Clark, D.M.: *Heriot Rugby* (Edinburgh 1948).

Clarke, M.L.: *Classical Education in Britain 1500–1900* (Cambridge 1959).

Copley, Terence: *Black Tom. Arnold of Rugby. The Myth and the Man* (London 2002).

Cowan, R.M.W.: *The Newspaper in Scotland. A Study of its First Expansion, 1815–1860* (Glasgow 1946).

Cozens-Hardy, Basil: *The Diary of Sylas Neville, 1767–1788* (London 1950).

Craigie, James: *A Bibliography of Scottish Education before 1872* (London 1970) pp. 128–133.

Craigie, Sir William A.: *Dictionary of the Older Scottish Tongue* (Chicago 1937).

Crawford, Donald (ed.): *Journals of Sir John Lauder, Lord Fountainhall* (Edinburgh 1900).

Croft, Pauline: *King James* (Basingstoke and New York 2003).

Cruft, Kirsty & Fraser, Andrew (eds): *James Craig, 1744–1795* (Edinburgh 1995).

Dalgleish, George and Maxwell, Stuart: *The Loveable Craft, 1687–1987* (Edinburgh 1987).

Devine, T.M. & Jackson, Gordon (eds): *Glasgow* vol. 1 *Beginnings to 1830* (Manchester 1995).

Dewar, William McL.: *George Heriot's School* (Edinburgh 1950).

Dietz, Frederick C.: *English Public Finance 1558–1641* (New York 1932).

Dingwall, Helen M.: *Late 17th Century Edinburgh: a demographic study* (Aldershot 1994).

Dingwall, Helen M.: *Physicians, Surgeons and Apothecaries. Medicine in 17th Century Edinburgh* (East Linton 1995).

Donaldson, Gordon: *All the Queen's Men. Power and politics in Mary Stewart's Scotland* (London 1983).

Dow, F. D.: *Cromwellian Scotland 1651–60* (Edinburgh 1979).

Dunbar, John G. (ed.): *Sir William Burrell's Northern Tour 1758* (East Linton 1997).

Dunlop, A.D.: *Hutchesons' Grammar: The History of a Glasgow School* (Glasgow 1992).

Dyer, Michael: *Men of Property and Intelligence. The Scottish Electoral System prior to 1884* (Aberdeen 1996).

Fawcett, Richard: *Scottish Architecture From the Accession of the Stewarts to the Reformation* (Edinburgh 1994).

Fawcett, Richard: *Argyll's Lodging, Stirling* (Edinburgh 1996).

Finley, Gerald: *Landscapes of Memory. Turner as Illustrator to Scott* (London 1980).

Fletcher, Bannister: *A History of Architecture on the Comparative Method* (7th ed. London 1961).

Fletcher, Sheila: *Feminists and Bureaucrats. A study in the development of girls' education in the nineteenth century* (Cambridge 1980).

Fraser, Duncan: *Edinburgh in Olden Times* (Montrose 1976).

Freeman, F.W.: *Robert Fergusson and the Scots Humanist Compromise* (Edinburgh 1984).

Fyfe, W.T.: *Edinburgh under Sir Walter Scott* (Edinburgh 1906).

Gardiner, Leslie: *Man in the Clouds. The Story of Vincenzo Lunardi* (Edinburgh 1963).

Gifford, John: *William Adam 1689–1748. A Life and Times of Scotland's Universal Architect* (Edinburgh 1989).

Gifford, John, McWilliam, Colin & Walker, David: *The Buildings of Scotland. Edinburgh* (London 1984).

Giuseppi, M.S. (ed.): *Calendar of State Papers (Scotland) 1595–7*, vol. XII (Edinburgh 1952).

Glendinning, Miles, MacInnes, Ranald & MacKechnie, Aonghus: *A History of Scottish Architecture. From the Renaissance to the Present Day* (Edinburgh 1996).

Goodare, Julian: *State and Society in Early Modern Scotland* (Oxford 1999).

Goodare, J & Lynch, M. (eds): *The Reign of James VI* (East Linton 2000).

Gordon, Robert C.: *Under Which King? A Study of the Scottish Waverley Novels* (Edinburgh

1969).

Gosden, P.H.J.H.: *The Development of Educational Administration in England and Wales* (Oxford 1966).

Green, Andy: *Education and State Formation. The Rise of Education Systems in England, France and the USA* (London 1990).

Gunn, Clement B.: *George Heriot's Hospital. Memoirs of a Modern Monk. Being Reminiscences of Life in the Hospital* (Edinburgh nd) prob. 1902.

Harris, Rose: *Sir Henry Raeburn 1756–1823* (Bristol 1966).

Harrison, John: *The Company of Merchants of the City of Edinburgh and its Schools 1694–1920* (Edinburgh 1920).

Hein, Jørgen & Kristianseni, Peter: *Rosenborg. Official guide* (Copenhagen, 3rd ed. 1994).

Hitchcock, Henry-Russell: *Netherlandish Scrolled Gables of the Sixteenth and early Seventeenth Centuries* (New York 1978).

Holmes, Heather (ed.): *Scottish Life and Society. Institutions of Scotland. Education* (East Linton 2000).

Honey, J.R. deS.: *Tom Brown's Universe* (London 1977).

Horn, D.B.: *A Short History of the University of Edinburgh, 1556–1889* (Edinburgh 1967).

Houston, R.A.: *Social Change in the Age of the Enlightenment. Edinburgh 1660–1760* (Oxford 1994).

Howard, Deborah: *Scottish Architecture from the Reformation to the Restoration 1560–1660* (Edinburgh 1995).

Imrie, John and Dunbar, John G. (ed.): *Accounts of the Master of Works, vol.II 1616–1649* (Edinburgh 1982).

Innes, Joseph: *Architectural History of Innes House*, nd (privately published).

Jamie, Revd David: John Hope: *Philanthropist and Reformer* (Edinburgh 1900).

Johnson, D.: *Music and Society in Lowland Scotland in the 18th Century* (London 1972).

Johnson, Edgar: *Sir Walter Scott. The Great Unknown*, vol. II, 1821–1832 (London 1970).

Kerr, John: *Scottish Education. School and University from Early Times to 1908* (Cambridge 1910).

King, David: *The Complete Works of Robert and James Adam* (Oxford 1991).

Knox, H.M.: *Two Hundred and Fifty Years of Scottish Education 1696–1946* (Edinburgh 1953).

Law, Alexander: *Education in Edinburgh in the Eighteenth Century* (London 1965).

Law, Alexander: *An Account of Five Aerial Voyages in Scotland by Vincent Lunardi 1759–1806. London 1786* (Edinburgh 1976).

Lee, Maurice Jr: *Great Britain's Solomon. James VI and I in His Three Kingdoms* (Urbana 1990).

Lynch, Michael: *Edinburgh and the Reformation* (Edinburgh 1981).

Lynch, Michael: *Scotland. A New History* (London 1991; Edinburgh 2000).

Macaulay, James: *The Gothic Revival 1745–1845* (Glasgow 1975).

MacDougall, Ian: *Minutes of Edinburgh Trades Council 1859–73* (Edinburgh 1968).

Mack, Edward C.: *Public Schools and British Opinion, 1780–1860. An Examination of the Relationship between Contemporary Ideas and the Evolution of an English Institution* (London 1938).

McKee, Alasdair: *Uncle Harry's Last Stand* (London 1989).

Mackie, J.D. (ed.): *Calendar of State Papers (Scotland) 1597–1603*, vol. XIII (1) (Edinburgh 1969).

McCrie, Thomas: *Life of Andrew Melville* (Edinburgh 1899).

McCrum, Michael: *Thomas Arnold. Head Master. A Reassessment* (Oxford 1989).

MacDonald, A.A., Lynch, Michael & Cowan, Ian B. (eds): *The Renaissance in Scotland. Studies in Literature, Religion, History and Culture* (Leiden 1994).

McElwee, William: *The Wisest Fool in Christendom. The Reign of James I and VI* (New York 1958).

McFarlane, I.D.: *Buchanan* (Bristol 1981).

MacLeod, Iain: *The Glasgow Academy. 150 Years* (Glasgow 1997).

MacQueen. Hector: *George Heriot's Former Pupils Cricket Club* (Edinburgh 1989).

MacQueen, John (ed.): *Humanism in Renaissance Scotland* (Edinburgh 1990).

Magnusson, Magnus: *The Clacken and the Slate. The Story of the Edinburgh Academy 1824–1974* (London 1974).

Mangan, J. A.: *Athleticism in the Victorian and Edwardian public school. The Emergence and Consolidation of an Educational Ideology* (Cambridge 1981).

Mann, Alastair J.: *The Scottish Book Trade 1500–1720. Print Commerce and Print Control in Early Modern Scotland* (East Linton, 2000).

Martin, Dennis R.: *The Operas and Operatic Style of John Frederick Lampe* (Detroit 1985).

Marwick, Sir James D.: *A Retrospect* (Glasgow 1905).

Mathew, David: *James I* (London 1967).

Morgan, Alexander: *Rise and Progress of Scottish Education* (Edinburgh 1927).

Morgan, Alexander: *Makers of Scottish Education* (London 1929).

Murray, Peter: *The Architecture of the Italian Renaissance* (London 1963).

O'Day, Rosemary: *Education and Society, 1500–1800: the Social Foundations of Education in Early Modern Britain* (London 1982).

Patterson, W.B.: *King James VI and I and the Reunion of Christendom* (Cambridge 1997).

Philip, Henry L.: *The Higher Tradition. A history of public examination in Scottish schools and how they influenced the development of secondary education* (Dalkeith 1992).

Piggott, Stuart (ed.): *Camden's 'Britannia', 1695 edition* (London 1971).

Prince, Alison: *Hans Christian Andersen. The Fan Dancer* (London 1997).

Pryde, David: *Heriot's Hospital. A Short History* (Edinburgh 1938).*

Purves, Sir William: *Revenue of the Scottish Crown 1681* (ed. D. Murray Rose) (Edinburgh 1897).

Reed, Joseph W. & Pottle, Frederick (ed): *Boswell. Laird of Auchinleck 1778–1782* (Edinburgh 1993).

Reid, Wemyss: *Memoirs and Correspondence of Lyon Playfair (1st Lord Playfair of St Andrews)* (London 1899).

RIIA: *The Architecture of the Scottish Renaissance* (Broxburn 1990).

Riis, Thomas: *Should Auld Acquaintance Be Forgot: Scottish–Danish relations c. 1450–1707*, vol. I (Odense 1988).

Roach, John: *A History of Secondary Education in England 1800–1870* (London 1986).

Roach, John: *Secondary Education in England 1870–1902. Public activity and private enterprise* (London 1991).

Robbins, K.: *Nineteenth Century Britain; Integration and Diversity* (Oxford 1988).

Robertson, David & Wood, Marguerite: *Castle and Town. Chapters in the History of the Royal Burgh of Edinburgh* (Edinburgh 1928).

Robertson, Forbes W.: *Early Scottish Gardeners and their Plants 1650–1750* (East Linton, 2000).

Robertson, Pamela (ed.): *Charles Rennie Mackintosh: The Architectural Papers* (London 1990).

Rodger, Richard: *The Transformation of Edinburgh. Land, Property and Trust in the Nineteenths Century* (Cambridge 2001).

Royal Commission on Ancient Monuments of Scotland: *Inventory of Ancient and Historical Monuments of the City of Edinburgh* (Edinburgh 1951).

Rush, Christopher & Shaw, John F.: *With Sharp Compassion. Norman Dott. Freeman Surgeon of Edinburgh* (Aberdeen 1990).

Scarisbrick, D.: *Anne of Denmark's Jewellery Inventory* (Devonshire 1991).

Scotland, J.: *The History of Scottish Education*, 2 vols (London 1969).

Selleck, R. J. W.: *James Kay-Shuttleworth: Journey of an Outsider* (Ilford, Essex 1994).

Shrosbree, Colin: *Public Schools and private education. The Clarendon Commission, 1861–64, and the Public Schools Acts* (Manchester 1988).

Simon, Brian: *The State and Educational Change. Essays in the History of Education and Pedagogy* (London 1994).

Smelser, Neil J.: *Social Paralysis and Social Change. British Working-Class Education in the Nineteenth Century* (Berkeley 1991).

Smith, Charles: *Historic South Edinburgh*, vol. 1 (Edinburgh 1978).

Smout, T.C. (ed.): *Scotland and Europe 1200–1850* (Edinburgh 1986).

Sommerville, Margaret K.B.: *The Merchant Maiden Hospital* (Oxford 1970).

Southey, Robert: *Journal of a Tour in Scotland in 1819* (Edinburgh 1972).

Stephen, W.B.: *Education in Britain 1750–1914* (London 1998).

Stevenson, David: *Scotland's Last Royal Wedding: The Marriage James VI and Anne of Denmark* (Edinburgh 1997).

Stewart, Alan: *The Cradle King. A Life of James VI and I* (London 2003).

Summerson, Sir John: *Architecture in Britain 1530–1830*, 7th edn (Frome, Somerset 1983).

Sutherland, Gillian: *Policy-Making in Elementary Education 1870–95* (London 1973).

Sutherland, John: *The Life of Sir Walter Scott. A Critical Biography* (Oxford 1995).

Sylvester, D. W.: *Robert Lowe and Education* (London 1974).

Taylor, Joseph: *1705 A Journey to Edenborough in Scotland* (Edinburgh 1903).

Thomson, Katrina: *Turner and Sir Walter Scott. The Provincial Antiquities and Picturesque Scenery of Scotland* (Edinburgh 1999).

Tranter, Neil: *Sport, economy and society in Britain 1750–1914* (Cambridge 1998).

Vincent, J. and Stenton, M. (eds): *McCalmont's Parliamentary Poll Book of All Elections 1832–1918*, 8th edn (Brighton 1971).

Walker, David M.: *The Scotish Jurists* (Edinburgh 1985).

Walker, David M.: *A Legal History of Scotland. Vol. IV. The Seventeenth Century* (Edinburgh 1996).

Walker, Dr Samuel (ed.): *Roll of Honour of George Heriot's School 1914–1919* (Edinburgh 1921).

Watt, Francis: *The Book of Edinburgh Anecdotes* (London 1913).

Waugh, Hector L. (ed.): *George Watson's College. History and Record 1724–1970* (Edinburgh 1970).

West, E.G.: *Education and the State. A Study in Political Economy*, 2nd edn (London 1970).

Whyte, Ian D.: *Scotland before the Industrial Revolution. An Economic and Social History c. 1050–c. 1750* (London 1995).

Williams, Ethel Carleton: *Anne of Denmark. Wife of James VI of Scotland. James I of England* (London 1970).

Wilson, Sir David: *Old Edinburgh*, vol 1

Wood, Marguerite (ed.): *Extracts from the Records of the Burgh of Edinburgh 1589–1603* (Edinburgh 1927).

Wood, Marguerite (ed.): *Extracts from the Records of the Burgh of Edinburgh, 1604–1626* (Edinburgh 1931).

Wood, Marguerite (ed.): *Extracts from the Records of the Burgh of Edinburgh, 1626–1641* (Edinburgh 1936).

Wood, Marguerite (ed*.): Extracts from the Records of the Burgh of Edinburgh, 1642–1655* (Edinburgh 1938).

Wood, Marguerite (ed.): *Extracts from the Records of the Burgh of Edinburgh, 1655–1665* (Edinburgh 1940).

Wood, Marguerite (ed.) *Extracts from the Records of the Burgh of Edinburgh, 1665–1680* (Edinburgh 1950).

Wood, Marguerite & Armit, Helen (eds): *Extracts from the Records of the Burgh of Edinburgh, 1681–1689* (Edinburgh 1954).

D. ARTICLES

Anderson, Robert: 'Secondary Schools and Scottish Society in the Nineteenth Century' in *Past and Present*, Nov. 1985, pp. 176–203.

Anderson, William: 'George Heriot' in *The Scottish Nation* (Edinburgh 1863), vol. II, pp. 469–70.

Anon.: 'Biographical Sketch of the Life of George Heriot', in *Scots Magazine*, 1802, LXIV, pp. 95–9.

Anon: 'Secondary Education in Scotland', in *Blackwood's Magazine*, March 1876, CXIX, pp. 283–96.

Anon: 'Sir Alexander Grant', in *Blackwood's Magazine*, January 1885, CXXXVII, pp. 133–43.

Anon: 'David Crawford. A forgotten poet of the Wark', *The Herioter*, April 1920, XIV no. 1.

Anon: 'Edinburgh Journal, 1823–33', in *The Book of the Old Edinburgh Club*, 1956, XXIX, pp. 143–84.

Balls, F.E.: 'The Endowed Schools Act 1869 and the Development of the English Grammar Schools in the Nineteenth Century', in *Durham Research Review*, vol. V, nos 19 and 20 (1967 and 1968).

Bedford, F.W.: 'The Hospital System of Scotland', in *Transactions of the National Association for the Promotion of Social Sciences*, ed. Hastings, George, pp. 340–8 (London 1864).

Blanc, Hippolyte J.: 'Heriot's Hospital and Contemporary Work' in *Transactions of the Edinburgh Architectural Association*, vol. II, pp. 3–11 (Edinburgh 1892).

Blanc, Hippolyte J.: 'George Heriot's Hospital described from an Architectural Viewpoint' in C.B. Gunn, H.J. Blanc and C.H. Bedford: *George Heriot's Hospital* (Edinburgh n.d.).

Blanc, Hippolyte J.: 'George Heriot's Hospital', in the *Book of the Old Edinburgh Club, 1911*, no. 4, pp. 4–10.

Brown, Keith M.: 'The Vanishing Emperor. British Kingship at its Decline 1603–1707', in Roger A Mason (ed.): *Scots and Britons. Scottish Political Thought and the Union of 1603* (Edinburgh 1994).

Byrom, Connie: 'The Development of Edinburgh's Second New Town', in the *Book of the*

Old Edinburgh Club, new series, 1994, vol. 3, pp. 37–61.

Chambers, Robert: 'George Heriot' in *Biographical Dictionary of Eminent Scotsmen* (Edinburgh 1834).

Cornforth, John: 'Ornamentally Scottish' in *Country Life*, 9 August, 1990, pp. 58–61.

Crawford, David: 'A Description of Heriot's Hospital', in *Poems, chiefly in the Scottish Dialect, on various Subjects*, pp. 6–9 (Edinburgh 1798).

Cruikshank, Margaret: 'The Argyll Commission Report 1865–8: A Landmark in Scottish Education', in *British Journal of Educational Studies*, pp. 133–47 (June 1967).

Dewar, William McL.: 'Heriot's' in *Scottish Field*, January 1959, vol. CVI, no. 678, pp. 34–39.

Erskine, David S. (Earl of Buchan): 'Sketch of the Life of George Heriot' in *The Bee (Literary Weekly Intelligencer)*, 9 November 1791, VI, p. 104.

Gaskell, E. 'Three Letters by Sir James Young Simpson', *British Medical Journal*, May 1970, 2.

Gentleman's Magazine: December 1745, Supplement, vol. XV, pp. 681–690.

Girouard, Mark: 'Drumlanrig Castle, Dumfriesshire', I and II, in *Country Life*, 25 August 1960, pp. 378–81 1 September 1960, pp. 434–7.

Goodare, Julian: 'Thomas Foulis and the Scottish Fiscal Crisis of the 1590s', pp. 170–97, in W.M. Ormrod, Margaret Bonney & Richard Bonney (eds): *Crises, Revolutions and Self-Sustained Growth: Essays in European Fiscal History, 1130–1830* (Stanford 1999).

Gow, Ian: 'Pugin and Trotter', pp. 60–73 in 'Caledonia Gothica. Pugin and the Gothic Revival in Scotland' (*Architectural Heritage*, VIII (Edinburgh 1997)).

Grage, Elsa-Brita: 'Scottish Merchants in Gothenburg 1621–1850', in T.C. Smout (ed.): *op. cit.* 1986.

Gray, William Forbes: 'George Heriot, Jeweller to James VI', in *An Edinburgh Miscellany*, pp. 55–66 (Edinburgh 1925).

Hodgkinson, George G.: 'Education, Endowments and Competition', in *Blackwood's Magazine*, CX, July 1871, pp. 81–99.

Inglis, John A.: 'Sir John Hay, the "Incendiary"', in *Scottish Historical Review*, 1918, XV, pp. 124–45.

Laing, David: 'Who was the Architect of Heriot's Hospital?' in *Transactions of the Architectural Institute of Scotland*, 2nd series, 1851–2, no. II, pp. 13–40.

Law, Alexander: 'Teachers in Edinburgh in the Eighteenth Century' in *The Book of the Old Edinburgh Club*, XXXII, 1966, pp. 109–57.

Lenman, Bruce P.: Jacobean Goldsmith-Jewellers as Credit-Creators. The Cases of James Mossman, James Cockie and George Heriot' in *Scottish Historical Review*, October 1995, LXXIV, 2, No. 198

Lilliehammer, Arnbid: 'The Scottish Norwegian Timber Trade in the Stavanger area in the 16th–17th centuries', in T.C. Smout (ed.): *op. cit.*, pp. 97–111.

Lockhart, Brian: 'George Heriot's Hospital and School. A Survey of the Buildings, 1628–1978', *The Herioter*, 1978.

Macaulay, James: 'The architectural collaboration between J. Gillespie Graham and A.W. Pugin', in *Architectural History*, 1984, vol. 27, pp. 406–20.

MacKechnie, Aonghus: 'Evidence of a post-1603 court architecture in Scotland?', in *Architectural History*, 1988, vol. 31, pp. 107–21.

Marwick, W.H.: 'Municipal Politics in Victorian Edinburgh', in *The Book of the Old Edinburgh Club*, XXXIII, 1969, pp. 31–41.

Meikle, Maureen: 'Holde her at the Oeconomicke Rule of the House: Anna of Denmark and

Scottish Court Finances, 1589–1603', in Elizabeth Ewan & Maureen M. Meikle: *Women in Scotland* c. *1100* to c. *1750* (East Linton 1999).

Morgan, Nicholas & Trainor, Richard: 'The Domestic Classes', in W. Hamish Fraser and R.J. Morris (eds): *People and Society in Scotland 1830–1914*, pp. 103–37.

Nissen, Hartvig: 'George Heriot's Hospital og Skoler', in *Beskrivelse over Skotlands Almueskolevaesen*, pp. 115–21 (Christiana 1854).

Parker, W.M.: 'The Amiable Dane. Han Christian Andersen's Visit to Scotland', *Evening Dispatch*, 8 September 1943.

Rhind, David: 'On the respective claims of Inigo Jones, Dr Balcanquall, Dean of Rochester, and William Wallace – to have been the Designer of Heriot's Hospital', in *The Transactions of the Architectural Institute of Scotland*, 1852, no. II, pp. 173–86.

Riis, Thomas: 'Scottish–Danish Relations in the 16th Century', in T.C. Smout (ed.): *Scotland and Europe 1200–1850*, pp. 112–27 (Edinburgh 1986).

Rowan, Alistair: 'George Heriot's Hospital, Edinburgh', in *Country Life*, 6 March & 13 March 1975, vol. CLVII, no. 4053.

Scots Magazine: February 1802, vol. LXIV, no. 64, pp. 95–8.

Scots Magazine: 'Heriot's Hospital', April 1809, no. LXXI, pp. 259–60

Scott, Paul H.: 'Walter Scott at the High School', in *Blackwood's Magazine* (October 1980).

Simpson, W. Douglas: 'George Heriot's Hospital', in *The Book of the Old Edinburgh Club*, vol. 31, pp. 33–42 (Edinburgh 1962).

Stenhouse, Lawrence: 'Hartvig Nissen's impressions of the Scottish educational system in the mid-nineteenth century', in *British Journal of Educational Studies*, 9, no. 2, pp. 143–54 (May 1961).

Tait, H.P. 'Two notable epidemics in Edinburgh and Leith', in *The Book of the Old Edinburgh Club*, XXXII, 1966.

Thompson, D'Arcy Wentworth: 'Jinglin' Geordie', in *Blackwood's Magazine*, pp. 390–6 (September 1935).

Towill, Revd Edwin S.: 'Minutes of the Trades Maiden Hospital', in *The Book of the Old Edinburgh Club*, vol. 28 (Edinburgh 1953).

Towill, Revd Edwin S.: 'Minutes of the Merchant Maiden Hospital', in *The Book of the Old Edinburgh Club*, vol. 29 (Edinburgh 1956).

Wood, Dr William: *Edinburgh Medical and Surgical Journal*, vol. xliii, pp. 32–49 (1835); vol. xlvii, pp. 97–141 (1839).

E. DISSERTATIONS

Balls, F.E.: 'The origins of the Endowed Schools Act and its operation in England from 1869–1895', University of Cambridge, 1964.

Brown, Rowan: 'The Evolution of Taymouth Castle', School of Art History, University of Aberdeen, 2001.

Dean, Leonard B.: 'William Henry Playfair and the Athens of the North 1807–1857', University of Edinburgh, 1999.

Dodge, Andrew Kenneth: James Gillespie Graham, University of St Andrews, 2000.

McGill, David: 'Heriot's Hospital', dissertation to RIBA, May 1974.

Robinson, Jane K.: 'An insight into the work of Hippolyte Jean Blanc. Architect. Edinburgh 1844–1917.' University of Edinburgh, 1999.

Scott, Alan J.: 'The History of George Heriot's Hospital, (unpublished Dip. Adv. Arch. Studies to Scott Sutherland School, Aberdeen), March 1978.

Index